Asian American
Studies
Now

Edited by

Jean Yu-wen Shen Wu

and Thomas C. Chen

RUTGERS UNIVERSITY PRESS

NEW BRUNSWICK, NEW JERSEY, AND LONDON

sian American Studies Now

A Critical Reader

Second paperback printing, 2011

Library of Congress Cataloging-in-Publication Data

Asian American studies now : a critical reader / edited by Jean Yu-wen Shen Wu and
Thomas C. Chen.
     p. cm.
   Includes bibliographical references and index.
    ISBN 978-0-8135-4574-5 (hardcover : alk. paper)—ISBN 978-0-8135-4575-2
  (pbk. : alk. paper)
     1. Asian Americans—History.   2. Asian Americans—Social conditions.
3. American literature—Asian American authors.
I. Wu, Jean Yu-wen Shen, 1948–   II. Chen, Thomas C.
E184.A75A8419   2009
973.′0495—dc22

                                    2009000771

A British Cataloging-in-Publication record for this book is available from the British Library.

Book design by Karolina Harris
Visit our Web site: http://rutgerspress.rutgers.edu
Manufactured in the United States of America

To Lucy Shen Wu, for her gumption,
and to Steve Marrone, for continued support,

To Aina and David Chen,
for their love, support, and encouragement,

and

In memory of Him Mark Lai (1925–2009)
and Ronald Takaki (1939–2009)

Contents

TWO: HISTORY AND MEMORY

THREE: CULTURE, POLITICS, AND SOCIETY

FOUR: PEDAGOGIES AND POSSIBILITIES

Acknowledgments

Were it not for our students, we would not have envisioned this project or embarked on it. It is their yearning for understanding Asian America that keeps us teaching, researching, and writing in the field. And it was our sense of their passion for shaping a more just society through their engagement with Asian America that kept us tenaciously focused on completing this project, especially in the moments when we wanted to give in to the many other demands in our lives. We thank Paul Spickard, whose enthusiastic support for "another Asian American anthology" at the proposal stage of this endeavor gave us the courage to go forward. We thank the following individuals who generously went out of their way to give very welcome assistance, advice, criticism, and support throughout this process: Jin Suk Bai, Doug Brugge, Sucheng Chan, Derrick Chao, Cecilia Chen, Annie Cho, Joel Cohen, Gill Frank, James Gatewood, Jessica Hunter, Kohei Ishihara, Jessica Johnson, Gregory Kornbluh, Erika Lee, Robert Lee, Andrew Leong, Steve Marrone, Ani Mukherji, Kim Park Nelson, Greg Robinson, Felicia Salinas, Elizabeth Samuels, Susan Smulyan, Saket Soni, Colette Tippy, Jane Jeong Trenka, Ben Tyler, and Chia Vang. At various points along the road, they made our journey bearable, even rewarding. We are thankful for the intellectual and institutional support of the Center for the Study of Race and Ethnicity in America at Brown University, where Thomas Chen was a graduate fellow while working on this project. We also recognize and thank the anti-racist social justice workers in our communities for their tireless efforts (and for keeping us honest). Last but not least, our gratitude and appreciation go to Leslie Mitchner at Rutgers University Press. Though there were a few moments near the end of the project when we were afraid to open her e-mails, we could not have asked for or worked with a better editor. The blame for any gaps, errors, or misjudgments in this book belongs solely to the editors.

Introduction

Ten years have passed since Jean Wu and Min Song edited *Asian American Studies: A Reader,* inspired by the idea that an interdisciplinary collection of foundational writings about Asian America would make course preparation easier for teachers of introductory level Asian American Studies courses.[1] Since then, Min Song has advanced from senior level graduate student to tenured professor of English at Boston College, and Jean Wu continues to teach at Tufts University, where she develops and teaches comparative race and Asian American Studies courses that involve students in racial and social justice projects in Asian American communities.

The Wu and Song *Reader* brought together essential readings in the field, and we believe that it remains an excellent resource for students and teachers of Asian America. All the same, in view of the flood of outstanding new scholarship on Asian America in the years since 2000, we have come to the conclusion that the time is right for supplementation. A new generation of scholars is responsible for much of the latest work in the field, and they are researching new topics, bringing new theoretical approaches to bear on familiar themes, and pushing the field in bold new directions. These recent developments have coincided with worldwide shifts that make the present moment very different from that at the end of the last century, when the first anthology was produced. We sense an emerging need to define the current shape of this rapidly changing field, one that has only recently established itself as a vibrant, mature, and thriving scholarly enterprise.

Asian American Studies Now: A Critical Reader attempts to meet this need by providing an updated introduction to Asian American Studies. It collects seminal articles and groundbreaking texts along with exciting new scholarship. We hope that it will be used as both a companion to the earlier anthology and a stand-alone introduction to the field.

Two major goals have governed our efforts in producing this new reader. First, we intend our anthology to be used as a primer and teacher's guide in introductory Asian American Studies classrooms and beyond. Students and teachers at the undergraduate, graduate, and secondary levels will find its contents useful both as a curriculum outline and as a resource for readings on Asian American history, culture, politics, and social issues. In the latter instance, it can even be excerpted for a wide range of classroom situations. And the reader will also provide a general audience with an introduction to the field's core issues and themes. We have selected essays for the significance of their contribution to the field, but also for their clarity, their brevity, and—just as important—their accessibility to readers with little or no prior knowledge of Asian American Studies.

Second, we thought we should use the compiling of a new anthology as an occasion to pause and reflect on the state of the field and to think about its future, particularly its pedagogical dimensions now that it is established as an interdisciplinary field with a significant presence in colleges and universities across the United States and a growing presence internationally. We likewise wanted to reflect on the relationship between Asian American Studies and ongoing social justice initiatives.[2] In doing so, we tried not only to consider the field's past and present but also to look toward its future.

Asian American Studies was initiated together with ethnic studies as part of the movements for social justice of the 1960s and 1970s. From the outset Asian American Studies included a commitment to working with and serving Asian American communities in their struggle for a more just and equitable present and future.[3] Since its foundation, the field has undergone significant transformation, reconfiguration, expansion, and crisis. Still, many academics engaged in Asian American Studies continue to pay homage to the field's origin in a context of social change, and they point to the way their work fits within that tradition.

Given the manifestly political nature of Asian American Studies from its very establishment as a scholarly endeavor, we have often found ourselves wondering aloud, "What impact has the field had on the world? How has the field contributed to fundamental social change?" We usually tell ourselves that, surely, decades of dialogue, research, and teaching in Asian American Studies have helped in some ways to promote social justice, to establish Asian America as an integral and vital part of our world, and to improve the conditions of all people. Yet we are reminded daily by what we witness, hear, and experience that the work of Asian American Studies as a political project has only just begun.

In her essay "Teaching *Who Killed Vincent Chin?* 1991 and 2001,"[4] Jean observes how the responses of students viewing the film for the first time in 2001 were indistinguishable from those of earlier students introduced to the film close to the time it first became available, ten years before. Students in 2001, just like students in 1991, were absolutely stunned to learn about Vincent Chin because they had never—up to the moment of learning about the Vincent Chin story in her course—encountered his story anywhere in their K–12 educations. As in 1991, a significant number of the 2001 students also found the realities of brutal anti-Asian violence—in large part (we are convinced) because of the near absence of Asian American history and experience in the popular consciousness.[5]

Sadly, teaching *Who Killed Vincent Chin?* in 2008 produces the same scenario. Even more troubling is that the reason does not seem to have changed. In fact, widespread ignorance of Asian America persists in all spheres of life, including the halls and corridors of our own educational institutions. It is a relatively common occurrence for us to encounter faculty and students who believe that the model minority myth is positive and rewarding. Others doubt that Asian American Studies constitutes a field, and many, even after having been convinced that it is, still question its legitimacy as *real* knowledge. Yet others continue to conflate Asian American Studies with Asian Studies, pigeonholing the former as a special-interest field relevant only to those interested in studying Asia. Meanwhile, as we prepare this anthology, Asian Americans are still being deported and still being targeted by hate violence. Asian American youth are still being denied their own histories and realities in K–12 education. Our communities are still being destroyed by gentrification, and we are still excluded and disenfranchised from innumerable activities and institutions—ranging from voting to emergency aid to proper legal representation—by policies and procedures that discriminate through race, language, gender, culture, sexuality, religion, class, and immigrant status.

The fact is that while Asian Americanist research and scholarship have been prolific in the past few decades, and while Asian American Studies programs have been established in a number of colleges and universities, the histories and realities of Asian Americans have yet to be seriously incorporated into K–16 educational curricula, openly acknowledged in the fabric of American society, and woven into public discourse. All the while, interlocking systems of oppression continue to structure Asian American life in important and often devastating ways. We recognize the painful irony that while Asian American Studies—a field founded on a social justice agenda—may indeed be doing very well in many respects, many social injustices in our communities remain constant and pervasive.[6] Moreover, we recognize that while Asian American Studies has produced far-reaching critical analyses and a powerful epistemological critique of American history and life, analysis and critique must be linked to broader efforts for social transformation. Even as changing circumstances present new challenges and contradictions, it is the enduring importance of this crucial link that compels us—forty years after the birth of the field—to stress how important it is now to reassess our efforts.

This essential relationship between intellectual and political work is reflected in our choice for the title of this anthology, "Asian American Studies Now." These words refer to two things at once: (1) the current state of what is in many respects a thriving academic field, and (2) the political impetus behind the field, which Movement activists expressed in their demand for "Asian American Studies *Now!*" The conspicuous absence of the exclamation point registers our sense that the urgency that once united pioneers of Asian American Studies in their demand for a relevant education has receded somewhat now that the field has gained a foothold in some pockets of higher education. We find this lack of urgency both ironic and alarming in light of the profound injustices occurring locally and globally in our communities. Our goal here is to urge those active in Asian Americanist research, writing, and teaching to consider with a new sense of urgency just how Asian American Studies relates—or should relate—to the work of anti-oppressive social transformation today. After four decades, what has Asian American Studies accomplished? What has it yet to achieve? Indeed, what do we want Asian Americanist research, writing, and teaching to achieve?

Questions like these played a decisive role in bringing Thomas Chen into Asian American Studies and leading him to collaborate on this update with Jean. When Thomas first encountered Asian American Studies as an undergraduate in Jean's courses, the experiences of anti-Asian racism referred to in the course material were familiar to him, as were the feelings of anger that reading the material stirred up inside him. Unfamiliar, on the other hand, were the vocabulary, the theories, and the analytical habits needed to make sense of these experiences both in his own life and in the world. Prior to enrolling in Asian American Studies courses, he, like so many of his peers, had felt powerless in the face of complex, overwhelming, and seemingly inevitable forces. He was skeptical of efforts for social change. The Asian American Studies courses he took in college enabled him to give a name to the instances of racism, blatant and subtle, that he had experienced and seen growing up in Connecticut. The same courses gave him the concepts and skills necessary for placing those experiences in historical context, connecting his memories to a larger social framework, and seeing the whole world anew. It was in those encounters with Asian American Studies that he first began to imagine himself as an agent of social change. Since that time, he has observed similar transformations take place in students he has taught as a graduate instructor at Brown University.

The experiences of both of us, Jean and Thomas, as teachers and students, have taught us that central to the power and promise of Asian American Studies is its ability to give voice to alternative and oppositional histories and realities, to make transparent the power structures that shape our lives, and to interrogate the dominant values and assumptions of American society. They have made plain to us the importance of the field's ability to historicize the taken-for-granted, to develop critical consciousness in socially marginalized and politically disenfranchised peoples, and to empower those engaged in the field to see themselves as active participants in history. Most critically, they have revealed to us how so much of this enormous potential lies in the classroom.

We firmly believe that pedagogy remains a—maybe *the*—critical site for Asian American Studies today. That this should be so stands, of course, as testimony to the great strides made over recent decades in the establishment of the field and in the production of cutting-edge scholarship. With all due respect to these laudable accomplishments, though, we are convinced that it is not just whether Asian American Studies is taught but *how* it is taught that will decide whether the field will more fully realize its potential for educational and social transformation in the decades to come.

We contend that for Asian American Studies to be effective in empowering students to work for a more just world, it must be recognized as the activist endeavor it was intended to be when the field was founded. In our view, Asian American Studies requires the kind of teaching that will equip students with the knowledge, habits of mind, skills, and vision to be agents of social change. As the pioneering ethnic studies scholar Ronald Takaki once told his students, critical thinking, writing, and an understanding of our multiracial past "can be revolutionary tools if we make them so."[7] No one can expect to transform the world overnight. But understanding of the self and understanding of the world, in which massively unequal power relationships shape all of our experiences, are what students will need if they are to feel empowered to work for change. We have in mind a critical pedagogy that demands of students not that they conform to a set image of political liberation, but that they see their education itself as a site of ongoing struggle over meaning and power. It is a pedagogy that inspires students to confront the nature of their own involvement with both institutions of learning and society at large and leads them to consider their roles and responsibilities in shaping the world in which they live.[8]

These pedagogical objectives have guided the design and arrangement of this anthology. Our hope is that students and teachers will find it useful in a range of educational settings. To this end, we have used Jean's interdisciplinary courses on race and Asian America as an organizational blueprint. Her courses often follow a four-part sequence: (1) Students learn to identify and name experiences of social inequality in their own lives and the lives of others. (2) Students then delve into history, analyzing historical events and developing an appreciation for how the past shapes the present. (3) Students examine a range of contemporary social and cultural issues from the perspectives of many different disciplines to develop their skills at identifying and critically analyzing patterns and structures of social inequality. (4) Students tackle the question of what can be done with the knowledge they have gained and explore possibilities for future learning and action.

The reader is divided into four broad sections, each corresponding to one step in the four-part sequence of Jean's courses. Part One assembles readings that examine Asian American experiences of social inequality and situate Asian America in the racial and social landscape of the United States and the world. Part Two analyzes major events and core themes in Asian American history. Part Three brings together writing from diverse disciplines including sociology, anthropology, literature, and cultural studies. This section broadly examines struggles over meaning and power that shape and define Asian America. Part Four critically addresses the purpose, pedagogies, and future directions of Asian Americans Studies. The pieces collected in this last section discuss critical pedagogies, provide models of effective social justice work, and raise questions with which we believe the field must grapple if it is to survive as an effective site for political struggle and social transformation. Although these questions may seem to be aimed only at professionals in the field, we believe that they also cut right to the heart of issues that students often confront in their own quests for meaning and direction.

NOTES

1. Jean Yu-wen Shen Wu and Min Song, eds., *Asian American Studies: A Reader* (New Brunswick, N.J.: Rutgers University Press, 2000).

2. These questions are explored further in Part Four of this volume; see especially Sucheng Chan, "Whither Asian American Studies?" and Glenn Omatsu, "Freedom Schooling: Reconceptualizing Asian American Studies for Our Communities." See also E. San Juan Jr., "The Ordeal of Ethnic Studies in the Age of Globalization," in *Displacements and Diasporas: Asians in the Americas*, ed. Wanni W. Anderson and Robert G. Lee (New Brunswick, N.J.: Rutgers University Press, 2005).

3. See Glenn Omatsu, "The 'Four Prisons' and the Movements of Liberation: Asian American Activism from the 1960s to the 1990s," this volume.

4. Jean Wu, "Teaching *Who Killed Vincent Chin?* 1991 and 2001," in *Asian Americans: Vulnerable Populations, Model Interventions, and Clarifying Agendas*, ed. Lin Zhan (Sudbury, Mass.: Jones & Bartlett, 2003).

5. While most Asian American students can, after some prodding, describe a variety of blatant, covert, and frequent targeting in their own experiences, they are often very hesitant to acknowledge that this targeting is raced and more specifically, anti-Asian.

6. George Lipsitz makes a similar point about ethnic studies in his essay, " 'To Tell the Truth and Not Get Trapped': Why Interethnic Antiracism Matters Now," in *Orientations: Mapping Studies in the Asian Diaspora*, ed. Kandace Chuh and Karen Shimakawa (Durham, N.C.: Duke University Press, 2001), 296.

7. Elaine Woo, "Ronald T. Takaki dies at 70; pioneer in the field of ethnic studies" (Los Angeles Times, May 29, 2009, A24).

8. See Glenn Omatsu, "Freedom Schooling: Reconceptualizing Asian American Studies for Our Communities," and Jean Y. Wu, "Race Matters in Civic Engagement Work," both in this volume. For other excellent discussions of critical pedagogy in Asian American Studies, see "Pedagogy, Social Justice, and the State of Asian American Studies," Special Issue of *Amerasia Journal*, 29.2 (2003); Lane Ryo Hirabayashi, ed., *Teaching Asian America* (Lanham, Md.: Rowman and Littlefield, 1998); Kevin Lam, "Relocating Critical Pedagogy," *Radical History Review* 2008.102 (2008), 12–14; Keith Osajima, "Pedagogical Considerations in Asian American Studies," *Journal of Asian American Studies* 1.3 (October 1998).

ne:
Situating
Asian America

notion whereby "individuals of all nations are melted into a new race of men," an idea later called the "melting pot," paralleled the building of networks of roads, railroads, and communications that unified and bound the nation.[9]

Although Asians helped to construct those iron links that connected East to West, they, along with other peoples of color, were excluded from the industrial, masculine, destroying melting pot. Ellis Island was not their port of entry; its statue was not their goddess of liberty. Instead, the square-jawed, androgynous visage of the "Mother of Exiles" turned outward to instruct, to warn, and to repel those who would endanger the good order of America's shores, both at home and abroad. The indigenous inhabitants of Africa, Asia, and the Americas were not members of the community but were more akin to the wilderness, which required penetration and domestication. Three years after the Constitution was ratified, the first Congress met and, through the Naturalization Act of 1790, restricted admission into the American community to "free white persons." Although the act was modified to include "persons of African nativity or descent" in 1870 and Chinese nationals in 1943, the racial criterion for citizenship was eliminated completely only in 1952, 162 years after the original delineation of the Republic's members, or, according to the Naturalization Act, the "worthy part of mankind."

In 1886, African American educator Anna Julia Cooper told a group of African American ministers: "Only the BLACK WOMAN can say 'when and where I enter . . . then and there the whole *Negro race enters with me.*' "[10] Cooper's confident declaration held profound meaning. African American men bore the stigma of race, but African American women bore the stigmata of race and gender. Her liberation, her access to the full promise of America, embraced the admission of the entire race. The matter of "when and where," accordingly, is an engendered, enabling moment. The matter of "when and where," in addition, is a generative, transformative moment. The matter of "when and where," finally, is an extravagant, expansive moment. That entry into the American community, however enfeebled by barriers to full membership, parallels the earlier entry into historical consciousness, and the "when and where" of both moments are engendered/enabling, generative/transformative, extravagant/expansive.

Asians entered into the European American historical consciousness long before the mid-nineteenth-century Chinese migration to "Gold Mountain" and, I believe, even before Yankee traders and American diplomats and missionaries traveled to China in the late eighteenth century. The "when and where" of the Asian American experience can be found within the European imagination and construction of Asians and Asia and within their expansion eastward and westward to Asia for conquest and trade.

Writing in the fifth or fourth century B.C.E., Hippocrates, Greek physician and "father of medicine," offered a "scientific" view of Asia and its people. Asia, Hippocrates held, differed "in every respect" and "very widely" from Europe.[11] He attributed those contrasts to the environment, which shaped the peoples' bodily conformations and their characters. Asia's mild, uniform climate supported lush vegetation and plentiful harvests, but under those conditions "courage, endurance, industry and high spirit could not arise" and "pleasure must be supreme." Asians reflected the seasons in their natures, exhibiting a "monotonous sameness" and "stagnation," and their form of government, led by kings who ruled as "despots," enfeebled them even more. Among Asians, Hippocrates reported, were "Longheads" and "Phasians." The latter had yellowish complexions "as though they suffered from jaundice." Because of the differing environments in which they lived, Hippocrates concluded, Europeans had a wider variety of physical types and were more courageous and energetic than Asians, "for uniformity engenders slackness, while variation fosters endurance in both body and soul; rest and slackness are food for cowardice, endurance and exertion for bravery."[12]

Aristotle mirrored Hippocrates' views of Asia during the fourth century B.C.E. In his *Politics*, Aristotle observed that northern Europeans were "full of spirit, but wanting in intelligence and skill," whereas Asians were "intelligent and inventive," but lacked spirit and were therefore "always in a state of subjection and slavery." The Greeks, in contrast, lived between those two groups and thus were both "high-spirited and . . . intelligent." Further, argued Aristotle, barbarians were by nature "more servile in character" than Greeks and he reported that some Asians practiced cannibalism.[13] The fourth-century B.C.E. conflict between Persia and Greece, between barbarism and civilization, between inferior and superior, tested the "great chain of being" idea propounded by Plato and Aristotle. Alexander the Great's thrust into India, to "the ends of the world," was a one-sided affair, according to the Roman historian Arrian, a chronicler of the expedition. Using contemporary accounts but writing some four hundred years after Alexander's death in 323 B.C.E., Arrian contrasted Alexander's ingenuity and dauntless spirit—"he could not endure to think of putting an end to the war so long as he could find enemies"—with the cowardice of the barbarian hordes, who fled pell-mell at the sight of the conqueror.[14] As recorded by Arrian, Alexander reminded his officers in a speech that they were "ever conquerors" and their enemies were "always beaten," that the Greeks were "a free people" and the Asians "a nation of slaves." He praised the strength and valor of the Greeks, who were "inured to warlike toils," and he declared that their enemies had been "enervated by long ease and effeminacy" and called them "the wanton, the luxurious, and effeminate Asiatics."[15]

Such accounts of Asia, based upon the belief in a generative relationship between the environment and race and culture, enabled an exotic, alienating construction of Asians, whether witnessed or simply imagined. Literary critics Edward W. Said and Mary B. Campbell have characterized that European conception of Asia and Asians—"the Other"—as "almost a European invention." According to Said, Europeans understood Asia as a place of "romance, exotic beings, haunting memories and landscapes, remarkable experiences"; for Campbell, that conception was "the ground for dynamic struggles between the powers of language and the facts of life."[16] Accordingly, the Greek historian Ctesias, writing probably in the fifth century B.C.E., reveled in the accounts of "dog-faced creatures" and "creatures without heads" that supposedly inhabited Africa, and he peopled his Asia with those same monstrous beasts. Likewise, the author of the early medieval account *Wonders of the East* described Asian women "who have boars' tusks and hair down to their heels and oxen's tails growing out of their loins. These women are thirteen feet tall, and their bodies have the whiteness of marble, and they have camels' feet and donkeys' teeth." Alexander the Great, hero of *Wonders of the East*, kills those giant, tusked, and tailed women "because of their obscenity" and thereby eliminates strangeness, making the world sane and safe again. Asia, in *Wonders of the East*, writes Campbell, "stands in opposition to the world we know and the laws that govern it," and is way beyond and outside the realm of order and sensibility.[17]

That otherworldliness, that flight from reality, pervades the earliest Christian European text to define Europe in opposition to Asia, the *Peregrinatio ad terram sanctam* by Egeria, probably written during the late fourth century C.E. Although her account of her journey to the Holy Land contained "moments of awe, reverence, wonder or gratitude," it described an exotic Asia that served to highlight the positive, the real, the substantial Europe. *De locis sanctis*, written during the late seventh century C.E. by Adamnan, abbot at Iona's monastery, recounted a similar Asia from the travels of Bishop Arculf to the Holy Land. Asia, according to *De locis sanctis*, was a strange, even demonic place, where people exhibited grotesque inversions and perversions of human nature, and where a prerational, stagnant configuration existed, "a world stripped of spirit and past."[18]

Asia, according to Campbell and Said, was Europe's Other.[19] Asia was the location of Europe's oldest, greatest, and richest colonies, the source of its civilization and languages, its cultural contestant, and the wellspring of one of its most persistent images of the Other. At the same time, cautions Said, the assumptions of Orientalism were not merely abstractions and figments of the European imagination but composed a system of thought that supported a "Western style for dominating, restructuring, and having authority over" Asia. Within Orientalism's lexicon, Asians were inferior to and deformations of Europeans, and Orientalism's purpose was to stir an inert people, raise them to their former greatness, shape them and give them an identity, and subdue and domesticate them. That colonization, wrote Said, was an engendered subordination, by which European men aroused, penetrated, and possessed a passive, dark, and vacuous "Eastern bride," imposing movement and giving definition to the "inscrutable Orient," full of secrecy and sexual promise.[20] The feminization of Asia was well under way before the colonization of Asia by Europe in the sixteenth century, as evident in the accounts of Hippocrates, Herodotus,[21] Aristotle, Arrian, Egeria, and Adamnan.

Arrian's account of Alexander's effortless victory over "effeminate" Asian men, for example, parallels his discussion of Greek men's easy conquest of erotic Asian women. Indian women, wrote the Roman historian, "who will suffer themselves to be deflowered for no other gift, will easily condescend, when an elephant is promised as the purchase," thinking it "an honour to have their beauty valued at so high a rate."[22] The conqueror took for himself several Asian wives, he "bestowed the daughters of the most illustrious" Persians on his friends, and more than 10,000 of his soldiers married Asian women. Further, commented Arrian, despite being "in the very heat of youth," Alexander curbed his sexual desires and thereby displayed the triumph of mind over body, rationality over sensuality, Greek over Asian. "The daughter of Oxyartes was named Roxana, a virgin, but very marriageable, and, by the general consent of writers, the most beautiful of all the Asiatic women, Darius's wife excepted," wrote Arrian. "Alexander was struck with surprise at the sight of her beauty; nevertheless, being fully resolved not to offer violence to a captive, he forbore to gratify his desires till he took her, afterwards, to wife . . . and herein showed himself no less a pattern of true continency, than he had before done of heroic fortitude." "As to those pleasures which regarded the body," wrote Arrian in eulogizing Alexander, "he shewed himself indifferent; as to the desires of the mind, insatiable."[23]

The Greek representation of Asia yielded not only soft men and erotic women but also hard, cruel men and virile, martial women. Fifth-century B.C.E. polarities of Greek/barbarian, male/female, and human/animal helped to define the citizens of the *polis*—Greek men—as the negation of their Other—barbarian, female, animal—who were linked by analogy such that barbarian was like female was like animal.[24] Athenian patriarchy held that men were the norm, were superior, and brought order, whereas women were abnormal, inferior, and brought chaos. Marriage domesticated women, civilizing their wild, untamed sexuality and disciplining them for admittance into the city. Amazons reversed the gender relations of the *polis* and stood in opposition to its androcentrism by being members of a society of women who refused to marry and become mothers to sons and who assumed the preeminent male characteristics of aggressiveness, leadership, and strength. Although the myth of Amazons originated before the Persian wars, the Greeks considered Asia to be the Amazons' homeland, and they equated Persians with Amazons, in that both Persians and Amazons were barbarians and, according to Isocrates in 380 B.C.E., Amazons "hated the whole Greek race" and sought "to gain mastery over all." Athenians, explained Isocrates, defended themselves against Amazon expansion, defeated them, and destroyed them "just as if they had waged war against all mankind."[25] Besides posing a political threat, Asia served as an object lesson of how, when men ceased to act as men, order and normalcy vanished, resulting in the topsy-turvy world of the Amazons.[26]

The Mongol invasions of the thirteenth century not only breached Alexander's wall but also made palpable a hitherto distant, alien people and culture. "Swarming like locusts over the face of the earth," Friar William of Rubruck wrote in 1255, the Mongols "have brought terrible devastation to the eastern parts [of Europe], laying waste with fire and carnage . . . it seemed that God did not wish them to come out; nevertheless it is written in sacred history that they shall come out toward the end of the world, and shall make a great slaughter of men."[27] The Mongols, of whom the Tatars were the most prominent group, appeared as avenging angels from hell, "Tartarus," and hence the corruption of their name to "Tartars."[28] Although in awe of the Mongols' military prowess and strength, Friar William saw little to admire in their filth and barbarism: "the poor provide for themselves by trading sheep and skins; and the slaves fill their bellies with dirty water and are content with this. They also catch mice, of which many kinds abound there; mice with long tails they do not eat but give to their birds; they eat doormice and all kinds of mice with short tails."[29]

The late-thirteenth-century account of Asia by the Venetian Marco Polo contains both feminine and masculine attributions, chaste women and diabolical men, and grotesque and wondrous objects and people, including unicorns, Amazons, dog-headed creatures, mountain streams flowing with diamonds, and deserts full of ghouls. His narrative is a distillation of the brew that had preceded him. John Masefield, in his introduction to the 1908 edition of Polo's *Travels*, wrote that "his picture of the East is the picture which we all make in our minds when we repeat to ourselves those two strange words, 'the East,' and give ourselves up to the image which that symbol evokes."[30] A prominent part of that image was the exotic and the erotic, highlighted in Polo's ample accounts of prostitutes, sex, and women, leading Henry Hart to speculate: "One may surmise that the numerous references to women—the intimate descriptions of their persons, their various aptitudes in sex relations and many other details not usually related even by hardy travelers of that or a later day . . . were largely, if not entirely, called forth by the frank curiosity and continual questionings of the stay-at-home Westerners for whom his tale was told and written." Polo wrote of the Chinese that "their ladies and wives are also most delicate and angelique things, and raised gently, and with great delicacy, and they clothe themselves with so many ornaments and of silk and of jewels, that the value of them cannot be estimated."[31]

In Europe, *The Travels of Sir John Mandeville* was the most influential book about Asia from its original publication in 1356 to the eighteenth century. "Mandeville" was a pseudonym for perhaps a number of authors, who claimed to have traveled from England to the Holy Land, Egypt, Arabia, and even to the court of the Great Khan in Cathay. Like Polo, Mandeville described the marvels and monsters of the East, from the bounties of gold, silver, precious stones, cloves, nutmeg, and ginger to the horrors of one-eyed and headless beasts, giants, pygmies, and cannibals. In a single passage, Mandeville poses an apparently curious juxtaposition of sexuality and war, but upon reflection, the feminine (sexuality) and masculine (war) so constructed are really two sides of the same coin: the dominance of men over women and territory, achieved through heterosexual sex and war, and, by extension, under imperialism, European men's superiority over Asian women and men and their control of reproduction and the state. On the island of "Calonak" near Java, wrote Mandeville, the king

> hath as many wives as he will. For he maketh search all the country to get him the fairest maidens that may be found, and maketh them to be brought before him. And he taketh one one night, and another another night, and so forth continually ensuing; so that he hath a thousand wives or more. And he lieth never but one night with one of them, and another night with another; but if that one happen to be more lusty to his pleasance than another. And therefore the king getteth full many children, sometime an hundred, some-time a two-hundred, and some-time more.

Without a paragraph break, Mandeville continued: "And he hath also into a 14,000 elephants or more that he maketh for to be brought up amongst his villains by all his towns. For in case that he had any war against any other king about him, then [he] maketh certain men of arms for to go up into the castles of tree made for the war, that craftily be set upon the elephants' backs, for to fight against their enemies."[32]

Christopher Columbus was a great admirer of "Mandeville" and, along with English explorers Martin Frobisher and Walter Raleigh and Flemish cartographer Gerhardus Mercator, read and believed Mandeville's account of Asia and his idea of a circumnavigable and universally inhabited world.[33] The fabulous East, the earthly paradise "discovered" and described by Columbus, was to him and his contemporaries Asia—the "Indies"—and its peoples were Asians—the "Indians." They were just as surely Asian as the lands and peoples in Polo's and Mandeville's travelogues. As Columbus noted in the preface to his ship's daily log, the expedition's purpose was to go "to the regions of India, to see the Princes there and the peoples and the lands, and to learn of their disposition, and of everything, and the measures which could be taken for their conversion to our Holy Faith."[34] Columbus compared the new lands to the virtuous Garden before the Fall, where people were like children, innocent and unselfconscious in their nakedness, and where the feminized land invited conquest. His log entry for October 12, 1492, reported: "At dawn we saw naked people, and I went ashore in the ship's boat, armed. . . . I unfurled the royal banner. . . . After a prayer of thanksgiving I ordered the captains of the Pinta and Nina . . . to bear faith and witness that I was taking possession of this island for the King and Queen."[35] Much of the land was bountiful and laden with fruit, and on his third voyage, Columbus described the mouth of the Orinoco River as shaped "like a woman's nipple," from whence "issued the waters of paradise into the sea."[36]

Some islanders, reported Columbus, were friendly, domestic, tractable, and even cowardly, but others were warlike, monstrous, and evil, even cannibalistic (a word derived from the name "Carib" Indians). "I also understand that, a long distance from here," wrote Columbus on November 4, 1492, "there are men with one eye and others with dogs' snouts who eat men. On taking a man they behead him and drink his blood and cut off his genitals."[37] The timid Indians were eager to submit to Europeans, being "utterly convinced that I and all my people came from Heaven," according to Columbus, whereas the fearless ones required discipline. Both kinds of Indians, "feminine" and "masculine," were fair game for capture, or, in Columbus's euphemism, "I would like to take some of them with me."[38] That, in fact, was what the admiral did, as easily as plucking leaves from the lush, tropical vegetation, intending them to serve as guides, servants, and specimens. Columbus's text and others like it helped to justify a "Christian imperialism" and were the means by which the invaders "communicated—and helped control—a suddenly larger world."[39]

That world grew even larger in about 1510, when a few Europeans questioned Columbus's "India" and proposed the existence of a new continent that stood between Europe and Asia, although cartographers continued to append American discoveries to the Asian coast until the late sixteenth century. Accompanying and justifying their expanded physical world was an ideology, articulated in texts, of a growing racial and cultural distance between Europeans and the peoples of Asia, Africa, and the Americas. The first cracks had appeared, in the perceptions of Asians by Europeans, in the fifth-century B.C.E. works of Hippocrates, who had posited "very wide" differences "in every respect" between Europeans and Asians. The fissures continued to widen thereafter to the degree that Asia, Africa, and the Americas became antipodes of Europe, the habitations of monstrous beasts and perversions of nature itself. That world, it seemed, needed to be appropriated, worked over, and tamed.

The process of colonization and the relationship between colonizer and colonized were incisively described by Albert Memmi, the twentieth-century Tunisian philosopher and author: "The colonialist stresses those things which keep him separate, rather than emphasizing that which might contribute to the foundation of a joint community." That focus on difference is not of itself racist, but it takes on a particular meaning and function within a racist context. According to Memmi: "In those differences, the colonized is always degraded and the colonialist finds justification for rejecting his subject. . . . The colonialist removes the factor [the colonized] from history, time, and therefore possible evolution. What is actually a sociological point becomes labeled as being biological or, preferably, metaphysical. It is attached to the colonized's basic nature."[40] Whether because of race or culture, of biology or behavior, of physical appearance or social construct, Asians appeared immutable, engendered, and inferior. These differences not only served to set Asians apart from the "joint community" but also helped to define the European identity as a negation of its Other.

Reflecting on works published on the five hundredth anniversary of Columbus's "discovery," anthropologist Wilcomb E. Washburn, noted interpreter of American Indian culture and director of the Office of American Studies at the Smithsonian Institution, reminded his readers that the initiative for discovery came from the West and not the East, and thus "Asia was more sharply etched on the European mind than on the Asian mind. . . . Both America and Asia were relatively stagnant," he explained, "being more wedded to their traditions than was the West, which found the novelty of other climes and other cultures stimulating. While the Western mind did not always move in directions that we would now applaud, it moved—indeed, darted here and there—as the Asian mind too often did not."[41]

Following Columbus's "great enterprise" and his "taking possession" of "Asia," the penetration of Asia proper began with the Portuguese, who seized parts of India and Southeast Asia during the early sixteenth century, established a colony at Macao in 1557, and controlled much of the trade with China and Japan. Despite Portugal's presumed sole possession of the hemisphere east of the 1493 papal line of demarcation, Spain, the Netherlands, France, and Britain also participated in the trade with and colonization of Asia. The conquest and colonization of the Americas was, of course, a product of that global expansion of Europeans, and the "when and where" of the Asian American experience must be similarly situated. I do not claim, however, that Orientalism's restructuring and domination of Asia simply migrated with Europeans to the Americas; nor am I arguing a necessary relationship between European and European American perceptions of Asians. My contention is that there is a remarkable familiarity to

Orientalism's face on both shores of the Atlantic and that its resemblance extends to European constructions of American Indians and Africans.[42]

Historian Stuart Creighton Miller, in his 1969 book, *The Unwelcome Immigrant: The American Image of the Chinese, 1785–1882*, argued that although it was sensible to assume that American attitudes toward Asians were rooted in the European heritage, he could find no direct connection between those views. Neither the writings nor the libraries of America's leading figures during the colonial period showed any interest in or even curiosity about Asians. Miller characterized that lacuna as indicative of an "innocent, unstructured perception of China in the American mind" and, as proof, pointed to George Washington, who was surprised to learn in 1785 that the Chinese were nonwhites. Further, Miller noted that the English failed to share the Continent's enthusiasm for Chinese government and law and for Confucian philosophy, made popular by Jesuit missionaries and by the iconoclasts of the Age of Reason. In fact, in Britain, Sinophobes such as Daniel Defoe, Samuel Johnson, Jonathan Swift, and Adam Smith launched a vitriolic attack against the Chinese. The American image of Asians, Miller concluded, took shape only after direct American trade with China began with the departure of the *Empress of China* from New York Harbor in 1784.[43]

Miller underestimates the malleability and mobility of racial attitudes and notions of the Other, characteristics that have been amply demonstrated by scholars. Europeans, as noted by historian Dwight W. Hoover, "did not approach new lands and new people devoid of preconceptions. Instead, they brought with them a whole set of ideas concerning both the natural and historical worlds."[44] Some of those preconceptions included the idea of a biological chain of being that evolved from ape to wild man to man and the biblical notion of postdiluvian degeneration and diversification originating with the Tower of Babel.[45] Despite their manifest variety, ideas of race distinguished Europeans from their shadow—non-Europeans—and claimed superiority for the civilized, Christian portion of humankind.

William Shakespeare's *The Tempest*, first performed in 1611, was likely set in Bermuda but might just as well have been an allegory of race relations during the age of European overseas expansion and colonization, or perhaps even an account of the sugar plantation system that was installed along the European Mediterranean coast and on islands like Cyprus and Crete and that by the late fourteenth century was driven mainly by Asian and African slave labor.[46] Prospero, "a prince of power" and lover of books, is set adrift with his daughter, Miranda, and lands on an enchanted island which he takes from Caliban, whom he enslaves and banishes to the island's wasteland. Caliban (anagram of the word "cannibal") is everything Prospero is not: he is dark and physically deformed; he is "poisonous," "lying," "filth," "capable of all ill," and begotten of "the devil himself." He is both African and Indian, his mother was from Algiers and he is descended from Brazilians, Patagonians, and Bermudans, but he is also part fish, part beast. Caliban's mother, Prospero said, was a "damn'd witch," a "hag," who had given birth to Caliban like an animal—"she did litter here" her son, who was "not honour'd with a human shape." Despite being excluded from their company and despite Miranda's abhorrence of him, Caliban is indispensable to

Prospero and Miranda, because he "does make our fire, fetch in our wood; and serves in offices that profit us." Prospero pities Caliban, tutors him, and takes "pains to make [him] speak"; Prospero gives meaning to Caliban's "gabble." Instruction, however, proves insufficient. The wild man is driven by savage lust and tries to kill Prospero and rape the virginal Miranda, but he is repulsed by Prospero's magic.[47]

Caliban, the "savage man of Inde," was African and Indian, but he was also Asian insofar as Indians came from Asia, as was contended by Samuel Purchas, scholar and chaplain to the archbishop of Canterbury, in his widely read book *Purchas his Pilgrimage*, published in 1613, and seconded by the astronomer Edward Brerewood in his 1614 book, *Enquiries touching the diversity of languages, and religions through the chiefe parts of the world*, and by Walter Raleigh in his 1614 *History of the World*. The fact that Indians were once Asians accounted for their barbarism, according to these English writers.[48] Thus, although a separate race, Indians were still Asians, both groups having descended from the biblical Shem; and Asians, Indians, and Africans all belonged to the darker races of men, the Calibans of the earth, who were ruled by beastly passions, sought to impregnate white women (to people "this isle with Calibans"), and, although given a language and trained in useful labor, still turned against their benefactors and had to be subdued.[49] Perhaps influenced by those European views, Thomas Jefferson hypothesized the kinship of Asians and America's Indians: "the resemblance between the Indians of America and the eastern inhabitants of Asia would induce us to conjecture that the former are descendants of the latter, or the latter of the former."[50]

Although they arrived in the New World carrying the baggage of the Old World, Americans developed their own projections and invented their own mythologies, peering from their "clearing" into the "wilderness." George Washington may have been reflecting the light of European ideology bent by the prism of American experience when he declared that "being upon good terms with the Indians" was based upon economy and expediency, and instead of driving them "by force of arms out of their Country; which . . . is like driving the wild Beasts of ye forest . . . the gradual extension of our settlements will as certainly cause the savage, as the wolf, to retire; both being beasts of prey, tho' they differ in shape."[51] And Jefferson might have defended Indians as "a degraded yet basically noble brand of white man," but he was also defending the American environment and its quadrupeds, those "other animals of America," against French naturalist Georges Buffon's claim of American inferiority. Having failed to assimilate and civilize the savage and childish Indians, Jefferson argued for their extermination, made "necessary to secure ourselves against the future effects of their savage and ruthless warfare."[52] Jefferson, having reached that conclusion about Indians, linked America's determination to clear the forests with a New World version of British expansion and colonization and predicted that the "confirmed brutalization, if not extermination of this race in our America is . . . to form an additional chapter in the English history of [oppression of] the same colored man in Asia, and of the brethren of their own color in Ireland."[53]

When Yankee traders arrived in China during the late eighteenth century, they saw the Chinese through lenses that had already been ground with the grit of European views of Asia and Asians and the rub of historical and contemporary relations between European Americans and American Indians and Africans. The traders' diaries, journals, and letters were mostly free of racial prejudice, reports Miller, and the negative images of the Chinese that did appear concerned China's government and the officials with whom the traders dealt, whom they saw as despotic, corrupt, barbarous, begging, and cowardly. But traders' accounts also revealed extreme ethnocentrism. According to a trader, the Chinese were "the most vile, the most cowardly and submissive of slaves"; another wrote that whites could bully even Chinese soldiers, whose "silly grunts and menaces mean nothing and are to be disregarded."[54] A prominent theme was the bizarre and peculiar nature of the Chinese in their alleged taste for dogs, cats, and rats; in their music, which was a "mass of detestible discord"; and in their theater, which was "ridiculous or disgracefully obscene." The records, wrote Miller, "portrayed him [the Chinese] as a ludicrous specimen of the human race and [were] not designed to evoke the admiration and respect for Chinese culture." The focus on the exotic, on "strange and curious objects," was complemented by a featuring of vice—gambling and prostitution—and practices showing the "moral debasement" of the people, including idolatry, polygamy, and infanticide. The Chinese, wrote a trader contemptuously, are "grossly superstitious . . . most depraved and vicious: gambling is universal . . . they use pernicious drugs . . . are gross gluttons," and are "a people refined in cruelty, bloodthirsty, and inhuman."[55]

The journey begun in New England and continuing around South America's Cape Horn was just the start of America's masculine thrust westward toward Asia's open shores.[56] Like those Yankee China trade vessels, the Conestoga wagons and prairie schooners pushed their way through "vacant, virgin" land to the Pacific and in the process built a continental empire that stretched "from sea to shining sea." In 1879, Robert Louis Stevenson rode the iron rails that bound the nation together, and his account, "Across the Plains: Leaves from the Notebook of an Emigrant between New York and San Francisco," might be read as the great American epic. America was "a sort of promised land" for Americans like Stevenson, who were immigrants from Europe and who found themselves among a diverse lot of fellow passengers, "a babel of bewildered men, women, and children." As the train carried them westward, Stevenson, like Crèvecoeur, described the beauties of the land, where "all times, races, and languages have brought their contribution." That equality, that melting pot, however, was broken at Chicago, at the frontier of civilization, where the travelers were placed on an "emigrant train" that consisted of segregated coaches: one for white men, another for white women and children, and yet another for Chinese. Stevenson reflected upon the hatreds that had prompted that racial, gender, and age segregation as the train "pushed through this unwatered wilderness and haunt of savage tribes." America, he wrote, was the meeting ground, where "hungry Europe and hungry China, each pouring from their gates in search of provender, had here come face to face," and where Europeans had come with preconceived hatreds of the Chinese that had moved them from one field of conflict to another. "They [Europeans] seemed never to have looked at them [Chinese], listened to them, or thought of them, but hated them a priori," observed Stevenson. "The Mongols were their enemies in that cruel and treacherous battle-field of money."[57]

Despite his contempt for those "stupid" (albeit modified) Old World prejudices, prejudices given further license once civilization had been left behind for the "unwatered wilderness" of the frontier, Stevenson was not entirely free of those same perceptions of the Chinese. His fellow Europeans, reported Stevenson, saw the Chinese as physically repulsive, such that the mere sight of them caused "a kind of choking in the throat." "Now, as a matter of fact," admitted the observant Scotsman, "the young Chinese man is so like a large class of European women, that on raising my head and suddenly catching sight of one at a considerable distance, I have for an instant been deceived by the resemblance"—although, he offered, "I do not say it is the most attractive class of our women." And while looking upon the Chinese with "wonder and respect," Stevenson saw them as creatures from "the other" world: "They [the Chinese] walk the earth with us, but it seems they must be of different clay." "They hear the clock strike the same hour, yet surely of a different epoch. They travel by steam conveyance, yet with such a baggage of old Asiatic thoughts and superstitions as might check the locomotive in its course. . . . Heaven knows if we had one common thought or fancy all that way, or whether our eyes, which yet were formed upon the same design, beheld the same world out of the railway windows."[58]

Stevenson's view of the Chinese as "different clay" might have been conditioned by his European origins, but Herman Melville, surely no stranger to the American metaphysics of race relations, cannot be similarly dismissed. His retelling of a story by James Hall, "Indian hating.—Some of the sources of this animosity.—Brief account of Col. Moredock," not only offered a stinging critique of inhumanity masked as morality, embodied in the "confidence-man" and Indian-hater John Moredock, but also foresaw, according to Richard Drinnon, that "when the metaphysics of Indian-hating hit salt water it more clearly became the metaphysics of empire-building." Although believed to be a barbarian, predicted Melville, "the backwoodsman would seem to America what Alexander was to Asia—captain in the vanguard of conquering civilization." Melville, Drinnon points out, correctly saw that the relentless westward advance of the Indian-hater would, after reaching the Pacific Ocean, continue on to Asia, and in Melville's words, his hatreds would ride "upon the advance as the Polynesian upon the comb of the surf."[59] And like Alexander, who had sought to conquer all of India, the "backwoodsman," the "barbarian," "could not endure to think of putting an end to the war so long as he could find enemies."

In truth, America's manifest destiny was "an additional chapter" in the Orientalist text of Europe's "dominating, restructuring, and having authority over" Asia. In July 1853, Commodore Matthew C. Perry pushed into Tokyo Bay carrying a letter from the U.S. president demanding the opening of trade relations. That "opening" of Japan was accomplished, like the "opening" of the American West, with the iron fist of industry and the might of military arms; Perry's "black ships" under full steam power and with matchless guns were complements of the iron horses and Kentucky rifles of the backwoodsmen, who were simultaneously taming the wilderness. Reflecting on the second period of America's manifest destiny, after the annexation of the Philippines and Hawai'i in 1898 and after Secretary of State John Hay's pronouncement of an "Open Door" with China, Theodore Roosevelt declared: "Of course our whole national history has been one of expansion. . . . That the barbarians recede or are conquered, with the attendant fact that peace follows their retrogression or conquest, is due solely to the power of the mighty civilized races which have not lost the fighting instinct, and which by their expansion are gradually bringing peace into the red wastes where the barbarian peoples of the world hold sway."[60]

The filling of those "red wastes," those empty spaces, was, of course, the white man's burden. John Hay, a son of the frontier of sorts, sought "to draw close the bonds" that united "the two Anglo-Saxon peoples" of Britain and America in a common destiny and mission: "All of us who think cannot but see that there is a sanction like that of religion which binds us to a sort of partnership in the beneficent work of the world. Whether we will it or not, we are associated in that work by the very nature of things, and no man and no group of men can prevent it. We are bound by a tie which we did not forge and which we cannot break; we are the joint Ministers of the same sacred mission of liberty and progress, charged with duties which we cannot evade by the imposition of irresistible hands."[61] China's "Open Door" and America's "splendid little war" with Spain, observed Hay, were of that beneficent quality. "We have done the Chinks a great service," wrote Hay of his policy, "which they don't seem inclined to recognize," and he admonished the next generation of backwoodsmen, "as the children of Israel encamping by the sea were bidden, to Go Forward." Indeed, noted Hay, America had gone forward and had charted a "general plan of opening a field of enterprise in those distant regions where the Far West becomes the Far East."[62] In becoming a Pacific power, America had fulfilled a European people's destiny and, like Columbus, had gone ashore, unfurled the royal banner, offered a prayer of thanksgiving, and taken possession of the land. America's Far West had become the Far East, where Indian-fighters became "goo-goo" fighters in the Philippines and Indian savages became Filipino "niggers," and where a war of extermination was pursued with no less determination than the chastising of the Iroquois urged by George Washington in 1779, when he instructed Major General John Sullivan: "but you will not, by any means, listen to any overture of peace before the total ruin of their settlement is effected. . . . Our future security will be in their inability to injure us . . . and in the terror with which the severity of the chastizement they receive will inspire them."[63]

Asians, it must be remembered, did not come to America; Americans went to Asia. Asians, it must be remembered, did not come to take the wealth of America; Americans went to take the wealth of Asia. Asians, it must be remembered, did not come to conquer and colonize America; Americans went to conquer and colonize Asia. And the matter of the "when and where" of Asian American history is located therein, in Europe's eastward and westward thrusts, engendered, transformative, expansive. But another context of the "when and where" is the historical moment in America where Prospero ruled over the hideous, the imperative Caliban. Asia not only provided markets for goods and outposts for military and naval bases, but also supplied pools of cheap labor for the development of America's "plantations" along its southern and western frontiers. In 1848, Aaron H. Palmer, a counselor to the U.S. Supreme Court, anticipated the nation's destiny in the American southwest and Asia when he predicted that San Francisco would become "the great emporium of our commerce on the Pacific; and so soon as it is connected by a railroad with the Atlantic States, will become the most eligible point of departure for steamers to . . . China." To build that rail link and to bring the fertile valleys of California under cultivation, Palmer favored the importation of Chinese workers, explaining that "no people in all the East are so well adapted for clearing wild lands and raising every species of agricultural product . . . as the Chinese."[64]

It was within those American "plantations" that Asians joined Africans, Indians, and Latinos in labor, making Prospero's fire, fetching his wood, and serving in offices that profited him. It was within those "plantations" that Europeans tutored Asians, Africans, Indians, and Latinos and gave meaning to their gabble. And it was within those "plantations" that Asians, Africans, Indians, and Latinos rose up in rebellion against their bondage and struck for their freedom.

In 1885, a Chinese American described his reaction to being solicited for funds for erecting the Statue of Liberty. He felt honored to be counted among "citizens in the cause of liberty," he wrote,

> but the word liberty makes me think of the fact that this country is the land of liberty for men of all nations except the Chinese. I consider it an insult to us Chinese to call on us to contribute toward the building in this land a pedestal for a statue of liberty. That statue represents liberty holding a torch which lights the passage of those of all nations who come into this country. But are the Chinese allowed to come? As for the Chinese who are here, are they allowed to enjoy liberty as men of all other nationalities enjoy it?[65]

For China's prodemocracy students in 1989 and for Asians in America, the "goddess of liberty," featured so prominently by the American news media, situated squarely within the mainstream, and lifting up her torch above the masses in Tiananmen Square, was not a symbol of liberation. Instead, their true symbol, relegated to the background as the camera panned the crowd, situated inconspicuously along the margins, was the declaration emblazoned by the Chinese students on the banners they waved, the shirts they wore, and the fliers they distributed: the words were "We Shall Overcome."

Notes

1. I have taken the title of this chapter from a narrative history of African American women by Paula Giddings, *When and Where I Enter: The Impact of Black Women on Race and Sex in America* (New York: William Morrow, 1984).
2. Poems published in Him Mark Lai, Genny Lim, and Judy Yung, *Island: Poetry and History of Chinese Immigrants on Angel Island, 1910–1940* (Seattle: University of Washington Press, 1991), 34, 52.

3. A third island, Sullivan's Island, was the point of entry for many African slaves during the eighteenth century. "Sullivan's Island," wrote historian Peter H. Wood, "the sandy spit on the northeast edge of Charlestown harbor where incoming slaves were briefly quarantined, might well be viewed as the Ellis Island of black Americans." Peter H. Wood, *Black Majority: Negroes in Colonial South Carolina from 1670 through the Stono Rebellion* (New York: Alfred A. Knopf, 1975), xiv.

4. The text of the 1882 Chinese Exclusion Act is quoted in Cheng-Tsu Wu, ed., *"Chink!" A Documentary History of Anti-Chinese Prejudice in America* (New York: World Publishing, 1972), 70–75.

5. John Higham, *Send These to Me: Jews and Other Immigrants in Urban America* (New York: Atheneum, 1975), 71–72, 74, 75.

6. Ibid., 75, 77, 79.

7. J. Hector St. John de Crèvecoeur, *Letters from an American Farmer* (New York: Fox, Duffield & Co., 1904), 54–55.

8. Higham, *Send These to Me*, 3.

9. Ibid., 199.

10. Giddings, *When and Where I Enter*, 81–82.

11. For Hippocrates, Asia meant Asia Minor, or the area between the Mediterranean and Black Seas. Depending upon who was writing and when, Asia meant variously Asia Minor (or Anatolia), the Levant, Southwest Asia, Central Asia, or India. Generally, during the fifth and fourth centuries B.C.E. the Greeks called the Persians "Asians."

12. *Hippocrates*, trans. W.H.S. Jones (Cambridge: Harvard University Press, 1923), 1:105–133.

13. *The Politics of Aristotle*, trans. Benjamin Jowett (Oxford: Clarendon Press, 1885), 96, 218, 248. "Barbarians," it should be noted, could refer to Europeans, such as Thracians and Illyrians, as well as to Asians.

14. Arrian's *History of the Expedition of Alexander the Great, and Conquest of Persia*, trans. John Rooke (London: W. McDowall, 1813), 112, 117, 123, 146.

15. Ibid., 42. Arrian was an Asian from Nicomedia in northern Turkey and wrote in Greek, despite serving as a Roman governor. See also Alexander's contrast of intelligent Greeks with Persian and Indian hordes in the influential work of late Greek literature *The Greek Alexander Romance*, trans. Richard Stoneman (London: Penguin Books, 1991), 105, 128, 181; and a similar representation of Persians by Romans during the third century C.E. in Michael H. Dodgeon and Samuel N. C. Lieu, comps. and eds., *The Roman Eastern Frontier and the Persian Wars (A.D. 226–363): A Documentary History* (London: Routledge, 1991), 19, 26.

16. Edward W. Said, *Orientalism* (New York: Random House, 1978), 1; and Mary B. Campbell, *The Witness and the Other World: Exotic European Travel Writing, 400–1600* (Ithaca, N.Y.: Cornell University Press, 1988), 3.

17. Campbell, *Witness*, 51, 63–65, 68–69, 84. See also *Greek Alexander Romance*, 124.

18. Campbell, *Witness*, 7–8, 21, 26, 44–45.

19. Ibid., 3; and Said, *Orientalism*, 1. See also Christopher Miller, *Blank Darkness: Africanist Discourse in French* (Chicago: University of Chicago Press, 1985), who contends that Africa was Europe's Other.

20. Said, *Orientalism*, 1, 59, 62, 72, 74, 86, 207–208, 211, 222. For a cautionary critique of Said, see Lisa Lowe, *Critical Terrains: French and British Orientalisms* (Ithaca, N.Y.: Cornell University Press, 1991).

21. The contest between Greece and Asia was a major theme in ancient Greek literature, as seen in the writings of Homer, Aeschylus, Euripides, Xenophon, and many others. The work of Herodotus, written in the fifth century B.C.E., is perhaps the best known example of this genre. I simply present a selection of the evidence.

22. *Arrian's History*, 220.

23. Ibid., 112–113, 181, 205. Arrian was a Stoic philosopher, which accounts for his stress on mind over body.

24. Page duBois, *Centaurs and Amazons: Women and the Pre-history of the Great Chain of Being* (Ann Arbor: University of Michigan Press, 1982), 4–5.

25. Quoted in W. Blake Tyrrell, *Amazons: A Study in Athenian Mythmaking* (Baltimore: Johns Hopkins University Press, 1984), 15–16. For another view of Amazons and their relation to Greek patriarchy, see duBois, *Centaurs and Amazons*, 4–5, 34, 70.

26. On the ambiguities of Greek attributions of male and female and the rhetoric of discourse and reality of practice, see John J. Winkler, *The Constraints of Desire: The Anthropology of Sex and Gender in Ancient Greece* (New York: Routledge, 1990).

27. Campbell, *Witness*, 88–89.

28. David Morgan, *The Mongols* (London: Basil Blackwell, 1986), 56–57.

29. Campbell, *Witness*, 114.

30. *The Travels of Marco Polo the Venetian* (London: J. M. Dent, 1908), xi.

31. Henry H. Hart, *Marco Polo: Venetian Adventurer* (Norman: University of Oklahoma Press, 1967), 117, 135.

32. *The Travels of Sir John Mandeville* (London: Macmillan, 1900), 127–128.

33. Campbell, *Witness*, 10, 161; and *The Log of Christopher Columbus*, trans. Robert H. Fuson (Camden, Maine: International Marine Publishing, 1987), 25.

34. *Log of Christopher Columbus*, 51.

35. Ibid., 75–76.

36. Campbell, *Witness*, 171, 247. Walter Raleigh also believed the Orinoco led to paradise (ibid., 246–247).

37. *Log of Christopher Columbus*, 102.

38. Ibid., 145, 173; and "Letter of Columbus," in *The Four Voyages of Columbus*, ed. and trans. Cecil Jane (New York: Dover Publications, 1988), 10.

39. Campbell, *Witness*, 166.

40. Albert Memmi, *The Colonizer and the Colonized* (Boston: Beacon Press, 1967), 71.

41. Wilcomb E. Washburn, "Columbus: On and off the Reservation," *National Review*, 5 October 1992, 57–58.

42. See chapter 5 for an elaboration of this theme. [Editors' note: This article is an excerpt from Gary Okihiro's *Margins and Mainstreams: Asians in American History and Culture* (University of Washington Press, 1994); this note refers to a chapter in Okihiro's book.]

43. Stuart Creighton Miller, *The Unwelcome Immigrant: The American Image of the Chinese, 1785–1882* (Berkeley and Los Angeles: University of California Press, 1969), 11–14.

44. Dwight W. Hoover, *The Red and the Black* (Chicago: Rand McNally, 1976), 4.

45. I merely allude to the vast literature on the history of racism and racist thought and cite as particularly helpful Arthur O. Lovejoy, *The Great Chain of Being: A Study of the History of an Idea* (Cambridge: Harvard University Press, 1936); and George L. Mosse, *Toward the Final Solution: A History of European Racism* (New York: Howard Fertig, 1978).

46. Hoover, *Red and Black*, 1–2; and David Brion Davis, *Slavery and Human Progress* (New York: Oxford University Press, 1984), 52–57.

47. *The Complete Works of William Shakespeare* (New York: Walter J. Black, 1937), 2–6; Ronald T. Takaki, *Iron Cages: Race and Culture in Nineteenth-Century America* (New York: Alfred A. Knopf, 1979), 11–12; and Leslie A. Fielder, *The Return of the Vanishing American* (New York: Stein & Day, 1968), 42–49. See O. Mannoni, *Prospero and Caliban: The Psychology of Colonization*, trans. Pamela Powesland (London: Methuen, 1956), for a more complex reading of the play, esp. 105–106.

48. Hoover, *Red and Black*, 35–37.

49. See Winthrop Jordan, *White over Black* (Chapel Hill: University of North Carolina Press, 1968), for British and American racial attitudes toward Indians and Africans from 1550 to 1812.

50. Frederick M. Binder, *The Color Problem in Early National America as Viewed by John Adams, Jefferson, and Jackson* (The Hague: Mouton, 1968), 83.

51. Quoted in Richard Drinnon, *Facing West: The Metaphysics of Indian-Hating and Empire-Building* (New York: New American Library, 1980), 65.

52. Ibid., 80–81, 98; and Jordan, *White over Black*, 475–481.

53. Drinnon, *Facing West*, 81.

54. Miller, *Unwelcome Immigrant*, 21, 25–27, 34.

55. Ibid., 27–32, 35.

56. The phrase "masculine thrust toward Asia" is from the title of chapter 11 of Takaki's *Iron Cages*, 253.

57. Robert Louis Stevenson, *Across the Plains, with Other Memories and Essays* (New York: Charles Scribner's Sons, 1900), 1, 11, 26–27, 48, 60, 62; and Drinnon, *Facing West*, 219–221.

58. Stevenson, *Across the Plains*, 62, 65–66.

59. Herman Melville, *The Confidence-Man: His Masquerade*, ed. Elizabeth S. Foster (New York: Hendricks House, 1954), lxv–lxx, 164, 334–341; and Drinnon, *Facing West*, 214–215.

60. Quoted in Drinnon, *Facing West*, 232.

61. Ibid., 267.

62. Ibid., 277, 278.

63. Ibid., 331.

64. Takaki, *Iron Cages*, 229.

65. Renqiu Yu, *To Save China, To Save Ourselves: The Chinese Hand Laundry Alliance of New York* (Philadelphia: Temple University Press, 1992), 199–200.

NEITHER BLACK NOR WHITE

Angelo N. Ancheta

In his 1989 feature film *Do the Right Thing*, filmmaker Spike Lee explores urban race relations by tracing the interplay of a set of characters during a sweltering day in the Bedford-Stuyvesant section of Brooklyn, New York. Lee's film tracks the life of a neighborhood during a twenty-four-hour span, punctuated by interracial tensions that culminate in violence and rioting.

A climactic scene near the end of the film features the movement of an angry mob outraged by the killing of a black youth by white police officers. The crowd's rage is turned on Sal's Famous Pizzeria, a neighborhood restaurant owned and operated by a white family. After Mookie, Sal's only black employee, throws a garbage can through the front window, others in the crowd rush into the restaurant, ransacking and setting fire to it. As flames engulf the pizzeria, the mob turns toward a new target: the grocery store across the street owned by Korean immigrants.

Tensions build as three men lead the others to confront the store's owner, Sonny. Anxious and confused, Sonny swings a broom wildly through the air in a desperate attempt to hold back the crowd. He shouts out:

> I not white! I not white! I not white!
> I black! I BLACK!

Several people laugh and scoff at Sonny's pleas. He responds, "You, me— same!" One of the men retorts incredulously: "Same? *Me* black! Open your eyes!" But others in the crowd begin sympathizing with the grocer. They nod their heads in agreement with Sonny and move closer to restrain the men who first challenged him. Sonny extends an open hand in friendship, as another man says, "He's all right. He's black." Tensions subside, and the crowd turns and moves on.

Real life is rarely as tidy as cinematic fiction, but the imagery and dialogue from *Do the Right Thing* offer a glimpse into the potential violence that many Asian immigrants encounter in the nation's inner cities. And since the film's original release, reality has proved to be far more dramatic than fiction. The country witnessed the destruction of thousands of Asian American-owned businesses during the civil unrest in Los Angeles and other cities in the spring of 1992, following the acquittal of Los Angeles Police Department officers on trial for the beating of Rodney King.

The scene illustrates the volatility of urban race relations, but it also encapsulates some of the distinctive problems that Asian Americans face as a racial group. On one level, the idealistic and convenient ending to the mob scene offers an insight into the parallels between Asian Americans and African Americans. The grocer identified himself as black and many in the crowd agreed with him because Asian Americans and African Americans share similar histories and experiences with racial subordination in the United States.

On another level, though, the scene portrays a more complex dynamic: the grocer, caught in the middle of a race riot, invoked an inaccurate but successful appeal to he treated as if black. The crowd initially equated the Korean grocer with the white pizzeria owner because of his store ownership and his economic stature within the neighborhood. But the grocer took on a new identity when confronted by the crowd. The entreaty "I black" placed him squarely on one side of the conflict, resolving any ambiguity about his alignment within the neighborhood's racial matrix.

The grocer's transformation is an extreme example but it illuminates a dilemma that Asian Americans typically encounter in matters involving race. When discourse is limited to antagonisms between black and white, Asian Americans often find themselves in a racial limbo, marginalized or unrecognized as full participants. The assertion of other experiences, different from black or white, can be misunderstood, become trivial or ineffectual, or even prove to be dangerous. Within a less perilous context, the grocer might have been expected to declare a different identity—Korean or Asian American. But placed within a conflict that had been reduced to black versus white, the grocer assumed the safety of a black identity.

RACE RELATIONS IN BLACK AND WHITE

"Are you black or are you white?" For Asian Americans the obvious answer would seem to be "neither." Yet, when questions of race relations arise, a dichotomy between black and white typically predominates. Formed largely through inequities and conflicts between blacks and whites, discourse on race relations provides minimal space to articulate experiences independent of a black–white framework. The representation of Asian Americans is especially elusive and often shifts, depending on context, between black and white.

Popular works on race suggest that expositions of Asian American experiences are peripheral, more often confined to the footnotes than expounded in the primary analyses. Studs Terkel's *Race* frames race relations through a dialogue about blacks and whites, confined almost entirely to the opinions of blacks and whites. Andrew Hacker's *Two Nations: Black and White, Separate, Hostile, Unequal* contains, as its subtitle implies, extensive discussions of inequality between blacks and whites, but only a minimal analysis of inequality among other racial groups.[1] The controversial books *The Bell Curve*, by Charles Murray and Richard Herrnstein, and *The End of Racism*, by Dinesh D'Souza, go to considerable length to expound arguments that blacks as a group are less intelligent than whites and suffer from cultural pathologies that inhibit advancement to the level of whites. When discussed at all, Asian Americans are offered as a "model minority" group, to be contrasted with blacks and likened to whites because of their higher IQ scores and cultural values stressing family, hard work, and educational achievement.

News media portrayals of racial minorities suffer from the same tendency to reduce race relations to a simple black–white equation. Popular television news shows such as ABC's *Nightline* offer recurring programming on race relations, but typically confine their analyses to black–white relations. Public opinion polls on race and civil rights usually exclude Asian Americans as subjects or as participants, or reduce them to the category of "Other." News coverage of racially charged events is most often framed by black versus white antagonisms. The murder trial of O. J. Simpson, for instance, provoked extensive dialogue on the impact of race and racism on the criminal justice system, but excluded for the most part any perspectives from Asian Americans or Latinos, which is ironic for a trial held in Los Angeles, a city where half of the population is Asian American and Latino.[2]

Public policies that reflect and reinforce race relations also approach race in terms of black and white. Historically, the major landmarks denoting both racial subordination and progress in racial rights have been measured through the experiences of African Americans. Slavery and its abolition, the black codes and the Reconstruction-era constitutional amendments, Jim Crow laws and the desegregation cases culminating in *Brown v. Board of Education*, the struggles of the civil rights movement and the federal legislation of the 1960s—these are the familiar signs that have dominated the landscape of civil rights in the United States. Debates on affirmative action have occasionally shone the spotlight on Asian Americans, but almost exclusively as unintended victims of affirmative action in higher education. Problems of ongoing racial discrimination and inequality among Asian American communities are largely ignored.

Not that focusing on black experiences is unjustified. African Americans have been the largest racial minority group in the United States since the country's birth, and continue to endure the effects of racial subordination. By any social or economic measure, African Americans suffer extensive inequality because of race. In describing the African American experience, the statement of the Kerner Commission resonates as strongly today as it did in 1968: "Our nation is moving toward two societies, one black, one white—separate but unequal."[3] But to say that our nation is moving toward two separate and unequal societies, however disconcerting, is fundamentally incomplete. Underlying the Kerner Commission's statement is the assumption that our nation's cities are divisible along a single racial axis. Cleavages between black and white persist but American race relations are not an exclusively black–white phenomenon and never have been. The civil unrest in Los Angeles in 1992 is just one example of the intricacy of contemporary racial dynamics, shedding light on a host of race-based and class-based conflicts, as well as an array of racial and ethnic groups—blacks, whites, Asians, Latinos—who were both victims and victimizers.

BLACK AND WHITE BY ANALOGY

Dualism is a convenient lens through which to view the world. Black or white, male or female, straight or gay—the categories help us frame reality and make sense of it. In matters of race, a black–white dichotomy has been the dominant model, based primarily on the fact that African Americans have been the largest and most conspicuous nonwhite racial group in the United States. But the legal history of the United States is punctuated by the abridgment of rights among other racial and ethnic groups such as Asian Americans, and the country's changing demographics are mandating new perspectives based on the experiences of immigrants. Still, the black–white model is the regnant paradigm in both social and legal discussions of race.

How can Asian Americans fit within a black–white racial paradigm? Historian Gary Okihiro poses the question this way: "Is yellow black or white?" Okihiro suggests that Asian Americans have been "near-blacks" in the past and "near-whites" in the present, but that "[y]ellow is emphatically neither white nor black."[4] Recognizing the dominance of the black–white paradigm in the law, Frank Wu adopts a similar view proposing that Asian Americans have been forced to fit within race relations discourse through analogy to either whites or blacks. He posits that American society and its legal system have conceived of racial groups as whites, blacks, honorary whites, or constructive (legal jargon for "implied") blacks.[5]

For most of the nation's history, Asian Americans have been treated primarily as constructive blacks. Asian Americans for decades endured many of the same disabilities of racial subordination as African Americans—racial violence, segregation, unequal access to public institutions and discrimination in housing, employment, and education. The courts even classified Asian Americans as if they were black. In the mid-nineteenth century, the California Supreme Court held in *People v. Hall* that Chinese immigrants were barred from testifying in court under a statute prohibiting the testimony of blacks, by reasoning that "black" was a generic term encompassing all nonwhites, including Chinese: "[T]he words 'Black person' . . . must be taken as contradistinguished from White, and necessarily excludes all races other than the Caucasian."[6]

Similarly, in *Gong Lum v. Rice*, decided twenty-seven years before *Brown v. Board of Education*, the United States Supreme Court upheld the constitutionality of sending Asian American students to segregated schools. Comparing its earlier rulings on the "separate but equal" doctrine, the Court stated: "Most of the cases cited arose, it is true, over the establishment of separate schools as between white pupils and black pupils, but we can not think that the question is any different or that any different result can be reached . . . where the issue is as between white pupils and the pupils of the yellow races."[7] In the eyes of the Supreme Court, yellow equaled black, and neither equaled white.

In more recent years, the inclusion of Asian Americans in civil rights laws and race-conscious remedial programs has relied on the historical parallels between the experiences of Asian Americans and African Americans. The civil rights protections available to Asian Americans are most often contingent upon the rights granted to African Americans. Civil rights laws that apply to Asian Americans, as constructive blacks, can usually trace their origins to a legislative intent to protect African Americans from racial discrimination.

The treatment of Asian Americans as "honorary whites" is more unusual. In the Reconstruction-era South, Asian Americans were initially afforded a status above blacks for a period of time during the nineteenth century; Louisiana, for example, counted Chinese as whites for census purposes before 1870.[8] The status was short-lived: the Chinese were soon reduced to constructive black status under systems of racial segregation. More contemporary race relations controversies appear to have elevated Asian Americans to the status of honorary whites, particularly in the minds of those who oppose race-conscious remedies such as affirmative action. Asian Americans are often omitted from protection in affirmative action programs as a matter of course, lumped with whites even in contexts where Asian Americans still face racial discrimination and remain underrepresented.

The rigidity of the legal system's treatment of race as either black or white is evident in civil rights litigation filed by Asian American plaintiffs in the earlier half of this century. Unlike the fictional grocer in Spike Lee's *Do the Right Thing*, Asian Americans sought, quite unsuccessfully, to be classified as white under the law, in recognition of the social and legal stigmas attached to being categorized as black. Gong Lum, for example, argued that his daughter Martha should not have to attend the school for colored children in Mississippi because "'[c]olored' describes only one race, and that is the negro."[9] Because his daughter was "pure Chinese," Gong Lum argued that she ought to have been classified with whites rather than blacks. The Court rejected this reasoning and held that yellow was black when it came to segregation.

During the late nineteenth and early twentieth centuries, Asian Americans sought to be classified as white in attempts to become naturalized citizens.[10] Congress enacted naturalization legislation in 1790 to limit citizenship to "free white persons." After the Civil War, the law was amended to allow persons of "African nativity" or "African descent" to naturalize, but Congress rejected extending naturalization to Asian immigrants. Asian immigrants sought relief through the courts, but had little success arguing that they were white: Burmese, Chinese, Filipino, Hawaiian, Japanese, and Korean plaintiffs were all held to be nonwhite; mixed-race plaintiffs who were half-white and half-Asian were also held to be nonwhite.[11] The United States Supreme Court laid to rest any questions about the racial bar in *Ozawa v. United States*, ruling that Japanese immigrants were not white, and in *United States v. Thind*, ruling that Asian Indian immigrants were not white.[12] Asian immigrants were prohibited by statute from naturalizing through the 1940s, and the racial bar on naturalization was not repealed until 1952.

From today's vantage point, these attempts by Asian immigrants to he classified as white may seem absurd and even subordinative, because they symbolically pushed blacks down the social ladder relative to whites and Asians. But when the legal paradigm limits options to black or white and nothing else, curious and unseemly choices inevitably arise. The solution, of course, is to develop and rely on theories that comprehend the complexity of race relations, which includes discerning that the experiences of Asian Americans are not the same as the experiences of African Americans.

RACISM IN CONTEXT: ANTI-ASIAN VIOLENCE

To better understand the experiences of Asian Americans, consider how racial subordination operates within a specific context: anti-Asian violence. Racial violence is not a new phenomenon, and the histories of all racial minorities include extensive violence, whether it is the genocide of Native American tribes during the expansion of the United States, the terrorism against blacks in the South, the military conquest and ongoing border violence against Latinos in the Southwest, or the attacks on Asian immigrant laborers in the West. Incidents of anti-Asian violence reveal unique themes of prejudice and discrimination that illustrate the dynamics of racism against Asian Americans.[13]

Chronicling the growth of anti-Asian violence in recent years, a 1986 report by the United States Commission on Civil Rights concluded that "anti-Asian activity in the form of violence, harassment intimidation, and vandalism has been reported across the nation."[14] The Asian American Justice Center (formerly the National Asian Pacific American Legal Consortium) has measured anti-Asian violence since the 1990s and has tracked a wide variety of crimes, including graffiti, vandalism, cross burnings, property damage, arson, hate mail, intimidation, physical assaults, homicides, and police misconduct. Calculating figures is difficult because of underreporting—many immigrants face language barriers or are fearful of the police—and because of major weaknesses in law enforcement's compilation of statistics. The numbers that are available are sobering. During the eight-year period from 1995 to 2002, audits of anti-Asian violence by the Asian American Justice Center reported a nationwide total of 3,581 incidents against Asian Americans and Pacific Islanders, with at least 400 incidents logged for almost every year during the period.[15]

The most notorious episode of recent anti-Asian violence was the killing of Vincent Chin in 1982. Chin, a twenty-seven-year-old Chinese American, was celebrating his upcoming wedding at a Detroit bar when he was approached by Ronald Ebens and Michael Nitz, two white automobile factory workers. Ebens and Nitz thought Chin was Japanese and blamed him for the loss of jobs in the automobile industry. After calling Chin a "jap," the two men chased him out of the bar. They eventually caught Chin and proceeded to beat him repeatedly with a baseball hat. Chin died from his injuries a few days later. Ebens and Nitz each pleaded guilty to manslaughter but received only probation and a fine.

Ebens was later convicted of federal civil rights violations, but his conviction was overturned on appeal and he was acquitted on retrial. Neither Ebens nor Nitz spent any time in prison for the killing.

A similar incident occurred in 1989 in Raleigh, North Carolina. Jim (Ming Hai) Loo had been playing pool with several friends when he was approached by Robert Piche and his brother Lloyd Piche, who began calling Loo and his friends "chinks" and "gooks" and blaming them for the death of American soldiers in Vietnam. Once outside, Robert Piche pistol-whipped Loo on the back of the head, causing Loo to fall onto a broken bottle that pierced his brain. Loo died from his injuries two days later. Robert Piche was convicted and sentenced to thirty-seven years in prison; Lloyd Piche was sentenced to six months in prison by a state court, and sentenced to four years in prison for federal civil rights violations.

Another tragic illustration of anti-Asian violence is the multiple killings of Asian American children at the Cleveland Elementary School in Stockton, California, in 1989. Patrick Purdy used an AK-47 assault rifle to spray bullets into a crowded schoolyard, killing five children and wounding over twenty others before turning the gun on himself. Although initially labeled the product of a disturbed mind obsessed with guns and the military, the shootings were later proved to be motivated by racial hatred. A report issued by the California attorney general's office found that Purdy targeted the school because it was heavily populated by Southeast Asian children.[16]

Perpetrators who are affiliated with hate groups have been responsible for many anti-Asian crimes. During the early 1980s, when tensions erupted between Vietnamese immigrant fishermen and native-born fishermen in several coastal states, the Ku Klux Klan engaged in extensive harassment and violence against Vietnamese fishermen along the Gulf Coast of Texas. Federal litigation was required to end a pattern of threats, cross burnings, arsons, and shootings.[17] In 1990, Hung Truong, a fifteen-year-old Vietnamese boy living in Houston, was attacked by two men who were later identified as white supremacist "skinheads." After following Truong and his friends as they walked down the street, the two assailants jumped out of their car, one wielding a club, and shouted "White power." They chased Truong and proceeded to kick and beat him, even as he pleaded for his life. The two men admitted at trial that they attacked Truong because he was Vietnamese.

In August 1999, Joseph Ileto, a Filipino American postal worker, was gunned down in California's San Fernando Valley by Buford Furrow, Jr., a white supremacist who earlier the same day had riddled the North Valley Jewish Community Center with over seventy rounds from a semi-automatic weapon and wounded several individuals, including three small children. Linked to anti-Semitic and white supremacist groups, Furrow shot Ileto nine times and admitted that he had targeted Ileto because he was a "chink or spic," terms that were no doubt tied to Furrow's perception that an individual like Ileto was somehow less than fully American. Ironically, Ileto was a wearing a clear symbol of membership in American society—the uniform of a U.S. Postal Service mail carrier—at the time he was killed. Pleading guilty to avoid the imposition of a federal death penalty,

Furrow was ultimately sentenced to multiple life sentences without possibility of parole.[18]

More common, however, are incidents that do not involve formal hate groups and that occur in day-to-day interactions among people at work, in schools, at home, and on the street. Here are some examples, all of which occurred during 2002:

- A Japanese American man in Rancho Santa Margarita, California was attacked in his front yard by a perpetrator who threw eggs at him and shouted "You dirty Jap!" while leaving the scene.
- While stalled in traffic, a Korean American woman, along with her young son, were approached by a man who slapped the woman, asked her if she was Korean several times, and shouted: "Why don't you go fuck some Japanese bastard?," "What are you doing in this country?," "Go back to your country," and "Go back to where you came from."
- In a supermarket parking lot in Fort Lee, New Jersey, a Korean American woman was verbally assaulted by a couple, one of whom yelled, "Where did you learn to drive? You chink!" After confronting the couple, the woman was threatened by another customer who yelled, "Yeah, go back to your own country!"
- While leaving a casino in Lake Tahoe, Nevada, three Chinese American families were verbally and physically assaulted by an individual who, after already having confronted a Latino security guard, shouted out, "This is America, you fucking chinks. Do you want some of me?" During the perpetrator's detention by security guards, he told one of the guards: "Hey man, I can respect you. Not like these fucking spics and slant-eyes who are just there to take our money."
- At a business in Los Angeles, a perpetrator brandished a knife and told a South Asian American victim, "I don't like Indians or Pakistanis and if you don't go back to your country, I'll kill you."
- A Filipino American's tax business in Castaic, California was vandalized by an unknown suspect who wrote in black ink on the doors of the business: "Fuck you Asians."
- In Beverly Hills, California, a South Asian American man working as a restaurant valet was accosted by an individual who called the man an "Indian mother fucker" and asked "Are you a terrorist?" before attempting to assault the victim.[19]

Even the virtual world of computer networks has been the site of anti-Asian intimidation. In September 1996, a threatening electronic message was sent to about sixty students at the University of California, Irvine—a college campus whose undergraduate student population is approximately one-half Asian American—accusing Asians of being responsible for all crimes on campus, ordering them to leave the university, and threatening to hunt them down and kill them if they did not leave. The e-mail was signed "Asian-hater."[20]

Many incidents of anti-Asian violence arise from conflicts among racial minorities. During the 1990s, Asian American tenants in San Francisco's public housing projects—primarily Southeast Asian refugees and their families—were subjected to harassment and violence by African American tenants. Inadequate institutional policies, including poor overall security and a flawed racial integration strategy, aggravated cultural differences and tensions among the tenants, resulting in intimidation and numerous assaults. Many families feared for their lives and became prisoners in their own homes, while others moved out of public housing altogether.[21]

Anti-Asian violence is even linked to political rhetoric and public policy making. During the 1994 campaign for California's Proposition 187, the ballot initiative designed to restrict the rights of undocumented immigrants, racial rhetoric and literature abounded. In Los Angeles, for example, mailboxes were stuffed with flyers that supported the passage of Proposition 187 and stated: "WE NEED A *REAL* BORDER. FIRST WE GET THE SPICS, THEN THE GOOKS, AND AT LAST WE GET THE NIGGERS. *DEPORTATION.* THEY'RE ALL GOING HOME." Other flyers pointed to the "invasion" of the "Gooks," stating "they had to go"; references to genocide and "taking back America" were also common.[22]

Attempting to solve anti-Asian violence is as difficult and troubling an exercise as reading the graphic reports of the violence itself. The Asian American Justice Center has identified several problems on both the national and local level that remain unaddressed by government and policy makers: incomplete reporting and monitoring mechanisms among law enforcement; the weakness or absence of hate crimes laws; inadequate training of law enforcement personnel; insufficient funding for civil rights agencies; and major barriers to reporting, including the absence of bilingual services for limited-English–speaking immigrants.[23]

Even where reporting mechanisms and laws are in place, prosecuting hate crimes is problematic: inadequately trained officers may not collect relevant evidence, and prosecutors may be reluctant to press charges because of the difficulty of proving intent on the part of the perpetrator.[24] The problem is compounded when the victims are recent immigrants who may speak little English and may be reluctant to report the crimes because of their distrust of law enforcement. In some areas of the country, such as New York City, police relations have been so poor that police misconduct itself became a major source of anti-Asian violence.[25] At its base, addressing anti-Asian violence means developing explanations and solutions to racial subordination against Asian Americans in general; violence is the most pernicious variation on several general themes.

RACIAL THEMES

Without question, the examples of anti-Asian violence demonstrate that overt racism is still a serious problem for Asian Americans, just as it has been for African Americans and other racial minorities. Some types of anti-Asian violence can thus be explained by treating violence against Asian Americans and other racial minority groups as expressions of white racism. Anti-Asian violence committed by white supremacists targeting anyone who is not white fits within a binary model of race that places all racial minorities in the same category of "nonwhite."

But many incidents of anti-Asian violence suggest that more complex dynamics are at work. Members of one Asian ethnic group are often mistaken for being members of other Asian ethnic groups. Racial and ethnic slurs are interlaced with nativist anti-immigrant rhetoric. Resentment about economic competition, both foreign and domestic, is often implicated. Even hostility rooted in the United States' previous military involvement in Asian countries may be a factor. And a white–nonwhite framework cannot explain racial violence in which members of one nonwhite group victimize members of another nonwhite group. Several basic themes can be gleaned from these and other examples of violence against Asian Americans.

Racialization

One theme is the importance of *racial* categorizing in anti-Asian violence. The killing of Vincent Chin is an example of how anti-Asian violence is racialized: based on his physical appearance, Chin, a Chinese American, was taken to be a Japanese national by his killers, who had made him the focus of their anger and frustration toward Japanese competition in the automobile industry. A perpetrator who makes the race-based generalization that all Asians look alike puts every Asian American at risk, even if the specific antagonisms are targeted against a smaller subset of people.

The attribution of specific ethnic characteristics to anyone falling within the racial category of "Asian" is common in anti-Asian violence. For example, when Luyen Phan Nguyen, a Vietnamese premedical student, was killed in Coral Springs, Florida, in 1992, he was taunted with slurs at a party and later chased down by a group of men who beat and kicked him repeatedly. Among the epithets directed at Nguyen during the beating were "chink," "vietcong," and "sayonara"—three separate and distinct ethnic slurs.

Nativism and Racism

Another theme manifested by anti-Asian violence is the centrality of nativism, which John Higham defines as "intense opposition to an internal minority on the ground of its foreign (i.e., 'un-American') connections."[26] Asian Americans are equated with foreigners, or they are at least presumed to he foreign-born. Race and nativism thus intersect to produce a distinctive form of subordination of Asian Americans—what Robert Chang labels "nativistic racism."[27]

In many incidents, Asian American victims are perceived and categorized as foreigners by their assailants: Vincent Chin was transformed into a Japanese national; Jim Loo became a Vietnamese adversary; immigrant merchants were remade as foreign investors and capitalists. Even Joseph Ileto, wearing the uniform of a U.S. Postal Service mail carrier, was reduced to the position of an outsider. Anti-immigrant epithets such as "Go home!" or "Why don't you go back to your own country?" frequently accompany anti-Asian violence, along with specific racial and ethnic slurs. And under the rubric of foreign outsider, Asian Americans fall into an array of unpopular categories: economic competitor, organized criminal, "illegal alien," or just unwelcome immigrant.

Patriotic racism is a peculiar and especially deep-seated form of nativist racism. American military conflicts against the Japanese during World War II, against Koreans and Chinese during the Korean War, and against the Vietnamese during the Vietnam War have generated intense animosity against Asian Americans. During World War II, the federal government's internment of Japanese Americans, most of whom were United States citizens, reflected patriotic racism at its worst, as a formal governmental policy. Intimidation and violence against Asian Americans is still common on December 7 because of the hostility that arises on the anniversary of the bombing of Pearl Harbor by Japan. And with the ongoing war against terrorism, South Asians, coupled with Arab Americans and Muslim Americans, have been subjected to extensive harassment, intimidation, and discrimination.

Racial Hierarchies and Interracial Conflict

A related theme made evident by anti-Asian violence revolves around the intermediate position that Asian Americans appear to occupy on a social and economic ladder that places whites on top and blacks at the bottom. Black-on-Asian hate crimes often contain strong elements of cultural conflict and nativism—blacks, like whites, treat Asians as foreigners. But black-on-Asian crimes also have strains traceable to resentment over the economic achievements of Asian Americans, particularly their entrepreneurial success in the inner cities. The destruction of Korean immigrants' businesses in 1992, many located in the historically black residential area of South Central Los Angeles, reflected a growing anger against Asian American prosperity.

In this context, the "model minority" stereotype of Asian Americans becomes a two-edged sword, breeding not only incomplete and inaccurate images of Asian American success but resentment and hostility on the part of other racial groups. Racial differentiation often places Asian Americans in a middle position within the racial hierarchy of the United Stares—neither black nor white, and somewhere between black and white.

THE LIMITS OF BLACK AND WHITE

Hate violence is the most extreme form of racial subordination against Asian Americans, but it sheds light on important differences between the subordination of Asian Americans and African Americans. A binary model of race based on relations between blacks and whites cannot fully describe the complex racial matrix that exists in the U.S. In terms of representation, a black–white model ignores or marginalizes the experiences of Asian Americans, Latinos, Native Americans, Arab Americans, and other groups who have extensive histories of discrimination against them. A black–white model discounts the role of immigration in race relations and confines discussion on the impact race has had on anti-immigrant policies that affect the nation's growing Asian American and Latino populations. A black–white model also limits any analysis of the relations and tensions between racial and ethnic groups, which are increasingly significant in urban areas where racial "minorities" are now becoming majorities.

In essence a black–white model fails to recognize that the basic nature of discrimination can differ among racial and ethnic groups. Theories of racial inferiority have been applied, often with violent force, against Asian Americans, just as they have been applied against blacks and other racial minority groups. But the causes of anti-Asian subordination can he traced to other factors as well, including nativism, differences in language and culture, perceptions of Asians as economic competitors, international relations, and past military involvement in Asian countries. Recent immigration from Asian countries has elevated culture and language to prominent places on the race relations landscape, challenging even the integrity of the racial category "Asian American." And the promotion in recent years of a "model minority" racial stereotype, based on the high education levels and incomes of some Asian Americans, represents a curious and distorted form of racism, denying the existence of Asian American poverty and inequality. All of these considerations point to the need for an analysis of race that is very different from the dominant black–white paradigm.

ASIAN AMERICANS AND THE CIVIL RIGHTS LAWS

Racial discourse finds expression in the civil rights laws—the sections of the federal Constitution and the anti-discrimination statutes designed to address racial discrimination. Hate crimes laws, for instance, create special crimes based on racial violence or augment the punishment for violent crimes when there is finding of racially discriminatory intent. Asian Americans are protected by these laws and other antidiscrimination laws from racial discrimination. But, like other manifestations of race, the antidiscrimination laws define most rights within a black–white framework, and the laws contain significant limitations in accommodating the full array of Asian American experiences. When questions of civil rights move beyond a black–white dichotomy, rights and remedies become problematic and Asian Americans are often left without the full protection of the law.

The laws fail to recognize the intersection of race and nativism found in anti-Asian discrimination. When United States–born Asian Americans suffer discrimination as perceived immigrants, antidiscrimination laws may provide relief, but only if the facts permit a finding of discrimination based on categories of race or national origin, and not on the basis of being perceived as a foreigner. Laws such as the Immigration Reform and Control Act of 1986, which requires employers to verify the immigration status of all newly hired employees, have actually caused more discrimination against Asian Americans because of the common perception that all Asian Americans are immigrants and are therefore more likely to be undocumented.

Governmental ambivalence toward anti-immigrant discrimination is a significant weakness in the system of civil rights enforcement. Most antidiscrimination laws protect immigrants from discrimination based on race or national origin, but they lack specific protections for immigrants as immigrants. Attempts to expand civil rights legislation to protect immigrants have been rebuffed in the past. In California, for instance, legislation to protect immigrants from intimidation and hate violence was introduced and passed twice by the state legislature during the mid-1990s, but was vetoed each time by Governor Pete Wilson.

Some laws, such as California's Proposition 187, openly discriminate against undocumented immigrants. Federal laws discriminating against immigrants have gone even further, because the federal laws related to immigration enjoy special constitutional status arising from deference to national sovereignty. Welfare reform legislation enacted in 1996 not only discriminated against undocumented immigrants but against lawful permanent residents—"green card" holders—by stripping many permanent residents of eligibility for entitlement programs such as Food Stamps and Supplemental Security Income, which remained available to citizens. The impact of anti-immigrant policies falls most heavily on Asian Americans and Latinos because of the large numbers of immigrants within their communities and because of the linkage between nativism and race.

Characteristics inherent to immigrants are often ignored in the law. Forms of language-based discrimination dealing with accent and the ability to speak a second language at work are problematic under the civil rights laws, which generally lack explicit protections for language minority groups. Language may serve as a proxy for race, but the nexus between language and race is usually absent in statutes and in judicial interpretations of the law. In addition, the ability to access important government services such as police and fire, emergency health care, and public education is often compromised because of the narrowness of rights related to language and ethnicity.

Within the broader race relations landscape, where Asian Americans are ignored or, increasingly, where they occupy a racial middle ground, civil rights laws are not well equipped to recognize variations in both discrimination and the remedies for discrimination. The "model minority" image often leads to the exclusion of Asian Americans from corrective civil rights programs; Asian Americans are even labeled, along with whites, as victims of affirmative action. The image also leads to antagonisms between Asian Americans and members of other racial groups because of the perceptions of relative inequality and the resentment arising from those perceptions. In the area of interethnic relations, as in other areas, the antidiscrimination laws do not go far enough in recognizing and addressing the problems of Asian Americans.

[handwritten: AshAm are both black & white but also non-black & white]

NOTES

1. Andrew Hacker, *Two Nations: Black and White, Separate, Hostile, Unequal,* rev. ed. (New York: Ballantine Books, 1995). Hacker even suggests that Asian Americans and Latinos, particularly second- and later-generation individuals, are "merging" into the white race, through intermarriage and assimilation (18–19).
2. Ishmael Reed. "O. J. Bias–Black and White," *San Francisco Chronicle,* 10 February 1997, p. A23.
3. *Report of the National Advisory Commission on Civil Disorders* (New York: Bantam, 1968), 1.
4. Gary Y. Okihiro, *Margins and Mainstreams: Asians in American History and Culture* (Seattle and London: University of Washington Press, 1994), 34.
5. Frank H. Wu, "Neither Black nor White: Asian Americans and Affirmative Action," *Boston College Third World Law Journal* 15 (Summer 1995): 225, 249–251.
6. 4 Cal. 399, 404 (1854).

[handwritten: black → exclusion   white → model minority]

7. 275 U.S. 78, 87 (1927).

8. James W. Loewen, *The Mississippi Chinese: Between Black and White* (Cambridge, Mass.: Harvard University Press, 1971).

9. *Gong Lum v. Rice,* 275 U.S. 78, 79 (1927).

10. Ian F. Haney López, *White by Law: The Legal Construction of Race* (New York and London: New York University Press, 1996).

11. Ibid., appendix A. As Haney López notes, a legal strategy arguing for whiteness rather than blackness may have had some tactical advantage at the time, because the 1870 naturalization statute employed a geographic test rather than a racial test of eligibility for blacks: the law referred to persons of "African nativity, or African descent," rather than to "black persons." More likely, though, Asian American plaintiffs sought to distinguish themselves from blacks because of the stigmas attached to being black, and sought the only available alternative—to be classified as white.

12. 260 U.S. 178 (1922); 261 U.S. 204 (1923).

13. Note, "Racial Violence against Asian Americans," *Harvard Law Review* 106 (June 1993): 1926.

14. United States Commission on Civil Rights, *Recent Activities against Citizens and Residents of Asian Descent,* Clearinghouse Publication No. 88 (Washington, D.C., 1986), 5.

15. National Asian Pacific American Legal Consortium, 2002 *Audit of Violence Against Asian Pacific Americans*: Tenth Annual Report (Washington, D.C.: National Asian Pacific American Legal Consortium. 2004), 11.

16. Nelson Kempsky, *A Report to Attorney General John K. Van de Kemp on Patrick Purdy and the Cleveland School Killings* (Sacramento: California Department of Justice, Office of the Attorney General, 1989).

17. *Vietnamese Fishermen's Association v. Knights of the Ku Klux Klan,* S43 F. Supp. 198 (S.D. Tex. 1982) (permanent injunction); *Vietnamese Fishermen's Association v. Knights of the Ku Klux Klan,* 518 F. Supp. 993 (S.D. Tex. 1981) (preliminary injunction).

18. "Moving Beyond the Past," *AsianWeek,* 25 May 2000; Henry Weinstein, "Furrow Gets 5 Life Terms for Racist Rampage Court: The White Supremacist Wounded Five People at a Valley Jewish Center and Murdered a Filipino American Postal Worker in 1999," *Los Angeles Times,* 27 March 2001, p. B1.

19. National Asian Pacific American Legal Consortium, 2002 *Audit of Violence against Asian Pacific Americans: Tenth Annual Report* (Washington, D.C.: National Asian Pacific American Legal Consortium, 2004), 14–23.

20. Davan Maharaj, "Ex-UC Student Indicted in Cyberspace Hate Crime Case," *Los Angeles Times,* 14 November 1996, p. Al.

21. Gen Fujioka, "Turning the Tide of Terror and Indifference," *The Reporter* (Asian Law Caucus newsletter), vol. 16, no. 3 (October 1994): 1.

22. National Asian Pacific American Legal Consortium, 1994 *Audit of Violence against Asian Pacific Americans* (Washington, D.C.: National Asian Pacific American Legal Consortium, 1995), 4.

23. National Asian Pacific American Legal Consortium, 1995 *Audit,* 26–27.

24. Aurelio Rojas, "Turning a Blind Eye to Hate Crimes: Most Attacks in California Go Unprosecuted," *San Francisco Chronicle,* 22 October 1996, p. Al.

25. The Asian American Legal Defense and Education Fund found that one-half of the incidents of anti-Asian violence in New York City during 1994 could be traced to police misconduct. National Asian Pacific American Legal Consortium, *1994 Audit,* 12.

26. John Higham, *Strangers in the Land: Patterns of American Nativism, 1860–1925* (New York: Atheneum, 1970), 4.

27. Robert S. Chang, "Toward an Asian American Legal Scholarship: Critical Race Theory, Post-Structuralism, and Narrative Space," *California Law Review* 81 (October 1993): 1241, 1255.

Detroit Blues

"Because of You Motherfuckers"

Helen Zia

I arrived in Detroit in 1976 with little more than my beat-up Chevy Vega, a suitcase, a few boxes, and about a hundred dollars. My first order of business was to find a job, preferably at an auto factory. I was on a mission, a grand adventure, to learn what it meant to be an American in America's heartland. I was finally doing what we had talked about endlessly in college—going to the grass roots, the workplaces and neighborhoods where we could learn from the people who were the real makers of history. This was not the road my ancestors had planned for me.

Like many Asian American immigrant parents, mine had instilled in me the virtues of education and scholarship. But our family's tiny baby novelty business offered little exposure to possible careers. My parents had few ideas of where my studies might take me. I was so unsure of what to do in my life beyond college that I did what any good Asian American child would do: I applied to medical school. Though I majored in public and international affairs, and minored in East Asian Studies and student activism, I also took a few pre-med courses—just to be safe. I even got accepted, and within days of starting on my M.D. I began to realize I had made a terrible mistake. But my filial obligation to my parents—and my entire line of ancestors—was a core part of my Chinese heritage, so I stayed on.

After struggling for two years, I finally mustered the courage to ruin forever my parents' dream—and that of nearly every Asian immigrant parent—to have an offspring who is a doctor, who will care for them in their old age. I quit medical school, spurning my path to respectability, wealth, and filial nirvana. But I was clueless about what to pursue instead. I still wanted to be part of the big social changes I discovered during the student protest years. My equally idealistic friends encouraged me to move to Detroit, which they viewed as the real America. My parents saw this as further evidence that I had lost my mind.

Almost immediately, I landed a job as a large-press operator at a Chrysler stamping plant, making car hoods, fenders, and other parts. I joined the United Auto Workers union. In a factory of several thousand workers, I was one of perhaps three Asian faces; I definitely stood out. I was a rarity on the streets of Detroit as well, with its 60 percent African American population and the rest mostly working-class whites, many from the South. At the time, Detroit had only 7,614 Asian Americans in a population of 1.2 million—not even one percent of the city.

I didn't go to Detroit to find a large Asian American population, but I had hoped to find some palatable Chinese food. I was unhappy with the restaurants in the diminutive and decaying Chinatown, whose residents seemed too old and fragile to move elsewhere. Desperate, I asked my co-workers at the stamping plant where to go.

"Stanley's is the happening place for Chinese food," the African American autoworkers unanimously told me. I wouldn't have been so trusting had I recalled that any dish more exotic than sweet and sour pork unnerved many of my black friends. At Stanley's, I wasn't surprised to find that the cocktails wore pink umbrellas. But I was stunned by the gigantic, flaky dinner rolls that accompanied my order. Rice was optional, and everything was smothered in heavy brown gravy. I didn't fault Stanley's—like Chinese everywhere in the diaspora, they had to survive and adapt to the environment. But if culinary influence was an indication of political status in Detroit, Asian Americans weren't even on the map.

Two years later, I was no longer a press operator. As easily as I found my job at the auto plant, I lost it, along with some 300,000 other autoworkers in the devastating collapse of the auto industry. I was learning more about "real Americans" than I ever imagined; my biggest lesson was that we were not so different. There was the occasional racial confrontation—like the drunken worker who pointed her finger in my face and said, "I don't care if you're from Jap-pan, the Philippeenes or Ha-wah-yeh, you're on my turf," but she was the rare exception. Standing together on the assembly line and the unemployment line, we shared our lives and recognized our common humanity.

In the midst of that social upheaval, I discovered journalism. I began writing for the *Detroit Metro Times* and other "alternative" news publications. I wrote about the auto industry and the labor movement for *Monthly Detroit* magazine, then joined the staff of a new city magazine, *Metropolitan Detroit*. I spent my days reporting on the life and trends that made Detroit dynamic. Asian American issues were not among them.

The last thing I expected to find in Detroit was an Asian American mandate that would compel the scattered groups across the nation into a broad-based pan-Asian movement. I was in for a big surprise.

In the years leading up to the summer of 1982, Detroit was a city in crisis. Long lines of despair snaked around unemployment offices, union halls, welfare offices, soup kitchens. Men and women lost homes, cars, recreational vehicles, summer cottages, and possessions accumulated from a lifetime of hard work in a once-thriving industry. They were named the "new poor." For many, gloom turned to anger as they searched for the cause of their miseries.

At first, the companies blamed the workers for incompetence and malaise, for wanting too much in exchange for too little. The workers, in turn, pointed to decrepit factories and machines that hadn't been upgraded since World War II, profits that had been squandered and not reinvested in plants and people. The government was faulted for the usual reasons. Before long, however, they all found a common enemy to blame: the Japanese.

While Detroit had once scoffed at the threat of oil shortages, Japan's automakers were busily meeting the demand for inexpensive, fuel-efficient cars. In 1978, a new oil crisis and subsequent price hikes at the gas pumps killed the market for the heavy, eight-cylinder dinosaurs made in Detroit, precipitating the massive layoffs and a crisis throughout the industrial Midwest. The Japanese auto imports were everything the gas-guzzlers were not—cheap to buy, cheap to run, well made and dependable. They were easy to hate.

Anything Japanese, or presumed to be Japanese, became a potential target. Japanese cars were easy pickings. Local unions sponsored sledge-hammer events giving frustrated workers a chance to smash Japanese cars for a dollar a swing. Japanese cars were vandalized and their owners were shot at on the freeways. On TV, radio, and the local street corner, anti-Japanese slurs were commonplace. Politicians and public figures made irresponsible and unambiguous racial barbs aimed at Japanese people. Lee Iacocca, chairman of the failing Chrysler Corporation and onetime presidential candidate, jokingly suggested dropping nuclear bombs on Japan, while U.S. Representative John Dingell of Michigan pointed his fury at "those little yellow men."

Bumper stickers threatened "Honda, Toyota—Pearl Harbor." It felt dangerous to have an Asian face. Asian American employees of auto companies were warned not to go onto the factory floor because angry workers might hurt them if they were thought to be Japanese. Even in distant California, Robert Handa, a third-generation Japanese American television reporter, was threatened by an autoworker who pulled a knife and yelled, "I don't likee Jap food . . . only like American food."

I had lost my job at Chrysler in the first round of layoffs, four years earlier, but every time I drove my car I was grateful that it was American-made. The tension was an ominous reminder of dangerous times past. It seemed only a matter of time before the anger turned to violence.

That summer, a twenty-seven-year-old man named Vincent Chin was destined to become a symbol for Asian Americans. Vincent was a regular Detroit guy who happened to be of Chinese descent. Cheerful and easygoing, Vincent was a recent graduate of Control Data Institute, a computer trade school, and worked as a draftsman during the day and a waiter on weekends. He liked nothing more than spending a lazy afternoon fishing with his buddies. He hadn't been touched by the Asian American movement and knew little of the violence endured by past generations of Asians in America. But he had felt the sting of racial prejudice and witnessed the hardships of his immigrant parents, who worked in the laundries and restaurants of Detroit.

On June 19, 1982, a week before his wedding, Vincent's pals took him out for the all-American ritual the bachelor party. They went to Fancy Pants, a raunchy striptease bar in Highland Park, a tattered enclave of Detroit, near the crumbling mansions once home to auto magnates and Motown stars and only blocks away from the abandoned buildings where Henry Ford manufactured the Model T. Vincent, who grew up in that neighborhood, had been to Fancy Pants several times before.

That night, his mother admonished him, "You're getting married, you shouldn't go there anymore."

"Ma, it's my last time," he replied.

"Don't say 'last time,' it's bad luck," she scolded, conjuring up old Chinese superstitions.

At the lounge, two white men sat across the striptease stage from Vincent and his three friends—two white men and one Chinese American. Ronald Ebens, a plant superintendent for Chrysler, and his stepson, Michael Nitz, a laid-off autoworker, soon made it clear that they found Vincent's presence distasteful. The friends of the groom-to-be were paying the dancers handsomely to shower their favors on Vincent. According to witnesses, Ebens seemed annoyed by the attention the Chinese American was receiving from the nude dancers. Vincent's friends overheard Ebens say "Chink," "Nip," and "fucker." One of the dancers heard him say, "It's because of motherfuckers like you that we're out of work." Vincent replied, "Don't call me a fucker," and a scuffle ensued. Nitz's forehead was cut, possibly by a punch or chair thrown by Vincent. Both groups were ejected from the bar.

Ebens and Nitz hunted for Chin and the other Chinese man in his group. In the dark summer night, they drove through the area for a half hour with a neighborhood man whom they paid to help them "get the Chinese." Finally they spotted Vincent and his friend in front of a crowded McDonald's on Woodward Avenue, Detroit's main central thoroughfare. Creeping up behind the Chinese Americans, Nitz held Vincent Chin down while his stepfather swung his Louisville Slugger baseball bat into Vincent's skull four times, "as if he was going for a home run." Two off-duty cops who were moonlighting as security guards witnessed the attack. The impact of the blows broke a jade pendant that Vincent wore—to some Chinese, a sign of bad luck. Mortally wounded, Vincent died four days later. His four hundred wedding guests attended his funeral instead.

The *Detroit Free Press* featured the bridegroom's beating death on its front page, telling of Vincent's life and hopes for his marriage, but offering no details of his slaying—none of the circumstances were yet known. Detroit's Asian Americans, unaccustomed to any media coverage, took notice. But they remained silent even though many believed that race was a factor in the killing. The community was small and unorganized. Conventional wisdom of the "don't make waves" variety admonished that visibility could bring trouble. Even if they wished to protest, they had no advocacy or watchdog group to turn to. It seemed that the matter would end there. I read the story with sadness and alarm, too aware of the racial tensions swirling around the region. I wondered how this Chinese American came to be killed, when there were so few Asian Americans in Detroit. As an enterprising young journalist, I clipped the story out and filed it, certain that there was a bigger story behind Vincent's death.

Nine months later, on March 18, 1983, new headlines appeared on the front pages of Detroit's two dailies: "Two Men Charged in '82 Slaying Get Probation" and "Probation in Slaying Riles Chinese." It seemed to be the courtroom conclusion to Vincent Chin's death. The two killers pleaded guilty and no contest to savagely beating Chin to death; each received three years' probation and $3,780 in fines and court costs to be paid over three years. The judge, Charles Kaufman, explained his reasoning: "These aren't the kind of men you send to jail," he said. "You fit the punishment to the criminal, not the crime." The lightness of the sentence shocked Detroit. Two white killers were set free in a city with a population more than 60 percent black, where African Americans routinely received harsher sentences for lesser crimes. The sentence of probation drew cries of outrage. Local pundits harshly criticized Judge Kaufman. "You have raised the ugly ghost of racism, suggesting in your explanation that the lives of the killers are of great and continuing value to society, implying they are of greater value than the life of the slain victim. . . . How gross and ostentatious of you; how callous and yes, unjust," wrote *Detroit Free Press* columnist Nikki McWhirter.

Detroit News reporter Cynthia Lee, herself a Chinese American from Hawaii, interviewed members of the Chinese American community, who voiced their disbelief. "You go to jail for killing a dog," said Henry Yee, a noted local restaurateur who was described as the "unofficial mayor of Chinatown." Vincent's life was worth less than a used car, cried a distraught family friend.

The reaction within the Detroit area's small, scattered Asian American population was immediate and visceral. Suddenly people who had endured a lifetime of degrading treatment were wondering if their capacity to suffer in silence might no longer be a virtue, when even in death, after such a brutal, uncontested killing, they could be so disrespected. Disconnected, informal networks of Asian Americans frantically worked the phones, trying to find some way to vent their frustrations and perhaps correct the injustice.

I, too, was stunned. Here was the incredible ending to the story I had clipped out for future reference. I felt distraught, betrayed—and furious. The probationary sentences seemed to echo the familiar taunt, "a China-man's chance," that grim reminder of the days when whites lynched Chinese with impunity. The lessons from my Asian American student movement days came rushing back to me. After I read the articles, I telephoned the person named in the *Detroit News* article. Introducing myself to Henry Yee, whose common Chinese American name was the same as my older brother's, I offered to help in any way I could. Henry invited me to meet him and some others that afternoon. At Carl's Steak House, I met Henry Yee and Kin Yee (not related), president of the Detroit Chinese Welfare Council. A woman named Liza Chan, a Hong Kong–born attorney of my own generation, joined us. We talked generally about possible actions. The first step would be to conduct a larger meeting that could include more members of the Chinese and Asian American community.

The Chinese Welfare Council was the public face of the local branches of the Chinese Consolidated Benevolent Association and the On Leong Merchants Association, a tong, a form of Chinatown organization often associated with the seamier side of Chinese American ghettoes. In Detroit it served a social func-tion. Both organizations had long histories in Chinatowns. The business associ-ation, also known as the Six Companies, began in San Francisco in the 1860s to provide public services denied to Chinese by local governments. The associa-tion arbitrated disputes, representing Chinese concerns to the city, state, and federal governments. The tongs, on the other hand, were alleged to conduct organized crime activities in Chinatowns, using their networks to run gambling, prostitution, drug-trafficking, and protection rackets. Some tongs performed legitimate community and civic functions; in Detroit, the Chinese Welfare Council and On Leong Merchants Association were well established, and both Henry Yee and Kin Yee were members.

Merchants were the Chinese pioneers in Detroit. In 1872, the first Chinese Detroiter, Ah Chee, arrived and set up a laundry business; subsequent arrivals did the same. The first Chinese restaurant opened in 1905. The Chinese busi-ness community hit its peak in the 1920s, when the city counted 300 Chinese laundries and 32 restaurants. Since that time, the Chinatown population and business base had dwindled, becoming a mere shadow of its peak days.

Over the years, the Asian American population in the Detroit area changed considerably. The Immigration Act of 1965 had ushered in a new generation of Chinese immigrants, as well as those from Korea, the Philippines, and South Asia. Because the new immigration regulations heavily favored educated pro-fessionals, the newer Asian immigrants included highly trained scientists, engi-neers, doctors, and nurses. Many of the top researchers for the Big Three automakers were Ph.D.'s from throughout Asia. The professionals lived in the suburbs, far from Detroit's urban core and Chinatown. By the 1980s, Chinatown's shrinking base reflected the diminished role of the merchants. The children of the laundry and restaurant owners had gone to college and moved to the sub-urbs or to other cities. The family businesses in Chinatown faded.

The 1980 census reported only 1,213 Chinese in the entire city; while that is surely an undercount, the population was unquestionably small. On Leong ran the Chinese Culture and Recreational Center, offering activities for youth and English-language instruction to new immigrants. It also assisted the aging bach-elor Chinese, settled disputes among immigrants, and maintained a cemetery plot for Chinese. If it had more nefarious pursuits, they weren't obvious, though the notorious Hong Kong–based chief of the national On Leong, Eddie Chan, was well known to the FBI and Interpol. The Detroit Chinese Welfare Council represented Chinatown interests to the city and at political functions. Both groups were run by the same aging elders who realized they needed to bolster their membership by attracting new, and younger, blood. The late Vincent Chin was one of their younger members.

Vincent's background was like that of many second-generation Chinatown Chinese. His father, David Bing Hing Chin, had worked in laundries all his life, from the time he arrived from China in 1922 at the age of seventeen until his death in 1981, the year before Vincent was slain. He had served in the Army dur-ing World War II, which earned him his citizenship and the right to find a wife in China. Lily came to the United States in 1948 to be married, like so many other Chinese women of her generation, including my mother. Lily knew her husband-to-be's family, and looked forward to joining him in America. Lily's father opposed the move because his grandfather had worked on the transcontinental railroad, but was driven out. He feared Lily might face similar bigotry. In Detroit, Lily worked in the laundries and restaurants alongside her new husband.

In 1961, Lily and David Bing Chin adopted a cheerful six-year-old boy from Guangdong Province in China. Vincent grew up into a friendly young man and a devoted only child who helped support his parents financially. He ran on his high school track team, but he also wrote poetry. Vincent was an energetic, take-charge guy who knew how to stand up for himself on the tough streets of Detroit. But friends and co-workers had never seen him angry and were shocked that he had been provoked into a fight.

For Chinese Americans, the identification with the Chin family was direct. The details of the Chins' family history mirrored those of so many other Chinese Americans, who, like Lily and David, came from Guangdong Province. So did the military service that made it possible for Chinese American men to get married, and their work in the restaurants and laundries. Vincent was part of an entire generation for whom the immigrant parents had suffered and sacrificed. Other Asian Americans also found a strong connection to the lives of Vincent, Lily, and David Chin. Theirs was the classic immigrant story of survival: work hard and sacrifice for the family, keep a low profile, don't complain, and, perhaps in the next generation, attain the American dream. For Asian Americans, along with the dream came the hope of one day gaining acceptance in America. The injustice surrounding Vincent's slaying shattered the dream.

But most of all, Vincent was everyone's son, brother, boyfriend, husband, father. Asian Americans felt deeply that what happened to Vincent Chin could have happened to anyone who "looked" Japanese. From childhood, nearly every Asian American has experienced being mistaken for other Asian ethnicities, even harassed and called names as though every Asian group were the same. The climate of hostility made many Asian Americans feel unsafe, not just in Detroit, but across the country, as the Japan-bashing began to emanate from the nation's capital and was amplified through the news media. If Vincent Chin could be harassed and brutally beaten to death, and his killers freed, many felt it could happen to them.

After the news of the sentences of probation for Vincent's killers, his mother, Lily, wrote a letter in Chinese to the Detroit Chinese Welfare Council: "This is injustice to the grossest extreme. I grieve in my heart and shed tears in blood. My son cannot be brought back to life, but he was a member of your council. Therefore, I plead to you. Please let the Chinese American community know, so they can help me hire legal counsel to appeal, so my son can rest his soul."

As phone calls and offers of help from Chinese Americans and others poured in from all over the Detroit area, Henry Yee and Kin Yee called for a meeting on March 20, 1983, under the auspices of the Detroit Chinese Welfare Council at the Golden Star Restaurant in Ferndale, a working-class suburb just north of

Detroit. Vincent had worked at the Golden Star as a waiter. The restaurant was three miles from the McDonald's on Woodward Avenue where he was killed.

One week after the sentencing, about thirty people crammed into the back dining room of the Golden Star. I had never been to the restaurant, but its familiar decor of red, black, and gold-speckled mirrors reminded me of Chinese restaurants everywhere. The lawyers stood at the front, fielding questions from the group. Barely a half dozen of them, they constituted the majority of Asian American attorneys in the entire state. Most were under thirty. None specialized in criminal law, but they agreed on one thing: once a sentence was rendered, little could be done to change it; the law offered few options. The impasse forced an uneasy quiet over the gathering, broken only by the low sounds of Lily Chin weeping at the back of the room.

Aside from Kin Yee, Henry Yee, and Liza Chan, whom I had just met, I knew no one at the meeting. At that moment I had to decide between being a reporter on the sidelines and being an active participant in whatever happened. I hesitated, then raised my hand. "We must let the world know that we think this is wrong. We can't stop now without even trying." At first there was no response. Then the weeping stopped. Mrs. Chin stood up and spoke in a shaky but clear voice. "We must speak up. These men killed my son like an animal. But they go free. This is wrong. We must tell the people, this is wrong."

With Mrs. Chin's words as a moral turning point, the group decided to press forward. The lawyers recommended a meeting with the sentencing judge, Charles Kaufman. But who would accompany Mrs. Chin and Kin Yee to meet the judge? Some of the lawyers stepped back, explaining how such an act might jeopardize their jobs. In a community with so little political clout, to be "the nail that sticks out" was an invitation to disaster. After another pause, a woman spoke up. "I'll meet with Kaufman." It was Liza Chan, the only Asian American woman practicing law in Michigan. I took on the task of publicizing the news that Asian Americans were outraged and preparing to fight the judge's sentence. From the beginning, women would play a major role in the case.

In the next few days, Liza and Kin attempted to meet with the judge, who by now was flooded by angry phone calls, letters, and media inquiries, as Asian Americans and others challenged his sentence. He skipped their appointment. When I joined Liza and Kin for the next scheduled meeting, we were told that the judge had suddenly decided to go on vacation. On a pro bono basis, Liza began the work of finding and interviewing witnesses to reconstruct what happened to Vincent Chin that fateful night, so that Mrs. Chin and the community could assess their legal options. It soon became clear that there were failures at every step of the criminal justice process. The police and court record was slipshod and incomplete. The police had failed to interview numerous witnesses, including the dancers at the bar and a man the killers hired outside the bar to help them "get the Chinese"; when Liza and I visited the arresting officer, he had the murder weapon, the Louisville Slugger baseball bat, sitting behind his desk. The first presiding judge had set the initial charges against the killers at second-degree murder, which other legal experts determined to be too low. Almost as outrageous as the sentence itself was the fact that no prosecutor was present when Judge Kaufman rendered his sentence of probation.

After the community meeting at the Golden Star, I issued our first press release. We were flooded with numerous requests for information and offers to help. Without an existing advocacy group to manage the community response, we decided some kind of organization would have to be formed. The founding meeting was set for the following week, after we contacted the various community groups, which were mostly religious, cultural, and professional in nature. The meeting would be held at the Detroit Chinese Welfare Council building.

On the evening of March 31, more than a hundred solidly middle-aged and mainly middle-class Asian Americans from towns surrounding Detroit packed the dingy, low-ceilinged hall. The threat of a Michigan frost still lingered, but the topic under debate this night was hot and unprecedented among Asian Americans: whether to form a pan-Asian organization that might seek a federal civil rights investigation in the slaying of Vincent Chin. There had never before been a criminal civil rights case involving anyone of Asian descent in the United States.

Once again, the gathering was mostly Chinese American, with a few other Asian ethnicities offering a thin slice of diversity. The imagery was staunchly conservative: a faded portrait of Chiang Kai-shek at the front, flanked by the red-white-and-blue—not Old Glory but the flag of Taiwan, the Republic of China.

The main order of business was to create an organization that could file petitions and legal actions, raise money, and organize the outcry for a response. The idea was to form an umbrella organization to coordinate the efforts of the area's varied Asian American groups. Members of some twenty groups had come that night, mostly Chinese, from the Association of Chinese Americans and the Greater Detroit Taiwanese Association, to such professional associations as the Detroit Chinese Engineers Association; cultural groups like the Chinese American Educational and Cultural Center; church organizations from the Chinese Community Church to the Detroit Buddhist Church; and a women's group, the Organization of Chinese American Women.

Detroit had not seen such a broad gathering of Chinese since the China War Relief effort of the 1930s. Non-Chinese were also represented, including the Japanese American Citizens League, the Korean Society of Greater Detroit, and the Filipino American Community Council.

The pan-Asian intent of the group became clear as the group discussed what to name the new organization. "Citizens for Fair Sentencing in the Cause of Vincent Chin" and "Justice Committee of the Chinese Welfare Council" were rejected as too narrow. "Chinese Americans for Justice" limited the concern to Chinese. The vote overwhelmingly went to "American Citizens for Justice," which offered an inclusive base and a vision for justice beyond a single case. The founding of the American Citizens for Justice, or ACJ, marked the formation of the first explicitly Asian American grass-roots community advocacy effort with a national scope. Third-generation Japanese American James Shimoura was the first, and at the time only, non-Chinese to serve on the executive board. Japanese, Filipino, and Korean American groups joined in support, assured that they would be welcome. As word of our efforts spread, both white and black individuals also volunteered, making the campaign for justice multiracial in character.

That night, the new pan-Asian American organization drafted its statement of principles:

ACJ BELIEVES THAT:

1. All citizens are guaranteed the right to equal treatment by our judicial and governmental system;

2. When the rights of one individual are violated, all of society suffers;

3. Asian Americans, along with many other groups of people, have historically been given less than equal treatment by the American judicial and governmental system. Only through cooperative efforts with all people will society progress and be a better place for all citizens.

ACJ's first mandate was unambiguous: to obtain justice for Vincent Chin, an Asian American man who was killed because he looked Japanese.

Hard questions came quickly as the newly formed ACJ sought to gain supporters outside the Asian American community. Our first efforts at mounting a national media campaign were crude and amateurish as we learned the process of getting our news out; in the days before fax machines, each press release was hand-delivered, often by a retired Chinese American couple, Ray and Mable Lim. ACJ held its first news conference at the Detroit Press Club on April 15, 1983. The entire spectrum of local media appeared—it was big news to see Asian Americans coming together to protest injustice. To the reporters and the people of Detroit, Asian Americans seemed to emerge from nowhere. Our task, and mine in particular, was to educate them quickly, in sound bites, about Asian Americans.

An appearance that Liza Chan and I made on a popular African American talk radio program drew numerous calls from black listeners. Some were pleased that Asian Americans would reach out to their community to talk about this injustice. Others asked if Asians were just trying to "ride the coattails" of African Americans, and still others accused Asian people of prejudice against blacks. We tried to answer questions frankly, acknowledging that anti-black prejudice exists among some, but not all, Asian Americans, and that ACJ was trying to address racial bias and injustice against any group, including attitudes held by Asians. The talk shows gave us an opportunity to point out the contributions of Asian Americans to the civil rights struggles. The listeners' comments also underscored the need for us to bring such discussions to the more recent Asian immigrants who had arrived after the 1965 Immigration Act with little awareness of the U.S. civil rights movement.

The growing prominence of the case gave Asian Americans our first direct entry on a national level into the white–black race dynamic with an Asian American issue. We tried to explain that we recognized and respected African

Americans' central and dominant position in the civil rights struggle; we wanted to show that we weren't trying to benefit from their sacrifices without offering anything in return. On the other hand, many European Americans were hostile or resistant to "yet another minority group" stepping forward to make claims. Underlying both concerns was the suggestion, a nagging doubt, that Asian Americans had no legitimate place in discussions of racism because we hadn't *really* suffered any.

Still, many did welcome Asian Americans into the civil rights fold, as a new voice from a previously silent neighbor. As ACJ began to make its case, African American organizations such as the umbrella Detroit-Area Black Organizations quickly endorsed ACJ's efforts. Its president, Horace Sheffield, became a dependable supporter at ACJ events, and Asian Americans reciprocated. The Detroit chapter of the NAACP, the largest chapter in the country, issued a statement about the sentence. Several prominent African American churches gave their support, as did the Anti-Defamation League of B'nai B'rith and the Detroit Roundtable of Christians and Jews. ACJ sought and won the support of other communities as well, including Latinos, Arab Americans, and Italian Americans. A diversity of women's groups from the Detroit Women's Forum to Black Women for a Better Society endorsed ACJ, as did a number of local political leaders from the president of the Detroit City Council to U.S. Representative John Conyers.

Many Asian Americans wanted to express their outrage, but were unsure how race fit in the picture. Their tentativeness about the issue of race was evident in ACJ's carefully crafted public positions. ACJ focused on Judge Kaufman's unjust sentence, deliberately not commenting on possible racial bias by the judge or the potential for a racial motivation in the killing of Vincent Chin. A few of us in the core organizing effort—attorneys Roland Hwang and Jim Shimoura, educator Parker Woo, and I—had an understanding of civil rights from the Asian American student movement days and felt that racism permeated the case on many levels. But we also knew that other Asian Americans would need to hear more conclusive evidence if they were to take a strong position on race.

ACJ waited to see if Liza Chan's interviews with witnesses would produce evidence of a racially motivated killing. I worded our press releases carefully to convey the context of our history with racism, while avoiding an outright accusation; one of the first ACJ press statements said: "This case has aroused the anger of the Asian community by recalling the days of 'frontier justice,' when massacres of Chinese workers were common-place." News reporters, on the other hand, wanted ACJ to call Kaufman a racist. Journalists discovered that Kaufman had been held in a Japanese prisoner-of-war camp during World War II. ACJ refused the bait.

Soon the smoking gun the community needed appeared. A private investigator hired by ACJ to uncover the facts leading to Vincent's death reported that Racine Colwell, a tough blond dancer at the Fancy Pants, overheard Ebens tell Chin, "It's because of you motherfuckers that we're out of work." At a time when bilious anti-Japanese remarks by politicians, public officials, and the next-door neighbors spewed forth regularly, Asian Americans knew exactly what Ebens meant. A nude dancer with nothing to gain from her testimony had produced the link to a racial motivation that the community was waiting for. ACJ attorneys and leaders realized it was enough to charge Ebens and Nitz with violating Vincent Chin's civil rights. It was time to talk about race.

The next meeting of the ACJ was held at Ford Motor Company World Headquarters, in Dearborn. David Hwang, who had worked at Ford as a research engineer for thirty-six years, secured the use of the company cafeteria on a Sunday evening. More than two hundred people packed the cavernous room to hear updates on the legal efforts and to coordinate the grass-roots, volunteer work. A quick roll call identified Asian American employee groups from the top corporations of the Detroit area, from Burroughs and Detroit Diesel to General Motors and Volkswagen. The meeting's featured speaker from the U.S. Department of Justice explained the difficult process of getting the federal government to conduct a civil rights investigation. The FBI would need to show that there was a conspiracy to deprive Vincent Chin of his civil rights, he advised. The strong public outcry would also be a factor in its decision to investigate.

After the Department of Justice official left the meeting, a gray-haired engineer from General Motors raised his hand. In the clipped English of a native Cantonese speaker, he voiced the uneasiness of the crowd. "If we try to pursue a civil rights case," he asked, "is it necessary for us to talk about race?"

The simple question captured the race conundrum bedeviling Asian Americans. Should Asian Americans downplay race to stay in the "safe" shadows of the white establishment? Or should they step out of the shadows and cast their lot with the more vulnerable position of minorities seeking civil rights? Was there a third, Asian American way that would take sides with neither?

"We may alienate our supporters," argued an earnest-looking businessman, who voiced his fears that a stand on racism might affect an already fragile existence between black and white. "Could we win the NAACP but lose the FBI?" asked another.

Behind the discomfort of "talking about race" was the question of where Asian Americans fit in America, and, more important, where we wanted to be. Asian Americans had never been included in broad discussions on race, nor had we interjected ourselves. The questions were many. If race was such a volatile subject for whites and blacks, why should Asian Americans step in, to face potential wrath from one or the other, or both? Organizing over race might make us seem like troublemakers, as African Americans were often perceived, but we lacked the numerical strength and political power of blacks; if we stepped out of the shadows to make waves, wouldn't we risk becoming targets again?

One by one, people discussed their uncertainties. Those of us who had been involved with Third World movements knew the political theories about race and racism, but making the argument to struggling restaurant workers or comfortable professionals was another matter. Even in 1983, fifteen years after the term "Asian American" first designated a pan-Asian identity, civil rights and their importance to Asian Americans were simply not familiar at the grass-roots level of the Asian ethnic communities. We tried to give direct, even practical answers: yes, a civil rights suit would involve race, and if we wanted to pursue a federal case, we would have to get comfortable educating people—including ourselves—about our experiences with race. But remaining silent would not protect us from the anti-Japanese racial hostility all around us and we could all become targets anyway, the way Vincent Chin had.

Suddenly people began talking about the anger and frustration that brought them to this meeting, why they were touched and outraged by what happened to Vincent Chin. "I've worked hard for my company for forty years," said a computer programmer, his voice shaking. "They always pass me over for promotion because I'm Chinese. I have trained many young white boys fresh out of college to be my boss. I never complain, but inside I'm burning. This time, with this killing, I must complain. What is the point of silence if our children can be killed and treated like this? I wish I'd stood up and complained a lot sooner in my life."

The outrage overcame the fear. "We want to win this case, and we want equal justice for all, including Asian Americans," David Hwang reminded the group. In the end, we reached a consensus: to fight for what we believed in, we would have to enter the arena of civil rights and racial politics. Welcome or not, Asian Americans would put ourselves into the white–black race paradigm.

ACJ began to publicize its findings of racial slurs and comments made by Vincent Chin's killers and to call for a civil rights investigation. The backlash that some had feared was immediate. Non-Asians, most particularly those in a position to make policy on civil rights and race matters, openly resisted claims by Asians of racial discrimination and prejudice. Angry white listeners called in to radio talk shows to complain: "What does race have to do with this?" and "Don't white people have civil rights?"

White liberals were the most skeptical. When Wayne State University constitutional law professor Robert A. Sedler met with Liza Chan and other ACJ attorneys about the legal issues in a civil rights case, he told them to forget it. In his opinion, civil rights laws were enacted to protect African Americans, not Asians. Asian Americans cannot seek redress using federal civil rights law; besides, he said, Asians are considered white.

Sedler wasn't alone in this view. The American Civil Liberties Union of Michigan initially dismissed the outcry from Asian Americans as a law-and-order, "mandatory sentencing" movement. Later, as the community outrage continued, Howard Simon, its executive director, issued a report absolving Judge Kaufman of bias and blaming the prosecutors for failing to prepare the facts of the case for sentencing. The Michigan ACLU wasn't interested in the civil rights aspects of Chin's slaying.

Nor did the Detroit chapter of the National Lawyers Guild, which defined itself as part of the political left, find any connection between Vincent Chin's killing and racism. But the Guild's West Coast chapters, more familiar with Asian Americans' history with racial violence, mustered the votes to give the national endorsement to ACJ's efforts. A near mutiny broke out in the Detroit chapter, but the national body prevailed.

To build a broad coalition of support, ACJ decided to approach the United Auto Workers union, and not just for its powerful presence in Detroit. We felt that if we could change some of its members' anti-Japanese rhetoric, we might be able to prevent future attacks on Asian Americans—and possibly save lives. The UAW department of fair practices was across from Solidarity House, the international headquarters, so it was impossible to avoid the racially inflammatory signs and bumper stickers adorning the parking lot entrance. "300,000 Laid-Off Autoworkers Say Park Your Import in Tokyo" proclaimed one large sign; Volvos, VWs, Saabs, and other European imports apparently presented no problem. I recognized Joe Davis, the fair practices director, from my days as a Chrysler press operator, when he was president of a militant UAW local. Davis told us that the UAW condemned the attack on Vincent Chin. "But if he had been Japanese," noted Davis, an African American, "the attack would be understandable, and we wouldn't give you our support." I had a similar encounter with Doug Fraser, the former president of the UAW, at a reception. I had just shown a city council member, Maryann Mahaffey, a supporter of ACJ, the photo of a poster at Auto World theme park in Flint, Michigan, that featured a buck-toothed, slant-eyed car dropping bombs on Detroit—an example of autoworkers' racial hostility. Mahaffey showed the photo to Fraser, who burst into gleeful laughter—until he saw me standing nearby. As a former UAW member, I was embarrassed and repulsed by the union's acquiescence in racism. I recalled the violent anti-Asian campaigns of Samuel Gompers and wondered when the chain would be broken.

In spite of the backlash, local, national, and international support for ACJ's efforts was growing daily. The legal twists and turns garnered steady local news coverage, and the mobilization of Detroit's Asian Americans was an interesting new phenomenon for reporters. The Vincent Chin case broke into national news by a strange twist of fate. I had rented a car while my American-made auto was in the shop; as I waited at the car rental agency, I stood in line behind a woman with a *New York Times* notebook and copies of the two Detroit daily newspapers, each open to a story about the Chin case. I happened to be carrying several ACJ press packets and asked her if she wanted more information. She turned out to be Judith Cummins, a *New York Times* reporter in town visiting relatives. She wrote a story about the killing and the controversy, even though the local bureau chief had shrugged us off. Perhaps Cummins recognized the story's importance because she was African American and the bureau chief missed it because he was white; in any case, the *New York Times* coverage brought other national media interest, including national network news, TV news magazine specials, and an appearance on the Phil Donahue show.

It was the first time that an Asian American–initiated issue was considered significant national news. Ethnic media from the Asian American community, as well as foreign-language news media from China, Hong Kong, Taiwan, and Japan, followed the case closely—sending to Asia images of Asian Americans raising political Cain over issues of race, racism, and racial unity. As the news of the case spread, groups from all over the country and the world contacted ACJ to extend their support. We developed an international following. Several Chinese Canadian groups offered assistance, as did the North American representative of

Taiwan; ACJ politely declined Taiwan's help, deciding not to accept money from foreign governments. Families of other hate crimes victims reached out from afar; a representative for the family of Steven Harvey, an African American musician who was killed by whites in Kansas City, came to an ACJ meeting. Asian Americans and African Americans pledged mutual support.

ACJ was pursuing a three-pronged legal effort. It called on Judge Kaufman, who finally heard arguments by Liza, to set aside his own sentence, since it was based on incomplete information. ACJ filed briefs with the Michigan Court of Appeals to overturn Kaufman's sentence. The third approach was the civil rights case. Kin Yee and Lily Chin went to Washington, D.C., to meet with William Bradford Reynolds, President Ronald Reagan's civil rights chief, about a federal civil rights investigation. As the local and state actions turned sour, the FBI began to take an interest in the case. To capture the mounting frustration of the community, the ACJ decided to hold a citywide demonstration at Kennedy Square in downtown Detroit, the site of many historic protests. We had held a number of noisy picket lines in front of City Hall, but there had never before been a protest in Detroit organized by the broad Asian American community. This would possibly be the first in the country outside the larger Asian American centers of New York City and the West Coast.

The "demonstration committee" was headed by David Chock, Michael Lee, and Man Feng Chang, all senior scientists from the General Motors Tech Center. They enlisted the help of other engineers, and joked that this would be the most precisely planned demonstration in history. The out-pouring of support was unprecedented. Waving American flags and placards that demanded equal justice, hundreds of professionals and housewives marched alongside waiters and cooks from Chinese restaurants across the region. The restaurant owners shut their doors during the busy weekday lunch rush to allow employees and their own families to participate in the demonstration. Children and seniors, hunched and wizened, walked or rode in wheelchairs. Chinese, Japanese, Koreans, and Filipinos marched in pan-Asian unity. Support statements were made by the city's major African American and religious organizations, local politicians, and even the UAW. At the rally's emotional end, Mrs. Chin appealed to the nation. Through her tears, she said haltingly, "I want justice for my son. Please help me so no other mother must do this." Finally, the demonstrators marched to the Federal Courthouse singing "We Shall Overcome," and hand-delivered to U.S. Attorney Leonard Gilman a petition with three thousand signatures seeking federal intervention.

ACJ used the demonstration to launch its call for a federal prosecution of the killers for violating Chin's civil right to be in a public place, even if that place was a sleazy nude bar. In his speech to the demonstrators, ACJ president Kin Yee read the group's carefully worded position on race: "Eye-witnesses have come forward to confirm something that we suspected all along: that Vincent Chin was brutally slain as a result of a racial incident. Ronald Ebens, a foreman at Chrysler, was so consumed with racial hatred toward Asian people that he started a fight, blaming Asians for the problems of the ailing auto industry. Even non-minority immigrant groups like the Irish and the Poles have faced violence from others who blamed them for their problems. This misguided view encourages attacks on Asian American people and it must be fought against by all who cherish justice and have respect for human dignity."

In direct yet subtle terms, ACJ showed the ways in which Asian Americans had been made scapegoats for the ills of the modern American economy, naming anti-Asian violence as a present-day phenomenon that should concern all people. This created a framework for Asian Americans to organize nationally, and was a first step toward placing Asian Americans in the center of domestic and international economic, political, and social policy contexts. Across the country, in Los Angeles, San Francisco, New York, and Chicago—cities with far greater Asian American populations than Detroit's—pan-Asian coalitions were being built to support the campaign and to address anti-Asian violence in the local community. Fund-raising efforts nationwide encompassed the entire spectrum of Chinese American society, from the National On Leong Association and local chapters, the Chinese Consolidated Benevolent Association and the Chinese Hand Laundry Alliance, to overtly left-leaning groups like the Chinese Progressive Association and the Chinese Association for Human Rights in Taiwan. In between were civil rights groups like the Organization of Chinese Americans, Asian American Law Students Association, Chinese restaurants and business enterprises, and church groups. Dozens of chapters of the Japanese American Citizens League sent money, as did the Korean American Association of Illinois and the American-Arab Anti-Discrimination Committee. The broad cross section showed that the Vincent Chin case was able to overcome the forces of tradition and fear of the unknown, particularly in the arena of race politics. Asian Americans were finally joining together to correct perceived injustices.

Such unity was difficult to maintain. It was rare for the highly educated suburbanites who spoke the Northern Chinese Mandarin dialect to be aligned so closely with Cantonese-speaking Chinatown merchants and workers whose roots were in Southern China. In addition to differences in language, class, and kinship bonds, there was the political gap. Many business owners were Chiang Kai-shek loyalists and fervent anti-Communists, while the more left-wing groups openly supported Mao Tse-tung and the People's Republic of China.

Partly to avoid fractious conflict over "homeland" politics, the charter of the Organization of Chinese Americans, for example, expressly prohibited taking stands on international issues—a policy that is still in effect. ACJ's policy was to admit all who supported its goals, as long as they also maintained an open and tolerant policy toward others. Vincent Chin's story had struck such a raw nerve that Asian American groups were competing to be affiliated with ACJ. In San Francisco, with its rich profusion of Asian American groups, near warfare broke out among various factions. The first cracks appeared when the Chinatown business groups, a powerful constituency in San Francisco, withdrew their support of the case because leftist, pro–People's Republic groups were involved. They used their influence over several Chinese-language newspapers to criticize the fund-raising efforts.

Meanwhile, the leftists were at odds with one another. The Reverend Jesse Jackson's presidential campaign manager for Northern California, Eddie Wong, arranged for Jackson to stop in San Francisco's Chinatown to meet Mrs. Chin, who was attending local support events in California. Jackson became the first national political leader of any race to speak out against racial violence toward Asians. During Jackson's speech in front of a swarm of national reporters and TV cameras at Chinatown's historic Cameron House, where assistance had been provided to Chinese immigrants since 1874, the leaders of two rival leftist groups pinched and shoved each other, trying to elbow the other off the stage just beyond Jackson's view.

Despite the rumblings among the Chinese, ACJ continued to actively reach out to other Asian ethnicities. The second non-Chinese board member was Minoru Togasaki, a second-generation Japanese American. The Chinese speakers on the board felt worried that they might insult Min by mispronouncing his polysyllabic name, difficult for Chinese speakers accustomed to single-syllable ones. A practice session was held, with a room full of Chinese Americans gingerly repeating the name "To-ga-sa-ki" until they got it right.

Detroit's growing Korean community was represented by two large groups: the Korean Society of Greater Detroit, and the Korean American Women's Association. The two groups had rarely worked together. The Korean women were the wives of non-Korean GIs and were often looked down upon by other Koreans—but their support for the Vincent Chin case brought them together. The Filipino and South Asian populations were larger than any of the others and had well-established connections with both Republican and Democratic parties. Their political savvy and access to politicians made it clear to other Asian American groups why they needed to get involved in politics, which many new immigrants tended to shun.

At ACJ's first fund-raiser dinner, a prominent local citizen appeared, the architect Minoru Yamasaki, designer of the World Trade Center towers in New York and other buildings of world renown. Yamasaki, then seventy-three years old, unexpectedly came to join the gathering as an ordinary citizen. Looking dignified but frail, he rose up slowly from his seat with the assistance of a companion. A hush fell over the banquet room as Yamasaki said in a strong, clear voice, "If Asian people in America don't learn to stand up for themselves, these injustices will never cease."

The civil rights investigations dragged on. In November 1983, a federal grand jury indicted Ronald Ebens and Michael Nitz for violating Vincent Chin's right to enjoy a place of public accommodation; the trial would take place the following June. During this period, other racial attacks drew the attention of the Asian American community. In Lansing, Michigan, a Vietnamese American man and his European American wife were harassed and repeatedly shot at by white men shouting racial slurs. In Davis, California, a seventeen-year-old Vietnamese youth was stabbed to death in his high school by white students, while in New York a pregnant Chinese woman was decapitated when she was pushed in front of an oncoming subway car by a European American teacher who claimed to have a fear of Asians.

In other cities, Asian Americans followed the Detroit Asian American community's example and organized to track such incidents. In Boston, a pan-Asian group called Asians for Justice was formed after an escalating number of anti-Asian attacks against Japanese Americans, Chinese Americans, and Cambodian Americans, as well as the stabbing death of a Vietnamese American man. As such new groups raised public awareness about the particular kind of racial hostility against Asians, they prompted more people to come forward to file hate crime reports. The growing list of cases underscored the existence of racism against Asian Americans.

ACJ expanded its civil rights work from anti-Asian hate crimes. It took on employment and discrimination referrals; successfully lobbied the governor to create a statewide Asian American advisory commission; campaigned against offensive media images, like the poster of the slant-eyed car displayed in Flint, Michigan, and a children's TV program whose host, Jim Harper, appeared in yellowface as a sinister Fu Manchu character with a phony Asian accent. To reach out to children and young people, ACJ members Pang Man and Marisa Chuang Ming sponsored a ten-kilometer Run for Justice, while Harold and Joyce Leon's three daughters, professional violinists and a cellist with the world's leading symphony orchestras, performed a special benefit concert for ACJ.

When the federal civil rights trial began on June 5, 1984, in the courtroom of Judge Anna Diggs Taylor, a dignified jurist who was one of the first African American women to serve on the federal bench, ACJ knew that the courtroom battle would be uphill. Many people had a hard time believing that Asian Americans experienced any kind of racial prejudice, let alone hate violence. What Asian Americans found to be racially offensive fighting words drew only shrugs from people who would otherwise never use racial epithets—at least not in public.

The words Racine Colwell, the stripper, heard—"It's because of you motherfuckers that we're out of work"—didn't contain a single racial slur. Asian Americans recognized that they were being singled out in that comment, but to others it was simply a true statement. Don Ball, the veteran *Detroit News* reporter covering the trial, wrote that such statements and the fact that Ebens and Nitz hunted for Vincent and his one Chinese buddy, while ignoring his white friends, were "flimsy evidence that Chin's slaying was racially motivated."

On June 28, the federal jury in Detroit disagreed, and found Ebens guilty of violating Vincent Chin's civil rights; Nitz was acquitted. The jury foreperson explained to filmmakers Christine Choy and Renee Tajima in their documentary *Who Killed Vincent Chin?* that Racine Colwell's testimony was the clincher—in Detroit, it was clear that "you motherfuckers" meant the Japanese, or people who looked like them. Ebens was sentenced to twenty-five years by Judge Taylor.

But the case won a retrial on appeal in 1986 because of pretrial publicity and evidentiary errors associated with audiotapes made of witnesses when ACJ was first investigating the case. It was a cruel irony that the very interviews that convinced Detroit's Asian American community and the U.S. Department of Justice of the killers' racial motivation would be used to grant Ebens's appeal. The new trial would be held in Cincinnati, where there was less chance that prospective jurors knew of the case.

Located across the Ohio River from Kentucky, Cincinnati is known as a conservative city with Southern sensibilities. Absent was the heightened racial consciousness of Detroit, with its black majority and civil rights history. If Asians were hard to find in Detroit, they were near-invisible in Cincinnati—but not completely invisible; on July 4, 1986, a gang of patriotic whites shot up the homes of Southeast Asian refugees in the city. When the jury selection process for the new trial began on April 20, 1987, potential jurors were interrogated on their familiarity with Asians. "Do you have any contact with Asians? What is the nature of your contact?" they were asked, as though they had been exposed to a deadly virus.

Their answers were even more revealing. Out of about 180 Cincinnati citizens in the jury pool, only 19 had ever had a "casual contact" with an Asian American, whether at work or the local Chinese takeout joint. A white woman who said she had Asian American friends was dismissed as though the friendship tainted her; also dismissed was a woman whose daughter had Asian friends, and a black man who had served in Korea.

The jury that was eventually seated looked remarkably like the defendant, Ronald Ebens—mostly white, male, and blue-collar. This time the jury foreperson was a fifty-something machinist who was laid off after thirty years at his company. This time the defense attorneys tried to argue that ACJ and the Asian American community had paid attorney Liza Chan to trump up a civil rights case; that argument was objected to by the prosecutors and overruled by the judge.

It was a terrible disappointment, but not a surprise, when the jury of this second civil rights trial reached its not-guilty verdict on May 1, 1987, nearly five years after Vincent Chin was killed. This jury, composed of people with so little contact with Asian Americans and knowledge of our concerns, couldn't see how "It's because of you motherfuckers" might contain a racial connotation.

Mrs. Chin was distraught. "Vincent's soul will never rest. My life is over," she said. She cried every day for Vincent, when she awoke in the morning and when she lay down at night. Soon after, she moved to New York, then San Francisco, to stay with relatives. Detroit had too many hard memories. Once the legal proceedings were over, Mrs. Chin, disheartened by the failure of the courts to bring her son's killers to justice, moved to her birthplace in Guangdong Province, China, after spending fifty of her seventy years in the United States.

In a civil suit against Ebens and Nitz for the loss of Vincent's life, a settlement judgment of $1.5 million was levied in September 1987 against Ebens, who later told documentary filmmaker Christine Choy that Mrs. Chin would never see the money. He stopped making payments toward the judgment in 1989. At no point did Ebens ever publicly express remorse for taking Chin's life; he never spent a full day in jail. He and his wife, Juanita, moved several times, leaving a trail in Missouri and Nevada en route to whereabouts unknown.

ACJ, however, vowed to continue in its mission of equal justice for all. After the Cincinnati trial, its president, Kim Bridges, a Korean American, announced that ACJ was founding a Midwest Asian American Center for Justice.

Losing the legal effort in its first national campaign of this magnitude after five years of intensive organizing did not devastate the Asian American community; instead, it had been transformed.

The legacy of the Vincent Chin case has lived on, in mainstream America as well as the Asian American community. The documentary *Who Killed Vincent Chin?* is a staple on college campuses, retelling the story to generations of students. Musicians from balladeer Charlie Chin to jazz artist Jon Jang have created songs and musical arrangements about the struggle for justice in the Vincent Chin case. The Contemporary American Theater Festival of Shepherdstown, West Virginia, near Washington, D.C., commissioned playwright Cherylene Lee to write the play *Carry the Tiger to the Mountain*; West Virginia Governor Cecil H. Underwood used the issues raised by the play to launch a statewide dialogue on race, modeled after President Clinton's Race Initiative. Consuelo Echeverria, a Latina sculptor at Carnegie Mellon University in Pittsburgh, welded a life-size installation from forged steel auto parts, portraying the baseball bat slaying, called *Because They Thought He Was . . .*

Los Angeles attorney and activist Stewart Kwoh, a MacArthur Fellowship "genius" award winner, attributes to the Vincent Chin case his inspiration for establishing the Asian Pacific American Legal Center of Southern California and the National Asian Pacific American Legal Consortium, which conducts an annual audit of anti-Asian hate crimes. New generations of Asian American activists, such as Victor M. Hwang, a civil rights attorney with the Asian Law Caucus in San Francisco, cite the influence of the Vincent Chin case on their desire to make a difference as Asian Americans.

Numerous scholars have studied the Vincent Chin case and its impact on the Asian American community. As Yen Le Espiritu, professor of Ethnic Studies at the University of California at San Diego, wrote in her book *Asian American Panethnicity:*

> Considered the archetype of anti-Asian violence, the Chin killing has "taken on mythic proportions" in the Asian American community (W. Wong 1989a). As a result of the Chin case, Asian Americans today are much more willing to speak out on the issue of anti-Asianism; they are also much better organized than they were at the time of Chin's death. . . . Besides combating anti-Asian violence, these pan-Asian organizations provide a social setting for building pan-Asian unity.

After a century of seeking acceptance by distancing from one another, Asian Americans were coming together to assert their right to be American.

A Dialogue on Racial Melancholia

David L. Eng and Shinhee Han

> *I wondered if whiteness were contagious. If it were, then surely I had caught it. I imagined this "condition" affected the way I walked, talked, dressed, danced, and at its most advanced stage, the way I looked at the world and at other people.*
>
> —Danzy Senna, *Caucasia*

The "Condition" of Whiteness

Configuring whiteness as contagion, Birdie Lee, the narrator of Danzy Senna's *Caucasia*, connects assimilation to illness and disease. Separated from her African American activist father, Birdie Lee and her blue-blooded mother flee from the law in a racialized and radicalized 1970s Boston. Eventually, the two take up residence in New Hampshire, where Birdie passes as "Jesse" and for white.[1] This assimilation into the whiteness of New Hampshire plagues Birdie, who wonders if she "had actually become Jesse, and it was this girl, this Birdie Lee who haunted these streets, searching for ghosts, who was the lie." This vexing "condition" of whiteness not only alters the narrator's physical world—the manner in which Birdie walks, talks, dresses, and dances. It also configures the sphere of the affective—the ways in which Birdie ultimately apprehends the world and its occupants around her. Physically and psychically haunted, Birdie/Jesse feels "contaminated."[2]

This is the condition of racial melancholia.

In Place of a Dialogue

This essay is the result of a series of sustained dialogues on racial melancholia that we recorded in the autumn and winter of 1998. We—a Chinese American male professor in the humanities and a Korean American female psychotherapist—transcribed, rewrote, and edited these dialogues into their present form. However, we hope that our distinct disciplinary approaches to psychoanalysis—from literary theory as well as from clinical practice—not only remain clear in this essay but also work to supplement each another. The pressing need to consider carefully methods by which a more speculative approach to psychoanalysis might enhance clinical applications, and vice versa, is urgent. This essay, in part, is a critical response to the disturbing patterns of depression that we have been witnessing in a significant and growing number of Asian American students with whom we interact on a regular basis. "A Dialogue on Racial Melancholia" provides, then, an opportunity for us to propose several ways of addressing race in psychoanalysis, a topic largely neglected in this field.

As Freud's privileged theory of unresolved grief, melancholia presents a compelling framework to conceptualize registers of loss and depression attendant to both psychic and material processes of assimilation.[3] Although Freud typically casts melancholia as pathological, we are more concerned with exploring this psychic condition as a depathologized structure of feeling. From this particular vantage, melancholia might be thought of as underpinning our everyday conflicts and struggles with experiences of immigration, assimilation, and racialization.[4] Furthermore, even though melancholia is often conceived of in terms of individual loss and suffering, we are interested in addressing group identifications. As such, some of our observations bring together different minority groups—people of color as well as gays and lesbians—from widely disparate historical, juridical, cultural, social, and economic backgrounds. We are wary of generalizing, but we also hope that, in forging theoretical links among these various minority groups, we might develop new intellectual, clinical, and political coalitions.

This essay is framed by two larger questions: How might psychoanalytic theory and clinical practice be leveraged to think about not only sexual but also racial identifications? How might we focus on these crossings in psychoanalysis to discuss, in particular, processes of immigration, assimilation, and racialization underpinning the formation of Asian American subjectivity?

ASSIMILATION AS/AND MELANCHOLIA

Freud's theory of melancholia provides a provocative model to consider how processes of assimilation work in this country and how the depression that characterizes so much of our contemporary culture at the turn of this century might be thought about in relation to particularly marked social groups. In the United States today, assimilation into mainstream culture for people of color still means adopting a set of dominant norms and ideals—whiteness, heterosexuality, middle-class family values—often foreclosed to them. The loss of these norms—the reiterated loss of whiteness as an ideal, for example—establishes one melancholic framework for delineating assimilation and racialization processes in the United States precisely as a series of failed and unresolved integrations.

Let us return for a moment to Freud's 1917 essay, "Mourning and Melancholia," in which he attempts to draw a clear distinction between these two psychic states through the question of "successful" and "failed" resolutions to loss. Freud reminds us at the start of this essay that "mourning is regularly the reaction to the loss of a loved person, or to the loss of some abstraction which has taken the place of one, such as one's country, liberty, an ideal, and so on. In some people the same influences produce melancholia instead of mourning and we consequently suspect them of a pathological disposition."[5] Mourning, unlike melancholia, is a psychic process in which the loss of an object or ideal occasions the withdrawal of libido from that object or ideal. This withdrawal cannot be enacted at once; instead, it is a gradual letting go. Libido is detached bit by bit so that, eventually, the mourner is able to declare the object dead and to invest in new objects. In Freud's initial definition of the concept, melancholia is pathological precisely because it is a mourning without end. Interminable grief is the result of the melancholic's inability to resolve the various conflicts and ambivalences that the loss of the loved object or ideal effects. In other words, the melancholic cannot "get over" this loss, cannot work out this loss in order to invest in new objects.

To the extent that ideals of whiteness for Asian Americans (and other groups of color) remain unattainable, processes of assimilation are suspended, conflicted, and unresolved. The irresolution of this process places the concept of assimilation within a melancholic framework. Put otherwise, mourning describes a finite process that might be reasonably aligned with the popular American myth of immigration, assimilation, and the melting pot for dominant white ethnic groups. In contrast, melancholia delineates an unresolved process that might usefully describe the unstable immigration and suspended assimilation of Asian Americans into the national fabric. This suspended assimilation—this inability to blend into the "melting pot" of America—suggests that, for Asian Americans, ideals of whiteness are continually estranged. They remain at an unattainable distance, at once a compelling fantasy and a lost ideal.

In configuring assimilation and melancholia in this particular manner, it is important to challenge Freud's contention that melancholia ensues from a "pathological disposition"—that it emerges from the disturbance of a one-person psychology rather than the disruption of an intersubjective relationship. In our model, the inability to "get over" the lost ideal of whiteness, we must emphasize, is less individual than social. For instance, Asian Americans are typically seen by the mainstream as perpetual foreigners on the basis of skin color and facial markings. Despite that they may be U.S.-born or may have resided here for many years, Asian Americans are continually perceived as eccentric to the nation. At other times, Asian Americans are recognized as hypermodel minorities—inhumanly productive—and hence pathological to the nation. In both scenarios, mainstream refusal to see Asian Americans as part and parcel of the American "melting pot" is less an individual failure to blend in with the whole than a socially determined interdiction. Indeed, Freud suggests in "Mourning and Melancholia" that melancholia may proceed from "environmental influences" rather than internal conditions that threaten the existence of the object or ideal.[6]

Freud goes on in "Mourning and Melancholia" to delineate the debilitating psychic consequences of melancholia. When faced with unresolved grief, he tells us, the melancholic preserves the lost object or ideal by incorporating it into the ego and establishing an ambivalent identification with it—ambivalent precisely because of the unresolved and conflicted nature of this forfeiture.

From a slightly different perspective, we might say that the melancholic makes every conceivable effort to retain the lost object, to keep it alive within the domain of the psyche. However, the tremendous costs of maintaining this ongoing relationship to the lost object or ideal are psychically damaging. Freud notes that the "distinguishing mental features of melancholia are a profoundly painful dejection, cessation of interest in the outside world, loss of the capacity to love, inhibition of all activity, and a lowering of the self-regarding feelings to a degree that finds utterance in self-reproaches and self-revilings, and culminates in a delusional expectation of punishment."[7]

In identifying with the lost object, the melancholic is able to preserve it but only as a type of haunted, ghostly identification. That is, the melancholic assumes the emptiness of the lost object or ideal, identifies with this emptiness, and thus participates in his or her own self-denigration and ruination of self-esteem. Freud summarizes the distinction between mourning and melancholia in this oft-quoted citation: "In mourning it is the world which has become poor and empty; in melancholia it is the ego itself."[8] He contends that melancholia is one of the most difficult of psychic conditions both to confront and to cure, because it is largely an unconscious process. Freud observes:

> In yet other cases one feels justified in maintaining the belief that a loss of the kind occurred, but one cannot see clearly what it is that has been lost, and it is all the more reasonable to suppose that the patient cannot consciously perceive what he has lost either. This, indeed, might be so even if the patient is aware of the loss which has given rise to his melancholia, but only in the sense that he knows *whom* he has lost but not *what* he has lost in him.[9]

Freud tells us that the depression often accompanying melancholia is extremely dangerous, characterized by the tendency to suicide.[10] Here, we must add, suicide may not be merely physical; it may also be a psychical erasure of one's identity—racial, sexual, or gender identity, for example.

NATIONAL MELANCHOLIA

For Asian Americans and other groups of color, suspended assimilation into mainstream culture may involve more than severe personal consequences; ultimately, it also constitutes the foundation for a type of national melancholia, a national haunting, with negative social effects. In Senna's *Caucasia*, the ambivalence characterizing whiteness leaves the narrator with the constant and eerie feeling of "contamination."[11] Writing about the nature of collective identifications, Freud notes in *Group Psychology and the Analysis of the Ego*: "In a group every sentiment and act is contagious, and contagious to such a degree that an individual readily sacrifices his personal interest to the collective interest. This is an aptitude very contrary to his nature, and of which a man is scarcely capable, except when he makes part of a group."[12] Our dialogue on racial melancholia insists on thinking what happens when the demand to sacrifice personal to collective interest is accompanied not by inclusion within but by exclusion from the larger group.

As we know, the formation of the U.S. nation-state quite literally entailed, and continues to entail, a history of institutionalized exclusions, from Japanese American internment to immigration exclusion acts, legislated by Congress, brokered by the executive, and upheld by the judiciary, against every Asian immigrant group.[13] For example, from 1882 to 1943, Chinese Americans experienced one of the longest juridical histories of immigration exclusion as well as bars to naturalization and citizenship. Yet, few people realize that the first exclusion laws passed against a particular ethnic group were passed against the Chinese. These laws were followed by a series of further exclusion acts culminating in the 1924 National Origins Act and the Tydings-McDuffie Act of 1934, which effectively halted all Asian immigration and naturalization. At the same time, other laws were instituted against miscegenation and ownership of private property.

Discourses of American exceptionalism and democratic myths of liberty, individualism, and inclusion force a misremembering of these exclusions, an enforced psychic amnesia that can return only as a type of repetitive national haunting—a type of negative or absent presence.[14] The popular model-minority stereotype that clings to Asian Americans is both a product—and productive— of this negative or absent presence.[15] In its compulsive restaging, the model minority stereotype homogenizes widely disparate Asian and Asian American racial and ethnic groups by generalizing them all as economically or academically successful, with no personal or familial problems to speak of. In this manner, the stereotype works not only to deny the heterogeneity, hybridity, and multiplicity of various Asian American groups who do not fit its ideals of model citizenry.[16] It also functions as a national tool that erases and manages the history of these institutionalized exclusions. The pervasiveness of the model minority stereotype in our contemporary vocabulary works, then, as a melancholic mechanism facilitating the erasure and loss of repressed Asian American histories and identities. These histories and identities can return only as a type of ghostly presence. In this sense, the Asian American model minority *subject* also endures in the United States as a melancholic national *object*—as a haunting specter to democratic ideals of inclusion that cannot quite "get over" the histories of these legislated proscriptions of loss.

Before moving on, we extend our observations on the psychic consequences that this model of national melancholia exacts on the individual Asian American psyche. One compelling example comes from Maxine Hong Kingston's *China Men* (1980). In Kingston's historical novel, the narrator wildly speculates about the disappearance of "The Grandfather of the Sierra Nevada Mountains" after he helps to complete the transcontinental railroad, the greatest technological feat of the nineteenth century: "Maybe he hadn't died in San Francisco, it was just his papers that burned; it was just that his existence was outlawed by Chinese Exclusion Acts. The family called him Fleaman. They did not understand his accomplishments as an American ancestor, a holding, homing ancestor of this place."[17] Kingston understands that the law's refusal to recognize Chinese Americans as citizens "outlaws" their existence, placing them under erasure. At the same time, she also underscores how this national refusal gains its efficacy through a simultaneous psychic internalization of its interdicting imperatives on the part of excluded Asian American subjects. That is, the grandfather's own family refuses to recognize him. They cannot perceive his accomplishments in building the railroad as legitimizing his membership in the American nation. How, in turn, can it be possible to see themselves as legitimate members of this society?

In this regard, racial melancholia might be described as splitting the Asian American psyche. This cleaving of the psyche might be productively thought about in terms of an altered, racialized model of classic Freudian fetishism.[18] That is, assimilation into the national fabric demands a psychic splitting on the part of the Asian American subject, who knows and does not know, at once, that she or he is part of the larger group. In the early 1970s, Asian American psychologists Stanley Sue and Derald W. Sue coined the term "Marginal Man" to describe an Asian American subject who desires to assimilate into mainstream American society at any cost. The Marginal Man faithfully subscribes to the ideals of assimilation only through an elaborate self-denial of the daily acts of institutionalized racism directed against him. In "Chinese-American Personality and Mental Health," the Sues write about the complex psychological defenses that the Marginal Man must necessarily employ in order to "function" within American society. The Marginal Man finds it "difficult to admit widespread racism since to do so would be to say that he aspires to join a racist society."[19] Caught in this untenable contradiction, the Marginal Man must necessarily become a split subject—one who exhibits a faithful allegiance to the universal norms of abstract equality and collective national membership at the same time as he displays an uncomfortable understanding of his utter disenfranchisement from these democratic ideals.

In Senna's *Caucasia*, Birdie's unresolved assimilation into the whiteness of New Hampshire gives us a final reflection on the psychic effects of splitting in racial melancholia on the level of the signifier. Through the twinning of her name, the impossible mulatta child is marked by doubleness: Birdie (mulatto) → Jesse (white). Here, Birdie/Jesse is the object of melancholia for a nation organized by an ecology of whiteness. At the same time, she is the subject of melancholia, a girl haunted by ghosts. It is difficult not to notice that much of contemporary ethnic literature in the United States is characterized by ghosts and by hauntings from both these perspectives—the objects and subjects of national melancholia. For instance, the subtitle of Maxine Hong Kingston's well-known *The Woman Warrior: Memoirs of a Girlhood among Ghosts*.[20] In "Unspeakable Things Unspoken: The Afro-American Presence in American Literature," the Nobel laureate Toni Morrison writes that the African American presence is "the ghost in the machine."[21]

Mimicry; or, The Melancholic Machine

Racial melancholia as psychic splitting and national dis-ease opens upon the interconnected terrain of mimicry, ambivalence, and the stereotype. Homi Bhabha's seminal essay, "Of Mimicry and Man: The Ambivalence of Colonial Discourse" (1984), is crucial here. Bhabha describes the ways in which a colonial regime impels the colonized subject to mimic Western ideals of whiteness.

At the same time, this mimicry is also condemned to failure. Bhabha writes, "Colonial mimicry is the desire for a reformed, recognizable Other, as *a subject of a difference that is almost the same, but not quite.* Which is to say, that the discourse of mimicry is constructed around an *ambivalence;* in order to be effective, mimicry must continually reproduce its slippage, its excess, its difference. . . . *Almost the same but not white.*"[22] Bhabha locates and labels the social imperative to assimilate as the colonial structure of mimicry. He marks not only this social imperative but also its inevitable, built-in failure. This doubling of difference that is almost the same but not quite, almost the same but not white, results in ambivalence, which comes to define the failure of mimicry.

Here we would like to connect Bhabha's observations on mimicry in the material space of the colonized with the psychic domain through the logic of melancholia. It is important to remember that, like Bhabha's analysis of mimicry, Freud marks ambivalence as one of melancholia's defining characteristics. In describing the genealogy of ambivalence in melancholia, Freud himself moves from the domain of the material to the register of the psychic. He notes that the "conflict due to ambivalence, which sometimes arises from real experiences, sometimes more from constitutional factors, must not be overlooked among the preconditions of melancholia."[23] Melancholia not only traces an internalized pathological identification with what was once an external and now lost ideal. In this moving from outside to inside (from Bhabha to Freud, as it were), we also get a strong sense of how social injunctions of mimicry configure individual psychic structures as split and dis-eased—another angle from which to consider the cleaving of the Marginal Man. The ambivalence that comes to define Freud's concept of melancholia is one that finds its origins in the social, in colonial and racial structures impelling systems of mimicry and man.

It is crucial to extend Bhabha's theories on colonial mimicry to domestic contexts of racialization in order to consider how we might usefully track this concept to explore further the material and psychic contours of racial melancholia for Asian Americans. One potential site of investigation is the stereotype. In an earlier essay entitled "The Other Question: Stereotype, Discrimination, and the Discourse of Colonialism" (1983), Bhabha also aligns ambivalence and splitting with the stereotype, suggesting that the process of mimicry and the phenomenon of the stereotype might be considered together. The stereotype, Bhabha writes, "is a form of knowledge and identification that vacillates between what is always 'in place,' already known, and something that must be anxiously repeated . . . for it is the force of ambivalence that gives the colonial stereotype its currency."[24]

If we conceptualize the model minority myth as a privileged stereotype through which Asian Americans appear as subjects in the contemporary social domain, then we gain a more refined understanding of how mimicry specifically functions as a material practice in racial melancholia. That is, Asian Americans are forced to mimic the model minority stereotype in order to be recognized by mainstream society—in order *to be* at all. To the extent, however, that this mimicry of the model minority stereotype functions only to estrange Asian Americans from mainstream norms and ideals (as well as from themselves), mimicry can operate only as a melancholic process. As both a social and a psychic malady, mimicry distances Asian Americans from the mimetic ideals of the nation. Through the mobilization and exploitation of the model minority stereotype, mimicry for Asian Americans is always a partial success as well as a partial failure to assimilate into regimes of whiteness.

Let us analyze this dynamic from yet another angle. While Asian Americans are now largely thought of as "model minorities" living out the "American Dream," this stereotyped dream of material success is partial, because it is at most configured as economic achievement. The "success" of the model minority myth comes to mask our lack of political and cultural representation. It covers over our inability to gain "full" subjectivities—to be politicians, athletes, and activists, for example—to be recognized as "All American." To occupy the model minority position, Asian American subjects must follow this prescribed model of economic integration and forfeit political representation as well as cultural voice. In other words, they must not contest the dominant order of things; they must not "rock the boat" or draw attention to themselves. It is difficult for Asian Americans to express any legitimate political, economic, or social needs, because the stereotype demands not only an enclosed but also a passive self-sufficiency.

From an academic point of view, the model minority stereotype also delineates Asian American students as academically successful but rarely "well-rounded"—well-rounded in tacit comparison to the unmarked (white) student body. Here is another example of Bhabha's concept of mimicry as nearly successful imitation. This near successful assimilation attempts to cover over that gap—the failure of well-roundedness—as well as that unavoidable ambivalence resulting from this tacit comparison in which the Asian American student is seen as lacking. This material failure leads to a psychic ambivalence that works to characterize the colonized subject's identification with dominant ideals of whiteness as a pathological identification. It is an ambivalence that opens upon the landscape of melancholia and depression for many of the Asian American students with whom we come into contact on a regular basis. Those Asian Americans who do not fit into the model minority stereotype (and this is probably a majority of Asian American students) are altogether erased from—not seen in—mainstream society. Like Kingston's grandfather in *China Men*, they are often rejected by their own families as well.[25]

The difficulty of negotiating this unwieldy stereotype is that, unlike most pejorative stereotypes of African Americans (but not unlike the myth of the black athlete), the model minority myth is considered to be a "positive" representation, an "exceptional" model for this racialized group. In this regard, not only mainstream society but also Asian Americans themselves become attached to, and split by, its seemingly admirable qualities without recognizing its simultaneous liabilities—what Wendy Brown terms a "wounded attachment."[26] According to Bhabha, in its doubleness the stereotype, like mimicry, creates a gap embedded in an unrecognized structure of material and psychic ambivalence. In Gish Jen's *Typical American*, for instance, we encounter Ralph Chang, who chases the American Dream through his attempts to build a fried-chicken kingdom, the Chicken Palace.[27] Eventually, the franchise fails, the *a* falling off the sign so that

"Chicken Palace" becomes "Chicken P lace." This falling-off is the linguistic corollary to the gap in the American Dream that Ralph unsuccessfully attempts to mime. Perhaps it is in this gap—in this emptiness—that Freud's theory of melancholia emerges and dwells. It is in this gap—this loss of whiteness—that the negotiation between mourning and melancholia is staged.

MOURNING/MELANCHOLIA/IMMIGRATION

This structure of mimicry gestures to the partial success and partial failure to mourn our identifications with whiteness. Moreover, it gestures to our partial success and partial failure to mourn our identifications and affiliations with our "original" Asian cultures. Thus far, we have been focusing on the loss of whiteness as an ideal structuring the assimilation and racialization processes of Asian Americans. However, the lost object can be multifaceted. Since the 1965 reformation of the Immigration and Nationality Act, there are more first-generation Asian American immigrants living in the United States today than any other generation of Asian Americans. A majority of Asian American college students are the offspring of this generation. Hence, many of our clinical observations lead us to a more concerted focus on the relationship of mourning and melancholia to questions of immigration and intergenerational losses involving Asian identity.

The experience of immigration itself is based on a structure of mourning. When one leaves one's country of origin, voluntarily or involuntarily, one must mourn a host of losses both concrete and abstract. These include homeland, family, language, identity, property, status in the community—the list goes on. In Freud's theory of mourning, one works through and finds closure to these losses by investing in new objects—in the American Dream, for example. Our attention to the problematics of mimicry, ambivalence, and the stereotype, as well as our earlier analysis of the history of juridical exclusions of Asian Americans, reveals a social structure that prevents the immigrant from fully assimilating. From another perspective, this structure might be said to deny him or her the capacity to invest in new objects. The inability to invest in new objects, we must remember, is part of Freud's definition of melancholia. Given our current discussion of the ways in which Asian American immigrants are foreclosed from fully assimilating, are they perpetually consigned to a melancholic status? If so, how do we begin to address Freud's notion of melancholia as pathological? Clearly not all Asian American immigrants are confined to melancholic or depressive states. If this is the case, how do Asian American immigrants negotiate their losses? And how do their offspring inherit and inhabit these losses?

If the losses suffered by the first generation are not resolved and mourned in the process of assimilation—if libido is not replenished by the investment in new objects, new communities, and new ideals—then the melancholia that ensues from this condition can be transferred to the second generation. At the same time, however, can the hope of assimilation and mastery of the American Dream also be transferred? If so, mourning and melancholia are reenacted and lived out by the children in their own attempts to assimilate and to negotiate the American Dream. Here, immigration and assimilation might be said to characterize a process involving not just mourning *or* melancholia but the inter-generational negotiation between mourning *and* melancholia. Configured as such, this notion begins to depathologize melancholia by situating it as the inherent unfolding and outcome of the mourning process that underwrites the losses of the immigration experience.

Let us turn to a clinical example. Elaine, a U.S.-born Korean American female college student, grew up in Texas. Her father is a professor and her mother is a homemaker. An academic dean referred Elaine to Ms. Han because she was at risk of failing her first year in college. In a tearful presentation, Elaine reported, "My parents have sacrificed everything to raise me here. If my parents had stayed in Korea, my mom would be so much happier and not depressed. She would have friends to speak Korean with, my father would be a famous profes-sor, and we would be better off socially and economically. I wouldn't be so pres-sured to succeed. They sacrificed everything for me, and now it's up to me to please them and to do well in school." When asked the reasons for her academic probation, she responded, "I didn't do well because at a certain point, I didn't care anymore, about myself or anything else."

Elaine's case is an illustration of an intergenerational transference between the immigrant parents and child, which might be usefully described through the logic of melancholia. The loss experienced by the parents' failure to achieve the American Dream—to achieve a standard of living greater than that which they could have putatively achieved in Korea—is a loss transferred onto and incorporated by Elaine for her to "work out" and to repair. In particular, Elaine reenacts these losses through her relationship with her mother. Elaine's depres-sion is a result of internalized guilt and residual anger that she not only feels toward but also identifies with in her mother. Through this incorporation, she also functions as the place-holder of her mother's depression. This mother–daughter predicament has been widely debated in feminist circles.[28] Here, the question is how racial difference comes to intersect what is a strongly gendered formation.

This crossing of sexual and racial difference is a narrative that is very com-mon in Asian American literature (especially Asian American women's writing). Numerous stories portray the first generation (or, alternately, the second gen-eration depending on the particular historical moment and ethnic group) as being a lost generation—bereft, traumatized, with few material or psychic resources.[29] Is it, however, only at the moment in which the first generation acknowledges its failure to achieve the American Dream that this theme of first-generation sacrifice then emerges to be retroactively projected onto the second generation? In other words, are Asian American parents as completely selfless as the theme of sacrifice suggests, or is this theme a compensatory gesture that attaches itself to the parents' losses and failures? Could the ambitions of Elaine's father to become a professor in an American university have motivated their family's immigration? Sacrifice, it is important to remember, is built upon the assumption of nonequivalence and the melancholic notion that what is for-feited and lost can never be recuperated. In turn, do children of immigrants "repay" this sacrifice only by repeating and perpetuating its melancholic logic—by berating and sacrificing themselves?

Yet can sacrifice also be considered the displaced residue of hope—a hope for the reparation of melancholia, of the American Dream? Can hope also be transferred from parent to child and from child to parent? Elaine's case evokes Rea Tajiri's stunning video *History and Memory*,[30] which is about a young Japanese American girl whose parents endure internment during World War II. While her mother has repressed all memories of the internment experience, the daughter has nightmares that she cannot explain: recurring images of a young woman at a watering well. The daughter is depressed, and the parents argue over the etiology of her depression. Eventually, the daughter discovers that these nightmares are reenactments of the mother's histories in the camp. Ironically, the mother has history but no memory, while the daughter has memory but no history. For both mother and daughter, history and memory do not come together until the daughter visits the former site of the internment camp, Poston. Here she realizes that it is her mother's history that she remembers.

Tajiri's video is a compelling example of the ways in which historical traumas of loss are passed down from one generation to another unconsciously. It illustrates Freud's maxim that the losses experienced in melancholia are often unconscious losses. Yet, at the same time, it also diverges from Freud's conception of the disease insofar as it posits a theory of melancholia that is not individually experienced but intergenerationally shared among members of a social group, Japanese Americans. It also departs from Freud's definition of melancholia as pathology and permanence. Here, the hope for psychic health is stitched into the fabric of melancholia but only as an optative gesture that must be redeemed by subsequent generations. In contrast with Freud's contention that melancholia is a classic, one-person psychology—a permanent psychic condition if not solved within a generation—Tajiri's version of melancholia approaches this condition from a different perspective. It refines our theory of racial melancholia as a psychic state focused on bonds among people—an intersubjective psychology—that might be addressed and resolved across generations. Indeed, in *History and Memory* the daughter's return to Poston initiates an incipient healing process in her mother.

In melancholia, the subject's turning from outside (intersubjective) to inside (intrapsychic) threatens to render the social invisible. What is striking in both these examples, of Elaine and of *History and Memory*, is the manner in which the daughters' bodies and voices become substitutes for those of the mothers—not just the mothers' bodies and voices but also something that is unconsciously lost in them. To return to Freud, the melancholic "knows *whom* he has lost but not *what* he has lost in him."[31] Elaine's narrative and the daughter's nightmares are not their own histories. These daughters have absorbed and been saturated by their mothers' losses. The mothers' voices haunt the daughters. These losses and voices are melancholically displaced from the external world into the internal world of the psyche. The anger that these daughters feel toward the loved object is internalized as depression. In "Mourning and Melancholia," Freud reminds us that the reproaches against the self are, in fact, displaced reproaches against the loved object that have been shifted onto the individual's own ego.[32]

In this respect, melancholia might be said to trace a trajectory from love to hate of the lost object. This hate is subsequently transformed into self-hate in the course of moving from the outside world into the internalized domain of the psyche. As such, the internal monologue that the daughters direct toward themselves should rightly be an external dialogue between daughter and mother. In *The Psychic Life of Power,* Judith Butler writes:

> The melancholic would have *said something*, if he or she could, but did not, and now believes in the sustaining power of the voice. Vainly, the melancholic now says what he or she would have said, addressed only to himself, as one who is already split off from himself, but whose power of self-address depends upon this self-forfeiture. The melancholic thus burrows in a direction opposite to that in which he might find a fresher trace of the lost other, attempting to resolve the loss through psychic substitutions and compounding the loss as he goes.[33]

This turning from outside to inside threatens to erase the *political* bases of melancholia. When Asian American students seek therapy, for example, their mental health issues—overwhelmingly perceived as intergenerational familial conflicts—are often diagnosed as being exclusively symptomatic of *cultural* (not political) conflicts. That is, by configuring Asian cultural difference as the source of all intergenerational dis-ease, Asian culture comes to serve as an alibi or a scapegoat for a panoply of mental health issues. These issues may, in fact, trace their etiology not to questions of Asian cultural difference but rather to forms of institutionalized racism and economic exploitation. The segregation of Asian American health issues into the domain of cultural difference thus covers over the need to investigate structural questions of social inequity as they circulate both inside and outside the therapeutic space of the clinic. For instance, not to recognize the history of Japanese internment when analyzing Tajiri's mother–daughter relationship serves not only to repress and to deny this history but also to redouble and to intensify the source of the daughter's melancholia. Lisa Lowe writes in *Immigrant Acts*:

> Interpreting Asian American culture exclusively in terms of the master narratives of generational conflict and filial relation essentializes Asian American culture, obscuring the particularities and incommensurabilities of class, gender, and national diversities among Asians. The reduction of the cultural politics of racialized ethnic groups, like Asian Americans, to first-generation/second-generation struggles displaces social differences into a privatized familial opposition. Such reductions contribute to the aestheticizing commodification of Asian American *cultural* differences, while denying the immigrant histories of material exclusion and differentiation.[34]

A therapeutic process that solely attributes cultural differences to intergenerational conflict may not only result in the failure to cure; it may also serve to endanger further the mental health of the Asian American patient.

MOURNING/MELANCHOLIA/LANGUAGE

This discussion on intergenerational immigration issues brings us to the corollary issue of language. Nelson, a first-generation Japanese American student who immigrated from Osaka to New Jersey when he was five, sought therapy with Ms. Han, presenting chronic struggles with depression associated with identity conflicts regarding race. Nelson's family history reveals that he is the eldest child and has two siblings, a brother and a sister, both of whom were born in the United States. Before Nelson entered school, his mother spoke only Japanese to the children. When Nelson started kindergarten, his teacher strongly advised the mother to replace Japanese with English at home if she wanted her children to assimilate and become successful students. Despite the mother's broken English, she followed the teacher's instruction assiduously, speaking only English to her children. Nelson recounts a story that later took place in grade school. During a reading lesson, he mispronounced *crooked* as though it had only one syllable: "crook'd." His teacher shamed him publicly for this failed mimicry and demanded to know where he learned to (mis) pronounce such a simple word. Nelson reluctantly replied that he learned this pronunciation from his mother. Nelson remembers, in particular, the social embarrassment and ridicule of his classmates.

What we learn about Nelson's case is that, although his original connection to the primary object (the mother) was through the Japanese language, this connection was abruptly interrupted by a foreign property, English. The mother's "poor" mimicry of English abandoned and revised the earliest mother-son attachment, one brokered in Japanese. As such, Nelson could no longer mirror himself from his mother, in Japanese or in English. This estrangement from language, native and foreign, is a double loss. While acquiring a new language (English) should be perceived as a positive cognitive development, what is not often acknowledged or emphasized enough is the concomitant psychic trauma triggered by the loss of what had once been safe, nurturing, and familiar to the young child (Japanese).

The loss of Japanese as a safe and nurturing object reveals another concrete way to think about racial melancholia in relation to Asian American immigration and assimilation. In Nelson's case, melancholia results not only from a thwarted identification with a dominant ideal of unattainable whiteness but also from a vexed relationship to a compromised Japaneseness. Nelson's analytic situation reveals how on two fronts ideals of whiteness and ideals of Asianness are lost and unresolved for the Asian American subject. In both instances, language is the privileged vehicle by which standards of successful assimilation and failed imitation are measured. In this sense, language itself might be thought of as a kind of stereotype, as demanding a flawless mimicry on the part of the young Nelson, whose poor performance leads him to shame and self-abasement.

Nelson's transition from Japanese to English is another good example of the negotiation between mourning and melancholia in the immigration and assimilation process. That is, although he suffers a loss and revaluation of his "mother" tongue, his transition into the "adopted" language (or ideal) of English is anything but smooth. We need to emphasize that the shaming ritual to which the grade school teacher subjects Nelson—one all too common in the Darwinian space of the classroom—is one that not merely makes his transition into English difficult but also demonizes the mother (the mother tongue and accent) at the same time. What was once a loved and safe object is retroactively transformed into an object of insecurity and shame. To the extent that the mother originally represents the safe notion of "home," Nelson's estrangement from his mother and his mother tongue renders it *unheimlich*—unhomely, unfamiliar, uncanny.[35]

The relationship between language and assimilation into national citizenry is developed in a short story by Monique T.-D. Truong. "Kelly" is about a young Vietnamese refugee girl, Thuy-Mai, who finds herself in the improbable space of a 1975 North Carolina classroom.[36] Truong's narrator writes a distressing epistolary monologue to Kelly, her one and only (and now absent) friend from that dark period of her life. In doing so, she mimes the melancholic logic discussed earlier. That is, an intersubjective external dialogue meant for two parties is melancholically internalized and transformed into an intrasubjective, interminable monologue of one, remarkable for its anger and depressed solipsism. What is an epistolary, after all, but an impassioned (though not necessarily answered) plea to the other?

Truong's narrator recalls their grade school teacher:

> Kelly, remember how Mrs. Hammerick talked about Veteran's Day? How about the Day of Infamy when the Japanese bombed Pearl Harbor? Mrs. Hammerick, you know, the mayor's wife always had a sweet something surrounding her like she had spent too much time pulling taffy. . . . Kelly, you only knew that she liked the Beths and the Susans cause they wore pink and never bulged and buckled out of their shirt plackets. I was scared of her like no dark corners could ever scare me. You have to know that all the while she was teaching us history she was telling, with her language for the deaf, blind, and dumb; she was telling all the boys in our class that I was Pearl and my last name was Harbor. They understood her like she was speaking French and their names were all Claude and Pierre.[37]

Truong's story expands our discussion of language and its effects on the constitution of good and bad national subjects. Here, Mrs. Hammerick's common language for the "deaf, blind, and dumb"—a language from which Thuy-Mai is emphatically excluded—is used to create good and bad students within the institutionalized space of the classroom. The Susans and the Beths, the Claudes and the Pierres, are all, as Louis Althusser would put it, "interpellated" by the mayor's wife as good citizen-subjects of the classroom and consequently the nation.[38] Truong emphasizes how education is a primary site through which narratives of national group identity are established, reinforced, and normalized. At the same time, the Vietnamese refugee Thuy-Mai is pathologized as Asian enemy, dismissively labeled "Pearl Harbor," erroneously conflated with the Japanese, and implicitly rendered a menace to the coherence of the U.S. nation-state. Mrs, Hammerick is, of course, not literally speaking French. However, Truong's attention to language underscores the ways in which an unconscious discourse of racism is circulated in the space of the classroom as a nationalizing tract.

Furthermore, as Lisa Lowe points out, Mrs. Hammerick's nationalizing tract is also a gendered discourse: "The narrator's observations that the teacher's history lesson addresses 'all the boys' further instantiates how the American nationalist narrative recognizes, recruits, and incorporates male subjects, while 'feminizing' and silencing the students who do not conform to that notion of patriotic subjectivity."[39] Racialized subjects, such as Nelson and Thuy-Mai, become "good" citizens when they identify with the paternal state and accept, as Lowe summarizes, "the terms of this identification by subordinating [their] racial difference and denying [their] ties with the feminized and racialized 'motherland.'"[40]

ON GOOD AND BAD RACIALIZED OBJECTS

In the case of Nelson, the teacher's shaming of the mother brings the mother's image into crisis, reconfiguring her return in the guise of a "bad" mother. Like Elaine, Nelson, as the Asian American child of immigrant parents, becomes the arbiter of not only his mother's ambitions and losses but also his own. His attempts to "reinstate" his first love-object and caretaker (the Japanese mother) as well as his first language (Japanese) are torturous and compromised.

Nelson's case history brings us to the work of Melanie Klein on good and bad objects, which might be usefully factored into our discussion of racial melancholia for Asian Americans. In "Mourning and Manic-Depressive States," Klein extends Freud's theory on mourning: "While it is true that the characteristic feature of normal mourning is the individual's setting up the lost loved object inside himself, he is not doing so for the first time but, through the work of mourning, is reinstating that object as well as all his loved *internal* objects which he feels he has lost. He is therefore *recovering* what he had already attained in childhood."[41] States of mourning in adult life are dealt with and resolved through the alignment of the lost object with all the loved internal objects of infancy. This clustering of the lost object with the good objects of the past is, as Klein points out, an attempt to recover and hence to reinstate the securities of infancy before the mother was split into good and bad (a necessary but impossible project). In this manner, the loved object is "preserved in safety inside oneself," and depression can be negotiated.[42]

Unlike Freud's theory, then, Klein's formulation for mourning, as well as her prescription for psychic health, depends upon the introjection of the lost object, on retaining it through a melancholic logic of internalization, but an internalization that attempts to reinstate the lost object by aligning it with a cluster of good internal objects.[43] Klein warns, however, of the difficulties often accompanying this rebuilding of the inner world, this recovery and reinstatement of the lost object as "good." Depression will surely ensue, Klein warns, when the lost object cannot be clustered with the good objects of the past. In particular, she writes about the advent of depression through the forfeiture of the "good" mother. In "The Psychogenesis of Manic-Depressive States," Klein observes that from

the very beginning of psychic development there is a constant correlation of real objects with those installed within the ego. It is for this reason that the anxiety I have just described manifests itself in a child's exaggerated fixation to its mother or whoever looks after it. The absence of the mother arouses in the child anxiety lest it should be handed over to bad objects, external and internalized, either *because* of her death or because of her return in the guise of a "*bad*" mother.[44]

Nelson's case illustrates what happens when the mother returns in the guise of a "bad" mother precisely through the loss—the death—of "Japaneseness." Nelson's "good" mother of infancy returns as a "bad" mother of childhood at the moment of the teacher's sudden linguistic interdiction. After this childhood trauma, Nelson cannot easily repair and realign an image of the mother as "bad" with his earlier perceptions of this nurturing figure. Klein summarizes:

> In some patients who had turned away from their mother in dislike or hate, or used other mechanisms to get away from her, I have found that there existed in their minds nevertheless a beautiful picture of the mother, but one which was felt to be a *picture* of her only, not her real self. The real object was felt to be unattractive—really an injured, incurable and therefore dreaded person. The beautiful picture had been dissociated from the real object but had never been given up and played a great part in the specific ways of their sublimations.[45]

Nelson's case history challenges us to consider what must be shorn away from the shamed Japanese mother in order to reinstate her to a world of loved internal objects, in order to create from her a "beautiful picture." In this instance, it would seem that it is racial difference—Japaneseness itself—that must be dissociated from the figure of the injured and dreaded mother in order for this reinstatement to occur. In turn, however, through the shaming of his mother and mother tongue as well as his attempts to repair them, Nelson's Japanese identity becomes dissociated from him, repressed into the unconscious and transformed into a bad object. Nelson's case history emphatically underscores the way in which good attachments to a primary object can be threatened and transformed into bad attachments *specifically through the axis of race.*

What we are proposing here is the refinement of Klein's theory into an account of "good" and "bad" *racialized* objects. Nelson and his mother are bound together as mourners. Nelson's mother becomes overwhelmed with guilt about her broken English. She transfers the burden of this trauma as well as the burden of hope onto Nelson's shoulders. As such, Nelson attempts to save himself by reinstating his mother (and thus his own ego) as good object. His fixation with perfecting his English is indicative of an obsessional mechanism that negotiates the depressive position for him. This process of perfecting English might be seen as Nelson's displaced attempt to preserve the image of the beautiful Japanese mother. Nelson's efforts to reinstate an image of beauty can never be fulfilled (for him or anyone). However, these attempts are a "necessary failure," for Klein warns that if this image of beauty is removed completely—if the death wish against the mother is fulfilled—then guilt is not reduced but in fact heightened. Were this to happen, the self-abasement accompanying melancholia's guilt and ambivalence would only redouble and heighten.

Indeed, the racial melancholia that underwrites Nelson's unresolved loss of the Japanese mother renders any attempt to reinstate this loved object extraordinarily tenuous. This compromising of Nelson's efforts vexes the "proper" work of mourning, leaving him depressed. Klein states, "The ego endeavours to keep the good apart from the bad, and the real from the phantasmatic objects."[46] However, it may be that the racial melancholia and depression that ensue for Nelson can be avoided only through the most difficult psychic process of dissociation—splitting of Japaneseness from the figure of the mother as well as segregating racial and sexual difference. Klein comments, "The attempts to save the loved object, to repair and restore it, attempts which in the state of depression are coupled with despair, since the ego doubts its capacity to achieve this restoration, are determining factors for all sublimations and the whole of the ego development."[47] Nelson's chronic depression and sustained ambivalence toward the figure of his mother indicate the torturous process of reinstatement that clearly impedes proper ego development. It is racial difference that must be attended to here.

At this point, we would like to return to Butler. In *The Psychic Life of Power*, Butler makes the observation that melancholia instantiates a psychic topography in which the ego constitutively emerges in relation to a superego that admonishes and judges it to be lacking. Melancholia, Butler states, "produces the possibility for the representation of psychic life."[48] She makes this claim through a deconstruction of mourning and melancholia. In his first account of the disease, Freud contrasts the pathological condition of melancholia to the normal work of mourning. Later, in *The Ego and the Id*, Freud revises this earlier distinction between mourning and melancholia. He reconceptualizes it, Butler notes, when he realizes that the ego itself is composed of abandoned object-cathexes internalized as constitutive identifications: "But let us remember that in *The Ego and the Id* Freud himself acknowledges that melancholy, the unfinished process of grieving, is central to the formation of identifications that form the ego. Indeed, identifications formed from unfinished grief are the modes in which the lost object is incorporated and phantasmatically preserved in and as the ego."[49] If the ego is composed of its lost attachments, then there would be no ego—indeed, no distinction between inside and outside—without the internalization of loss along melancholic lines. Melancholia thus instantiates the very logic by which the ego and its psychic landscape are constituted. It is only after this partition of internal and external worlds that the work of mourning—that subjectivity itself—becomes possible.[50]

Butler aligns this deconstruction of mourning and melancholia with the social emergence of gender and a system of compulsory heterosexuality. She focuses on Freud's contention, in *The Ego and the Id*, that the primary lost object of desire for the little boy is the father. As such, Butler argues that heterosexual male subjectivity is created melancholically through the father's forfeiture as an object of desire and his internalization as a primary and constitutive identification. She writes that heterosexual identity is thus

purchased through a melancholic incorporation of the love that it disavows: the man who insists upon the coherence of his heterosexuality will claim that he never loved another man, and hence never lost another man. That love, that attachment becomes subject to a double disavowal, a never having loved, and a never having lost. This "never-never" thus founds the heterosexual subject, as it were; it is an identity based upon the refusal to avow an attachment and, hence, the refusal to grieve.[51]

Butler concludes that in opposition to a conception of (hetero)sexuality that is said to reflect a natural gendered order, gender in this case is understood to be composed of precisely what remains melancholically disavowed in sexuality.

Klein's theory of good and bad objects is a useful theoretical supplement here, because she addresses something unaddressed by Butler. If a system of gender melancholy instantiates compulsory male heterosexuality, we neverthe-less do not typically describe the normative male subject as melancholic or depressed. In other words, as Adam Phillips suggests, if the normative hetero-sexual male claims to be relatively untroubled by this disavowal, is it the task of the psychoanalyst to engineer its undoing?[52] Here, the clinical implications of this undoing diverge from the speculative payoff of rethinking a system of com-pulsory heterosexuality.

In both cases, however, Klein's notion of the good and the bad object—of "recovery" and "reinstatement"—allows us to understand how certain losses are grieved because they are not, perhaps, even seen as losses but are seen as social gains. These include access to political, economic, and cultural privilege; align-ment with whiteness and the nation; and "full" subjectivity and a sense of belonging. In other words, the loss of the father as object of desire for the little boy can be more acceptably mourned than other losses, for this "forfeiture" has widespread social support and approbation. Indeed, it provides the very foun-dation of oedipalization. As such, this "forfeiture" is seen not as an abandon-ment but as a culturally rewarded transaction. To return to Phillips, we must continue to ask why it is that the normative heterosexual white male can claim to be untroubled by his melancholic disavowals.

Let us contrast this normative story of oedipalization and the "loss" of the father with Nelson's compromised loss of the mother and the mother tongue. Our present deconstruction of mourning and melancholia tells us that it is cru-cial to recognize that all identities are built on loss. Loss is symptomatic of ego formation, for both dominant as well as marginalized subjects. The crucial point to investigate, then, is the social and psychic status of that lost object, idealized or devalued, and the ways in which that lost object can or cannot be reinstated into the psychic life of the individual in order to rebuild an internal world. It is Klein who lends us a theoretical account to make these distinctions.

DEPATHOLOGIZING MELANCHOLIA

The process of assimilation is a negotiation between mourning and melancholia. The ethnic subject does not inhabit one or the other—mourning *or* melancholia—but mourning *and* melancholia coexist at once in the process of assimilation. This continuum between mourning and melancholia allows us to understand the negotiation of racial melancholia as *conflict* rather than *damage*. Indeed, might we consider damage the intrasubjective displacement of a necessarily intersubjective dynamic of conflict? This attention to racial melancholia as conflict rather than damage not only renders it a productive category but also removes Asian Americans from the position of solipsistic "victims." We are dissatisfied with the assumption that minority subjectivities are *permanently* damaged—forever injured and incapable of ever being "whole." Our theory of intersubjective conflict, intergenerationally shared, evokes Klein's notion of rebuilding on a communal level. This notion of communal rebuilding provides the foundation for the reparation of individual psyches as well as group identities.

Our discussion of immigration, assimilation, and racialization pursued here develops them as issues involving the fluid negotiation between mourning and melancholia. In this manner, melancholia is neither pathological nor permanent but, as José Esteban Muñoz, following Raymond Williams, eloquently suggests, "a structure of feeling," a structure of everyday life. In *Disidentifications: Queers of Color and the Performance of Politics*, Muñoz states that, for queers as well as for people of color, melancholia is not a pathology but an integral part of daily existence and survival. He provides a corrective to Freud's vision of melancholia as a destructive force and states that it is instead part of the

> process of dealing with all the catastrophes that occur in the lives of people of color, lesbians, and gay men. I have proposed a different understanding of melancholia that does not see it as a pathology or as a self-absorbed mood that inhibits activism. Rather, it is a mechanism that helps us (re) construct identity and take our dead with us to the various battles we must wage in their names—and in our names.[53]

Within the continuum of mourning and melancholia is a productive gap inhabited by the various issues under discussion here: immigration, assimilation, and racialization; mimicry, ambivalence, and the stereotype; sacrifice, loss, and reinstatement. The material and psychic negotiations of these various issues are the conflicts with which Asian Americans struggle on an everyday basis. This struggle does not necessarily result in damage but is finally a productive and a necessary process. It is the work of rebuilding. "Suffering," Klein adds, "can become productive":

> It seems that every advance in the process of mourning results in a deepening in the individual's relation to his inner objects, in the happiness of regaining them after they were felt to be lost ("Paradise Lost and Regained"), in an increased trust in them and love for them because they proved to be good and helpful after all. This is similar to the way in which the young child step by step builds up his relations to external objects, for he gains trust not only from pleasant experiences, but also from the ways in which he overcomes frustrations and unpleasant experiences, nevertheless retaining his good objects (externally and internally).[54]

We would like to think about the numerous difficulties of Asian American immigration, assimilation, and racialization processes in terms of "Paradise Lost and Regained."

In the work of racial melancholia there, too, lies a nascent ethical and political project. In "Mourning and Melancholia," Freud originally describes in rather negative terms the melancholic's inability to "get over" loss. We instead focus on the melancholic's absolute refusal to relinquish the other—to forfeit alterity—at any costs. In his essay, Freud lays out the provocative idea that in melancholia "the shadow of the object fell upon the ego."[55] In most of the Freudian oeuvre, it is indubitably the ego that holds sway; his majesty the ego's narcissism reigns supreme. Throughout his writings, Jacques Lacan, even more, emphasizes the narcissism of the ego, reversing this particular formulation by insisting that it is always the shadow of the ego that falls upon the object.[56] In this present formulation, however, we have the loved object, not the ego, holding sway. Racial melancholia thus delineates one psychic process in which the loved object is so overwhelmingly important to and beloved by the ego that the ego is willing to preserve it even at the cost of its own self. In the transferential aspects of melancholic identifications, Freud suggests, "is the expression of there being something in common which may signify love."[57]

This community of love—as W.R.D. Fairbairn, Jessica Benjamin, Christopher Bollas, and others have noted—is possible only through the aggressive and militant preservation of the loved and lost object.[58] Hence, the melancholic process is one way in which socially disparaged objects—racially and sexually deprivileged others—live on in the psychic realm. This behavior, Freud remarks, proceeds from an attitude of "revolt" on the part of the ego. It displays the ego's melancholic yet militant refusal to allow certain objects to disappear into oblivion. In this way, Freud tells us, "love escapes extinction."[59] This preservation of the threatened object might be seen, then, as a type of ethical hold on the part of the melancholic ego. The mourner, in contrast, has no such ethics. The mourner is perfectly content with killing off the lost object, declaring it to be dead yet again within the domain of the psyche.

While the ambivalence, anger, and rage that characterize this preservation of the lost object threaten the ego's stability, we do not imagine that this threat is the result of some ontological tendency on the part of the melancholic; it is a *social* threat. Ambivalence, rage, and anger are the internalized refractions of an ecology of whiteness bent on the obliteration of cherished minority subjectivities. If the loved object is not going to live out there, the melancholic emphatically avers, then it is going to live here inside me. Along with Freud, "we only wonder why a man has to be ill before he can be accessible to a truth of this kind."[60] It is the melancholic who helps us come face to face with this social truth. It is the melancholic who teaches us that "in the last resort we must begin to love in order not to fall ill."[61]

Both Judith Butler and Douglas Crimp isolate the call of melancholia in the age of AIDS as one in which the loss of a public language to mourn a seemingly endless series of young male deaths triggers the absolute need to think about melancholia and activism. Muñoz highlights the communal nature of this activist project—the community-oriented aspect of group rather than individual losses, of group rather than individual identifications, and of group rather than individual activism: "Communal mourning, by its very nature, is an immensely complicated text to read, for we do not mourn just one lost object or other, but we also mourn as a 'whole'—or, put another way, as a contingent and temporary collection of fragments that is experiencing a loss of its parts."[62] A series of unresolved fragments, we come together as a contingent whole. We gain social recognition in the face of this communal loss.

There is a militant refusal on the part of the ego—better yet, a series of egos—to let go, and this militant refusal is at the heart of melancholia's productive political potentials. Paradoxically, in this instance, the ego's death drive may be the very precondition for survival, the beginning of a strategy for living and for living on. Butler asks of melancholia: "Is the psychic violence of conscience not a refracted indictment of the social forms that have made certain kinds of losses ungrievable?"[63] And Crimp ends his essay "Mourning and Militancy" with this simple and moving call: "Militancy, of course, then, but mourning too: mourning *and* militancy."[64] We pause here to insert yet another permutation of this political project in relation to the Asian American immigration, assimilation, and racialization processes we have been discussing throughout this essay: "mourning *and* melancholia."

EPILOGUE: LIVING MELANCHOLIA

This essay is an engagement with psychoanalysis and racial difference that belongs neither in the speculative nor in the clinical arena proper. Rather, this essay, like our theory of racial melancholia, exists in a gap between two spheres and seeks to establish a productive relationship between them. We wrote this essay with the hope of proffering a number of new critical interventions significant to both realms and with the desire to understand better our students, our communities, ourselves.

It also occurs to us that our dialogue—crossing into the often disparate realms of the literary and the clinical—is an exercise in new models of communal interaction that we advocate in our various discussions on the everyday living out of racial melancholia by Asian Americans. Much of this essay reexamines the ways in which the genealogy of racial melancholia as individual pathology functions in terms of larger social group identities—as a type of "psychic citizenship." Indeed, it is our belief that the refusal to view identities under social erasure as individual pathology and permanent damage lies in the communal appropriation of melancholia, its refunctioning as a structure of everyday life that annuls the multitude of losses continually demanded by an unforgiving social world.

To that end, we conclude with a few words on one strategy of community-building within the space of the university. A recent, albeit contested, trend in the academy is the establishing of Asian American studies programs. In the face of this trend, the model minority stereotype is consistently marshaled by university administrations as proof that Asian Americans neither are in want of any special recognition nor have any particular needs as a distinct and socially marked group. The popular vision of Asian Americans as model minorities, as having the best of both worlds (two cultures, two languages), is a multicultural fantasy in the age of diversity management. Our investigation here of immigration, assimilation, and racialization as conflicted and unresolved processes of mourning and melancholia reveals the link between East and West as less than fluid. For Asian Americans, the reparation of these unresolved processes requires a public language. It requires a public space where these conflicts can be acknowledged and negotiated.

In their ideal form, Asian American studies programs provide this publicity, a physical and psychic space to bring together various fragmented parts (intellectual, social, political, cultural) to compose, borrowing from Winnicott, a "holding environment," a "whole" environment.[65] This type of public space ultimately facilitates the creation of new representations of Asian Americans emerging from that gap of ambivalence between mourning and melancholia. These new representations not only contest conventional ways in which Asian Americans have been traditionally apprehended but also refunction the very meanings of "Asian American" within the public sphere.

In the final analysis, this essay has been an exercise for us to mourn the various passings of Asian American students who no longer felt tied to our present world, such as it is. However, this dialogue—this production of new ideas about the conditions and constraints of racial melancholia—should not be taken as a summary moment. Instead, it might be understood as only an initial engagement in the continued work of mourning and melancholia and the rebuilding of new communities.

NOTES

This essay was originally published in *Psychoanalytic Dialogues* 10, no. 4 (2000): 667–700. We would like to thank The Analytic Press, Inc., for allowing us to reproduce it here. The epigraph is from Danzy Senna, *Caucasia* (New York: Riverhead Books, 1998), 329.

1. "Jesse" presents herself as Jewish (and not black), significantly complicating the racial complexities of "whiteness" in Senna's novel. Although Jesse is marked differently from the WASPs populating her New Hampshire environment, her part-Jewish background is mobilized so that she can "pass." It is ostensibly used as an explanation for her darker skin tone and hair.
2. Senna, *Caucasia*, 329.
3. It is important to remember that melancholia and depression are not synonymous psychic conditions, although they often coexist and can trigger one another.
4. The relationship between melancholia and processes of immigration, assimilation, and racialization is underdeveloped in both Asian American studies and clinical practice. We suggest that those interested in this intersection read Asian American literature by authors such as Frank Chin (*The Chinaman Pacific and Frisco R.R. Co.*, 1988), Maxine Hong Kingston (*The Woman Warrior*, 1976), Wendy Law-Yone (*The Coffin Tree*, 1983), Chang-rae Lee (*Native Speaker*, 1995), Fae Myenne Ng (*Bone*, 1993), Hualing Nieh (*Mulberry and Peach*, 1981), and Chay Yew (*Porcelain*, 1997). For a discussion of Asian American immigration, see Sucheng Chan, ed., *Entry Denied: Exclusion and the Chinese Community in America, 1882–1943* (Philadelphia: Temple University Press, 1991); Bill Ong Hing, *Making and Remaking Asian America through Immigration Policy, 1850–1990* (Stanford, Calif.: Stanford University Press, 1993); and Lisa Lowe, *Immigrant Acts: On Asian American Cultural Politics* (Durham, N.C.: Duke University Press, 1996).

For a discussion of Asian American immigration and mental health issues, see Salman Akhtar, "A Third Individuation: Immigration, Identity, and the Psychoanalytic Process," *Journal of the American Psychoanalytic Association* 43, no. 4 (1995): 1051–84; and Yu-Wen Ying, "Psychotherapy for East Asian Americans with Major Depression," in *Working with Asian Americans: A Guide for Clinicians*, ed. Evelyn Lee (New York: Guilford Press, 1997), 252–64.

5. Sigmund Freud, "Mourning and Melancholia," in *The Standard Edition of the Complete Psychological Works of Sigmund Freud*, vol. 14, trans. and ed. James Strachey (London: Hogarth Press, 1953), 243.

6. Freud, "Mourning and Melancholia," 243.

7. Freud, "Mourning and Melancholia," 244.

8. Freud, "Mourning and Melancholia," 246.

9. Freud, "Mourning and Melancholia," 245; emphasis in original.

10. Freud, "Mourning and Melancholia," 252.

11. Here, Senna is reconfiguring a long history of "contamination" that racializes individuals with "one drop of black blood" as colored. There is also a long history that configures immigrants as diseased and contaminated, carriers of illness that infects the national body politic. Contamination is thus one theme for thinking about the intersections of African American and Asian American racialization processes.

12. Sigmund Freud, *Group Psychology and the Analysis of the Ego*, in *The Standard Edition*, vol. 18, 75.

13. For a history of these immigration exclusion acts see Chan, *Entry Denied;* Hing, *Making and Remaking Asian America;* and Lowe, *Immigrant Acts.*

14. See Anne Anlin Cheng, "The Melancholy of Race," *Kenyon Review* 19, no. 1 (1997): 51–52.

15. For a history of the model minority stereotype, see Bob H. Suzuki, "Education and the Socialization of Asian Americans: A Revisionist Analysis of the Model Minority Thesis," *Amerasia Journal* 4, no. 2 (1977): 23–51. For a critique of the model minority thesis in terms of Asian, white, and black relations, see Mari Matsuda, "We Will Not Be Used: Are Asian Americans the Racial Bourgeoisie?" in *Where Is Your Body? And Other Essays on Race, Gender, and the Law* (Boston: Beacon Press, 1996), 149–59.

16. For an elaboration of the concepts of "heterogeneity, hybridity, and multiplicity," see Lowe, *Immigrant Acts*, chapter 3, 60–83, from which this phrase is drawn.

17. Maxine Hong Kingston, *China Men* (New York: Vintage, 1989; originally published 1980), 151.

18. See Freud's essays "Fetishism," in *The Standard Edition of the Complete Psychological Works of Sigmund Freud*, vol. 21, trans. and ed. James Strachey (London: Hogarth Press, 1927), 152–57; and the "Splitting of the Ego in the Defensive Process," in *The Standard Edition*, vol. 23 (1938), 271–78. This argument on racial fetishization and the following discussion on the "Marginal Man" come from David L. Eng, *Racial Castration: Managing Masculinity in Asian America* (Durham, N.C.: Duke University Press, 2001).

19. Stanley Sue and Derald W. Sue, "Chinese-American Personality and Mental Health," *Amerasia Journal* 1, no. 2 (July 1971): 42.

20. Maxine Hong Kingston, *The Woman Warrior: Memoirs of a Girlhood among Ghosts* (New York: Vintage, 1989; originally published 1976).

21. Toni Morrison, "Unspeakable Things Unspoken: The Afro-American Presence in American Literature," *Michigan Quarterly Review* 28 (winter 1989): 11. The phrase was coined by Gilbert Ryle.

22. Homi Bhabha, "Of Mimicry and Man: The Ambivalence of Colonial Discourse," *October* 28 (spring 1984): 126, 130; emphasis in original.

23. Freud, "Mourning and Melancholia," 251.

24. See Homi K. Bhabha, "The Other Question: Stereotype, Discrimination, and the Discourse of Colonialism," in *The Location of Culture* (London: Routledge, 1994), 66; reprinted from *Screen* 24, no. 6 (November–December 1983).

25. Tazuko Shibusawa points out that we must also consider how the model minority stereotype dovetails with a Confucian tradition within East Asian societies. This tradition mandates

a strict hierarchical relationship among members of individual family units and between individual family units and the political representatives of the state.

26. For an elaboration of this concept, see Wendy Brown, *States of Injury: Power and Freedom in Late Modernity* (Princeton, N.J.: Princeton University Press, 1995). In particular, see chapter 3, "Wounded Attachments," 52–76, in which Brown writes:

> But in its attempts to displace its suffering, identity structured by *ressentiment* at the same time becomes invested in its own subjection. This investment lies not only in its discovery of a site of blame for its hurt will, not only in its acquisition of recognition through its history of subjection (a recognition predicated on injury now righteously revalued), but also in the satisfactions of revenge, which ceaselessly reenact even as they redistribute the injuries of marginalization and subordination in a liberal discursive order that alternately denies the very possibility of these things and blames those who experience them for their own condition. Identity politics structured by *ressentiment* reverse without subverting this blaming structure; they do not subject to critique the sovereign subject of accountability that liberal individualism presupposes, nor the economy of inclusion and exclusion that liberal universalism establishes. (70)

27. Gish Jen, *Typical American* (Boston: Houghton Mifflin, 1991).

28. See, for example, Julia Kristeva, *Desire in Language: A Semiotic Approach to Literature and Art* (New York: Columbia University Press, 1980).

29. The question of generational sacrifice is historically as well as ethnically specific. For example, during the exclusion era, many first-generation Asian immigrants barred from naturalization and citizenship exhibited a strong identification with their home country as "sojourners." Consequently, it was the second generation during this historical period (especially those born on U.S. soil) who exhibited the stronger characteristics of a lost generation—for instance, the Nisei interned during World War II. After the 1965 reformation of the Immigration and Nationality Act, Asian immigrants were legally guaranteed— and in much larger numbers—access to the space of the nation-state as citizens. The narrative of sacrifice thus attaches itself more strongly to these first-generation immigrants, whose hopes for assimilation and integration into the national fabric are more evident.

30. Rea Tajiri, dir., *History and Memory* (New York: Women Make Movies, 1991).

31. Freud, "Mourning and Melacholia," 245.

32. Freud, "Mourning and Melancholia," 248.

33. Judith Butler, *The Psychic Life of Power: Theories in Subjection* (Stanford, Calif.: Stanford University Press, 1997), 182; emphasis in original.

34. Lowe, *Immigrant Acts*, 63; emphasis in original.

35. See Freud's essay "Uncanny." For a discussion of the uncanny and nation-building, see Sau-ling Wong, *Reading Asian American Literature, from Necessity to Extravagance* (Princeton, N.J.: Princeton University Press, 1993), chapter 2; and Priscilla Wald, *Constituting Americans: Cultural Anxiety and Narrative Form* (Durham, N.C.: Duke University Press, 1995), chapter 1.

36. Monique Thuy-Dung Truong, "Kelly," *Amerasia Journal* 17, no. 2 (1991): 41–48.

37. Truong, "Kelly," 42.

38. See Louis Althusser, "Ideology and Ideological State Apparatuses (Notes toward an Investigation)," in *Lenin and Philosophy and Other Essays*, trans. Ben Brewster (New York: Monthly Review Press, 1971), 127–86.

39. Lowe, *Immigrant Acts*, 55.

40. Lowe, *Immigrant Acts*, 56.

41. Melanie Klein, "Mourning and Manic-Depressive States," in *The Selected Melanie Klein*, ed. Juliet Mitchell (New York: Free Press, 1987), 165–66; emphasis in original.

42. Melanie Klein, "The Psychogenesis of Manic-Depressive States," in *The Selected Melanie Klein*, 119.

43. It might be useful here to consider Freud's notion of mourning and melancholia against Abraham and Torok's concept of "introjection" versus "incorporation." See Nicolas

Abraham and Maria Torok, *The Shell and the Kernel*, vol. 1, trans. Nicholas T. Rand (Chicago: University of Chicago Press, 1994), chapter 5, "Mourning *or* Melancholia: Introjection *versus* Incorporation," 125–38.

44. Klein, "The Psychogenesis of Manic-Depressive States," 121; emphasis in original.
45. Klein, "The Psychogenesis of Manic-Depressive States," 125; emphasis in original.
46. Klein, "The Psychogenesis of Manic-Depressive States," 123.
47. Klein, "The Psychogenesis of Manic-Depressive States," 124.
48. Butler, *The Psychic Life of Power*, 177.
49. Butler, *The Psychic Life of Power*, 132.
50. Butler writes that in melancholia, the

> inability to declare such a loss signifies the "retraction" or "absorption" of the loss by the ego. Clearly, the ego does not literally take an object inside itself, as if the ego were a kind of shelter prior to its melancholy. The psychological discourses and its various "parts" miss the crucial point that melancholy is precisely what interiorizes the psyche, that is, makes it possible to refer to the psyche through such topographical tropes. The turn from object to ego is the movement that makes the distinction between them possible, that marks the division, the separation or loss, that forms the ego to begin with. In this sense, the turn from the object to the ego fails successfully to substitute the latter for the former, but does succeed in marking and perpetuating the partition between the two. The turn thus produces the divide between ego and object, the internal and external worlds that it appears to presume. (*The Psychic Life of Power*, 170)

51. Butler, *The Psychic Life of Power*, 139–40.
52. Adam Phillips, "Keep It Moving: Commentary on Judith Butler's 'Melancholy Gender/Refused Identification,'" in Butler, *The Psychic Life of Power*, 155.
53. José Esteban Muñoz, *Disidentifications: Queers of Color and the Performance of Politics* (Minneapolis: University of Minnesota Press, 1999), 74.
54. Klein, 'The Psychogenesis of Manic-Depressive States," 163–64.
55. Freud, "Mourning and Melancholia," 249.
56. See Jacques Lacan, *The Seminar of Jacques Lacan*, book 2: *The Ego in Freud's Theory and in the Technique of Psychoanalysis, 1954–1955*, ed. Jacques-Alain Miller (New York: W. W. Norton, 1991).
57. Freud, "Mourning and Melancholia," 250.
58. See W.R.D. Fairbairn, *An Object-Relations Theory of the Personality* (New York: Basic Books, 1954); Christopher Bollas, *The Shadow of the Object: Psychoanalysis of the Unthought* (New York: Columbia University Press, 1987); and Jessica Benjamin, *The Shadow of the Other: Intersubjectivity and Gender in Psychoanalysis* (New York: Routledge, 1998).
59. Freud, "Mourning and Melancholia," 248, 257.
60. Freud, "Mourning and Melancholia," 246.
61. Sigmund Freud, "On Narcissism: An Introduction," in *The Standard Edition*, vol. 14, 85.
62. Muñoz, *Disidentifications*, 73.
63. Butler, *The Psychic Life of Power*, 185.
64. Douglas Crimp, "Mourning and Militancy," *October* 51 (1989): 18; emphasis in original.
65. See D. W. Winnicott, *The Maturation Process and the Facilitating Environment* (New York: International Universities Press, 1965).

HOME IS WHERE THE *HAN* IS

A KOREAN AMERICAN PERSPECTIVE ON
THE LOS ANGELES UPHEAVALS

Elaine H. Kim

About half of the estimated $850 million in material losses incurred during the Los Angeles upheavals was sustained by a community no one seems to want to talk much about. Korean Americans in Los Angeles, suddenly at the front lines when violence came to the buffer zone they had been so precariously occupying, suffered profound damage to their means of livelihood.[1] But my concern here is the psychic damage which, unlike material damage, is impossible to quantify.

I want to explore the questions of whether or not recovery is possible for Korean Americans, and what will become of our attempts to "become American" without dying of *han*. *Han* is a Korean word that means, loosely translated, the sorrow and anger that grow from the accumulated experiences of oppression. Although the word is frequently and commonly used by Koreans, the condition it describes is taken quite seriously. When people die of *han*, it is called dying of *hwabyong*, a disease of frustration and rage following misfortune.

Situated as we are on the border between those who have and those who have not, between predominantly Anglo and mostly African American and Latino communities, from our current interstitial position in the American discourse of race, many Korean Americans have trouble calling what happened in Los Angeles an "uprising." At the same time, we cannot quite say it was a "riot." So some of us have taken to calling it *sa-i-ku*, April 29, after the manner of naming other events in Korean history—3.1 (*sam-il*) for March 1, 1919, when massive protests against Japanese colonial rule began in Korea; 6.25 (*yook-i-o*) for June 25, 1950, when the Korean War began; and 4.19 (*sa-il-ku*) for April 19, 1960, when the first student movement in the world to overthrow a government began in South Korea. The ironic similarity between 4.19 and 4.29 does not escape most Korean Americans.

Los Angeles Koreatown has been important to me, even though I visit only a dozen times a year. Before Koreatown sprang up during the last decade and a half,[2] I used to hang around the fringes of Chinatown, although I knew that this habit was pure pretense.[3] For me, knowing that Los Angeles Koreatown existed made a difference; one of my closest friends worked with the Black–Korean Alliance there,[4] and I liked to think of it as a kind of "home"—however idealized and hypostatized—for the soul, an anchor, a potential refuge, a place in America where I could belong without ever being asked, "Who are you and what are you doing here? Where did you come from and when are you going back?"

Many of us watched in horror the destruction of Koreatown and the systematic targeting of Korean shops in South Central Los Angeles after the Rodney King verdict. Seeing those buildings in flames and those anguished Korean faces, I had the terrible thought that there would be no belonging and that we were, just as I had always suspected, a people destined to carry our *han* around with us wherever we went in the world. The destiny (*p'aljja*) that had spelled centuries of extreme suffering from invasion, colonization, war, and national division had smuggled itself into the United States with our baggage.

AFRICAN AMERICAN AND KOREAN AMERICAN CONFLICT

As someone whose social consciousness was shaped by the African American–led civil rights movement of the 1960s, I felt that I was watching our collective dreams for a just society disintegrating, cast aside as naive and irrelevant in the bitter and embattled 1990s. It was the courageous African American women and men of the 1960s who had redefined the meaning of "American," who had first suggested that a person like me could reject the false choice between being treated as a perpetual foreigner in my own birthplace, on the one hand, and relinquishing my identity for someone else's ill-fitting and impossible Anglo-American one on the other. Thanks to them, I began to discern how institutional racism works and why Korea was never mentioned in my world history textbooks. I was able to see how others besides Koreans had been swept aside by the dominant culture. My American education offered nothing about Chicanos or Latinos, and most of what I was taught about African and Native Americans was distorted to justify their oppression and vindicate their oppressors.

I could hardly believe my ears when, during the weeks immediately following *sa-i-ku,* I heard African American community leaders suggesting that Korean American merchants were foreign intruders deliberately trying to stifle African American economic development, when I knew that they had bought those liquor stores at five times gross receipts from African American owners, who had previously bought them at two times gross receipts from Jewish owners after Watts.[5] I saw anti-Korean flyers that were being circulated by African American political candidates and read about South Central residents petitioning against the reestablishment of swap meets, groups of typically Korean immigrant-operated market stalls. I was disheartened with Latinos who related the pleasure they felt while looting Korean stores they believed "had it coming," and who claimed that it was because of racism that more Latinos were arrested during *sa-i-ku* than Asian Americans.[6] And I was filled with despair when I read about Chinese Americans wanting to dissociate themselves from us. According to one Chinese American reporter assigned to cover Asian American issues for a San Francisco daily, Chinese and Japanese American shopkeepers, unlike Koreans, always got along fine with African Americans in the past.[7] "Suddenly," admitted another Chinese American, "I am scared to be Asian. More specifically, I am afraid to be mistaken for Korean."[8] I was enraged when I overheard European Americans discussing the conflicts as if they were watching a dogfight or a boxing match. The situation reminded me of the Chinese film "Raise the Red Lantern," in which we never see the husband's face. We only hear his mellifluous voice as he benignly admonishes his four wives not to fight among themselves. He can afford to be kind and pleasant because the structure that pits his wives against each other is so firmly in place that he need never sully his hands or even raise his voice.

BATTLEGROUND LEGACY

Korean Americans are squeezed between black and white and also between U.S. and South Korean political agendas. Opportunistic American and South Korean presidential candidates toured the burnt ruins, posing for the television cameras but delivering nothing of substance to the victims. Like their U.S. counterparts, South Korean news media seized upon *sa-i-ku*, featuring sensational stories that depicted the problem as that of savage African Americans attacking innocent Koreans for no reason.[9] To give the appearance of authenticity, Seoul newspapers even published articles using the names of Korean Americans who did not in fact write them.[10]

Those of us who chafe at being asked whether we are Chinese or Japanese as if there were no other possibilities or who were angered when the news media sought Chinese and Japanese but not Korean American views during *sa-i-ku* are sensitive to an invisibility that seems particular to us. To many Americans, Korea is but the gateway to or the bridge between China and Japan, or a crossroads of major Asian conflicts.[11]

Although little known or cared about in the Western world, Korea has been a perennial battleground. Besides the Mongols and the Manchus, there were the *Yŏjin* (Jurched), the *Koran* (Khitan), and the *Waegu* (Wäkö) invaders. In relatively recent years, there was the war between China and Japan that ended in 1895 and the war between Japan and Russia in 1905, both of which were fought on Korean soil and resulted in extreme suffering for the Korean people. Japan's thirty-six years of brutal colonial rule ended with the United States and what was then the Soviet Union dividing the country in half at the 38th parallel. Thus, Korea was turned into a cold war territory that ultimately became a battleground for world superpowers during the conflict of 1950–53.

BECOMING AMERICAN

One of the consequences of war, colonization, national division, and super-power economic and cultural domination has been the migration of Koreans to places like Los Angeles, where they believed their human rights would be protected by law. After all, they had received U.S.-influenced political educations. They started learning English in the seventh grade. They all knew the story of the poor boy from Illinois who became president. They all learned that the U.S. Constitution and Bill of Rights protected the common people from violence and injustice. But they who grew up in Korea watching "Gunsmoke," "Knight Rider," and "McGyver" dubbed in Korean were not prepared for the black, brown, red, and yellow America they encountered when they disembarked at the Los Angeles International Airport.[12] They hadn't heard that there is no equal justice in the United States. They had to learn about American racial hierarchies. They did not realize that, as immigrants of color, they would never attain political voice or visibility but would instead be used to uphold the inequality and the racial hierarchy they had no part in creating.

Most of the newcomers had underestimated the communication barriers they would face. Like the Turkish workers in Germany described in John Berger and Jean Mohr's *A Seventh Man*,[13] their toil amounted to only a pile of gestures and the English they tried to speak changed and turned against them as they spoke it. Working fourteen hours a day, six or seven days a week, they rarely came into sustained contact with English-speaking Americans and almost never had time to study English. Not feeling at ease with English, they did not engage in informal conversations easily with non-Koreans and were hated for being curt and rude. They did not attend churches or do business in banks or other enterprises where English was required. Typically, the immigrant, small-business owners utilized unpaid family labor instead of hiring people from local communities. Thanks to Eurocentric American cultural practices, they knew little or nothing good about African Americans or Latinos, who in turn and for similar reasons knew little or nothing good about them. At the same time, Korean shop owners in South Central and Koreatown were affluent compared with the impoverished residents, whom they often exploited as laborers or looked down upon as fools with an aversion to hard work.[14] Most Korean immigrants did not even know that they were among the many direct beneficiaries of the African American–led civil rights movement, which helped pave the way for the 1965 reforms that made their immigration possible.

Korean immigrant views, shaped as they were by U.S. cultural influences and official, anticommunist, South Korean education,[15] differed radically from those of many poor people in the communities Korean immigrants served: unaware of the shameful history of oppression of nonwhite immigrants and other people of color in the United States, they regarded themselves as having arrived in a meritocratic "land of opportunity" where a person's chances for success are limited only by individual lack of ability or diligence. Having left a homeland where they foresaw their talents and hard work going unrecognized and unrewarded, they were desperate to believe that the "American dream" of social and economic mobility through hard work was within their reach.

SA-I-KU

What they experienced on April 29 and 30 was a baptism into what it really means for a Korean to "become American" in the 1990s.[16] In South Korea, there is no 911, and no one really expects a fire engine or police car if there is trouble. Instead, people make arrangements with friends and family for emergencies. At the same time, guns are not part of Korean daily life. No civilian in South Korea can own a gun. Guns are the exclusive accoutrement of the military and police, who enforce order for those who rule the society. When the Korean Americans in South Central and Koreatown dialed 911, nothing happened. When their stores and homes were being looted and burned to the ground, they were left completely alone for three horrifying days. How betrayed they must have felt by what they had believed was a democratic system that protects its people from violence. Those who trusted the government to protect them lost everything; those who took up arms after waiting for help for two days were able to defend themselves. It was as simple as that. What they had to learn was that, as in South Korea, protection in the United States is by and large for the rich and powerful. If there were a choice between Westwood and Koreatown, it is clear that Koreatown would have to be sacrificed. The familiar concept of privilege for the rich and powerful would have been easy for the Korean immigrant to grasp if only those exhortations about democracy and equality had not obfuscated the picture. Perhaps they should have relied even more on whatever they brought with them from Korea instead of fretting over trying to understand what was going on around them here. That Koreatown became a battleground does seem like the further playing out of a tragic legacy that has followed them across oceans and continents. The difference is that this was a battle between the poor and disenfranchised and the invisible rich, who were being protected by a layer of clearly visible Korean American human shields in a battle on the buffer zone.

This difference is crucial. Perhaps the legacy is not one carried across oceans and continents but one assumed immediately upon arrival, not the curse of being Korean but the initiation into becoming American, which requires that Korean Americans take on this country's legacy of five centuries of racial violence and inequality, of divide and rule, of privilege for the rich and oppression of the poor. Within this legacy, they have been assigned a place on the front lines. Silenced by those who possess the power to characterize and represent, they are permitted to speak only to reiterate their acceptance of this role.

SILENCING THE KOREAN AMERICAN VOICE

Twelve years ago, in Kwangju, South Korea, hundreds of civilians demonstrating for constitutional reform and free elections were murdered by U.S.-supported and -equipped South Korean elite paratroopers. Because I recorded it and played it over and over again, searching for a sign or a clue, I remember clearly how what were to me heartrendingly tragic events were represented in the U.S. news media. For a few fleeting moments, images of unruly crowds of alien-looking Asians shouting unintelligible words and phrases and wearing white headbands inscribed with unintelligible characters flickered across the screen. The Koreans were made to seem like insane people from another planet. The voice in the background stated simply that there were massive demonstrations but did not explain what the protests were about. Nor was a single Korean ever given an opportunity to speak to the camera.

The next news story was about demonstrations for democracy in Poland. The camera settled on individuals' faces, which one by one filled the screen as each man or woman was asked to explain how he or she felt. Each Polish person's words were translated in a voiceover or subtitle. Solidarity leader Lech Walesa, who was allowed to speak often, was characterized as a heroic human being with whom all Americans could surely identify personally. Polish Americans from New York and Chicago to San Francisco, asked in man-on-the-street interviews about their reactions, described the canned hams and blankets they were sending to Warsaw.

This was for me a lesson in media representation, race, and power politics. It is a given that Americans are encouraged by our ideological apparatuses to side with our allies (here, the Polish resisters and the anticommunist South Korean government) against our enemies (here, the communist Soviet Union and protesters against the South Korean government). But visual-media racism helps craft and reinforce our identification with Europeans and whites while distancing us from fearsome and alien Asiatic hordes.

In March 1992, when two delegates from North Korea visited the Bay Area to participate in community-sponsored talks on Korean reunification, about 800 people from the Korean American community attended. The meeting was consummately newsworthy, since it was the first time in history that anyone from North Korea had ever been in California for more than twenty-four hours just passing through. The event was discussed for months in the Korean-language media—television, radio, and newspapers. Almost every Korean-speaking person in California knew about it. Although we sent press releases to all the commercial and public radio and television stations and to all the Bay Area newspapers, not a single mainstream media outfit covered the event. However, whenever there was an African American boycott of a Korean store or whenever conflict surfaced between Korean and African Americans, community leaders found a dozen microphones from all the main news media shoved into their faces, as if they were the president's press secretary making an official public pronouncement. Fascination with interethnic conflicts is rooted in the desire to excuse or minimize white racism by buttressing the mistaken notion that all human beings are "naturally" racist, and when Korean and African Americans allow themselves to be distracted by these interests, their attention is deflected from the social hierarchies that give racism its destructive power.

Without a doubt, the U.S. news media played a major role in exacerbating the damage and ill will toward Korean Americans, first by spotlighting tensions between African Americans and Koreans above all efforts to work together and as opposed to many other newsworthy events in these two communities, and second by exploiting racist stereotypes of Koreans as unfathomable aliens, this time wielding guns on rooftops and allegedly firing wildly into crowds.[17] In news programs and on talk shows, African and Korean American tensions were discussed by blacks and whites, who pointed to these tensions as the main cause of the uprising. I heard some European Americans railing against rude and exploitative Korean merchants for ruining peaceful race relations for everyone else. Thus, Korean Americans were used to deflect attention from the racism they inherited and the economic injustice and poverty that had been already well woven into the fabric of American life, as evidenced by a judicial system that could allow not only the Korean store owner who killed Latasha Harlins but also the white men who killed Vincent Chin and the white police who beat Rodney King to go free, while Leonard Peltier still languishes in prison.

As far as I know, neither the commercial nor the public news media has mentioned the many Korean and African American attempts to improve relations, such as joint church services, joint musical performances and poetry readings, Korean merchant donations to African American community and youth programs, African American volunteer teachers in classes for Korean immigrants studying for citizenship examinations, or Korean translations of African American history materials.

While Korean immigrants were preoccupied with the mantra of day-to-day survival, Korean Americans had no voice, no political presence whatsoever in American life. When they became the targets of violence in Los Angeles, their opinions and views were hardly solicited except as they could be used in the already constructed mainstream discourse on race relations, which is a sorry combination of blaming the African American and Latino victims for their poverty and scapegoating the Korean Americans as robotic aliens who have no "real" right to be here in the first place and therefore deserve whatever happens to them.

THE *NEWSWEEK* EXPERIENCE

In this situation, I felt compelled to respond when an editor from the "My Turn" section of *Newsweek* magazine asked for a 1,000-word personal essay.[18] Hesitant because I was given only a day and a half to write the piece, not enough time in light of the vastness of American ignorance about Koreans and Korean Americans, I decided to do it because I thought I could not be made into a sound bite or a quote contextualized for someone else's agenda.

I wrote an essay accusing the news media of using Korean Americans and tensions between African and Korean Americans to divert attention from the roots of racial violence in the United States. I asserted that these lie not in the Korean-immigrant–owned corner store situated in a community ravaged by poverty and police violence, but reach far back into the corridors of corporate and government offices in Los Angeles, Sacramento, and Washington, D.C. I suggested that Koreans and African Americans were kept ignorant about each other by educational and media institutions that erase or distort their experiences and perspectives. I tried to explain how racism had kept my parents from ever really becoming Americans, but that having been born here, I considered myself American and wanted to believe in the possibility of an American dream.

The editor of "My Turn" did everything he could to frame my words with his own viewpoint. He faxed his own introductory and concluding paragraphs that equated Korean merchants with cowboys in the Wild West and alluded to Korean/African American hatred. When I objected, he told me that my writing style was not crisp enough and that as an experienced journalist, he could help me out. My confidence wavered, but ultimately I rejected his editing. Then he accused me of being overly sensitive, confiding that I had no need to be defensive—because his wife was a Chinese American. Only after I had decided to withdraw the piece did he agree to accept it as I had written it.

Before I could finish congratulating myself on being able to resist silencing and the kind of decontextualization I was trying to describe in the piece, I started receiving hate mail. Some of it was addressed directly to me, since I had been identified as a University of California faculty member, but most of it arrived in bundles, forwarded by *Newsweek*. Hundreds of letters came from all over the country, from Florida to Washington state and from Massachusetts to Arizona. I was unprepared for the hostility expressed in most of the letters. Some people sent the article, torn from the magazine and covered with angry, red-inked obscenities scratched across my picture. "You should see a good doctor," wrote someone from Southern California, "you have severe problems in thinking, reasoning, and adjusting to your environment."

A significant proportion of the writers, especially those who identified themselves as descendants of immigrants from Eastern Europe, wrote *Newsweek* that they were outraged, sickened, disgusted, appalled, annoyed, and angry at the magazine for providing an arena for the paranoid, absurd, hypocritical, racist, and childish views of a spoiled, ungrateful, whining, bitching, un-American bogus faculty member who should be fired or die when the next California earthquake dumps all of the "so-called people of color" into the Pacific Ocean.

I was shocked by the profound ignorance of many writers' assumptions about the experiences and perspectives of American people of color in general and Korean and other Asian Americans in particular. Even though my essay revealed that I was born in the United States and that my parents had lived in the United States for more than six decades, I was viewed as a foreigner without the right to say anything except words of gratitude and praise about America. The letters also provided some evidence of the dilemma Korean Americans are placed in by those who assume that we are aliens who should "go back" and at the same time berate us for not rejecting "Korean-American identity" for "American identity."

How many Americans migrate to Korea? If you are so disenchanted, Korea is still there. Why did you ever leave it? Sayonara.

Ms. Kim appears to have a personal axe to grind with this country that has given her so much freedom and opportunity. . . . I should suggest that she move to Korea, where her children will learn all they ever wanted about that country's history.

[Her] whining about the supposedly racist U.S. society is just a mask for her own acute inferiority complex. If she is so dissatisfied with the United States why doesn't she vote with her feet and leave? She can get the hell out and return to her beloved Korea—her tribal afinity [*sic*] where her true loyalty and consciousness lies [*sic*].

You refer to yourself as a Korean American and yet you have lived all your life in the United States . . . you write about racism in this country and yet you are the biggest racist by your own written words. If you cannot accept the fact that you are an American, maybe you should be living your life in Korea.

My stepfather and cousin risked their lives in the country where your father is buried to ensure the ideals of our country would remain. So don't expect to find a sympathetic ear for your pathetic whining.

Many of the letter writers assumed that my family had been the "scum" of Asia and that I was a college teacher only because of American justice and largesse. They were furious that I did not express gratitude for being saved from starvation in Asia and given the opportunity to flourish, no doubt beyond my wildest dreams, in America.

Where would she be if her parents had not migrated to the United States? For a professor at Berkeley University [*sic*] to say the American dream is only an empty promise is ludicrous. Shame, shame, shame on Elaine!

[Her father and his family] made enough money in the USA to ship his corpse home to Korea for burial. Ms. Kim herself no doubt has a guaranteed life income as a professor paid by California taxpayers. Wouldn't you think that she might say kind things about the USA instead of whining about racism?

At the same time some letters blamed me for expecting freedom and opportunity: "It is wondrous that folks such as you find truth in your paranoia. No one ever promised anything to you or your parents."

Besides providing indications of how Korean Americans are regarded, the letters revealed a great deal about how American identity is thought of. One California woman explained that although her grandparents were Irish immigrants, she was not an Irish American, because "if you are not with us, you are against us." A Missouri woman did not seem to realize that she was conflating race and nationality and confusing "nonethnic" and "nonracial," by which she seems to have meant "white," with "American." And, although she insists that it is impossible to be both "black" and "American," she identifies herself at the outset as a "white American."

I am a white American. I am proud to be an American. You cannot be black, white, Korean, Chinese, Mexican, German, French, or English or any other and still be an American. Of course the culture taught in schools is strictly American. That's where we are and if you choose to learn another [culture] you have the freedom to settle there. You cannot be a Korean American which assumes you are not ready to be an AMERICAN. Do you get my gist?

The suggestion that more should be taught in U.S. schools about America's many immigrant groups and people of color prompted many letters in defense of Western civilization against non-Western barbarism:

> You are dissatisfied with current school curricula that exclude Korea. Could it possibly be because Korea and Asia for that matter has [*sic*] not had . . . a noticeable impact on the shaping of Western culture, and Korea has had unfortunately little culture of its own?

> Who cares about Korea, Ms. Kim? . . . And what enduring contributions has the Black culture, both here in the US and on the continent contributed to the world, and mankind? I'm from a culture, Ms. Kim, who put a man on the moon 23 years ago, who established medical schools to train doctors to perform open heart surgery, and . . . who created a language of music so that musicians, from Beethoven to the Beatles, could easily touch the world with their brilliance forever and ever and ever. Perhaps the dominant culture, whites obviously, "swept aside Chicanos . . . Latinos . . . African-Americans . . . Koreans," because they haven't contributed anything that made—be mindful of the cliche—a world of difference?

> Koreans' favorite means of execution is decapitation. . . . Ms. Kim, and others like her, came here to escape such injustice. Then they whine at riots to which they have contributed by their own fanning of flames of discontent. . . . Yes! Let us all study more about Oriental culture! Let us put matters into proper perspective.

> Fanatical multiculturalists like you expect a country whose dominant culture has been formed and influenced by Europe . . . nearly 80% of her population consisting of persons whose ancestry is European, to include the history of every ethnic group who has ever lived here. I truly feel sorry for you. You and your bunch need to realize that white Americans are not racists. . . . We would love to get along, but not at the expense of our own culture and heritage.

> Kim's axe-to-grind confirms the utter futility of race-relations—the races were never meant to live together. We don't get along and never will. . . . Whats [*sic*] needed is to divide the United States up along racial lines so that life here can finally become livable.

What seemed to anger some people the most was their idea that, although they worked hard, people of color were seeking handouts and privileges because of their race, and the thought of an ungrateful Asian American siding with African Americans, presumably against whites, was infuriating. How dare I "bite the hand that feeds" me by siding with the champion "whiners who cry 'racism'" because to do so is the last refuge of the "terminally incompetent"?

> The racial health in this country won't improve until minorities stop erecting "me first" barriers and strive to be Americans, not African-Americans or Asian-Americans expecting privileges.

Ms. Kim wants preferential treatment that immigrants from Greece-to-Sweden have not enjoyed. . . . Even the Chinese . . . have not created any special problems for themselves or other Americans. Soon those folk are going to express their own resentments to the insatiable demands of the Blacks and other colored peoples, including the wetbacks from Mexico who sneak into this country then pilfer it for all they can.

The Afroderived citizens of Los Angeles and the Asiatic derivatives were not suffering a common imposition. . . . The Asiatics are trying to build their success. The Africans are sucking at the teats of entitlement.

As is usual with racists, most of the writers of these hate letters saw only themselves in their notions about Korea, America, Korean Americans, African Americans. They felt that their own sense of American identity was being threatened and that they were being blamed as individuals for U.S. racism. One man, adept at manipulating various fonts on his word processor, imposed his preconceptions on my words:

Let me read between the lines of your little hate message:
        . . . "The roots . . . stretch far back into the corridors of corporate and government offices in Los Angeles, Sacramento, and Washington, D.C."
    All white America and all American institutions are to blame for racism.
        . . . "I still want to believe the promise is real."
    I have the savvy to know that the American ideals of freedom and justice are a joke but if you want to give me what I want I'm willing to make concessions.
        Ms. Kim . . . if you want to embody the ignorant, the insecure, and the emotionally immature, that's your right! just stop preaching hate and please, please, quit whining.
                                Sincerely, A proud White-American
                                teaching my children not to be prejudicial

Especially since my essay had been subdued and intensely personal, I had not anticipated the fury it would provoke. I never thought that readers would write over my words with their own. The very fact that I used words, and English words at that, particularly incensed some: one letter writer complained about my use of words and phrases like "manifestation" and "zero-sum game," and "suzerain relationship," which is the only way to describe Korea's relationship with China during the T'ang Dynasty. "Not more than ten people in the USA know what [these words] mean," he wrote. "You are on an ego trip." I wondered if it made him particularly angry that an Asian American had used those English words, or if he would make such a comment to George Will or Jane Bryant Quinn.

Clearly I had encountered part of America's legacy, the legacy that insists on silencing certain voices and erasing certain presences, even if it means deportation, internment, and outright murder. I should not have been surprised by what happened in Koreatown or by the ignorance and hatred expressed in the letters to *Newsweek*, any more than African Americans should have been surprised by the Rodney King verdict. Perhaps the news media, which constituted *sa-i-ku* as news, as an extraordinary event in no way continuous with our everyday lives, made us forget for a moment that as people of color many of us simultaneously inhabit two Americas: the America of our dreams and the America of our experience.

Who among us does not cling stubbornly to the America of our dreams, the promise of a multicultural democracy where our cultures and our differences might be affirmed instead of distorted in an effort to destroy us?

After *sa-i-ku*, I was able to catch glimpses of this America of my dreams because I received other letters that expressed another American legacy. Some people identified themselves as Norwegian or Irish Americans interested in combating racism. Significantly, while most of the angry mail had been sent not to me but to *Newsweek*, almost all of the sympathetic mail, particularly the letters from African Americans, came directly to me. Many came from Korean Americans who were glad that one of their number had found a vehicle for self-expression. Others were from Chinese and Japanese Americans who wrote that they had had similar experiences and feelings. Several were written in shaky longhand by women fervently wishing for peace and understanding among people of all races. A Native American from Nashville wrote a long description of cases of racism against African, Asian, and Native Americans in the U.S. criminal justice system. A large number of letters came from African Americans, all of them supportive and sympathetic—from judges and professors who wanted better understanding between Africans and Koreans to poets and laborers who scribbled their notes in pencil while on breaks at work. One man identified himself as a Los Angeles African American whose uncle had married a Korean woman. He stated that as a black man in America, he knew what other people feel when they face injustice. He ended his letter apologizing for his spelling and grammar mistakes and asking for materials to read on Asian Americans. The most touching letter I received was written by a prison inmate who had served twelve years of a thirty-five-to-seventy-year sentence for armed robbery during which no physical injuries occurred. He wrote:

> I've been locked in these prisons going on 12 years now . . . and since being here I have studied fully the struggles of not just blacks, but all people of color. I am a true believer of helping "your" people "first," but also the helping of all people no matter where there at or the color of there skin. But I must be truthful, my struggle and assistance is truly on the side of people of color like ourselves. But just a few years ago I didn't think like this.
>
> I thought that if you wasn't black, then you was the enemy, but . . . many years of this prison madness and much study and research changed all of this. . . . [I]t's not with each other, blacks against Koreans or Koreans against blacks. No, this is not what it's about. Our struggle(s) are truly one in the same. What happened in L.A. during the riot really hurt me, because it was no way that blacks was suppose to do the things to your people, my people (Koreans) that they did. You're my sister, our people are my people. Even though our culture may be somewhat different, and even though we may worship our God(s) different . . . white-Amerikkka [doesn't] separate us. They look at us all the same. Either you're white, or you're wrong. . . . I'm just writing you to let you know that, you're my sister, your people's struggle are my people's struggle.

This is the ground I need to claim now for Korean American resistance and recovery, so that we can become American without dying of *han*.

Although the sentiments expressed in these letters seemed to break down roughly along racial lines—that is, all writers who were identifiably people of color wrote in support—and one might become alarmed at the depth of the divisions they imply, I like to think that I have experienced the desire of many Americans, especially Americans of color, to do as Rodney King pleaded on the second day of *sa-i-ku*: "We're all stuck here for awhile. . . . Let's try to work it out."

In my view, it's important for us to think about *all* of what Rodney King said and not just the words "we all can get along," which have been depoliticized and transformed into a Disneyesque catchphrase for Pat Boone songs and roadside billboards in Los Angeles. It seems to me the emphasis is on the being "stuck here for awhile" together as we await "our day in court."[19]

Like the African American man who wrote from prison, the African American man who had been brutally beaten by white police might have felt the desire to "love everybody," but he had to amend—or rectify—that wish. He had to speak last about loving "people of color." The impulse to "love everybody" was there, but the conditions were not right. For now, the most practical and progressive agenda may be people of color trying to "work it out."

FINDING COMMUNITY THROUGH NATIONAL CONSCIOUSNESS

The place where Korean and American legacies converge for Korean Americans is the exhortation to "go home to where you belong."

One of the letters I received was from a Korean American living in Chicago. He had read a translation of my essay in a Korean-language newspaper. "Although you were born in the U.S.A.," he wrote, noticing what none of the white men who ordered me to go back to "my" country had, "your ethnical background and your complexion belong to Korea. It is time to give up your U.S. citizenship and go to Korea."

Some ruined merchants are claiming that they will pull up stakes and return to Korea, but I know that this is not possible for most of them. Even if their stores had not been destroyed, even if they were able to sell their businesses and take the proceeds to Korea, most of them would not have enough to buy a home or business there, since both require total cash up front. Neither would they be able to find work in the society they left behind because it is plagued by recession, repression, and fierce economic competition.

Going back to Korea. The dream of going back to Korea fed the spirit of my father, who came to Chicago in 1926 and lived in the United States for sixty-three years, during which time he never became a U.S. citizen, at first because the law did not allow it and later because he did not want to. He kept himself going by believing that he would return to Korea in triumph one day. Instead, he died in Oakland at eighty-eight. Only his remains returned to Korea, where we buried him in accordance with his wishes.

Hasn't the dream of going back home to where you belong sustained most of America's unwanted at one time or another, giving meaning to lives of toil and making it possible to endure other people's hatred and rejection? Isn't the attempt to find community through national consciousness natural for people refused an American identity because racism does not give them that choice?

Korean national consciousness, the resolve to resist and fight back when threatened with extermination, was all that could be called upon when the Korean Americans in Los Angeles found themselves abandoned. They joined together to guard each other's means of livelihood with guns, relying on Korean-language radio and newspapers to communicate with and help each other. On the third day after the outbreak of violence, more than 30,000 Korean Americans gathered for a peace march in downtown L.A. in what was perhaps the largest and most quickly organized mass mobilization in Asian American history. Musicians in white, the color of mourning, beat traditional Korean drums in sorrow, anger, and celebration of community, a call to arms like a collective heartbeat.[20] I believe that the mother of Edward Song Lee, the Los Angeles–born college student mistaken for a looter and shot to death in the streets, has been able to persevere in great part because of the massive outpouring of sympathy expressed by the Korean American community that shared and understood her *han*.

I have been critical lately of cultural nationalism as detrimental to Korean Americans, especially Korean American women, because it operates on exclusions and fosters intolerance and uniformity of thought while stifling self-criticism and encouraging sacrifice, even to the point of suicide. But *sa-i-ku* makes me think again: what remains for those who are left to stand alone? If Korean Americans refuse to be victims or political pawns in the United States while rejecting the exhortation that we go back to Korea where we belong, what will be our weapons of choice?

In the darkest days of Japanese colonial rule, even after being stripped of land and of all economic means of survival, Koreans were threatened with total erasure when the colonizers rewrote Korean history, outlawed the Korean language, forced the subjugated people to worship the Japanese emperor, and demanded that they adopt Japanese names. One of the results of these cultural-annihilation policies was the fierce insistence on the sanctity of Korean national identity that persists among Koreans to this day. In this context, it is not difficult to understand why nationalism has been the main refuge of Koreans and Korean Americans.

While recognizing the potential dangers of nationalism as a weapon, I for one am not ready to respond to the antiessentialists' call to relinquish my Korean American identity. It is easy enough for the French and Germans to call for a common European identity and an end to nationalisms, but what of the peoples suppressed and submerged while France and Germany exercised their national prerogatives? I am mindful of the argument that the resurgence of nationalism in Europe is rooted in historical and contemporary political and economic inequality among the nations of Europe. Likewise, I have noticed that many white Americans do not like to think of themselves as belonging to a race, even while thinking of people of color almost exclusively in terms of race. In the same way, many men think of themselves as "human beings" and of women as the ones having a gender. Thus crime, small businesses, and all Korean–African American interactions are seen and interpreted through the lens of race in the same dominant culture that angrily rejects the use of the racial lens for viewing yellow/white or black/white interactions and insists suddenly that we are all "American" whenever we attempt to assert our identity as people of color. It is far easier for Anglo-Americans to call for an end to cultural nationalisms than for Korean Americans to give up the national consciousness that makes it possible for us to survive the vicious racism that would deny our existence as either Korean Americans or Americans.

Is there anything of use to us in Korean nationalism? During one thousand years of Chinese suzerainty, the Korean ruling elite developed a philosophy called *sadaejui*, or reliance of the weak on the strong. In direct opposition to this way of thought is what is called *jaju* or *juche sasang*, or self-determination.[21] Both *sadaejui* and *juche sasang* are ways of dealing with unequal power relationships and resisting the transformation of one's homeland into a battlefield for others, but *sadaejui* has never worked any better for Koreans than it has for any minority group in America. *Juche sasang*, on the other hand, has the kind of oppositional potential needed in the struggle against silence and invisibility. From Korean national consciousness, we can recover this fierce refusal to accept subjugation, which is the first step in the effort to build community, so that we can work with others to challenge the forces that would have us annihilate each other instead of our mutual oppression.

What is clear is that we cannot "become American" without dying of *han* unless we think about community in new ways. Self-determination does not mean living alone. At least for now, that may mean mining the rich and haunted lode of Korean national consciousness while we struggle to understand how our fate is entwined with the fate of others lying prostrate before the triumphal procession of the winners of History.[22] During the past fifteen years or so, many young Korean nationalists have been studying the legacies of colonialism and imperialism that they share with peoples in many Asian, African, and Latin American nations. At the same time that we take note of this work, we can also try to understand how nationalism and feminism can be worked together to demystify the limitations and reductiveness of each as a weapon of empowerment. If Korean national consciousness is ever to be such a weapon for us, we must use it to create a new kind of nationalism-in-internationalism to help us call forth a culture of survival and recovery, so that our *han* might be released and we might be freed to dream fiercely of different possibilities.

NOTES

1. According to a September 1992 Dun and Bradstreet survey of 560 business owners in Koreatown in South Central Los Angeles, an estimated 40 percent of the businesses damaged during *sa-i-ku* have closed their doors permanently. Moreover, almost 40 percent had no insurance or were insured for 50 percent or less of their total losses ("L.A. Riot Took Heavy Toll on Businesses," *San Francisco Chronicle*, 12 September 1992).
2. Following quota changes in U.S. immigration laws in 1965, the Korean population in America increased more than eightfold to almost one million. Between 1970 and 1990, Los Angeles Koreatown grew from a few blocks of stores and businesses into a community base for all sorts of economic and cultural activities.

3. Pretense, of course, because I was only passing for Chinese. The temporary comfort I experienced would come to an end whenever it was discovered that I could speak no Chinese and that I had no organic links to Chinese Americans, who frequently underscored both our commonalities and our differences by telling me that everything Korean—even *kimchi*, that quintessentially Korean vegetable eaten at every Korean meal—was originally Chinese.

4. The Black–Korean Alliance (BKA) was formed, with the assistance of the Los Angeles County Human Relations Commission, to improve relations between the Korean and African American communities after four Korean merchants were killed in robberies during April 1986. The BKA sponsored activities and events, such as joint church services, education forums, joint cultural events, and seminars on crime prevention and community economic development. The BKA never received political or financial support from the public or private sectors. The organization had neither its own meeting place nor a telephone. Grassroots participation was not extensive, and despite the good intentions of the individuals involved, the BKA was unable to prevent the killing of a dozen more Korean merchants in southern California between 1990 and *sa-i-ku*, or to stop the escalation of tensions between the two communities after the shooting of fifteen-year-old Latasha Harlins by Korean merchant Soon Ja Du in March 1991. By June of that year, after police declared the killing of an African American man by a Korean liquor store owner "justifiable homicide," African American groups began boycotting the store, and the BKA failed to convince African American boycotters and Korean merchants to meet together to negotiate an end to the conflict. Nor were the members of the BKA successful in obtaining the help of members of the Los Angeles City Council or the California State Legislature, who might have been instrumental in preventing the destructive violence of *sa-i-ku* if they had had the integrity and farsightedness to address the intensifying hostilities before it was too late. After *sa-i-ku*, the BKA was in disarray, and as of this writing, its members are planning to dissolve the group.

5. According to John Murray, founder of the southern California chapter of Cal-Pac, the black beverage and grocers' association, African American liquor store owners "sold stores they had bought in the mid-1960s for two times monthly gross sales—roughly $80,000 at the time, depending on the store—for five times monthly gross, or about $300,000." After the Jews fled in the wake of the Watts riots, African Americans were enabled by civil rights legislative mandates to obtain for the first time credit from government-backed banks to start a number of small businesses. But operating liquor stores, although profitable, was grueling, dangerous, and not something fathers wanted their sons to do, according to interviews with African American owners and former owners of liquor stores in African American communities. Former liquor merchant Ed Piert exclaimed: "Seven days a week, 20 hours a day, no vacations, people stealing. That's slave labor. I wouldn't buy another liquor store." When liquor prices were deregulated in 1978 and profit margins shrank in the face of competition from volume buyers, many African American owners sold out to Korean immigrants carrying cash collected in rotating credit clubs called *kye* (Susan Moffat, "Shopkeepers Fight Back: Blacks join with Koreans in a Battle to Rebuild Their Liquor Stores," *Los Angeles Times*, 15 May 1992).

6. In a newspaper interview, Alberto Machon, an eighteen-year-old junior at Washington Preparatory High School who had moved to South Central Los Angeles with his family from El Salvador ten years ago, said that he was laughing as he watched every Korean store looted or burned down because "I felt that they deserved it for the way they was treatin' people . . . the money that we are giving to the stores they're taking it to their community, Koreatown." Thirty-two-year-old Arnulfo Nunez Barrajas served four days in the Los Angeles County jail for curfew violation. He was arrested while going from Santa Ana to Los Angeles to see his aunt, whose son had been killed during the upheavals. According to Nunez, "[T]he ones they've caught are only from the black race and the Latin race. I haven't seen any Koreans or Chinese. Why not them? Or white? Why only the black race and the Latinos? Well, it's racism" (*Los Angeles Times*, 13 May 1992).

7. L. A. Chung, "Tensions Divide Blacks, Asians," *San Francisco Chronicle*, 4 May 1992.
8. *Los Angeles Times*, 5 May 1992.
9. They were also given to gloating over the inability of American authorities to maintain social order as well as the South Korean government can. In an interview, a South Korean diplomat in Los Angeles remarked to me that he was astonished at how ill-prepared the Los Angeles police and the National Guard were for "mass disturbances." They did not react quickly enough, they were very inefficient, they had no emergency plan, and even their communications network broke down, he observed. He could not imagine "riots" getting out of control in South Korea, which was ruled by the military from 1961 to 1987; there, he commented, "the police are very effective. They work closely with the military."
10. For example, a story about the "black riots" in the 6 May 1992 *Central Daily News* in Seoul listed the writer as Korean-American sociologist Edward T'ae-han Chang, who was astonished when he saw it because he hadn't written it (personal communication).
11. In 1913, a group of Korean American laborers was run out of Hemet Valley, California by a mob of anti-Japanese whites. The Koreans responded by insisting that they were Korean, not Japanese. What might seem a ludicrous response to racist expulsion has to be viewed in light of the fact that the United States sanctioned Japan's 1909 annexation of Korea, closing all Korean delegations and placing Korean immigrants under the authority of Japanese consulates. Since they were classified as Japanese, Korean Americans were subject to the Alien Land Acts that, in California and nine other states, targeted Japanese by denying them the right afforded all others regardless of race, nativity, or citizenship: the right to own land. Also, foreign-born Koreans were able to become naturalized U.S. citizens only after the McCarran-Walter Act of 1952 permitted naturalization of Japanese. I have heard some Asian Americans equate the Chinese and Japanese American use of signs and buttons reading "I Am Not Korean" during *sa-i-ku* with the Korean American (and, not coincidentally, Chinese American) practice of wearing buttons saying "I Am Not Japanese" during World War II. But, in light of the specificities of Korean and Korean American history, this cannot be a one-to-one comparison.
12. In a 23 July 1992 interview, a fifty-year-old Korean immigrant woman whose South Central Los Angeles corner grocery store had been completely destroyed during *sa-i-ku* told me, "The America I imagined [before I arrived here] was like what I saw in the movies—clean, wide streets, flowers everywhere. I imagined Americans would be all big, tall . . . with white faces and blond hair. . . . But the America here is not like that. When I got up to walk around the neighborhood the morning after we arrived in Los Angeles from Korea, it was as if we had come to Mexico."
13. John Berger and Jean Mohr, *A Seventh Man: A Book of Images and Words about the Experiences of Migrant Workers in Europe* (New York: Penguin Books, 1975). I want to thank Barry Maxwell for bringing this work to my attention.
14. I am not grappling directly with social class issues here because, although I am cognizant of their crucial importance, I am simply not qualified to address them at the present time. The exploited "guest workers" in Europe described by Berger and Mohr, unlike the Korean immigrants to the United States, brought with them their laboring bodies but not capital to start small businesses. Because they are merchants, the class interests of Korean American shop owners in Los Angeles differ clearly from the interests of poor African American and Latino customers. But working with simple dyads is impossible, since Korean American shop owners are also of color and mostly immigrants from a country colonized by the United States. At the same time, it seems to me that class factors have been more important than race factors in shaping Korean American immigrants' attitudes toward African American and Latino populations. Perhaps because of the devastation caused by Japanese colonization and the Korean War, many Koreans exhibit intensely negative attitudes toward the poor and indeed desperately fear being associated with them. I have often marveled at the importance placed on conspicuous consumer items, especially clothing, in South Korean society, where a shabbily dressed person can expect only shabby treatment. In the 1960s, a middle-class American could make a social

statement against materialistic values by dressing in tattered clothing without being mistaken for a homeless person. Now that this is no longer true, it seems to me that middle-class Americans exhibit some of the fears and aversions I witnessed in South Korea. Ironically, in the society where blackness and brownness have historically been almost tantamount to a condemnation to poverty, prejudice against the poor brought from Korea is combined with homegrown U.S. racism, and the results have been explosive.

At the same time, I have also noticed among Korean merchants profound empathy with the poor, whose situation many older immigrants know from firsthand past experiences. I personally witnessed many encounters between Korean merchants who lost their stores and African American neighbors in South Central during July 1992, when I accompanied the merchants as they visited their burned-out sites. None of the encounters were hostile. On the contrary, most of the African American neighbors embraced the Korean shop owners and expressed concern for them, while the merchants in turn asked warmly after the welfare of their neighbors' children. Although Korean–African American interaction has been racialized in the dominant culture, the quality of these relationships, like the quality of all human relationships, proved far more individual than racial schematizing allows for.

15. Every South Korean middle school, high school, and college student is required to take a course in "National Ethics," formerly called "Anticommunism." This course, which loosely resembles a civics class on Western civilization, government, constitutionalism, and political ideology, emphasizes the superiority of capitalism over communism and the importance of the national identity and the modern capitalist state. From the early 1960s through the 1970s, when most of the Los Angeles Korean immigrant merchants studied "Anticommunism" or "National Ethics," they were taught that "capitalism" and "democracy" are the same, and that both are antithetical to "communism" or "socialism." According to this logic, criticisms of the United States, a "democracy," are tantamount to praise of "communism." Such a view left little room for acknowledgment of racism and other social problems in American society. Indeed, the South Korean National Security Law formerly prosecuted and jailed writers who depicted Americans negatively and filmmakers who portrayed North Koreans as good-looking or capable of falling in love. Today, however, the interpretation of what constitutes antistate activity is far narrower, and although the South Korean government maintains that "pro–North Korea" activities are against the law, anti–U.S. sentiments have been common in South Korea since the mid-1980s.

16. I cannot help thinking that these violent baptisms are an Asian American legacy of sorts, for in some sense it was the internment that forced the Japanese Americans to "become American" half a century ago.

17. Many Korean Americans have criticized the *Los Angeles Times* and local television news, and the ABC network in particular, for repeatedly running stories about Soon Ja Du shooting Latasha Harlins (the tape was the second-most-played video during the week of the riots, according to the media-watch section of *A Magazine: An Asian American Quarterly* 1, no. 3 [1991]: 4). They complained that the Los Angeles ABC affiliate aired the store videotape in tandem with the King footage. ABC even inserted the Du–Harlins tape segment into its reportage of the height of the *sa-i-ku* upheavals. Korean Americans have also protested the media focus on armed Korean American merchants. In particular, they objected to the repeated use of the image of a Korean merchant pointing a gun at an unseen, off-camera target. They knew that he was being shot at and that he was firing only at the ground, but they felt that the image was used to depict Korean immigrants as violent and lawless. They argued that by blocking out the context, the news media harmed Korean Americans, about whom little positive was known by the American public. Tong S. Suhr wrote in a Korean American newspaper:

> The Harlins killing is a tragic but isolated case. . . . This is not to condone the
> Harlins killing; nor is it to justify the death by countering with how many merchants

in turn have been killed. Our complaint is directed to the constant refrain of "the Korean-born grocer killing a black teen-ager," which couldn't help but sow the seeds of racial hatred . . . [and make me wonder]: Was there any conspiracy among the . . . white-dominated media to pit one ethnic group against another and sit back and watch them destroy one another? . . . Why were the Korean American merchants portrayed as gun-toting vigilantes shooting indiscriminately when they decided to protect their lives and businesses by arming themselves because no police protection was available? Why wasn't there any mention of the fact that they were fired upon first? Why such biased reporting? ("Time for Soul Searching by Media," *Korea Times*, 29 June 1992)

I would challenge representatives of the news media who argue that visual images of beatings and shootings, especially when they are racialized or sexualized, are "exciting" and "interesting," even when they are aired hundreds or thousands of times, when compared with "boring" images of the everyday. Three months after *sa-i-ku*, I visited a videotape brokerage company in search of generic footage that could be used in a documentary about the Korean immigrant experience of losing their means of livelihood. Almost every inch of the stringers' footage contained images of police cars, fire engines, and uniformed men heroically wiping their brows as they courageously prepared to meet the challenges before them. Since there were neither police nor firemen anywhere in sight in South Central or Koreatown during the first three days of *sa-i-ku*, none of this footage was of use to me. No doubt the men who shot these scenes chose what seemed to them the most "interesting" and "exciting" images. But if I, a woman and a Korean American, had had a camera in my hands, I would have chosen quite different ones.

18. *Newsweek*, 18 May 1992.

19. The text of King's statement was printed in the *Los Angeles Times* (2 May 1992) as follows:

People I just want to say . . . can we all get along? Can we get along? Can we stop making it horrible for the older people and the kids? . . . We've got enough smog here in Los Angeles, let alone to deal with the setting of those fires and things. It's just not right. It's not right, and it's not going to change anything.

We'll get our justice. They've won the battle but they haven't won the war. We will have our day in court and that's all we want. . . . I'm neutral. I love everybody. I love people of color. . . . I'm not like they're . . . making me out to be.

We've got to quit. We've got to quit. . . . I can understand the first upset in the first two hours after the verdict, but to go on, to keep going on like this, and to see a security guard shot on the ground, it's just not right. It's just not right because those people will never go home to their families again. And I mean, please, we can get along here. We all can get along. We've just got to, just got to. We're all stuck here for awhile. . . . Let's try to work it out. Let's try to work it out.

20. The news media that did cover this massive demonstration invariably focused on the Korean musicians because they looked and sounded alien and exotic. Ironically, most of them were young, American-born or at least American-educated Korean Americans who learned traditional music as a way to recover their cultural heritage. They perform at many events: I remember them in the demonstrations against the 1991 Gulf War.

21. *Juche sasang*, the concept of self-determination, was attractive to Koreans before the division of the country after the defeat of Japan in World War II. However, since the term *juche* is central to the official political ideology in communist North Korea, the synonym *jaju* is used in South Korean officialdom.

22. I borrow this image from Walter Benjamin, "Theses on the Philosophy of History," in *Illuminations* (New York: Schocken Books, 1969), 256. I would like to thank Shelley Sunn Wong for helping me see its relevance to Korean Americans in the 1990s.

Recognizing Native Hawaiians

A Quest for Sovereignty

Davianna Pomaika'i McGregor

Native Hawaiians comprise a distinct and unique indigenous people with a historical continuity to the original inhabitants of the Hawaiian archipelago who exercised sovereignty as a nation centuries before the beginning of continuous European and American contact in 1778.

—Native Hawaiian Health Care Improvement Act of 1992
(42 U.S.C. 1994)

The Hawaiian people remain determined to preserve, develop and transmit to future generations their ancestral territory, and their cultural identity in accordance with their own spiritual and traditional beliefs, customs, practices, language, and social institutions.

—Public Law 103–150, Senate Joint Resolution of Apology,
November 23, 1993

The truth and significance of these statements of findings by the U.S. Congress in the Native Hawaiian Health Care Improvement Act and Public Law 103–150 is at the heart of the most important human rights issue facing Hawai'i's people in the new millennium.

The U.S. Supreme Court, in the *Rice v. Cayetano* case, ruled on February 23, 2000 that elections for the trustees of the State of Hawai'i Office of Hawaiian Affairs (OHA), in which only Native Hawaiians were allowed to vote, used unconstitutional race-based qualifications.[1] The majority of the members of the court ruled that the Native Hawaiian OHA election violated the 15th Amendment of the U.S. Constitution which states that the right to vote cannot be denied on account of race or color.[2] Subsequently, in the November 2000 election for the trustees of the Office of Hawaiian Affairs, all registered voters, regardless of Native Hawaiian ancestry, were allowed to cast votes and to run for these offices.

The U.S. Supreme Court, in its ruling, stated that Native Hawaiians have a shared purpose with the general public in the islands and that the Constitution of the United States has become the heritage of all the citizens of Hawai'i, including Native Hawaiians. In addition, the court raised questions about whether or not Native Hawaiians are, in fact, a distinct and unique indigenous people with the right of self-governance and self-determination under the U.S. law or whether they are, instead, an ethnic or racial minority. Under the U.S. Constitution, indigenous Native American tribes are recognized as domestic dependent nations, with inherent powers of self-governance and self-determination, for whom the U.S. federal government sustains a trust responsibility.[3] This status has been extended to Eskimos, Aleuts, and Native Alaskans under the Alaskan Native Claims Act. However, ethnic and racial minorities within the fifty U.S. states do *not* enjoy the status of nationhood, they do *not* have the right of self-governance and self-determination, and the federal government does *not* have a trust responsibility for them.

In the ruling, a majority of the Supreme Court justices also raised, but did not resolve, four fundamental questions regarding the status of Native Hawaiians. May Congress treat the Native Hawaiians as it does the Indian tribes? Has Congress in fact determined that Native Hawaiians have a status like that of Indians in organized tribes? May Congress delegate to the State of Hawai'i the authority to preserve that status? Has Congress delegated to the State of Hawai'i the authority to preserve that status?[4] A negative answer to any of these questions could result in a determination that Native Hawaiians do not qualify under U.S. law for the rights and protection afforded other indigenous peoples within the fifty states. The majority of the Supreme Court Justices also seemed to open the door to future legal challenges on the status of Native Hawaiians when it stated,

> It is a matter of some dispute, for instance, whether Congress may treat the native Hawaiians as it does the Indian tribes. Compare Van Dyke, The Political Status of the Hawaiian People, 17 Yale L. & Pol'y Rev. 95 (1998), with Benjamin, Equal Protection and the Special Relationship: The Case of Native Hawaiians, 106 Yale L.J. 537 (1996). We can stay far off that difficult terrain however.

Suddenly, the status, rights and entitlements which Native Hawaiians had enjoyed throughout the 20th century could be legally challenged out of existence. Moreover, the Supreme Court ruling seemed to contradict the policy of the U.S. Congress toward Native Hawaiians.

Beginning in 1906 and through 1998 the U.S. Congress, in effect, recognized a trust relationship with the native people of Hawai'i through the enactment of 183 federal laws that explicitly included Native Hawaiians in the class of Native Americans.[5] Some of the laws extended federal programs set up for Native Americans to Native Hawaiians, while other laws represented recognition by the U.S. Congress that the United States bore a special responsibility to protect

Native Hawaiian interests.[6] Although the operational policy of the U.S. Congress has been to exercise a trust responsibility with Native Hawaiians similar to Native Americans, none of the laws passed extended an explicit and formal recognition that Native Hawaiians are a sovereign people, with the right of self-governance and self-determination. Without such an explicit law, Native Hawaiians stand to lose the special benefits, entitlements, and protection that the U.S. Congress has extended to Native Hawaiians beginning in 1906.

In light of the ruling by the U.S. Supreme Court, Hawai'i's congressional delegation, led by Senators Daniel Akaka and Daniel Inouye, drafted and introduced legislation (called The Akaka Bill) to explicitly and unambiguously clarify the trust relationship between Native Hawaiians and the United States. Although the bill failed to pass in 2000, the Hawai'i congressional delegation reintroduced the bill for passage in 2001. When passed, the bill would formally and directly extend the federal policy of self-determination and self-governance to Native Hawaiians, as Hawai'i's indigenous native people. The legislation provides a process for the recognition by the United States, under the Secretary of the Department of Interior, of a Native Hawaiian governing entity.[7]

Opponents of Native Hawaiian recognition successfully lobbied Republican congressmen to oppose the bill in 2000. They continued their efforts to prevent its passage in 2001. Calling themselves "Aloha For All," the group is supported by the National Coalition for a Color Blind America. On their Web page, which lists four members, they state that they are "creating web pages, speaking to Rotary clubs, Exchange Clubs and other organizations, writing letters to the editor and presenting op/ed articles to the media, testifying before legislative bodies, and litigating."[8] The Web page also states their opposition to the Akaka Bill, as follows:

> This legislation is dangerous to the people of Hawai'i and to the sovereignty of the United States. It is an attempt to divide the thoroughly integrated people of Hawai'i along racial lines. It would partition the State of Hawai'i by setting up an apartheid regime to which only *kanaka maoli* (the name Native Hawaiians prefer to call themselves) could belong . . . One of the most troubling aspects of the Akaka bill is its attempt to create an Indian tribe where none currently exists. It would be the first time in history when Congress recognizes a currently non-existent political entity and then puts in place a procedure to populate it.[9]

The Aloha For All group claims that all residents of Hawai'i are Hawaiian and that the limitation of any benefits to those who are "racially Hawaiian" is discriminatory and violates the 14th Amendment of the U.S. Constitution.[10]

The developments outlined above, which challenge Native Hawaiian status, rights, and entitlements, set the scene for this article. In the first part of this article, I review the indicators which show that Native Hawaiians continue to be a distinct people with a unique language, culture, economic life, and national lands. In the second part of this article I review the historical and political basis for the recognition of Native Hawaiian sovereignty and the organized efforts of Native Hawaiians to re-establish a government to exercise sovereignty.

CONTEMPORARY CONDITIONS
OF NATIVE HAWAIIANS

In 1988, approximately 218,000 Native Hawaiians comprised 20.7 percent of the overall Hawai'i population. Of that amount, only 10,000 were pure Hawaiian and another 70,000 were estimated to have half Hawaiian ancestry or more. Thirty-two percent of all Native Hawaiians still lived outside of O'ahu on neighboring islands.[11]

In 1990, Native Hawaiians earned low incomes comparable to the most recently arrived immigrant groups, held low-status jobs, and had the highest rate of unemployment of all the ethnic groups in the islands. By contrast, the descendants of Caucasian, Japanese, and Chinese immigrants earned high incomes and held a greater portion of the managerial and professional jobs in Hawai'i. Moreover, a significant portion of the Native Hawaiians earned incomes that were insufficient to provide for their families and thus received public assistance to supplement their incomes. Among these, some depended entirely upon welfare support to meet their day-to-day needs.[12]

In 1992, 35 percent of the adult inmate population in state correctional facilities were of Native Hawaiian ancestry.[13]

In 1980, Native Hawaiians had the lowest life expectancy among the ethnic groups in Hawai'i, at 67.6 years compared to 73 for Caucasians, 77 for Japanese, 72 for Filipinos, and 76 for Chinese.[14] In 1989, the Native Hawaiian infant mortality rate was 11.8 per thousand. This represented 44 percent of the infant deaths in the state in 1989. Heart disease was the major cause of death among Native Hawaiians. While Native Hawaiians did not have the highest incidence of cancer, they had the highest mortality rates for most cancers. Native Hawaiian men had the highest incidence of lung cancer and Hawaiian women had the highest rates of breast cancer. Native Hawaiians over age 65 had the highest incidence of chronic diseases and were disproportionately afflicted by diabetes.[15]

These socioeconomic statistics reflect a disparity in the standard of living between Native Hawaiians and Caucasians, Japanese, and Chinese in Hawai'i. They also indicate a high degree of alienation from the social system and the political power structure of modern Hawai'i. On one hand, it represents the effect of institutionalized cultural barriers that prevent equal access to opportunities in the educational system, equal access to health care delivery systems, and adequate representation in the judicial system.[16] On the other hand, it reflects the persistence of Native Hawaiian cultural customs and practices in rural-based Hawaiian communities where Native Hawaiians did not assimilate into Westernized Hawai'i society.

These statistics reflect the individual and collective pain, bitterness and trauma of a people whose sovereignty has been and remains suppressed; who are dispossessed in their own homeland; and who lack control over the resources of their ancestral lands to provide for the welfare of their people. Sovereignty is looked to as a means of providing control over key resources to enable the Native Hawaiian people to be uplifted.

SURVIVAL OF THE NATIVE HAWAIIAN CULTURE

The present generation of Native Hawaiians stand upon the threshold of history as no previous generation of Native Hawaiians. Since first contact with Europeans and Americans, generation after generation of Native Hawaiians have faced the specter of decline, displacement, and impoverishment. However, the possibility of extinction as a people with a distinct language, culture, and land base has never been so imminent and real as it is for Native Hawaiians today. Action or inaction on their part will determine whether the Native Hawaiian language, culture, religion, subsistence farming, and fishing and land base will survive or gradually disappear with the passing away of their *kupuna* (elders).

At each critical juncture of Hawai'i's history, Native Hawaiians were challenged by changes that would undermine their traditional culture. Some Native Hawaiians chose to accept those changes. They passively accommodated and adjusted to Western society. Many actively assimilated and participated in Western political, social, and economic activities. Others chose to stand firm, reject, and resist change—actively or by withdrawing from mainstream economic and political activities.

Of singular importance to the perpetuation of the Native Hawaiian people are isolated and undeveloped rural communities that were historically bypassed by the mainstream of social and economic development. Native Hawaiians in these rural areas did not fully assimilate into the changing social system. Instead, they pursued traditional subsistence livelihoods in which they applied cultural customs, beliefs, and practices. They also sustained extended family networks through sharing and exchange of food, work, and services.

Rural Hawaiians still acquire the basic necessities for their families through subsistence activities upon the land by employing traditional knowledge and practices passed down to them from their *kupuna*. Family knowledge about prime fishing grounds and the types of fish that frequent the ocean in their district at different times of year usually assure Native Hawaiian fishermen of successful fishing expeditions.

Many Native Hawaiians in rural districts continue to cultivate fish in ponds and the open ocean by regularly feeding the fish in conjunction with making offerings at the *ku'ula* (fish deity) shrines that marked their ocean fishing grounds. Taro and other domestic crops are planted by the moon phase to assure excellent growth. Rural families take advantage of seasonal fruits and marine life for their regular diet. Native plants are still utilized for healing of illness by traditional methods that involve both physical and spiritual cleansing and dedication.

Cultural knowledge attached to the traditional names of places, winds, and rains of their district informed rural Hawaiians about the effect of the dynamic forces of nature upon the ocean and the land in their area. Legends and chants inform them about how their ancestors coped with such elements.

Thus, in these rural communities, Native Hawaiian custom, belief, and practice continue to be a practical part of everyday life, not only for the old people, but also for the middle-aged and the young. By contrast, such customs and beliefs have assumed an air of mystery and superstition for urban Native Hawaiians whose day-to-day lives depend solely upon wage-earning activities in a modern commercial economic system.

An analogy that conveys a sense of the significance of these areas can be found in the natural phenomena in the volcanic rainforest. Botanists who study the volcanic rainforest have observed that eruptions which destroy large areas of forest land leave oases of native trees and plants which are called *kipuka*. From these natural *kipuka* come the seeds and spores for the eventual regeneration of the native flora upon the fresh lava. Rural Native Hawaiian communities are cultural *kipuka* from which Native Hawaiian culture can be regenerated and revitalized in the contemporary setting.

Beginning in the 1970s Native Hawaiians engaged in a cultural renaissance that reaffirmed the consciousness of, pride in, and practice of Native Hawaiian cultural and spiritual customs and beliefs. In rallying around protection of the island of Kaho'olawe from bombing by the U.S. military, the traditional practice of *aloha 'aina* gained prominence and the importance of these rural Hawaiian communities as strongholds of traditional Native Hawaiian subsistence lifestyles was recognized.

Rural Hawaiian communities threatened with development organized to protect their landholdings and the surrounding natural resources in their districts from the assault of proposed tourist, commercial and industrial development. On the island of Hawai'i, Ka'u Hawaiians formed the Ka 'Ohana O KaLae to protect the natural and cultural resources of their district from a planned spaceport to launch missiles.[17] The Pele Defense Fund formed to protect the volcano deity Pele from the development of geothermal energy and electric plants.[18] On Moloka'i, the Hui Ala Loa, Ka Leo O Mana'e, and Hui Ho'opakela 'Aina are community groups which formed to protect the natural and cultural resources of Moloka'i for farming and fishing rather than for tourist resort development. On the island of Maui, the Hui Ala Nui O Makena organized to keep access to the ocean open for traditional fishing and gathering as well as recreation; Hana Pohaku developed community-based economic development projects on their *kuleana* lands in Kipahulu; and the Ke'anae Community Association worked to keep the water flowing to their taro patches rather than being diverted for development in Kula and Kihei or for hydroelectric plants. On Kaua'i island, the Native Hawaiian Farmers of Hanalei initiated community-based projects at Waipa and Ka Wai Ola organized to protect the shoreline of Hanalei from ruin by numerous tour boat operations. On O'ahu, community-based economic development projects were pursued on the Wai'anae Coast by Ka'ala Farms, the Opelu Project and Na Hoa'aina O Makaha. Malama I Na Kupuna O Hawai'i Nei, a statewide group, formed to protect and provide proper treatment of traditional Native Hawaiian burials.

Traditional navigational arts and skills were revived with the transpacific voyages of the Polynesian Voyaging Society on the *Hokule'a*, the *Hawai'i Loa*, and the *Makali'i*. *Halau hula*, the schools that teach traditional Hawaiian dance and chant, increased and flourished. *La'au Lapa'u*, traditional herbal and spiritual healing practices, were recognized as valid holistic medicinal practices. Hawaiian

Studies from the elementary to university level was established as part of the regular curricula. Hawaiian music evolved into new forms of expression and gained greater popularity.

Perhaps the most remarkable development was the rejuvenation of the Hawaiian language. In 1987 there were only 2,000 native speakers of Hawaiian.[19] Most were in their sixties and seventies. Only thirty were under five years old. Extinction of the language because of America's colonial policy was imminent. However, Hawaiian language professors and students at the University of Hawai'i visited Aotearoa (New Zealand) and were inspired with the efforts of the Maori people to rescue their language through Maori language immersion preschools. They began Punana Leo Hawaiian language immersion preschools in Hawai'i and went on to establish Hawaiian language immersion classes in state schools throughout the islands. In the 1999–2000 school year, 1,750 students were enrolled in eighteen Hawaiian language immersion public schools.

All of these efforts, combined, reaffirmed the continuity and perpetuation of Native Hawaiians as unique and distinct with their own cultural and spiritual beliefs, customs, practices, language and ancestral national lands.

HISTORICAL AND POLITICAL BASIS OF NATIVE HAWAIIAN SOVEREIGNTY

Centuries before the beginning of continuous European and American contact, the Native Hawaiian people lived in a highly organized, self-sufficient, subsistence social system based on communal land tenure with a sophisticated language, culture, and religion. Hawaiian ancestral chants trace the origins from Papa, the earth; Wakea, the sky; Kane, springs and streams; Kanaloa, the ocean; and Pele, the volcano. *He Hawai'i kakou*: We are Hawai'i. Native Hawaiians are inseparable from the *'aina*, earth, sea, sky and the magnificent power of these life forces. Family genealogies link contemporary Native Hawaiians to astronomers, navigators, planters, fishermen, engineers, healers, and artisans who settled Hawai'i and constructed great walled fishponds, irrigated taro terraces, dryland agricultural systems, *heiau* (temples), *pu'uhonua* (refuge areas), adze quarries, coastal and inland trails, and extended family settlements. Native Hawaiians were a nation of people living in harmony and balance with the land, the *akua* (gods), and each other: *lokahi* (balance and harmony). Each *ahupua'a* valley system provided the families living within them the necessities of life: from abundant marine life in the ocean, to fresh water streams and springs, gentle sloping fertile lands for cultivation, and forests with trees for building houses and canoes, as well as plants for healing.[20]

After contact with the west, islanders began trading in cultivated food crops and sandalwood. As trade increased the Native Hawaiian people suffered periodic famine and were continuously exposed to devastating epidemics of foreign disease. A unified monarchial government of all the Hawaiian Islands was established in 1810 under Kamehameha I, the first King of Hawai'i (1779–1819). Trade was conducted with China, England, and the United States on a regular basis. In 1819, Kamehameha died and his successors abolished formal observance of traditional religious ritual and ceremony. Rival chiefs defended the traditional gods but were defeated. In the following year, American missionaries began to settle Hawai'i and convert Native Hawaiians to Christianity. By 1823, after only forty-five years of contact, the Native Hawaiian people had declined from 400,000 to 135,000. Commercial whaling attracted increasing numbers of foreign settlers who demanded rights of citizenship and private ownership of land.[21]

By 1840, King Kamehameha II transformed the government into a constitutional monarchy, having signed a Bill of Rights in 1839 and a Constitution for the Kingdom of Hawai'i in 1840. In 1845, despite petitions of protest signed by 5,790 Native Hawaiians, foreigners were allowed to become naturalized citizens and to hold public office. Ka Mahele in 1848 established a system of private land ownership which concentrated 99.2 percent of Hawai'i's lands among 245 chiefs, the Crown, and the government. Less than one percent of the lands were given to 28 percent of the people, leaving 72 percent of the people landless. In 1850, foreigners were given the right to own land. From this point on foreigners, primarily Americans, continued to expand their interests, eventually controlling most of the land, sugar and pineapple plantations, banks, shipping, and commerce.[22]

Throughout the 19th century until 1893, the United States recognized the independence of the Hawaiian Nation and extended full and complete diplomatic recognition to that government. The United States government entered into treaties and conventions with the Hawaiian monarchs to govern commerce and navigation in 1826, 1842, 1850, 1855, 1875 and 1887.[23]

By 1887, Hawai'i had treaties and conventions with Belgium, Bremen, Denmark, France, the German Empire, Great Britain, Hamburg, Hong Kong, Italy, Japan, the Netherlands, New South Wales, Portugal, Russia, Samoa, Spain, the Swiss Confederation, Sweden, Norway, Tahiti, and the United States.[24] On November 28,1843, Great Britain and France signed a joint declaration recognizing the independence of Hawai'i and pledging never to take possession of Hawai'i.[25] Hawai'i was also a member of one of the first international governmental organizations, the Universal Postal Union. It had established approximately a hundred diplomatic and consular posts around the world.[26]

In 1887, American planter interests organized a coup d'etat against King David Kalākaua, forcing him to sign the Bayonet Constitution, which took away his sovereign powers as king and the civil rights of Hawaiians. In 1889, eight men were killed, twelve wounded, and seventy were arrested in the Wilcox Rebellion, which attempted to restore the Hawaiian Constitution. By 1890, non-Hawaiians controlled 96 percent of the sugar industry and Native Hawaiians were reduced to only 45 percent of the population due to the importation of Chinese, Japanese, and Portuguese immigrant laborers by the sugar planters.

In the year 1893, the United States Minister assigned to the Kingdom of Hawaii, John L. Stevens, conspired with a small group of non-Hawaiian residents of the Kingdom, including citizens of the United States, to overthrow the indigenous and lawful Government of Hawai'i.[27] In pursuance of that conspiracy, the United States Minister and the naval representative of the United States caused 162 armed naval forces of the United States to invade the sovereign Hawaiian Nation in support of the overthrow of the indigenous and lawful

Government of Hawai'i and the United States Minister thereupon extended diplomatic recognition to a provisional government declared by eighteen conspirators, mostly American, without the consent of the native people of Hawai'i or the lawful government of Hawai'i, in violation of treaties between the two nations and of international law.[28]

Without warning or a declaration of war, this surprise attack upon a friendly and peaceful nation caught the government and its citizens totally unprepared to respond. Protesting the U.S. role in this conspiracy and receiving assurances of an immediate and fair investigation, the Queen, on January 17, 1893, trusted the "enlightened justice" of the United States and yielded, under protest, to the U.S. forces until an investigation could be completed and she could be restored. She wrote:

I Lili'uokalani, by the Grace of God and under the Constitution of the Hawaiian Kingdom, Queen, do hereby solemnly protest against any and all acts done against myself and the Constitutional Government of the Hawaiian Kingdom by certain persons claiming to have established a Provisional Government of and for this Kingdom.

That I yield to the superior force of the United States of America whose Minister Plenipotentiary, His Excellency John L. Stevens, has caused United States troops to be landed at Honolulu and declared that he would support the Provisional Government.

Now to avoid any collision of armed forces, and perhaps the loss of life, I do under this protest and impelled by said force yield my authority until such time as the Government of the United States shall, upon the facts being presented to it, undo the action of its representative and reinstate me in the authority which I claim as the Constitutional Sovereign of the Hawaiian Islands.

Done at Honolulu this 17th day of January, A.D. 1893.[29]

Queen Lili'uokalani, the lawful monarch of Hawai'i, and the Hawaiian Patriotic League, representing the aboriginal citizens of Hawai'i, promptly petitioned the United States for redress of these wrongs and for restoration of the indigenous government of the Hawaiian nation, but this petition was not acted upon.

In a message to Congress on December 18, 1893, then President Grover Cleveland reported fully and accurately on these illegal actions, and acknowledged that by these acts, described by the President as acts of war, the government of a peaceful and friendly people was overthrown, and the President concluded that a "substantial wrong has thus been done which a due regard for our national character as well as the rights of the injured people requires that we should endeavor to repair." The following are excerpts from his report:

The lawful Government of Hawaii was overthrown without the drawing of a sword or the firing of a shot by a process every step of which, it may safely be asserted, is directly traceable to and dependent for its success upon the agency of the United States acting through its diplomatic and naval representatives . . .

But for the lawless occupation of Honolulu under false pretexts by the United States forces, and but for Minister Stevens' recognition of the provisional government when the United States forces were its sole support and constituted its only military strength, the Queen and her Government would never have yielded to the provisional government, even for a time and for the sole purpose of submitting her case to the enlightened justice of the United States. . . .

Believing, therefore, that the United States could not, under the circumstances disclosed, annex the islands without justly incurring the imputation of acquiring them by unjustifiable methods, I shall not again submit the treaty of annexation to the Senate for its consideration. . . . I instructed Minister Willis to advise the Queen and her supporters of my desire to aid in the restoration of the status existing before the lawless landing of the United States forces at Honolulu on the 16th of January last, if such restoration could be effected upon terms providing for clemency as well as justice to all parties concerned.[30]

The Provisional Government refused to acquiesce to President Cleveland's request to restore the Queen to the throne. They continued to hold state power and lobby for annexation to the United States. Cleveland, not ready to shed American blood for the Hawaiian people and their Queen, took no further action.[31]

On July 4, 1894, the provisional government proclaimed the Republic of Hawai'i under a new constitution.[32]

On January 7, 1895, royalists organized an armed insurrection aimed at restoring the Queen to the throne. The restoration was crushed; 220 royalists, including the Queen herself, were arrested and charged as prisoners of war for treason and concealment of treason.[33]

On January 24, 1895, while being held prisoner in 'Iolani Palace, Queen Lili'uokalani was forced to sign a statement of abdication in favor of the Republic of Hawai'i. Once free, the Queen renounced the abdication, contending that she had signed the statement because it had been falsely represented to her that the royalists who had been arrested would be immediately released.[34]

In 1898, the United States annexed Hawai'i through the Newlands Resolution without the consent of or compensation to the Native Hawaiian people or their sovereign government. Native Hawaiians were thereby denied the mechanism for expression of their inherent sovereignty through self-government and self-determination, their lands and ocean resources.[35]

Through the Newlands Resolution and the 1900 Organic Act, the United States Congress received 1.75 million acres of lands formerly owned by the Crown and Government of the Hawaiian Kingdom and exempted the lands from then existing public land laws of the United States by mandating that the revenue and proceeds from these lands be "used solely for the benefit of the inhabitants of the Hawaiian Islands for education and other public purposes," thereby establishing a special trust relationship between the United States and the inhabitants of Hawai'i.[36]

From 1900 through 1959, Hawai'i was governed as a Territory of the United States. The official U.S. policy was to Americanize the multiethnic society of the Hawaiian Islands, beginning with the children through the American public school system. Hawaiian and other languages except English were banned as official languages or as a medium of instruction. An elite group of Americans who were the owners and managers of what was called the Big Five factories had monopoly control over every facet of Hawai'i's economy and social system.[37]

In 1921, Congress enacted the Hawaiian Homes Commission Act, which designated 200,000 acres of the ceded public lands for exclusive homesteading by Native Hawaiians, thereby affirming the trust relationship between the United States and the Native Hawaiians, as expressed by then Secretary of Interior Franklin K. Lane. Lane was cited in the Committee Report of the United States House of Representatives Committee on Territories as stating, "One thing that impressed me . . . was the fact that the natives of the islands who are our wards, I should say, and for whom in a sense we are trustees, are falling off rapidly in numbers and many of them are in poverty."[38]

In 1938 the United States Congress again acknowledged the unique status of the Native Hawaiian people by including in the Kalapana Extension Act a provision to lease lands within the extension to Native Hawaiians and to permit fishing in the area "only by native Hawaiian residents of said area or of adjacent villages and by visitors under their guidance."[39]

A plebiscite on statehood was held in 1940 by the territorial government. The question posed was, "Do you favor statehood for Hawai'i?"; 67 percent of the voters answered "yes." Almost one-third of the voters opposed statehood. In 10 of the 162 precincts the majority voted "no." Slightly more than 20 percent of those eligible did not vote.[40]

In 1946, the United States, as required under Chapter XI, Article 73 of the U.N. Charter, "Declaration Regarding Non-Self-Governing Territories," included Hawai'i on the list of its non-self-governing territories together with Alaska, American Samoa, Guam, Panama Canal Zone, Puerto Rico, and the Virgin Islands. By this action the U.S. accepted responsibility to assist the Territory of Hawai'i in achieving self-government. This was to be achieved when the inhabitants voted for one of the following three alternative statuses:

Complete independence from any other state.
Free association with another state.
Complete integration into another state.[41]

In 1959, in accordance with the Admission Act of March 18, 1959, a second statehood plebiscite was held. The plebiscite provided that the qualified voters of Hawai'i adopt or reject three propositions, all of which had to be adopted for Hawai'i to become a state: (a) "Shall Hawai'i immediately be admitted into the Union as a state?" (b) acceptance of the boundaries of the State, and (c) acceptance of all the provisions contained in the Statehood Bill. Any American citizen who had resided in Hawai'i for one year was eligible to vote. The result of the plebiscite was: 132,938 voters in favor of statehood and 7,854 opposed.[42]

For a plebiscite to be considered free and fair it must meet the criteria of (1) neutrality of the plebiscite area; (2) freedom from foreign occupation; and (3) control of the administration of the plebiscite by a neutral authority. Given these criteria, advocates of independence for Hawai'i charge that the 1959 plebiscite cannot be considered an adequate exercise in self-determination by the true residents of Hawai'i.

First, those who participated in the plebiscite could not be considered the correct "self," reflecting those citizens of Hawai'i or descendants of them who had been denied the continued exercise of their independent nation by the U.S. invasion in 1893. The U.S. government defined the qualifications for voting in such a way that it resulted in the exercise of an altered "self"-determination. By 1959, Hawai'i had been Americanized by years of transmigration from the United States of America and socialization through control over the media, the economy, and the educational, social, legal, and political system of Hawai'i. Following four generations of U.S. control over the society, the United States permitted the "qualified" voters in Hawai'i to become equal American citizens. Qualified voters were American citizens who were residents of Hawai'i for at least one year. Only U.S. declared citizens could vote. Those who resisted the American domination and insisted on their Hawaiian citizenship could not vote.

Second, the question, "Shall Hawai'i immediately be admitted into the Union as a State?" was unfair and fell short as a measure of self-determination. It failed to afford the people the range of choices from integration within the United States or to reemerge as an independent nation. The question, "Should Hawai'i be a free and independent nation?" should have been but was never asked.

Additional factors that make the 1959 plebiscite fraudulent as an exercise of self-determination were that the United States stated the question to be asked; supervised the plebiscite process; and counted the votes. The United States military maintained a strong presence in the territory when the plebiscite was conducted. Many in the U.S. military also participated in the plebiscite. The United States failed to carry out or to see that others carried out an educational program on the right to independence. In fact, the United States caused fear within the society by promoting a communist scare and a nuclear arms race scare which later proved, on both fronts, to have been fabrications of the government of the day. The United States did not inform the people of their right to self-determination or of the responsibility of the United States to the people regarding decolonization as called for under Chapter XI, Article 73 of the U.N. Charter.[43]

In 1959, after the Hawai'i statehood plebiscite, the U.S. removed Hawai'i from the U.N. list of Non-Self-Governing Territories. As evidence, the U.S. submitted a memorandum to the Secretary General, the text of the Congressional Act admitting Hawai'i into the U.S. as a state (1959 Admission Act),[44] a Presidential Proclamation, and the text of Hawaii's Constitution. In response, the U.N. General Assembly, through Resolution 1469 (XIV), expressed the opinion that Hawai'i had effectively exercised the right of self-determination and had freely chosen its status as a state of the Union. This relieved the United States of further responsibility to report to the U.N.[45]

While the 1959 Admission Act incorporated Hawai'i and its multiethnic population into the United States of America as the fiftieth state, it also recognized and reaffirmed a trust relationship with the Native Hawaiian people.

Under the Admission Act, the United States mandated the new State of Hawai'i to assume responsibility for administration of 200,000 acres of Hawaiian

Home Lands for the exclusive benefit of native Hawaiians. It also reaffirmed the trust relationship which existed between the United States and the Native Hawaiian people by retaining exclusive power to enforce the trust, including the power to approve land exchanges and legislative amendments affecting the rights of beneficiaries under the act.

Under the Admission Act, the United States also transferred responsibility for administration over portions of the ceded public lands trust not retained by the United States (approximately 1,200,000 acres) to the State of Hawai'i but reaffirmed the trust relationship which existed between the United States and the Native Hawaiian people by retaining the legal responsibility of oversight over the State for the betterment of the conditions of Native Hawaiians under section 5(f) of the Admission Act.

After 1959, Congress enacted over 100 pieces of legislation that addressed the special needs of Native Hawaiians ranging from healthcare and education, to economic development and cultural and natural resource preservation. Some examples of these include the Native Hawaiian Study Commission Act, Pub. L. No. 98–139, 97 Stat. 871 (1983); Native Hawaiian Health Care Act of 1988, Pub. L. No. 100–579,102 Stat. 4181; and the Native Hawaiian Education Act, Pub. L. No. 103–382, 108 Stat. 3518 (1994).[46]

These laws culminated with the Apology Resolution of November 23, 1993, which directly acknowledged the inherent sovereignty of Native Hawaiians at the time of the overthrow of the Kingdom of Hawai'i. The Apology Resolution also acknowledged the vested rights of the Native Hawaiian people in the crown and government lands of the Kingdom of Hawai'i; and that Native Hawaiians continue to be a distinct people determined to preserve, develop, and transmit to future generations their ancestral territory and their cultural identity in accordance with their own spiritual and traditional beliefs, customs, practices, language, and social institutions.[47]

GOALS AND STRATEGIES

There are two distinct goals for Hawaiian governance: achieving nation-within-nation status, like other Native Americans, and achieving independence from the United States, under free-association status like the republics in Micronesia or as an independent state like island nations of the South Pacific.

Hawaiian groups tend to pose "nation-within-nation" and "independence" as two competing goals. However, it is my contention that these are actually complementary. In fact, we are really looking at one status that will address the unique and special conditions of the indigenous Hawaiian people and one status that will address the broader issues of the decolonization of Hawai'i as a whole for the indigenous Hawaiians in partnership with the "local" multi-ethnic population.

What is called nation-within-nation status is what has thus far been accorded to more than 550 Native American nations in the United States. It is important to emphasize that this status can and should be accorded to the indigenous Hawaiian nation whether Hawai'i is a part of or independent from the United States.

The process of decolonization toward total independence is a status for indigenous Hawaiians to pursue in conjunction with the broader "local" population, those who primarily identify culturally, socially, economically, and politically with Hawai'i as their homeland. This would include Hawai'i residents who distinguish themselves from America as well as from the nation from which their ancestors originated.

By the end of the twentieth century, the majority of indigenous Hawaiians seemed prepared to begin a process to re-establish Hawaiian sovereignty, but the broader local population appeared to need more time and education to unite in a process building toward decolonization.

A survey on support for sovereignty was conducted by SMS Research in February 1994. The survey asked the question, "Some Hawaiians have said that sovereignty can only be realized by declaring independence from the state, but others feel they can achieve sovereignty by working within the state and federal government. Which do you believe?" In response, 74 percent favored working within the system and 12 percent favored independence, while 14 percent were undecided.[48] Table 1 shows the breakdown by ethnic group.

TABLE 1

	Total	Hawaiian	Caucasian	Japanese	Filipino
Within System	74%	73%	79%	70%	71%
Independent	12%	11%	8%	15%	14%
Undecided	14%	16%	13%	15%	15%

This poll is one indication of the broad support for recognition of Native Hawaiian sovereignty and the lack of support among the broad spectrum of Hawai'i's population, including Native Hawaiians, for the total independence of Hawai'i. If a vote had been taken in 1994, the majority of people born and raised in Hawai'i would probably have voted for Hawai'i to remain a state and for the recognition of Native Hawaiian sovereignty.

In July 1996 the Hawaiian Sovereignty Elections Council organized a Native Hawaiian Vote with funding from the Hawai'i State Legislature. The Council mailed out 81,507 ballots to registered Native Hawaiian voters which asked, "Shall the Hawaiian people elect delegates to propose a Native Hawaiian government?" A total of 30,423 ballots were cast, representing 37 percent of the registered voters. Of these, 22,294 (73.28 percent of the ballots cast) voted "yes" and 8,129 (26.72 percent of the ballots cast) voted "no."

There are numerous Native Hawaiian organizations working for the re-establishment and recognition of a sovereign Native Hawaiian nation. Native Hawaiians involved in these organizations seek to improve and uplift Hawaiian health, education, and standard of living. They also seek to protect and perpetuate the natural and cultural resources essential for religious, cultural, and subsistence custom, belief, and practice. Ultimately, Native Hawaiians seek full redress for past injustices; restitution of all of the territory of the Native Hawaiian nation;

compensation for mismanagement and destruction of national lands and natural resources; and most significant, the re-establishment and recognition of a government to exercise sovereignty and self-determination.[49]

CONCLUSION

In the recognition of the status, rights, and entitlements of Native Hawaiian people as just lies the future of human rights in Hawai'i. Many non-Hawaiians claim they bear no obligation to reconcile with the descendants of Native Hawaiians for the injustices that occurred decades ago by persons to whom they bear no relation. However, non-Hawaiians in Hawai'i benefit, while Native Hawaiians bear the burden of the results of those historical injustices. Moreover, the U.S. Congress and the President of the United States in Public Law 103–150 outlined a series of historical injustices for which they acknowledge responsibility and apologized "to Native Hawaiians on behalf of the people of the United States." The Apology Resolution also committed the Congress and all the people of the United States to a process of reconciliation with the Native Hawaiian people.

Among the reasons given by those who oppose Native Hawaiian entitlements is that the privileging of one ethnic group over the others is unfair and will cause resentment and undermine the spirit of *aloha* in contemporary Hawai'i: *Aloha mai no, aloha aku* (when love is given, love should be returned).[50] However, this *'olelo no'eau* means that *aloha* is reciprocal. Native Hawaiian people have given *aloha* to newcomers and their descendants for generations. Now is the time for *aloha* to be acknowledged and returned to the Native Hawaiian people and their descendants. The Akaka Bill introduced by Hawai'i's congressional delegation would provide an avenue for both the people of Hawai'i and the U.S. Congress to correct the historic injustices they have suffered collectively as a people, and enable them to exercise self-determination through self-governance to heal as a people. While federal recognition would represent a culmination of a century-old trust relationship between Native Hawaiians and the U.S. Congress, it would really constitute a small first step in the re-establishment of a Native Hawaiian government since the overthrow of the Hawaiian monarchy in 1893.

NOTES

1. In the Apology Resolution, a Native Hawaiian (both words capitalized) is defined as "any individual who is a descendant of the aboriginal people who, prior to 1778, occupied and exercised sovereignty in the area that now constitutes the State of Hawai'i." The Hawaiian Homes Commission Act and the Admission Act use the term native Hawaiian (lower case n, capital H) to mean "Any descendant of not less than one-half part of the blood of the races inhabiting the Hawaiian Islands previous to 1778." The term *"Kanaka Maoli"* is promoted as the indigenous name for Native Hawaiians. However, *"Kanaka Maoli"* simply means native or indigenous, while *"Kanaka Maoli Hawai'i"* means native or indigenous Hawaiian. In the 1859 Civil Code of the Kingdom of Hawai'i, Chapter VIII, *"kanaka Hawai'i"* is used to translate "native of the Hawaiian Islands" and *"ke kanaka maoli"* is used to translate "native." In the 1878 Census of the Kingdom of Hawai'i, *"He kane kanaka maoli (Hawai'i)"* was used for "Native Male" and *"He wahine kanaka maoli (Hawai'i)"* was

used for "Native Female." However, this must have referred to pure Hawaiians only, as there was a category for "Half-Caste Male" ("He *hapahaole kane*") and "Half-Cast Female" (*"He hapahaole wahine"*). In this article, I will use "Native Hawaiian" to refer anyone who has Hawaiian ancestry, that is, who is descended from a *"Kanaka Maoli Hawai'i"* ancestor, and "native Hawaiian" to refer to those who are of half or more Hawaiian ancestry. Under the law, thus far, only "native Hawaiians" are the beneficiaries of the Hawaiian Home Lands and the ceded public lands trusts, as discussed below.

2. No. 98–818, February 23, 2000. Kennedy, J. delivered the opinion of the Court, in which Rehnquist, C. J., O'Connor, Scalia, Thomas, J.J. joined. Breyer, J. filed an opinion concurring in the result, in which Souter, J. joined. Stevens, J. filed a dissenting opinion in which Ginsburg, J. joined as to Part II. Ginsburg, J. filed a dissenting opinion.

3. 1993–1998/Federal Indian Policies/June 12, 1998.

4. These questions were raised in the following statement: "If Hawaii's restriction were to be sustained under Mancari we would be required to accept some beginning premises not yet established in our case law. Among other postulates, it would be necessary to conclude that Congress, in reciting the purposes for the transfer of lands to the State—and in other enactments such as the Hawaiian Homes Commission Act and the Joint Resolution of 1993—has determined that native Hawaiians have a status like that of Indians in organized tribes, and that it may, and has, delegated to the State a broad authority to preserve that status. These propositions would raise questions of considerable moment and difficulty."

5. List of laws include the Older Americans Act; the Developmental Disabilities Assistance and Bill of Rights Act Amendments of 1987; the Veterans' Benefits and Services Act of 1988; the Rehabilitation Act of 1973, as amended in 1988; the Native Hawaiian Health Care Act of 1988; the Health Professions Reauthorization Act of 1988; the Nursing Shortage Reduction and Education Extension Act of 1988; the Handicapped Programs Technical Amendments Act of 1988; the Indian Health Care Amendments of 1988; and the Disadvantaged Minority Health Improvement Act of 1990.

6. Department of Interior and Department of Justice, "From Mauka to Makai: The River of Justice Must Flow Freely, Report on the Reconciliation Process Between the Federal Government and Native Hawaiians," Washington, D.C., October 23, 2000, p. 56.

7. Statements on Introduced Bills and Joint Resolutions—April 6, 2001 (Senate—April 06, 2001) by Mr. Akaka (for himself and Mr. Inouye).

8. www.angelfire.com/hi2/hawaiiansovereignty; www.aloha4all.org.

9. Ibid.

10. Ibid., KITV News, June 4, 2001; *Honolulu Advertiser,* June 5, 2001, p. B-2.

11. The difference in the two sources is due to the difference in handling persons of mixed parentage. The census did not have a mixed category and assigned persons of mixed ancestry to one of the categories on the basis of self-identification or the race of the father. The Health Surveillance Program bases it on birth statistics. The figure of 70,000 is from Office of Hawaiian Affairs, "Population Survey/Needs Assessment, Final Report" (Honolulu: Office of Hawaiian Affairs, 1986). In a study of the Health Surveillance Program data, the Office of Hawaiian Affairs estimated that there were 208,476 Hawaiians in Hawai'i in 1984, out of which 72,709 had 50 percent to 99 percent Hawaiian ancestry and 8,244 had 100 percent Hawaiian ancestry.

12. Health Surveillance Program, 1988. According to the 1988 Health Surveillance Program, 18.9 percent of the Hawaiian families earned less than $15,000 per year as compared to 12.5 percent of families in other ethnic groups. In the $60,000 or more category, only 13.6 percent of the Hawaiian families earned incomes at that level, while 21.4 percent of the families in other ethnic groups earned incomes at that level. According to the Research and Evaluation Division of the Department of Human Services, 20,487 Hawaiian families received public financial assistance and Medicaid in 1990. This represented 26 percent of all of the families in Hawai'i who received financial assistance and Medicaid in 1990. The same source reported that 14,956 Hawaiian families received Aid

to Families with Dependent Children (AFDC) in 1990. This represented one-third (33.4 percent) of all of the families in Hawaii who received AFDC in 1990.

13. Department of Public Safety—Corrections Division, "Distribution of the Inmate Population By Ethnicity and Facility As Of June 30, 1992." The ethnic breakdown of the adult inmate population was as follows: Black (5.3 percent), Caucasian (22.9 percent), Chinese (0.9 percent), Filipino (7.9 percent), Hawaiian/Part Hawaiian (35 percent), Japanese (3.4 percent), Korean (0.9 percent), Samoan (3.9 percent), Other (16.1 percent)

14. George S. Kanahele, *Current Facts and Figures About Hawaiians* (Honolulu: Project WAIAHA, 1982), p. 8.

15. *Native Hawaiian Health Data Book* (Honolulu: Papa Ola Lokahi, 1992).

16. Alu Like, "Summary of the Analysis of the Needs Assessment Survey and Related Data," 1976. Kamehameha Schools/Bishop Estate, 1983. Native Hawaiian Health Research Consortium, Mental Health Task Force, Alu Like, Inc. *E Ola Mau: Native Hawaiian Health Needs Study: Mental Health Task Force Report* (Honolulu: Native Hawaiian Health Research Consortium, Alu Like, Inc., 1985).

17. "Sociocultural Impact Assessment" in the Environmental Impact Statement for the Commercial Satellite Launching Facility, Palima Point, Ka'u, Hawai'i, with Jon Matsuoka, 1991.

18. Davianna McGregor, "Pele vs. Geothermal: A Clash of Cultures," in *Bearing Dreams, Shaping Visions: Asian Pacific Americans Facing the 90's* (Seattle: Washington State University Press, 1993).

19. John Heckathorn, "Ua Hiki Anei Ke Ola Ka 'Olelo Hawai'i?—Can the Hawaiian Language Survive?" *Honolulu Magazine* 21, no. 10 (April 1987).

20. E. S. Craighill Handy, "The Hawaiian Planter—Volume I: His Plants, Methods and Areas of Cultivation," *Bernice Pauahi Bishop Museum Bulletin* 161 (Honolulu: Bernice P. Bishop Museum, 1940); E. S. Craighill Handy and Mary Kawena Pūku'i, *The Polynesian Family System in Ka'u, Hawai'i* (Wellington: Polynesian Society, 1958; reprint, Tokyo: Charles E. Tuttle Company, 1976); Samuel Kamakau, *Ruling Chiefs of Hawaii* (Honolulu: Kamehameha Schools Press, 1961); Samuel Kamakau, "Ka Po'e Kahiko: The People of Old," *BPBM Spec. Publ.* 51., 1964; Samuel Kamakau, "The Works of the People of Old," *BPBM Spec. Publ.* 61, 1976; David Malo, *Hawaiian Antiquities*, trans. Dr. Nathaniel B. Emerson (Honolulu: Bishop Museum Press, 1971); T. G. Thrum (ed.), "Fornander Collection of Hawaiian Antiquities and Folk-Lore," *BPBM Memoirs* 4, 5, 6 (1916–1920); Martha W. Beckwith, *Hawaiian Mythology* (Honolulu: University of Hawai'i Press, 1970); David Kalākaua, King of Hawaii, *The Legends and Myths of Hawaii: The Fables and Folklore of a Strange People* (Tokyo & Rutland: Charles E. Tuttle, 1973).

21. Kamakau 1961; Ralph S. Kuykendall, *The Hawaiian Kingdom, Volume I, 1778–1854: Foundation and Transformation* (Honolulu: University of Hawai'i Press; 1938; reprint, Honolulu: The University Press of Hawai'i, 1980).

22. Kuykendall 1980; Davianna McGregor, "Voices of Today Echo Voices of the Past," in *Malama Hawaiian Land and Water*, edited by Dana Naone Hall (Honolulu: Bamboo Ridge Press, 1985).

23. A convention negotiated December 24, 1826, a Treaty of Commerce, declared that the "peace and friendship" between the United States and Hawai'i was "confirmed and declared to be perpetual." The Tyler Doctrine of 1842 included Hawai'i within the U.S. sphere of influence by stating that it "could not but create dissatisfaction on the part of the United States at any attempt by another power, should such attempt be threatened or feared, to take possession of the islands, colonize them, and subvert the native government." There was also the Treaty of Friendship, Commerce and Navigation, August 24, 1850; Rights of Neutrals at Sea, March 25, 1855; Treaty of Commercial Reciprocity, September 1876; Treaty of Commercial Reciprocity, November 9, 1887. See *Treaties and Other International Agreements of the United States of America*, V. 8.

24. *Treaties and Conventions Concluded Between the Hawaiian Kingdom and Other Powers Since 1825.*

25. Senate Ex. Doc. 52 Cong. 2 Sess., No. 57, p. 12.

26. F. M. Hustat, *Directory and Handbook of the Kingdom of Hawai'i* (Honolulu: Polk, 1892).

27. U.S. Congress, House, Report No. 243, "Intervention of United States Government in Affairs of Foreign Friendly Governments," 53rd Congress, 2nd Session, December 21, 1893 (Washington, D.C.: Government Printing Office, 1893); U.S. Congress, Senate, Committee on Foreign Relations, "Hawaiian Islands," Report of the Committee on Foreign Relations With Accompanying Testimony and Executive Documents Transmitted to Congress from January 1, 1893 to March 19, 1894, Volumes I and II (Washington, D.C.: Government Printing Office, 1894. Also referred to as "The Morgan Report"); U.S. Congress, Senate, Committee on Foreign Relations, Report No. 227, "Report from the Committee on Foreign Relations and Appendix in Relation to the Hawaiian Islands, February 26, 1894," 53rd Congress, 2nd Session (Washington, D.C.: Government Printing Office, 1894); U.S. Department of State, "Papers Relating to the Mission of James H. Blount, United States Commissioner to the Hawaiian Islands" (Washington, D.C.: Government Printing Office, 1893).

28. Close to 5:00 P.M. on January 16, 1893, 162 U.S. naval forces with 80 rounds of ammunition each, one Gatling gun and one 37-millimeter revolving gun, landed at the foot of Nu'uanu Avenue and marched up Fort Street to Merchant Street. They were accompanied by a hospital corps with stretchers and medical supplies. Some troops were deployed to guard the U.S. consulate and some were sent to the U.S. legation. The main body of three companies ultimately took up quarters at Arion Hall near the government building and the palace. William De Witt Alexander, *History of the Later Years of the Hawaiian monarchy and the Revolution of 1893* (Honolulu: Hawaiian Gazette Co., 1896).

In a report to Congress on December 11, 1893 President Cleveland observed that:

> There is as little basis for the pretense that such forces were landed for the security of American life and property. If so, they would have been stationed in the vicinity of such property and so as to protect it, instead of at a distance and so as to command the Hawaiian Government building and palace. Admiral Skerrett, the officer in command of our naval force on the Pacific station, has frankly stated that in his opinion the location of the troops was inadvisable if they were landed for protection of American citizens whose residences and places of business, as well as the legation and consulate, were in a distant part of the city, but the location selected was a wise one if the forces were landed for the purpose of supporting the provisional government. (Grover Cleveland, "Message of the President," December 18, 1893, in 53rd Congress 2nd Session, House of Representatives, Report 243, p. 7)

29. Queen Lili'uokalani, *Hawaii's Story By Hawaii's Queen* (Boston: Lothrop, Lee & Shepard, Co., 1898; reprint, Tokyo: Charles E. Tuttle Company, 1977), pp. 387–388.

30. U.S. House of Representatives, 53rd Congress, 2nd Session, December 21, 1893, pp. 13–14.

31. Alexander 1896; Lili'uokalani 1898.

32. Ibid.

33. Hawai'i State Archives, 1895 Insurrection File; Albertine Loomis, *For Whom Are the Stars?* (Honolulu: University of Hawai'i Press and Friends of the Library of Hawai'i, 1976).

34. Lili'uokalani, 1898.

35. Robert M.C. Littler, *The Governance of Hawaii: A Study in Territorial Administration* (Stanford, Calif.: Stanford University Press, 1929).

36. U.S. Congress. 56th Congress, 1st Session 1899–1900. "Congressional Debates on Hawaii Organic Act, Together With Debates and Congressional Action on Other Matters Concerning the Hawaiian Islands." Washington, D.C. (photostat reproduction from the Congressional Record, v. 33, pts. 1–8), 1899–1900.

37. Lawrence Fuchs, *Hawaii Pono: A Social History* (San Diego, Calif.: Harcourt, Brace & World, Inc., 1961); Noel Kent, *Hawaii, Islands Under the Influence* (New York: Monthly Review

Press, 1983); Andrew Lind, *An Island Community: Ecological Succession in Hawaii* (Chicago: The University of Chicago, 1938; reprint, New York: Greenwood Press, 1968).

38. U.S. Congress, House, Committee on the Territories, Report No. 839, 66th Congress 2nd Session. Seen in Hawai'i State Archives, Delegate Kalanianaole File on Rehabilitation.

39. Act of June 20, 1938 (52 Stat. 781 et seq.).

40. Roger J. Bell, *Last Among Equals: Hawaiian Statehood and American Politics* (Honolulu: University of Hawai'i Press, 1984).

41. Rob Williams, esq., working paper for "Status and Entitlements of Hawaiian Natives" study, funded by the Ford Foundation, to the Native Hawaiian Advisory Council, 1992–1993; Hawaiian Sovereignty Advisory Council Report To The Legislature, January 1992; Presentation of Russell Barsh, esq., to the Hawaiian Sovereignty Advisory Commission, November 5–6, 1993, Hawai'i State Tower.

42. Ibid.

43. Ibid.

44. "An Act to provide for the admission of the State of Hawai'i into the Union," approved March 18, 1959 (Pub.L. 86–3, 73 Stat. 4)

45. Hawaiian Sovereignty Advisory Council Report To The Legislature, January 1992.

46. Department of Interior and Department of Justice, "From Mauka to Makai: The River of Justice Must Flow Freely, Report on the Reconciliation Process Between the Federal Government and Native Hawaiians," Washington, D.C., October 23, 2000, pp. 56–57.

47. Apology Resolution, Public Law 103–150.

48. *Honolulu Advertiser*, February 22, 1994, pp. A-1 and A-4.

49. Ka Lahui Hawai'i, claiming to represent 20,000 members, has held four constitutional conventions to establish their own national legislature, governor, and council of elders. As strong advocates for nation-within-nation status, Ka Lahui Hawai'i seeks recognition from the U.S. Congress and the State of Hawai'i as the nation of Hawaiians to exist within the nation of the United States of America. In the 1993 legislative session they introduced a bill calling for the transfer to their nation of all of the Hawaiian national lands controlled by the state government. The State Hawaiian Homes Association claims to represent 30,000 Hawaiians who are settled on Hawaiian Homelands. They seek immediate and direct control over the homestead lands they live on and use, seeking home rule over the Hawaiian Homelands. The statewide Association of Hawaiian Civic Clubs has traditionally represented the more conservative sector of the Native Hawaiian community. The clubs support Native Hawaiian sovereignty. There are several organizations that seek to totally decolonize Hawai'i. Smaller in number than the advocates of nation-within-nation status, they nevertheless comprise a very eloquent, determined, and militant sector of the community. Included among the organizations seeking total independence from the United States are the Institute for the Advancement of Hawaiian Affairs, the Nation State of Hawai'i, Ka Pakaukau, the Sovereign Kingdom of Hawai'i, the Hawaiian Patriotic League, and the Lawful Kingdom of Hawai'i.

50. Pūku'i, 1983, no. 113, p. 15. *Aloha mai no, aloha aku; o ka huhu ka mea e ola 'ole at.* When love is given, love should be returned; anger is the thing that gives no life.

Situating Asian Americans in the Political Discourse on Affirmative Action

Michael Omi and Dana Takagi

The hegemonic "black/white" paradigm of race relations has fundamentally shaped how we think about, engage, and politically mobilize around racial issues. Historical narratives of racialized minorities in the United States are cast in the shadows of the black/white encounter. Contemporary conflicts between a number of different racial/ethnic groups are understood in relationship to this bipolar model, which the media then utilize as a master frame to present such conflicts. During the Los Angeles "riots" of 1992, for example, various racial subjects were identified (for example, Koreans, Guatemalans), but the popular interpretation of the civil disorder was fundamentally shaped by the hegemonic paradigm.

This prevailing bipolar model of race significantly obscures the complex patterns of race over time. Tomás Almaguer, in his study of race in nineteenth-century California, breaks from the dominant mode of biracial theorizing by illustrating how Native Americans, Mexicans, Chinese, and Japanese are racialized and positioned in relation to one another by the dominant Anglo elite.[1] His discussion draws attention to how the Asian American historical experience is essential to a full comprehension of racial dynamics in the West.

We want to suggest that a more complex and nuanced understanding of the affirmative action debate needs to be attentive to how distinct political positions socially construct and represent Asian Americans. Our intent is to locate Asian Americans within the political discourse on affirmative action, a move that would serve to deepen a critical analysis of the black/white paradigm, and, in doing so, reveal some intriguing aspects about racial politics in the current period.

Gary Y. Okihiro, in a collection of essays on Asian American history and culture, asks: "Is yellow black or white?"[2] His discussion of this question highlights how Asian Americans have historically been located somewhere between black and white. Depending on the period in question, Asian Americans have been seen as racially "black"[3] or as a group "outwhiting the whites."[4]

The question of how to situate Asian Americans on a spectrum—close to African Americans at one end or closer to whites on the other—helps to critically define the distinctive political positions on affirmative action. Both the Right and the Left of the political spectrum implicate, in varying degrees, Asian Americans in the ongoing debate. Unlike "black" and "white" as racial categories, there is a greater fluidity to "Asian American" that can be manipulated in particular ways to suit particular positions. It may not matter whether specific claims about Asian Americans are empirically correct or not. In fact, much of what both the Left and the Right claim about Asian Americans is contestable. Thus, the "truth" of the claims is immaterial. What matters are the kinds of rhetorical constructions, and their emotional impacts, that the Right and the Left deploy.

RIGHT POLITICAL DISCOURSE AND ASIAN AMERICAN VICTIMS

In January 1996, Governor Pete Wilson upheld his support for the July 1995 decision by the University of California (UC) Regents to eliminate race as a consideration for admissions, hiring, and contracting. It was the "right decision," he argued, one premised on the principles of equal opportunity: "Racial preferences are by definition racial discrimination. They were wrong 30 years ago when they discriminated against African-Americans. And they're wrong today, when they discriminate against *Asian* or Caucasian Americans" (emphasis ours).[5] Wilson's strategic assignment of Asian Americans to the white side of the battle lines is noteworthy. The UC Regents' questioning of affirmative action was precipitated by a complaint lodged by Jerry and Ellen Cook, a white San Diego couple who began examining statistical information on the five medical schools in the UC system when their son was denied admission to the UC San Diego Medical School. The Cooks claimed that at UC Davis, for example, Chicanos were offered admission at five times the rate of whites and *nineteen times* the rate of Japanese Americans.[6] The signal was clear. "Preferential policies" victimized Asian Americans as much as, perhaps more than, whites.

Deploying this particular social construction serves an important political purpose. By raising the issue of Asian American victimization, the Right could deflect the charge levied against them by their critics that their opposition to affirmative action represents merely a thinly veiled attempt to preserve white skin privilege. At work here is a specific *rearticulation* of the issue of affirmative action.[7]

This rearticulation has several interesting effects that creatively engage the existing field of racial meanings. One effect, as we suggested above, is to disrupt the understanding of the racial issue as an expression of white/nonwhite difference and conflict. The Right evokes Asian Americans to demonstrate that another nonwhite, racialized minority is being hurt by such policies. This representation of Asian Americans as disadvantaged by affirmative action plays into popular constructions of Asian Americans as "friends" of whites and "foes" of African Americans. The specter of black/Asian American conflict, evident in numerous cinematic portrayals of ghetto life,[8] is elevated to a national level of policy debate.

The historical experience of Asian Americans becomes a particularly convenient narrative to exploit. Asian Americans are presented as a group that has been subject to extreme forms of racial discrimination in the past (including immigration exclusion, the denial of naturalization rights, and, in the case of Japanese Americans, incarceration). Despite these obstacles, they have become a "model minority," not by means of state assistance, but through their own hard work and efforts. This narrative questions the efficacy of state intervention to change patterns of racial inequality, and feeds into the reductionist accounts that claim that a group's "culture" is the key to their mobility and success.[9]

The Right also takes pains to note that Asian Americans are not active discriminators in the present. There is, so it seems, no "yellow skin privilege." Given the weight of the past and their location in the present, it is truly unfair, the Right argues, that Asian Americans must now confront a new and pernicious form of discrimination under the guise of equality. Dinesh D'Souza makes this clear:

> One can hardly maintain that preferential policies strictly serve the goals of social justice. Take the case of Asian Americans: Members of this minority group have experienced both *de facto* and *de jure* discrimination, and they have played no part in any of the historical crimes that affirmative action was designed to remedy. In fairness, why should the burden of preferential policies be placed on historically innocent parties?[10]

In June 1995, Governor Wilson stated that "it is not just the 'angry white males' who think the time has come for change." He went on to describe his conversation with a Vietnamese senior at prestigious Lowell High School in San Francisco. The young woman was "deeply troubled" that Vietnamese students were admitted with lower scores than Chinese students.[11] Many of the Right's principal themes are condensed in this example. The "troubled" Vietnamese student bears more than a passing resemblance to that African American student evoked by numerous conservative political commentators, the student whose self-esteem and sense of worth is shaken by the belief that she or he is an affirmative action case. The example also reveals that the Right's construction of Asian Americans as the victims of affirmative action does not necessarily rely on treating the group as undifferentiated and monolithic. The Right's argument is nuanced and attentive to the diversity among Asian Americans and the different political claims that can potentially surface.

The Right's representation of Asian Americans with respect to affirmative action is full of irony. We read it as the strategic use of race to deflect the issue of race. The Right has rearticulated the racial meanings embedded in the affirmative action debates by representing Asian Americans as an "innocent" group wronged by racial preferences. Race has been rendered more complex, but in so doing, attention has been distracted from the hegemonic position of whites on the playing field. Such an ideological sleight of hand allows racial privilege to be sidelined while an agenda based on individual merit, social justice, and the creation of a "colorblind" society is promoted.

LEFT POLITICAL DISCOURSE AND ASIAN AMERICAN INVISIBILITY

On 18 January 1996, student advocates for affirmative action staged a dramatic and emotional protest inside the UC Board of Regents meeting in San Francisco. During a brief public comment session on SP-1 and SP-2, approximately fifty students applied whiteface and pasted stickers reading "Reclaim Our Education" over their mouths.[12] Their "white" faces, they explained, represented the increasing whiteness of the University of California, and the corresponding lack of racial diversity that would result when the resolutions took effect. The mouth stickers were worn to underscore the students' lack of voice in UC policy. The visual symbols deployed by the students were a stunning display of what many progressives believe is the future of UC without affirmative action.[13]

Outside the meeting, some four hundred students from across the nine-campus system supported the (mostly but not always) silent protesters inside with a loud and enthusiastic rally. The student protesters were galvanized by chants of "no University without diversity" and "UC diversity, we see hypocrisy." Somewhat predictably, the gaggle of TV news cameras and reporters organized their feature stories and news coverage by juxtaposing images of painted faces and silent protest inside the meeting with those of noisy demonstrators outside the meeting. The imagery and representations of the January meeting, resonant with past debate and demonstrations about affirmative action at UC, prompt us to think about how Asian Americans are positioned in pro–affirmative action and Left discourses on racial preferences.

If Asian Americans assume the status of newfound victims of discrimination in Right narratives, they occupy a kind of racial pariah position in Left and progressive accounts of affirmative action. Left discursive practices have been organized in two ways, both problematic. In the first, Asian Americans are simply left out of the affirmative action debate. Part of this is attributable to the hegemonic, bipolar model of race relations we emphasized earlier. Many pro–affirmative action statements from major organizations, for instance, focus entirely on black/white inequalities, with nary a whisper about Asian Americans. Their absence from the debate can also be accounted for in the argument that historically Asian Americans have not been the beneficiaries of racial preferences. Hence, the debate about SP-1 and SP-2 does not concern Asian Americans per se. Perhaps another explanation for the deletion of Asian Americans from Left discourses concerns the numerical size of the Asian American population. At three percent of the national population in 1990, Asians are arguably a tiny minority—and hence expendable in the "big" picture of race relations. Yet another explanation might be that many progressives worry that Asian Americans, because they see themselves benefiting from the end of affirmative action, are likely to oppose racial preferences. Hence, the less said about Asian Americans, the better.

A second discursive practice, and one that we believe is more prevalent than the first, includes Asian Americans as relatively unproblematic partners in a wider coalition politics. The chant "no University without diversity" is suggestive of a broad phalanx of diverse constituencies, including Asian Americans. Here, while we are sympathetic to the politics of a "united front" of opposition to SP-1 and SP-2, we remain concerned that such a politics presumes that Asian American interests are similar enough to other interests to make the coalition claims viable and rhetorically persuasive. In our view, the assumption that Asian Americans share a similar social location as, for example, African Americans in the affirmative action debate, is wrong. Rather, it is precisely the difference between these groups that has played an important part in the mobilization of the Right. While the Right has capitalized on Asian American achievement in higher education, the Left has weakly insisted on the "shared interests" model of politics.

Interrogating the concept of "shared interests" among people of color raises a host of questions, including that of the nature of racism in the United States. We tend to think of racism as hostility directed against those of a different skin color believed to be "inferior"—in terms of class and status, in intellectual ability, or in cultural orientation. This hostility is coupled with structural forms of discrimination—in the job market, in politics, in residential patterns—and negative cultural representations. Clearly African Americans are subject to this type of racism.

Asian Americans, however, are subject to a different form of racism. They are often the objects of *resentment* by other groups who perceive that they do "too well," that they secure wealth and other material resources and social advantages unfairly. This resentment has resulted historically in political disenfranchisement and exclusionary laws in the late nineteenth to early twentieth century, and in "English-only" initiatives and more stringent curbs on immigration and foreign capital investment today.

The status of Asian Americans in higher education and projections regarding their increased growth renders the "shared interest" model of coalition politics quite problematic. In the midst of debate about UC admissions policy in July 1995, the University's Office of the President projected that Asian Americans would be the only nonwhite group to benefit from passage of SP-1 and SP-2. The estimate that Asian enrollment would increase by twenty percent, while other racial minority enrollments would decline, presented an interesting dilemma for Left and pro–affirmative action activists. While some groups would support racial preferences on the grounds of self-interest in admissions, Asian Americans would presumably support preferences on the basis of altruistic sentiments about the needs of, and rights owed to, other racial minorities.

We wish to emphasize our agreement with the students in whiteface that declining diversity is an inevitable consequence of SP-1 and SP-2. But we also wish to open up a nagging question about the racial narrative conveyed by the dramatic student protest: will the University become primarily *white*? How will the discursive politics about preferences shift and change if, as the projections suggest, the University becomes increasingly *Asian American*?

BLACK, WHITE, OR "OTHER"?

Both the Right and the Left are vying for custody of the political "interests" of Asian Americans. For the Right, the Asian American "model minority" figures as the Allan Bakke replacement for the 1990s assault on affirmative action. On the other hand, Left and progressive forces hope that Asian Americans will broaden the political coalition of pro–affirmative action and pro-diversity forces and thereby expand the unified front of opposition to the Right. One side pits Asian Americans against whites, the other pits Asian Americans against racial minorities. From there, the discussion descends into quibbles over whether Asian Americans are more like African Americans or, alternatively, more like whites in the politics of race in the United States. In our view, neither the Left nor the Right has custodial rights to the experiences of Asian Americans. Attempts on both sides to meld Asian America into a vision of "whiteness" or "racial diversity" will always be problematic given the unique racial formation of Asian Americans.

Asian American educational achievement, for example, threatens to subvert both Right and Left versions of preferential policies. Members of the Right, including Regent Ward Connerly and Governor Pete Wilson, have argued for the substitution of class preferences for race in UC admissions. Parts of the Left as well have hinged the viability of affirmative action on class, with the assumption that underrepresented racial minorities would continue to be given preference through class variables. But the use of class preferences will present a clear *racial* advantage for Asian American applicants to all UC campuses. If socioeconomic status is used as an admissions criterion instead of race, UC officials predict that Asian American enrollment will *increase* by fifteen to twenty-five percent while African American enrollment will drop forty to fifty percent, Latino enrollment will fall five to fifteen percent, and white enrollment will stay about the same.[14]

The class-based initiatives presented above serve as one example of the tendency to delete race from both sides of the rhetorical divide about affirmative action. For the Right, opposition to affirmative action is premised on ideas of individual merit and the advancement of a colorblind society, and any hints of "color consciousness" are suspiciously viewed as forms of racial discrimination. For part of the Left, there is a tendency to keep the Pandora's box of race closed to avoid the messy racial issues that threaten to emerge from it. The UC faculty challenge to the Regents' decision, for example, emphasizes threats to faculty governance and the intrusion of partisan politics into the academy, rather than the desirability of racial preferences.

What is missing from the conversations about affirmative action—on the Left *and* the Right—is an explicit discussion of the nature of race and racism in the United States today. Both the Right and Left have wrestled with how to situate Asian Americans in affirmative action debates and how to frame particular strategic representations of them. Their attempts reveal the complexity of race in the current period when the bipolar model of race relations has revealed an increasing inability to comprehend the patterns of conflict and accommodation that now occur between, and among, many different racialized groups. Race in the United States can no longer, if it ever could, be adequately understood by narrowly assessing the relative situations of whites and blacks.

We need a new framework that is attentive to a complex understanding of racial location and interest, one that does not essentialize race but interrogates how groups are constructed and represented, one that understands that social policies—regarding immigration, welfare, crime, as well as affirmative action—have a differential impact on different groups and the way they are defined. This framework will be crucial to an understanding of politics in a period when the traditional discourse of civil rights is being rearticulated by the Right in ways that preserve the structure of racial privilege. A post–civil rights perspective will have to grapple with the increased visibility of Asian Americans and how they are implicated in a range of racial issues. Asian Americans can no longer be cast in the shadows of black/white relations. Yet observers continue to do just that. Andrew Hacker, for example, needs to talk extensively about Asian Americans in order to examine race-based admissions policies in higher education.[15] Unfortunately his analysis does not lead him to consider that the United States, in this area as well as in many others, may be more than "two nations," black and white.

Asian Americans as a group are, we think, a crucial barometer of the contemporary racial climate. It will indeed be interesting to see how the issue of affirmative action is recast by both the Right and the Left if, as a consequence of SP-1 and SP-2, the student bodies of the two UC flagship campuses—Berkeley and Los Angeles—become overwhelmingly Asian.

NOTES

1. Tomás Almaguer, *Racial Fault Lines: The Historical Origins of White Supremacy in California* (Berkeley, 1994).
2. Gary Y. Okihiro, *Margins and Mainstreams: Asians in American History and Culture* (Seattle, 1994), chap. 2.
3. Dan Cauldwell, "The Negroization of the Chinese Stereotype in California," *Southern California Historical Quarterly* 1 (June 1971).
4. "Success Story: Outwhiting the Whites," *Newsweek*, 21 June 1971.
5. Pete Wilson, "Why Racial Preferences Must End," *San Francisco Chronicle*, 18 January 1996, A21.
6. Richard Bernstein, "Moves Under Way in California to Overturn Higher Education's Affirmative Action Policy," *New York Times*, 25 January 1995, B8.
7. By rearticulation we mean "the process of redefinition of political interests and identities through a process of recombination of familiar ideas and values in hitherto unrecognized ways." Michael Omi and Howard Winant, *Racial Formation in the United States: From the 1960s to the 1990s*, 2d ed. (New York, 1994), 163 n. 8.
8. A particularly explosive example is the Allen Hughes and Albert Hughes film *Menace II Society* (1993).
9. This position is best articulated by Thomas Sowell in his numerous publications. For the most current example, see his *Race and Culture: A World View* (New York, 1994).
10. Dinesh D'Souza, "The Failure of the 'Cruel Compassion,'" *The Chronicle of Higher Education*, 15 September 1995, Bl.
11. Yumi Wilson, "Wilson Explains His Affirmative Action Plans," *San Francisco Chronicle*, 1 June 1995, A16.

12. SP-1 and SP-2 are the two UC Regents resolutions passed on 20 July 1995 that ban the use of race and gender preferences in, respectively, admissions and employment practices at the University of California.

13. Indeed, this imagery of the meeting was carried by all the major newspapers the following day—the *New York Times*, the *San Francisco Examiner*, the *San Francisco Chronicle*—and depicted in television reports as well.

14. "Affirmative-Action Aftermath," *The Chronicle of Higher Education*, 4 August 1995, A18.

15. Andrew Hacker, *Two Nations: Black and White, Separate, Hostile, Unequal* (New York, 1992), chap. 8, esp. 9–10. Hacker justifies his bipolar framework by suggesting that over time Asian Americans may be absorbed into a new expansive definition of what "white" is.

Racism

From Domination to Hegemony

Howard Winant

At the turn of the twenty-first century the world has largely dispensed with the overt racial hierarchies that existed before the post–World War II racial break: colonialism, racially demarcated labor reserves, explicit policies of segregation and apartheid, and candid avowals of racial superiority and inferiority all appear today as hopeless atavisms, relics of a benighted past. International organizations like the UN have for decades made opposition to racism a central priority. And the globalized "culture industry"—from Hollywood to Bollywood, from Disney to Globo to Benneton—has produced a continuing stream of anti-racist messages: legitimating interracial romance and friendship, stigmatizing prejudice and discrimination, and fostering the hybridization of cultures and styles.

Yet as all this anti-racist policy-making, multiculturalism, and hybridization proceeds, the vast gaps between North and South, haves and have-nots, whites and "others," also persist. Pick any relevant sociological indicator—life expectancy, infant mortality, literacy, access to health care, income level—and apply it in virtually any setting, global, regional, or local, and the results will be the same: the worldwide correlation of wealth and well-being with white skin and European descent, and of poverty and immiseration with dark skin and "otherness." Sure, there are exceptions: there are plenty of exploited white workers, plenty of white welfare mothers both urban and rural, plenty of poor whites throughout the world's North; and there are a smattering of wealth-holders "of color" around the world too. But these are outliers in the planetary correlation of darkness and poverty.

In analyzing patterns of inequality, of stratification, it is impossible fully to distinguish the effects of race and class. These factors interact both locally and globally; they have shaped each other over historical time and continue to do so in the present. For instance, is the black worker at General Motors' plant in Ohio, or at Volkswagen's plant in the ABC region of São Paulo for that matter, so much worse off than the white worker beside him (or her) on the assembly line? Not so much. The real local discrepancies are between those who have fairly reliable, even unionized jobs, and those relegated to poverty and the informal economy.[1] And then there are the global discrepancies: auto workers' wages in the ABC, heartland of the highly developed Brazilian manufacturing economy, home base of the *Confederação Unificado dos Trabalhadores* (CUT—the militant Brazilian trade union confederation), and site of some of the most desirable jobs in the national economy, average about 10 percent of U.S. wages for the same work.[2]

Nor do we have to look at stratification to recognize the continuing significance of race. When we turn to the world political system, to the social structure of domination and subjugation, to the allocation of voice and voicelessness, the point is confirmed again. A worldwide political class exercises power from corporate boardrooms and government ministries alike: how multiracial, how committed to racial equality, is this select group? Of course at the commencement of the twenty-first century, after the end of colonialism and the conclusion of the Cold War, political rule can claim to be democratic almost everywhere. But democracy now means little more than that the citizenry "periodically enjoys the right to withhold their acclaim," as Jürgen Habermas remarked (Habermas 1997; see also Habermas 1996).[3]

In such a system the racial gradations of power and powerlessness can sometimes be confusing, but long-standing patterns of racial hierarchy still hold. Do citizens of the core nations of the metropolitan North, do the whites of the world, exercise much political power? No, they do not. How much "freedom" (in the sense of the relative absence of coercion, the availability of personal autonomy) do they possess relative to the racialized "others" both in the northern metropoles and "down home" in the world's South? There are two answers. First, in a given local/national setting—in Los Angeles or Frankfurt, Fortaleza or Durban—whites experience a sense of belonging, a sense of entitlement, that blacks, immigrants, racialized "others," rarely if ever enjoy. Second, on a global level, however disfranchised, however yoked to a low-skilled and inadequately paid job, however resentful of those in command, however manipulable by racists both "old" and "new," the ordinary *schmo* in the world's North—in the still largely white bastions of Europe and North America and ("honorary white") Japan—disposes of a greater basket of life chances, greater freedom, than most of his or her southern brothers and sisters could even imagine.[4]

Culturally too the old system rules. Whence cometh the ideals, the near universal representations, the recognizable icons and idols: where do Michael Jordan and Michael Jackson and Michael Mouse live? In Hollywood, of course (or perhaps in Orlando)! Whose names adorn the canonical bookshelves, whose artworks hang in the museums, whose films does the world stand in line to see? Yes, here again there are exceptions: there is the vast treasurehouse of black music that rules the audio world from Bensonhurst to Bahia,[5] even if it is harnessed to the profit-making imperatives of global media conglomerates; there is not only

Hollywood but also Bollywood; there is Chris Ofili, who scandalized New York Mayor Giuliani with his painting *Black Madonna.* But "McWorld" (Barber 1995) is still a largely northern place.

To make sense of these developments and dilemmas, we must rethink the concept of racism. Just as the meaning of race has proved to be malleable and fungible, changing dramatically in the years since World War II, for example, so too the meaning of *racism* has changed over time. The attitudes, practices, and institutions of the epochs of colonialism, segregation, or apartheid may not have been entirely eliminated, but neither do they operate today in the same ways that they did half a century ago. Employing a similar logic, it is reasonable to question whether concepts of racism that were developed in the early postwar period, when the limitations of both nationalist revolution and moderate programs of reform had not yet been encountered, could possibly remain adequate to explain racial dynamics and conflicts in the twenty-first century.

Today racism operates in societies and institutions that explicitly condemn prejudice and discrimination. In the era that succeeded the post–World War II racial break, the conflicts between anti-racist movements and reform-oriented regimes resulted in a new pattern of racial rule, one that makes concessions without surrendering fundamental power. Put somewhat differently: after half a millennium in which global power and capitalist development had been based on racial domination, opposition to the coercive rule required by this old-world racial system simply became too strong. Faced with increasingly assertive demands for democracy and national liberation—demands that sometimes reached revolutionary levels of mobilization and involved prolonged armed conflict—the world racial system underwent a transition *from domination to hegemony.* Segregation and colonialism—at least in their explicit, state-enforced forms—were abandoned as the principal instrumentalities of racial rule.

But having conceded this much, northern rule, metropolitan rule, capitalist rule, found its stability largely restored. The new world racial system could maintain much of the stratification and inequality, much of the differential access to political power and voice, much of the preexisting cultural logic of collective representation and racial hierarchy, without recourse to comprehensive coercion or racial dictatorship. Since the political energy and support available to its movement adversaries was limited, a new era of world racial equilibrium could be proclaimed. Opposition was now effectively reduced: since the moderates had been effectively satisfied by reforms, only radical groups remained restive; they could be contained by a combination of marginalization and repression.

In the age of racial hegemony, then, what forms does racism take? To the extent that the transition from domination to hegemony has been accomplished, it is racism's reinforced structural role, its "cleaned-up," "streamlined," and "mainstream" manifestations, that allow it to survive and indeed go largely politically unchallenged at the dawn of the twenty-first century.[6]

Today racism must be identified by its consequences. Racism has been largely—although not entirely, to be sure—detached from its perpetrators. In its most advanced forms, indeed, it has no perpetrators; it is a nearly invisible, taken-for-granted, commonsense (Gramsci) feature of everyday life and global social structure.[7]

Under these conditions—racial hegemony—racism may be defined as *the routinized outcome of practices that create or reproduce hierarchical social structures based on essentialized racial categories.*[8] This definition seeks a comprehensiveness that may not be fully attainable. It leaves enough room to contain the old, instrumental forms of racism—such as prejudice and discrimination, racial code words, and the like—but focuses attention on new, structural forms that can operate more or less automatically. It incorporates the analyses that critiqued the European new racism (Barker 1981; Taguieff 2001 [1988]; Miles 1993; Wieviorka 1995; Ansell 1997; Gilroy 1999), but seeks to place that important work in a global framework.

There can be no timeless and absolute standard for what constitutes racism, because social structures undergo reform (and reaction) and discourses are always subject to rearticulation. The concept of racism should not be invested with any permanent content. Instead racism should be seen as a property of certain—but by no means all—political projects that link the *representation* and *organization* of race, that engage in the "work" of racial formation. Such an approach focuses on the "work" essentialism does for domination, and the "need" domination displays to essentialize the subordinated.[9] It allows comparison of different national/regional cases of racial formation, such as those I have presented here. All these countries/regions are in transition from racial domination to racial hegemony. The case study settings both overlap and diverge: each has a unique location and genealogy, yet all partake in the world racial system; all were reshaped during the post–World War II racial break.

Of Our Political Strivings

The tremendous accomplishments of the anti-racist and anti-colonial movements that succeeded World War II have now been incorporated. In the decades after the war it seemed at times that these movements might not only found independent post-colonial states, but that they might reorganize global society, even demolish capitalism. At the start of the twenty-first century, however, the outlook is far less promising. At the local/national level many formerly powerful anti-racist movements have lost their adherents and some their political moorings. Some are reduced to defending the limited racial reforms won in earlier moments, for example, affirmative action policies, against the specious claims of public institutions that they are now color-blind, meritocratic, post-racial. Other movements and activists put their energies into multicultural projects, which (again defensively) advocate pluralism and tend to reduce racism to a strictly cultural phenomenon. At the global level the still-impoverished nations of the former Third World, even the formerly revolutionary and still officially communist ones, seek direct private investment and curry favor from the gnomes of London, Zurich, and the IMF.

In earlier times and places—say, during the later 1960s in the United States—it seemed that the "Third World within" might finally achieve the power and claim the wealth so long denied it: redistribution of resources, community control, massive rebuilding of the inner cities, black power (and red power, brown power, yellow power) would accomplish in a "second reconstruction" what had been denied and betrayed one hundred years earlier. But today, at the turn of the twenty-first century, the ghettos, barrios, and reservations are still neglected, still occupied by trigger-happy police, still immiserated; and no serious political movement is in sight.

The vast social movements that democratized the old world racial system, that did away with official policies of racial exclusion, disfranchisement, segregation, and degradation, have now lost a great deal of their support. Formerly they could lead whole peoples in the direction of emancipation; now they struggle to define their purpose. The disruption of the old world racial system during and after the post–World War II racial break has given rise to a "new world racial system" characterized not by racial domination, but instead by racial hegemony. This new system can maintain white supremacy better than the old one could. This system of racial hegemony can present itself as colorblind and multicultural, not to mention meritocratic, egalitarian, and differentialist, all the while restricting immigration, exporting industry (and pollution) to the low-waged South, and doing away with the welfare state in the North.

So while some racial mobility has been achieved, fierce racial inequalities persist: globally they mirror the North-South patterns that colonial rule developed and the *Pax Americana* has continued. In local settings, racial inequalities also continue to operate: by and large the descendants of slaves, indigenous and occupied peoples, refugees, and migrants continue to be subjugated to the descendants of landholders and slavemasters, occupiers and European settlers.

While some political power has passed from colonialists' and segregationists' hands into darker hands, both the global political system and its local variants have survived and prospered in the transition to a new world racial system. Contemporary political systems of rule—both global and local—descend rather directly from the old world racial system. How independent are the rulers of southern nation-states, even relatively developed ones like South Africa and Brazil, from the discipline of world financial markets and institutions like the IMF? How effective is political representation—black, immigrant, indigenous—even in settings where those formerly excluded on racial grounds can now vote?

Culturally too the transition to hegemony has been contradictory. Well before the post–World War II break the world's "others" were crucial sources of signification: artistic, musical, philosophical, religious, and scholarly insights and techniques were deeply rooted outside the West, even though the "big heads" of Europe laid claim to sole possession of advanced knowledge in all these areas. Already adept at reworking these cultural riches, in the period after the break the metropolitan "culture industries" moved to take possession of them, to commodify and purvey them on a global scale. But although ready, willing, and able to market reggae, soka, or samba, say, anywhere in the world, the metropolitan powers still claimed to possess the superior cultures, to live in the home of reason and the center-stage of history (Sen 2000b; Davidson 1992). They still required the *difference* of the world's "others," whose cultures they purported now to value far more than in the past, in order to define their own identities.[10]

So what's left after all this conflict and accommodation? Is the picture so bleak that the legacy of half a millennium of resistance to racial rule must now be abandoned? After the tremendous upsurge of the break, after the partial but real triumphs of recent decades, has the worldwide movement for racial equality and justice, for emancipation and self-determination, finally been defeated, not by force and repression, but by co-optation and incorporation? How should racial hegemony be confronted politically, or even politically understood?

The definitive answer to this question cannot be given on paper. Only in political action, in organization and mobilization, will present-day racial dilemmas and contradictions be resolved. Researchers and writers, even those who identify with movements for social justice, are ultimately led by those movements. They cannot, and I cannot, presume to offer political prescriptions.

Yet it is clear that despite recent setbacks, fertile ground remains for new antiracist initiatives. However successfully the new world racial order was able to incorporate the anti-racist and anti-colonial demands asserted during the break, it was not able fully to transform the inequalities and injustices that generated those demands. It could defuse and blunt the basis of racial opposition, but it could hardly eliminate it. Under no circumstances could the system move "beyond race," despite its claims to post-raciality, color-blindness, multiculturalism, and so on.

So what's left? The fundamental elements of resistance to racial injustice and inequality that remain intact, that have been largely untouched by the incorporative initiatives of the new world racial system, may form building-blocks for the new anti-racist movements. Both in the case study countries/regions and more generally, counter-hegemonic movements may emerge as significant challenges to the world racial system.

There are three fundamental reasons, three ineluctable social facts, that suggest that the struggle against white supremacy will continue around the world: first, *global racial inequality and injustice remain*; second, *race-consciousness endures*; and third, *racial politics is pervasive*. In what follows I present the arguments for these three claims, necessarily in a brief and schematic way. I then conclude with some notes on the Duboisian legacy.

GLOBAL RACIAL INEQUALITY AND INJUSTICE REMAIN

Indeed, they are more visible now, in the age of the Internet and globalized media, than ever before. Where there is injustice and oppression, there is resistance. A powerful argument can be made that opposition to injustice is the main form that political opposition takes in the modern world (Moore 1978).

In all the national/regional case studies examined here, racial stratification remains a significant issue: that unemployment levels are higher and income levels lower for those with dark faces across the world is hardly news. The complex phenomenon known as globalization is itself a major mechanism of resource redistribution—but mainly in a regressive direction.

In the world's North globalization tends toward deindustrialization. The work that can be exported consists of the less skilled factory jobs that are held by immigrants and the working poor—who are disproportionately people "of color." Much of the low-waged work that remains in the metropolitan countries is located in sweatshops, in agriculture, in the service sector, and in the informal economy. Assaults on the welfare state—both on the spending and revenue side—also have regressively redistributive consequences. Many of these developments—competition for jobs, association of immigrants and non-whites with crime, objections to the welfare state and calls for tax reduction—are framed racially.

In the world's South globalization takes the form of neo-liberal economic discipline. The ability to extract primary resources at low cost, unburdened by government regulation, labor organization, or environmental restrictions, is the primary force driving globalization here. Often the importation of factory work doesn't mean serious industrial development or foreign direct investment: more likely it involves an ongoing search for easy acquisition of resources and for cheap and submissive labor. Such policies combine with the austerity and compulsory debt-service enforced upon the South by the International Monetary Fund to maintain much of the population of the South—not only those in countries decolonized only after World War II but even the great majority in an industrially developed country like Brazil—in a state of impoverishment (Greider 1997).

This is an outline—very schematically summarized here—of current world patterns of economic inequality and injustice. Although often seen in terms of global *social* stratification, in terms of environmental destruction, and in terms of gender inequalities (sweatshops and *maquilas*, for example, tend to exploit women at high levels), these injustices are rarely characterized as *racial*. Yet is it not clear that they flow fairly continuously from patterns established in the now-departed colonial epoch?

A movement against the depredations of globalization has begun to appear, drawing on a range of supporters: chiefly environmentalists, trade unions, and religious groups (as well as assorted radical groups committed to direct action). In demonstrations against the World Trade Organization (WTO) in Seattle in 1999, and against the IMF and World Bank in Washington, DC in 2000, this coalition first attracted major attention. Protests in Geneva, Paris, Bangkok, and Prague have also taken place. Real questions have been raised as to how much support the anti-WTO (or anti-globalization) movement can count on from the world's South, where impoverishment is severe enough to make even employment in a sweatshop or *maquila* seem desirable, and where even relatively progressive governments sympathetic to trade unionism—such as the ANC government in South Africa—are subject to immense pressure from the world's financial power-centers.[11] As of yet this movement has exhibited relatively little racial awareness. It remains to be seen if this initiative will acquire the depth and organizational strength needed to operate on a global scale, but it is already achieving limited results (somewhere between substantive and symbolic) in respect to its demands for debt relief.

RACE-CONSCIOUSNESS ENDURES

One of the most important accomplishments of the worldwide racial mobilizations that confronted colonialism and white supremacy during and after World War II was their reinterpretation (or if one prefers this term, their rearticulation) of the meaning of race and the significance of racial identity. Building upon the immense labors of their ancestors and predecessors, these movements systematically fostered awareness and pride among the world's subjugated and subaltern peoples. To be sure, the creation and nurturing of race-consciousness is a highly uneven and contradictory process. It combines potentially emancipatory elements, such as rejection of stereotypes and "internalized racism," with potentially chauvinistic and even fascist ones (Gilroy 1996). Although in many cases it was the work of revolutionary nationalism to awaken and enunciate concepts of pride, solidarity, and cultural awareness among the racially subordinated, these projects were themselves undertaken by insurgent elites, as we have learned from subalternity theory (see Chapter Five, Winant 2001). They did not preclude, and in some cases actively fostered, new forms of subordination and voicelessness among black, native, or colonized peoples. They could not avoid, and in some cases actively participated in, the degradation of race-consciousness into a commodified and depoliticized form (dashikis, kente cloth, blaxploitation films, etc.).

Yet with all these limitations there has been an indisputably enormous increase in racial awareness throughout the world as a consequence of the upheavals of the break and its aftermath. This awareness is open to further articulation, and by no means inherently emancipatory. There can be no permanent formulas here.[12] Yet the vastly augmented presence of race-consciousness in the world, although contradictory and flexible, still works as a sort of transnational inoculation against post-racialism in all its forms: notably the color-blind viewpoint in the United States and the racial differentialism evident in Europe.

This expanded awareness also acts as a reminder to those on the left who have remained committed to an outmoded notion of anti-racism as integration pure and simple—for example, some in the South African ANC who remain diehard adherents to the vision of non-racialism articulated in the 1955 Freedom Charter—that the old world racial system is definitively dead, and that a new vision of racial justice and equality must be developed. The fact that race-consciousness has expanded so much in the aftermath of the break also has consequences in Brazil, where it works to erode the tenacious ideology of racial democracy. The old charge that to criticize or even to acknowledge the presence of racism was ipso facto to perpetuate it, is less tenable today, due to the growing debates and discussions about race in the political sphere, in popular media, in religious venues, and in everyday life.

RACIAL POLITICS IS PERVASIVE

Despite the decline of anti-racist movements in the new world racial order, a significant legacy of the break and its aftermath remains relatively intact. It is the pervasiveness of racial politics, the recognition that racial hierarchies and systems of signification permeate social institutions from the most comprehensive and global to the most small-scale and experiential. A notable and intriguing feature of race is its ubiquity, its presence in both the "smallest" and the "largest" features of social relationships, institutions, and identities. Much of the impetus behind the "politicization of the social," the reconceptualization of politics that has occurred in recent, decades, was derived from anti-racist social movements. The democratizing challenge posed after World War II to "normal" systems of domination and power, "accepted" divisions of labor, and "rational-legal" means of legitimation, all had inescapable racial dimensions. Racially based movements, then (and the "second wave" feminism that followed and was inspired by them), problematized the public-private distinction basic to preexisting political cultures. After World War II, the range of political issues that existed, and the number and sorts of political actors afforded any voice, was greatly expanded beyond the political norms of the years before the break.[13]

These transformations were also reflected in political theory and political sociology, where older approaches to democratic theory, social movements, and the state were challenged, for example, by "political process" models (McAdam 1982; Morris and Mueller 1992). Recognition of the pervasiveness of politics also appears in the revival of interest in pragmatist sociology, in symbolic interactionism, in "constitution" theories of society (Joas 1996; Giddens 1984), and in the belated revival of interest in the work of W.E.B. Du Bois (West 1989; Lewis 1993, Winant 1997).[14]

Mention of Du Bois brings me to the final points I want to make. Du Bois's astonishing career stretched from the eventide of the U.S. Civil War to the aftermath of the postwar racial break. He lived to see the sun set on the great colonial empires whose ravages he had opposed for seventy years, and to greet the dawn of the modern civil rights movement in the United States, for which he had laid so much groundwork. In a less well-known speech, given at a conference in 1960, Du Bois (then 92 years of age) contemplated the consequences of these victories, and of the new political situation that black people would find themselves in in their aftermath:

[W]hat we must now ask ourselves is when we become equal American citizens what will be our aims and ideals and what we will have to do with selecting these aims and ideals. Are we to assume that we will simply adopt the ideals of Americans and become what they are or want to be and that we will have in this process no ideals of our own?

That would mean that we would cease to be Negroes as such and become white in action if not completely in color. We would take on the culture of white Americans doing as they do and thinking as they think.

Manifestly this would not be satisfactory. Physically it would mean that we would be integrated with Americans losing first of all, the physical evidence of color and hair and racial type. We would lose our memory of Negro history and of those racial peculiarities which have long been associated with the Negro. We would cease to acknowledge any greater tie with Africa than with England or Germany. We would not try to develop Negro music and Art and Literature as distinctive and different, but allow them to be further degraded as is the case now. We would always, if possible, marry lighter-hued people so as to have children who are not identified with the Negro race, and thus solve our racial problem in America by committing race suicide. (Du Bois 1973 [1960], 149–150)

Du Bois confronted this tendency, not very different from the color-blind position of the present day, with the same radical democratic alternative he had been proposing over the course of the entire century. He recognized at its dawning the outlines of the new world racial system that would not be fully realized for many decades. He identified very early the limits of the moderate civil rights vision: the United States could not undo its deep commitment to white supremacy, at least not without a fundamental social upheaval. Blacks would be asked to absorb the costs of their inclusion, not whites. The price black people would be asked to pay in return for full inclusion was self-negation: the repudiation of their particularity and the unlearning of their history. Determined to maintain both the demand for full equality and the integrity of black identity, Du Bois *refused to choose* between the two terms of "American" and "Negro."

Du Bois ends his talk with a series of revolutionary commitments: the world, he says, is "going socialist." Black people should support a socialist transition in the United States as the only route to full equality; they should also dedicate their resources to self-determination and autonomous development for their own community. Du Bois also reiterates his long-standing commitments to pan-Africanism and the well-being (again, within the socialist framework) of the formerly colonized peoples of the South.

What can we take from this talk today? As I have noted, the injunction against race "suicide" remains convincing. The socialist alternative that Du Bois embraced (and about which he was perhaps willfully naive) is dead: the Stalinist and Maoist systems were certainly no democratic alternative for blacks in the United States or the "wretched of the earth" in general. Without repudiating the ideals of socialism—of cooperation, egalitarianism, and democratic self-rule—we probably have to reject Du Bois's complacency about the "actually existing forms" that socialism took at this time.[15]

Yet at the same time the contours of the Duboisian political formula of racial dualism—what he calls "the possibility of black folk and their cultural patterns existing in America without discrimination and on terms of equality" (150)—seems, if extrapolated to a global level, a good starting-point for revisioning a political program for the next century or so. This vision remains strong. It continues as a radical pole of attraction. It is a "North Star" that shines yet.

To return to the Duboisian dictum with which I began this chapter: at the start of the twenty-first century the world as a whole, and various national societies as well, are far from overcoming the tenacious legacies of colonial rule, apartheid, and segregation. All still experience continuing confusion, anxiety, and contention about race. Yet the legacies of epochal struggles for freedom, democracy, and human rights persist as well.

Despite the enormous vicissitudes that demarcate and distinguish national conditions, historical developments, roles in the international market, political tendencies, and cultural norms, racial differences still operate as they did in centuries past: as a way of restricting the political influence, not just of racially subordinated groups, but of all those at the bottom end of the system of social stratification. In the contemporary era, racial beliefs and practices have become far more contradictory and complex. The old world racial order has not disappeared, but it has been seriously disrupted and changed. The legacy of democratic, racially oriented movements,[16] and anti-colonialist initiatives throughout the world's South, remains a force to be reckoned with. But the incorporative (or if one prefers this term, hegemonic) effects of decades of reform-oriented state racial policies have had a profound result as well: they have removed much of the motivation for sustained, anti-racist mobilization.

In this unresolved situation, it is unlikely that attempts to address worldwide dilemmas of race and racism by ignoring or transcending these themes, for example, by adopting so-called color-blind or differentialist policies, will have much effect. In the past the centrality of race deeply determined the economic, political, and cultural configuration of the modern world. Although recent decades have seen an efflorescence of movements for racial equality and justice, the legacies of centuries of racial oppression have not been overcome. Nor is a vision of racial justice fully worked out. Certainly the idea that such justice has already been largely achieved—as seen in the color-blind paradigm in the United States, the non-racialist rhetoric of the South African Freedom Charter, the Brazilian rhetoric of racial democracy, or the emerging racial differentialism of the European Union—remains problematic.

Will race ever be transcended? Will the world ever "get beyond" race? Probably not. But the entire planet still has a chance of overcoming the stratification, the hierarchy, the taken-for-granted injustice and inhumanity that so often accompanies the race-concept. Like religion or language, race can be accepted as part of the spectrum of the human condition, while it is simultaneously and categorically resisted as a means of stratifying national or global societies. Nothing is more essential in the effort to strengthen our commitments to democracy and social justice, and indeed to global survival and prosperity, as we enter a new millennium.

NOTES

1. This is not to deny that discrimination persists in the internal labor markets of manufacturing firms and in trade unions as well. Nor is it to assert that black and white workers receive the same treatment from the police, in the housing market, at their children's schools, and so on.

2. On the international dynamics of the automobile industry, see Maynard 1998. On the ABC and CUT, see French 1992.

3. In the German elections that Habermas was analyzing, a major theme voiced by the Christian Democrats of Helmut Kohl was so-called *ausländerkriminalität*: the charge that it was (largely racialized) immigrants and non-German denizens who were responsible for crime.

4. The tendency to view indices of well-being as measures of class—as quantifiable Weberian life chances—itself must be looked at critically. In an important intervention in this area, Amartya Sen has argued that the dominant optic in the field of ("welfare"

and "development") economics systematically neglects the qualitative dimensions of human well-being, which he links to the attainment of *freedom* and the achievement of *capability*. See Sen 2000a.

5. Indeed, Bahia is not only the birthplace of Caetano Veloso (whose fierce critique of global racism serves as this book's epigraph), but the home of Olodum, a musical/political organization that has dedicated itself to black political education on a national scale. See their website at http://www.e-net.com.br/olodum/.

6. Certainly prejudice and discrimination are still very much present, even if they are no longer overtly advocated. In particular spheres—for example, among many police forces and prison guards (see Parenti 1999), in many corporate boardrooms, in certain "smoke-filled" political campaign headquarters—explicitly racist discourse is still the norm.

7. For a more detailed discussion focused on the United States, see Winant 1998. This approach has much in common with the theoretical current known as *critical race theory*. A valuable collection of writings from that general perspective is Crenshaw et al. 1995.

8. I am sorry to offer such a mouthful as a definition, but it seems to be unavoidable.

9. It is also important to distinguish racial awareness from racial essentialism. Attribution of merits or faults, allocation of values or resources, and/or representations of individuals or groups on the basis of racial categories should not be considered racist in and of themselves. Such projects may in fact be quite benign. Of course, any of these projects may be considered racist, but only if they meet the criteria I have just outlined: in other words, a combination of essentialization and subordination must be present.

10. The foremost theorist of the rearticulations of racial difference is Pierre-André Taguieff 2001 [1988].

11. See Singh 1999; *Race and Class* 1998–99. Organizations that can provide information on these topics are Global Exchange (website: www.globalexchange.org); Focus on the Global South (website: www.focusweb.org); and Jubilee 2000 (website: www.j2000usa.org).

12. To attempt to answer these questions even in part is to plunge into the theoretical and practical endeavors of racial formation. For my own efforts in this area, see Omi and Winant 1994.

13. In non-U.S. settings, the "new social movement" phenomenon has not always been so clearly recognized as racially structured. This is particularly notable in Europe, where its study was prompted by the vicissitudes of the new left, the resurgence of feminism, the rise of green politics, and the upsurge of terrorism in the 1970s (Melucci 1989). But in the Third World the rethinking of political theory and political sociology in terms of issues of subjectivity and of "identity" often took on a racial dimension. Consider the legacy of Fanon, for example.

14. For the past few decades all three of these themes have been developed in a body of theoretical work that goes under the general heading *of racial formation theory*. As one of the founders of this approach, I must admit to the lack of consensus, as well as the overall incompleteness, of this theoretical current. Still, racial formation theory at least begins to provide the theoretical tools needed to make sense of the new world racial order described here. Indeed, this book is no more than an attempt to use such tools in a comparative historical framework.

To summarize the racial formation approach: (1) it views the meaning of race and the content of racial identities as unstable and politically contested; (2) it understands racial formation as the intersection/conflict of racial "projects" that combine representational/discursive elements with structural/institutional ones; (3) it sees these intersections as iterative sequences of interpretations ("articulations") of the meaning of race that are open to many types of agency, from the individual to the organizational, from the local to the global (Omi and Winant 1994).

15. Obviously I cannot engage this issue profoundly here. I simply note that the question of new forms of socialism remains theoretically open, and that emerging global conflicts over the inequalities in the global economic system (see above) retain links with the socialist tradition.

16. For example, the U.S. civil rights movement, anti-apartheid struggles, *SOS-Racisme* in France, the *Movimento Negro Unificado* in Brazil.

REFERENCES

Ansell, Amy Elizabeth. *New Right, New Racism: Race and Reaction in the United States and Britain.* New York: New York University Press, 1997.

Barber, Benjamin R. *Jihad vs. McWorld.* New York: Times Books, 1995.

Barker, Martin. *The New Racism: Conservatives and the Ideology of the Tribe.* London: Junction, 1981.

Crenshaw, Kimberlé, et al., eds. *Critical Race Theory: The Key Writings that Formed the Movement.* New York: New Press, 1995.

Davidson, Basil. *The Black Man's Burden: Africa and the Curse of the Nation-State.* New York: Random House, 1992.

Du Bois, W.E.B. "Whither Now and Why" [1960]. In idem., *The Education of Black People: Ten Critiques 1906–1960.* Edited by Herbert Aptheker. Amherst: University of Massachusetts Press, 1973.

French, John D. *The Brazilian Workers' ABC: Class Conflict and Alliances in Modern São Paulo.* Chapel Hill: University of North Carolina Press, 1992.

Giddens, Anthony. *The Constitution of Society: Outline of the Theory of Structuration.* Berkeley: University of California Press, 1984.

Gilroy, Paul. "Revolutionary Conservatism and the Tyrannies of Unanimism." *New Formations* 28 (Spring 1996).

———. "The End of Anti-Racism." In Martin Bulmer, and John Solomos, eds. *Racism.* New York: Oxford University Press, 1999.

Gramsci, Antonio. *Selections from the Prison Notebooks.* Edited by Quinton Hoare and Geoffrey Nowell-Smith. New York: International Publishers, 1971.

Greider, William. *One World, Ready or Not: The Manic Logic of Global Capitalism.* New York: Touchstone, 1997.

Habermas, Jürgen. *Between Facts and Norms: Contributions to a Discourse Theory of Law and Democracy.* Translated by William Rehg. Cambridge, Mass.: MIT Press, 1996.

———. *A Berlin Republic: Writings on Germany.* Translated by Steven Rendall. Lincoln: University of Nebraska Press, 1997.

Joas, Hans. *The Creativity of Action.* Translated by Jeremy Gaines and Paul Keast. Chicago: University of Chicago Press, 1996.

Lewis, David Levering. *W.E.B. Du Bois: Biography of a Race, 1868-1919.* New York: Henry Holt, 1993.

Maynard, Micheline. *The Global Manufacturing Vanguard: New Rules from the Industry Elite.* New York: Wiley, 1998.

McAdam, Doug. *Political Process and the Development of Black Insurgency, 1930–1970.* Chicago: University of Chicago Press, 1982.

Melucci, Alberto. *Nomads of the Present: Social Movements and Individual Needs in Contemporary Society.* Philadelphia: Temple University Press, 1989.

Miles, Robert. *Racism after "Race Relations."* London: Routledge, 1993.

Moore, Barrington, Jr. *Injustice: The Social Bases of Obedience and Revolt.* White Plains, N.Y.: M. E. Sharpe, 1978.

Morris, Aldon, and Carol McClurg Mueller, eds. *Frontiers in Social Movement Theory.* New Haven, Conn.: Yale University Press, 1992.

Omi, Michael, and Howard Winant. *Racial Formation in the United States: From the 1960s to the 1990s.* Rev. ed. New York: Routledge, 1994.

Parenti, Christian. *Lockdown America: Police and Prisons in the Age of Crisis.* New York: Verso, 1999.

Race and Class 40, nos. 2–3 (October 1998/March 1999). Special Issue: "The Threat of Globalism."

Sen, Amartya. *Development as Freedom.* New York: Knopf, 2000a.

Sen, Amartya. "East and West: The Reach of Reason." *The New York Review of Books,* July 20, 2000b.

Singh, Kavaljit. *The Globalization of Finance: A Citizen's Guide.* London: Zed, 1999.

Taguieff, Pierre-André. *The Force of Prejudice: On Racism and Its Doubles.* Translated by Hassan Melehy. Minneapolis: University of Minnesota Press, 2001; original French edition 1988.

West, Cornel. *The American Evasion of Philosophy: A Genealogy of Pragmatism.* Madison: University of Wisconsin Press, 1989.

Wieviorka, Michel. *The Arena of Racism.* Translated by Chris Turner. Thousand Oaks, Calif.: Sage, 1995.

Winant, Howard. "Racial Dualism at Century's End." In Wahneema Lubiano, ed., *The House that Race Built: Black Americans, US Terrain.* New York: Pantheon, 1997.

———. "Racism Today: Continuity and Change in the Post–Civil Rights Era." *Ethnic and Racial Studies* 21, no. 4 (July 1998).

———. *The World Is a Ghetto: Race and Democracy Since World War II.* New York: Basic Books, 2001.

wo:
History
and Memory

THE CHINESE ARE COMING. HOW CAN WE STOP THEM?

CHINESE EXCLUSION AND THE ORIGINS OF AMERICAN GATEKEEPING

Erika Lee

In 1876, H. N. Clement, a San Francisco lawyer, stood before a California State Senate Committee and sounded the alarm: "*The Chinese are upon us.* How can we get rid of them? *The Chinese are coming.* How can we stop them?"[1] Panicked cries such as these and portrayals of Chinese immigration as an evil, "unarmed invasion" had been shared by several witnesses before the committee, which was charged with investigating the "social, moral, and political effects" of Chinese immigration. Testimony like Clement's was designed to reach a broad audience, and the committee hearings themselves were part of a calculated political attempt to bring the question of Chinese immigration to a national audience.[2] Many Californians had long felt beleaguered by the influx of Chinese immigrants into the state and now believed that it was time that the federal government took action. As the committee's "Address to the People of the United States upon the Evils of Chinese Immigration" stated, the people of California had "but one disposition upon this grave subject . . . and that is an open and pronounced demand upon the Federal Government for relief."[3]

At the time of the committee hearings, the United States was just beginning to exert federal control over immigration. Its first efforts had begun one year earlier in response to the California lobby to exclude Asian contract labor and women (mostly Chinese) suspected of entering the country for "lewd or immoral purposes." The resulting Page Law, passed in 1875, represented the country's first—albeit limited—regulation of immigration on the federal level and served as an important step toward general Chinese exclusion.[4] The U.S. Congress eventually heeded the call of Californians and other westerners to protect them from the so-called Chinese invasion with the 1882 Chinese Exclusion Act.

Historians have often noted that the Chinese Exclusion Act marks a "watershed" in U.S. history. Not only was it the country's first significant restrictive immigration law; it was also the first to restrict a group of immigrants based on their race, nationality, and class. As Roger Daniels has written, the Chinese Exclusion Act was "the hinge upon which the legal history of immigration turned."[5] This observation has become the standard interpretation of the anti-Chinese movement, but until recently, most accounts of Chinese exclusion have focused more on the anti-Chinese movement preceding the Chinese Exclusion Act than on the six decades of the exclusion era itself.[6] Moreover, there has been little attempt to explain the larger impact and legacies of Chinese exclusion. For example, how did the effort to exclude Chinese influence the restriction and exclusion of other immigrant groups? How did the racialization of Chinese as excludable aliens contribute to and intersect with the racialization of other Asian, southern and eastern European, and Mexican immigrants? What precedents did the Chinese Exclusion Act set for the admission, documentation, surveillance, and deportation of both new arrivals and immigrant communities within the United States?

When the Page Law and the Chinese Exclusion Act serve as the beginning rather than the end of the narrative, we are forced to focus more fully on the enormous significance of Chinese exclusion. It becomes clear that its importance as a "watershed" goes beyond its status as one of the first immigration policies to be passed in the United States. Certainly, the Page Law and the Chinese Exclusion Act provided the legal architecture for twentieth-century American immigration policy.[7] Chinese exclusion, however, also introduced gatekeeping ideology, politics, law, and culture that transformed the ways in which Americans viewed and thought about race, immigration, and the United States' identity as a nation of immigrants. It legalized the restriction, exclusion, and deportation of immigrants considered to be threats to the United States. It established Chinese immigrants—categorized by their race, class, and gender relations as the ultimate example of the dangerous, degraded alien—as the yardsticks by which to measure the desirability (and "whiteness") of other immigrant groups. Lastly, the Chinese exclusion laws not only provided an example of how to contain threatening and undesirable foreigners, they also set in motion new modes and technologies of immigration regulation, including federal immigration officials and bureaucracies, U.S. passports, "green cards," and illegal immigration and deportation policies. In the end, Chinese exclusion forever changed America's relationship to immigration.

THE ANTI-CHINESE MOVEMENT AND THE PASSAGE OF THE 1882 CHINESE EXCLUSION ACT

Chinese immigrants began to arrive in the United States in significant numbers following the discovery of gold in California in 1848. Most came from the Pearl River delta region in Guangdong, China, and, like the majority of newcomers to

California, the Chinese community was comprised mostly of male laborers. They were only a small fraction of the total immigrant population of the United States. From 1870 to 1880, a total of 138,941 Chinese immigrants entered the country, 4.3 percent of the total number of immigrants (3,199,394) who entered the country during the same decade.[8]

Their small numbers notwithstanding, Chinese immigrants were the targets of racial hostility, discriminatory laws, and violence. This racism was grounded in an American Orientalist ideology that homogenized Asia as one indistinguishable entity and positioned and defined the West and the East in diametrically opposite terms, using those distinctions to claim American and Anglo-American superiority. Americans first learned to identify Chinese through reports from American traders, diplomats, and missionaries in China. Their portrayals of Chinese as heathen, crafty, and dishonest "marginal members of the human race" quickly set Chinese apart. At first seen as exotic curiosities from a distant land, Chinese immigrants came to be viewed as threats, especially as Chinese immigration increased throughout the gold rush period.[9]

Orientalist fears of the Asian "other" intersected and overlapped with domestic fears about American race, class, and gender relations. During the 1870s, massive population growth, coupled with economic dislocation in California in general, and San Francisco in particular, helped fan the fires of early anti-Chinese sentiment. By 1871, historians estimate, there were four workers for every job, but Chinese laborers were producing 50 percent of California's boots and shoes. By 1882, Chinese made up between 50 and 75 percent of the farm labor in some California counties.[10] Blaming Chinese workers for low wages and the scarcity of jobs, anti-Chinese leaders first charged that the Chinese were imported under servile conditions as "coolies" and were engaged in a new system of slavery that degraded American labor.[11] Chinese immigrants' purported diet of "rice and rats" was also cited as a clear sign that they had a lower standard of living, one that white working families could not (and should not) degrade themselves by accepting.[12] Samuel Gompers, president of the American Federation of Labor, framed this issue explicitly by asking, "Meat vs. Rice—American Manhood vs. Asiatic Coolieism. Which Shall Survive?"[13] Such rhetoric heightened the appeal of groups like the Workingmen's Party of California. Founded in 1877 and headed by Irish immigrant Denis Kearney, the party's rallying cry was "The Chinese Must Go!" Local and national politicians alike used race- and class-based economic arguments to nationalize the Chinese question. As Gwendolyn Mink has illustrated, the anti-Chinese movement in California was a "building block of national trade-union politics" that "transposed anti-capitalist feeling with anti-immigrant hostility."[14]

Many of the arguments in favor of restricting Chinese immigrants also hinged explicitly on gender and sexuality. As Sucheta Mazumdar argues, a specific kind of Orientalism emerged in the West, with Chinese women symbolizing some of the most fundamental differences between the West and the "Far East."[15] The almost 900 Chinese prostitutes in California in 1870 came to represent a sexualized danger with the power to subvert both the domestic ideal and the existing relations between white heterosexual men and women. Their mere presence made possible the crossing of racial and class lines and renewed fears of "moral and racial pollution."[16] Chinese prostitutes were also believed to carry more virulent strains of venereal disease that had the power to "poison Anglo-Saxon blood." They allegedly not only threatened the morals of the larger society but, as exclusionists argued, could also cause its downfall.[17]

Historian Karen Leong reminds us that the ways in which both American and Chinese masculinity were constructed in the anti-Chinese debates were also central arguments for Chinese exclusion. Exclusionists claimed that Chinese men exploited women (by supporting the Chinese trade in prostitution) and immigrated alone, failing to establish families. Both actions, they argued, pointed to their lack of manhood.[18] Chinese men also did not abide by the rules that divided labor by gender in American society. Expelled from mining camps, excluded from industrial and agricultural labor, Chinese men had established an economic niche for themselves in laundries, restaurants, and domestic service, all occupations traditionally assigned to women.[19] Their physical appearance and choice of clothing also disturbed American perceptions of proper gender roles. Prior to the Chinese Revolution in 1911, Chinese men shaved their foreheads and wore their hair in a queue as a symbol of loyalty to the Qing Empire. The loose garments that Chinese men often wore were also cause for scrutiny. In 1901, a California agricultural journal complained that "the good dollars which ought to be going into a white man's pocket" were instead going to the "Chinaman" and "that garment of his which passes for 'pants.'" Both the queue and the garments were seen as sexually ambiguous at a time when strict gender codes generally dictated short hair and pants for men, long hair and dresses for women.[20]

Such class- and gender-based arguments for Chinese exclusion merged with charges that Chinese were racially inferior and would worsen America's existing race problems. Underlying the anti-Chinese movement was a larger campaign to impose and sustain white supremacy in the West. Californians had long envisioned their state to be an Edenic, unspoiled land where free labor might thrive. This image was disrupted by the "Chinese Problem."[21] Alexander Saxton has demonstrated how the heirs to the Jacksonian Democratic Party—committed to territorial expansion, defense of slavery, and a belief in the racial inferiority of Africans and Native Americans—systematically nourished and exploited anti-Chinese sentiment and turned the Chinese immigration question into a centerpiece of California politics.[22] When Chinese immigrants began arriving in America, the conquest of American Indians and Mexicans in the West had been accomplished only recently. Moreover, white anti-Chinese residents of California and other Pacific Coast states felt that the future of "their society" was particularly endangered because of their proximity to Asia.[23] In order to highlight the alleged racial threat that Chinese posed, the similarities between African Americans and Chinese immigrants were drawn most explicitly. Both the "bought" Chinese prostitute and the "enslaved" Chinese coolie were conflated with African American slaves. Racial qualities commonly assigned to African Americans were used to describe Chinese immigrants. Both were believed to be heathen, inherently inferior, savage, depraved, and lustful.[24] Chinese, like African Americans, were "incapable of attaining the state of civilization [of] the Caucasian." And while some believed the Chinese were "physiologically and mentally" superior to African Americans, they were more of a threat, because they were less assimilable.[25]

Anti-Chinese activists' charges that Chinese were unwilling and, in fact, incapable of assimilating were repeatedly used to introduce and support the idea of closing America's gates to Chinese immigration. Chinese immigrants were first set apart from both European immigrants and native-born white Americans. One witness before the 1876 California State Committee on Chinese Immigration described Chinese immigration as an unwelcome "invasion" of "new" and "different" immigrants, while the earlier classes of (European) immigrants were "welcome visitors." In this way, the country's immigrant heritage and identification as a nation of immigrants was largely preserved. Even more important, the witnesses continued to emphasize how Chinese were "permanently alien" to America, unable to ever assimilate into American life and citizenship.[26]

These interrelated threats justified that legal barriers be established and that metaphorical gates be built and closed against the Chinese in order to protect Americans. Western politicians effectively claimed the right to speak for the rest of the country and to assert American national sovereignty in the name of Chinese exclusion. They argued that it was nothing less than the duty and the sovereign right of Californians and Americans writ large to exclude the Chinese for the good of the country. H. N. Clement, the San Francisco lawyer, explicitly combined the themes of racial difference, the closed gate/closed door metaphor, and national sovereignty to articulate this philosophy. "Have we any right to *close our doors* against one nation and open them to another?" he asked. "Has the Caucasian race any better right to occupy this country than the Mongolian?" He answered with an emphatic "Yes." Citing contemporary treatises on international law, Clement argued that the greatest fundamental right of every nation was self-preservation, and the Chinese immigration question was nothing less than a battle for America's survival. "A nation has a right to do *everything* that can secure it from threatening danger and to *keep at a distance* whatever is capable of causing its ruin," he continued. "We have a great right to say to the half-civilized subject from Asia, '*You shall not come at all.*'"[27]

Both the West's history of extending and reinforcing white supremacy in the region and its unique relationship with the federal government paved the way toward Chinese exclusion and the larger development of a gatekeeping nation. The language and politics of the anti-Chinese movement closely followed other western campaigns of territorial expansion, expropriation of Native American lands, and the subjugation of African Americans and Mexicans. The exclusion of Chinese immigrants became a "natural" progression in the region's history of racial oppression and segregation, but because immigration was recognized as a federal, rather than state or regional, issue, westerners could not achieve their directives alone. As one of the best examples of what historians have identified as a "quintessentially western story" of westerners relying upon the federal government to solve the region's racial and class problems, anti-Chinese activists designed a special plea for assistance to the U.S. Congress.[28] Their message was clear: Chinese immigration was both a "local grievance" and a "national question," the "darkest cloud" not only on California's horizon but on the republic's as well.[29] The threats, pleas, and cajoling worked. In 1880, unrelenting lobbying resulted in a revision of the Burlingame Treaty that had protected Chinese immigration since 1868. By March of 1882, midwestern congressman Edward K. Valentine (R-Nebraska) had articulated western exclusionists' message perfectly. "In order to protect our laboring classes," he proclaimed in the halls of Congress, *the gate must be closed.*"[30] With the passage of the Chinese Exclusion Act in 1882, the federal government rode to the rescue of the West once again. The exclusion of Chinese became yet one more chapter in the region's consolidation of white supremacy, but with enduring, national consequences.

THE EXAMPLE OF CHINESE EXCLUSION: RACE AND RACIALIZATION

One of the most significant consequences of Chinese exclusion was that it provided a powerful framework to be used to racialize other threatening, excludable, and undesirable aliens. After the Chinese were excluded, calls to restrict or exclude other immigrants followed quickly, and the rhetoric and strategy of these later campaigns drew important lessons from the anti-Chinese movement. For example, the class-based arguments and restrictions in the Chinese Exclusion Act were echoed in campaigns to bar contract laborers of any race. Southern and eastern European immigrants—like Chinese—were denounced as "coolies, serfs, and slaves." Such connections were persuasive. In 1885, the Foran Act prohibited the immigration of all contract laborers.[31]

The gender-based exclusions of the Page Act were also duplicated in later government attempts to screen out immigrants, especially women, who were perceived to be immoral or guilty of sexual misdeeds. The exclusion of Chinese prostitutes led to a more general exclusion of all prostitutes in the 1903 Immigration Act.[32] Signifying a larger concern that independent female migration was a moral problem, other immigration laws restricted the entry of immigrants who were "likely to become public charges" or who had committed a "crime involving moral turpitude."[33] As Donna Gabaccia has pointed out, such general exclusion laws were theoretically "gender-neutral." In practice, however, "any unaccompanied woman of any age, marital status, or background might be questioned" as a potential public charge. Clauses in the 1891 Immigration Act excluded women on moral grounds. Sexual misdeeds such as adultery, fornication, and illegitimate pregnancy were all reasons for exclusion. Lastly, echoes of the "unwelcome invasion" of Chinese and Japanese immigration were heard in nativist rhetoric focusing on the high birthrates of southern and eastern European immigrant families. Immigrant fecundity, it was claimed, would cause the "race suicide" of the Anglo-American race.[34]

Race clearly intersected with these class- and gender-based arguments and played perhaps the largest role in determining which immigrant groups were admitted or excluded. The arguments and lessons of Chinese exclusion were resurrected over and over again during the nativist debates over the "new" immigrants from Asia, Mexico, and southern and eastern Europe, further refining and consolidating the racialization of these groups. David Roediger and James Barrett have suggested that African Americans provided the racial model for southern and eastern European immigrants. The terms "guinea," to refer to Italians, and "hunky," to refer to Slavic immigrants, were especially connected to these two groups often laboring in industries and jobs previously dominated by African Americans.[35] In terms of immigration restriction, however, new immigrants were more closely racialized along the Chinese immigrant model, especially in the Pacific Coast states. There, whiteness was defined most clearly in opposition to Asian-ness or "yellowness."[36] The persistent use of the metaphor of the closed gate, combined with the rhetoric of "unwelcome invasions," most clearly reveals the difference. African Americans, originally brought into the nation as slaves, could never really be "sent back" despite their alleged inferiority and threat to the nation. Segregation and Jim Crow legislation was mostly aimed at keeping African Americans "in their place." Chinese, who were racialized as polar opposites to "Americans," also clearly did not belong in the United States and were often compared to blacks. But unlike African Americans, they could be kept at bay through immigration laws. Later, immigration restrictions were expanded to include southern and eastern European and Mexican immigrants but never applied to African Americans.

As early-twentieth-century nativist literature and organization records illustrate, the language of Chinese restriction and exclusion was quickly refashioned to apply to each succeeding group. These connections—though clear to contemporary intellectuals, politicians, and nativists—have not been made forcefully enough by immigration historians, who too often study European, Asian, or Latino immigrants in isolation from one another. John Higham, the leading authority on American nativism, has claimed that the anti-Asian movements were "historically tangential" to the main currents of American nativism. Edith Abbott, who authored one of the first comprehensive studies of immigration, argued that "the study of European immigration should not be complicated for the student by confusing it with the very different problems of Chinese and Japanese immigration." Carl Wittke, considered a founder of the field, devoted much attention to Asians in his important survey of American immigration history but argued that their history was "a brief and strange interlude in the general account of the great migrations to America."[37] Continued intellectual segregation within immigration history is a fruitless endeavor.[38] In the case of immigration restriction, it is now clear that anti-Asian nativism was not only directly connected to American nativist ideology and politics in the early twentieth century; it was in fact their dominant model.

Following the exclusion of Chinese, Americans on the West Coast became increasingly alarmed about new immigration from Asia, particularly from Japan, Korea, and India. Californians portrayed the immigrants as comprising another "Oriental invasion," and San Francisco newspapers urged readers to "step to the front once more and battle to hold the Pacific Coast for the white race."[39] Like the Chinese before them, these new Asian immigrants were considered threats because of their race and labor. The Japanese were especially feared because of their great success in agriculture. Moreover, unlike the Chinese community, which had a large proportion of single male sojourners,

Japanese tended to settle and start families in the United States. The political and cultural ideology that came to be used in the anti-Japanese movement immediately connected the new Japanese threat with the old Chinese one. Headlines in San Francisco newspapers talked of "another phase in the Immigration from Asia" and warned that the "Japanese [were] taking the place of the Chinese." Similar charges that the Japanese were unassimilable and exploitable cheap labor were made. And because the Japanese were supposedly even more "tricky and unscrupulous," as well as more "aggressive and warlike," than the Chinese, they were considered even "more objectionable."[40] Political leaders made the connections explicit. Denis Kearney, the charismatic leader of the Workingmen's Party, which spearheaded the anti-Chinese movement in San Francisco during the 1870s, found the Chinese and Japanese "problems" to be synonymous. A Sacramento reporter recorded Kearney in 1892 berating the "foreign Shylocks [who] are rushing another breed of Asiatic slaves to fill up the gap made vacant by the Chinese who are shut out by our laws. . . . Japs . . . are being brought here now in countless numbers to demoralize and discourage our domestic labor market." Kearney rousingly ended his speech with "The Japs Must Go!"[41] In 1901, James D. Phelan, mayor of San Francisco, spearheaded the Chinese Exclusion Convention of 1901 around the theme "For Home, Country, and Civilization." Later, in 1920, he ran for the U.S. Senate under the slogan "Stop the Silent Invasion" (of Japanese).[42]

The small population of Asian Indian immigrants also felt the wrath of nativists, who regarded them as the "most objectionable of all Orientals" in the United States.[43] In 1905, the San Francisco-based Japanese-Korean Exclusion League renamed itself the Asiatic Exclusion League in an attempt to meet the new threat. Newspapers complained of "Hindu Hordes" coming to the United States. Indians were "dirty, diseased," "the worst type of immigrant . . . not fit to become a citizen . . . and entirely foreign to the people of the United States." Their employment by "moneyed capitalists" as expendable cheap labor and India's large population "teeming with millions upon millions of emaciated sickly Hindus existing on starvation wages" also hearkened back to the charges of a cheap labor invasion made against Chinese and Japanese immigrants.[44]

Racialized definitions of Mexican immigrants also referred back to Chinese immigration. Long classified as racially inferior, Mexican immigrants often served as replacement agricultural laborers following the exclusion of Asian immigrants.[45] Although their immigration was largely protected by agricultural and industrial employers through the 1920s, Mexican immigrants were long-standing targets of racial nativism, and many of the arguments directed toward Mexicans echoed earlier charges made against the Chinese. Because the legal, political, and cultural understandings of Chinese immigrants as permanent foreigners had long been established, nativists' direct connections between Chinese and Mexicans played a crucial role in racializing Mexicans as foreign. As Mae Ngai has shown for the post-1924 period, the characterization of Mexicans as foreign, rather than as the natives of what used to be their former homeland, "*distanced* them both from Anglo-Americans culturally and from the Southwest as a region" and made it easier to restrict, criminalize, and deport Mexicans as "illegal."[46]

Nativists used the Chinese framework to characterize Mexicans as foreign on the basis of two main arguments: racial inferiority and racial unassimilability. George P. Clemens, the head of the Los Angeles County Agricultural Department, explained that Asians and Mexicans were racially inferior to whites because they were physically highly suitable for the degraded agricultural labor in which they were often employed. The tasks involved were those "which the Oriental and Mexican due to their crouching and bending habits are fully adapted, while the white is physically unable to adapt himself to them."[47] While Chinese were considered to be biologically inferior because of their status as heathens and their alleged inability to conform to an Anglo-American mold, Mexicans were degraded as an ignorant "hybrid race" of Spanish and Native American origin.[48] As Mexican immigration increased, fears of a foreign invasion of cheap, unassimilable laborers similar to the Chinese one permeated the nativist literature. Major Frederick Russell Burnham warned that "the whole Pacific Coast would have been Asiatic in blood today except for the Exclusion Acts. Our whole Southwest will be racially Mexican in three generations unless some similar restriction is placed upon them."[49] (Burnham, of course, conveniently ignored the fact that the Southwest—as well as most of the American West—had already been "racially Mexican" long before he himself had migrated west.) V. S. McClatchy, editor of the *Sacramento Bee*, warned that the "wholesale introduction of Mexican peons" presented California's "most serious problem" in the 1920s.[50] Increased Mexican migration to Texas was an especially contested issue, and nativists there pointed to the example of California and Chinese immigration to warn of their state's future. "To Mexicanize Texas or Orientalize California is a crime," raged one nativist.[51] Chester H. Rowell argued that the Mexican invasion was even more detrimental than the Chinese one because at least the "Chinese coolie"—"the ideal human mule"—would not "plague us with his progeny. His wife and children are in China, and he returns there himself when we no longer need him." Mexicans, he argued, might not be so compliant or easy to send back.[52]

Other nativists extended the racial unassimilability argument to Mexicans by claiming that they "can no more blend into our race than can the Chinaman or the Negro."[53] Anti-Mexican nativists increasingly called for restriction by framing the new Mexican immigration problem within the old argument for Chinese exclusion. Major Burnham blamed the reliance on cheap Mexican labor on the immigration promoters of the 1920s, just as Denis Kearney had blamed the capitalists and their "Chinese pets" during the 1870s. "It is the old Chinese stuff, an echo of the [18]70s, word for word!" wrote Burnham. Moreover, Burnham believed that immigration law—and specifically the same types of exclusionary measures used against the Chinese—were the only remedy: "Let us refuse cheap labor. Let us restrict Mexican immigration and go steadily on to prosperity and wealth just as we did after the Asiatic Exclusion Acts were passed."[54]

At the same time, some of the race- and class-based theories and arguments used against Asians and Mexicans were being applied to certain European immigrant groups, especially in the northeastern United States, where most European immigrants first landed and settled. The sense of "absolute difference" that already divided white Americans from people of color was extended to certain European nationalities. Because distinctive physical differences between native white Americans and European immigrants were not readily apparent, nativists "manufactured" racial difference. Boston intellectuals like Nathaniel Shaler, Henry Cabot Lodge, and Francis Walker all promoted an elaborate set of racial ideas that marked southern and eastern Europeans and others as different and inferior, a threat to the nation. In 1894, they formed a new nativist group, the Immigration Restriction League (IRL), in Boston.[55]

Both Italians and French Canadians, for example, were often compared with Chinese immigrants. Italians were called the "Chinese of Europe," and French Canadians were labeled the "Chinese of the Eastern States." As Donna Gabaccia has argued, Chinese and Italians "occupied an ambiguous, overlapping and intermediary position in the binary racial schema." Neither black nor white, both were seen as in-between, or "yellow," "olive," or "swarthy." Their use as cheap labor also linked the two together. Italians were often called "European coolies" or "padrone coolies."[56] French Canadians were compared to Chinese immigrants because of their alleged inability to assimilate to Anglo-American norms. An 1881 Massachusetts state agency report charged that French Canadians were the "Chinese of the Eastern States" because "they care nothing for our institutions. . . . They do not come to make a home among us, to dwell with us as citizens. . . . Their purpose is merely to sojourn a few years as aliens."[57] In 1891, Henry Cabot Lodge opined that the Slovak immigrants—another threatening group—"are not a good acquisition for us to make, since they appear to have so many items in common with the Chinese."[58] Lothrop Stoddard, another leading nativist, went even further by arguing that eastern Europeans were not only "like the Chinese"; they were, in fact, part Asian. Eastern Europe, he explained, was situated "next door" to Asia and had already been invaded by "Asiatic hordes" over the past two thousand years. As a result, the Slavic peoples were mongrels, "all impregnated with Asiatic Mongol and Turki blood."[59]

Such explicit race- and class-based connections to Chinese immigration were effective in defining and articulating nativists' problems with newer immigrants. The old Chinese exclusion rhetoric was one with which Americans were familiar by the 1910s, and it served as a strong foundation from which to build new nativist arguments on the national level. The Immigration Restriction League used this tactic masterfully. In a 1908 letter to labor unions, the organization affirmed that Chinese immigration was the ultimate evil but warned that the Orient was "only one source of the foreign cheap labor which competes so ruinously with our own workmen." The IRL charged that the stream of immigrants from Europe and western Asia was "beginning to flow," and without proper measures to check it, it would "swell, as did the coolie labor, until it overwhelms one laboring community after another."[60]

In a letter to politicians, the IRL defined the issues and the sides even more clearly. The letter asked congressmen and senators across the country to identify the "classes of persons" who were desired and not desired in their state. The IRL made this task simple by offering them pre-set lists of groups they themselves deemed "desirable" and "undesirable." The politicians needed only to check the groups in order of preference. In the "desired" categories, "Americans, native born," topped the list. The generic category of "persons from northern Europe" came second. Then, the specific groups of British, Scandinavians, and Germans followed. Asiatics, southern and eastern Europeans, illiterates, and the generic "foreign born" were all lumped together in the second list of supposed unwanted and excludable immigrants.[61] The IRL could make no clearer statement: the new threat from Europe and the old threat from Asia were one.

Because of different regional politics and dynamics of race relations, divergent opinions about the connections between the old Asian immigration problem and the new European one existed on the West Coast. On the one hand, the parties behind the virulent anti-Asian campaigns broadened their appeals to preserve "America for all Americans" and called into question just who was a "real American." The San Francisco-based Asiatic Exclusion League implied that all aliens were dangerous to the country and passed a resolution that required aliens to disarm in order to prevent insurrection.[62] Other nativists in California expressed fears of the degraded immigrants entering the country from both Asia and Europe. Homer Lea, the author and leading proponent of the Yellow Peril theory of Japanese domination of America, warned that the growing immigration from Europe augmented the Japanese danger by "sapping America's racial strength and unity."[63] The California branch of the Junior Order of United American Mechanics, a well-established nativist group, allied itself with the Asiatic Exclusion League and announced that southern Europeans were semi-Mongolian.[64]

On the other hand, western nativists continued the West's campaign to preserve a "white man's frontier" by emphasizing the differences between Europeans and Asians and by privileging whiteness at the expense of people of color. Significantly, many of the leading nativists were European immigrants and second-generation Americans themselves.[65] Denis Kearney, leader of the anti-Chinese Workingmen's Party, was an Irish immigrant. James D. Phelan, leader of the anti-Japanese movement, was Irish American. By leading racist campaigns against Asian immigration, Kearney and Phelan reaffirmed their own status as whites. In the multiracial West, such consolidations of whiteness were central to sustaining the existing racial hierarchy. The best expression of this sentiment occurred during the 1901 Chinese Exclusion Convention, an event organized to lobby for the permanent exclusion of Chinese immigrants. While attendees rallied around the convention theme of protecting the American "home, country, and civilization," keynote speakers strongly defended an open-door policy toward all European immigrants. In an impassioned speech, A. Sbarboro (an Italian immigrant/Italian American himself), president of the Manufacturers' and Producers' Association, declared that in California,

> we want the Englishman, who brings with him capital, industry and enterprise; the Irish who build and populate our cities; the Frenchmen, with his vivacity and love of liberty; the industrious and thrifty Italians, who cultivate the fruit, olives, and vines—who come with poetry and music from the classic land of Virgil; the Teutonic race, strong, patient, and frugal; the Swedes, Slavs, and Belgians; we want *all good people from all parts of Europe*. To these, Mr. Chairman, we should never close our doors, for although when the European immigrant lands at Castle Garden he may be uncouth and with little money,

yet soon by his thrift and industry he improves his condition; he becomes a worthy citizen and the children who bless him mingle with the children of those who came before him, and when the country calls they are always ready and willing to defend the flag to follow the stars and stripes throughout the world.[66]

Sbarboro, by explicitly including Italians and Slavs, indeed, all immigrants from all parts of Europe, with the older stock of immigrants from France, Sweden, Germany, and Belgium, made clear that the distinction to be made was not among European immigrants but between European and, in this case, Asian immigrants. Membership in the white race was tantamount. Southern and eastern European immigrants had the potential to become worthy citizens. Even the European immigrant's children would be American patriots some day. The belief that second-generation Chinese would do the same was unimaginable.

An increasing number of politicians and policy makers across the country disregarded Sbarboro's pleas to keep America's doors open to Europeans and instead supported restrictions on immigration from southern and eastern Europe. Nevertheless, Sbarboro's attempts to distinguish European immigrants from Asians pointed to significant differences in the ways in which European, Asian, and Mexican immigrants were racially constructed and regulated by immigration law. First, southern and eastern European immigrants came in much greater numbers than did the Chinese, and their whiteness secured them the right of naturalized citizenship, while Asians were consistently denied naturalization by law and in the courts. Whiteness permitted European immigrants more access to full participation in the larger American polity, economy, and society. Although they were eventually greatly restricted, they were never excluded. As Mae Ngai has shown, the 1924 Immigration Act restricted European immigrants according to their "national origins" (rather than race), presuming their shared whiteness with white Americans and separating them from non-Europeans. The act thus established the "legal foundations . . . for European immigrants [to] becom[e] Americans." Chinese, Japanese, Korean, Filipino, and Asian Indian immigrants were codified as "aliens ineligible to citizenship."[67]

Mexican immigration differed from both southern and eastern European and Asian immigration on several levels. First was Mexico's proximity to the United States and the relatively porous U.S.-Mexican border, which facilitated migration "to and from the United States." As historians have shown, Mexican immigrants were treated differently, even considered "safe" from mainstream nativism, because of their status as long-term residents and their propensity to be "birds of passage," returning home after the agricultural season ended rather than settling in the United States permanently.[68] In addition, Mexico's contentious history with the United States and the latter country's "legacy of conquest" aggravated already tense U.S.-Mexican relations, racialized Mexicans as inferiors, and structured Mexican immigrant and Mexican American life within the United States in ways that contrasted sharply with the lives of other immigrant groups. In the post-1924 period, Mexicans were categorized as "illegal," an all-encompassing racial category that not only negated any claim of Mexicans belonging in a conquered homeland but also extended to both Mexican immigrants and Mexican Americans.[69]

The significant differences in the ways that these immigrant groups were viewed functioned to shape both immigration regulation and immigrant life in distinct ways. Still, the rhetoric and tools of gatekeeping were instrumental in defining the issues for all immigrants and set important precedents for twentieth-century immigration. Each group held its own unique position within the hierarchy of race and immigration, but all eventually became subjected to an immigration ideology and law designed to limit their entry into the United States. By the early twentieth century, the call to "close the gates" was sounded in relation not only to Chinese immigration but to immigration in general. Thomas Bailey Aldrich, poet and former editor of the *Atlantic Monthly*, reacted to the new immigrants from southern and eastern Europe arriving in Boston in 1892 by publishing "The Unguarded Gates," a poem demonizing the new arrivals as a "wild motley throng . . . accents of menace alien to our air."[70] Just as H. N. Clement had suggested "closing the doors" against Chinese immigration in 1876, Madison Grant, the well-known nativist and leader of the Immigration Restriction League, called for "closing the flood gates" against the "new immigration" from southern and eastern Europe in 1914.[71] At the same time, Frank Julian Warne, another nativist leader, warned that unregulated immigration from Europe was akin to "throwing open wide our gates to all the races of the world."[72]

The solution, all agreed, lay in immigration policy, and a succession of federal laws were passed to increase the control and regulation of threatening and inferior immigrants. The Immigration Act of 1917 required a literacy test for all adult immigrants, tightened restrictions on suspected radicals, and, as a concession to politicians on the West Coast, denied entry to aliens living within a newly conceived geographical area called the "Asiatic Barred Zone." With this zone in place, the United States effectively excluded all immigrants from India, Burma, Siam, the Malay States, Arabia, Afghanistan, part of Russia, and most of the Polynesian Islands.[73] The 1921 and 1924 Immigration Acts drastically restricted immigration from southern and eastern Europe and perfected the exclusion of all Asians, except for Filipinos.[74] In 1934, Filipinos were also excluded, and both Filipinos and Mexicans were singled out for massive deportation and repatriation programs during the Great Depression.[75] By the 1930s, exclusion, restriction, and deportation had been extended to other immigrant groups and codified into law and immigration service practices. The cycle that had begun with Chinese exclusion was completed.[76]

THE EXAMPLE OF CHINESE EXCLUSION: IMMIGRATION REGULATION

The concepts of race that developed out of Chinese exclusion provided the ideological structure within which other immigrant groups were compared and racialized. The passage of the Chinese Exclusion Act also ushered in drastic changes in immigration regulation and set the foundation for twentieth-century policies designed not only for the inspection and processing of newly arriving immigrants but also for the control of potentially dangerous immigrants already in the country. Written into the act itself were several major changes in immigration regulation. All would become standard means of inspecting, processing, admitting, tracking, punishing, and deporting immigrants in the United States. First, the Exclusion Act paved the way for the appointment of the country's first federal immigrant inspectors. Years before a federal immigration agency was established in 1891, the inspectors of Chinese immigrants (under the auspices of the U.S. Customs Service) were the first to be authorized to enforce U.S. immigration law on behalf of the federal government.[77] Prior to the passage of the Page Law and the Chinese Exclusion Act, there was neither a trained force of government officials and interpreters nor the bureaucratic machinery with which to enforce the new law. The U.S. collector of customs and his staff had been granted the authority to examine Chinese female passengers and their documents under the Page Law, but the Chinese Exclusion Act extended the duties of these officials to include the examination of all arriving Chinese.[78] Under the new act, inspectors were also required to examine and clear Chinese laborers departing the United States.[79]

Second, the enforcement of the Chinese exclusion laws set in motion the federal government's first attempts to identify and record the movements, occupations, and familial relationships of immigrants, returning residents, and native-born citizens. Because of the complexity of the laws and immigration officials' suspicions that Chinese were attempting to enter the country under fraudulent pretenses, the government's enforcement practices involved an elaborate tracking system of registration documents and certificates of identity and voluminous interviews with individuals and their families.[80] Section 4 of the Exclusion Act also established "certificates of registration" for departing laborers. Such certificates were to contain the name, age, occupation, last place of residence, and personal description of the Chinese laborer. This information was also recorded in specific registry books kept in the customhouse. The certificate entitled the holder to "return and reenter the United States upon producing and delivering the [document] to the collector of customs." The laborer's return certificate was the first document of its kind issued to an immigrant group by the federal government, and it served as a passport facilitating reentry into the country. Chinese remained the only immigrant group required to hold such reentry permits (or passports) until 1924, when the new immigration act of that year issued—but did not require—reentry permits for other aliens.[81]

The documentary requirements established for Chinese women emigrating under the Page Law and for exempt-class Chinese (merchants, teachers, diplomats, students, travelers) applying for admission under the exclusion laws also set in motion an "early . . . system of 'remote control' involving passports and visas" through which U.S. consular officials in China and Hong Kong verified the admissibility of immigrants prior to their departure for the United States. The Exclusion Act of 1882 placed this responsibility in the hands of Chinese government officials alone, but an 1884 amendment gave U.S. diplomatic officers the responsibility of verifying the facts on the so-called Section 6 certificates required of exempt-class Chinese so that the documents could be considered "*prima facie* evidence of right of reentry."[82]

Eventually, in an effort to crack down on illegal entry and residence, the Chinese exclusion laws were amended to require all Chinese already in the country to possess "certificates of residence" and "certificates of identity" that served as proof of their legal entry into and lawful right to remain in the country. The rules regarding these precursors to documents now commonly known as green cards were first outlined in the 1892 Geary Act and 1893 McCreary Amendment, which required Chinese laborers to register with the federal government. The resulting certificates of residence contained the name, age, local residence and occupation of the applicant (or "Chinaman," as the act noted), as well as a photograph. Any Chinese laborer found within the jurisdiction of the United States without a certificate of residence was to be "deemed and adjudged to be unlawfully in the United States" and would be vulnerable to arrest and deportation.[83] The Bureau of Immigration used its administrative authority to demand a similar "certificate of identity" for all exempt-class Chinese, including merchants, teachers, travelers, and students, beginning in 1909. Although such certificates were supposed to serve as "indubitable proof of legal entry," they failed to protect legal immigrants and residents from government harassment. The requirement that all Chinese possess the certificates subjected the entire community—including immigrants and residents who were supposed to be exempt from the exclusion laws—to the same system of registration and scrutiny governing Chinese laborers. Apparently, the plan was an extension of an existing system of registration used for Chinese Americans entering the mainland from Hawaii.[84] No other immigrants were required to hold documents proving their lawful residence until 1928, when "immigrant identification cards" were first issued to any new immigrants arriving for permanent residence. These were eventually replaced by the "alien registration receipt cards" (that is, "green cards") after 1940.[85]

The institution of these documentary requirements verifying Chinese immigrants' rights to enter, reenter, and remain in the country codified a highly organized system of control and surveillance over the Chinese in America. Much of the rationale behind them stemmed from the prejudiced belief that it was, as California congressman Thomas Geary explained, "impossible to identify [one] Chinaman [from another]."[86] This unprecedented method of processing and tracking immigrants eventually became central to America's control of all immigrants and immigration in the twentieth century.

The Chinese Exclusion Act set another precedent by defining illegal immigration as a criminal offense. It declared that any person who secured certificates of identity fraudulently or through impersonation was to be deemed guilty of a misdemeanor, fined $1,000, and imprisoned for up to five years. Any persons who knowingly aided and abetted the landing of "any Chinese person not lawfully entitled to enter the United States" could also be charged with a misdemeanor, fined, and imprisoned for up to one year.[87] Defining and punishing illegal immigration directly led to the establishment of the country's first modern deportation laws as well, and one of the final sections of the act declared that "any Chinese person found unlawfully within the United States shall be caused to be removed therefrom to the country from whence he came."[88] These initial forays into federal regulation of immigration would be even further codified and institutionalized seven years later in the Immigration Act of 1891.[89]

THE CLOSED GATE: RENEWING AND EXPANDING CHINESE EXCLUSION, 1882–1904

The first result of exclusion was that Chinese immigration dropped dramatically. In 1882, before the Chinese Exclusion Act went into effect, 39,579 Chinese rushed to enter the United States. Thereafter, the numbers fell to an all-time low in 1887, when immigration officials admitted only ten Chinese immigrants into the United States.[90] Other immigrants gained admission through the courts, but over all, Chinese exclusion was extremely effective in limiting Chinese immigration in the first two decades of the exclusion era. The number of Chinese departing from the United States also greatly increased (probably a result of a burst of anti-Chinese violence throughout the West after 1882). Statistics for most years are not available, but the Chinese Bureau in San Francisco recorded a total of 11,434 departures of Chinese residents in the first fourteen months after the Exclusion Act was passed, and the trend apparently continued throughout the 1880s.[91] For the period from 1888 to 1890, the bureau's records indicate a total of 11,312 departures of Chinese residents.[92] In 1888, the number of departures was still extremely high, and S. J. Ruddell, the chief inspector at the port, remarked that the excess of departures was "very noticeable." "The number of stores [in Chinatown] are decreasing every day," he testified before a congressional committee in 1890. The passage of the Exclusion Act, he continued, had made a "very marked difference" among the Chinese population, and if the trend continued, he predicted, the community might "completely disappear."[93] While some of the departing immigrants might have reentered the United States at a later date, immigration officials overwhelmingly agreed that the Chinese Exclusion Act itself prevented most Chinese from even attempting to immigrate to the United States.[94]

The Chinese Exclusion Act was clearly successful in reducing Chinese immigration to the United States. Californians and other proponents of exclusion, however, believed that the 1882 act was a failure. Chinese immigration was not completely halted, and many believed that employers, the Chinese, and the federal courts took advantage of loopholes in the laws that, in their minds, made a mockery of the exclusion laws. As Lucy Salyer has shown, until 1903, federal district courts were indeed much more lenient in enforcing the exclusion laws than were the immigration officials at the ports of entry.[95]

Calls to amend the laws were almost immediate. One and a half years after President Arthur had signed the Chinese exclusion bill, San Franciscans clamored for more laws and outlined a registration policy for all Chinese immigrants. In December 1884, the San Francisco Board of Supervisors unanimously passed a resolution that explained that while the Chinese Exclusion Act had "to some extent prevented the Chinese hordes from coming into this State as heretofore . . . the ingenuity of these people in contriving means to land on our shores is almost incredible." The resolution called upon California senators and representatives to pass legislation instituting a strict registration and deportation system in order to "protect our people."[96] (Significantly, the registration provisions were later adopted by the federal government as part of the Geary Act of 1892.) In response, Congress passed a bill in 1884 that strengthened the existing exclusion law. Chinese laborers from any foreign country (not just China) were excluded, and immigration officials were required to record extensive identification information for all Chinese immigrants. The documentary requirements and the terms of criminal punishment for illegal immigration were also affirmed.[97]

In 1888, Congress refined the terms of exclusion. Instead of explicitly prohibiting only Chinese laborers, the new provisions excluded *all* Chinese except "teachers, students, merchants, or travelers for pleasure or curiosity." The law also prohibited any returning Chinese laborer from entering the country unless he had a lawful wife, child, or parent in the United States, or had property or debts due him worth at least $1,000. This aspect of the 1888 act was particularly harsh because it stipulated that the returning laborer's marriage had to have taken place at least a year prior to the laborer's application to depart and return to the United States and that the marriage had to be characterized as a "continuous cohabitation of the parties as man and wife."[98] The Scott Act of the same year nullified 20,000 return certificates already granted and immediately denied entrance to returning Chinese laborers.[99] Some California exclusionists even introduced legislation that called for the exclusion of all Chinese except for diplomatic officials.[100] Although these bills failed, they reflected the long-range goals of exclusionists.

The original Chinese Exclusion Act suspended the immigration of Chinese laborers for a period of ten years. When the act came up for renewal in 1892, Congress readily passed the Geary Act, sponsored by Thomas Geary, a California Democrat in the U.S. Senate. The amended act renewed the exclusion of laborers for another ten years.[101] By 1898, the original Chinese Exclusion Act was extended to Hawaii. In 1901, the Chinese Exclusion Convention brought together 2,500 anti-Chinese delegates who represented not only laboring men but also business and professional groups united by the desire to "prevent the threatened invasion of Mongol hordes to the peril and degradation of American labor."[102] The expiration of the Geary Act was a major topic of discussion. One of the stars of the convention was San Francisco mayor James Phelan, who highlighted California's citizens' role in "sounding the alarm" and serving as the "wardens of the Golden Gate" in the face of an onslaught of undesirable and dangerous Chinese immigrants.[103] Again, the metaphor of the gate—both as a San Francisco geographical landmark and as a symbolic barrier against Chinese immigration—remained central to exclusionists' arguments. In 1902, Congress passed a bill that renewed the exclusion of Chinese laborers and extended exclusion to all insular possessions of the United States, including the Philippines.[104] In 1904, the Chinese Exclusion Act was extended without time limit, and it remained in effect until its repeal in 1943.[105]

CONCLUSION

For Chinese immigrants, the year 1882 marked the end of one chapter in history and the beginning of a new one. From 1882 to 1904, the exclusion laws were expanded in scope and across geographic regions. Chinese immigrants felt the effects of these laws immediately, and Chinese immigration dropped dramatically. However, Chinese immigrants challenged and evaded the exclusion laws throughout the exclusion era.[106]

The United States' relationship with immigrants reached a similar turning point. The Chinese Exclusion Act instituted the first of many restriction and exclusion laws, but its significance goes far beyond the legal realm. Chinese exclusion helped redefine American politics; race, class, and gender relations; national identity; and the role of the federal government in controlling immigration. The result was a nation that embraced the notion of building and guarding America's gates against "undesirable" foreigners in order to protect white Americans. Rooted in a western American desire to sustain white supremacy in a multiracial West, gatekeeping became a national reality and was extended to other immigrant groups throughout the early twentieth century. Both the rhetoric and the tools used to exclude the Chinese were repeated in later debates over immigration. In many ways, Chinese immigrants became the models against which others were measured. Nativists repeatedly pointed to ways in which other Asians, Mexicans, and Europeans were "just like" the Chinese and argued that similar restrictions should be extended to them as well. By the 1930s, immigration inspections, passport and other documentary requirements, the surveillance and criminalization of immigration, and the deportation of immigrants found to be in the country illegally all became standard operating procedures in the United States. Nativists no longer needed to ask "*how* can we stop immigrants?" They had found the answer in Chinese exclusion.

NOTES

1. California State Senate, *Chinese Immigration*, 275.
2. Gyory, *Closing the Gate*, 78; Mink, *Old Labor and New Immigrants*, 73.
3. California State Senate, *Chinese Immigration*, 4.
4. Act of Mar. 3,1875 (18 Stat. 477); Peffer, *If They Don't Bring Their Women Here*, 28; Hutchinson, *Legislative History*, 65–66; Salyer, *Laws Harsh as Tigers*, 5.
5. Daniels, "No Lamps Were Lit for Them," 4. See also Gyory, *Closing the Gate*, 1, 258–59, on the significance of the Chinese Exclusion Act.
6. Recent exceptions are Salyer, *Laws Harsh as Tigers*; Chan, ed., *Entry Denied*; Chan and Wong, eds., *Claiming America*; Ngai, "Legacies of Exclusion"; Hsu, *Dreaming of Gold*; and McKeown, *Chinese Migrant Networks*.
7. Lucy Salyer (*Laws Harsh as Tigers*, xvi–xvii) has demonstrated how Chinese exclusion shaped the doctrine and administration of modern immigration law.
8. U.S. Department of Commerce and Labor, *Annual Reports of the Commissioner-General of Immigration* (1906), 43; Liu, "Comparative Demographic Study," 223; H. Chen, "Chinese Immigration," 201.
9. Said, *Orientalism*, 55; Gotanda, "Exclusion and Inclusion," 129–32; Tchen, *New York before Chinatown*, xx; Miller, *Unwelcome Immigrant*, 36, 83–94; Robert Lee, *Orientals*, 28.
10. Mink, *Old Labor and New Immigrants*, 74–75; Chan, *This Bittersweet Soil*, 51–78; Salyer, *Laws Harsh as Tigers*, 10.
11. As Sucheng Chan notes, the coolie trade in Asian Indian and Chinese laborers sprang up in response to the end of slavery in the Americas in the early nineteenth century. These individuals often traveled and labored under extremely coercive and exploitative conditions. The Chinese who migrated to the United States did not come as coolies. Instead,

they usually came using their own resources or under a credit-ticket system that financed their passage. Opponents of Chinese immigration often made no distinction between the free and semifree migration of Chinese to the United States and coerced coolies to other parts of the Americas. Labeling all Chinese immigration as a coolie migration helped to galvanize the anti-Chinese movement (*This Bittersweet Soil*, 21, 26, 31).

12. On anti-Chinese arguments in general, see Gyory, *Closing the Gate*; Saxton, *Indispensable Enemy*; Mink, *Old Labor and New Immigrants*; and Leong, " 'Distant and Antagonistic Race.' "

13. Gompers, "Some Reasons for Chinese Exclusion."

14. Mink, *Old Labor and New Immigrants*, 72, 96. On labor's role in California, see Saxton, *Indispensable Enemy*, 261–65.

15. Mazumdar, "Through Western Eyes," 158–59.

16. Scholars differ on the exact number of prostitutes in California in 1870. See Chan, "Exclusion of Chinese Women," 141 n. 44; Cheng, "Free, Indentured, Enslaved," 23–29; Robert Lee, *Orientals*, 88–89; and Peffer, *If They Don't Bring Their Women Here*, 28–42.

17. Miller, *Unwelcome Immigrant*, 163, 171; Robert Lee, *Orientals*, 90; Leong, " 'Distant and Antagonistic Race,' " 141.

18. Leong, " 'Distant and Antagonistic Race,' " 133.

19. Ibid., 142; Robert Lee, *Orientals*, 104.

20. *Pacific Rural Press*, Nov. 9, 1901, 292. My thanks to Linda Ivey for this citation.

21. Robert Lee, *Orientals*, 47.

22. Saxton, *Indispensable Enemy*, 94–96; Almaguer, *Racial Fault Lines*, 153–82.

23. Daniels, *Asian America*, 3–4.

24. Mazumdar, "Through Western Eyes," 164; Takaki, *Iron Cages*, 216–17.

25. U.S. Congress, Joint Special Committee, *Chinese Immigration*, 289–92; K. Scott Wong, "Cultural Defenders and Brokers," 6.

26. California State Senate, *Chinese Immigration*, 260, 10.

27. Ibid., 276–77 (emphasis original).

28. White, "Race Relations in the American West," 396–416; Friday, " 'In Due Time,' " 308.

29. California State Senate, *Chinese Immigration*, 280, 288.

30. Gyory, *Closing the Gate*, 238 (emphasis original).

31. Mink, *Old Labor and New Immigrants*, 109. Act of Feb. 26, 1885 (23 Stat. 332).

32. Act of Mar. 3, 1903 (32 Stat. 1222).

33. The 1882 Regulation of Immigration Act (Act of Aug. 3,1882 [22 Stat. 214]) also excluded lunatics, convicts, and idiots. The 1891 Immigration Act added polygamists and "persons suffering from a loathsome or dangerous contagious disease" (Act of Mar. 3, 1891 [26 Stat. 1084]).

34. Gabaccia, *From the Other Side*, 37.

35. Barrett and Roediger, "Inbetween Peoples," 8–9.

36. Recent studies on racial formation in the West illustrate the importance of moving beyond the white and black binary. See Foley, *White Scourge*; Almaguer, *Racial Fault Lines*; and Friday, " 'In Due Time.' "

37. Higham, *Strangers in the Land*, preface and afterword; Abbott, *Historical Aspects of the Immigration Problem*, ix; Wittke, *We Who Built America*, 458. Many of these oversights were first pointed out by Roger Daniels in "Westerners from the East," and "No Lamps Were Lit for Them," 3–18.

38. Sánchez, "Race, Nation, and Culture," 66–84; Gabaccia, "Is Everywhere Nowhere?," 1115–35.

39. *San Francisco Examiner*, June 16, 1910; *San Francisco Post*, May 24, 1910.

40. *San Francisco Bulletin*, May 4, 1891, as cited in Daniels, *Asian America*, 111; Asiatic Exclusion League, "Proceedings," July 1911.

41. Daniels, *Politics of Prejudice*, 20.

42. Chan, *Asian Americans*, 44.

43. *San Francisco Examiner*, Aug. 7, 1910, as cited in Salyer, *Laws Harsh as Tigers*, 127.

44. *San Francisco Daily News*, Sept. 20, 1910.

45. Sánchez, *Becoming Mexican American*, 19.

46. Ngai, "Architecture of Race," 91.

47. Hoffman, *Unwanted Mexican Americans*, 10.

48. Foley, *White Scourge*, 54.

49. Burnham, "Howl for Cheap Mexican Labor," 48.

50. McClatchy, "Oriental Immigration," 197.

51. Foley, *White Scourge*, 55.

52. Rowell, "Why Make Mexico an Exception?" and "Chinese and Japanese Immigrants," 4, as cited in Foley, *White Scourge*, 53.

53. Burnham, "Howl for Cheap Mexican Labor," 45.

54. Ibid., 48.

55. Higham, *Strangers in the Land*, 132–33.

56. Gabaccia, "'Yellow Peril,'" 177–79.

57. Massachusetts Bureau of Statistics of Labor, *Twelfth Annual Report*, 469–70. My thanks to FlorenceMae Waldron for this citation.

58. Lodge was quoting the U.S. Consul in Budapest (Lodge, "Restriction of Immigration," 30–32, 35, as cited in Jacobson, *Barbarian Virtues*, 76–77).

59. Stoddard, "Permanent Menace from Europe," 227–78.

60. J. H. Patten, Asst. Secretary, Immigration Restriction League, Letter to Unions, Oct. 15, 1908, Immigration Restriction League Scrapbooks.

61. J. H. Patten, Asst. Secretary, Immigration Restriction League, to Congressmen and Senators, n.d., ibid.

62. Asiatic Exclusion League, "Proceedings," Feb. 1908, 19, 71, and Dec. 1908, 17, 19.

63. Lea, *Valor of Ignorance*, 124–28; Higham, *Strangers in the Land*, 166, 172.

64. *Congressional Record*, 61st Cong., 1st sess., 9174; Asiatic Exclusion League, "Proceedings," Feb. 1908, 55, 57; Higham, *Strangers in the Land*, 174.

65. As David Roediger, Matthew Frye Jacobson, and Noel Ignatiev have shown, Irish and southern and eastern European immigrants commonly constructed and asserted their "whiteness" by allying themselves (and sometimes leading) other racist campaigns against African Americans, Native Americans, and Asian and Mexican immigrants (Roediger, *Wages of Whiteness*; Jacobson, *Whiteness of a Different Color*; Ignatiev, *How the Irish Became White*).

66. *San Francisco Call*, Nov. 22, 1901.

67. Ngai, "Architecture of Race," 70.

68. Cardoso, *Mexican Emigration*, 22; Sánchez, *Becoming Mexican American*, 20; Hoffman, *Unwanted Mexican Americans*, 30–32.

69. Ngai, "Architecture of Race," 91.

70. Solomon, *Ancestors and Immigrants*, 82–88; Jacobson, *Barbarian Virtues*, 181.

71. Grant and Davison, eds., *Alien in Our Midst*, 23.

72. Warne, *Immigrant Invasion*, 295.

73. Immigration Act of 1917 (39 Stat. 874).

74. The Quota Act of 1921 (42 Stat. 5, sec. 2); Immigration Act of 1924 (43 Stat. 153). On the 1924 act, see generally Higham, *Strangers in the Land*, 308–24.

75. Divine, *American Immigration Policy*, 60; Melendy, "Filipinos in the United States," 115–16, 119–25.

76. One estimate places the number of Mexicans, including their American-born children, deported to Mexico at one million. See Balderrama and Rodriguez, *Decade of Betrayal*, 122.

77. The Immigration Act of 1891 established the Superintendent of Immigration (26 Stat. 1084). In 1894, the Bureau of Immigration was established (28 Stat. 390). The immigration service dates its inception to 1891.

78. Peffer, *If They Don't Bring Their Women Here*, 58–59; W. Chen, "Chinese under Both Exclusion and Immigration Laws," 91. The Page Law was also enforced by U.S. Consuls in Hong Kong (Act of Mar. 3, 1875 [18 Stat. 477]).

79. Act of May 6, 1882 (22 Stat. 58), secs. 4, 8.

80. See, for example, the Chinese Arrival Files, San Francisco, Records of the U.S. Immigration and Naturalization Service, National Archives.

81. Act of May 6, 1882 (22 Stat. 58), sec. 4; Act of May 26, 1924: the Immigration Act of 1924 (43 Stat. 153); e-mail communication with Marian Smith, historian, INS, Oct. 24, 2000. See also Torpey, *Invention of the Passport*, 97–99.

82. Act of May 6, 1882 (22 Stat. 58), sec. 4; Act of July 5, 1884 (23 Stat. 115); Coolidge, *Chinese Immigration*, 183–85; Peffer, *If They Don't Bring Their Women Here*. I borrow the description of "an early . . . system of 'remote control' involving passports and visas" from Torpey, *Invention of the Passport*, 97–99.

83. Act of May 5, 1892, "Geary Act" (27 Stat. 25), sec. 7, and Act of Nov. 3, 1893, "McCreary Amendment" (28 Stat. 7), sec. 2.

84. U.S. Department of Commerce and Labor, *Annual Reports* (1903), 156; U.S. Department of Commerce and Labor, *Annual Reports* (1909), 131.

85. The use of "immigrant identification cards" was first begun under U.S. consular regulations on July 1, 1928. Green cards were the product of the Alien Registration Act of 1940 and the corresponding INS Alien Registration Program (Act of June 28, 1940 [54 Stat. 670]; e-mail communication with Marian Smith, historian, INS, Oct. 26, 2000; Smith, "Why Isn't the Green Card Green?").

86. Coolidge, *Chinese Immigration*, 209–33; Torpey, *Invention of the Passport*, 100.

87. Act of May 6, 1882 (22 Stat. 58), secs. 7 and 11.

88. Ibid., sec. 12.

89. Act of Mar. 3, 1891 (26 Stat. 1084), and Act of Aug. 18, 1894 (28 Stat. 390).

90. U.S. Department of Commerce and Labor, *Annual Reports* (1903), 32.

91. Collector of Customs to Secretary of the Treasury, Dec. 3, 1883, Customs Case File No. 3358d Related to Chinese Immigration, 1877–91, Records of the U.S. Immigration and Naturalization Service, National Archives

92. U.S. Congress, House, Select Committee, *Investigation of Chinese Immigration*, 270–71.

93. Ibid.

94. Ibid., 279.

95. Salyer, *Laws Harsh as Tigers*, 69–93.

96. Resolution No. 17,673, Office of the Clerk of the Board of Supervisors, San Francisco, Dec. 10, 1884, Customs Case File No. 3358d Related to Chinese Immigration, 1877–91, Records of the U.S. Immigration and Naturalization Service, National Archives.

97. 23 Stat. 115. See Tsai, *Chinese Experience*, 66.

98. Act of Sept. 13, 1888 (25 Stat. 476, sec. 6, at 477).

99. Act of Oct. 1, 1888 (25 Stat. 504, sec. 2). The United States acted in retaliation in response to a rumor that China would not sign the new U.S.-China treaty.

100. Sandmeyer, *Anti-Chinese Movement in California*, 102.

101. Act of May 5, 1892 (27 Stat. 25).

102. Act of July 7, 1898 (30 Stat. 750); Act of Apr. 30, 1900 (31 Stat. 141); *San Francisco Call*, Nov. 22, 1901.

103. *San Francisco Call*, Nov. 22, 1901.

104. Act of Apr. 29, 1902, "Chinese Immigration Prohibited" (32 Stat. 176).

105. Act of Apr. 27, 1904 (33 Stat. 428).

106. See Erika Lee, *At America's Gates*, especially pp. 111–146.

REFERENCES

Abbott, Edith. *Historical Aspects of the Immigration Problem*. Chicago: University of Chicago Press, 1926.

Almaguer, Tomás. *Racial Fault Lines: The Historical Origins of White Supremacy in California*. Berkeley: University of California Press, 1994.

Asiatic Exclusion League of North America. "Proceedings of the Asiatic Exclusion League," February 1908. San Francisco: Allied Printing, 1908.

———. "Proceedings of the Asiatic Exclusion League," December 1908. San Francisco: Allied Printing, 1908.

———. "Proceedings of the Asiatic Exclusion League," July 1911. San Francisco: Allied Printing, 1911.

Balderrama, Francisco E., and Raymond Rodriguez. *Decade of Betrayal: Mexican Repatriation in the 1930s*. Albuquerque: University of New Mexico Press, 1995.

Barrett, James, and David Roediger. "Inbetween Peoples: Race, Nationality and the 'New Immigrant' Working Class." *Journal of American Ethnic History* 6, no. 3 (1997): 3–44.

Burnham, Frederick Russell. "The Howl for Cheap Mexican Labor." In *The Alien in Our Midst or Selling Our Birthright for a Mess of Pottage*, edited by Madison Grant and Charles Stewart Davison. New York: Galton Publishing, 1930.

California State Senate. Special Committee on Chinese Immigration. *Chinese Immigration: Its Social, Moral, and Political Effect*. Sacramento, Calif.: State Office of Printing, 1878.

Cardoso, Lawrence. *Mexican Emigration to the United States, 1891–1931*. Tucson: University of Arizona Press, 1980.

Chan, Sucheng. *Asian Americans: An Interpretive History*. Boston: Twayne, 1991.

———. "The Exclusion of Chinese Women, 1875–1943." In *Entry Denied: Exclusion and the Chinese Community in America, 1882–1943*, edited by Sucheng Chan, 94–146. Philadelphia: Temple University Press, 1991.

———. *This Bittersweet Soil: The Chinese in California Agriculture, 1860–1910*. Berkeley: University of California Press, 1986.

———, ed. *Entry Denied: Exclusion and the Chinese Community in America, 1882–1943*. Philadelphia: Temple University Press, 1991.

Chan, Sucheng, and K. Scott Wong, eds. *Claiming America: Constructing Chinese American Identities during the Exclusion Era*. Philadelphia: Temple University Press, 1998.

Chen, Helen. "Chinese Immigration into the United States: An Analysis of Changes in Immigration Policies." Ph.D. dissertation, Brandeis University, 1980.

Chen, Wen-hsien. "Chinese under Both Exclusion and Immigration Laws." Ph.D. dissertation, University of Chicago, 1940.

Cheng, Lucie. "Free, Indentured, Enslaved: Chinese Prostitutes in 19th Century America." *Signs: Journal of Women in Culture and Society* 5 (1979): 23–29.

Coolidge, Mary Roberts. *Chinese Immigration*. New York: Henry Holt and Co. 1909.

Daniels, Roger. *Asian America: Chinese and Japanese in the United States since 1850*. Seattle: University of Washington Press, 1988.

———. *Coming to America: A History of Immigration and Ethnicity in American Life*. New York: Harper Collins, 1990.

———. "No Lamps Were Lit for Them: Angel Island and the Historiography of Asian American immigration." *Journal of American Ethnic History* 17, no. 1 (fall 1997): 3–18.

———. *The Politics of Prejudice: The Anti-Japanese Movement in California and the Struggle for Japanese Exclusion*. Berkeley: University of California Press, 1962.

———. "Westerners from the East: Oriental Immigrants Reappraised." *Pacific Historical Review* 35 (1966): 373–83.

Divine, Robert A. *American Immigration Policy, 1924–1952*. New York: Da Capo Press, 1957.

Foley, Neil. *The White Scourge: Mexicans, Blacks, and Poor Whites in Texas Cotton Culture*. Berkeley: University of California Press, 1997.

Friday, Chris. "'In Due Time': Narratives of Race and Place in the Western U.S." In *Race, Ethnicity, and Nationality in the United States: Toward the Twenty-first Century*, edited by Paul Wong, 102–52. Boulder, Colo.: Westview Press, 1999.

Gabaccia, Donna. *From the Other Side: Women, Gender, and Immigration Life in the U.S., 1820–1990*. Bloomington: Indiana University Press, 1994.

———. "Is Everywhere Nowhere? Nomads, Nations, and the Immigrant Paradigm of United States History." *Journal of American History* 86, no. 3 (1999): 1115–34.

————. "The 'Yellow Peril' and the 'Chinese of Europe': Global Perspectives on Race and Labor, 1815–1930." In *Migration, Migration History, History: Old Paradigms and New Perspectives*, edited by Jan Lucassen and Leo Lucassen, 177–96. Bern, N.Y.: Peter Lang, 1999.

Gompers, Samuel. "Some Reasons for Chinese Exclusion—Meat vs. Rice—American Manhood against Asiatic Coolieism—Which Shall Survive?" Washington, D.C.: American Federation of Labor, GPO, 1902.

Gotanda, Neil. "Exclusion and Inclusion: Immigration and American Orientalism." In *Across the Pacific: Asian Americans and Globalization*, edited by Evelyn Hu-DeHart, 129–51. Philadelphia: Temple University Press, 1999.

Grant, Madison, and Charles Stewart Davison, eds. *The Alien in Our Midst or Selling Our Birthright for a Mess of Pottage*. New York: Galton Publishing, 1930.

Gyory, Andrew. *Closing the Gate: Race, Politics, and the Chinese Exclusion Act*. Chapel Hill: University of North Carolina Press, 1998.

Higham, John. *Strangers in the Land: Patterns of American Nativism, 1860–1925*. 2d ed. New York: Atheneum, 1978.

Hoffman, Abraham. *Unwanted Mexican Americans in the Great Depression: Repatriation Pressures, 1929–1939*. Tucson: University of Arizona Press, 1974.

Hsu, Madeline. *Dreaming of Gold, Dreaming of Home: Transnationalism and Migration between the United States and South China, 1882–1943*. Stanford, Calif.: Stanford University Press, 2000.

Hutchinson, E. P. *Legislative History of American Immigration Policy, 1798–1965*. Philadelphia: University of Pennsylvania, 1981.

Ignatiev, Noel. *How the Irish Became White*. New York: Routledge, 1995.

Immigration Restriction League Scrapbooks, 1894–1912. Boston Public Library, Boston, Massachusetts.

Jacobson, Matthew Frye. *Barbarian Virtues: The United States Encounters Foreign Peoples at Home and Abroad, 1876–1917*. New York: Hill and Wang, 2000.

————. *Whiteness of a Different Color: European Immigrants and the Alchemy of Race*. Cambridge, Mass.: Harvard University Press, 1998.

Lea, Homer. *The Valor of Ignorance*. New York: Harper and Brothers, 1909.

Lee, Erika. *At America's Gates: Chinese Immigration during the Exclusion Era, 1882–1943*. Chapel Hill: University of North Carolina Press, 2003.

Lee, Robert. *Orientals: Asian Americans in Popular Culture*. Philadelphia: Temple University Press, 1999.

Leong, Karen J. "'A Distant and Antagonistic Race': Constructions of Chinese Manhood in the Exclusionist Debates, 1869–1878." In *Across the Great Divide: Cultures of Manhood in the American West*, edited by Laura McCall, Matthew Basso, and Dee Garceau, 131–48. New York: Routledge, 2000.

Liu, Fu-ju. "A Comparative Demographic Study of Native-Born and Foreign-Born Chinese Populations in the United States." Ph.D. dissertation, University of Michigan, 1953.

Lodge, Henry Cabot. "The Restriction of Immigration." *North American Review* 152 (January 1891): 27–36.

Massachusetts Bureau of Statistics of Labor. *Twelfth Annual Report of the Bureau of Statistics of Labor*. Boston: Wright and Potter, 1881.

Mazumdar, Sucheta. "Through Western Eyes: Discovering Chinese Women in America." In *A New Significance: Re-envisioning the History of the American West*, edited by Clyde Milner, 158–67. New York: Oxford University Press, 1996.

McClatchy, V. S. "Oriental Immigration." In *The Alien in Our Midst or Selling Our Birthright for a Mess of Pottage*, edited by Madison Grant and Charles Stewart Davison. New York: Galton Publishing, 1930.

McKeown, Adam. *Chinese Migrant Networks and Cultural Change: Peru, Chicago, Hawaii, 1900–1936*. Chicago: University of Chicago Press, 2001.

Melendy, H. Brett. "The Filipinos in the United States." In *The Asian-American: The Historical Experience*, edited by Norris Hundley, 101–28. Santa Barbara, Calif.: American Bibliography Center, CLIO Press, 1976.

Miller, Stuart Creighton. *The Unwelcome Immigrant: The American Image of the Chinese, 1785–1882*. Berkeley: University of California Press, 1969.

Mink, Gwendolyn. *Old Labor and New Immigrants in American Political Development: Union, Party, and State, 1875–1920*. Ithaca, N.Y.: Cornell University Press, 1986.

National Archives, Pacific Region, San Bruno California. Records of the U.S. Immigration and Naturalization Service. RG 85. Chinese Arrival Files, San Francisco and Honolulu.

National Archives, Washington D.C. Records of the U.S. Immigration and Naturalization Services. RG 85. Customs Case File No. 3358d Related to Chinese Immigration, 1877–91.

Ngai, Mae. "The Architecture of Race in American Immigration Law: A Reexamination of the Immigration Act of 1924." *Journal of American History* 86, no. 1 (1999): 67–92.

———. "Legacies of Exclusion: Illegal Chinese Immigration during the Cold War Years." *Journal of American Ethnic History* 18, no. 1 (1998): 3–35.

Peffer, George Anthony. *If They Don't Bring Their Women Here: Chinese Female Immigration before Exclusion*. Urbana: University of Illinois Press, 1999.

Roediger, David. *The Wages of Whiteness: Race and the Making of the American Working Class*. New York: Verso, 1991.

Rowell, Chester H. "Chinese and Japanese Immigrants—A Comparison." *Annals of the American Academy of Political and Social Sciences* 34, no. 2 (September 1909): 3–10.

———. "Why Make Mexico an Exception?" *Survey*, May 1, 1931, 180.

Said, Edward. *Orientalism*. New York: Vintage, 1979.

Salyer, Lucy. *Laws Harsh as Tigers: Chinese Immigrants and the Shaping of Modern Immigration Law*. Chapel Hill: University of North Carolina Press, 1995.

Sánchez, George J. *Becoming Mexican American: Ethnicity, Culture, and Identity in Chicano Los Angeles, 1900–1945*. New York: Oxford University Press, 1993.

———. "Race, Nation, and Culture in Recent immigration Studies." *Journal of American Ethnic History* 18, no. 4 (1999): 66–84.

Sandmeyer, Elmer C. *The Anti-Chinese Movement in California*. Urbana: University of Illinois Press, 1939.

Saxton, Alexander. *The Indispensable Enemy: Labor and the Anti-Chinese Movement in California*. Berkeley: University of California Press, 1971.

Smith, Marian L. "Why Isn't the Green Card Green?" <http://www.ins.usdoj.gov/graphics/aboutins/history/articles/Green.htm>. January 3, 2001.

Solomon, Barbara Miller. *Ancestors and Immigrants: A Changing New England Tradition*. Cambridge: Harvard University Press, 1956.

Stoddard, Lothrop. "The Permanent Menace from Europe." In *The Alien in Our Midst or Selling Our Birthright for a Mess of Pottage*, edited by Madison Grant and Charles Stewart Davison. New York: Galton Publishing, 1930.

Takaki, Ronald. *Iron Cages: Race and Culture in Nineteenth Century America*. New York: Oxford University Press, 1979.

Tchen, John Kuo Wei. *New York before Chinatown: Orientalism and the Shaping of American Culture, 1776–1882*. Baltimore: Johns Hopkins University Press, 1999.

Torpey, John. *The Invention of the Passport: Surveillance, Citizenship, and the State*. New York: Cambridge University Press, 2000.

Tsai, Shih-Shan Henry. *The Chinese Experience in America*. Bloomington: Indiana University Press, 1986.

U.S. Congress. House. Select Committee on Immigration and Naturalization. *Investigation of Chinese Immigration*. 51st Cong., 2d sess. H. Doc. 4048, serial 2890. Washington, D.C.: GPO, 1890.

U.S. Congress. Joint Special Committee to Investigate Chinese Immigration. *Chinese Immigration*. 44th Cong., 2d sess., S. Rept. 689. Washington, D.C.: GPO, 1877.

U.S. Department of Commerce and Labor. *Annual Reports of the Commissioner-General of Immigration*. Washington, D.C.: GPO, 1903–11.

Warne, Frank Julian. *The Immigrant Invasion*. New York: Dodd, Mead, and Co., 1913.

White, Richard. "Race Relations in the American West." *American Quarterly* 38 (1986): 396–416.

Wittke, Carl. *We Who Built America: The Saga of the Immigrant.* New York: Prentice-Hall, 1939.

Wong, K. Scott. "Cultural Defenders and Brokers: Chinese Responses to the Anti-Chinese Movement." In *Claiming America: Constructing Chinese American Identities during the Exclusion Era,* edited by Sucheng Chan and K. Scott Wong, 3–40. Philadelphia: Temple University Press, 1998.

PUBLIC HEALTH AND THE MAPPING OF CHINATOWN

Nayan Shah

Nineteenth-century San Francisco journalists, politicians, and health officials feared an impending epidemic catastrophe festering in the tenements of what was then labeled as Chinatown. In the press coverage of public health inspections, newspaper reporters described the Chinatown labyrinth as hundreds of underground passageways connecting the filthy "cellars" and cramped "garrets" where Chinese men lived. In their salacious portrayals, journalists related how dozens of Chinese men slept on narrow wooden shelves squeezed into claustrophobic rooms, "which was considered close quarters for a single white man." Opium fumes, tobacco smoke, and putrefying waste pervaded the atmosphere in these windowless and unventilated rooms, and "each cellar [was] ankle-deep with loathsome slush, with ceilings dripping with percolations of other nastiness above, [and] with walls slimy with the clamminess of Asiatic diseases."[1]

Periodic public health investigations—both informal midnight journeys and official fact-finding missions—fed the alarm about the danger Chinese men and women posed to white Americans' health. Seizing upon the suspected causes of contamination, health officials emphasized the "overcrowded" tenements, "unventilated underground habitations," and stale "nauseating" air.[2] These investigations produced a "knowledge" of Chinese women and men's seemingly unhygienic habits, the unsanitary conditions in which they lived, and the dangerous diseases they carried. The widespread publicity of the horrors of percolating waste, teeming bodies, and a polluted atmosphere in Chinese habitations underscored the vile and infectious menace of Chinatown spaces. Almost at once the threat of illness became the legitimate grounds for the city government's intervention and shaped health policy toward Chinatown and Chinese residents.

How did these revolting images become the incontestable truth about Chinese residents of San Francisco? How did the descriptions offered by health officers and journalists achieve the stature of scientific knowledge and pervasiveness of common sense? In order to understand how quickly public-health knowledge came to identify a place and its inhabitants as dangerous, it is necessary to examine the process by which description became policy through scientific knowledge. The category of Chinese race and place created the field of study for investigations; strategies of scientific knowing generated the rich descriptive data that were then interpreted by medical reasoning. This formation of scientific knowledge shaped regulatory policy that in turn spurred further investigations, and the process of knowledge creation intensified.

The investigations targeted Chinatown, identifying its location and its boundaries and surveying the spaces within it. In the nineteenth and early twentieth centuries, "Chinatown" ghettos proliferated in both cities and small towns throughout North America. The generic naming of a Chinatown in some locations referred to a handful of buildings and in others to a set of streets. Although the physical boundaries of these "Chinatowns" constantly shifted, the name signaled a potent racial designation of Chinese immigrant inhabitation. The cartography of Chinatown that was developed in government investigations, newspaper reports, and travelogues both established "knowledge" of the Chinese race and aided in the making and remaking of Chinatown. The idea of Chinatown as a self-contained and alien society in turn justified "recurring rounds" of policing, investigation, and statistical surveys that "scientifically" corroborated the racial classification.[3]

The creation of "knowledge" of Chinatown relied upon three key spatial elements: dens, density, and the labyrinth. The enclosed and inhuman spaces of dens were where the Chinese lived. High density was the condition in which they lived. And the labyrinth was the unnavigable maze that characterized both the subterranean passageways within the buildings and the streets and alleys aboveground. These spatial elements established the basic contours of the representation of Chinatown and provided the canvas for detailed renderings of Chinese living styles, conditions, and behaviors. The investigations and the accompanying publicity not only established the Chinatown spatial elements of dens, density, and the labyrinth but also generated the stereotyped imagery that would be used more intensively over the decades and that illuminates how racial categories in the United States were produced in the late nineteenth century and persisted in the twentieth century.

Five government-sponsored investigations were both emblematic and politically pivotal in defining the Chinatown menace: the 1854 inquiry by the San Francisco Common Council (the precursor to the San Francisco Board of Supervisors) that reestablished the municipal Board of Health; the investigation that resulted in the 1869 report of the San Francisco health officer C. M. Bates; the 1871 investigation by Dr. Thomas Logan, the secretary of the California State Board of Health; the 1880 inspection by the Board of Health that declared Chinatown a "nuisance"; and the 1885 survey of Chinatown by the San Francisco Board of Supervisors. Although these expeditions were not always led by physicians, medical expertise shaped their findings and implicitly supported the "truth" they exposed. From 1854 to 1885, reports of every official investigation recycled these spatial metaphors and both consistently and uncritically channeled the imagery of "dense" and "enclosed" living conditions into the interpretive framework of epidemic danger for white San Francisco residents.

Over the span of forty years, four strategies of scientific knowing developed that transformed the knowledge of Chinatown. These strategies were scientific observation, standards of normalcy and deviance, statistics, and mapping. Scientific observation emphasized firsthand descriptions. These descriptions were offered in a realist style, evoking a travel narrative rich in visceral sensory details. The strategy of creating standards of normalcy and deviance was especially critical to evaluating density in residential space. This primarily involved the calculation of room dimensions in relation to the number of inhabitants. Against the yardstick of the middle-class white ideal, Chinese residential practices were, therefore, designated as deviant and a sign of inhumanity. The strategy of using statistics stipulated the frequency of health violations and census enumeration of the inhabitants. The enumeration demonstrated both the ordinariness and the extensiveness of the dangerous conditions in Chinatown. Finally, through the regularity and thoroughness of sanitary surveillance, the public health authorities developed a map that identified every business and residence in Chinatown.[4] It was the combined weight of all four strategies that enhanced the intensity of scientific knowledge formation and substantiated claims to objective truth.

By 1880, the understanding of Chinatown as the site of filth, disease, and inhuman habitation had achieved a pervasiveness in public discourse as both scientific truth and common sense. Political discourse, travel writing, journalism, and public health reports all shared these strategies of scientific knowledge and interpretation. Public health alone did not invent this knowledge of Chinatown but rather organized it. The persuasive power of public health knowledge was its capacity to identify, intensify, and relentlessly classify popular representations into a limited array of mutually sustaining racial and medical meanings. The shared knowledge of Chinatown produced explanations that tenaciously connected the Chinese race to place, behavior, and cultural differences and framed the endurance of the Chinatown ghetto as a living repository of the strange, peculiar, and unassimilable in San Francisco.[5]

INVESTIGATING CHINESE SETTLEMENT

Medical interest and municipal investigation of Chinese settlement began in 1854, when it was first possible to see and describe a San Francisco street as being predominantly "Chinese." The Chinese population had grown rapidly from a handful in 1848 to more than 2,000 Chinese residents six years later. The first substantial number of Chinese immigrants had entered the port of San Francisco in 1849. Chinese men, mostly from the southeastern province of Guangdong, emigrated in large numbers to California in the early 1850s. In California overall, the Chinese population leaped from 450 in 1850 to 20,026 in 1852. The Cantonese men called their destination *Gamsaan*, or Gold Mountain. Lured by the 1848 gold strike in the Sierra, most Chinese men traveled to the hinterlands to seek their fortunes. Even so, Chinese men accounted for 12 percent of San Francisco's total population, and a visible cluster of Chinese businesses emerged on Sacramento Street, between Kearny Street and Dupont Street. Chinese residents and travelers themselves recognized the cluster of their compatriots' businesses and in time called Sacramento Street *Tongyan gaai,* or "Street of the Chinese."[6]

In August 1854 a local physician, Dr. William Rabe, was perturbed by the "filthy" conditions on Sacramento Street and demanded that the Common Council immediately investigate the Chinese settlement in the city. The unhealthy living conditions of Chinese residents aggravated council members' concerns about Chinese immigration.[7] The council's official investigation of the nascent Chinese district became the model for the next half century's expeditions. These expeditions presumed first that discrete racial territories existed, and then that their features could be known through direct observation and expert analysis. In 1854, city council officials enlisted a police officer to conduct a tour and ferret out the hidden dangers of the settlement. The party was accompanied by Dr. Rabe, who provided medical expertise to diagnose the territory's problems.[8]

The political atmosphere around the 1854 investigation was charged, however, with the tensions of escalating anti-Chinese politics and the specter of epidemic disease. The *Daily Alta California,* an avowed opponent of Chinese immigration and the leading daily in the city, claimed that the Chinese were "notoriously filthy," an assertion that could be validated by "taking a walk through any of the Chinese quarters of the City."[9] News of a cholera epidemic heightened worries about Chinese filth. The newspaper issued frequent reports of a national cholera epidemic, detailing weekly death tolls in major Eastern cities and the rapid spread of cholera westward.[10] This coverage revisited the history of nineteenth-century cholera epidemics; the October 1850 outbreak was responsible for forty deaths in San Francisco.

The *Daily Alta* editors warned their readers that despite overall improvements in sanitation, cholera could erupt in "filthy localities like the Chinese quarters" because "cholera delights in filth, in decaying garbage, and stagnant water, and dirty clothing and filthy bodies: particularly when all of these are united in crowded localities." The editors employed popularized medical knowledge about the causes of cholera—waste, contaminated water, and filth—and combined it with an abhorrence of "crowded" and impoverished localities and bodies. The wave of cholera epidemics in Europe and in the United States since 1832 had generated intense medical and popular debate about the causes and spread of the disease. Although there was recognition that social status offered no immunity to the disease, there was a widespread moral and medical belief that the living conditions of society's poor and marginal were responsible for the spread of cholera. The *Daily Alta* had characterized the spaces inhabited by the Chinese as "dirty, filthy dens" where "sickly" Chinese were "piled together like pigs in a pen." The editors called upon municipal authorities to enforce sanitary regulations to eliminate these "dens" and expel the Chinese population from the city.[11]

These images of filth, density, and sickliness reappeared in the Common Council's investigation. The report identified the most intense dangers as being in the boardinghouses owned by the so-called Chinese Companies and depicted them as the "filthiest places that could be imagined." In some of these dormitories "hundreds of Chinamen are crowded together . . . and the stench which pervade [s] the air is insupportable." The crowding and filth generated rampant disease and resulted in high illness rates that affected 10 to 15 percent of the occupants of each house on average. Physicians and middle-class commentators in the period perceived the unsanitary living conditions as both evidence of moral turpitude and an incubator of fatal epidemics. The filth and density of the homes of the poor and working classes enfeebled the occupants, making them unusually susceptible to common illnesses and even more vulnerable to epidemics. The investigating committee concluded that the Chinese settlement posed a health menace to the rest of the city's inhabitants; for example, the "excessive" number of Chinese was "dangerous to the health of the inhabitants owing to the crowded state of the houses of Chinamen, the sickness which they introduce and the extreme and habitual filthy condition of their persons and their habitations."[12]

The Chinese were characterized repeatedly in terms of "excess"—of their number, of their living densities, of the diseases they spawned, and of the waste they produced. The references to excess and extremes stood in menacing contrast to the presumed norms of the white middle class. The danger of excess lay in its perceived capacity to expand across class and racial differences and spatial boundaries, carrying lethal contagion. The investigators feared not only that cholera would "make short work of the Chinese in their quarters" but also that it would strike "our own citizens." The differentiation between Chinese "aliens" and the municipal "citizens" enabled the committee to entertain the suggestion of taking "extraordinary measures" to suppress the epidemic by expelling the Chinese and thereby "removing from our midst the germs of pestilence." In their rhetoric, the committee members shifted from attributing the health threat to collective Chinese *behavior* to denouncing the Chinese as the very *embodiment* of disease. Their substitution revealed how effortlessly the classification of racial difference could shift from social to biological attributes. Despite the interest in radical removal, the committee endorsed a plan to revive the Board of Health, implement health regulations, and appoint a public health officer to enforce them. Although the committee failed to remove the Chinese population, whom they regarded as disease carriers, they demanded that the Chinese Companies make provisions to take "their sick countrymen outside the city limits."[13]

Early in the history of Chinese settlement, Chinese merchants took the lead in establishing associations, known in Chinese as *huiguan* (literally, meeting halls), which translated into English as "company." The immigrants from each of the districts of Guangdong province spoke different dialects of Cantonese and identified strongly with places of origin. The district *huiguan* served as a mutual-aid umbrella group that comprised various subgroups organized around village origins and surnames. These associations were run by elected officers, usually merchants, and they provided their members with accommodations, work and business opportunities, and when necessary, health care and burial assistance. Although relations between the district *huiguan* were often strained, these *huiguan* banded together to respond to local and national political, immigration, and legal challenges. In the 1870s, the coordinating council of six *huiguan*—the Zhonghua (Chinese) Huiguan—adopted a formal English name, the Chinese Consolidated Benevolent Association (CCBA), and was commonly known as the "Six Companies."[14]

In 1854 leaders of several district *huiguan*, who referred to themselves as "respectable Chinese residents," convened the day before the Common Council hearings to respond to the report's recommendations. Supporting the public health concerns about the deleterious relationship between filth, crowding, and disease, the Chinese merchants developed a series of resolutions intended to "remove the causes of complaints which have been made recently against the Chinese." These resolutions included assurances that boardinghouses would be "cleaned and renovated" and "excess boarders" immediately removed, that "all Chinamen present will take immediate steps to have their premises cleaned," and that a hospital would be built on the outskirts of the city. Seeking to develop moral distinctions within the Chinese population, these Chinese merchants invited the intervention of inspectors to "force" noncompliant Chinese to abate "nuisances." They were eager to claim that the merchants represented at the meeting were law-abiding and responsive to the concerns of the city government. The business elite represented at the meeting served to further establish its "respectable" status by differentiating its members from those merchants engaged in illicit business. They requested that the police suppress Chinese brothels and gambling houses, "which the meeting considers to be a great grievance to the Chinese residents." In every regard, the merchants who petitioned the city council sought to ensure that the "innocent shall not suffer with the guilty."[15]

The "respectable merchants" retreated from a class condemnation of the Chinese laborers living in boardinghouses. Instead they denounced the brothel keepers and gambling-den owners. They conflated the operation of illicit businesses with sanitary negligence. Since the respectable merchants operated the boardinghouses, they were eager to prove compliance with city regulations and their good intentions. In the mid-nineteenth century, service delivery in the city was uneven and garbage collection and even police protection were transacted privately by businesspeople and residence owners. Merchants complained that white police officers collected weekly payments from merchants on Sacramento and Dupont Streets to "clean their respective quarters" and provide protection, but these same merchants rarely received proper trash removal or sanitary services. They felt helpless to redress the police extortion and fraud in light of the absence of regular city services.

The Chinese merchants' pledge to build a "suitable" hospital for Chinese immigrants outside city limits raised questions about the civic ambivalence toward providing services to the Chinese and especially about the unwillingness to include Chinese residents in the body politic. The city council's unusual requirement that they build outside city limits expressed the fear that "sick Chinese" would radiate contagion and the belief that they must be removed beyond city boundaries. City council members further questioned the effectiveness of Chinese medical treatment and hospital care and in the end refused any plans for a Chinese hospital. These suspicions belied the unwillingness of city and state officials to take any responsibility for providing health care and for opening the public hospitals to Chinese patients. The *Daily Alta* editor argued that the state of California was responsible for ill Chinese immigrants. In 1852 the state legislature had passed a tax on passengers arriving at the port of San Francisco, in order to pay the costs of the State Marine Hospital in San Francisco and public hospitals in Sacramento and Stockton. Although Chinese immigrants contributed substantial tax receipts, these immigrants were not entitled to medical care and treatment in public facilities.[16]

The cholera panic quickly subsided in September 1854, and in its wake emerged a new city health authority in the revived Board of Health and a new perception of space, race, and contagion. The *Daily Alta* disingenuously criticized the "unnecessary alarm among the nervous portion of our citizens." Without acknowledging the newspaper's own responsibility in fanning the hysteria with reports of "authenticated [Chinese] cases" of cholera the week before, the *Daily Alta* editor admonished those who would rely upon "rumors."[17] The hysteria and rumors created fears based on a new articulation of space and race. Chinatown had become a singular and separate place that henceforth could be targeted in official inspections and popular commentary.

From a single block on Sacramento Street in 1854, the territory described as Chinatown expanded by 1885 to a fifteen-square-block region bounded by Kearny, Broadway, Sacramento, and Powell Streets. The growth to the west and north was shaped by the hilly topography, exponential population growth, and the rapid articulation of other zones of the city. The Chinese businesses and residences spread rapidly west up the hill to Powell Street and north to the relatively flat streets as far as Broadway. The sharp ridges on California Street limited the expansion south. Although in the 1850s the businesses and residences occupied by the Chinese immigrants were located throughout the city, by the 1870s these businesses and residences had been consolidated in the Chinatown zone. In the last third of the century, the borders of Chinatown abutted four defined zones of the city: the elite residential district of Nob Hill on the west; the main commercial and business districts on the south and east; and the Latin Quarter (which in the twentieth century became known as North Beach) to the north.

The number of Chinese residents remained stable during the decade of the 1850s, but like San Francisco's population as a whole, the number of Chinese residents climbed rapidly in the 1860s. The total population of San Francisco nearly tripled in size, to 149,473, and the Chinese population quadrupled to over 12,000 in 1870. By the 1880 census the Chinese population stood at 21,745, out of a total of 233,979. In the 1860s, Chinese commercial enterprises and labor contractors set up business in San Francisco. Workers often circulated through the city between work contracts for rural agriculture and construction. After the completion of the Central Pacific Railroad, Chinese immigrant workers migrated to San

Francisco, where they found work in the growing manufacturing industries and service trades.[18] The Chinese were the largest racial minority group in San Francisco at the time. By comparison, the population of blacks hovered between 1,100 and 1,800 throughout the nineteenth century.[19]

Although throughout the late nineteenth century the area called Chinatown had a variety of inhabitants, the predominance of Chinese residents meant the entire location had only one racial identity. Businesses and residences occupied by Irish, Italian, Portuguese, Mexican, Canadian, and Anglo Americans continued to thrive in so-called Chinatown, but they were of little interest to the health inspectors. These inspectors imagined the preeminent site of contagion as the spaces of Chinese residence, particularly the bunking houses of Chinese bachelor workers.

In the late 1860s and 1870s the increase in Chinese population exacerbated white fear of Chinese spaces. Health officials continued to identify Chinese behavior as the cultural cause of the perceived medical menace. In 1869 the city health officer C. M. Bates issued his report stating that Chinese "habits and manner of life are of such a character as to breed and engender disease wherever they reside." In the report, Bates warned that "unless their style of life is changed[,] . . . some disease of a malignant form may break out among them and communicate itself to our Caucasian population." Bates feared the perceived lethal consequences of Chinese living standards and styles: "As a class, their mode of life is the most abject in which it is possible for human beings to exist. The great majority of them live crowded together in rickety, filthy and dilapidated tenement houses, like so many cattle or hogs. Considering their mode of life, it is indeed wonderful that they have so far escaped every phase of disease. In passing through that portion of the city occupied by them, the most absolute squalidness and misery meets one at every turn. Vice in all its hideousness is on every hand."[20]

The "abjectness" of the Chinese "mode of life" was manifested in the comparisons to farm animals, feeding a perception not only of Chinese immigrants' inferiority but also of their inhumanity. In health reports and journalistic reports of health inspections, Chinese were likened to a wide array of animals, including rats, hogs, and cattle. The choice of animals underscored a relationship to waste and an imperviousness to crowding. As David Sibley has observed, rats and pigs especially have had a "particular place in the racist bestiary because all are associated with residues—food waste, human waste—and in the case of rats there is an association with spaces which border civilized society, particular subterranean spaces like sewers, which also channel residues and from which rats occasionally emerge to transgress the boundaries of society."[21] The insinuations that the Chinese were wallowing in cesspools and in possession of an instinct for crowded, decaying environments made the metonyms of reviled creatures all the more menacing and transgressive to the readers. Like pigs and cattle herded into pens, the living densities of Chinese "dens" demonstrated Chinese indifference to human comforts. Bates claimed that "apartments that would be deemed small for the accommodation of a single American [were] occupied by six, eight or ten Mongolians, with seeming indifference to all ordinary comforts."[22] The Chinese were presumed to relish these "miserable" circumstances of poverty, squalor, and filth.

As city health officer, a position created in the 1870 reorganization of the Board of Health, Bates held responsibility for the daily enforcement of sanitary regulations. Therefore, his pronouncements carried the weight of regulative authority. He carefully cultivated the professional objectivity of a physician to buttress this authority and distanced himself from the opportunistic "politicians and demagogues" who had manipulated hostility toward the Chinese for political advantage. Bates was particularly concerned that his conclusions would be dismissed by the city's business community and elected officials because they appeared similar to those of the Anti-Coolie Association, a white labor group who opposed Chinese immigration and settlement.

The tension between the white manufacturers and white laborers was exacerbated by a devastating commercial panic and depression in the late 1860s. After the completion of the transcontinental railroad, San Francisco's population increased 30 percent in two years, but manufacturing output plummeted once trade from the East Coast made the price of consumer goods plunge. Thousands of white workingmen were unemployed, and they blamed white capitalists and the Chinese workers for their troubles. The Anti-Coolie Association formed in March 1867 and coordinated boycotts of manufacturers who employed Chinese workers. The organization engaged in selective industrial sabotage citywide and persistently harassed and assaulted Chinese men. Its rapid growth and frequently violent mobilization of anxious white tradesmen and unemployed workers alarmed San Francisco's commercial elite.[23]

The Anti-Coolie Association deftly borrowed and elaborated upon the medical menace of Chinese settlement. In 1869 the organization outlined the threat posed by Chinese immigrants to white labor, national prosperity, and the general health of American citizens. The 1868 smallpox epidemic, which had left 760 dead in its wake, served as an ominous sign of the extreme health dangers posed by Chinese immigration. The virulent strain of smallpox "baffled the skill of our medical men" and was "unknown among the Caucasian race." The Chinese allegedly bred disease as a result of the "density of their population and their peculiar mode of living." To the medical causality that Chinese living densities and habits contributed to infection, the Anti-Coolie Association added the ominous assertion that Chinese immigrants carried peculiar disease strains.[24]

This problem of the Chinese possessing potentially innate dispositions to illness was taken up by Thomas Logan, secretary of the California State Board of Health and a nationally reputed physician who was elected in 1872 as president of the American Medical Association. For the California State Board of Health, Logan had commissioned in 1871 an investigation of San Francisco's Chinatown, charging not only that Chinese habits and living conditions had vital implications for all San Francisco inhabitants but also that Chinatown's conditions could "spread dismay and desolation throughout the land." Logan was attentive to environmental conditions and behavior but feared the contagious consequences of Chinese innate racial propensities. Logan predicted that their "hereditary vices" or "engrafted peculiarities" preordained the Chinese to chronic and unusual illness. In Logan's assessment, Chinese cultural behavior was not shaped by historical context but rather emerged from hereditary traits that were naturalized in their very bodies. This conflation of behavior and body as both the cultural and biological heritage of the Chinese "race" powerfully influenced the public-health knowledge of Chinatown and Chinese people.[25]

Logan's investigation not only contributed new explanations of medical causality but also advanced a key strategy of accumulating knowledge about the Chinatown "underworld." Logan popularized the eyewitness journey into Chinatown's dens and proclaimed the journey's narrative as the primary evidence of its hidden horrors. The vivid and visceral narration of the midnight journey through Chinatown became one of the standard forms of knowledge used in both medical and popular accounts to establish the truth of Chinatown as the preeminent site of vice, immorality, degradation, crime, and disease.[26] By visiting and surveying Chinatown, individual doctors, journalists, and middle-class tourists delineated the utter foreignness, exoticism, and evil of the place. The firsthand account and the narration of visual and olfactory sensations provided authoritative and seemingly transparent evidence of the true nature of the Chinese problem. The eyewitness account became indispensable to the social diagnosis and policy advanced by health officers like Bates, who had concluded that "nothing short of an ocular demonstration can convey an idea of Chinese poverty and depravity."[27] Investigators later in the century recommended a visit to Chinatown for skeptics in order to ensure that the official findings were not considered an "exaggeration" or a fictional "sketch." These investigators were confident that an excursion through the Chinatown labyrinth would produce sufficient "ocular and olfactory proofs."[28]

The question of "proof" and "evidence" shaped the procedures and itinerary of the eyewitness investigation and its narrative report. Logan's journey emphasized all the characteristic procedures and features of the investigation. Despite the confidence that visual scrutiny would provide proof, Logan and other investigators simultaneously held a keen appreciation that the "truth" of Chinatown was hidden from public view. The most revealing journeys, then, had to be conducted at night, when the "true character" of the quarter—with its gambling houses, opium dens, and brothels—revealed itself. Logan solicited the services of a police escort to navigate the serpentine and subterranean passageways—the labyrinth— and to provide physical protection from routine threats of violence. His party also included the local medical expert, Bates, who could interpret the consequences of "vice and abominations." Although the itinerary of the investigation could include the "tangled maze of narrow streets" and "dark alleys," the crucial objective was to penetrate underground and visit the labyrinth of bunking houses, opium dens, and barricaded gambling houses. Logan's itinerary ignored other Chinatown spaces—the merchants' homes, dry goods stores, temples, meeting rooms, and Chinese opera theaters included in other kinds of travelogues—since these more visible sites offered little evidence of filth, sickness, and pathology that demanded medical evaluation.[29]

The narrative of Logan's midnight journey dispensed with the posture of professional objectivity and disinterested observation. His narrative featured a dramatic selection of circumstances, details, and medical explanation that passionately yielded the author's own personal and immediate sensations and reactions. Logan offered his medical colleagues and the curious public some instances of his momentary disorientation, horror, disgust, and fascination. He described his visit to the "lowest dens of degraded bestiality," where he saw opium smokers, prostitutes, and furtive gamblers. The investigators crept through "foul labyrinthine passages" that would occasionally "open into a dimly lit room," where they saw "dusky human beings lying on tiers of broad shelves . . . with a foul opium pipe, and dirty little oil lamp used for lighting the pipe." In other rooms, female prostitutes "with painted lips and rosy-tipped fingers" solicited the visitors, or male gamblers would "hurry and scuffle to conceal" their illicit games. In their inspection of large lodging houses, Logan discovered tiny rooms that had been "cut up and divided into what might be called pens."[30]

Logan's medical authority transformed sensational observations into somber appraisals of environmental conditions that necessitated immediate public health surveillance and redress. His medical scrutiny fixed on the insupportable "stench" that made his party feel "enveloped in a physical atmosphere as tainted and disgusting, from superadded stale opium smoke, as the moral one was degraded." Logan conflated the unventilated physical atmosphere with the moral degradation of opium smoking, gambling, and prostitution. Unventilated space that locked in stale smoke and produced a horrible "stench" violated "sanitary law," requiring "immediate redress." The "absolute absence of ventilation" provided the pretext for the intervention of the health officials. Influenced by the miasma theory of disease that remained popular in the 1870s, Logan regarded Chinatown, with its "foul and disgusting vapors" and unsanitary conditions, as the primary source of atmospheric pollution.[31]

Logan was assured in his ability to faithfully narrate the "real" conditions and offer authoritative diagnosis of social ills. This self-confident medical authority made it possible for him to draw freely from both literary and political sources and to repackage fictional and partisan rhetoric into irreproachable medical diagnosis. For instance, he borrowed literary allusions to heighten the drama of an opium den encounter. In subterranean dormitory "pens," Logan encountered "half naked" Chinese "inmates . . . reposing on shelves—some sleeping, others blowing out curling puffs of narcotic fumes from their broad nostrils." The immodesty, lethargy, and unabashed narcotic addiction recalled for Logan the figure of the "opium-smoking hag" in Charles Dickens's novel *Edwin Drood,* which presented a "graphic instance of civilization touching barbarism."[32] The dramatic literary scene amplified the dangers of Oriental "barbarism" in the midst of the "civilized," modern city of San Francisco, particularly with the horrifying possibility of white American men and women being discovered among the addicts. Logan worried about both the physical and moral dangers to the body and society that opium addiction posed.

Logan's ready use of literary analogy did not confound his purpose of exposing the "real" conditions of Chinatown. Logan used realist narrative devices and evoked Dickens's "morally-ordered universe" to effectively communicate the hidden dangers of Chinese habitation. Nineteenth-century realist narratives appeared in a range of forms—newspapers, government inquiry, autopsy reports, and novels. The popularity of represented and sensationalized reality offered readers melodramatic experiences, naturalistic details, and the disclosure of private truth to a public world. Logan's description of sensations and realist narrative secured his authority as the eyewitness observer. His revulsion and his unfaltering judgment, however, demonstrated his distance from his object of study and bolstered his claims to comprehensive knowledge of the true nature of the Chinese residents. Logan applied both medical and moral discernment in his prognosis of the dens and showed little concern that his readers would mistake his literary allusions for the facts of Chinatown's dangers.[33]

Logan was equally unfazed by the potential taint of political partisanship. In a discussion of density in the boardinghouses, Logan supplemented his analysis with a quote from the Anti-Coolie Association deputation to the San Francisco Board of Health: "Some houses have five hundred lodgers—some one thousand; and in the Globe Hotel—standing on ground sixty by sixty, and three stories high—there are twenty five hundred tenants." Once Logan had marshaled the Anti-Coolie Association anecdote about the Globe Hotel, he propelled that description into a popular and credible shorthand for the condition of all Chinese boardinghouses and a poignant example of the degeneration that followed Chinese habitation of any site. White travelogue writers and labor politicians freely seized on the devolution of the Globe Hotel at 1001 Dupont Street from the most opulent hotel for Gold Rush prospectors to a decaying and filthy tenement for the "flotsam and jetsam of Chinatown." All the official and popular accounts of the Globe Hotel shared a description of how, over the course of thirty years, the spacious and luxurious accommodations had been subdivided into congested and claustrophobic bunkrooms. Estimates of the number of inhabitants ranged from eight hundred to twenty-five hundred Chinese "crammed" inside.[34] The itinerary of this example—from Anti-Coolie deputation to Dr. Logan's report to the myriad popular travelogues—raises questions about precisely who investigated the building, what they saw, and how they arrived at the wide range of estimates. Was it even important to distinguish between the facts and an exaggeration in this migration from political anecdote to commonsense truth? The number of inhabitants reported simply accentuated the shared idea that Chinatown boardinghouses were extraordinarily crowded and overpopulated.

The sensationalist imagery overpowered the range of estimates, and all writers were quick to emphasize the typical and pervasive nature of the problem of density and crowding. The Anti-Coolie anecdote in 1869 claimed that "Chinamen have burrowed dens, even beneath the streets, holes that would 'not admit a coffin.'" The images of cramped, hidden, and subterranean living quarters that resembled "pens," "dens," "coffins," and "dungeons" was an imagery common to both physicians and political activists, reflecting ubiquitous anxiety and an abhorrence for crowded and dark spaces. These spaces were fit for animals, criminals, and the dead, not for human habitation.[35] In 1886, the travelogue writer Walter Raymond claimed that the general character of Chinese boardinghouses was a "noisome density in the atmosphere, which cannot be received into the system without great nausea. . . . Here can be experienced all the horrors of a catacomb, packed with living, disease-breeding flesh, slowly drifting into their graves."[36] The atmosphere Raymond related gave white readers every indication of the experience of being trapped alive in a grave. He detailed the horrors of visiting a place that lacked light, oxygen, and free space, the opposite of the sun-drenched, ventilated, airy, and clean middle-class home—the presumed type of home inhabited by the visitors and the readers.

However, these startling assessments of unhealthy Chinatown conditions raise the question of why such "gross violations" had not resulted in more frequent epidemic disaster. Unbelievably, Logan explained that the city was blessed by natural ventilation: "Were it not for the strong oceanic winds which prevail during the summer months, San Francisco would . . . have suffered the heaviest penalties." Over the years, many of the city's public health officials and physicians would evoke the presence of good crosswinds to explain the city population's relative good health despite the dangers posed by Chinatown. This explanation demonstrated how the environment could both contribute to epidemic and suppress it. In the miasma theory of infection, festering waste would breed disease in enclosed rooms, and natural ventilation could air out rooms with windows. Yet it remained a mystery as to how winds could quickly decontaminate the vapors that rose from the rotting waste in Chinatown's unventilated cellars before it infected its white neighbors in other parts of the city.[37]

The mysteries of infection and contamination had not, however, dissuaded white labor politicians from elaborating on discourses of racial hygiene in their struggles for political power. In the late 1860s complicated relationships had emerged between white working-class political mobilization, anti-Chinese ideology, public health, and municipal politics in San Francisco. These interests became increasingly entangled by the end of the decade. In 1877, at a moment of financial panic and the conclusion of a widespread smallpox epidemic, new political and social arrangements emerged that attributed economic distress and death to the Chinese "race." At the same time, workers organized the Workingmen's Party of California (WPC), which appropriated this "knowledge" in their political rhetoric and action.

The party became an increasingly potent political force in local and statewide politics. By the September 1879 general elections, the WPC had absorbed much of the Democratic Party's electoral constituency and swept dozens of candidates into office. On the state level, the Working-men's Party and the Republican Party split election results; a Republican became California's governor, while a WPC candidate won the seat of chief justice on the California Supreme Court. In San Francisco, after an extraordinary mayoral campaign punctuated by assassination attempts and accusations of sexual impropriety, the WPC candidate and pastor of the Baptist Metropolitan Temple, Issac Kalloch, won the mayoral race.[38] Kalloch's campaign swept into office WPC candidates for sheriff, auditor, tax collector, district attorney, and public administrator as well. The labor organizer Frank Roney speculated years later in his memoirs that a deal had been made between the WPC and the bipartisan establishment to divide municipal administration. The Workingmen's Party won the mayoralty and a number of posts controlling patronage, while the real power centers—the board of supervisors and the police—remained in the hands of the establishment Republicans and Democrats. The divided administration created intractable government deadlocks.[39]

In his inaugural address, Mayor Kalloch outlined a WPC mandate to use the powers of city government to remedy the Chinese problem, provide relief for unemployed white workers, and reduce the tax burden by a voluntary salary cut for all elected officials. Although the work relief and tax abatement programs required the approval of the hostile board of supervisors, Kalloch could directly influence the Board of Health in his capacity of presiding officer. The health officer John Meares and the other state-appointed physicians on the board—Henry Gibbons Jr., William Douglass, James A. Simpson, and Hugh Huger Toland—were already sympathetic to the idea that Chinatown was a threat to public health.[40] Immediately after Kalloch's inauguration, Meares and Gibbons conducted a rapid investigation of Chinatown. The WPC was eager to supplement the findings of the official investigation; in January its Anti-Chinese Council commissioned a committee of physicians and other sympathetic members to conduct their own investigation of Chinatown's sanitary conditions.[41]

In the 1880 Board of Health report on the living conditions in the Chinese quarter, Logan's images of slime, filth, and underground habitations were reapplied with even more horrifying detail than before. Gibbons, Meares, and Kalloch had conducted the investigation, concluding that "unnatural overcrowding" was detrimental to the health of the Chinese and endangered the "health of the city." They gave a detailed description of several of the subterranean dwellings:

> Near the entrance to this underground den there are large waste pipes running from the water-closets and sinks of the building above ground, which empty into open wooden boxes above the sewer, and the mass of filth is so great that the sewer is frequently choked and the troughs run over. The crowded occupants of the underground regions are hardly to blame for avoiding such wretched apologies as their "water-closets" for the purpose of nature. . . . Amongst all this smoke and stench and rottenness, in rooms barely 10×12, feet, 12 persons eat and sleep. . . . In another basement near by, thirteen Chinamen . . . live in a room eight feet square. In a room 6×6 feet ten Chinese men and women huddled together in beastly promiscuousness. . . . [These rooms] are absolutely without proper ventilation, and it seems unaccountable how human beings can live in them for a single night.[42]

These descriptions emphasized the sheer physicality of the "sickening filth" and "slime" and reiterated the animality and inhuman living density of the Chinese residents. In a boardinghouse where two hundred "Chinamen" lived, the report described "its inmates [as] having a ghastly look, and [they] are covered with a clammy perspiration. On the other side the rooms appeared to be filled with sick Chinamen, and ranged around the walls are chicken-coops, filled with what appeared to be sick chickens." [43] The equation of Chinese men with sick animals heightened perceptions of the intolerable, horrific living conditions and continued the comparison of Chinese to animals started by Bates.

The process of inspection and regulation of living conditions generated detailed knowledge of the location and nature of individual aberrations. Regulation, with its legal rules, standards, and threat of routine surveillance, generated knowledge that could be quantified and compared over time and against circumstances in other buildings and neighborhoods. The report catalogued dozens of health ordinances that the "Chinese people" habitually violated. During the 1870s, the city had passed ordinances regulating housing density, garbage disposal, the quarantine of contagious disease victims, the sanitary condition of food vendors, the condition of sewage systems, the construction of toilets, and the condition and location of hospitals. The report detailed a litany of stopped-up sewers, stench, and slime, all of which provided yardsticks by which to judge the unsanitary living conditions.[44]

When the committee catalogued the public health infractions in the Chinese quarter, they were quick to repudiate the idea that their investigation was biased by "race prejudice or class hatred," neglecting to consider how both race and class discrimination had forced Chinese immigrants to live in crowded and dilapidated tenements. They complimented some Chinese for "living quite decently and cleanly as any people could do who have to live under similar circumstances." The committee members emphasized that Chinatown—not necessarily the Chinese people—was a nuisance. The Board of Health unanimously adopted the report and the motion to declare Chinatown a nuisance to the public's health arid welfare. The investigating members of the board adamantly advocated that the "Chinese cancer must be cut out of the heart of the city." They reasoned that such radical action would benefit "the Chinese themselves" as well as "our people." However, their rhetoric revealed that their disgust of Chinatown actually did extend to the "health-defying" and "law-defying" Chinese women and men themselves.[45]

At the February 25, 1880, meeting, the Republican-dominated board of supervisors initially supported the Board of Health's condemnation of Chinatown as a "sanitary nuisance." However, the board of supervisors expressed concern that the health notice would fuel an extralegal "incendiary" response by white workingmen, and promptly gave orders to the police to hire four hundred additional officers. Supported by the local business establishment, the board of supervisors feared a recurrence of the 1877 riot, where a white working-class mob threatened to torch Chinatown. Not only were the businessmen and the supervisors concerned with maintaining the general social order, many of the white business elite were protecting their own interests: the majority of property leased by Chinese businesses and residents was owned by white businessmen. The WPC suspected that the bipartisan establishment that controlled the police would resist executing any orders that would eradicate Chinatown, knowing that East Coast capitalists feared that such summary use of police powers would disrupt manufacturing and trade on the West Coast. Sheriff Thomas Desmond, elected on the WPC ticket, assured the party's rank and file that he would execute the Board of Health's orders and warned that, if the police refused to comply, the city authorities "would call on the Workingmen to clear out Chinatown." And the WPC issued resolutions warning that, if there were any interference in the "abatement of the

Chinese nuisance," the WPC would "visit upon low-designing minions of power, backed up though they may be by cowardly capitalists and corporations, a punishment so swift and terrible that the reader of the history will shudder at the record."[46]

In light of these threats, Kalloch had difficulty convincing the board of supervisors that there was "nothing revolutionary or radical" in the removal of the Chinese from the city center and the razing of Chinatown for sanitary reasons. Many of the board's constituents among the elite commercial establishment feared that property they leased to the Chinese would be destroyed and they would lose their tenants. On February 28, the board of supervisors decided to rescind its earlier endorsement of the Board of Health's declaration of "Chinatown [as] a nuisance."[47] Although the mayor and the WPC organized mass meetings and pamphlet campaigns to marshal support for the Board of Health's order, the WPC rank and file remained orderly, and the city administration remained politically deadlocked—until the end of Mayor Kalloch's term and the dissolution of the WPC in 1881. No legal or extralegal action on the Board of Health's condemnation of Chinatown ever occurred. However, the Board of Health did continue to impose routine sanitary surveillance, vaccination campaigns, and fumigation of dwellings in Chinatown.

In 1882 the U.S. Congress passed the Chinese Exclusion Act, which disallowed Chinese workers to immigrate. Although the law exempted Chinese merchants, students, diplomats, and their families, it consolidated the disenfranchisement of all Chinese people by prohibiting any state or federal court from admitting Chinese immigrants to naturalized citizenship. Subsequent legislation virtually cut off Chinese immigration and that of other East and South Asian immigrants—as well as abridged opportunities to win citizenship and the right to political participation—by branding Chinese and other Asian immigrants as perpetual "aliens ineligible for citizenship." Throughout the western states, local white vigilantes drove out Chinese settlers. Many Chinese laborers sought safety in San Francisco along with the white laborers who flocked to the city because of a severe economic downturn in the eastern United States.[48]

Three years later, the Republican-dominated board of supervisors under the Democratic mayor Washington Bartlett revisited the issue of Chinese residents in San Francisco and commissioned a special committee to survey Chinatown. In May 1885, supervisors Willard Farwell and John Kunkler presented their comprehensive report to the public. They confined their investigation to the area bounded by California, Kearny, Broadway, and Stockton Streets, a twelve-block area. Although the supervisors recognized that the Chinese population had "drifted" into the blocks west of Stockton Street, they restricted the report to the popularly assumed boundaries of Chinatown because of fiscal considerations.[49]

The zeal of health officials to know the spaces within Chinatown culminated in a report that also produced the cartography of Chinatown. Nearly two decades of systematic surveillance and normalizing public health codes had aided in producing a map of the street-level Chinatown settlement. The special committee employed surveyors who accompanied them on visits of "every floor and every room." The detailed report of the "conditions of occupancy of every room"—its use, number of inhabitants, and sanitary condition—enabled the committee to make a map of the district, specifying the "character of occupancy" of the first floor of each of the buildings as well as providing a detailed accounting of all the basements, the subbasements, and the floors above the street level. Titled the *Official Map of "Chinatown" in San Francisco*, it was color coded to distinguish "General Chinese Occupancy," "Chinese Gambling Houses," "Chinese Prostitution," "Chinese Opium Resorts," "Chinese Joss Houses," and "White Prostitution." The "General Occupancy" sections were further identified by the type of factory, store, or lodging, which were tagged by street number. The white sections sprinkled throughout the district and on its edges were identified as "white" groceries, saloons, bakeries, and residences.

This explicit map of Chinatown represented a new strategy of knowledge.[50] This cartography substantiated the 1885 report's goal of obtaining a "correct idea of the general condition of things there and the ordinary mode of life and practices of its inhabitants" by providing precise dimensions and visual representations of the extent of Chinatown. The map ordered and made intelligible at least the street level of the heretofore impenetrable and labyrinthine geography of Chinatown. Thorough inventories of sanitary infractions, indices of manufactures, and catalogues of the secret exits and entrances of "barricaded gambling dens," in combination with the precise map of Chinatown, injected the "medium of crystallized fact and the inexorable logic of demonstrated truth" into the heated political debate about the condition of Chinatown. It also served to further "crystallize" the seemingly transparent relationship between race and place.[51]

The map and inventories were the products and tools of extensive surveillance, but they also ensured that more intensive surveillance would occur in the future. The report emphasized the scores of public health violations throughout Chinatown, knowledge of which had been reaped from the systematic investigation. The report presented an image of a normative regulatory apparatus that employed inspectors, police, and judges who forced all habitations in the city to comply with standard regulations. Although the surveillance and investigation of Chinatown were extraordinary, the violations were quite ordinary. A five-page catalogue of the most egregious, most frequent infractions merely cited inadequate plumbing and drainage, including clogged water closets, urinals, and sinks; stagnant cesspools; and the lack of plumbing connections to street sewers. As a catalogue, however, these violations were no longer individual or singular anomalies but were interpreted as a collective manifestation—evidence of collective behavior. They were perceived as evidence of "lawlessness" and resolute disregard by the Chinese population.

The precise mapping of vice onto Chinatown buildings and the perception of Chinese "lawlessness" inflamed fears of municipal corruption. For instance, in the early twentieth century an anonymous individual scribbled on one copy of the 1885 map of Chinatown a handwritten annotation that demonstrated acute political cynicism and grave doubts about police and public health enforcement: "This 'Official Map' of Chinatown shows official knowledge of the illegal gambling resorts, houses of prostitution, opium dens and houses of white prostitutes, which by the payment of blackmail have secured immunity from prosecution etc. and continue collecting filth and unhealthy surroundings which provided the ostensible excuse for the fraudulent quarantine and plague scare of 1900 by the Board of Health." The accumulation of knowledge through surveillance and mapping did not necessarily result in effective prosecution and long-term reform. The anonymous critic's allegations of police corruption also underscored a suspicion that the Board of Health would overreact to its own negligence in enforcing sanitary regulations. During the 1900 bubonic plague crisis, according to the writer's accusation, the Board of Health freely spent "public money to clean up nuisances that it was their duty to compel owners and tenants to do at their own expense." The writer emphasized a breakdown in governance, in which municipal officials were unwilling to curb vice that bred both unsanitary conditions and lawlessness. For some investigators and political commentators, the evidence of unabated vice and filth in Chinatown exacerbated fears of widespread government corruption and social anarchy that could spread beyond Chinatown borders.[52]

Officials had long worried that within Chinatown no respectable society existed that put moral and social checks on the culture of vice, lawlessness, and disease. The 1885 investigation included a population census that numerically demonstrated this presumed absence of respectable nuclear families in Chinatown. The enumeration of persons, within households and classified by their social relations, created an assessment of Chinese society driven by statistical evidence, not anecdote. These numbers revealed that the Chinese were at odds with the social structures and classification that organized the dominant white society. In their tabulations of women and children, Farwell and Kunkler observed that more than 40 percent of the women and more than 90 percent of the children were "herded together with apparent indiscriminate parental relations, and no family classification, so far as can be ascertained."[53] Like the late-nineteenth-century surveyors of urban England and colonial Africa who attributed disease and disorder to the improper social and spatial distribution of bodies, Kunkler and Farwell were horrified by the lack of distinctive and discernible nuclear families.[54] Many women and children lived together without the presence of a male head of household. And among "professional prostitutes," mothers and children lived "in adjoining apartments and intermingle freely," which for Farwell made it impossible to tell "where the family relationship leaves off and prostitution begins." This vision of middle-class domesticity and morality, which favored the presence of well-bounded and visibly distinct persons, families, and habitations, was widespread among European and American public health reformers in their imposition of proper sanitary practices.[55]

Not only did investigators want to prove collective activity, but they also intended to present the systematic nature of Chinese living conditions. In order to substantiate the assertion that the Chinese lived in "constant and habitual violation" of the cubic air ordinance, the report presented "some instances illustrating the *ordinary* habits of the Chinese laboring classes in the matter of sleeping and living accommodations," rather than providing "extreme cases" as investigators had repeatedly done in the past. Through statistical tables, the committee listed the addresses of more than two dozen locations, comparing the number of actual occupants with the allowable number of occupants. In every case, more than three times as many people lived in housing than could be legally accommodated. Farwell and Kunkler followed up their establishment of statistical "proof" with a more typically lurid and extreme description of an underground den. It featured all the conventions of previous medical trave-logues; however, the statistical preface substantiated the description's claim to represent "ordinary" conditions:

> Descend into the basement of almost any building in Chinatown at night; pick your way by the aid of the police-man's candle along the dark and narrow passageway, black and grimy with a quarter of a century's accumulation of filth; step with care lest you fall into a cesspool of sewage abominations with which these subterranean depths abound. Now follow your guide through a door, which he forces, into a sleeping room. The air is thick with smoke and fetid with an indescribable odor of reeking vapors. . . . It is a sense of a horror you have never before experienced, revolting to the last degree, sick-ening and stupefying. Through this semi-opaque atmosphere you discover perhaps eight or ten—never less than two or three—bunks, the greater part or all of which are occupied by two persons, some in a state of stupefaction from opium, some rapidly smoking themselves into that condition, and all in dirt and filth.

According to Farwell and Kunkler, the statistics and the description combined to provide authoritative "proof" for their assertion that the "mode of life among the Chinese here are [sic] not much above 'those of the rats of the waterfront.'"[56]

Following the now popular logic of medical discourse, the report predicted that dire health consequences would result from the presence of filthy, over-crowded, and inhuman conditions. These conditions presented "a constant menace to the welfare of society as a slumbering pest, likely at any time to gen-erate and spread disease should the city be visited by an epidemic in any virulent form." Not only was Chinatown characterized as "the rankest growth of human degradation that can be found upon this continent," outstripping all other slums in "filth, disease, crime and misery," but, authorities suggested, no amount of cleansing would improve these conditions. The Chinese were expected to "relapse" into a "more dense condition of nastiness, in which they apparently delight to exist." Since its inhabitants were walking, seemingly unaf-fected, disease carriers, Chinatown constituted a constant and continual "source of danger." Disease was conceived as organic to every Chinese racialized space. Inhuman living conditions appeared to be "inseparable from the very nature of the race," and city authorities warned that Chinatown would remain a "cesspool" so "long as it is inhabited by people of the Mongolian race."[57]

The knowledge of Chinatown spaces, conditions, and social relations pro-vided a material and representational terrain to explore the extreme contrasts between the "Chinese race" and the "American people." In public health reports the contrast fed the tension between aberrant and normal and the racial difference that separated the Chinese aliens from white Americans. In trave-logues, this binary opposition of two irreconcilable peoples generated the underlying dramatic tension that propelled the narratives. G. B. Densmore's central "argument" that drove his *Chinese in California* travelogue was the "radical difference between Caucasian and Mongolian civilization."[58] These differences of civilization and "standard of living" emerged from the obsessive descriptions of Chinatown as a space of difference antagonistic to the rest of the city. The editor of a local newspaper, Curt Abel-Musgrave, took the popular idea of Chinatown as a "subterranean world" to its logical extreme. In a bracing fantasy about a cholera epidemic unleashed in San Francisco, Abel-Musgrave conceptualized the territory of San Francisco as two distinctive cities—the "healthy paradise" of the true San Francisco above-ground and the "hell" of Chinatown underground. He explained that Chinatown below was impervious to the city's natural cleansing features: "Sunbeams that shine on us don't penetrate 50 feet deep into the pestilential dens of the Chinese population, and the fresh breezes which purify the air of our streets and our houses leave the sepulchres untouched in which for 30 years foul and disgusting vapors have been gathering."[59] Curiously, city officials offered detailed Chinatown maps to the street level only; it was up to travelogue writers to imagine and sketch out maps of the underground passageways and dens. Only Walter Raymond in his *Horrors of a Mongolian Settlement* offered a diagram of the subterranean roads and passageways of his journey.[60]

The public-health knowledge of dens, density, and the labyrinth cast Chinatown as a deviant transplantation of the traditional East in the modern Western city. This contrast emphasized the uneasy coexistence of growing, progressive San Francisco and decaying, regressive Chinatown. Chinatown was impervious to progress and was instead liable to rot and regress like the enervated Chinese empire across the Pacific. The environmental conditions of Chinatown could only harm the rest of the city.[61] The representation of the Chinese inhabitants was that of a race and culture apart and unaffected by the forces of modernity. City officials and travelogue writers represented the Chinese as burdened by the weight of an ancient civilization and impervious to beneficial change. These officials and writers conceived of time, in relation to Chinatown and the Chinese people, as a passage in which the physical environment was decaying and regressing while the residents lived without past or future. They perceived among the inhabitants of Chinatown ancient racial habits and proclivities that caused the Chinese to live in a "timeless present where all 'his' actions and reactions are repetitions of 'his' usual habits."[62] As with comparable racial formations, there was an insistent repetition of images that gave an ahistorical and unchanging quality to the represented reality of Chinatown and its inhabitants.[63] What propelled the endless, obsessive repetition of the idealized representation was the inherent impossibility to achieve the stereotyped racial category. The project of naturalizing race identity involved the production of effects that posed as "reality," a daunting but compulsive task for those invested in the reproduction of racial "truths."[64]

In the racial formation of Chinese and Chinatown, medical discourses employed and adapted prevailing political and social discourses of Chinese "vice," "criminality," "immorality," "slavery," and "subversiveness" and, in turn, informed these popular discourses with the threat of Chinese "dirt" and "disease."[65] However, the reports of threats of disease originating in the social conduct of Chinese immigrants and the spaces in which they dwelled did not appear originally or exclusively in public health records or at the insistence of physicians. The *Daily Alta* newspaper and the anti-Chinese labor organizations from the very beginning of this period articulated concern about the unsanitary environment in Chinatown and the spatial elements of dens, density, and the labyrinth, which preoccupied city and state officials during the second half of the nineteenth century.

Medical discourse lent scientific weight to the project and turned every one of these stylized features of Chinatown into a cause of pathology and source of disease. The keepers of public health had broad powers, and over time they developed the authority to put these "ideas" about race into practice. Health officials and politicians justified the idea of Chinatown as inherently pestilent, and they invested this idea, through the accumulation of these stereotyped images in their reports and rhetoric, with the value of a natural truth.[66]

During the late nineteenth century, the imagery of Chinatown and the Chinese race as pestilent intensified to such an overwhelming pitch that any contradictions and inconsistencies were bent into and subsumed by the prevailing interpretations of the Chinese medical menace. The practices of "scientific" investigations and fact-finding missions persuasively defined the "truth" of Chinatown in terms of constricted, crowded, immoral, unsanitary, and unnavigable space. These discursive practices profoundly affected the lives of Chinese men and women in San Francisco. Disease-producing and death-engendering threats defined Chinatown as a civic problem and emboldened the nascent Board of Health to intervene decisively to regulate Chinese space and, more generally, to manage the environment and inhabitants of San Francisco. Race and public health had become inextricably linked, producing a combination that would have profound and far-reaching consequences for every inhabitant of the city.

NOTES

1. "The Chinese Quarter: Chinatown Overhauled by Health Inspectors—a Terrible State of Affairs Found to Exist—Crowded into Garrets and Cellars—Radical Sanitary Regulations Needed," *Daily Alta California*, May 16, 1870; "Moving on Their Works: Health Officer Dr. J. L. Meares Notifies the Chinese to Set Their Houses in Order," *San Francisco Examiner*, February 24, 1880.

2. SFBH, *Annual Report*, 1880–81, p. 5; SFBH, *Annual Report*, 1881–82, p. 9; SFBH, *Annual Report*, 1879–80, p. 2.

3. K. J. Anderson, *Vancouver's Chinatown: Racial Discourse in Canada, 1875–1980* (Montreal: McGill-Queen's University Press, 1991), p. 31.

4. Thomas W. Laqueur, "Bodies, Details, and the Humanitarian Narrative," in *The New Cultural History*, ed. Lynn Hunt (Berkeley and Los Angeles: University of California Press, 1989); Mary Poovey, *Making a Social Body: British Cultural Formation, 1830–1864* (Chicago: University of Chicago Press, 1995); Thomas Osborne, "Security and Vitality: Drains, Liberalism, and Power in the Nineteenth Century," in *Foucault and Political Reason: Liberalism, Neo-Liberalism, and the Rationalities of Government*, ed. Andrew Barry, Thomas Osborne, and Nikolas Rose (Chicago: University of Chicago Press, 1996), pp. 99–122; Margaret Cohen, ed., *Spectacles of Realism: Body, Gender, and Genre* (Minneapolis: University of Minnesota Press, 1995).

5. Stuart Hall, "Gramsci's Relevance for the Study of Race and Ethnicity," *Journal of Communicative Inquiry* 10, no. 2 (1986): 5–27; Lorraine Daston, "Historical Epistemology," in *Questions of Evidence: Proof, Practice, and Persuasion across the Disciplines*, ed. James Chandler, Arnold I. Davidson, and Harry Harootunian (Chicago: University of Chicago Press, 1994), pp. 282–89; Thomas C. Holt, "Reflections on Race-Making and Racist Practice: Toward a Working Hypothesis" (paper prepared for the Newberry Seminar in American Social History, Chicago, May 30, 1991), pp. 17–18; Stuart Hall, "Race, Articulation, and Societies Structured under Dominance," in *Sociological Theories: Race and Colonialism* (Paris: UNESCO, 1980); T. J. Jackson Lears, "The Concept of Cultural Hegemony: Problems and Possibilities," *American Historical Review* 56 (June 1985). For another example of the conflation of race, culture, behavior, and a ghetto location, see Robin D. G. Kelley, *Yo Mama's Disfunktional: Fighting the Culture Wars in Urban America* (Boston: Beacon Press, 1998), particularly chapter 1.

6. *Gamsaan* was the Yale Cantonese transliteration, and *Jinshan* the Mandarin pinyin transliteration. Similarly, *Tongyan gaai* is *Tangren jie* in pinyin. Dupont Street was renamed Grant Avenue in 1908 during the reconstruction of San Francisco. *Daily Alta California*, November 21, 1853; Thomas W. Chinn, Him Mark Lai, and Philip P. Choy, *A History of the Chinese in California: A Syllabus* (San Francisco: Chinese Historical Society of America, 1969), pp. 10–11; Paul M. Ong, "Chinese Labor in Early San Francisco: Racial Segmentation and Industrial Expansion," *Amerasia* 8, no. 1 (1981): 70–75.

7. "Common Council," *Daily Alta California*, August 19, 1854.

8. *Daily Alta California*, August 15, 19, and 22, 1854.

9. Ibid., August 17 and 22, 1854.

10. Ibid., August 15, 1854; and "Spread of the Cholera," *Daily Alta California*, August 19, 1854. Cholera epidemics in the early nineteenth century became the occasion for intense debates about the administration of public health and national borders, and, more generally, about the role of government in ensuring social and political order in France and the United States. See Charles E. Rosenberg, *The Cholera Years: The United States in 1832, 1849, and 1866* (Chicago: University of Chicago Press, 1962); François Delaporte, *Disease and Civilization: The Cholera in Paris*, trans. Arthur Goldhammer (Boston: MIT Press, 1986).

11. *Daily Alta California*, August 15 and 22, 1854; Rosenberg, *The Cholera Years*; Delaporte, *Disease and Civilization*; Cathy Kudlick, *Cholera in Postrevolutionary Paris* (Berkeley and Los Angeles: University of California Press, 1996).

12. "Common Council, Board of Aldermen, August 21," *Daily Alta California*, August 22, 1854.

13. Ibid.

14. Him Mark Lai, "Historical Development of the Chinese Consolidated Benevolent Association/Huiguan System," in *Chinese America: History and Perspectives* (San Francisco) (1987): 13–51; Shih-shan Henry Tsai, *China and Overseas Chinese in the U.S., 1868–1911* (Fayetteville: University of Arkansas Press, 1983), pp. 31–38; William Hoy, *Chinese Six Companies* (San Francisco: Chinese Consolidated Benevolent Association, 1942); Yong Chen, *Chinese San Francisco, 1850–1943: A Trans-Pacific Community* (Stanford: Stanford University Press, 2000), pp. 71–73.

15. The meeting was chaired by the Chinese merchant A Hing; a white journalist, William Howard, editor of the *Golden Gate News*, served as secretary and submitted the petition as part of the Common Council's official record. Letter to William Rabe from William Howard, August 21, 1854, with petition, printed in *Daily Alta California*, August 22, 1854.

16. Editorial, *Daily Alta California*, August 17, 1854.

17. "More Chinese Emigrants," *Daily Alta California*, August 15, 1854; "The Exchange Chinamen," *Daily Alta California*, August 22, 1854; "Health of the City," *Daily Alta California*, August 26, 1854.

18. Sucheng Chan, *This Bittersweet Soil: The Chinese in California Agriculture, 1860–1910* (Berkeley and Los Angeles: University of California Press, 1986), pp. 37–78; Ronald Takaki, *Strangers from a Different Shore* (New York: Little, Brown and Co., 1989), esp.

pp. 86–94; Roger Daniels, *Asian American: Chinese and Japanese in the United States since 1850* (Seattle: University of Washington Press, 1988), pp. 9–69.

19. Census records did not account for the range of Spanish-speaking migrants (from Chile, Peru, Mexico, Spain, and the Caribbean), but they were not a significant portion of the population in the period 1860 to 1920. William Issel and Robert Cherny, *San Francisco, 1865–1932: Politics, Power, and Urban Development* (Berkeley and Los Angeles: University of California Press, 1986), p. 56; Douglas Henry Daniels, *Pioneer Urbanites: A Social and Cultural History of Black San Francisco* (Berkeley and Los Angeles: University of California Press, 1990), p. 13.

20. C. M. Bates, "Health Officer's Report," included in San Francisco Board of Supervisors (SFBS hereafter), *San Francisco Municipal Report* (San Francisco, 1869–70), p. 233.

21. David Sibley, *Geographies of Exclusion: Society and Difference in the West* (London: Routledge, 1995), p. 28; Peter Stallybrass and Allon White, *The Politics and Poetics of Transgression* (London: Methuen, 1986), pp. 132–33.

22. Bates, "Health Officer's Report," 1869–70, p. 233.

23. Alexander Saxton, *The Indispensable Enemy: Labor and the Anti-Chinese Movement in California* (Berkeley and Los Angeles: University of California Press, 1971), pp. 72–77; Neil Larry Shumsky, "Tar Flat and Nob Hill: A Social History of Industrial San Francisco during the 1870s" (Ph.D. diss., University of California at Berkeley, 1972).

24. "The Chinese on the Pacific Coast. The Statement of the Anti-Coolie Association," *Daily Alta California,* June 24, 1869.

25. California State Board of Health (CSBH hereafter), *Biennial Report of the State Board of Health of California* (Sacramento, 1870–71), pp. 44–47 and the appendix, p. 55.

26. Among the most famous popular accounts are B. E. Lloyd, *Lights and Shades in San Francisco* (San Francisco: A. L. Bancroft and Co., 1876), pp. 236–66; Walter Raymond, *Horrors of the Mongolian Settlement, San Francisco, California: Enslaved and Degraded Race of Paupers, Opium Eaters, and Lepers* (Boston: Cashman, Keating, and Co., 1886); Rudyard Kipling's series of articles for the *Allahbad "Pioneer"* (1889), reprinted in Rudyard Kipling, *Rudyard Kipling's Letters from San Francisco* (San Francisco: Colt Press, 1949), pp. 31–32; William Walter Bode, *Lights and Shadows of Chinatown* (San Francisco: Crocker, 1896); G. B. Densmore, *The Chinese in California: Description of Chinese Life in San Francisco. Their Habits, Morals, Manners* (San Francisco: Petit and Russ, 1880), pp. 20, 23, 117; J. W. Buel, *Metropolitan Life Unveiled; or, the Mysteries and Miseries of America's Great Cities* (St. Louis, Mo.: Historical Publishing Company, 1882).

27. Bates, "Health Officer's Report," 1869–70, p. 233.

28. SFBS, *Report of the Special Committee of the Board of Supervisors of San Francisco on the Condition of the Chinese Quarter and the Chinese in San Francisco, July 1885* (San Francisco, 1885), p. 19.

29. CSBH, *Biennial Report*, pp. 44–47. Logan's medical explanations of the dangers of underground spaces reappeared in popular travelogues through the late nineteenth century. See Lloyd, *Lights and Shades in San Francisco*, p. 257; Bode, *Lights and Shadows of Chinatown*, pp. 7, 13; Kipling, *Letters from San Francisco*, pp. 31–32; Buel, *Metropolitan Life Unveiled*, p. 276.

30. CSBH, *Biennial Report*, p. 46.

31. Ibid., p. 47.

32. Ibid., p. 46.

33. Judith Walkowitz, *City of Dreadful Delight: Narratives of Sexual Danger in Late Victorian London* (Chicago: University of Chicago Press, 1992); Margaret Cohen and Christopher Prendergast, eds., *Spectacles of Realism: Body, Gender, and Genre* (Minneapolis: University of Minnesota Press, 1995); Laqueur, "Bodies, Details, and the Humanitarian Narrative," pp. 176–204.

34. Bode, *Lights and Shadows of Chinatown*, p. 14; Densmore, *The Chinese in California*, p. 25.

35. CSBH, *Biennial Report*, pp. 44–47; SFBS, *San Francisco Municipal Report*, 1869–70, p. 233.

36. Raymond, *Horrors of the Mongolian Settlement*, pp. 52–53.

37. CSBH, *Biennial Report*, p. 47; M. P. Sawtelle, "The Plague Spot," *Medico-Literary Journal* 1, no. 4 (December 1878): 10–12; SFBH, *Annual Report*, 1871–72, p. 4; SFBH, *Annual Report*, 1872–73, p. 21; SFBH, *Annual Report*, 1879–80, p. 2.

38. This narrative of Kalloch's 1879 election relies on the historical research and analysis of Saxton, *The Indispensable Enemy*; Issel and Cherny, *San Francisco, 1865–1932*, pp. 127–30; Sandmeyer, *The Anti-Chinese Movement in California*, pp. 73–75.

39. Frank Roney, *Frank Roney, Irish Rebel and California Labor Leader*, ed. Ira Cross (Berkeley and Los Angeles: University of California Press, 1931), cited in Saxton, *Indispensable Enemy*, pp. 141–42.

40. Doctor Hugh Huger Toland was a prominent figure in the development of an understanding of the Chinese medical threat. In the mid-1870s his testimony to the California State Senate and U.S. congressional committees on the transmission of syphilis from Chinese female prostitutes to white adolescent males became the authoritative medical opinion on the subject and was cited in almost every subsequent report on Chinese female prostitution. See chapter 3 of Nayan Shah, Contagious Divides: Epidemics and Race in San Francisco's Chinatown (Berkeley and Los Angeles: University of California Press, 2001). Toland died on February 27, 1880, in the midst of the controversial declaration that Chinatown was a sanitary nuisance. Letter to the Board of Supervisors from I. S. Kalloch, February 27, 1880, printed in the *San Francisco Examiner*, February 28, 1880.

41. "Moving on Their Works: Health Officer Dr. J. L. Meares Notifies the Chinese to Set Their Houses in Order."

42. The report of the committee has been reprinted in Workingmen's Party of California, Anti-Chinese Council, comp. (WPC hereafter), "Board of Health: Resolutions of Condemnation," in *Chinatown Declared a Nuisance!* (San Francisco: Workingmen's Party of California, 1880), pp. 3–4. Curiously I have not found a reference to this report in the SFBH, *Annual Report*, 1879–80; or SFBS, *San Francisco Municipal Report*, 1879–80.

43. WPC, *Chinatown Declared a Nuisance!* p. 4.

44. Ibid., p. 6.

45. Ibid., pp. 5–6.

46. "The Workingmen in Session," *San Francisco Examiner*, February 26, 1880.

47. "Again Solicited to Cooperate," *San Francisco Examiner*, February 28, 1880.

48. Andrew Gyory, *Closing the Gate: Race, Politics, and the Chinese Exclusion Act* (Chapel Hill: University of North Carolina Press, 1998); Charles J. McClain, *In Search of Equality: The Chinese Struggle against Discrimination in Nineteenth-Century America* (Berkeley and Los Angeles: University of California Press, 1994), pp. 145–220; S. Chan, *Asian Americans*; Elmer Sandmeyer, *The Anti-Chinese Movement in California* (Urbana: University of Illinois Press, 1973).

49. SFBS, *Report of the Special Committee*, p. 3.

50. J. B. Harley, "Deconstructing the Map," *Cartographica* 26 (1989): 1–20; Harley, "Maps, Knowledge, and Power" in *The Iconography of Landscape: Essays on the Symbolic Representation, Design, and Use of Past Environments*, ed. Denis Cosgrove and Stephen Daniels (New York: Cambridge University Press, 1988), pp. 277–312.

51. SFBS, *Report of the Special Committee*, pp. 3, 4, 32.

52. SFBS, *Official Map of "Chinatown" in San Francisco* (San Francisco: Bosqui Engraving and Printing, 1885), in Maps Collection, Bancroft Library. Copy 1 has manuscript annotation.

53. Ibid., p. 8.

54. Jean Comaroff and John Comaroff, *Ethnography and the Historical Imagination* (Boulder, Colo.: Westview Press, 1992), pp. 265–94; Gareth Stedman Jones, *Outcast London: A Study of the Relationship between the Classes in Victorian Society* (Oxford: Clarendon Press, 1971).

55. SFBS, *Report of the Special Committee*, p. 9.

56. Ibid., pp. 18–25.

57. Ibid., pp. 4–5, 67.

58. Densmore, *The Chinese in California*, pp. 117–21.

59. Curt Abel-Musgrave, *The Cholera in San Francisco: A Contribution to the History of Corruption in California* (San Francisco: San Francisco News Company, 1885), p. 5.

60. Raymond, *Horrors of the Mongolian Settlement*, p. 2.

61. Fernando Coronil, "Beyond Occidentalism: Toward Nonimperial Geohistorical Categories," *Cultural Anthropology* 11, no. 1 (February 1996): 51–87; Frederick Cooper and Ann Stoler, *Tensions of Empire: Colonial Cultures in a Bourgeois World* (Berkeley and Los Angeles: University of California Press, 1997).

62. Mary Louise Pratt, *Imperial Eyes: Travel Writing and Transculturation* (New York: Routledge, 1992), p. 64.

63. Robert Miles, *Racism* (London: Routledge, 1989); David Theo Goldberg, *Racist Culture: Philosophy and the Politics of Meaning* Cambridge: Blackwell, 1993); Winthrop D. Jordan, *White over Black: American Attitudes toward the Negro, 1550–1812* (New York: W. W. Norton, 1968).

64. For a theoretical elaboration of the processes of representation and repetition in relation to the performative and incomplete production of identity, see Homi K. Bhabha, "Signs Taken for Wonders: Questions of Ambivalence and Authority under a Tree outside Delhi, May 1817," in *"Race," Writing and Difference*, ed. Henry Louis Gates Jr. (Chicago: University of Chicago Press, 1986) pp. 163–84; Homi K. Bhabha, *The Location of Culture* (New York: Routledge, 1994); Judith Butler, "Imitation and Gender Insubordination," in *Inside/Out: Lesbian Theories/Gay Theories*, ed. Diana Fuss (New York: Routledge, 1991) pp. 13–31.

65. Stuart Creighton Miller, *The Unwelcome Immigrant: The American Image of the Chinese, 1785–1882* (Berkeley and Los Angeles: University of California Press, 1969), pp. 145–204; Sandmeyer, *The Anti-Chinese Movement in California*, pp. 25–39.

66. K. J. Anderson, *Vancouver's Chinatown*, pp. 81–82.

THE SECRET MUNSON REPORT

Michi Nishiura Weglyn

One important difference between the situation in Hawaii and the mainland is that if all the Japanese on the mainland were actively disloyal they could be corralled or destroyed within a very short time.

—CURTIS B. MUNSON, NOVEMBER 7, 1941

I

By fall of 1941, war with Japan appeared imminent. For well over a year, coded messages going in and out of Tokyo had been intercepted and decoded by Washington cryptoanalysts. With relations between Tokyo and Washington rapidly deteriorating, a desperate sense of national urgency was evidenced in messages to Ambassador Nomura, then carrying on negotiations in the nation's capital. On July 25, Japan had seized south French Indo-China. The activation the following day of the Morgenthau-Stimson plan, calling for the complete cessation of trade with Japan and the freezing of her assets in America—Great Britain and the Netherlands following suit—had resulted in the strangulation and near collapse of the island economy.

By late September, Tokyo's coded messages included demands for data concerning the Pacific Fleet stationed at Pearl Harbor. Of great implication for U.S. Army and Naval Intelligence was the September 24 dispatch directed to Consul Nagao Kita in Honolulu:

HENCEFORTH, WE WOULD LIKE TO HAVE YOU MAKE REPORTS CONCERNING VESSELS ALONG THE FOLLOWING LINES IN SO FAR AS POSSIBLE:

1. THE WATERS OF PEARL HARBOR ARE TO BE DIVIDED ROUGHLY INTO FIVE SUB-AREAS. WE HAVE NO OBJECTION TO YOUR ABBREVIATING AS MUCH AS YOU LIKE. AREA A. WATERS BETWEEN FORD ISLAND AND THE ARSENAL. AREA B. WATERS ADJACENT TO THE ISLAND SOUTH AND WEST OF FORD ISLAND. THIS AREA IS ON THE OPPOSITE SIDE OF THE ISLAND

FROM AREA A. AREA C. EAST LOCH. AREA D. MIDDLE LOCH. AREA E. WEST LOCH AND THE
COMMUNICATING WATER ROUTES.

2. WITH REGARD TO WARSHIPS AND AIRCRAFT CARRIERS WE WOULD LIKE TO HAVE YOU
REPORT ON THOSE AT ANCHOR (THESE ARE NOT SO IMPORTANT), TIED UP AT WHARVES,
BUOYS, AND IN DOCK. DESIGNATE TYPES AND CLASSES BRIEFLY. IF POSSIBLE, WE WOULD
LIKE TO HAVE YOU MAKE MENTION OF THE FACT WHEN THERE ARE TWO OR MORE VESSELS
ALONGSIDE THE SAME WHARF.[1]

With all signs pointing to a rapid approach of war and the Hawaiian naval
outpost the probable target,[2] a highly secret intelligence-gathering was immediately ordered by the President.[3] Mandated with *pro forma* investigative powers as
a special representative of the State Department was one Curtis B. Munson.[4] His
mission: to get as precise a picture as possible of the degree of loyalty to be
found among residents of Japanese descent, both on the West Coast of the
United States and in Hawaii.

Carried out in the month of October and the first weeks of November,
Munson's investigation resulted in a twenty-five-page report of uncommon significance, especially as it served to corroborate data representing more than a
decade of prodigious snooping and spying by the various U.S. intelligence services, both domestic and military. *It certified a remarkable, even extraordinary degree*
of loyalty among this generally suspect ethnic group.

Yet, for reasons that still remain obscured, this highest level "double-checking"
and confirmation of favorable intelligence consensus—that *"there is no Japanese*
problem"—was to become one of the war's best-kept secrets. Not until after the
cessation of hostilities, when the report of the secret survey was introduced in
evidence in the Pearl Harbor hearings of 1946, did facts shattering all justification for the wartime suppression of the Japanese minority come to light.

What is more remarkable, perhaps, is that to this very day, the unusual significance of these findings has been strangely subdued.

Evidence would indicate that the Munson Report was shared only by the
State, War, and Navy departments; yet, paradoxically, Cordell Hull, Henry L.
Stimson, and Frank Knox, who then headed up these Cabinet posts, were to end
up being the most determined proponents of evacuation. Researchers and historians have repeatedly—and with justification—leveled an accusatory finger at
Stimson's War Department cohorts as being the Administration's most indus-
trious evacuation advocates. The question naturally arises: Were aides of the
Secretary kept in the dark regarding the "bill of health" given the vast majority
of the Japanese American population?

On February 5, 1942, a week before the go-ahead decision for the evacuation
was handed down, Stimson informed the Chief Executive in a letter sent along
with the President's personal copy of the Munson Report: "In response to your
memorandum of November 8 [see Appendix 10], the Department gave careful
study and consideration to the matters reported by Mr. C. B. Munson in his
memorandum covering the Japanese situation on the West Coast." This meant
that the General Staff had had fully three months to study, circulate, review, and
analyze the contents of the report before it was returned to the President.[5]

Owing to the wartime concealment of this important document, few, if any, realized how totally distorted was the known truth in pro-internment hysterics emanating from the military, with the exception of those in naval intelligence and the FBI, whose surveillance of the Japanese minority over the years had been exhaustive. Both services, to their credit, are on record as having opposed the President's decision for evacuation.[6]

To the average American, the evacuation tragedy, well shrouded as it remains in tidied-up historical orthodoxy and in the mythology spawned by the "total-war" frenzy, remains no more than a curious aberration in American history. Only during the civil rights turbulence of the sixties, when personal liberties of unpopular minorities were once again in jeopardy, was interest sharply rekindled in this blurred-out episode in America's past. A generation of the nation's youth, who had grown up knowing nothing or little of so colossal a national scandal as American-style concentration camps, suddenly demanded to know what it was that had happened. Noticed also was an upsurge of interest among the "Sansei" (the children of the second-generation "Nisei"), some of whom had been born in these camps, who now wanted to be told everything that their parents and grandparents, the "Issei," had tried so hard to forget.[7]

Yet the enormity of this incredible governmental hoax cannot begin to be fathomed without taking into consideration the definitive loyalty findings of Curtis B. Munson, especially in relation to the rationale that in 1942 "justified" the sending of some 110,000 men, women, and children to concentration camps: namely, that an "unknown" number of Japanese Americans presented a potential threat of dire fifth-column peril to the national security; that it would be difficult to sort out the dangerous ones in so short a time, so to play it safe all should be locked up.

II

Behind it all was a half century of focusing anti-Asian hates on the Japanese minority by West Coast pressure groups resentful of them as being hyperefficient competitors. An inordinate amount of regional anxiety had also accompanied Japan's rapid rise to power. Years of media-abetted conditioning to the possibility of war, invasion, and conquest by waves and waves of fanatic, emperor-worshiping yellow men—invariably aided by harmless-seeming Japanese gardeners and fisherfolk who were really spies and saboteurs in disguise—had evoked latent paranoia as the news from the Pacific in the early weeks of the war brought only reports of cataclysmic Allied defeats.

In 1941, the number of Japanese Americans living in the continental United States totaled 127,000. Over 112,000 of them lived in the three Pacific Coast states of Oregon, Washington, and California. Of this group, nearly 80 percent of the total (93,000) resided in the state of California alone.

In the hyperactive minds of longtime residents of California, where antipathy toward Asians was the most intense, the very nature of the Pearl Harbor attack provided ample—and prophetic—proof of inherent Japanese treachery. As the Imperial Army chalked up success after success on the far-flung Pacific front, and as rumors of prowling enemy submarines proliferated wildly, the West

Coast atmosphere became charged with a panicky fear of impending invasion and a profound suspicion that Japanese Americans in their midst were organized for coordinated subversive activity. From the myriad anti-Oriental forces and influential agriculturists who had long cast their covetous eyes over the coastal webwork of rich Japanese-owned land, a superb opportunity had thus become theirs for the long-sought expulsion of an unwanted minority.[8]

By enlisting the support of civic leaders, politicians, and their powerful mass-media allies, with special emphasis on those important in the military, the tide of tolerance which had surprisingly followed the news of attack was reversed by what soon appeared like a tidal wave of cries for evacuation. In the more inflammatory journals, the switch-over from tolerance to mistrust had been as simple as juxtaposing news of the bestial, despised enemy with that of "Japs" in their own backyards. The public became totally confused in their hatred.

Because little was known about the minority which had long kept itself withdrawn from the larger community in fear of rebuff, it was possible to make the public believe anything. The stereotype of the Oriental of supercunning and sly intent was rekindled and exploited in such a manner that Chinese Americans and other Asians began wearing "I am a Chinese" buttons in fear of being assaulted and spat upon. The tactics used in manipulating public fears were hardly different from those used to achieve the cutoff in Chinese immigration in 1882 and in bringing a halt to all Japanese immigration in 1924.

Significant for those maximizing this once-in-a-lifetime opportunity was that although the Japanese minority comprised only a minuscule 1 percent of the state's population, they were a group well on their way to controlling one-half of the commercial truck crops in California. Centuries-old agricultural skills which the Japanese brought over with them enabled Issei farmers not only to turn out an improved quality of farm produce but also to bring down prices. The retail distribution of fruits and vegetables in the heavily populated Southern California area was already a firmly entrenched monopoly of Japanese Americans.

And it was in the name of the citizen Nisei that much of the rich growing acreage belonged to the immigrants.

Like the Chinese before them, the immigrant Japanese were denied the right to become American citizens. Because they lacked this right of naturalization, they could not own land. Even the leasing of land was limited by a 1913 land law to three years. But the Issei found ways to get around such laws devised to drive Orientals away from California, the most popular of which was for the Issei to purchase property in the name of their citizen offspring.

It was a common practice among the Issei to snatch up strips of marginal unwanted land which were cheap: swamplands, barren desert areas that Caucasians disdained to invest their labor in. Often it included land bordering dangerously close to high-tension wires, dams, and railroad tracks. The extraordinary drive and morale of these hard-working, frugal Issei who could turn parched wastelands, even marshes, into lush growing fields—usually with help from the entire family—became legendary. In the course of the years, notably during period of economic crisis, a hue and cry arose of "unfair competition" and accusations that "the Japs have taken over the best land!"

Then, with the wild tales of resident Japanese perfidy that Pearl Harbor unleashed, rumors flew back and forth that Issei landowners had settled in stealth and with diabolical intent near vital installations. Their purpose: a "second Pearl Harbor." At the Tolan Committee hearings, then ostensibly weighing the pros and cons of evacuation, impressive documentation was unfurled by the top law officer of California, Attorney General Earl Warren (later to become the Chief Justice of the U.S. Supreme Court), purporting to support his theory of a possible insurrection in the making: that, with malice aforethought, Japanese Americans had "infiltrated themselves into every strategic spot in our coastal and valley counties." Substantiation of this county-by-county penetration read, in part, as follows:

ALAMEDA COUNTY
Japs adjacent to new Livermore Military Airport.
Japs adjacent to Southern Pacific and Western Pacific Railroads.
Japs in vicinity of Oakland Airport.
Japs in vicinity to Holt Caterpillar Tractor Co., San Leandro. . . .

SAN DIEGO COUNTY
Thirty miles of open coast broken by small water courses with a Jap on
    every water course.
Thirty miles of main railroad and highway easily blocked by slides, etc.,
    with Japs throughout their entire length. . . .
Japs adjacent to all dams supplying water to San Diego and vicinity. . . .
Japs adjacent to all power lines supplying the city of San Diego and
    vicinity.[9]

There was no possible way of separating the loyal from the disloyal, insisted the Attorney General: "when we are dealing with the Caucasian race we have methods that will test the loyalty of them. . . . But when we deal with the Japanese we are in an entirely different field and we cannot form any opinion that we believe to be sound." Warren urged speedy removal.

Unfortunately for the Nisei and Issei, it was an election year. The tide of "public opinion"—the ferocity of the clamor, at least—indicated total unconditional removal, citizen or not. And all politicians were falling in line.

In a desperate last-ditch effort to halt the mass uprooting, Nisei leaders proposed the formation of a volunteer suicide battalion, with parents as hostages to insure their good behavior. Just one opportunity to demonstrate the depth of Nisei integrity, implored Mike Masaoka, the mystic mainspring behind the audacious proposal. How else could they disprove Attorney General Warren's outrageous assertion that "there is more potential danger among the group of Japanese who were born in this country than from the alien Japanese who were born in Japan"?

Though Masaoka's brash proposal was summarily rejected at the time, it would later be reconsidered and implemented by the military, notwithstanding their initial insistence that America did not believe in the concept of hostages or of a segregated battalion—except, of course, for blacks.

Being one of the outstanding members of the xenophobic brotherhood of the "Native Sons of the Golden West" and not having access to Munson's intelligence summation, Attorney General Warren may have been merely vociferating some widely held concepts of supremacist groups as he readied himself for the gubernatorial race in the fall. But the army, which did have the facts, went on to interpret the surprising lack of disloyal activity among the Japanese minority as proof positive of intended treachery: "The very fact that no sabotage has taken place to date is a disturbing and confirming indication that such action will be taken."

Because the decision for concentrating the Japanese American population was one made in total isolation from the American people, the justifications given for it were often conflicting, varying from authority to authority. Humanitarian groups and civil libertarians who sharply protested the stamping out of due process were assured that it was merely a "protective custody" measure deemed necessary to shelter "these admirable people" from mob action. Yet when violence and intimidation were encountered by families who attempted voluntarily to relocate themselves in the "Free Zone" of California (the eastern half) and in intermountain areas of the American interior, not one move was made by federal authorities to help stem the harassment and vigilantism so that an orderly resettlement might have been made possible. The proven failure of this voluntary movement, halted by a military freezing order on March 27, 1942, was given as one more justification why "drastic measures" were called for. The Nisei who pleaded to be allowed to remain free, and Caucasian friends who attempted to aid them, were reduced to helplessness, since Washington and the military insisted they had knowledge of certain facts not known to the average person, that only the authorities were equipped to know what was best for the "Japanese."

To explore such facts not then known to the U.S. citizenry—indeed, to cut through the morass of long-nurtured, still-persisting myths—is therefore the primary objective of this chapter.

III

Apart from occasional brief references to the Munson Report in works of scholarly research, the eye-opening loyalty findings of Curtis B. Munson have yet to receive merited exposure in the pages of history. As it is a document which brings into better perspective the often grievously misunderstood and misinterpreted 1942 federal action, its more pertinent passages have been excerpted for examination in the pages which follow. For readers interested in studying the report in its entirety, a reprint of the document may be found in the Pearl Harbor hearings of the 79th Congress, 1st session. The original copy of the report may be found at the Franklin D. Roosevelt Library, Hyde Park, New York.

A duplicate copy may be found in the files of the assistant Secretary of War, National Archives.

A far greater portion of the allotted investigatory time had been spent by Curtis Munson in probing the West Coast Issei and Nisei; for the three naval districts (11th, 12th, and 13th) covered in Munson's coastal survey encompassed the full length of the West Coast—Southern California, Northern California, Washington, and Oregon. The report on the findings of the Special Investigator began as follows:

JAPANESE ON THE WEST COAST
Ground Covered
In reporting on the Japanese "problem" on the West Coast the facts are, on the whole, fairly clear and opinion toward the problem exceedingly uniform. . . . Your reporter spent about a week each in the 11th, 12th, and 13th Naval Districts with the full cooperation of the Naval and Army Intelligence and the FBI. Some mention should also be made of the assistance rendered from time to time by the British Intelligence. Our Navy has done by far the most work on this problem, having given it intense consideration for the last ten or fifteen years. . . .

Opinions of the various services were obtained, also for business, employees, universities, fellow white workers, students, fish packers, lettuce packers, farmers, religious groups, etc. The opinion expressed with minor differences was uniform. Select Japanese in all groups were sampled. To mix indiscriminately with the Japanese was not considered advisable chiefly because the opinions of many local white Americans who had made this their life work for the last fifteen years were available. . . .

In other words, long before the bombs began to fall on Pearl Harbor, efficient counterintelligence activity along the West Coast of the United States had resulted in all necessary loyalty-disloyalty information on Japanese Americans being evaluated, correlated, and catalogued—an impressive amount of amassed data representing more than a decade's worth of surveillance and intelligence-gathering. What is equally impressive is that this vast accumulation of military and domestic intelligence estimates (including opinions of private organizations, individuals, and informers) was, "with minor differences," in the estimation of the presidential sleuth, "exceedingly uniform."

Yet, with amazing aplomb, the army, whose own intelligence service had been an integral part of the investigative teamwork, was to maintain baldly throughout that the loyalties of this group were "unknown" and that "time was of the essence." If the time factor had, indeed, been so critical as to prevent holding hearings to separate the loyal from the disloyal, it is curious that some eleven months were to elapse before the last of such men, women, and children constituting a special menace were removed from restricted areas.

For the benefit of executive officers deficient in knowledge of the "Japanese background," historical and sociological background data "as [they have] a bearing on the question" were then briefly summarized by Munson. "No estimate of the elements characteristics of the Japanese is complete without a word about 'giri,'" explained the Special Investigator, displaying a keen power of observation for a nonspecialist working under obvious pressure:

> There is no accurate English word for "giri." The nearest approach to an understanding of the term is our word "obligation," which is very inadequate and altogether too weak. Favors of kindnesses done to a Japanese are never forgotten but are stored up in memory and in due time an adequate quid pro quo must be rendered in return. . . . "Giri" is the great political tool. To understand "giri" is to understand the Japanese.

Individuals aware of this ingrained character trait of the Japanese were even then attempting to convince the President that the strategy of tact and civility would prove more constructive than threats, sanctions, and affronts to Japan's pride. Among such individuals concerned for peace was the eminent theologian E. Stanley Jones, who sought repeatedly in the months preceding the attack to convince the President that if America were to revoke its punitive protectionist stance and accord discretionary treatment to a "have-not" nation vexed by problems of an exploding population, Japan would not only doubly reciprocate but also might possibly end up as an ally.

Severely damaging then to the Nisei was the habit of being lumped as "Japanese," or the pejorative "Japs," which also meant "the enemy." Munson was careful to point out to policy makers that "in the United States there are four divisions of Japanese to be considered." A brief definition of each followed:

1. The *ISSEI*—First generation Japanese. Entire cultural background Japanese. Probably loyal romantically to Japan. They must be considered, however, as other races. They have made this their home. They have brought up children here, their wealth accumulated by hard labor is here, and many would have become American citizens had they been allowed to do so. [The ineligibility of Orientals to acquire citizenship through naturalization had been determined by a Supreme Court decision: *Ozawa v. U.S.*, 260 U.S. 178(1922).] They are for the most part simple people. Their age group is largely 55 to 65, fairly old for a hard-working Japanese.

2. The *NISEI*—Second generation who have received their whole education in the United States and usually, in spite of discrimination against them and a certain amount of insults accumulated through the years from irresponsible elements, show a pathetic eagerness to be Americans. They are in constant conflict with the orthodox, well disciplined family life of their elders. Age group—1 to 30 years.

3. The *KIBEI*—This is an important division of the *NISEI*. This is the term used by the Japanese to signify those American born Japanese who received part or all of their education in Japan. In any consideration of the *KIBEI* they should be again divided into two classes, i.e. those who received their education in Japan from childhood to about 17 years of age and those who received their early formative education in the United States and returned to Japan for four or five years Japanese education. The Kibei are considered

the most dangerous element and closer to the Issei with special reference to those who received their early education in Japan. It must be noted, however, that many of those who visited Japan subsequent to their early American education come back with added loyalty to the United States. In fact it is a saying that all a Nisei needs is a trip to Japan to make a loyal American out of him. The American educated Japanese is a boor in Japan and treated as a foreigner. . . .

4. The *SANSEI*—The Third [*sic*] generation Japanese is a baby and may be disregarded for the purpose of our survey.

One of the gross absurdities of the evacuation was that a preponderance of those herded into wartime exile represented babes-in-arms, school-age children, youths not yet of voting age, and an exhausted army of elderly men and women hardly capable of rushing about carrying on subversion. The average age of the Nisei was eighteen. The Issei's average age hovered around sixty.

The Nisei generation, the American-born and -educated, had appeared relatively late on the scene, for only after years of saving up from his meager earnings did the early male immigrant send back to Japan for a bride. "Between these first and second generations there was often a whole generation missing," notes sociologist William Petersen in a January 9, 1966, *New York Times Magazine* article, "for many of the issei married so late in life that in age they might have been their children's grandparents." Owing largely to this generational chasm which separated the Issei from their fledgling offspring, the Nisei suffered not only from a serious communication gap—neither group speaking the other's language with any facility—but from the severe demands of an ancestral culture totally alien to the Americanizing influence of the classroom: a culture which emphasized strict conformity as opposed to individuality, duty more than rights.

The Kibei, the return-to-America Nisei, were an extreme product of this paradox. Some 8,000 of these native-born Americans had received three or more years of schooling in prewar Japan, often a desperate and sacrificial move on the part of parents at a time when even the highest level of educational preparation could not break down white employment barriers on the West Coast. Severe maladjustment problems were usually the lot of the Kibei on their return to a Caucasian-dominated society, causing some to withdraw into a shell of timidity. Ostracized not only by whites but also by their more Americanized peers as being too "Japanesey," the Kibei (often the older brothers and sisters in the family) suffered in angry isolation, feeling contemptuous of the Nisei as being a callow, culturally deprived generation whose "kowtowing" to whites they found distasteful. Marched into concentration camps before many had had a chance to readjust to the culture shock, and where the Kibei were subjected to stricter security surveillance, the more strident camp firebrands and disruptive deviants were inevitably to emerge from this group of misfits.

The factor of ethnicity, or "racial guilt" for the crime of adhering to old world cultural patterns, had been another of the bizarre arguments advanced by the military in justification for the preventive detention of a minority. In the words of Colonel Karl Bendetsen, the army architect-to-be of the racial uprooting, it was highly suspect that Japanese Americans were then part of a "national group almost wholly unassimilated and which had preserved in large measure to itself its customs and traditions." In the event of a Japanese invasion, he determined, the Issei and Nisei would hardly be able to "withstand the ties of race."

And for Secretary of War Stimson, mere racial identification with the fiendish Asiatic foe, whose military might had been woefully miscalculated, was cause enough to have little confidence in the American-born Nisei: "The racial characteristics are such that we cannot understand or trust even the citizen Japanese."[10]

In striking contradiction to such insinuations and untruths fabricated of prejudice, a far kindlier assessment of Issei and Niesi acculturation, aspirations, and value priorities had been documented for the President in the weeks prior to the outbreak of hostilities. Munson's prewar assessment had been strongly positive; his commendation of the Nisei was glowing:

> Their family life is disciplined and honorable. The children are obedient and the girls virtuous. . . .
>
> There are still Japanese in the United States who will tie dynamite around their waist and make a human bomb out of themselves. We grant this, but today they are few. Many things indicate that very many joints in the Japanese set-up show age, and many elements are not what they used to be. The weakest from a Japanese standpoint are the Nisei. They are universally estimated from 90 to 98 percent loyal to the United States if the Japanese-educated element of the Kibei is excluded. The Nisei are pathetically eager to show this loyalty. They are not Japanese in culture. They are foreigners to Japan. Though American citizens they are not accepted by Americans, largely because they look differently [*sic*] and can be easily recognized. The Japanese American Citizens league should be encouraged, the while an eye is kept open, to see that Tokio does not get its finger in this pie—which it has in a few cases attempted to do. The loyal Nisei hardly knows where to turn. Some gesture of protection or wholehearted acceptance of this group would go a long way to swinging them away from any last romantic hankering after old Japan. They are not oriental or mysterious, they are very American and are of a proud, self-respecting race suffering from a little inferiority complex and a lack of contact with the white boys they went to school with. They are eager for this contact and to work alongside them.

Noting the "degrees to which Americans were willing to believe almost anything about the Japanese," Professor Roger Daniels (*Concentration Camps USA*: Holt, Rinehart and Winston) wonders whether Munson's apocryphal reference to the fanatic-minded Japanese "who will tie dynamite around their waist and make a human bomb out of themselves" might not have contributed to alarming the President.

In 1941, the Japanese American Citizens League (JACL) was still a politically unsophisticated neophyte organization preoccupied with the problems of how to better the status of their own minority in the United States; most Nisei were not yet old enough to belong to it. In an eagerness to gain white approbation, and moved by the deep and unselfish ideals of the Republic, the League had early taken the route of superpatriotism, leading in time to a near-systematic disavowal of things Japanese. This marked compulsion on the part of the minority's youth generation to demonstrate an extraordinary allegiance may have accounted for the excellent bill of health given the Nisei, generally, and the Investigator's positive recommendation to policy makers: "the Japanese American Citizens League should be encouraged." Which military and civilian authorities proceeded to do to such a discriminatory degree that the manifest partiality shown JACL leaders in the stressful removal and adjustment period was to later become the fundamental cause of intracamp ferment.

Contradicting widely held assumptions to the contrary, Munson's following assessment of the immigrant group reveals the personal esteem in which many Issei had been held as individuals, even in the face of mounting prewar feelings:

> The Issei, or first generation, is considerably weakened in their loyalty to Japan by the fact that they have chosen to make this their home and have brought up their children here. They expect to die here. They are quite fearful of being put in a concentration camp. Many would take out American citizenship if allowed to do so. The haste of this report does not allow us to go into this more fully. The Issei have to break with their religion, their god and Emperor, their family, their ancestors and their after-life in order to be loyal to the United States. They are also still legally Japanese. Yet they do break, and send their boys off to the Army with pride and tears. They are good neighbors. They are old men fifty-five to sixty-five, for the most part simple and dignified. Roughly they were Japanese lower middle class, about analogous to the pilgrim fathers.

A strong factor in the Issei's ability to adapt to their inhospitable environment was that most of the immigrants had come from the lower rung of the social and economic ladder of their highly class-conscious homeland, thus were inured to inequalities in rights. Their self-effacing, uncritical admiration of America despite obvious repudiation was something "short of miraculous," recalls the Reverend Daisuke Kitagawa, an Episcopal priest from Japan who had worked among them in the less populous Pacific Northwest, where a lesser degree of discrimination was experienced than in California.

The Issei's admiration of, and ever-increasing attachment to, their adopted land was profoundly reinforced as the Nisei began to be inducted into the army under the Selective Service Act of 1939, Father Dai notes discerningly:

> When he saw his son standing proudly in a U.S. Army uniform, he knew that he had been wedded to the United States for all these years, even though there had been many in-laws, as it were, who mistreated him. . . . At that moment the Issei was in a frame of mind that would easily have led him to fight the Japanese forces, should they invade the Pacific Coast. Emotionally it would have been an extremely painful thing for him to do, but he would have done it just the same, for he saw quite clearly that it was the only thing for him to do as one who had been "wedded" to the United States. The traditional Japanese ethic, when faithfully adhered to, would not only justify, but more positively demand, his taking the side of the United States.[11]

The Nisei "show a pathetic eagerness to be Americans" had been Munson's perceptive summation, and it was an apt one; for it described the state of mind of a substantial majority of draft-age Japanese Americans when pridefully answering their nation's call to arms as a heaven-sent opportunity to prove that, first and foremost, they were Americans—that their love and loyalty were for the Stars and Stripes.

The report continued: "Now that we have roughly given a background and description of the Japanese elements in the United States, the question naturally arises—what will all these people do in case of a war between the United States and Japan?" In other words, could Japanese Americans be trusted to withstand the ties of "blood" and "race" in the ultimate test of loyalty, of being pitted against their own kind? Would there be the *banzai* uprisings, the espionage and sabotage long prophesied and propagandized by anti-Oriental hate exploiters? "As interview after interview piled up," reported Investigator Munson, "those bringing in results began to call it the same old tune."

> The story was all the same. There is no Japanese "problem" on the Coast. There will be no armed uprising of Japanese. There will undoubtedly be some sabotage financed by Japan and executed largely by imported agents. . . . In each Naval District there are about 250 to 300 suspects under surveillance. It is easy to get on the suspect list, merely a speech in favor of Japan at some banquet being sufficient to land one there. The Intelligence Services are generous with the title of suspect and are taking no chances. Privately, they believe that only 50 or 60 in each district can be classed as really dangerous. The Japanese are hampered as saboteurs because of their easily recognized physical appearance. It will be hard for them to get near anything to blow up *if it is guarded.* There is far more danger from Communists and people of the Bridges type on the Coast than there is from Japanese. The Japanese here is almost exclusively a farmer, a fisherman or a small businessman. He has no entree to plants or intricate machinery.

Despite the restrained intelligence estimate that "only 50 or 60 in each district can be classed as really dangerous," the ferocity of the sneak attack which followed provided apparent justification for a ruthless sweep for suspects, made possible by the blanket authority given the Attorney General by Presidential Proclamation No. 2525, of December 7, 1941. Over 5,000 Issei and Nisei were pulled in by the FBI, most of whom were subsequently released after interrogation or examination before Alien Enemy hearing boards. Over 2,000 Issei suspects bore the anguish of having businesses and careers destroyed, reputations defiled in being shipped to distant Department of Justice detention camps for an indefinite stay.

Herbert V. Nicholson, a former Quaker missionary to Japan who then headed up a Japanese American congregation in Los Angeles, recalls the haphazardness of the indiscriminate pickups—that the FBI, with the help of law enforcement officers,

> . . . picked up anybody that was the head of anything. The same thing they did when Lenin and the Communists took over in Russia. . . . Anybody that was a *cho*—that

means "head"—he was picked up. Heads of prefectural organizations were picked up. Just because we come from the same country, we get together occasionally, see, and just have a social time and talk about our friends back in Japan. But everybody that was head of anything was picked up, which was a crazy thing. . . . Because of public opinion and pressure, others were picked up later for all sorts of things. Buddhist priests and Japanese language schoolteachers were all picked up later . . . because of public opinion, they picked up more and more.[12]

Since it was assumed that years of social and legislative slights had hopelessly estranged the Japanese American minority, little did authorities then realize that with all their zealotry, not one instance of subversion or sabotage would ever be uncovered among the Issei, or a single case involving the Nisei. James Rowe, Jr., then second-in-command at the Justice Department as the Assistant Attorney General (today a prominent Washington attorney) recently admitted with candor that "we picked up too many . . . some of this stuff they were charged on was as silly as hell."[13]

The four-week probe of the West Coast "problem" had ended up putting the Nisei entirely in the clear. Munson was positive the enemy would look elsewhere for agents: "Japan will commit some sabotage largely depending on imported Japanese as they are afraid of and do not trust the Nisei."

There will be no wholehearted response from Japanese in the United States. They may get some helpers from certain Kibei. They will be in a position to pick up information on troop, supply and ship movements from local Japanese. . . . [Another salient passage that may have alarmed the President.]

For the most part the local Japanese are loyal to the United States or, at worst, hope that by remaining quiet they can avoid concentration camps or irresponsible mobs. We do not believe that they would be at the least any more disloyal than any other racial group in the United States with whom we went to war. Those being here are on a spot and they *know* it.

IV

A total of nine days were spent by the Special Investigator in Honolulu. As had been done in the Pacific Coast probe of the Japanese minority, an independent check was made with "the full cooperation of Army and Navy Intelligence and the FBI" on intelligence estimates of each agency, culled from years of accumulated surveillance data. Munson's assessment of the Hawaiian-Japanese problem began as follows:

The consensus of opinion is that there will be no racial uprising of the Japanese in Honolulu. The first generation, as on the Coast, are ideologically and culturally closest to Japan. Though many of them speak no English, or at best only pigeon-English, it is considered that the big bulk of them will be loyal. . . . The second generation is estimated as approximately ninety-eight percent loyal. However, with the large Japanese population in the Hawaiian Islands, giving this the best interpretation possible, it would mean that fifteen hundred were disloyal. However, the F.B.I. state that there are about four hundred suspects, and the F.B.I.'s private estimate is that only fifty or sixty of these are sinister. . . .

Following the Pearl Harbor assault, 980 suspects from the Hawaiian Japanese community were to be pulled in by authorities and penned up at the Hawaiian Detention Center before their removal to mainland Justice Department camps. It is worth noting that the Honolulu-based FBI appears to have exercised far more restraint than its West Coast counterparts, considering that twice as many mainland Issei were to end up in Justice's custody.

A marked difference between the kind of discrimination being practiced on the Islands as compared to that on the mainland caught the attention of the Special Investigator. On the West Coast, there was no mistaking that racial attitudes were at the root of the animosity against the Issei and Nisei: "there are plenty of 'Okies' to call the Japanese a 'Yellow-belly,' when economically and by education the Japanese may not only be their equal but their superior." On the other hand, discrimination as practiced in Hawaii (where the Japanese "fit in" because "the bulk are dark-skinned of one kind or another") struck Munson as being based more on one's financial standing—on whether one fitted in on a social and economic basis.

> The result of this is that the Hawaiian Japanese does not suffer from the same inferiority complex or feel the same mistrust of the whites that he does on the mainland. While it is seldom on the mainland that you find even a college-educated Japanese-American citizen who talks to you wholly openly until you have gained his confidence, this is far from the case in Hawaii. Many young Japanese there are fully as open and frank and at ease with a white as white boys are. In a word, Hawaii is more of a melting pot because there are more brown skins to melt—Japanese, Hawaiian, Chinese and Filipino. It is interesting to note that there has been absolutely no bad feeling between the Japanese and the Chinese in the islands due to the Japanese-Chinese war. Why should they be any worse toward us?

More than a few Nisei and Kibei detained by Hawaiian authorities were to end up, with family members, in mainland "relocation centers," where the breezy outspokenness of Hawaiian youths and their uninhibited tendency to be openly resentful of insult was to come as a shock and special vexation to administrators—accustomed, as they were, to the docile, more taciturn mainland Nisei.

However marked the difference in personality makeup, the compelling need to demonstrate love of country and loyalty to the flag was a character trait shared in common by both the Hawaiian and mainland Nisei, or one might gather as much by their positive attitude toward army enlistment—no doubt a moral imperative—"country before self"—passed on to them by their duty-conscious parents. Noted the Investigator:

> Due to the preponderance of Japanese in the population of the Islands, a much greater proportion of Japanese have been called to the draft than on the mainland. As on the

mainland they are inclined to enlist before being drafted. The Army is extremely high in its praise of them as recruits. . . . They are beginning to feel that they are going to get a square deal and some of them are really almost pathetically exuberant.

Postwar statistics were to dramatize this remarkable *esprit de corps* more tellingly. A higher percentage of Americans of Japanese ancestry ended up serving in the U.S. Army during World War II than any other racial group, divided almost equally between the mainland Nisei (13,528) and those in Hawaii (12,250). "The final count of Hawaiian war casualties revealed that 80 percent of those killed and 88 percent of those wounded throughout the war were of Japanese descent," states Andrew Lind, writing in *Hawaii's Japanese.*

V

Los Angeles, California: December 20, 1941 (or some two weeks *after* the Pearl Harbor attack).

Munson offered no comments or post-mortems on the "surprise" attack which finally came—in obvious anticipation of which he had warned Washington from his Hawaiian vantage point in the early part of November: *"The best consensus of opinion seemed to agree that martial law should be proclaimed now in Hawaii."*

From his post-Pearl (December 20) Los Angeles vantage point, Munson volunteered some strong private opinions on a fast-developing situation which augured no good for the Coastal Japanese.

We desire respectfully to call attention to a statement of the Secretary of the Navy evidently made to some reporter on his return to Washington after the Pearl Harbor attack as printed in the *Los Angeles Times* of December 18. . . . We quote, "I think the most effective Fifth Column work of the entire war was done in Hawaii with the possible exception of Norway," Secretary of the Navy Knox said. . . . Fifth Column activities, such as in Norway, impugns [*sic*] the loyalty of a certain large proportion of a population. Your observer still doubts that this was the case in Honolulu. . . .

Some reaction of an undesirable nature is already apparent on the West Coast due to this statement of the Secretary's. In Honolulu your observer noted that the seagoing Navy was inclined to consider everybody with slant eyes bad. This thought stems from two sources: self-interest, largely in the economic field, and in the Navy usually from pure lack of knowledge and the good old "eat 'em up alive" school. It is not the measured judgment of 98% of the intelligence services or the knowing citizenry either on the mainland or in Honolulu. . . .

Knox's allegations of foul play were providing the opening wedge for racist forces to begin reactivating slumbering anti-Oriental prejudices along the Pacific Coast. Subsequently, the climate was to take an abrupt turn toward intolerance, notably when the Roberts Commission Report on the attack, released on January 25, 1942, reinforced the misleading impression that the aid of resident traitors had been received by the spy operation then centered in the Japanese Consulate: "some were consular agents and others were persons having no open relations with the Japanese foreign service." Yet Washington was to remain remarkably silent about it. By the time official denials reached the mainland public, the developing fear hysteria had become irreversible.

Even as Munson sought to set the record straight, the President and his Cabinet had agreed, as early as December 19, 1941, to concentrate all aliens of Japanese ancestry on an island other than Oahu.[14] Navy Secretary Knox doubted that the measure went far enough and sought, from the outset, to convince the President that citizens, too, should be included. In a memorandum of February 26, a supremely confident President assured Knox that there would be no problem in removing "most of the Japanese": "I do not worry about the constitutional question, first because of my recent order [West Coast evacuation], second because Hawaii is under martial law. The whole matter is one of immediate and present war emergency. I think you and Stimson can agree and then go ahead and do it as a military project."[15]

Had the island roundup involved only aliens, as originally agreed upon, the Hawaiian evacuation might have proceeded swiftly, without hindrance. Approximately 20,000 aliens and 98,000 citizens then lived on the island of Oahu, the Japanese minority then making up one-third of the total island population. The small Issei population might have been readily replaced by an equivalent work force.

But because of Knox's stubborn insistence on a large-scale evacuation, which would have involved some hundred thousand Nisei and Issei (recommended by the Joint Chiefs of Staff on March 11, 1942, and approved by the President on March 13, 1942),[16] the project was to end up becoming unwieldly and unworkable, especially since the Joint Chiefs of Staff ruled on removal to the mainland "utilizing empty ships returning to the west coast" at a time when shipping facilities were being taxed to their utmost.

The Hawaiian evacuation, to begin with the removal of 20,000 of "the most dangerous" aliens and citizens, was vigorously opposed—later thwarted—by island army and navy authorities closer to the problem as being too costly, logistically complex, and self-defeating. As Munson had prophetically forewarned in his pre–Pearl Harbor report, "it would simply mean that the Islands would lose their vital labor supply by so doing, and in addition to that we would have to feed them . . . it is essential that they should be kept loyal."

Accordingly—and paradoxically—it had become a veritable military necessity for authorities to retain, *not detain,* Hawaii's Japanese population in a battle zone thousands of miles closer to the enemy mainland than the jittery state of California and to do everything possible to encourage their loyalty so that all would stay at their tasks.

It was in sharp contrast to the policy pursued on the West Coast in reference to a people then posing an increasing threat to the prosperity of native farmers and merchants though still an infinitesimal percentage of the population—thus expendable, both politically and economically. Should the "Japanese" on the mainland "prove actively disloyal *they could be corralled or destroyed within a very short time,*" the Special Investigator, in his prewar assessment, had dramatically punctuated this expendability.

But on the basis of the highly favorable impression he had gained during the hurried survey, Munson was moved to submit to the President his own well-considered recommendations with the reassurance "Your reporter, fully believing that his reports are still good after the attack, makes the following observations about handling the Japanese 'problem' on the West Coast."

A. The loyal Japanese citizens should be encouraged by a statement from high government authority and public attitude toward them outlined.

B. Their offers of assistance should be accepted through such agencies as:
1. Civilian Defense
2. Red Cross
3. U.S.O., etc., etc.

C. This assistance should not be merely monetary, nor should it even be limited to physical voluntary work in segregated Nisei units. The Nisei should work with and among white persons, and be made to feel he is welcome on a basis of equality.

D. An alien property custodian should be appointed to supervise Issei (first generation-alien) businesses, *but* encouraging Nisei (second generation-American citizen) to take over.

E. Accept investigated Nisei as workers in defense industries such as shipbuilding plants, aircraft plants, etc.

F. Put *responsibility* for behavior of Issei and Nisei on the leaders of Nisei groups such as the Japanese American Citizens League.

G. Put the *responsibility* for production of food (vegetables, fish, etc.) on Nisei leaders.

In essence, Munson's power-to-the-Nisei policy was to involve federal control:

In case we have not made it apparent, the aim of this report is that all Japanese Nationals in the continental United States and property owned and operated by them within the country be immediately placed under absolute Federal control. The aim of this will be to squeeze control from the hands of the Japanese Nationals into the hands of the loyal Nisei who are American citizens. . . . It is the aim that the Nisei should police themselves, and as result police their parents.

Munson's suggested course of governmental action, which would have catapulted the Nisei into a position of leadership and control, might have proved sound had both the Issei and Nisei been permitted to remain at liberty as in Hawaii. But the power-to-the-Nisei policy was to become the root cause of resentment and conflict, when imposed behind barbed wire, in abortively speeding up the process whereby the still fledgling Nisei were taken out from under the control of elders, a generation to whom they owed unlimited deference and obedience.

Regrettably ignored was Munson's strong recommendation that the public's attitude toward the minority be positively led with a reassuring statement by the "President or Vice President, or at least [someone] almost as high"—as was the adopted policy in Hawaii, where the newly appointed military governor acted swiftly to squelch fifth-column rumors while assuring justice and equitable treatment to aliens and citizens alike, if they would remain loyal.

But on the U.S. mainland, where other pressing considerations apparently outweighed justice for so inconsequential a minority, fear and fiction were allowed to luxuriate as part of the total war propaganda. And for reasons that defy easy explanation, Secretary of the Navy Knox was to further crucify a powerless minority by reporting to the Tolan Committee in a letter of March 24, 1942:

> . . . There was a considerable amount of evidence of subversive activity on the part of the Japanese prior to the attack. This consisted of providing the enemy with the most exact possible kind of information as an aid to them in locating their objectives, and also creating a great deal of confusion in the air following the attack by the use of radio sets which successfully prevented the commander in chief of the fleet from determining in what direction the attackers had withdrawn and in locating the position of the covering fleet, including the carriers. . . .[17]

It can only be assumed that Knox's tissue of fallacies impugning the fidelity of the resident Japanese was meant merely to divert, to take political "heat" off himself and the administration for the unspeakable humiliation that Pearl Harbor represented. By the convenient redirection of public rage, a nation on the verge of disunity and disaster was finally—and purposefully—united as one.

The actions of Knox and the wartime suppression of the Munson papers, like the more familiar Pentagon Papers, once again make evident how executive officers of the Republic are able to mislead public opinion by keeping hidden facts which are precisely the opposite of what the public is told—information vital to the opinions they hold.

In the case of Japanese Americans, data regarding their character and integrity were positive and "exceedingly uniform," the facts clear-cut. But as once observed by Nobel Peace Prize recipient Sir Norman Angell: "Men, particularly in political matters, are not guided by the facts but by their opinions about the facts." Under the guise of an emergency and pretended threats to the national security, the citizenry was denied the known facts, public opinion was skillfully manipulated, and a cruel and massive governmental hoax enacted. According to one of the foremost authorities on constitutional law, Dr. Eugene V. Rostow: "One hundred thousand persons were sent to concentration camps on a record which wouldn't support a conviction for stealing a dog."

NOTES

1. For documentation of key enemy message decoded in the weeks and months preceding the attack, see Admiral Robert A. Theobald's *The Final Secret of Pearl Harbor*. The book's Foreword, written by Admiral William F. Halsey, hero of the Pacific War, reads in part: "Had we known of Japan's minute and continued interest in the exact location and movement of our ships in Pearl Harbor, as indicated in the 'Magic Messages,' it is only logical that we would have concentrated our thought on meeting the practical certainty of an attack on Pearl Harbor. . . . I have always considered Admiral Kimmel and General Short [commanders at Pearl Harbor] to be splendid officers who were thrown to the wolves as scapegoats . . . They had to work with what they were given, both in equipment

and information. They are our outstanding military martyrs." Works of historians William L. Langer, Roberta Wohlstetter, and Thomas A. Bailey might be consulted for a defense of Roosevelt's conduct of foreign policy leading up to the attack.

2. According to the findings of the Army Pearl Harbor Board investigating the attack: " . . . Washington was in possession of essential facts as to the enemy's intentions and proposals. This information showed clearly that war was inevitable and late in November absolutely imminent. . . . It would have been possible to have sent safely, information ample for the purpose of orienting the commanders in Hawaii, or positive directive for an all-out alert." U.S. Army. The Army Pearl Harbor Board. *Report to the Secretary of War,* October 20, 1944, Vol. 39, pp. 103–4 of the *Hearings before the Joint Committee on the Investigation of the Pearl Harbor Attack.*

3. " . . . the State Department and the President were not satisfied with intelligence of the Army and the Navy and the FBI and they sent out their own intelligence agents to get certain information in relation to the Japanese both in Hawaii and the Japanese on the west coast," declared Senator Homer Ferguson on making the Munson document public for the first time as Chairman of the Congressional Investigation into the Pearl Harbor Attack (November 15, 1945, to May 31, 1946). The operation had been set up by John Franklin Carter (Jay Franklin), a journalist-radio-commentator-friend of FDR. See Appendix 10 for Carter's covering memorandum on the report. [Editor's Note: This chapter is an excerpt from Michi Nishiura Weglyn's *Years of Infamy: The Untold Story of America's Concentration Camps* (Seattle: University of Washington Press, 1976); this note refers to an Appendix in Weglyn's book.]

4. Confidential investigative assignments for the State Department were taken on by Curtis Burton Munson whenever called upon. Examples: Assignments in 1941 included "Investigation into German interests of Anaconda and of General Motors" and, in September, a report on the "Attitude of French-Canadians toward the European War." From July 1942 to November 1943, Lieutenant Commander Munson served as Assistant Naval Attaché and Assistant Naval Attaché for Air to the Embassy in London. See name card index, 1940–44, of the Department of State.

5. The General Staff had also received about this time a copy of a ten-page report of Commander K. D. Ringle—intelligence chief of the Southern California naval district—strongly opposing the evacuation as "unwarranted," as the problem had been "magnified out of its true proportion because of the physical characteristics of the people." (All three West Coast naval districts had received copies of the Munson Report.) Ringle declared, moreover, that he "heartily agrees with the reports submitted by Mr. Munson." Report, Lieutenant Commander K. D. Ringle to the Chief of Naval Operations, undated (submitted "around February 1, 1942," according to Army historian Conn), Records of the Office of the Secretary of War (hereafter cited as "ASW," denoting the "Assistant Secretary of War," who then had been given charge of all matters relating to the Japanese problem), ASW 014.311 WDC, RG 107, National Archives.

6. J. Edgar Hoover believed that the demand for evacuation was "based primarily upon public political pressure rather than upon factual data" and that the FBI was fully capable of handling the small number of suspects then under surveillance. Naval authorities favored the use of hearing boards and the policy of selective internment.

7. "Issei" means "first generation"; "Nisei" means "second generation"; and "Sansei" is "third generation" in the Japanese language. As is done with other nationalities in the U.S., author will use the term "Japanese" to refer to the Japanese American minority whenever there is no possibility of confusion. Also, author will tread lightly on areas treated exhaustively in other evacuation works.

8. For a listing of pressure groups and organizations strongly anti-Japanese American, see Bosworth's *America's Concentration Camps,* pp. 30–32 in paperback edition.

9. Statements attributed to Earl Warren are taken from *Hearings,* 77th Congress, 2nd sess. Select committee Investigating National Defense Migration (Washington: Government Printing Office, 1942). The Tolan Committee hearings (conducted from February 21

through March 7, 1942) were a sham. Executive Order of February 19 had already given the evacuation go-ahead to the Army, yet the "road show," with stops in San Francisco, Los Angeles, Portland, and Seattle, was allowed to go on—with exclusionist groups well in control of all the hearings. Assistant War Secretary McCloy had instructed General John L. DeWitt to "cooperate" with the Tolan Committee "insofar as it was compatible with military interests. . . . You might therefore suggest to Mr. Tolan that he should quietly conduct his investigations . . . into the dislocations which would be caused by the removal of these elements and into the best methods of dealing with the problem of their resettlement. There is no need for any investigation of the military aspect of the problem." Memorandum, John J. McCloy to General DeWitt, February 18, 1942, ASW 014.311 *Aliens*, Enemy Aliens on WC, RG 107, National Archives.

10. Burns, p. 215.
11. Kitagawa, pp. 32–33. Copyright © 1967 by The Seabury Press, Inc. Used by permission.
12. Mitson, p. 31.
13. *Ibid.*, see fn. 19.
14. Conn, Engelman, Fairchild, p. 207
15. Memorandum, Roosevelt to Frank Knox, February 26, 1942, OF 18, Franklin D. Roosevelt Library, Hyde Park, New York. Knox was then advocating the removal of 140,000 from Oahu. See Appendix 1 in Weglyn, *Years of Infamy.*
16. Conn, Engelman, and Fairchild, *op. cit.*, p. 210. See Appendix 2 in Weglyn, *Years of Infamy* for the Joint Chiefs of Staff directive of March 11, 1942.
17. Letter, Frank Knox to John H. Tolan, March 24, 1942. House of Representatives, *Fourth Interim Report of the Select Committee Investigating National Defense Migration*, 77th Congress, 2nd sess. (Washington: Government Printing Office, 1942), pp. 48–49.

REFERENCES

Bosworth, Allan R. *America's Concentration Camps.* New York: W. W. Norton, 1967.

Burns, James MacGregor. *Roosevelt: The Soldier of Freedom.* New York: Harcourt Brace Jovanovich, Inc., 1970.

Conn, Stetson; Engelman, Rose C.; and Fairchild, Byron. *The United States Army in World War II: The Western Hemisphere: Guarding the United States and Its Outposts.* Washington, D.C.: Department of the Army, 1964.

Daniels, Roger. *Concentration Camps USA: Japanese Americans and World War II.* New York: Holt, Rinehart and Winston, 1970.

Kitagawa, Daisuke. *Issei and Nisei, The Internment Years.* New York: Seabury Press, 1967.

Lind, Andrew W. *Hawaii's Japanese: An Experiment in Democracy.* Princeton: Princeton University Press, 1946.

Mitson, Betty E. "Looking Back in Anguish: Oral History and Japanese-American Evacuation." New York: The Oral History Association, Inc., 1974.

Munson, Curtis B. "Report on Japanese on the West Coast of the United States," in *Hearings*, 79th Congress, 1st sess., Joint Committee on the Investigation of the Pearl Harbor Attack. Washington, D.C.: Government Printing Office, 1946.

Peterson, William. "Success Story, Japanese-American Style." *New York Times Magazine,* January 9, 1966.

Rostow, Eugene V. "Our Worst Wartime Mistake." *Harper's* 191 (1945): 193–201.

Theobald, Robert A. *The Final Secret of Pearl Harbor.* New York: Devin-Adair, 1954.

Asian American Struggles for Civil, Political, Economic, and Social Rights

Sucheng Chan

In the last century and a half, Asian immigrants and Asian Americans who have fought for various rights in the United States have sometimes succeeded and at other times failed in their efforts. The history of their struggles can be divided into four periods: (1) the 1860s to the 1880s, (2) the 1890s to the 1920s, (3) the 1940s to the 1970s, and (4) the late 1970s to the present. In the first period, Chinese immigrants acquired important civil rights. In the second period, aspiring Asian immigrants lost the legal battles they waged against laws that barred them from immigrating to the United States, while those who had managed to enter before exclusion went into effect failed to gain the right to become naturalized citizens and to own, or even lease, agricultural land. In the third period, they gained political rights in the 1940s and 1950s, and economic rights in the 1960s and 1970s. In the present, fourth period, the results of their attempts to win social rights have been mixed. To understand why there has been a vacillation between advances and retrenchments, we must examine the larger historical contexts in which those successes and failures have occurred. We must also recognize the differences among civil, political, economic, and social rights.

THE 1860s TO THE 1880s

During the first period, Reconstruction dominated American national life.[1] Between 1865, when the Civil War ended, and 1877, when Reconstruction was formally terminated, the federal government tried to ensure that the recently freed Black people would be accorded certain basic rights. However, these efforts ended when a political deal was struck. In the Compromise of 1877, Northern Republicans agreed to withdraw the federal troops that had been sent to occupy the South if Southern Democrats would let Rutherford B. Hayes, the Republican presidential candidate in the closely contested elections of 1876, take office. Troops had been used to enforce the changes that the North tried to impose on the South because the South, though defeated, resisted efforts to give African Americans the freedom they had been promised during the Civil War.

Despite the fact it was short-lived, Reconstruction did leave an enduring legacy in the form of the Thirteenth, Fourteenth, and Fifteenth Amendments and several laws that provided the doctrinal basis on which African Americans, Asian immigrants, and other minorities have legally challenged the discrimination against them. The Thirteenth Amendment abolished slavery and other forms of involuntary servitude, thereby codifying the Emancipation Proclamation within the amendments to the U.S. Constitution. The Fourteenth Amendment declared that "all persons born or naturalized in the United States, and subject to the jurisdiction thereof, are citizens of the United States and of the State wherein they reside." This endowed persons of African ancestry born on American soil with birthright citizenship,[2] thereby nullifying the majority opinion of the U.S. Supreme Court in the 1857 Dred Scott case, which had stated that Black people, whether enslaved or free, "had no rights which the white man was bound to respect" and were not and could not become U.S. citizens.[3] The 1870 Naturalization Act extended the right of naturalization to persons of African nativity or descent.[4] Up to that point, only "free, white persons" could become naturalized citizens. During the debates over the bill, Senator Charles Sumner of Massachusetts, a great advocate of equal rights for all human beings regardless of their skin color, had argued vigorously that the word "white" should be deleted from the text. However, he failed in his efforts. Had he succeeded, Chinese immigrants would have gained the right of naturalized citizenship at the same time that African Americans did. The Fifteenth Amendment declared that "the rights of citizens of the United States to vote shall not be denied or abridged by the United States or any State on account of race, color, or previous condition of servitude," but female citizens did not gain the right to vote in national elections until 1920. A series of civil rights acts passed in 1866, 1870, 1871, and 1875 further elaborated the rights of the recently freed people.[5] Although the effectiveness of these laws would depend on how judges and Supreme Court justices interpreted them, and on how politicians dealt with them, their enactment nevertheless provided a legal starting point from which those who had been discriminated against could challenge their subordination.

Although the Reconstruction legislation was not meant to benefit Asian immigrants, the Chinese living in the United States at that time successfully used selected doctrines enunciated in these laws to win some significant civil rights for themselves. A seldom recognized fact is that Chinese immigrants began fighting for civil rights long before they acquired any political rights. Political rights refer to the rights to which the *citizens* of a country are entitled. In the United States, the most important political rights are the right to vote, the right to run for office, and the right to serve on juries. Immigrant Chinese did not gain the right to become naturalized citizens, and hence the right to vote, until 1943. That means they had no political rights for almost a century after they set foot on American soil. Yet they somehow learned that in this country there are rights that are even more fundamental than political rights. Those rights are called civil rights—the rights that *individuals*, regardless of their national origins or citizenship status, can expect to enjoy in a democratic society.[6]

The main civil rights that Americans possess are listed in the first ten amendments to the Constitution—the so-called Bill of Rights—adopted in 1791, and in the Fourteenth Amendment, adopted in 1868.[7] Civil rights are a fundamental part of democracy because they protect individuals against their own government by limiting the ability of that government to act tyrannically. People living in the United States are supposed to have freedom of religion, freedom of speech, freedom of the press, and freedom of assembly. They can also petition the government for a redress of grievances. They have the right to be secure from unreasonable searches and seizures, to not be held for a capital crime without an indictment, to decline to testify against themselves, to have a speedy and public trial, and, in many cases, to be tried by a jury of their peers. Moreover, excessive bail or fines and cruel and unusual punishment are not supposed to be imposed. No one is supposed to be deprived of life, liberty, or property without due process.

The Bill of Rights, at the time it was adopted, aimed to safeguard individuals, as well as the constituent states of the United States, against the power of the *federal* government to oppress them. But a significant shift occurred after the adoption of the Fourteenth Amendment. Henceforth, individuals would be protected not only against the potential encroachments of the federal government but also against the possible oppressive actions of *state* governments and of the dominant majority population.[8] For the newly freed Black people, as well as for Chinese immigrants, this shift was of monumental importance, because in the United States, state governments have a great deal of power, and it is individual states that have played a leading role in depriving people of color of their civil and political rights. Specifically, after President Abraham Lincoln issued the Emancipation Proclamation to abolish slavery at the beginning of 1863, the Southern states, one after another, enacted "Black Codes" to prevent the freed African Americans from gaining any true freedom. During the same period, the State of California and some of its municipalities made one attempt after another to oppress Chinese immigrants in many ways. Had the Fourteenth Amendment not been adopted, federal courts would not have been able to overturn such discriminatory state and municipal statutes by declaring them unconstitutional.

Even though Asian immigrants were not the population that the Reconstruction legislation was designed to protect and empower, Chinese were able to take advantage of certain clauses in the Fourteenth Amendment because these clauses addressed the civil rights not only of U.S. citizens but also of "persons"—a much broader category than "citizens." While the amendment's "privileges and immunities" clause guaranteed the rights of citizens, its "due process" and "equal protection" clauses safeguarded the rights of persons.[9] And Chinese, though aliens, were definitely persons. Other legislation enacted during Reconstruction likewise proved useful to the Chinese—most notably Section 16 of the 1870 Civil Rights Act, which stated that all persons within U.S. jurisdiction shall have "full and equal benefit of all laws and proceedings for the security of persons and property as is enjoyed by white citizens."[10] Attorneys for the Chinese also relied on a treaty signed during these years: the 1868 Burlingame Treaty between China and the United States, which proclaimed that Chinese were to "enjoy the same privileges, immunities, and exemptions in respect to travel or residence, as may there be enjoyed by the citizens or subjects of the most favored nation."[11]

The Chinese filed thousands of cases in municipal, state, and the lower federal courts using the above doctrines to fight against discrimination. More than 150 of their cases reached the U.S. Supreme Court.[12] Although most Chinese who came to earn a living in the United States in the nineteenth century were peasants who knew nothing about the fine points of constitutional law, they did understand the concept of justice. When they felt they had been unjustly treated, they did not hesitate to challenge the wrongs done them. The most important avenue of which they availed themselves was the American judicial system. It is not known how they learned about lawyers and courts, but within a few short years of their arrival, they began going to court not only to sue non-Chinese, and in some instances their fellow Chinese, but also to contest the discriminatory laws themselves. They hired some of the best trial lawyers of the day, who argued that the laws passed to empower African Americans were also applicable to the Chinese.

Two of these decisions were absolutely critical. *Ho Ah Kow v. Nunan* involved a Chinese attempt to strike down two obnoxious statutes—one, a San Francisco municipal ordinance that made it a crime to sleep in a room with less than 500 cubic feet of air space per person, and the other, a California state law based on an earlier San Francisco municipal ordinance that allowed jail wardens to cut off the hair of prisoners to within an inch of the scalp. Chinatown was indeed overcrowded, but so were other residential quarters in the poorer neighborhoods. What made the "cubic air ordinance" discriminatory was that it was enforced only against Chinese. As for the "queue ordinance," authorities knew that Qing-dynasty Chinese men were required to keep their hair long and wear it in a braid. Thus, cutting off their hair was a way to harass and punish them. *Ho Ah Kow v. Nunan*, decided in 1879 in the Circuit Court for the District of California, declared both statutes unconstitutional. Its historical significance lies in the fact that it was the first federal case to state clearly that the "equal protection" clause of the Fourteenth Amendment and Section 16 of the 1870 Civil Rights Act were applicable to Chinese as *persons*. This decision was crucial because just a year earlier Chinese had been denied the right to acquire naturalized citizenship in the *In re Ah Yup* case—a denial that would be reiterated in the 1882 Chinese Exclusion Law.[13]

The civil rights of Chinese were further expanded by the landmark 1886 U.S. Supreme Court decision in *Yick Wo v. Hopkins*. That ruling affirmed the right of Chinese laundrymen—and, by extension, other workers—to pursue a profession or trade without being subjected to the arbitrary power of governments. In the 1870s and 1880s, the license applications of hundreds of Chinese laundry-men in San Francisco had been systematically turned down on the pretext that their laundries were housed in wooden buildings and that they dried clothes on the roofs of these buildings, thereby creating public health and fire hazards. But the justices ruled in favor of the Chinese. They concluded that the rights protected by the Fourteenth Amendment applied to aliens also, and that a law that may be "fair on its face" can be discriminatory if it is administered in an unequal way.[14] Chinese immigrants would not have won such victories had there been no efforts to accord African Americans certain basic rights.

The 1890s to the 1920s

The fates of Asian immigrants and African Americans were again intertwined during the second period, which lasted from the 1890s to the 1920s. During those years, people of color suffered severe repression as the advances gained in the preceding period were repudiated and reversed. Three developments that shaped American national life during these decades are pertinent to our analysis: (a) the establishment of a racist system called Jim Crow, (b) the Progressive movement, and (c) the U.S. acquisition of an overseas empire. Jim Crow, a name borrowed from a minstrel song that depicted Black people as inferior and childlike, grew out of the Reconstruction-era "Black Codes" and lasted well into the mid–1950s. It not only legalized segregation in all public facilities—with this segregation upheld by the U.S. Supreme Court in the 1896 *Plessy v. Ferguson* decision—but also sanctioned acts of extreme violence, including lynching and arson, against African Americans.[15]

Moreover, to reduce the political power that African Americans had gained during Reconstruction, poll taxes, literacy tests, discriminatory voter-registration requirements, erratic hours at polling places manned by hostile elections offi-cials in areas with a large Black population, outright intimidation, and other methods were used to prevent the freed Black people from voting. Even in cities where African Americans were not kept away from polling places, various tactics were used to dilute their vote. For example, to minimize the number of seats that African American political candidates might win in areas where they com-prised a significant percentage of the voters, racial gerrymandering was used to redraw election district boundaries to reduce the Black demographic concen-tration. In some instances, citywide at-large elections replaced an electoral structure with single-candidate districts to ensure that no African American can-didates (or European American candidates sympathetic to Blacks) could be elected.[16] In addition to political disenfranchisement, African Americans suf-fered severe economic deprivation. A vast majority of the former slaves contin-ued to be kept on Southern plantations as tenants or sharecroppers, eking out a living under conditions no less exploitative than those under slavery. In these myriad ways, racial subordination remained an intrinsic part of American soci-ety even after a civil war had been fought to end slavery.[17]

The Progressive movement emerged around the same time that the Jim Crow system was consolidated.[18] This movement was called "progressive" because it brought about many reforms to improve people's lives. But if we look beneath the surface, we discover that it, too, had a racist thrust. The main Progressive reformers were well-educated middle-class professionals and businessmen who were concerned about the nation's problems—particularly problems related to the maturation of industrial capitalism, urbanization, and a rise in the number of new immigrants. Progressives had great faith in science. They believed that scientific methods could be used to impose order on a society that seemed increasingly chaotic. They thought progress would be possible only if human beings intervened to control the forces of nature as well as of society. They carried out municipal projects to improve public health and education. They introduced the initiative, the referendum, and the recall in order to place control of the government back in the hands of the common people. But their view of who comprised "the people" was extremely restricted: the moniker included mainly White Anglo-Saxon Protestant men. Progressives apparently saw no contradiction between their efforts to enlarge the arena of liberty for European American men and their support of Southern efforts to segregate, disenfranchise, and exploit African Americans. They also supported the anti-Japanese movement in the West. As historian Roger Daniels has put it, "The middle-class progressive liked to think of himself as enlightened and free of prejudice; yet at the same time he insisted that separate races could not mix."[19]

Progressive reformers desired a homogeneously White, Anglo-Saxon, Protestant society because they thought it would be more manageable. To them, race relations, like other aspects of society, should definitely be managed. In the words of Chester Rowell, a leading Progressive intellectual, "The only time to solve a race problem is before it begins."[20] Thus, even though Progressives did not initiate the anti-Japanese movement in California, once it began they did not hesitate to support it. Reducing the number of Japanese immigrants in the state suited their purpose of creating a manageable society. Furthermore, Progressive politicians were concerned about having to compete with anti-Asian Democrats for votes in California's 1910 and 1912 state elections.[21] Adopting an anti-Japanese stance was a way to reduce the advantage that their opponents enjoyed in an age rife with anti-Japanese antipathy.

Although the campaign to exclude selected groups of aspiring immigrants began long before the Progressives appeared on the scene, it thrived in the decades when they were trying most actively to reshape society. The Chinese had been the first group targeted for immigration restriction. A series of increasingly stringent laws was enacted between 1882 and 1904 to keep out Chinese laborers,[22] but Chinese of all socioeconomic backgrounds, including those "exempted" from exclusion, found it increasingly difficult to enter the United States. Initially, judges granted most of the writs of *habeas corpus* that Chinese filed whenever they were forbidden to land, but the courts eventually deferred to the executive branch of the federal government—specifically, its immigration officials—when control of the nation's borders was concerned.

Four U.S. Supreme Court cases explicitly linked the concept of national sovereignty to the issue of who could enter the United States as immigrants. In *Chae Chan Ping v. United States*, decided in 1889, the justices upheld the constitutionality of the Act of October 1, 1888 (the so-called Scott Act), which unilaterally abrogated the right of Chinese laborers to reenter the United States when they returned from visits to China. Six years earlier, the right to reenter had been granted to Chinese laborers who had resided in the United States before the 1882 Chinese Exclusion Law was passed: they could return without impediment if they obtained a certificate before their departure and could produce this document upon their return. Chae Chan Ping had such a certificate with him when he arrived but was nevertheless forbidden to land because the Scott Act, which went into effect the day it was passed, had been enacted while he was at sea, en route to the United States. He challenged this denial. His case was eventually heard in the U.S. Supreme Court, but he failed in his efforts. The court declared that when treaty obligations or earlier laws conflicted with later congressional legislation, the latter took precedence over the former, and, moreover, that the right to choose which aliens to admit was one of the nation's sovereign powers.[23]

The second case involved Ekiu Nishimura, a Japanese woman who was denied entry when she came to join her husband who was living in the United States. Because he did not come to pick her up when she arrived, she was deemed a person "likely to become a public charge"—one of the categories of excludable immigrants listed in the 1891 Immigration Act. Nishimura's case was the very first one filed by a Japanese to reach the U.S. Supreme Court. In *Ekiu Nishimura v. United States*, decided in 1892, the court ruled that "every sovereign nation has the power . . . to forbid the entrance of foreigners," and that executive officers were the "sole and final" decision-makers in immigration cases. Moreover, it ruled, the decisions of immigration officials, in and of themselves, satisfied the "due process" requirement of the Fourteenth Amendment.[24]

In the third case, *Fong Yue Ting v. United States*, decided in 1893, the high court upheld the power of the federal government not only to exclude but also to deport aliens. A year earlier, Congress had extended the 1882 Chinese Exclusion Act by passing the so-called Geary Act, which required all alien Chinese then residing in the United States to register. Thereafter, any Chinese caught without such a registration form on his or her person could be arrested and deported. The most important organization in the Chinese immigrant community—the Chinese Consolidated Benevolent Association (CCBA), commonly called the Chinese Six Companies—advised Chinese to participate in a massive act of civil disobedience by refusing to register. The Chinese took their case all the way to the Supreme Court, but they lost when the justices decided that "the right of a nation to expel or deport foreigners . . . is as absolute as the right to prohibit and prevent their entrance into the country."[25]

Then, in *United States v. Ju Toy*, decided in 1905, the U.S. Supreme Court gave up its right to judicial review over immigration matters altogether.[26] As civil rights lawyer Angelo N. Ancheta has pointed out, in these Asian immigration cases, the Supreme Court had enlarged the plenary powers of Congress to such an extent that the latter gained more power than the Constitution had intended.[27] The only victory won by the Chinese during the exclusion era was the decision made by the U.S. Supreme Court in 1898 in *Wong Kim Ark v. United States*, which determined that the birthright citizenship of individuals born in the United

States, including those whose parents were not eligible for naturalized citizenship, could not be stripped from them.[28]

Anti-immigrant forces also tried to limit the entry of groups other than the Chinese. The 1917 Immigration Act introduced a literacy test to keep out less educated and non-English-speaking immigrants, and delineated a "barred zone" (encompassing most of Asia) from which people could not come. Immigrants from India were the main victims of this clause.[29] In 1921, Congress passed another immigration act that limited the number of immigrants from any particular country to 3 percent of the number of persons of that national origin residing in the United States in 1910. Three years later, the 1924 Immigration Act reduced the quotas even further, limiting the number of immigrants from each country to only 2 percent of the number of persons of that national origin residing in the United States in 1890.[30] The date was moved back because the main targets of the 1924 law were aspiring immigrants from Eastern, Central, and Southern Europe, and there were far fewer people from those areas of Europe residing in the United States in 1890 than in 1910. Though Poles, Hungarians, Italians, Greeks, various Slavic peoples, and Russian Jews were Europeans, they were neither Anglo-Saxon nor Protestant, and thus were deemed less desirable than people from Northwestern Europe.

The main group of Asian immigrants affected negatively by the 1924 law was the Japanese, even though they were not explicitly named in the act. Rather, no quota at all was allotted to aliens who were "ineligible to (*sic*) citizenship." This phrase was a code for Asians. Chinese had already been barred from naturalized citizenship in 1878 and 1882; now it was the turn of the Japanese and Asian Indians. In its 1922 decision in *Takao Ozawa v. United States*, the U.S. Supreme Court decided that Japanese could not be naturalized because racially they were neither white nor of African ancestry—these being the only two eligible groups explicitly named in the 1870 Naturalization Act.[31] In 1923, the U.S. Supreme Court, in *United States v. Bhagat Singh Thind*, came up with yet another basis for denying naturalized citizenship to Asian immigrants. Thind claimed that, as a native of India, he was an Aryan, and hence a Caucasian, and so was eligible to become a naturalized citizen. The justices disagreed. They said that even though he might be an Aryan ethnographically, he was not "white" in the understanding of the common man.[32]

Additional disabilities were imposed in 1923 on those Asian immigrants who managed to remain on American soil. Four U.S. Supreme Court decisions handed down that year upheld laws that prohibited aliens "ineligible to citizenship" from owning or even leasing farmland in California and in the State of Washington (and, later, in a dozen other states). The high court upheld the constitutionality of the 1920 California Alien Land Law in *Porterfield v. Webb*, and that of the 1921 Washington Alien Land Law in *Terrace v. Thompson*. The court ruled in *Webb v. O'Brien* that even sharecropping contracts with aliens "ineligible to citizenship" were illegal, while *Frick v. Webb* forbade such aliens from owning stocks in any corporation formed for the purpose of farming.[33] These laws deprived Japanese and other Asian immigrants of an important source of livelihood. The right of non-citizens to pursue a trade or profession without harassment, as stated in the 1886 *Yick Wo* decision, was not extended to the right to farm.

The anti-Asian sentiments that undergirded the above decisions and other anti-Asian actions were part of a larger ideological framework that both condoned violence and legally sanctioned racial discrimination against people of color. However, in justifying anti-Asian measures, an additional theme emerged—namely, that the national sovereignty of the United States must be forcefully asserted and defended. This concern over sovereignty reflects the fact that the United States had become an imperialist power during the last decade of the nineteenth century. In 1898, in one fell swoop, the United States acquired Hawai'i, Guam, the Philippines, and Puerto Rico as "insular possessions"—a euphemism for island colonies—beyond its continental borders. Furthermore, from that year onward, the United States repeatedly intervened in Cuba and in various Central American countries, landing Marines on their shores and taking over the governance of those countries for years at a time.[34] The crusade against leftists during the "Red Scare" that occurred after the Bolsheviks came to power in Russia was yet another manifestation of the wariness and fear with which many Americans regarded foreigners and their cultural practices and political ideologies.

There was an interregnum between the second and third periods because the Great Depression preoccupied Americans during the 1930s more than race relations or immigration did. The only significant law passed in the 1930s that affected Asian immigrants negatively was the 1934 Tydings-McDuffie Act. Its main purpose was to spell out the steps that had to be followed before independence could be granted to the Philippines, but it also contained a clause that reduced the number of Filipino immigrants to the U.S. to fifty persons a year.

THE 1940S TO THE 1970S

The third period in the history of the Asian American struggle for civil rights was by far the most complex of the four periods I have identified. It began in the summer of 1941 and ended with the 1978 U.S. Supreme Court decision, *Regents of the University of California v. Bakke.* The period can be subdivided into two segments. During the first segment, which stretched from 1941 to 1952, Asian immigrants and Asian Americans won *political* rights for the first time. These rights were granted by the federal government through executive orders, legislative action, and judicial decisions. World War II was the crucial factor that brought about the changes. During the second segment, which lasted from the early 1950s to the late 1970s, the Cold War (and one of its offshoots, the war in Vietnam), the Civil Rights movement, and the Black Power movement provided the crucial backdrops. Sit-ins, mass demonstrations, and "direct action" were the tactics of choice while the Civil Rights movement was unified, but when it splintered in 1966, one component of the movement retained racial integration as its goal and nonviolence as its main tactic, while other components—Black Power and various cultural nationalist currents—adopted more militant and separatist outlooks and actions.

Relatively few Asian Americans were involved in the civil rights protests of the early 1960s, although they nevertheless benefited from the legislation passed in response to the political and moral pressures exerted by the Civil Rights movement. What turned some Asian American high-school and college students into political activists was the antiwar movement against American involvement in Vietnam. Then, in 1969, Asian American college students joined their African American, Mexican American, and Native American peers in two massive student strikes at San Francisco State College (now University) and at the University of California, Berkeley, to demand a more relevant education and the establishment of Ethnic Studies programs. Asian American professionals also set up social service agencies to improve service delivery to Asian American communities in the name of "community control."[35] In terms of timing, therefore, these components of the multifaceted Asian American movement took shape after ethnic separatism became the defining characteristic of minority protest. Ethnic Studies programs and community service agencies have not only endured to this day—through many ups and downs—but have grown substantially in some localities, having survived longer than any of the other reforms instituted during this tumultuous period.

Long before protest movements in America captured the world's attention, tentative steps had been taken to change the state of race relations in the United States. In July 1941, several months before the United States declared war against the Axis powers—Japan, Germany, and Italy—President Franklin D. Roosevelt issued Executive Order 8802 to prohibit employment discrimination both by defense industries holding federal contracts and within the federal government itself. He did so to dissuade African American civil-rights pioneer A. Philip Randolph, president of the Sleeping Car Porters Union, from organizing a mass demonstration in Washington, D.C., to protest racial discrimination. Roosevelt also realized that, should the United States enter the war, the nation would need to maximize wartime production by calling forth the utmost effort from every American—men and women, whites and non-whites. Apparently he hoped that by ending employment discrimination, at least in certain public sectors, the loyalty and dedication of non-white Americans would be ensured during wartime. But he did not go very far in his efforts: during World War II, the contradiction between American ideals and American practices was starkly revealed by the fact that African American and Japanese American inductees called upon to defend democracy and liberty against fascism had to serve in segregated military units. Yet Roosevelt made no attempt to desegregate the armed forces. Instead, in 1943, he signed Executive Order 9346 to extend the earlier anti-discrimination order to all business and manufacturing enterprises holding federal contracts.[36]

The main group of Asian Americans who benefited from these executive orders were Chinese American college graduates, several thousand of whom found jobs commensurate with their education for the first time. The men worked mainly as scientists, engineers, and technicians, while most of the women worked at secretarial jobs, though a small number found jobs in the shipyards building "Liberty Ships," alongside significant numbers of European American and African American women.[37]

A large number of college-educated Japanese Americans was also available for employment, but the wartime labor market did not open its doors to them. Instead, simply because they looked like the enemy, some 120,000 persons of Japanese ancestry, two-thirds of them U.S.-born American citizens, were incarcerated in camps enclosed by barbed wire and guarded by armed troops. Four Japanese Americans—Gordon Hirabayashi, Min Yasui, Fred Korematsu, and Mitsuye Endo—challenged the constitutionality of their detention, but in each of these test cases, the U.S. Supreme Court rested its decision on the narrowest legal grounds and avoided making any pronouncements about whether or not the evacuation itself was constitutional. These decisions were finally vacated in the 1980s, through the brilliant litigation of young Asian American attorneys who helped the plaintiffs petition to have their cases reopened.[38]

The exigencies of World War II prompted the nation's leaders to offer Asian immigrants a modicum of political rights. To ensure that China, an ally of the United States during World War II, would fight strenuously against Japan, Congress repealed all the Chinese exclusion laws in late 1943.[39] Chinese were given a token annual immigration quota of 105 persons, plus the right to become naturalized citizens. Filipinos and Asian Indians gained the same rights in 1946, as a reward for also having been America's allies during the war. Japanese and Koreans did not acquire these rights until 1952—the same year the United States ended its seven-year military occupation of Japan, whose unconditional surrender in 1945 had brought an end to World War II. Acquiring the franchise meant that Asian immigrants were no longer barred from membership in the American polity.

Even Japanese Americans, more than twenty thousand of whom proved their loyalty in blood during World War II, gained something in the immediate postwar years: the courts overturned a number of prewar and wartime discriminatory statutes affecting them. In 1948, in *Oyama v. California*, the U.S. Supreme Court decided that California's Alien Land Law was unconstitutional. In the same year, in *Takahashi v. Fish and Game Commission*, the high court also struck down a 1943 California law that prohibited aliens "ineligible to citizenship" from fishing in the waters off the California coast. The state supreme courts of Oregon and California declared their states' alien land laws unconstitutional in 1949 and 1952, while the Washington legislature threw out that state's alien land law in 1967.[40] In this same period, discriminatory housing ordinances and anti-miscegenation laws also fell by the wayside.[41]

The Cold War[42] and the Civil Rights movement,[43] both of which began in the late 1940s, dominated the 1950s and 1960s. Scholars who have studied the two have generally treated them as unrelated phenomena, but as law professor Mary L. Dudziak has chronicled, a close relationship in fact existed between them.[44] Most accounts of the Civil Rights movement date it from the mid–1950s, but it actually began earlier, albeit quietly, without the kind of media exposure that protest activities in the 1960s received. In 1948, in response to another threat by A. Philip Randolph to organize a mass campaign of civil disobedience, President Harry S. Truman issued Executive Order 9981 to end segregation in the armed forces. Truman also created a Fair Employment Board within the federal civil service and a Government Contract Compliance Committee. His successors, Presidents Dwight D. Eisenhower and John F. Kennedy, likewise issued executive orders to promote racial equality,[45] not so much because they were good liberals as because they were pragmatic leaders who did not want domestic conditions to hamper their conduct of foreign relations during the Cold War.

The landmark civil-rights decision came in 1954, when *Brown v. Board of Education* mandated school desegregation by declaring the "separate but equal" doctrine laid down in the 1896 *Plessy* case unconstitutional.[46] In an *amicus curiae* brief filed by the U.S. Justice Department in connection with this case, the government's lawyers—quoting the U.S. State Department, which had received communications from many countries criticizing the inhumane way African Americans were being treated—told the court that America's troubled race relations were having a harmful effect on the country's standing in the international arena. The brief stated that "racial discrimination furnishes grist for the Communist propaganda mills, and it raises doubts even among friendly nations as to the intensity of our devotion to the democratic faith."[47] Since both the United States and the Soviet Union were trying strenuously to win the allegiance of countries in Asia, Africa, and Latin America during the Cold War, America's discrimination against African Americans was a black mark against it in the eyes of non-white peoples in the Third World.

When Southern leaders tried to defy the orders to desegregate education, the federal government sent troops into Little Rock, Arkansas, in 1957 to safeguard the courageous Black students who attempted to enroll in that city's high school. In the early 1960s, federal troops had to be sent once again to the South to protect Black Americans, as well as their white supporters, from brutal assaults. Pictures of police dogs attacking demonstrators and of policemen shooting jets of water out of fire hoses so powerful that they knocked their targets off their feet were seen around the world and had a truly deleterious impact. Condemnations appeared in the world press, and these were clipped and sent to the State Department by foreign service officers in American embassies and consulates.[48] Such adverse publicity convinced federal officials that they had no choice but to support the Civil Rights movement. As the United States Information Agency put it in one of its reports, "a successful outcome of this revolution in American society" would be "basic to its leadership in world affairs."[49]

President Lyndon B. Johnson, who knew Congress intimately, having served for years as Senate majority leader before he became vice president in the Kennedy administration, succeeded in persuading Congress to pass the most sweeping civil-rights legislation in U.S. history, partly as a tribute to President Kennedy, his assassinated predecessor. The 1964 Civil Rights Act, passed only after a compromise was reached following more than eighty days of filibuster by Southern senators, guaranteed people of all racial origins equal access to public accommodations, strengthened existing mechanisms for preventing employment discrimination, authorized the federal government to file school desegregation lawsuits, and allowed funds to be cut off from federal contractors who were found to discriminate.[50] Foreigner observers hailed it as "an historic advance" and "a vindication of the U.S. democratic system."[51] The act's Title VII established the Equal Employment Opportunity Commission, which can hear complaints, investigate allegations of violations, attempt to get the parties to reconcile, and, should no conciliation be possible, file lawsuits against the offending party. In a case decided in 1971, *Griggs v. Duke Power Company*—a decision reminiscent of the 1886 *Yick Wo* decision—the U.S. Supreme Court ruled that Title VII not only prohibits outright discrimination but also forbids employment policies and practices that have a "disparate impact" on minorities.[52]

The 1965 Voting Rights Act suspended the use of literacy tests and other devices to prevent people of color from voting, authorized the appointment of federal examiners to register people to vote, empowered the federal courts to enforce the Fifteenth Amendment, and provided criminal penalties against people who intimidate others in order to deny them the franchise.[53] The ability of minorities to exercise real political power was further increased after the U.S. Supreme Court, in the 1973 *White v. Regester* decision, ruled that at-large elections violate the "equal protection" clause of the Fourteenth Amendment because such an electoral format or structure reduces, or even completely eliminates, the chances of non-white candidates winning elections, thereby denying minorities equal participation in the political process.[54] As a result of this decision, the enfranchisement of non-white citizens now entails more than the right to vote; it also includes the ability to "elect legislators of their choice."

Even though Asian Americans were not meant to be the chief beneficiaries of these two laws, they successfully used Title VI of the 1964 Civil Rights Act to argue, in the *Lau v. Nichols* case, decided by the U.S. Supreme Court in 1974, that a school system that does not take the needs of limited-English-speaking students into account is denying equal educational opportunity to such students.[55] The high court did not suggest any specific remedies, but its decision "implicitly mandated bilingual education," according to L. Ling-chi Wang, one of the key strategists in the campaign to secure educational equity for language minority students.[56] Following the *Lau* decision, Congress passed the Equal Educational Opportunity Act in 1974 to enable federal agencies to monitor how schools were complying with the *Lau* decision.[57]

Asian immigrants with limited proficiency in English also benefited from the 1965 Voting Rights Act when its coverage was extended in 1975 to include language minorities.[58] A statutory basis was thereby created for multilingual ballots and election information brochures. Just as importantly, in *United Jewish Organizations v. Carey*, decided in 1977, the U.S. Supreme Court declined to overturn redistricting boundaries drawn to increase the likelihood of minority candidates winning elections.[59] As a result of this decision, some politically active Asian Americans in localities with sizable numbers of Asian American voters have participated in the redistricting efforts that occurred after the results of the 1980 and 1990 censuses became known.[60]

Historic as the 1964 Civil Rights Act and the 1965 Voting Rights Act have been, their impact on Asian Americans pales in comparison with a third piece of legislation passed in the same period—the 1965 Immigration Act, which abolished the discriminatory "national origins" quota system and replaced it with a system that puts immigrants from all countries of the world on an equal footing. Since 1965, two basic principles have guided the selection of immigrants: family reunification, and preferences given to individuals with skills needed by the U.S. economy.[61] Aspiring Asian immigrants have been able to make use of both selection criteria. As a result, the Asian-ancestry population in the United States has burgeoned in the last thirty-five years, transforming Asian communities in America.

Asian immigrants who have entered the United States since 1965 fall broadly into two groups. One consists of well-educated, highly trained professionals who have adapted relatively easily to life in the United States. Many of them find jobs in high-technology industries and in the various professions. Some bring sufficient capital to open their own businesses. A second, larger group consists of people entering through the family-reunification provisions of the 1965 and 1990 immigration laws. Many of them are less well-educated and lack both relevant job skills and fluency in English. In addition to immigrants, over a million people from Vietnam, Laos, and Cambodia have entered as refugees since 1975. Though the refugee population also falls into these two groups, the overwhelming majority belongs to the poorer segment of the Asian-ancestry population. Many of them hold low-paying jobs with few, if any, fringe benefits and no long-term job security, while others rely on welfare payments to survive.

The two kinds of Asian newcomers fill two different needs in the contemporary American labor market. Some scholars have called the present economy an "hourglass economy," first, because the two sectors that have grown fastest in the last few decades have been high-tech industries and personal services, and second, because it is now extremely difficult to climb up the occupational ladder from the lower tier to the upper one.[62] (In contrast, heavy industries manufacturing durable goods have declined in importance—a process that some observers have called "de-industrialization." In the past, the blue-collar jobs in these industries paid relatively high wages and served as a channel of upward mobility—a phenomenon that validated the existence of "the American Dream.") Today, the well-educated Asian immigrants meet the economy's need for technicians, engineers, and scientists in the top part of the hourglass, while the less-educated ones fill the bottom part's job openings. They become janitors, house cleaners, cooks, dishwashers, and nannies—such "woman's work" being increasingly done by hired help as more and more middle-class women of all ethnic backgrounds join the labor force.

Since the 1960s, Asian Americans have also benefited from affirmative action regulations and programs. Those programs that address employment discrimination have provided them with a statutory basis on which to demand *economic* rights. The term "affirmative action" was first used by President John Kennedy in 1961 in Executive Order 10925, which required companies with federal contracts to take positive action to prevent any employment discrimination based on race, color, creed, or national origin. The term appeared again in Title VII of the 1964 Civil Rights Act. In 1967, President Lyndon Johnson, in Executive Order 11375, extended the coverage to women by prohibiting discrimination on account of sex. Two years later, the Nixon administration established the

"Philadelphia Plan" to require the construction industry in Philadelphia and several other cities to come up with goals and timetables for hiring a specified number of minority workers. In subsequent years, federal guidelines indicated that tests could be used by employers only if they can be shown to be valid predictors of job performance.[63] One affirmative-action program that has benefited a significant number of Asian Americans economically is administered by the Small Business Administration, which has interpreted Section 8(a) of the 1953 act that established the agency in such a way as to allow set-asides for minority businesses. The Nixon administration created the Office of Minority Business Enterprises in 1969 to coordinate state and local resources for, and technical assistance to, minority businesses.[64]

It is important to understand how affirmative action differs from civil rights. Affirmative action programs aim not only to remedy past discrimination but also to prevent present or future discrimination. Whereas civil rights focus on equality of *opportunity*, affirmative action attempts to bring about equality of *results*. While civil rights are couched in terms of *individuals*, affirmative action programs are meant to affect *groups*. The importance of these differences, and the problems that have arisen because of them, will become clear as we examine the fourth period in the history of Asian American struggles for various kinds of rights.

THE LATE 1970S TO THE PRESENT

This fourth period is characterized by globalization and a conservative backlash. Economic globalization began with a phenomenon called "capitalist restructuring," which emerged in the 1970s with the rise of the "four little tigers," or "mini-dragons"—South Korea, Taiwan, Hong Kong, and Singapore.[65] These countries, following the example of Japan, adopted an export-led path of economic development. They succeeded so well that their exports began to compete with products from the United States, Western European countries, and Japan, where industrial production had been concentrated before the 1970s. (Countries in the Communist bloc had also become industrialized, but their products were seldom sold outside of their own bloc.) Today, transnational companies increasingly locate their manufacturing plants in Asian and Latin American countries with cheap labor and few environmental protection laws. Global capitalism recognizes no national borders: technology, raw materials, workers, and managers all roam the world in search of profits. However, control over research and development, as well as overall planning, has remained in corporate headquarters still located mainly in the United States, Western Europe, Japan, and the more developed of the newly industrializing countries.

During the contemporary period, Asian American rights-activists have focused on gaining *social* rights—namely, rights regarding education, the lack of English proficiency, anti-Asian violence, and racial profiling. The efforts to gain social rights, to ensure that Asian Americans continue to make headway in achieving economic rights, and to beat back attempts to diminish Asian American political rights are far more challenging than the earlier struggles for civil rights, for several reasons. First, when the Cold War ended in 1990, with the demise of Communism in

Eastern European countries and the political disintegration of the former Soviet Union itself, the powerful impetus that the Cold War had given the Civil Rights movement disappeared as well. Today, discrimination no longer "costs" the United States in the same way that it did from the late 1940s through the 1980s.

Second, because the U.S. Constitution and its pertinent amendments do not specify economic and social rights as such, there are no clear constitutional doctrines that Asian American activists can employ to make the social rights claims they are trying to make. Unfortunately, the distinction between civil and political rights, on the one hand, and economic and social rights, on the other, is widely accepted. The former set of rights carries far greater moral authority than does the latter. Even the United Nations has had to recognize the difference. In the first years of its existence, the UN's Human Rights Commission set about crafting a Universal Declaration of Human Rights. Mrs. Eleanor Roosevelt, who represented the United States in this effort and who chaired the commission, argued vigorously that the different kinds of rights should be treated as a unity. But as Mary Ann Glendon has revealed in a recent book, the U.S. State Department and other American officials strongly opposed her views: they thought that advocating for economic and social rights was Communistic and un-American.[66] Within the commission itself, members compromised by creating two separate enabling covenants for the Universal Declaration of Human Rights adopted in 1948. The first addresses civil and political rights, while the second deals with economic and social rights. Even with the two sets of rights now separated, the United States treated the Declaration only as "a non-binding statement of principles" until 1977, when President Jimmy Carter finally signed and forwarded it to Congress. However, Congress did not ratify the Declaration until 1992. Meanwhile, the economic and social rights covenant has languished and provides very little moral imperative, whether in the United States or anywhere else.

Third, conservatives opposed to the enlargement of rights for minorities have used extremely sophisticated tactics to erode the gains made during the Civil Rights era. They have argued that the programs established in those years not only have not solved any problems but have actually been the causes of the nation's current multiple ills. Three U.S. Supreme Court decisions have narrowed the reach of affirmative action. The first case involved Allan Bakke, a white student who had been denied admission to the medical school at the Davis campus of the University of California, which reserved sixteen out of one hundred slots in each year's incoming class for minority applicants. He sued the UC Regents for discriminating against him. In *Regents of the University of California v. Bakke*, the U.S. Supreme Court ruled in 1978 that such set-aside quotas violated the 1964 Civil Rights Act. However, the court left a crack open by allowing race-conscious criteria to continue to be used in a very limited way.[67] Two subsequent decisions have further severely limited the potential impact of affirmative action programs. In 1989, in *City of Richmond v. Croson*, the high court struck down the business affirmative-action plan of Richmond, Virginia, because its affirmative action net had been cast too widely and included too many groups. As Justice Sandra Day O'Connor wrote, "There is absolutely no evidence of past discrimination against Spanish-speaking, Oriental, Indian, Eskimo, or Aleut persons in any aspect of the Richmond construction industry."[68] (This list refers to the fact that in the 1960s, African Americans, "Spanish Americans," "Orientals," and "American Indians" were deemed eligible for affirmative action programs, but the categories were later expanded, so that the "African American" category now also includes Black people from the Caribbeans and Africa; the "Spanish American" category now refers to persons from Latin America, the Spanish-speaking Caribbeans, and Spain itself; the "Oriental" rubric now covers persons from East, Southeast, and South Asia—but not Afghanistan, countries in the Middle East, or the Asian part of the Soviet Union; and the "American Indian" category now takes in Eskimos and Aleuts.)[69] Then, in the 1995 *Adarand Constructors, Inc. v. Pena* decision, the Supreme Court ruled that affirmative action programs—whether they deal with education, employment, or federal contracts—must meet a judicial review standard of "strict scrutiny," which means that they can continue to exist only if the remedy is "narrowly tailored" to meet a "compelling" government interest.[70]

In light of these decisions, at present a remedy can be used only if there is concrete evidence that the allegedly guilty party (and not just society in general) specifically discriminated against a particular class of persons in the past or is still doing so at present. Today, an educational institution or an employer wishing to establish an affirmative action program must first carry out a "disparity study" to document the history of discrimination against a specific group. Proposed remedies must be of limited duration, benefit only the group(s) that had been discriminated against, and not impose undue burdens on white Americans.[71]

In recent years, anti-affirmative-action efforts have merged with anti-immigrant campaigns.[72] One consequence is that the fate of Asian immigrants has become more closely tied to that of Latino immigrants than to the situation of African Americans. Immigrants, both legal and illegal, have been the main targets of California's Proposition 187, the 1996 Personal Responsibility and Work Opportunity Reconciliation Act (the "Welfare Reform Act"), and the 1996 Illegal Immigration Reform and Immigrant Responsibility Act. In contrast, the main victims of the 1995 decision by the Regents of the University of California to stop using race-conscious methods to increase the number of underrepresented students—a policy in effect for six years until it was rescinded in May 2001—and of Proposition 209, passed in California in 1996, have been people of color, both immigrants and American-born.[73]

As journalism professor Lydia Chavez has documented, voters supported Proposition 209 for complex reasons. The most important reason was that many voters were unaware of the proposition's true intention—to end affirmative action—because its text made no reference at all to "affirmative action," claiming instead that its purpose was to end discrimination of any kind and against any person. Just as important, the groups opposing it were badly splintered and lacked financial support. In contrast, California Governor Pete Wilson and the Republican Party poured large sums of money into the pro-209 campaign. To avoid being sucked into a racial "wedge issue," the Democratic Party played only a lukewarm role in opposing it. Polls have shown that Americans in general are against discrimination; at the same time, they strongly oppose "preferential treatments" or "quotas" intended to benefit only certain specified groups.[74]

Efforts have also been made to undermine the growing political power of non-white Americans. In its 1993 decision in *Shaw v. Reno,* the U.S. Supreme Court affirmed that white Americans have the right to sue if race is the "predominant factor" in drawing electoral district boundaries.[75] In the 1994 *Holder v. Hall* decision, the court declared that neither the Fourteenth and Fifteenth Amendments nor the 1965 Voting Rights Act can be used to challenge the phenomenon of "vote dilution"—that is, the use of various mechanisms to minimize the impact of minority voters.[76] In a third case, *Miller v. Johnson,* decided in 1995, the court threw out the newly drawn boundaries of certain electoral districts, the aim of which was to enhance the clout of minority voters.[77] In light of these decisions, attempts to redraw electoral district boundaries after the results of the 2000 census become available will doubtless engender many conflicts.

The 1990s witnessed the unfolding of a great historical irony. Just as a successful African American businessman, Ward Connerly, led the effort to eliminate affirmative action at the University of California and played a key role in the Proposition 209 campaign, so another prominent African American, Supreme Court Justice Clarence Thomas, led the judicial attack against minority voting rights in the above three decisions. Connerly and Thomas represent a new phenomenon—the emergence of conservative individuals among African, Latino, and Asian Americans who are playing a leadership role in dismantling the gains of the Civil Rights era.

Yet individuals alone, no matter how firmly committed to retrenching various rights, could not succeed in their efforts were it not for the sea change brought about by the "Reagan Revolution" in the country's political and social climate—a change that the New Democrats during the Clinton administration attempted to domesticate and coopt in their own contest for political power. In the last two decades, the anti-affirmative-action and anti-immigrant campaigns succeeded because they tapped into the growing resentment that many European Americans have felt since the late 1960s. Not only has the average American worker experienced a decline in his or her real wages in the last thirty-some years, but he or she has also found that channels for upward socioeconomic mobility in today's globalized "hourglass economy" have become severely constricted. The gap between the richest and the poorest segments of the American population has grown alarmingly. Instead of attributing their downward slide to the phenomenal profits that giant corporations now make or expect to make, many working-class Americans blame their fall from grace on post–1965 immigrants from Asia and Latin America who compete with them for jobs, and on poorly paid (also non-white) workers overseas. They also blame affirmative action for favoring members of domestic minority groups, and the nation's liberal immigration laws for letting in so many non-white people. In other words, class antagonism is being deflected and is, instead, perceived in racial terms. However, since overt racism is no longer socially acceptable in the United States, at least not in public, theorists of the conservative cause have cynically but cleverly used the rhetoric of "preferences," "set-asides," "quotas," and "reverse discrimination" to get their message across to a receptive audience.[78]

Fourth, the most formidable hurdle that Asian American rights-activists now face comes, ironically, from within their own ranks. Affirmative action has been a highly controversial issue within Asian American communities because the Asian-ancestry population is now so heterogeneous. It is divided by national origin, language, religion, nativity, citizenship status, years of residence in the United States, class, sex, and, most important of all, political ideology. There are now numerous answers to such questions as: Who among the Asian-ancestry population should qualify for affirmative action? Should well-to-do Asian immigrants, including those who are not U.S. citizens, enjoy the benefits originally intended for historically oppressed racial minorities, particularly African Americans? Should high-achieving Asian American students be allowed to enroll in unlimited numbers at elite schools such as San Francisco's Lowell High School or the Berkeley and Los Angeles campuses of the University of California? Can it be argued that all Asian Americans are still "minorities"? Do Asian Americans want to be "minorities"? Are Asian American employers themselves practicing discrimination when they use word-of-mouth to recruit co-ethnic workers, thereby shutting out potential applicants from other groups? Debates over these questions have been heated, and Asian American rights-activists today are truly caught in a bind.

Politicians and others opposed to affirmative action have taken advantage of the ideological cleavages among Asian Americans by telling them that they are victimized when places are set aside for African, Latino, and Native Americans. Conservatives argue that affirmative action programs are a form of "reverse discrimination" against European Americans, particularly white men. They point out that the group basis of affirmative action violates the most deeply rooted American value: individualism. In American society, they say, people are supposed to be rewarded according to their individual merit. Moreover, the U.S. Constitution was designed to limit the ability of the government to regulate private behavior. Therefore, when federal or state agencies monitor businesses or schools to see whether or not they are complying with affirmative action guidelines, the government is intruding into the private realm in an unconstitutional manner. The struggle against conservative ideology and actions is so difficult because, in their efforts to demolish affirmative action, conservatives are using the very same rhetoric—and, more importantly, the same judicial doctrines—that oppressed groups have used in the past to fight for greater equality.

Some Asian Americans have bought such conservative arguments, partly because some of them agree with the principles voiced by European American and African American conservatives, partly because some hold negative views of African Americans and Latino Americans, and partly because many individuals are concerned mainly with their own advancement. Yet Asian Americans adopt such a stance at their own peril, for their status in American society, though greatly improved in recent years, remains a precarious one, subject to the changing winds of politics. The much-touted Asian American "success" did not prevent Asian-named donors from being singled out for investigation when the campaign finance scandal broke out during the 1996 elections. Neither did it prevent Dr. Wen Ho Lee from being incarcerated and held in solitary confinement when no real proof existed of his alleged guilt.

In my opinion, we Asian Americans really cannot afford to set ourselves apart from or above other groups who are also struggling for civil, political, economic, and social rights. We must not forget or minimize the fact that, historically, whatever rights we have gained have depended largely on the rights African Americans have won. In these days when critics of affirmative action are using a "divide and conquer" tactic to roll back the advances made during the Civil Rights era, we cannot afford to be racists ourselves. Although many Asians now residing in the United States tend to think of themselves not as minority Americans but as transnational members of various Asian diasporas who maintain ties with, and loyalty to, co-ethnics around the world, we must never forget that whatever rights we have acquired in the last century and a half have been contingent on our ability to claim membership in *American society*—claims we began making long before Asian immigrants were allowed to become naturalized citizens.

NOTES

This essay is revised from a keynote address given by the author on June 8, 2001 in San Francisco, at a dinner commemorating the thirty-second anniversary of the civil rights organization Chinese for Affirmative Action.

1. The literature on Reconstruction is voluminous. Eric Foner, *Reconstruction: America's Unfinished Revolution, 1863–1877* (New York: Harper & Row, 1988) provides an excellent overview. William Gillette, *Retreat from Reconstruction, 1869–1879* (Baton Rouge: Louisiana State University Press, 1979) discusses why the radical Republicans failed to complete the task they had set themselves. On the role of the army, see James Sefton, *The United States Army and Reconstruction, 1865–1877* (Baton Rouge: Louisiana State University Press, 1967). Two works by prominent African American historians are of critical importance: W.E.B. Du Bois, *Black Reconstruction in America, 1860–1880: An Essay Toward a History of the Part Which Black Folk Played in the Attempt to Reconstruct Democracy in America* (New York: Russell & Russell, 1935; Atheneum, 1972) remains a classic, while John Hope Franklin, *Reconstruction After the Civil War* (Chicago: University of Chicago Press, 1961; 2nd ed., 1994) assesses the accomplishments and failures of Reconstruction.
2. On birthright citizenship and people of color, see James H. Kettner, *The Development of American Citizenship, 1608–1870* (Chapel Hill: University of North Carolina Press, 1978), 287–333.
3. *Dred Scott v. Sanford,* 60 U.S. 393 (1857).
4. Act of July 14, 1870, 16 Stat. 254.
5. Civil Rights Act of 1866, 14 Stat. 27; Civil Rights Act of 1870, 16 Stat. 140; Civil Rights Act of 1871, 17 Stat. 13; and Civil Rights Act of 1875, 18 Stat. 335. These acts are discussed in Rogers M. Smith, *Civil Ideals: Conflicting Visions of Citizenship in U.S. History* (New Haven, Conn.: Yale University Press, 1997), 305–08, 317, and 325–27, while Charles J. McClain, *In Search of Equality: The Chinese Struggle against Discrimination in Nineteenth-Century America* (Berkeley and Los Angeles: University of California Press, 1994), 32–42, shows how they affected Chinese immigrants.
6. Akhil Reed Amar, *The Bill of Rights: Creation and Reconstruction* (New Haven, Conn.: Yale University Press, 1998), 48.
7. Amar, *Bill of Rights,* provides a systematic exposition of each amendment in the Bill of Rights and of the Fourteenth Amendment.
8. Amar, *Bill of Rights,* 181–86.

9. McClain, *In Search of Equality*, 31–36; Amar, *Bill of Rights*, 163–74; and Smith, *Civil Ideals*, 308–12.

10. McClain, *In Search of Equality*, 38–40.

11. The Burlingame Treaty, July 28, 1868, 16 Stat. 739. For the story of how Anson Burlingame, an American diplomat, came to lead a mission to the United States on behalf of the Chinese government, see Frederick Wells Williams, *Anson Burlingame and the First Chinese Mission to Foreign Powers* (New York: Russell & Russell, 1912; repr. 1972).

12. McClain, *In Search of Equality*, contains the most analytical discussion of the key cases. (McClain's many journal articles are not listed here because they became chapters in his book.) A very lengthy unpublished dissertation, Hudson N. Janisch, "The Chinese, the Courts, and the Constitution: A Study of the Legal Issues Raised by Chinese Immigration, 1850–1902" (J.S.D. dissertation, University of Chicago Law School, 1971), is a veritable treasure-trove of information about not only the landmark federal cases but also a large array of cases heard in local and state courts. Lucy E. Salyer, *Laws Harsh as Tigers: Chinese Immigrants and the Shaping of Modern Immigration Law* (Chapel Hill: University of North Carolina Press, 1995), offers an excellent analysis of the interplay among Chinese immigrants, the law, and politics in the making of U.S. immigration law. Four chapters in Sucheng Chan, ed., *Entry Denied: Exclusion and the Chinese Community in America, 1882–1943* (Philadelphia: Temple University Press, 1991), are also pertinent: Charles J. McClain and Laurene Wu McClain, "The Chinese Contribution to the Development of American Law," 3–24; Christian G. Fritz, "Due Process, Treaty Rights, and Chinese Exclusion, 1882–1891," 25–46 (which is a revised version of "A Nineteenth-Century 'Habeas Corpus Mill': The Chinese Before the Federal Courts in California," *Journal of American Legal History* 32 [1988]:347–72); Lucy E. Salyer, "'Laws Harsh as Tigers': Enforcement of the Chinese Exclusion Laws, 1891–1924," 57–93 (an earlier version of which appeared as "Captives of Law: Judicial Enforcement of the Chinese Exclusion Laws, 1891–1905," *Journal of American History* 76 [Sept. 1989]: 91–117); and Sucheng Chan, "The Exclusion of Chinese Women, 1870–1943," 94–146. See also Ralph James Mooney, "Matthew Deady and the Federal Judicial Response to Racism in the Early West," *Oregon Law Review* 63 (1984): 561–637; Louis Henkin, "The Constitution and United States Sovereignty: A Century of Chinese Exclusion and Its Progeny," *Harvard Law Review* 100 (1987): 853–86; Linda C. A. Przybyszewski, "Judge Lorenzo Sawyer and the Chinese: Civil Rights Decisions in the Ninth Circuit," *Western Legal History* 1 (1988): 23–56; David Beeseley, "More than *People v. Hall:* Chinese Immigrants and American Law in a Sierra Nevada County, 1850–1920," *Locus* 3 (1991): 123–39; Malik Simba, "Gong Lum v. Rice: The Convergence of Law, Race, and Ethnicity," *Explorations in Ethnic Studies* 15 (July 1992): 1–17; David C. Frederick, *Rugged Justice: The Ninth Circuit Court of Appeals and the American West, 1891–1941* (Berkeley and Los Angeles: University of California Press, 1994), chap. 3: "Testing Tolerance: Chinese Exclusion and the Ninth Circuit," 52–77; Ellen D. Katz, "The Six Companies and the Geary Act: A Case Study in Nineteenth-Century Civil Disobedience and Civil Rights Litigation," *Western Legal History* 8 (Summer/Fall 1995): 227–71; and the following articles by John R. Wunder: "Law and the Chinese in Frontier Montana," *Montana* 30 (July 1980): 18–31; "The Courts and the Chinese in Frontier Idaho," *Idaho Yesterday* 25 (Spring 1981): 23–32; "The Chinese and the Courts in the Pacific Northwest: Justice Denied?" *Pacific Historical Review* 52 (May 1983): 191–211; "Chinese in Trouble: Criminal Law and Race on the Trans-Mississippi West Frontier," *Western Historical Quarterly* 17 (January 1986): 25–41; "Law and the Chinese on the Southwest Frontier, 1850s–1902," *Western Legal History* 2 (Summer/Fall 1989): 139–58; and "*Territory of New Mexico v. Yee Shun:* A Turning Point in Chinese Legal Relationships in the Trans-Mississippi West," *New Mexico Historical Review* 65 (1990): 305–18.

13. *Ho Ah Kow v. Nunan*, 12 F.Cas. 252 (1879); *In re Ah Yup*, 1 F.Cas. 223 (1878).

14. *Yick Wo v. Hopkins*, 118 U.S. 356 (1886).

15. *Plessy v. Ferguson*, 163 U.S. 537 (1896). For the impact of Jim Crow on African Americans, see C. Vann Woodward, *The Strange Career of Jim Crow* (New York: Oxford University Press,

1955; 2nd rev. ed., 1966), and Leon Litwack, *Trouble in Mind: Black Southerners in the Age of Jim Crow* (New York: A. K. Knopf, 1998; New York: Vintage Books, 1999).

16. J. Morgan Krousser, *Colorblind Injustice: Minority Voting Rights and the Undoing of the Second Reconstruction* (Chapel Hill: University of North Carolina Press, 1999), 1–68.

17. Jay Mandle, *Not Slave, Not Free: The African American Economic Experience Since the Civil War* (Durham, N.C.: Duke University Press, 1992).

18. Writings on the Progressive movement are substantial. Richard Hofstadter, *The Age of Reform: From Bryan to FDR* (New York: Vintage Books, 1955); Gabriel Kolko, *The Triumph of Conservatism: A Reinterpretation of American History, 1900–1916* (Chicago: Quadrangle Books, 1963); Christopher Lasch, *The New Radicalism in America* (New York: A. K. Knopf, 1965; New York: W. W. Norton, 1986); Robert Wiebe, *The Search for Order, 1877–1920* (New York: Hill and Wang, 1967; Westport: Greenwood Press, 1980); John W. Chambers II, *The Tyranny of Change: America in the Progressive Era, 1900–1917* (New York: St. Martin's Press, 1980); and Robert Crunden, *Ministers of Reform* (New York: Basic Books, 1982; Urbana: University of Illinois Press, 1984), offer different interpretations of the movement. John D. Buenker, John C. Burnham, and Robert M. Crunden, *Progressivism* (Cambridge, Mass: Schenkman Pub. Co., 1967, 1977), and Arthur S. Link and Richard L. McCormick, *Progressivism* (Arlington Heights, Ill.: Harlan Davidson, 1983), emphasize its internal diversity. Steven J. Diner, *A Very Different Age: Americans of the Progressive Era* (New York: Hill and Wang, 1998), focuses on the lives of common people during the Progressive era. Jack Temple Kirby, *Darkness at the Dawning: Race and Reform in the Progressive South* (Philadelphia: Lippincott, 1972); Dewey W. Grantham, *Southern Progressivism: The Reconciliation of Progress and Tradition* (Knoxville: University of Tennessee Press, 1983); and William Link, *The Paradox of Southern Progressivism, 1880–1930* (Chapel Hill: University of North Carolina Press, 1992), examine the contradiction between racism and reform in the South. William Deverell and Tom Sitton, eds., *California Progressivism Revisited* (Berkeley and Los Angeles: University of California Press, 1994), contains revisionist essays on the phenomenon in California.

19. Roger Daniels, *The Politics of Prejudice: The Anti-Japanese Movement in California and the Struggle for Japanese Exclusion* (Berkeley and Los Angeles: University of California Press, 1962), 49.

20. Quoted in Daniels, *Politics of Prejudice*, 49. For an assessment of Chester Rowell, see Frank W. Van Nuys, "A Progressive Confronts the Race Question: Chester Rowell, the California Alien Land Act of 1913, and the Contradictions of Early Twentieth-Century Racial Thought," *California History* 73 (Spring 1994): 2–13 and 84–85.

21. Daniels, *Politics of Prejudice*, 49–50.

22. The following comprise the Chinese exclusion acts: Act of May 6, 1882, 22 Stat. 60; Act of July 5, 1884, 23 Stat. 116; Act of September 13, 1888, 25 Stat. 476; Act of October 1, 1888, 25 Stat. 504; Act of May 5, 1892, 27 Stat. 25; Amendatory Act of November 3, 1893, 28 Stat. 7; Act of April 9, 1902, 32 Stat. 176; and Act of April 27, 1904, 33 Stat. 394.

23. *Chae Chan Ping v. United States*, 130 U.S. 581 (1889).

24. *Nishimura Ekiu v. United States*, 142 U.S. 651 (1892).

25. *Fong Yue Ting v. United States*, 149 U.S. 698 (1893).

26. *United States v. Ju Toy*, 198 U.S. 253 (1905). Salyer, *Laws Harsh as Tigers*, 94–216, meticulously traces the process by which immigration officials, step by step, eclipsed the judicial system.

27. Angelo N. Ancheta, *Race, Rights, and the Asian American Experience* (New Brunswick, N.J.: Rutgers University Press, 1998), 88–92.

28. *United States v. Wong Kim Ark*, 169 U.S. 649 (1898).

29. 1917 Immigration Act, 39 Stat. 874.

30. 1924 Immigration Act, 43 Stat. 153.

31. *Takao Ozawa v. United States*, 260 U.S. 178 (1922).

32. *United States v. Bhagat Singh Thind*, 261 U.S. 204 (1923).

33. *Porterfield v. Webb*, 263 U.S. 225 (1923); *Terrace v. Thompson*, 263 U.S. 197 (1923); *Webb v. O'Brien*, 263 U.S. 313 (1923); and *Frick v. Webb*, 263 U.S. 326.

34. The writings on the growth of the American empire in the latter part of the nineteenth century are voluminous. Robert L. Beisner, *From the Old Diplomacy to the New, 1865–1900*

(Arlington Heights, Ill.; Harlan Davidson, 1975; 2nd ed. 1986), and Thomas Paterson, J. Garry Clifford, and Kenneth J. Hagen, *American Foreign Relations: A History* (Lexington, Mass.: D. C. Heath, 1977; 1983; 1988; 1991; 1995), offer useful introductions. Classics in the field include: two books by William Appleman Williams, *The Tragedy of American Diplomacy* (Cleveland: World Pub. Co., 1959; New York: Dell Pub. Co., rev. ed., 1962; rev. and enl. ed. 1972; New York: W. W. Norton, new ed., 1988), and *The Roots of the Modern American Empire: A Study of the Growth and Shaping of Social Consciousness in a Marketplace Society* (New York: Random House, 1969); two books by Walter LaFeber, *The New Empire: An Interpretation of American Expansion, 1860–1898* (Ithaca, N.Y.: Cornell University Press, 1963; 1983; 100th anniversary ed., 1998), and *The American Age: United States Foreign Policy at Home and Abroad Since 1750* (New York: W. W. Norton, 1989; 1994); two books by Ernest R. May, *Imperial Democracy: The Emergence of America as a Great Power* (New York: Harcourt Brace Jovanovich, 1961; New York: Harper & Row, 1973), and *American Imperialism: A Speculative Essay* (New York: Atheneum, 1968); and David Healy, *United States Expansionism: The Imperialist Urge in the 1890s* (Madison: University of Wisconsin Press, 1968; 1970). Newer works that examine the nonpolitical aspects of American imperialism include two books by Emily Rosenberg, *Spreading the American Dream: American Economic and Cultural Expansion, 1890–1945* (New York: Hill and Wang, 1982), and *Financial Missionaries to the World: The Politics and Culture of Dollar Diplomacy, 1900–1930* (Cambridge, Mass.: Harvard University Press, 1999). Michael Hunt, *Ideology and U.S. Foreign Policy* (New Haven, Conn.: Yale University Press, 1987), and Alexander DeConde, *Ethnicity, Race, and American Foreign Policy: A History* (Boston: Northeastern University Press, 1992), are especially pertinent to my discussion here because they examine the role of racial ideology in American foreign policies and practices.

35. See the essays in the 20th anniversary (of the Third World student strikes) commemorative issue of *Amerasia Journal*, vol. 15, no. 1 (1989); Yen Le Espiritu, *Asian American Panethnicity: Bridging Institutions and Identities* (Philadelphia: Temple University Press, 1992); and William Wei, *The Asian American Movement* (Philadelphia: Temple University Press, 1993).

36. Ward Thomas and Mark Garrett, "U.S. and California Affirmative Action Policies, Laws, and Programs," in *Impacts of Affirmative Action: Policies and Consequences in California*, ed. Paul Ong (Walnut Creek, Calif.: Alta Mira Press, 1999), 25–58.

37. Xiaojian Zhao, "Chinese American Women Defense Workers in World War II," *California History* 75 (Summer 1996): 138–53 and 182–84.

38. Dozens of books have been published about the forcible removal and incarceration of Japanese Americans during World War II. Roger Daniels, *Prisoners Without Trial: Japanese Americans in World War II* (New York: Hill and Wang, 1993), provides the most succinct introduction. For more details, see Jacobus tenBroek, Edward Barnhart, and Floyd W. Matson, *Prejudice, War and the Constitution: Causes and Consequences of the Evacuation of the Japanese Americans in World War II* (Berkeley and Los Angeles: University of California Press, 1954); and Commission on Wartime Relocation and Internment of Civilians, *Personal Justice Denied* (Washington, D.C.: U.S. Government Printing Office, 1982). For how the cases were reopened, see Peter Irons, *Justice at War: The Story of the Japanese American Internment Cases* (New York: Oxford University Press, 1983). Peter Irons, ed., *Justice Delayed: The Record of the Japanese American Internment Cases* (Middletown, Conn.: Wesleyan University Press, 1989), contains the texts of the Supreme Court decisions.

39. Fred W. Riggs, *Pressure on Congress: A Study of the Repeal of Chinese Exclusion* (New York: King's Crown Press, 1950).

40. *Oyama v. California*, 332 U.S. 633 (1948); *Takahashi v. Fish and Game Commission*, 334 U.S. 410 (1948); *Kenji Namba v. McCourt*, 185 Ore. 579 (1949); *Sei Fujii v. State of California*, 38 Cal. 2d 718 (1952); *Haruye Masaoka v. State of California*, 39 Cal. 2d 883 (1952); and 1967 Washington Laws, ch. 163, sec. 7. For a discussion of these cases, see Frank F. Chuman, *The Bamboo People: The Law and Japanese-Americans* (Del Mar, Calif.: Publisher's Inc., 1976), 198–223.

41. *Perez v. Sharp*, 32 Cal. 2d 711 (1948); and *Shelley v. Kramer*, 334 U.S. 1 (1948).

42. Thousands of books have been published about the many conflicts related to the Cold War. The following books offer useful introductions to the topic: Herbert Feis, *From Trust to Terror: The Onset of the Cold War, 1945–1950* (New York: W. W. Norton, 1970); John Lewis Gaddis, *The United States and the Origins of the Cold War, 1941–1947* (New York: Columbia University Press, 1972; new ed., 2000); Norman A. Graebner, ed., *The Cold War: A Conflict of Ideology and Power* (Lexington, Mass.: D. C. Heath, 1976); Thomas G. Paterson, *On Every Front: The Making of the Cold War* (New York: W. W. Norton, 1979); Jeff McMahan, *Reagan and the World: Imperial Policy in the New Cold War* (New York: Monthly Review Press, 1985); and John Lewis Gaddis, *We Now Know: Rethinking Cold War History* (New York: Oxford University Press, 1997).

43. A great deal has been written about each of the many facets of the Civil Rights movement, but there are few overviews of the movement as a whole. A good starting point consists of two books produced in conjunction with a six-part television series on the topic: Juan Williams, *Eyes on the Prize: America's Civil Rights Years, 1954–1965* (New York: Viking Penguin, 1987), and Clayborn Carson, et al., *Eyes on the Prize Civil Rights Reader: Documents, Speeches, and Firsthand Accounts from the Black Freedom Struggle, 1954–1990* (New York: Viking Penguin, 1987; 1991). Additional documents can be found in Leon Friedman, ed., *The Civil Rights Reader: Basic Documents of the Civil Rights Movement* (New York: Walker and Co., 1967; rev. ed., 1968). Key events are chronicled in William H. Chafe, *Civilities and Civil Rights: Greensboro, North Carolina, and the Black Struggle for Freedom* (New York: Oxford University Press, 1980); Elizabeth Huckaby, *Crisis at Central High, Little Rock, 1957–1958* (Baton Rouge: Louisiana State University Press, 1980); David J. Garrow, ed., *The Montgomery Bus Boycott and the Women Who Started It: The Memoir of Jo Ann Gibson Robinson* (Knoxville: University of Tennessee Press, 1987); idem, ed., *Birmingham, Alabama, 1956–1963: The Black Struggle for Civil Rights* (Brooklyn, N.Y.: Carlson Press, 1989); and idem, *Protest at Selma: Martin Luther King, Jr., and the Voting Rights Act of 1965* (New Haven, Conn.: Yale University Press, 1978). The different strands within the African American struggle for freedom in the 1950s and 1960s are discussed in David J. Garrow, *Bearing the Cross: Martin Luther King, Jr., and the Southern Christian Leadership Conference* (New York: William Morrow, 1986; New York: Vintage Books, 1988; 1993; New York: Quill Books, 1999); Taylor Branch, *Parting the Waters: America in the King Years, 1954–1963* (New York: Simon and Schuster, 1988); idem, *Pillars of Fire: America in the King Years, 1963–1965* (New York: Simon and Schuster, 1998); Clayborne Carson, *In Struggle: SNCC and the Black Awakening of the 1960s* (Cambridge, Mass.: Harvard University Press, 1981; 1995); Stokely Carmichael and Charles V. Hamilton, *Black Power: The Politics of Liberation in America* (New York: Vintage Books, 1967; 1992); William L. Van DeBurg, *New Day in Babylon: The Black Power Movement and American Culture, 1965–1975* (Chicago: University of Chicago Press, 1992); Malcolm X and Alex Haley, *The Autobiography of Malcolm X* (New York: Grove Press, 1965; New York: Ballantine Books, 1973; 1988; 1992); Gerald Horne, *Fire This Time: The Watts Uprising and the 1960s* (Charlottesville: University Press of Virginia, 1995); James W. Button, *Black Violence: The Political Impact of the 1960s Riots* (Princeton, N.J.: Princeton University Press, 1978); and Belinda Rohnett, *How Long? How Long? African-American Women in the Struggle for Civil Rights* (New York: Oxford University Press, 1997).

44. Mary L. Dudziak, *Cold War Civil Rights: Race and the Image of American Democracy* (Princeton, N.J.: Princeton University Press, 2000).

45. Thomas and Garrett, "U.S. and California Affirmative Action," 27–28; Robert F. Burk, *The Eisenhower Administration and Black Civil Rights* (Knoxville: University of Tennessee Press, 1984); Mark Stern, *Calculating Visions: Kennedy, Johnson, and Civil Rights* (New Brunswick, N.J.: Rutgers University Press, 1992); James W. Riddlesperger, Jr., and Donald W. Jackson, *Presidential Leadership and Civil Rights Policy* (Westport, Conn.: Greenwood Press, 1995); and Hugh Davis Graham, *Civil Rights and the Presidency: Race and Gender in American Politics, 1960–1972* (New York: Oxford University Press, 1992), which is an abridgement of his *The Civil Rights Era: Origins and Development of National Policy, 1960–1972* (New York: Oxford University Press, 1990).

46. *Plessy v. Ferguson*, 163 U.S. 537 (1896); *Brown v. Board of Education* 349 U.S. 483 (1954). For details, see Richard Kruger, *Simple Justice: The History of* Brown v. Board of Education *and Black America's Struggle for Equality* (New York: A. K. Knopf, 1975).

47. Dudziak, *Cold War Civil Rights*, 100.

48. Dudziak, *Cold War Civil Rights*, 115–202.

49. Dudziak, *Cold War Civil Rights*, 207.

50. Civil Rights Act of 1964, 78 Stat. 241. For discussions of the Congressional debates over the bills that became the 1964 Civil Rights Act, see Charles Whalen and Barbara Whalen, *The Longest Debate: The Legislative History of the 1964 Civil Rights Act* (Cabin John, Md.: Seven Locks Press, 1985); Robert D. Loevy, ed., *The Civil Rights Act of 1964: The Passage of the Law that Ended Racial Segregation* (Albany: State University of New York Press, 1997); and Bernard Grofman, ed., *Legacies of the 1964 Civil Rights Act* (Charlottesville: University Press of Virginia, 2000).

51. Dudziak, *Cold War Civil Rights*, 211.

52. *Griggs v. Duke Power Company*, 401 U.S. 424 (1971).

53. Voting Rights Act of 1965, 79 Stat. 437. The essays in Bernard Grofman and Chandler Davidson, eds., *Controversies in Minority Voting: The Voting Rights Act in Perspective* (Washington, D.C.: The Brookings Institution, 1992), examine various aspects of the act and its impact.

54. *White v. Regester*, 412 U.S. 755 (1973).

55. *Lau v. Nichols*, 414 U.S. 563 (1974).

56. Ling-chi Wang, "*Lau v. Nichols*: The Right of Limited English-Speaking Students," *Amerasia Journal* 2 (Fall 1974): 16–45. Additional details are found in L. Ling-chi Wang, "*Lau v. Nichols*: History of a Struggle for Equal and Quality Education," in Emma Gee et al., ed., *Counterpoint: Perspectives on Asian America* (Los Angeles: Asian American Studies Center, University of California, Los Angeles, 1976), 240–63.

57. Ancheta, *Race, Rights, and the Asian American Experience*, 104–05.

58. The 1975 amendments to the 1965 Voting Rights Act are found in 89 Stat. 400.

59. *United Jewish Organizations of Williamsburg v. Carey*, 430 U.S. 144 (1977).

60. Carole Jean Uhlaner, "Political Activity and Preferences of African Americans, Latinos, and Asian Americans," in Gerald D. Jaynes, ed., *Immigration and Race: New Challenges for American Democracy* (New Haven, Conn.: Yale University Press, 2000), 217–54.

61. 1965 Immigration Act, 79 Stat. 111.

62. Alejandro Portes and Min Zhou, "The New Second Generation: Segmented Assimilation and Its Variants," *The Annals of the American Academy of Political and Social Sciences* 530 (November 1993): 74–96.

63. Paul Ong, "An Overview of Affirmative Action," in Ong, ed., *Impacts of Affirmative Action*, 12–13; and Thomas and Garrett, "U.S. and California Affirmative Action," 31–32.

64. Thomas and Garrett, "U.S. and California Affirmative Action," 34. For a more detailed discussion, see Thomas J. Sugrue, "Breaking Through: The Troubled Origins of Affirmative Action in the Workplace," in John David Skrentny, ed., *Color Lines: Affirmative Action, Immigration, and Civil Rights Options for America* (Chicago: University of Chicago Press, 2001), 31–52.

65. Paul Ong, Edna Bonacich, and Lucie Cheng, "The Political Economy of Capitalist Restructuring and the New Asian Immigration," in Ong, Bonacich, and Cheng, eds., *The New Asian Immigration in Los Angeles and Global Restructuring* (Philadelphia: Temple University Press, 1994), 3–44.

66. Mary Ann Glendon, *A World Made New: Eleanor Roosevelt and the Universal Declaration of Human Rights* (New York: Random House, 2001).

67. *Regents of the University of California v. Bakke*, 438 U.S. 265 (1978).

68. *City of Richmond v. Croson*, 488 U.S. 469 (1989).

69. John David Skrentny, "Introduction," in Skrentny, ed., *Color Lines*, 8.

70. *Adarand Constructors, Inc. v. Pena*, 115 S. Ct. 2097 (1995).

71. Deborah C. Malamud, "Affirmative Action and Ethnic Niches: A Legal Afterword," in Skrentny, ed., *Color Lines*, 313–45.

72. Hugh Davis Graham, "Affirmative Action for Immigrants? The Unintended Consequences of Reform," in Skrentny, ed., *Color Lines*, 53–70.

73. Debra L. DeLaet, *U.S. Immigration Policy in an Age of Rights* (Westport, Conn.: Praeger, 2000), chap. 5: "U.S. Immigration Policy in the 1990s: A New Era of Restrictions?" 103–18; Thomas J. Espenshade, Jessica L. Baraka, and Gregory A. Huber, "Restructuring Incentives for U.S. Immigration," in Kavita Pandit and Suzanne Davies Withers, eds., *Migration and Restructuring in the United States: A Geographic Perspective* (Lanham, Md.: Rowman & Littlefield, 1999), 113–36; and Paul Ong, "Proposition 209 and Its Implications," in Ong, ed., *Impacts of Affirmative Action*, 197–209.

74. Lydia Chavez, *The Color Bind: California's Battle to End Affirmative Action* (Berkeley and Los Angeles: University of California Press, 1998).

75. *Shaw v. Reno*, 509 U.S. 630 (1993).

76. *Holder v. Hall*, 114 S. Ct. 2581 (1994).

77. *Miller v. Johnson*, 115 S. Ct. 2475 (1995). All three cases are discussed in detail in Krousser, *Colorblind Injustice.*

78. Terry Eastland and William J. Bennett, *Counting by Race: Equality from the Founding Fathers to Bakke and Weber* (New York: Basic Books, 1979), was one of the earliest attempts by conservative intellectuals to theorize their position. A more sophisticated effort is found in Andrew Kull, *The Color-Blind Constitution* (Cambridge, Mass.: Harvard University Press, 1992). Neil Gotanda, "A Critique of 'Our Constitution Is Color-Blind,'" *Stanford Law Review* 44 (November 1991): 1–68, analyzes the hypocrisy of the color-blind doctrine. The different strands within conservative ideology are clarified in Michael Omi and Howard Winant, *Racial Formation in the United States: From the 1960s to the 1990s* (New York: Routledge, 1994, 2nd ed.). For current public attitudes toward affirmative action and immigration, see Lawrence D. Bobo, "Race, Interests, and Beliefs about Affirmative Action: Unanswered Questions and New Directions," and Carol M. Swain, Kyra R. Greene, and Christine Min Wotipka, "Understanding Racial Polarization on Affirmative Action: The View from Focus Groups," both in Skrentny, ed., *Color Lines*, 191–213 and 214–238; and Grace A. Rosales, Mona D. Navarro, and Desdemona Cardosa, "Variation in Attitudes toward Immigrants Measured among Latino, African American, Asian, and European American Students," in Marta Lopez-Garza and David R. Diaz, eds., *Asian and Latino Immigrants in a Restructuring Economy: The Metamorphosis of Southern California* (Stanford, Calif.: Stanford University Press, 2001), 353–67.

OUT OF THE SHADOWS

CAMPTOWN WOMEN, MILITARY BRIDES, AND KOREAN (AMERICAN) COMMUNITIES

Ji-Yeon Yuh

A group of women wanted to participate in the life of their church, whose congregants, like themselves, were Korean immigrants to the United States. After much discussion, the women decided that they wanted to help prepare the food for the annual Thanksgiving dinner. Their proposal, however, was rejected by the church women's group. The church women's group was composed of Korean women married to Korean men, but the women who wanted to participate in the annual church event were Korean women who had married American soldiers. The Korean wives of Korean men believed that the Korean wives of American soldiers were dirty, unclean, unsanitary, and just not fit to prepare food. The message to the so-called "internationally married women" was clear: "You are not really one of us. We will tolerate your presence, but only as long as we can ignore you" (Yeo, personal interview).

Activists who work with Korean women in the camptowns surrounding U.S. military bases in South Korea often link militarized prostitution with Japan's militarized sex slavery. Along with scholars like Lynn Thiesmeyer, they argue that today's camptown women are a modern-day version of Japan's comfort women. But when they tried to expand the protest against militarized sex slavery to include militarized prostitution, they met with profound resistance. Comfort women, they were told, were innocent victims of Japanese colonial aggression, but camptown women were, well, weren't they just loose women looking to make easy money? (Kim, personal interview.)

Although these stories take place on opposite sides of the vast Pacific Ocean and involve two different groups of Korean women—those who married American soldiers and immigrated to the United States, and those who service American soldiers in camptowns—they are intimately linked, for it can be said that Korean military wives are to the Korean immigrant community in the United States what camptown women are to Korean society in South Korea: pariahs to be kept away from "respectable" society.

Korean military brides are among the tens of thousands of Asian women who married U.S. soldiers after World War II, immigrating to the U.S. in what can be called a silent, unnoticed and ignored phenomenon. Most Koreans assume that the so-called military brides or "internationally married women" have come from the camptowns, even though many of the women—perhaps most of them— have not. Many camptown women, influenced by Korean societal norms regarding marriage and motherhood, perceive marrying an American soldier as their best hope for leaving the camptown life and approximating what they see as a "normal" life as a wife and mother.[1] Camptown women often talk about the women they know who have taken that route, wondering how so-and-so is doing in her new life, or perhaps passing around a letter written by a former camptown woman. Thus the camptown woman and the military bride are linked as if they were each other's missing half, the one representing an assumed past and the other a hoped-for future. In this way, the camptown has a larger-than-life presence for Korean military brides, and they live with its ever-present shadow. Camptown women, who live with the camptown reality every day, are in turn living with the as-yet-unrealized possibility of becoming a military bride. Few other Koreans, however, whether in Korea or in America, are aware that camptown women and military brides are pervasive presences in their lives as well. Indeed, most Koreans either consciously or unconsciously dismiss both camptown women and military brides as outside the realm of Korean society.

This paper argues that such a dismissal allows Koreans to negate the realities of their subjugation under the United States and to glorify the United States as the object of desire.[2] This in turn allows immigrants to affirm their new American identity even as they assert their Koreanness, and allows Koreans to imagine the South Korean nation as the equal partner of the United States.

The history of the camptowns has been sketched primarily by journalists such as Oh Yun Ho, workers with Korea Church Women United, and activists with My Sister's Place, a community center for camptown women in Uijongbu. The following discussion is based on their work. Camptowns emerged with the arrival of U.S. forces in Korea in September 1945. By the end of that year, the first camptown was established in Bupyong near the western port city of Inchon. The growth of the camptowns followed the trajectory of the U.S. military presence; as the number of bases and troops increased, so did the number of camptowns and camptown women.

In addition to Bupyong, some of the earliest and largest camptowns include Itaewon in Seoul; areas of the southern port city of Pusan called Hialeah and Texas; Tongduchon; and Songtan. The camptowns in Pusan were among the most stable, as U.S. soldiers were stationed there throughout the Korean War. (This was possible because Pusan, a port city located at the southeastern tip of Korea, left UN control—virtually synonymous with U.S. control—only briefly during the war.) The U.S. military used Pusan as a landing port, and the camp-towns of Hialeah (next to Camp Hialeah) and Texas soon appeared. Hialeah remains a camptown today, while Texas (located next to the Pusan train station) has become a camptown serving not only the U.S. military but also sailors and other itinerant travelers passing through the port.

The 1960s were the heyday of the camptowns, when more than 30,000 women earned their living entertaining some 62,000 U.S. soldiers stationed in virtually every corner of South Korea. The Paju area northwest of Seoul, militarily impor-tant due to its proximity to the Demilitarized Zone approximating the 38th Parallel and serving as the dividing line between North and South Korea, contained the highest concentration of U.S. troops until 1971. Nicknamed the GI's Kingdom, the area was home to the 1st Marine Division and the 24th, 7th and 2nd Infantry Divisions. The largest camptown during this period was Tongduchon, nicknamed Little Chicago and located just east of Paju and north of Seoul. When Camp Casey was established at the end of the Korean War in 1953 as the main infantry base, Tongduchon was transformed from a remote farming village into a chaotic world of drugs, sex, crime and black market deals in PX goods. During its height in the mid-1960s, some 7,000 women in Tongduchon worked as prostitutes serving the U.S. military.

Because U.S. bases were one of the few steady sources of income in the poverty-stricken years of the 1940s through 1970s, the camptowns attracted not only poor women, including war widows, and orphans seeking to make a living, but also entrepreneurs and criminals. In collusion with American GIs, Korean civilians smuggled military supplies and PX goods out of the bases, selling them for a handsome profit on the black market. Pimps and madams established clubs catering to the soldiers, hiring women at starvation wages to work as hostesses cum prostitutes. Villagers opened laundries, restaurants, stores and other busi-nesses serving the more mundane needs of the soldiers and the camptown women. The newspaper *Dong-A Ilbo* reported on the development of these camptowns, using as a model Uijongbu, a camptown just north of Seoul but south of the larger Tongduchon. Before the war, Uijongbu had about 10,000 residents and one silk mill as the sole industry. But with the war, hundreds of unemployed people, UN forces and criminals literally invaded the town, bring-ing with them various underworld activities. About 2,000 women worked as camptown women, and the small town was suddenly filled with cabarets, bars, tailor and dress shops and other stores. By the 1960s, an estimated 60 percent of the 65,000 Koreans in Uijongbu were engaged in some form of business cater-ing to the U.S. military.[3]

With the construction of U.S. military bases came not only the transformation but also the literal destruction of Korean villages. In July of 1951, Songtan—about an hour south of Seoul by bus—was invaded by the bulldozers of the 417th Squadron of the U.S. Air Force. The squadron built an airfield, causing 5,000 people (1,000 families) to lose their homes. These families had farmed the same plots of land in Songtan for generations, making their living from the annual rice harvest and the charcoal they made from the wood they chopped. As they left their ancestral lands, each family held a piece of paper from the U.S.

military promising—in neatly typed Korean and English—monetary compensation for their loss. The promised compensation, which was much less than the market value of the land, never materialized despite years of legal battles. The issue was resolved in favor of the U.S. military with the 1966 Status of Forces Agreement (SOFA), which stipulated that the United States can use without charge any and all land necessary for its military operations in South Korea (Oh 140–142). Over the years, more residents were displaced as Osan Air Base expanded to become the largest base in Korea and the second largest Air Force base in Asia.[4] Journalist Oh Yun Ho describes the transformation of Songtan:

> Oblivious to the local residents' resentment, the airfield was completed at top speed within six months. The surrounding area became the land of the Stars and Stripes. Thatched-roof houses gave way to all kinds of stores with English signs, aluminum cans replaced gourds, and a village full of shy maidens with their long braided hair instantly became a village full of yang gongju.[5] (142)

With the construction of the airfield, Songtan became home to a major hub of U.S. military activity in Asia and a thriving camptown. When the United States began to reduce its land forces in 1971, camptowns such as Tongduchon suffered, but Songtan grew as the United States continued to emphasize air power. In addition to the air squadron stationed there, soldiers regularly fly in from Okinawa for weekend training sessions (*Korea Church Women United* 33). Songtan today is one of the largest camptowns, with about 1,500 prostitutes. The projected move to Osan of the Eighth Army and the headquarters for the U.S. forces in Korea (currently located in Seoul) is likely to make Songtan Korea's camptown capitol.

American Town is a camptown developed with the collusion of both the South Korean and American governments. Built by a South Korean general and a landowner in 1969 during the height of the Park Chung Hee regime, American Town turned farm fields in North Cholla Province into a sanctioned red-light district for U.S. soldiers. Distinctly marked off from the nearby civilian town of Kunsan and the surrounding countryside by chain-link fences, American Town at first was wholly owned by the two developers, but later became a corporation with shareholders. During the 1970s business was so good that the clubs opened even during the day and a fleet of buses ferried soldiers between Kunsan Air Force Base and the town. Today, two buses operate daily between the camptown and the base. The town includes dormitory-like housing for the women, about 20 clubs, a dozen stores, and a government-run health clinic where the women receive mandatory testing for sexually transmitted diseases (My Sister's Place, 33–34).

For the South Korean government, these camptowns and the regulation of camptown women have been crucial to maintaining smooth relations with the U.S. government. Katharine Moon points out that making sure that camptown women played their proper role as entertainers and sexual playmates who would foster good will toward Korea among American soldiers was essential for the South Korean government. Thus the South Korean government embarked on an official program during the 1970s that praised the women as patriots for earning foreign exchange and boosting the economy, and for contributing to the national defense by serving as personal ambassadors to U.S. troops. At monthly meetings in camptowns across South Korea, high-ranking government officials thanked the women for their hard work and assured them that their sacrifice for the sake of the nation would not be forgotten. But the official rhetoric of camptown women as patriots and civilian ambassadors is a thin cover-up for the exploitation of the women as sacrificial lambs, so to speak, to the United States. Although prostitution is illegal in South Korea, several hundred "special entertainment districts" are set aside where prostitution is regulated by the government. Not coincidentally, these districts correspond to the camptowns. The United States, for its part, takes it for granted that its soldiers "need" paid sexual companions for high morale and demands that camptown women be kept free of venereal disease so that soldiers do not become infected. Thus, as Moon describes, the South Korean government and the U.S. military have engaged in a decades-long collaboration to regulate camptown women and their behavior. The regulation, which appears likely to continue for as long as the United States stations troops in Korea, includes licensing camptown women to work in the clubs, requiring regular checkups for sexually transmitted diseases, and forcing the women to wear numbers so that their customers can easily identify them. Both Korean and U.S. military authorities also routinely stop women in the camptowns to check for valid licenses. Furthermore, while soldiers are encouraged to identify the women they believe caused their infection, women are not allowed to similarly identify the soldiers (Sturdevant and Stoltzfus, 176–179).

The presence of the U.S. military and the consequent development of camptowns have had profound effects on Koreans. For some, it has meant life as a prostitute serving foreign soldiers, struggling to survive in the harsh world of the camptowns. For others, it has meant immigration to America through marriage with a soldier. For still others, seeing a daughter or sister live and work in a camptown or immigrate to America as a military bride. For residents near camptowns, it has meant business opportunities catering to the needs of soldiers and camptown women. For the general Korean populace, it has meant access to U.S. goods, smuggled out of the bases via the camptowns and sold on the black market. It has also meant contact with American culture as conveyed by GIs, AFKN (Armed Forces Korea Network, the U.S. military's television station in Seoul, until recently accessible through any television set in the Seoul area), and the black market goods themselves. In short, as Nancy Abelmann and John Lie point out when they write that "GIs carried the United States to South Korea," American soldiers (and by extension the camptowns) have been the first point of contact with American culture for Koreans (56).

GIs, camptowns, *yang gongju* and military brides are thus intricately intertwined for Koreans. They also hold dual meanings. On the one hand, they are despised for what is seen as their immorality and corrupting influence. GIs and *yang gongju* frequently appear in Korean novels and short stories, for example, in story lines and descriptions that leave little doubt as to the cruelty and crassness of the GIs and the tawdry, tragic lives of the *yang gongju*. As one middle-aged man who grew up in rural southwestern Korea notes, "We all knew about the *yang gongju*, but it wasn't part of our lives. We just knew that they were dirty. Everyone knew that." But on the other hand, they can be imbued with an alluring glow by their link to America's modernity and material abundance. The term *yang gongju* itself embodies that duality, as does the term *yang saeksi*. Although both are derogatory terms for camptown women, the literal meaning of the first is western princess and of the second, western bride. (Another derogatory term, *yang galbo*, is more straightforward. The term simply means western whore, and is clearly the most insulting of the three terms.) One camptown woman explains how her longing to enter the luxurious America pictured in the movies and on television led her to naively seek out a camptown:

> When I watched TV and the movies during my youth, I wanted to go live in America. When I was a little older, I wanted to have some luxuries, but that was impossible in our poor household. So I came to the camptown to meet Americans and earn lots of money. But once I got here, I found that many things were different from what I had expected. I never imagined that I would have to do this kind of work. And it doesn't even earn lots of money. If I had known that it was this kind of place, I would never have come. (*My Sister's Place*, 17)

Despite America's direct connection to the despised camptowns, *yang gongju*, and military brides, however, America remains the object of envy and admiration. This seeming contradiction stems from the unequal, neo-colonial relationship between South Korea and the United States. The lure that America exerted (and to a large extent still exerts) on Koreans is the lure of the metropole on the colony. Abelmann and Lie discuss this lure in the context of transnationalism, pinpointing the ways in which American culture enters Korea and serves to promote a longing for that culture (49–84). This lure is all the stronger because America has been seen as a liberator, not a colonizer. As scholars such as Kang Hyeon-Dew and Manwoo Lee have pointed out, under the dominant discourse of America as the savior who rescued Korea from Japanese imperialism and then saved Korea from communism, American heroism and generosity joins with American material abundance into an image of utopia. The same Korean man who spoke of everyone knowing that camptown women are dirty continued by saying, "But America was like our big brother, our ally. And we felt gratitude to the soldiers for helping us defend our country." Although a countering image of America as a corrupting influence, even an imperial power, has run parallel with this Utopia image, the positive image has been dominant. Only since the 1980 Kwangju massacre and the persistent unearthing of post-1945 history by Korean scholars that details American acts of atrocity and imperialism in Korea has anti-Americanism become a persistently voiced opinion in South Korea.[6] Still, the power, wealth and modernity that America symbolizes have largely overshadowed the negative consequences of America's dominance over Korea.

Their connection to the envied and admired America, however, does not save camptown women and military brides from contempt and ostracism. Traditional patriarchal mores emphasizing female chastity and a centuries-old pride in what

Koreans consider to be a homogeneous culture and race has worked against these women. Those who, like the camptown woman quoted above, come to camptowns seeking the America of their dreams are quickly disillusioned by a reality they never imagined. But patriarchal mores and extremes of cultural/racial pride alone cannot account for the contempt heaped on camptown women and military brides. Those same mores and that same pride kept the issue of comfort women a secret for decades, but while comfort women are now held up as innocent victims of an imperialist aggressor, camptown women remain pariahs. Indeed, former comfort women themselves disdain any links with camptown women. What can account for this difference? Part of the answer lies in the identity of the aggressor. Japan is seen as a former colonizer who has yet to fully come to terms with its history, who may yet have designs on its former colony. The United States, however, is still primarily seen as an ally and a friend who deserves thanks, whose freedoms and material abundance are ideals to be envied and pursued. To see the camptown women as victims of militarized prostitution, as modern-day comfort women, would be to shatter that vision of America. It would force Koreans to confront the myriad humiliations and brutalities committed by Americans and the U.S. military, incidents tucked away in small print in obscure corners of the newspaper, hidden in half-forgotten memories. Land seized by force and farmers forced out to make room for U.S. military installations; American troops firing into small groups of unarmed civilians peacefully demonstrating against the division of their country and against the U.S. military government; workers thrown out of factories they had begun to operate on their own after the Japanese owners left in the wake of Japan's defeat in 1945; countless Korean civilians murdered or brutalized by American soldiers who are given little more than slaps on the wrist by U.S. military authorities. Memories and newspaper accounts of numerous such incidents, painstakingly researched by journalist Oh Yun Ho, testify to an America that is imperialist, cavalier and ruthlessly self-centered in its dealings with "junior partners" such as South Korea. In addition, recent revelations about not only the 1980 Kwangju massacre but also the 1948 Chejudo massacre reveal an America brutal in its treatment of Korea—an image that directly contradicts the dominant discourse.[7] Seeing camptown women as victims of U.S.-sponsored militarized prostitution would shatter a self-conception of Korea as a sovereign nation. It would force a realization of the ways in which the United States oppresses Korea and Koreans, of the fact that Korea is at best a junior, a very junior, partner, and at worst a victim, even a pawn, of an imperialist America. Koreans would be forced to examine their own relationships to America, to see how U.S. aggression affects and has affected Koreans. They would have to acknowledge the reality of their own subjugations, subjugations which only begin with the military occupation of their nation by a foreign power. The U.S. military presence in South Korea has meant, for example, that whole towns have grown economically dependent on the local U.S. military base, their fortunes waxing and waning with the number of troops. In short, towns such as Uijongbu, Songtan and Tongduchon are economically dependent on decisions made thousands of miles away by the leaders of a foreign country. But if such realities are faced, a national self-identity as a sovereign nation in partnership with the United States against the evil of communism (read: North Korea) would be in tatters.

The projection of camptown women as an other who then affirms the self-identity of the Korean nation follows a gendered pattern discussed by numerous scholars such as Susan Jeffords and Cynthia Enloe. The self-identity as a sovereign nation is a distinctly masculine one. To keep itself masculine and sovereign, it must banish the feminine and the subordinate. Camptown women, as prostitutes servicing the soldiers of a foreign power, are emblematic of the feminine and the subordinate. They serve to symbolize all the humiliations that Korea suffers at the hands of the United States. Indeed, political radicals in South Korea are increasingly using the image of the camptown woman as a metaphor for a nation brutalized under imperialism.[8] But for Koreans in the mainstream, it is necessary to condemn these women as whores and/or cynically praise them for patriotism as civilian ambassadors and earners of foreign exchange, all the while relegating them to the shadows. Only by doing so can they ignore/deny subjugation under a foreign power and the consequent shame, thus allowing the officially sanctioned discourse of Korean sovereignty and American benevolence to remain dominant. America's golden image is left relatively untainted, allowing Koreans to despise camptowns and camptown women even as they believe in America's rhetoric of freedom and opportunity and long for the material wealth, power and modernity that America symbolizes. In effect, the realities of U.S. influence on Korean society are interpreted as individual depravity—the women are prostitutes not because of Korea's circumstances and relations with the U.S., but because the women are morally corrupt. The logic of national pride requires this interpretation.[9]

Camptown women are well aware of their pariah status in Korean society. Interviews with camptown women conducted by My Sister's Place (Report) and by Saundra Pollock Sturdevant and Brenda Stoltzfus show that they believe that they too have rights as human beings and should not be condemned for being prostitutes. But most, if not all, view coming to the camptowns as a mistake. For camptown women, the concept of sex work as a legitimate profession is literally foreign. Many dream of a "normal" life as a wife and mother, and since this life is impossible to achieve with a Korean man due to Korean society's ostracism of camptown women, they dream of marrying an American soldier. How to survive and how to escape the camptown is the daily concern of most camptown women. The historical and social conditions underpinning camp town prostitution render largely irrelevant the arguments of some Western feminists and activist prostitutes who claim that prostitution can be an empowering occupation and a way out from under patriarchal domination.[10] Instead, I would argue that the converse is true in the case of militarized prostitution in Korea: the camptown women live under extremes of patriarchal domination literally practiced on their bodies by both Korea and the United States. This domination takes not only the form of rhetorical and social "othering" that serves to ostracize the women in order to affirm a masculine identity as a sovereign nation, as I have shown above, but it also takes the form of the daily policing and regulation of their behavior, restrictions that are placed upon them by masculine nation-states for the sake of their masculine national security interests and the masculine morale of soldiers.

The pariah status of camptown women extends to military brides. Because marriages between Korean women and American soldiers are made possible by the continued U.S. military presence in Korea, the military bride, like the camptown woman, is a potent reminder of that presence. In other words, she reminds other Koreans that a foreign military occupies their nation, as well as of some of the personal and social consequences of that occupation. As such, military brides stand as another emblem of South Korea's subjugation under the United States, and thus become another object of condemnation and ostracism. Most Koreans also assume that military brides were once camptown women, thus making a neat link between the two. This link allows Koreans to rationalize their condemnation of military brides as justified moral approbation of prostitutes, eliminating the need to further interrogate their motivations. Some military brides did indeed once work in camptowns. But while camptowns are one place where Korean women and American soldiers meet and then get married, it is not the only place. And although it may have been the primary place in the past for the blossoming of such international marriages, it can no longer be assumed that that remains the case. Yet the phenomenon of militarized prostitution is critically important to the phenomenon of marriages between Korean women and American soldiers. The very existence of militarized prostitution deeply affects the lives of Korean women who marry American soldiers, even when those marriages began in locales other than camptowns. The stereotype of the camptown woman often prompts military wives to censor the behavior of themselves and their fellows, to go out of their way to prove that they are good wives and mothers and not loose women. Older military brides at the church I attended for some two years, for example, would sometimes take aside a younger military bride and tell her to stop wearing short skirts or clothing that they deemed flamboyant and reminiscent of camptowns. These women took pains to dress modestly, keep an orderly house and raise their children. In an apparent reference to camptown women, a number of the military brides whom I interviewed complained that the behavior and backgrounds of a few "bad women" tainted the image of military brides in general. For some women, a desire to distance themselves from the stereotype leads them to distance themselves from other military brides, to prove that they are not "one of them," thus depriving them of one source of community. And of course, the stereotype works to keep Korean military wives isolated from both mainstream American society and mainstream Korean society, whether in South Korea itself or in Korean immigrant communities in America, for it makes the women an easy target for contempt. Combined with language and cultural barriers that make interaction with non-Korean Americans difficult, this in effect leaves most women isolated within tightly restricted social circles where their only relationships are with their immediate family and other Korean military wives.

And yet, just as camptown women have played critical roles in South Korea, military brides have been crucial in the formation of Korean immigrant communities. By inviting their family members under the family reunification provision of U.S. immigration law, it is estimated that military brides are responsible (directly and indirectly) for bringing 40 to 50 percent of all Korean immigrants since 1965. (Lee, 1997, 97) Some women are the beginning of chain migrations that include dozens of extended family members. Nearly every military bride I met had invited at least one family member to the United States.

The first Korean military brides began arriving in the 1950s. Of the women I interviewed, the earliest to arrive came in 1951. As wives of U.S. citizens, they were able to immigrate during a time when immigration from Korea and most of Asia was legally blocked. Thus they make up the largest group of Korean immigrants between 1945 and 1965, when immigration laws were liberalized after some five decades of strict, anti-Asian immigration restrictions. With the exception of small communities of immigrant Koreans in Hawaii and California, many of whom came during the first few years of the 20th century to work the Hawaiian sugar plantations, most other Koreans in the United States during that time period were international students. The students, mostly male, generally came from prominent, well-to-do families in Seoul, in contrast to most military brides, who came from relatively poor families in the provinces. The two populations also had little substantive contact in America. The world of colleges and universities in which the students traveled rarely connected with the military brides' world of bases, poor rural communities and urban neighborhoods. Thus in addition to the camptown shadow, class differences kept these two groups of Korean immigrants apart. These differences can be seen in many Korean immigrant communities today, where those immigrants who came as students and have attained professional status often keep their distance from those immigrants who came through the sponsorship of relatives—perhaps a military bride—and labor in small businesses and factories.[11]

Daniel B. Lee notes that between 1962 and 1968, Korean women who immigrated as wives of U.S. citizens accounted for 39.4 percent, the largest single immigration category, of all Korean immigration to the United States. Lee estimates that between 1950 and 1989, some 90,000 Korean women have immigrated to America as wives of U.S. soldiers (1997, 96–97).[12] They followed their husbands to every corner of the United States, from rural Kansas to urban Philadelphia, to places where they were the only Korean, if not the only Asian. A Korean immigrant presence in rural America is often the presence of military brides and their families. In most cases, a U.S. military base is nearby. This is true in Colorado, for example, where until recently the Korean community was primarily composed of military brides who had followed their husbands to Fort Collins. When the women invite their family members—usually parents and siblings—to immigrate to the United States, the relatives often first settled nearby. The women help their relatives adjust to U.S. society, find jobs, work their way through U.S. bureaucracy, put children in schools and find places to live. Often, the women provide these services for other immigrants as well.

But almost without exception, the women find that they are shunned once they outlast their usefulness. They are shunned even by their siblings, cousins and extended family members. One Korean American woman, a college student, recalled that one of her aunts had married an American soldier. This aunt had sponsored their immigration to the United States, and through that link, most members of the extended family came to America. But this aunt was rarely invited to family gatherings. Furthermore, the student said, the adults in the family made it clear to the children that having a military bride in the family was to be kept a secret. While ethnocentrism is certainly part of the dynamic of this kind of shunning, it is also a way for Korean immigrants to become American, much the same way that shunning camptown women allows Korea to be a sovereign nation in partnership with the United States. At the same time, it also allows Korean immigrants to affirm a Koreanness that seems threatened in the context of lives lived in America.

Lisa Lowe argues that Asian immigrants are forced to negate their own histories—of war, of oppression under imperialist and neo-imperialist powers, of racial discrimination—in order to become American. Post-1965 Asian immigrants, she argues, are in contradiction with the American sense of national identity precisely because of that history. Becoming American, then, requires negating that history and adopting the U.S. national narrative that disavows American imperialism (1–36). For Korean immigrants, negating their history of subjugation under the United States begins even before they step on American soil, for the ostracism of camptown women is nothing less than that negation. This negation continues with their shunning of military brides. By shunning her, the Korean immigrant simultaneously denies the history of subjugation, thus adopting the U.S. national narrative, and denies that he/she is like her in any way, thus affirming their Koreanness.

In the Korean (immigrant) imaginary, the military bride is figured as a lost soul—someone who has turned her back on her culture and her people in favor of an American and an American life. The military bride is thus seen as somehow not really Korean, as someone who has crossed a racial/ethnic border delineating Koreans and non-Koreans. That her children are not full-blooded Koreans only serves to underscore this otherness within a culture and society that prizes the alleged purity of the Korean bloodline. She is also figured as a pathetic wretch, a victim of domestic abuse, betrayal and abandonment by an American husband, someone who may "return" to prostitution, or an easy sexual conquest. Her status as victim—mostly at the hands of American men—serves to warn that crossing that border over into non-Korean territory leads only to disaster. But this characterization of military brides is not only a gross stereotype, it also serves to deflect attention away from the otherness of Korean immigrants themselves in relation to Koreans in Korea. Korean immigrants, like the military bride, have crossed a border by crossing the Pacific Ocean to live in a foreign land, raise their children as citizens of that land, and die in that land. To Koreans who have remained in Korea, the *jae mi gyopo* (a term for people of Korean descent in America) is a dual figure, someone to be envied for having achieved access to the American Utopia, but also someone who has forsaken the homeland. Portrayals of Korean Americans in the popular media, in television dramas such as *L.A. Arirang* and *1.5*, illustrate this duality. In the wake of the 1992 Los Angeles civil unrest, which was widely reported in Korea, "American beggar" has become the popular term for Korean Americans, one that highlights the immigrants' failure to find success. Thus for Korean immigrants who may be insecure about their identity, who may be ambivalent about their own history of immigration and who may question whether coming to America was the right thing to do, shunning military brides is one way to affirm an identity as Koreans.

This ostracism from Korean immigrant society does not mean, however, that the women are left without community. They have formed their own communities among themselves, and while these communities are not as large or as institutionalized or as strong as mainstream Korean immigrant communities, they are a valuable resource for military brides. The communities are often more akin to loose networks or groups of friends. They center around regional organizations of military brides, around churches near military bases whose congregations are composed almost exclusively of military brides, and around networks of friends and fictive sister relations. Their primary activities include helping each other in times of need, providing opportunities to socialize in a Korean atmosphere, doing charity work on behalf of Amerasian children in Korea, and publicizing Korean culture to the American public, usually through participating in multicultural festivals or international days.

One organization of military brides, Korean International Daughters Society (KIDS), was founded specifically to help Amerasian children in Korea. This organization holds an annual fundraising banquet, with the proceeds going to orphanages. The women also sponsor adult Amerasians who wish to immigrate to the United States. Although most military brides eschew any relationship to the camptowns, many of their organizations do similar charity work on behalf of Amerasian children, most of whom come from the camptowns. According to several of the women I interviewed, the women feel a connection with Amerasian children in Korea because their own children are also Amerasian.

Other clubs formed by military brides are primarily social. They meet once a month at the home of a member, eat a potluck dinner of Korean foods, and socialize. For some women, this is their only chance to speak Korean, eat Korean food, and be with other Korean women.

Communities also form around churches whose congregants are primarily military brides.[13] As is the case with Korean immigrant churches in general, the church becomes a place not only for religious expression, but also for cultural expression and social connection with fellow Koreans.[14] Much of that expression centers on food. At the church I attended for nearly two years, whose 100-some congregants were all military brides and their family members, the Sunday service was followed by lunch, always Korean food. The church women's club made *kimchee*, and each year also did *kimjang*, the making of winter *kimchee* that would last until early spring. These are communal activities that in Korea would be done by the women of an extended family, by close friends, or by a mother/daughter or mother-in-law/daughter-in-law combination. For many of the women, these are activities that they cannot do at home, simply because their American husbands and children do not like Korean food and/or because there are no other Korean family members with whom to share such an activity.

The women at this church also participate each year in the multicultural festival at the local school. Wearing traditional Korean clothes, the women prepare and sell Korean foods such as stuffed dumplings, barbecued beef, glass noodles with meat and vegetables, and rice/seaweed rolls. They also display their prized valuables to show Americans Korean cultural goods—lacquered jewelry boxes, embroidered screens, ceramic vases, jade jewelry.

The communities formed by the military brides serve other practical functions as well. They exchange information about jobs, often referring each other to job openings. They take in newcomers and teach them how to survive in America. They baby-sit each other's children and cook each other's food.

These communities, I argue, are primarily based on a sense of sisterhood that flows from shared identities as Koreans and as "internationally married women." To put it another way, these women reject the notion that they are no longer "really" Korean due to their outmarriage and immigration to the United States, and have created their own forms of Korean ethnic identity. This identity—gender specific, often class specific, and particular to their situation—challenges the validity of a monolithic Korean identity and opens up spaces for difference within Korean communities. Their experiences of sisterhood also demonstrate that shared gender, even when combined with shared ethnicity, is not enough to create bonds, but that sisterhood requires other commonalities grounded in concrete experiences.

The military brides' insistence on their Korean identity challenges the dominant self-identity for both Koreans and Korean Americans. This self-identity is based on notions of racial and cultural homogeneity which fail to recognize the diversity within Korean/American society. For example, as anthropologist Kyeyoung Park has shown, 1.5-generation Korean Americans have their own distinct sense of identity, one that incorporates and transforms elements of their Korean and American upbringings. Korean adoptees and many second-generation Korean Americans may not seem recognizably "Korean" to South Koreans or to the immigrant generation, but they too are part of Korean/American society. Mixed race people who are part Korean are increasingly claiming their Korean heritage and insisting that "full-blooded" Koreans recognize their claims to inclusion. This diversity—marginalized, suppressed and ignored—belies the dominant discourse of homogeneity.

Whether consciously or not military brides are refusing this marginalization by insisting on their Korean identity. They are pressing for a new definition of who and what is Korean, for an acknowledgment of the ways in which the United States has shaped Korean identity both in Korea and in the United States, and for recognition that they are also daughters of Korea, to borrow from the title of one internationally married woman's autobiography (Edwards). To engage this challenge, Koreans in Korea must face the reality of camptowns in their midst and must acknowledge the possibility that all of South Korea may be one huge camptown, that the degradation endured by camptown women is something that extends to all Koreans and something for which all Koreans are partially responsible. For Korean Americans, it means recognizing that their immigrant paths are linked to military brides, that their immigrant lives are intimately connected to the immigrant lives of military brides. What this requires are new conceptualizations of nation and peoplehood and community, conceptualizations that are open-ended and inclusive rather than closed and exclusive. I would argue also that these re-conceptualizations must take place simultaneously on both sides of the Pacific.

As a start, it may be useful to begin post-1945 Asian American history with the history of military brides. For although my work has examined only the case of Korean military brides, Asian military brides as a whole have been left out of Asian American communities and of Asian American studies.[15] Narratives of Asian American immigration history, if they mention Asian military brides at all, focus on immigration statistics for Asian wives of U.S. citizens, ignoring military bride experiences and their importance in Asian American history.[16] Perhaps ignoring the history of Asian military brides has been one way to occlude those experiences with imperialism that contradict the dominant American narrative. Putting Asian military brides—from Korea, Japan, the Philippines, Vietnam, all countries where the United States has acted as an imperial power—back into Asian American history requires us to look at the history of U.S. intervention in Asia and the ways in which relations between Asia and the United States influence Asian immigration. It requires us to do precisely what Oscar Campomanes, in a recent essay, calls on Asian American studies to do: begin to develop and use a "more radical epistemology that accounts for the problematics of nationalist narrativity and twentieth-century U.S. imperial power" (526–527). This means recognizing and exploring the ways in which Asian American history is intertwined with U.S. imperialism. It means recognizing that military brides are Asian immigrants whose lives are part of Asian American histories. It means recognizing that these women are among our Asian American forebears. It also means re-examining Asian American communities today, and asking, where are the military brides? How to begin making the links between mainstream Asian American communities and Asian military brides?

Finally, I want to go back to the church incident regarding Thanksgiving dinner. Faced with blatant rejection, the military brides at that church did not quietly return to the shadows assigned to them. They went ahead and prepared food. In a direct response to stereotypes of dirt and uncleanliness, they wore pure white aprons and chefs' hats to serve up a Thanksgiving meal of turkey with all the trimmings. It was a hit with the children at the church, and the food prepared by the military brides ran out while the food prepared by the other Korean women was left over (Yeo, personal interview).

NOTES

1. The "normal" and "respectable" path for women in Korea remains marriage and motherhood. Few camptown women view themselves as rebelling against this societal norm. Rather, the overwhelming majority see themselves as having been forced into camptown life due to unfortunate circumstances and desire to find a way out. Knowing that they have little to no chance of marriage with a Korean man due to societal prejudice against camptown women, many view marriage with an American as a desirable alternative.

2. This paper is drawn from a larger study of Korean military brides using oral history interviews with Korean military brides, participation/observation in Korean immigrant communities, and research in a camptown in South Korea.

3. *Dong-A Ilbo*, 7/22/1962, as cited in Moon, p. 42.

4. Since the closing of Clark Air Base in the Philippines in 1992, Osan is now the largest.

5. This is a derogatory term for camptown women.

6. The 1980 Kwangju massacre was a brutal, military crackdown on pro-democracy protesters in which the United States has been implicated. For a discussion of U.S. government documents that confirms long-standing suspicions about the U.S. role in the massacre, see Shorrock, Tim, "Ex-Leaders Go On Trial In Seoul." *Journal of Commerce.* Five Star Edition, Feb. 27, 1996. A1, and Shorrock, Tim, "Debacle in Kwangju." *The Nation.* Dec. 9, 1996. 19–22.

7. See Bruce Cumings' 1998 address, "The Question of American Responsibility for the Suppression of the Chejudo Uprising," presented at the 50th Anniversary Conference of the April 3, 1948 Chejudo Rebellion, Tokyo, March 14, 1998.

8. While this may appear to be a more sympathetic reading of the camptown woman, it has its own problems, not least among them that this usage of the figure of the camptown woman is yet another way that these women are objectified and their voices silenced, their life experiences used for someone else's purpose.

9. As violent crimes committed by American soldiers—such as the 1992 murder of Yoon Geum-yi, in which she was sexually tortured and beaten to death—are widely publicized, Koreans are becoming increasingly willing to condemn America and American soldiers. Nevertheless, this does not seem to be accompanied by a corresponding increase in understanding or sympathy for the camptown women.

10. See, for example, Pheterson, Gail. Ed. *A Vindication of the Rights of Whores.* (Seattle: Seal Press, 1989), and Delacoste, Frederique, and Priscilla Alexander. Eds. *Sex Work: Writings by Women in the Sex Industry.* (San Francisco: Cleis Press, 1998).

11. Bong-Youn Choy discusses class characteristics of post-1945 (mainly post-1965) *Korean Immigrants in America* (Chicago: Nelson-Hall, 1979). He does not, however, discuss military brides, giving them only a brief mention on page 218.

12. Statistics on the actual number of Korean women who entered the United States as wives of U.S. military personnel are not kept by any agency, but must be teased out of records kept by the U.S. Immigration and Naturalization Service, the City of Seoul's records of marriages between Korean citizens and citizens of foreign countries, and records kept by the South Korean Emigration Office. With these sources and others, Lee has compiled the most complete figures available on this subject.

13. See Daniel Y. Moon, "Ministering to 'Korean Wives' of Servicemen," in *Korean Women in a Struggle for Humanization,* edited by Harold Hakwon Sunoo and Dong Soo Kim, (Memphis, Tenn.: Assocation of Korean Christian Scholars in North America, 1978), pp. 97–116, for a discussion of the role that churches can play in the lives of military brides.

14. Korean immigrant churches have been a favorite topic of research for many Korean American scholars and most, if not all, anthologies of the Korean American experience include one or more articles on the subject. Jung-Ha Kim's *Bridge-makers and Cross-bearers: Korean American Women and the Church* (Atlanta: Scholars Press, 1997) is a recent book-length study that looks at Korean American women's church lives.

15. Few studies of Asian Americans include substantive discussions of Asian military brides. An exception is Evelyn Nakano Glenn's *Issei, Nisei, War Bride* (Philadelphia: Temple University Press, 1986). To my knowledge, no book-length study has focused on military brides from Asia other than Bok-Lim C. Kim, et al.'s *Women in Shadows: A Handbook for Service Providers Working with Asian Wives of U.S. Military Personnel* (La Jolla, Calif.: National Committee Concerned With Asian Wives of U.S. Servicemen, 1981). Like other studies of Asian military brides conducted by social work scholars and social service providers, this book focuses primarily on issues of marital conflict, dysfunctionality, and other problems, rather than linking military bride histories to Asian American histories.

16. This is the case, for example, in both Ronald Takaki's *Strangers from a Different Shore* (Boston: Little Brown, 1989) and Sucheng Chan's *Asian Americans: An Interpretative History* (Philadelphia: Temple University Press, 1991).

WORKS CITED

Abelmann, Nancy, and John Lie. *Blue Dreams: Korean Americans and the Los Angeles Riots.* Cambridge, MA: Harvard University Press, 1995.

Campomanes, Oscar V. "New Formations of Asian American Studies and the Question of U.S. Imperialism." *positions: east asia cultures critique* 5.2 (fall 1997): 523–550.

Chan, Sucheng. *Asian Americans: An Interpretive History.* Philadelphia: Temple University Press, 1989.

Choy, Bong-Youn. *Koreans in America.* Chicago: Nelson-Hall, 1979.

Cumings, Bruce. "The Question of American Responsibility for the Suppression of the Chejudo Uprising." Paper presented at the 50th Anniversary Conference of the April 3, 1948 Chejudo Rebellion. Tokyo. March 14, 1998.

Delacoste, Frederique, and Priscilla Alexander, eds. *Sex Work: Writings by Women in the Sex Industry.* Pittsburgh: Cleis Press, 1987.

Durebang and Korea Church Women United, eds. *Great Army, Great Father: Militarized Prostitution in South Korea; Life in GI Towns.* Seoul, Korea: Juhanmigun Beomjoi Geunjeoleulwihan Undongbonbu, 1995.

Edwards, Chon S. (Song Jun-Gi). *Na-do Hangug-ui Ddal (I Am Also a Daughter of Korea).* Seoul: Mirae Munhwasa Press, 1988.

Enloe, Cynthia. *Bananas, Beaches and Bases: Making Feminist Sense of International Politics.* Berkeley: University of California Press, 1989.

Glenn, Evelyn Nakano. *Issei, Nisei, War Bride: Three Generations of Japanese American Women in Domestic Service.* Philadelphia: Temple University Press, 1986.

Jeffords, Susan. *The Remasculinization of the United States.* Bloomington: Indiana University Press, 1989.

Kang, Hyeon-Dew. "Changing Image of America in Korean Popular Literature: With An Analysis of Short Stories Between 1945–1975." *Korea Journal* October, 1976. 19–33.

Kim, Bok-Lim C., et al. *Women in Shadows: A Handbook for Service Providers Working with Asian Wives of U.S. Military Personnel.* La Jolla, Calif.: National Committee Concerned with Asian Wives of U.S. Servicemen, 1981.

Kim, Jung-Ha. *Bridge-makers and Cross-bearers: Korean American Women and the Church.* Atlanta: Scholars Press, 1997.

Kim, M.B. (Staff member at My Sister's Place, Uijongbu, Korea.) Personal interview. March 1997.

Lee, Daniel B. "Korean Women Married to Servicemen." In *Korean American Women Living in Two Cultures.* Eds. Young In Song and Ailee Moon. Los Angeles: Academia Koreana-Keimyung-Baylo University Press, 1997. 94–123.

Manwoo Lee. "Anti-Americanism and South Korea's Changing Perception of America." In *Alliance under Tension: The Evolution of South Korea-U.S. Relations.* Eds. Manwoo Lee, Ronald D. McLaurin and Chung-in Moon. Boulder, Colo.: Westview Press, 1988. 7–27.

Lowe, Lisa. *Immigrant Acts: On Asian American Cultural Politics.* Durham, N.C.: Duke University Press, 1996.

Moon, Daniel Y. "Ministering to 'Korean Wives' of Servicemen." In *Korean Women in a Struggle for Humanization.* Ed. Harold Hakwon Sunoo and Dong Soo Kim. Memphis, Tenn.: Association of Korean Christian Scholars in North America, 1978.

Moon, Katharine H.S. "International Relations and Women: A Case Study of United States-Korea Camptown Prostitution, 1971–1976." Diss. Princeton University, 1995.

My Sister's Place. Report on camptowns and camptown prostitution in South Korea. Draft. Uijongbu, Korea. 1997.

Oh, Yun Ho. *Sikminji-ui Adul-ae-gae* (To The Sons of the Colony). 3rd ed. Seoul: Baiksan Sudang, 1994.

Pheterson, Gail, ed. *A Vindication of the Rights of Whores.* Seattle: Seal Press, 1989.

Shorrock, Tim. "Ex-Leaders Go on Trial in Seoul," *Journal of Commerce.* Five Star Edition, Feb. 27, 1996. A1.

————. "Debacle in Kwangju," *The Nation*, Dec. 9, 1996. 19–22.

Sturdevant, Saundra Pollock, and Brenda Stoltzfus. *Let the Good Times Roll: Prostitution and the U.S. Military in Asia.* New York: The New Press, 1992.

Takaki, Ronald. *Strangers from a Different Shore.* Boston: Little, Brown and Company, 1989.

Thiesmeyer, Lynn. "U.S. Comfort Women and the Silence of the American Other." *Hitting Critical Mass: A Journal of Asian American Cultural Criticism* 3.2 (Spring 1997) 47–67.

Yeo, Geumhyun. (Director of the Rainbow Center, Flushing, N.Y.) Personal interview. December, 1997.

The Cold War Origins
of the Model Minority Myth

Robert G. Lee

Racist Love

In 1974, the writer Frank Chin expressed it this way: "Whites love us because we're not black."[1] The elevation of Asian Americans to the position of model minority had less to do with the actual success of Asian Americans than with the perceived failure—or worse, refusal—of African Americans to assimilate. Asian Americans were "not black" in two significant ways: They were both politically silent and ethnically assimilable.

The Cold War construction of Asian America as a model minority that could become ethnically assimilated, despite what *U.S. News and World Report* euphemistically called its "racial disadvantage," reveals the contradiction between the continuing reproduction of racial difference and the process of ethnic assimilation. The representation of Asian Americans as a *racial* minority whose apparently successful *ethnic* assimilation was a result of stoic patience, political obedience, and self-improvement was a critically important narrative of ethnic liberalism that simultaneously promoted racial equality and sought to contain demands for social transformation. The representation of the Asian American as the paragon of ethnic virtue, who the *U.S. News and World Report* editors thought should be emulated by "Negroes and other minorities," reflected not so much Asian success as the triumph of an emergent discourse of race in which cultural difference replaced biological difference as the new determinant of social outcomes. Although the deployment of Asian Americans as a model minority was made explicit in the mid-1960s, its origins lay in the triumph of liberalism and the racial logic of the Cold War.

The narrative of Asian ethnic assimilation fit the requirements of Cold War containment perfectly. Three specters haunted Cold War America in the 1950s: the red menace of communism, the black menace of race mixing, and the white menace of homosexuality. On the international front, the narrative of ethnic assimilation sent a message to the Third World, especially to Asia where the United States was engaged in increasingly fierce struggles with nationalist and communist insurgencies, that the United States was a liberal democratic state where people of color could enjoy equal rights and upward mobility. On the home front, it sent a message to "Negroes and other minorities" that accommodation would be rewarded while militancy would be contained or crushed.

The successful transformation of the Oriental from the exotic to the acceptable was a narrative of Americanization, a sort of latter-day *Pilgrim's Progress*, through which America's anxieties about communism, race mixing, and transgressive sexuality might be contained and eventually tamed. The narrative of Asian ethnic assimilation helped construct a new national narrative for the atomic age that Walter Lippman had dubbed the American Century.

WORLD WAR II AS PRELUDE

Ironically, it was Japan's attack on Pearl Harbor and America's entry into the Second World War that began the unraveling of the Yellow Peril myth. The Second World War was a watershed event for Asian Americans. The treatment of Asian American ethnic groups brought into sharp focus the contradiction between their exclusion as racial subjects arid the promise of their assimilation as ethnic citizens.

America's entry into the war against Nazi Germany and Imperial Japan made it increasingly difficult to sustain national policies based on theories of white racial supremacy. After Dunkirk, the United States and its allies depended on support from their colonial subjects in India, China (not, strictly speaking, a colony), southeast Asia, and north Africa. The very nationalist movements whose representatives had been summarily dismissed by Woodrow Wilson at Versailles were now actively courted by the United States as allies against the Axis powers. In August 1941, four months before the United States entered the war, Roosevelt and Churchill signed the Atlantic Charter recognizing the right of "peoples" to decide their own form of government. Later that year, in response to the threat by civil rights leader A. Phillip Randolph to lead a massive protest march on Washington, Roosevelt signed an Executive Order outlawing racial discrimination by companies doing business with the federal government and established a Committee on Fair Employment Practices.

Official pronouncements of racial equality notwithstanding, the wholesale and brutal incarceration of the Japanese American population on the west coast underscored, in no uncertain terms, the willingness of the U.S. government to invoke race as a category of subordination to achieve its goals.[2] This willingness to use racial categories would result in physical hardship, economic ruin, family disintegration, and psychological trauma for more than 120,000 Japanese Americans, men and women, elderly and infant, citizen and immigrant.

After Pearl Harbor, the United States found itself allied with a weak and divided China. The Yellow Peril, that alliance of Japanese brains and Chinese bodies that had fired the racial nightmares of turn-of-the-century strategists of empire from Kaiser Wilhelm to Sax Rohmer, had remained imaginary. Japan's plans for empire, though couched in Pan-Asian anticolonial rhetoric, met with resistance in China and elsewhere in Asia. For the first time, being able to tell one Asian group apart from another seemed important to white Americans. Two weeks after the Japanese attack on Pearl Harbor brought the United States into the War, *Life* magazine ran a two-page pictorial entitled "How to Tell Japs from the Chinese." The reporter for *Life* magazine wrote:

> U.S. citizens have been demonstrating a distressing ignorance on the delicate question of how to tell a Chinese from a Jap. Innocent victims in cities all over the country are many of the 75,000 U.S. Chinese, whose homeland is our stanch [*sic*] ally. . . .
>
> To dispel some of this confusion, *Life* here adduces a rule of thumb from the anthropomorphic conformations that distinguish friendly Chinese from enemy alien Japs.[3]

On the right side of the article, two facial portraits of Orientals are juxtaposed one above the other. The top picture (of the Minister of Economic Affairs of the Chinese Nationalist government) is captioned "Chinese public servant" while the one below (of Admiral Tojo, the Japanese Prime Minister) is captioned "Japanese Warrior." Although the pictures are the same size and the proportions of the facial features virtually identical, the notes tell a vastly different story. The Chinese, *Life* told its readers, has "parchment yellow complexion, more frequent epicanthic fold, higher bridge, never has rosy cheeks, lighter facial bones, longer narrower face and scant beard." Tojo, "representative of the Japanese people as whole . . . betrays aboriginal antecedents, has an earthy yellow complexion, less frequent epicanthic fold, flatter nose, sometimes rosy cheeks, heavy beard, broader shorter face and massive cheek and jawbone."

In addition, the *Life* article showed two pictures whose captions read, respectively, "Tall Chinese Brothers" and "Short Japanese Admirals." *Life*, taking no chances with its racial taxonomy, supplied the following "field" notes: The Chinese brothers were "tall and slender" with "long legs" while the admirals were "short and squat" with "shorter legs and longer torso." Had *Life* only added blonde hair and blue eyes, it might have created the perfect Aryan Chinaman.

Not wanting to appear unlearned in the matter of racial anthropology, *Life* pointed out that its illustrations were drawn from Northern Chinese. Southern Chinese (at that time, the overwhelming majority of Chinese residents of the United States), the magazine noted, were short, and "when middle aged and fat, they look more like Japs." The *Life* editors went on to tell the reader that

> Southern Chinese have round, broad faces, not as massively boned as the Japanese. Except that their skin is darker, this description fits the Filipinos who are [also] often mistaken for Japs. Chinese sometimes pass for Europeans, but Japs more often approach the Western types.[4]

Lest this confusing racial taxonomy fail Americans in this time of crisis, *Life* reassured its audience that cultural difference could also be identified visually. "An often sounder clue is facial expression, shaped by cultural, not anthropological, factors. Chinese wear the rational calm of tolerant realists. Japs, like General Tojo, show the humorless intensity of ruthless mystics."[5]

Aware that readers might be suspicious that this exercise in racial cataloguing was similar to that being practiced by Nazi social scientists, *Life* assured its audience that American physical anthropologists were "devoted debunkers of race myths." Debunking notwithstanding, *Life* asserted that the ability to measure the difference between the Chinese and Japanese "in millimeters" enabled American scientists to "set apart the special types of each national group." To lend an air of precision, scientific objectivity, and authority to the photos and the accompanying text, *Life*'s editors festooned the pictures with handwritten captions and arrows simulating anthropological field notes.

The same disjuncture between the newly articulated ideals of racial egalitarianism and the practice of racial discrimination can be seen in the Supreme Court's decisions in the Japanese American internment cases. In the case of Gordon Hirabayashi, a student at the University of Washington who had challenged the right of military authorities to establish a curfew applicable only to persons of Japanese ancestry, the court stated that discrimination on the sole basis of race was "odious to a free people." Nevertheless, the court refused to curb the authority of the military in times of national emergency and upheld Hirabayashi's conviction (he had refused to leave the university library at the hour appointed for Japanese Americans to be in their homes). Likewise in the case of Fred Korematsu, a house painter from Oakland who had evaded relocation, the court held that while race was an "inherently invidious" category for discrimination by the state and subject to "strict scrutiny," the court accepted the state's claim of military necessity for the incarceration of Japanese Americans.[6]

Despite its massive mistreatment of Japanese Americans, the still rigidly enforced segregation of African Americans throughout most of American society (not least in the Armed Forces), and the deadly anti-Semitic policy of denying refuge to Europe's Jews, the U.S. government condemned the Nazi's doctrine of racial superiority and identified the defeat of racism as one of the reasons "Why We Fight." While Japanese Americans were singled out on the basis of their "race," other Asian American ethnic groups began to receive favorable treatment from the federal government.

In 1943, Congress voted to repeal the Chinese Exclusion Act, which had for sixty years forbidden Chinese, with few exceptions, to enter the United States. Repeal of exclusion had been a foreign policy goal of successive Chinese governments for more than half a century. Repeal was pushed through the U.S. Congress on the grounds that it would keep the wavering Nationalist Chinese government of Chiang Kai-shek in the war against Japan.[7]

In the next year, two bills were introduced in Congress to establish immigration quotas for India and the Philippines. These two bills were passed in 1946, on the eve of Philippine independence. The repeal of Chinese Exclusion and the effective dismantling of the Asiatic Barred Zone of 1917 had greater symbolic value than immediate demographic effect, since the number of visas issued to Asian countries was still severely restricted. Nevertheless, the ideological statement implied by the dismantling of racially specific barriers signaled an erosion of white supremacy as a national doctrine.[8]

MAKING THE MODEL MINORITY MYTH

In January 1966, the *New York Times Magazine* published an article with the title "Success Story: Japanese-American Style," and in December *U.S. News and World Report* published an article focusing on Chinese Americans, "Success Story of One Minority in the US."[9] As their titles suggest, both articles told the story of Asians in America as a narrative of triumphant ethnic assimilation.

This new popular representation of Asian Americans as the model of successful "ethnic assimilation" was created in the crisis of racial policy that had surfaced at the highest levels of the federal government the previous year. The policy debate, that emerged in 1965 reflected deep ideological division over responses to the demands for racial equality that had developed in the two decades since the end of the Second World War.

The Watts riot in the summer of 1964 and the growing demands of African Americans for economic equity as well as formal political rights, along with the gradual dismantling of Jim Crow segregation in the South, plunged racial policy into crisis. The contours of the crisis can be seen in the conflicting responses of the Johnson Administration to black demands for racial equality. In March 1965, Lyndon Johnson's assistant secretary of Labor, Daniel Patrick Moynihan, published a *Report on the Black Family*, which laid much of the blame for black poverty on the "tangle of pathology" of the black family. He admonished African Americans to rehabilitate their dysfunctional families in order to achieve economic and social assimilation. In June, at commencement exercises at all-black Howard University in Washington, D.C., the president articulated a vision of racial equality through sweeping social reconstruction in a massive War on Poverty. Both men genuinely claimed to support racial equality and civil rights, but their two documents could not have been further apart in their analysis and proposed solutions. The conflict between Johnson's response and Moynihan's response forms the ideological context in which the Asian Americans emerged as the model minority.

Johnson's speech emphasized the historical reality of race in America as compelling logic for extending civil rights into the economic sphere. Referring to the disadvantaged position of many blacks in the American economic structure, Johnson declared, "You do not take a person who for years has been hobbled by chains and liberate him, bring him up to the starting line of a race and then say, 'You are free to compete with all the others,' and still justly believe that you have been completely fair."[10] The president went on to lay the principal responsibility for black poverty on white racism, both historical and present, and he outlined an agenda of government-sponsored social change to ameliorate discrimination and poverty.

Moynihan took a radically different political tack. Quoting his former Harvard colleague, sociologist Nathan Glazer, Moynihan complained that "the demand for economic equality is now not the demand for equal opportunities for the equally qualified; it is now the demand for equality of economic results. . . . The demand for equality in education . . . has also become a demand for equality of results, of outcomes."[11]

Moynihan left implicit Glazer's ominous threat that American society, despite a commitment toward the former, would be "ruthless" in suppressing the latter. Moynihan went on to describe a black culture of poverty as a "tangle of pathology" born in slavery but "capable of perpetuating itself without assistance from the white world."[12] In particular, Moynihan identified the prevalence of female-headed households as a barrier to economic success. For Moynihan, the key to both racial integration and economic mobility was not in structural changes or social reorganization that might correct past injustice, but in the rehabilitation of "culturally deprived" black families.

The *U.S. News* article was quite explicit about the political context of its report when it asserted, "At a time when it is being proposed that hundreds of billions be spent on uplifting Negroes and other minorities, the nation's 300,000 Chinese Americans are moving ahead on their own with no help from anyone else." Foreshadowing an obsession that was to shape Richard Nixon's campaign rhetoric a year later, the writer of the *U.S. News* article described America's Chinatowns as "havens for law and order" and made no fewer than six references to low rates of delinquency among Chinese American youth.[13]

MAKING THE SILENT MINORITY

The construction of the model minority was based on the political silence of Asian America. An often cited example of Asian American self-reliance was the underutilization of welfare programs in 1970. Despite the fact that 15 percent of Chinese families in New York city had incomes below the federal poverty level, only 3.4 percent had enrolled to receive public assistance. This statistic has often been used as an example of a cultural trait of self-reliance and family cohesion. An alternative explanation, grounded in recent Asian American history, would stress apprehension and mistrust of the state's intentions toward them.

Wartime incarceration had left deep wounds in the Japanese American communities. The removal to fairgrounds and racetracks, the relocation to remote, barbed-wired camps, the uncertainty of loyalty oaths, the separation of family members, all traumatized the Japanese American community. The Japanese American Citizens League's policy of accommodation with the War Relocation Authority and its role in suppressing dissent within the camps had left bitter divisions among many Japanese Americans. Japanese Americans, for the most part, were anxious to rebuild their lives and livelihoods and reluctant to relive their experience. In particular, the American-born Nisei generation remained remarkably silent about its camp experience until the emergence of the Asian American movement in the 1970s and the Redress Movement of the 1980s.

Social psychologists have likened the response of Japanese Americans who had been unjustly incarcerated to that of victims of rape or other physical violation. They demonstrated anger, resentment, self-doubt, and guilt, all symptoms of post-traumatic stress syndrome.[14]

While postwar Japan became America's junior partner, the People's Republic of China became its principal enemy. After the Korean War broke out in 1950, and especially after China entered the war in 1951, the United States made every effort to isolate communist China, economically and diplomatically, and embarked on a military policy of confrontation aimed at "containing" the expansion of Chinese influence throughout Asia and the Third World.

The fear of Red China extended to the Chinese American community. In 1949, Chinese communities in the United States were divided in their attitudes toward the communist revolution. Although the number of communists in Chinese American communities was tiny, many who were not communist or even leftist nonetheless found some satisfaction in the fact that a genuinely nationalist, reputedly honest, and apparently more democratic government had finally united China after a century of political chaos, weakness, and humiliation. On the other hand, Chiang Kai-shek's Kuomintang Party had long enjoyed the support of the traditional elites in the larger Chinatowns.[15]

When the Korean War broke out in 1950, Congress passed the Emergency Detention Act, which vested the U.S. Attorney General with the authority to establish concentration camps for any who might be deemed a domestic threat in a national emergency. The mere authorization of such sweeping powers of detention served as a stark warning to Chinese Americans that what had been done to Japanese Americans a decade earlier could also be done to them without effort.

The pro–Chiang Kai-shek Chinatown elite, working with the FBI, launched a systematic attempt to suppress any expression of support for the new communist regime in China. The Trading with the Enemy Act, which prohibited any currency transfers to the Peoples Republic of China, including remittances to family, was used as a tool to attempt to deport suspected communist sympathizers. Although only a few leftists and labor leaders were actually deported, the threat of deportation had a deeply chilling effect, since many hundreds of Chinese had come to the United States as "paper sons" during the long decades of exclusion and were in the United States under false pretenses.

In 1952 Congress passed the McCarran-Walter Immigration and Nationality Act, which dismantled racial prohibitions on immigration and established an Asian-Pacific Triangle with an immigration quota cap of two thousand visas. Even though McCarran-Walter still strictly limited Asian immigration, the red scare that was its impetus was contagious. In 1955, Everett F. Drumwright, the U.S. consul in Hong Kong, issued a report warning that Communist China was making use of "massive" fraud and deception to infiltrate agents into the United States under cover as immigrants. Drumwright's hysterical and largely unsubstantiated report provided the rationale for massive FBI and INS raids into Chinatowns around the country to search out pro-China subversives. Chinatowns were flooded with public notices and street flyers warning of potential spies and subversives, while "innocent residents" were encouraged to report suspected subversives to the FBI.

In 1957 Congress authorized the Chinese Confession Program. Chinese Americans who had come as paper sons were encouraged to confess their illegal entry. In return for consideration for an appropriate (but not guaranteed) adjustment of their status, the applicant had also to make a full disclosure on every relative and friend. The information gathered in the Chinese Confession Program was used to try to deport those who were identified by the FBI's informants as supporters of China or as domestic troublemakers. Membership in leftist support organizations, in labor unions, in "pro-China" organizations melted away in the face of the sustained harassment and attack from the conservative elite within Chinatowns, and the FBI and INS from without.[16]

CONTAINING THE RED MENACE: THE FORDIST COMPROMISE

At the close of the Second World War, American labor was infused with a renewed militancy. During the war years union membership had grown from nine million in 1940 to about fifteen million in 1945. This represented almost thirty-six percent of the non-agricultural work force, the highest proportion of unionized labor in the country's history. During the war years, organized labor had agreed to a no strike policy and to curb wage demands as a patriotic obligation to the war effort. However, at the war's end pent-up wage demands and the problems of reabsorption of millions of men leaving the service led to a resurgence of demands for wages and a reassertion of control over work conditions. Labor strife soon boiled over at General Motors and in the oil industry. In 1945 forty-five hundred work stoppages, mainly wildcat strikes and sit-downs, involved five million workers. Some of these work stoppages took the form of hate strikes aimed at driving women and black workers from the factory positions they had earned during the war.[17]

In 1946, the steelworkers went on strike, then the miners. Strike fever spread when a general strike was called in Stamford, Connecticut. In 1947 militant labor called general strikes to shut down business in Houston, Rochester, Pittsburgh and Oakland.

In May 1946, President Truman seized the railroads to prevent a strike. Altogether Truman would seize and operate nine industries under powers granted the executive branch by the War Labor Disputes Act. Management launched a massive attack on radical, particularly Communist Party, leadership within the labor movement. Their most effective tool was the Taft-Hartley Act, passed in 1948, which outlawed the closed shop, secondary boycotts, and jurisdictional strikes in violation of decisions of the National Labor Relations Board; jointly administered welfare funds; and made unions subject to suit in federal courts for violation of contracts. The Taft-Hartley law stripped collective bargaining rights from unions having communists among their leadership and resulted in successive purges of the labor movement. Employers and employees could petition for decertification elections, and federal employees were forbidden to strike. State right-to-work laws were legalized, and the president was given power to enforce eighty-day cooling off periods during which labor would be compelled to return to work.

The long period of economic growth that sustained America's rise to hegemonic power depended on a sustained accord between labor and management. This pattern of cooperation has been called the Fordist Compromise, since it seemed to usher in that stage of capitalism which Henry Ford had envisioned, in which working-class demand for durable consumer goods would drive economic growth. The Fordist Compromise permanently institutionalized many of the features of "scientific management" that had been introduced during the war. Under the new production-oriented union leadership, labor contracts developed a pattern of close collaboration between labor leadership and management on issues of supervision, productivity, and work rules.[18] In return, management and the state worked together to create a working class that had the social characteristics of a middle class. Real income rose by 30 percent between 1945 and 1960. The Fordist Compromise also called for a relatively high degree of state intervention, from the mediation of labor relations through the National Labor Relations Board, to the regulation of working conditions through agencies such as the Occupational Safety and Health Administration, to the organization of a "welfare state" of permanent entitlements for the new "middle" class, such as social security, subsidized housing, educational financing, unemployment insurance, and increased public higher education. The state also took on an expanded role in intervening in the economy through an ever-wider range of fiscal control policies and by exercising its economic power as the purchaser of last resort.

The sustained economic growth on which the Fordist Compromise depended was fueled by several sources, but initially it was $40 billion in wartime personal savings and a pent-up demand for durable consumer products that drove production. This required the reinvigoration of the patriarchal nuclear family. Wartime production had increased the number of women in the labor force from just under fourteen million in 1940 to just over nineteen million in 1945.[19] Both management and federal agencies worked to encourage and sometimes force women back into the home while work assignments in many plants were resegregated along racial lines.[20] As men returned from war and started families, the birth rate in the United States grew for the first time in several decades, leading to the sustained growth of a domestic market for housing, education, and durable consumer goods. The nuclear family was the necessary social unit of consumption for durable goods—the automobiles (fifty-eight million sold in the 1950s), refrigerators, toasters, and televisions whose production drove the economy.

The realization of the Fordist Compromise could only be imagined in a world in which the United States had reconstructed a sphere of influence based on free trade and open markets. In the late 1930s and '40s, American policy planners in the State Department and the Council on Foreign Relations had initially imagined a "Grand Area" of American influence, to include the Western Hemisphere and the Asia-Pacific area. By the end of the war, the United States was in position to supplant Britain, France, and the Netherlands in many, if not all, of their colonial territories.[21] The American postwar project of global transformation supplanted European colonial administrations in Asia with nationalist elites whose economic interests and political allegiances were aligned with American interests. By the end of the 1940s, one-third of all manufactured goods in the world were made in America, and U.S. officials emphasized a high level of exports as a critical factor in avoiding a postwar depression.[22] American policy-makers therefore took it as an article of faith that the reconstruction of a stable, multilateral, capitalist economic system would rely on the unobstructed movement of capital and labor.

America's strategy for global reconstruction required the reconstruction of both western Europe and Japan as major industrialized trading partners. In Europe, the Marshall Plan funneled millions of dollars into the rebuilding of western Europe. Financing the reconstruction of Europe could not be funded solely through European-American trade, however; imports from Europe only amounted to one third of one percent of the U.S. gross national product. The United States therefore looked to Asia and the Pacific to close the "dollar gap."

The development of a Pacific Rim economic strategy therefore became a central requirement for American policy planners directly at the war's end. Although MacArthur had begun to dismantle prewar cartels such as Mitsui and Mitsubishi as a means of democratizing the Japanese economy along with its political system, by 1947 the reverse decision was made to reconstruct Japan's prewar economic machine as a foil to a possible revolutionary China. Japanese manufacturing was to become what the Council on Foreign Relations called "the workshop of the American lake." Japan was to play a critical role as a junior partner in the Pacific Rim strategy. After the "loss" of China, Japan, with American encouragement, focused its economic attention on southeast Asia. In its report on Asian economic development in 1952, the Institute for Pacific Relations spelled out the role that Japan was to play between the United States and the Southeast Asian market.

> There can be little question that . . . the best area for Japanese economic expansion is in Southeast Asia, with its demands for capital and consumer goods, its raw materials and rice surplus. . . . It would seem that Japan should be encouraged to develop trading outlets there in the interest of the overall structure of Pacific security. Japan has herself shown keen interest in these trade possibilities, especially in Thailand, Malaysia, Indonesia, and India.[23]

The Pacific Rim was not only a crucial market for American goods but also a highly profitable region for export of capital. In addition to the redeployment of Japanese capital, direct U.S. investment in the Pacific Rim was a major source of profits for American corporations. While overseas investments grew at about 10 percent per annum—twice the growth rate of domestic investment—American investment in the Pacific Rim outside Japan brought a 25.5 percent return on investment, and investment in the Japanese economy brought in 11.3 percent. Between 1951 and 1976, the book value of American investments in the Pacific Rim grew from $16 billion to $80.3 billion.[24]

CONTAINING THE BLACK MENACE: ETHNIC ASSIMILATION

In 1944, the same year in which the Supreme Court heard the Japanese internment cases, Gunnar Myrdal published *An American Dilemma: The Negro Problem and Modern Democracy*, a massive collaborative study of American race relations. Drawing on the work of a generation of American liberal social scientists, notably sociologist Robert E. Park and his students, *An American Dilemma* signaled the intellectual discrediting of biological theories of racial superiority and the triumph of the concept of ethnicity as the dominant paradigm for explaining and transforming race relations. Myrdal's report to the Carnegie Foundation focused on the disparity between the egalitarian ethos articulated in the nation's founding documents and the practice of racial discrimination in American society. Myrdal was clear about the implications of the "American dilemma" for America's role as the principal organizer of the postwar world order: "If America in actual practice could show the world a progressive trend by which the Negro finally became integrated into modern democracy, all mankind would have reason to believe that peace, progress, and order are feasible."[25]

Myrdal's hope was a statement of liberal faith. The triumph of liberalism, including ethnic liberalism, was made possible by the victory of the United States and its allies over the Axis powers and necessary to the rise of a *Pax Americana* in the postwar era.

The Cold War provided a national security dimension to the "race problem." Although Soviet communism was perceived as the greatest threat to the established order, after the Soviet Union exploded its own atomic bomb in 1949 the struggle against the Soviet Union was limited to a war of containment.[26] Since the establishment of relatively stable opposing blocs in Europe in the mid-1950s, the struggle between the U.S. and the Soviet Union was played out principally in Asia, Africa, and Latin America. In 1954, the term "Third World" was coined as India, the People's Republic of China, and Indonesia (with the tacit support of the Soviet Union) sponsored a conference of non-aligned nations at Bandung, Indonesia. The demands of the Third World nations, largely peoples of color, for independence, self-determination, and economic development became the ideological arena in the contest between the Soviet Union and the United States.

It is not surprising, then, to find federal intervention on behalf of civil rights expressed in the language and logic of the Cold War. As early as 1948, in *Shelley v. Kraemer*, a case involving restrictive covenants in real estate, the federal government's brief supporting the dismantling of racial restrictions on housing "relied" on the State Department's view that "the United States has been embarrassed in the conduct of foreign relations by acts of [racial] discrimination in this country."[27] In the most significant postwar desegregation case, *Brown v. Board of Education*, both the Justice Department and the NAACP briefs emphasized the important foreign policy implications of the case. The Justice Department's amicus brief stated the foreign policy case explicitly:

> The existence of discrimination against minority groups in the U.S. has an adverse effect upon our relations with other countries. . . . Racial discrimination furnishes grist

for the Communist propaganda mills and it raises doubts even among friendly nations as to the intensity of our devotion to the democratic faith.[28]

A decade later, in the aftermath of the Watts riots, both Johnson's Howard University speech and the preface to Moynihan's *Report* referred to this ideological struggle and framed the problem of civil rights and social justice in the United States within the global context of the Cold War. Both initially emphasized the need to provide the world with a model of the "true American revolution" as an alternative to communism. The president opened his speech by declaring,

> Our earth is the home of revolution. . . . Our enemies may occasionally seize the day of change. But it is the banner of our movement which they take. And our own future is linked to this process of change in many lands in the world. But nothing in any country touches us more profoundly, nothing is freighted with meaning for our own destiny, than the revolution of the Negro American.[29]

Moynihan opened his report with the observation that "the [Black] movement has profound international implications . . . [and that] it was not a matter of chance that the Negro movement caught fire in America at just that moment when the nations of Africa were gaining their freedom."[30] He went on to invoke the threat of perceived separatist Black Muslim doctrines or the "attractiveness of Chinese communism" to American blacks.

Anxious to replace the invidious category of race, for which there was little scientific justification and significant political cost, liberal theorists subsumed race relations to ethnicity. Ethnicity theory was grounded in the belief that while certain historically anachronistic patterns of racial segregation persisted, modern American society was open to the full participation of all who were willing to participate. Liberal social scientists who promoted the ethnicity paradigm argued that the desired assimilation of blacks into modern American society could be achieved in two steps. The barriers of Jim Crow segregation had to be dismantled (over the objections of "pre-modern" segregationists like the Klan, the White Citizens Councils, and an entrenched Southern power structure), and non-whites had to accommodate themselves to the "universal" demands of modernity.

The blueprint for ethnic assimilation was Robert Park's theory of a four-stage ethnic or race relations cycle. Park identified four stages in a natural and irreversible process of ethnic assimilation: initial contact between the outsider and the host society, economic and political competition, economic and cultural accommodation of the ethnic to the host society, and finally, assimilation into the host society. These patterns of cultural assimilation and integration were assumed to be universally applicable to all "newcomers" into the modern city and applicable to racial as well as ethnic relations. This was a narrative of modernization drawn from studies of the historical experiences of European immigrant groups in American cities. The ethnic component of cultural identity was identified with the Old World. Seen as pre-modern and dysfunctional, ethnic differences of language, custom, and religion were transcended as the immigrant became modern and American.

Since the stages of assimilation were based on a narrative of universal modernization and not on a theory of subordination, the burden was on the latecomer to modernization to accommodate the host society. It did not occur to assimilation theorists that racially subordinated people might be reluctant to abandon cultures of survival that had been developed over centuries of oppression. The black sociologist E. Franklin Frazier, a student of Park and one of the most important contributors to *The American Dilemma*, wrote:

> Since the institutions, the social stratification, and the culture of the Negro community are essentially the same as those of the larger community, it is not strange that the Negro minority belongs among the assimilationist rather than the pluralist, secessionist, or militant minorities. It is seldom that one finds Negroes who think of themselves as possessing a different culture from whites and that their culture should be preserved.[31]

Assimilationists supported the civil rights movement in the dismantling of Southern Jim Crow segregation and encouraged voting rights and electoral political participation. Assimilation theory, however, suggested that the duty of the state was limited to the dismantling of formal, legislated barriers to participation. Since the greater part of assimilation rested on the accommodation of the minority to the host society, state regulation of private activity in the interest of equal condition was seen to have little positive and possibly greater negative effect. The sociologist Milton Gordon, who in the early 1960s elaborated and refined Park's race relations cycle into a seven-stage theory of ethnic assimilation, warned explicitly:

> The government *must not* use racial criteria positively in order to impose desegregation upon public facilities in an institutional area where such segregation is not a function of racial discrimination directly, but results from discrimination operating in another institutional area or from some other causes.[32] [Emphasis added]

In the 1950s and early 1960s, liberalism, with its universalist claims on science and progress, became the hegemonic ideology of the American imperium. The political requirements of the Cold War and the logic of liberal universalism required an adherence to a doctrine of racial equality. Liberal social scientists articulated a theory of modernization that could be deployed as an ideological alternative to communism in resolving the problem of the Third World. Its domestic version, ethnic assimilation, would provide a similar nonradical solution to the "Negro problem."

Ethnicity theory met the requirements of liberalism by articulating a doctrine of individual competition in a "colorblind" society or, in Milton Gordon's view, a society in which the state played a neutral role. Ethnicity theory articulated a vision of the colorblind society but evaded a critique of the historical category of race altogether. Ethnicity theory offered a promise of equality that could be achieved, not through political organization and community empowerment, but only through individual effort, cultural assimilation, and political accommodation. For liberals who sought both to develop the Negro and to contain black demands for the systematic and structural dismantling of racial discrimination, the representation of Asian-American communities as self-contained, safe, and politically acquiescent became a powerful example of the success of the American creed in resolving the problems of race.

In 1955, less than a year after the Supreme Court had shocked the system of Southern segregation by declaring separate but equal education inherently unequal and unconstitutional, the torture, lynching, and mutilation of Emmett Till, a black fourteen-year-old who was accused of flirting with a white woman, shocked the world. The exoneration of Till's killers by a jury of their white peers signaled a strategy of "massive resistance" to racial equality in the South. The murder of Emmett Till served as the counternarrative of racial intolerance and violence that threatened to undermine the liberal narrative of Myrdal's American creed so painstakingly assembled and elaborately articulated.

CONTAINING THE WHITE MENACE:
THE NUCLEAR FAMILY AS CIVIL DEFENSE

In 1948, Alfred Kinsey shocked America by reporting that a third of American men had engaged in some homosexual activity during the course of their lives and that a majority had experienced homoerotic desire. The news should not have come as a surprise. The 1940s had witnessed a marked expansion of sexual freedom and experimentation with new definitions of gender relations. During the war years, millions of young men went into the armed forces and millions of young women went into the factories. These young people established new patterns of dating and had a more relaxed attitude toward premarital sex than did their parents. During the same period, gay and lesbian public cultures emerged in cities around the country.[33]

Kinsey's study, *The Sexual Behavior of the Human Male*, a dry sociological survey of 12,000 respondents, became an immediate best seller. It also drew the ire of conservative churchmen and politicians. For reporting these activities of Americans, Kinsey was accused of aiding and abetting the communist cause and was investigated by the House Committee on Un-American Activities.

In the Cold War search for traitors and subversives, homophobia and anticommunism went hand in hand. Following on the heels of Senator Joe McCarthy's search for communist agents, the Senate launched investigations to root out homosexuals in the federal government. Nonreproductive sexuality, homosexuality in particular, was seen as a threat to the national security. Anticommunist crusaders warned that homosexuality weakened the nation's "moral fiber," making it susceptible to both sexual and political seduction. Just as communism was considered a perversion of the natural economic order, homosexuality was considered a perversion of the natural biological order. When the sudden turn from World War to the high anxiety of the Cold War could only be explained by treason, homosexuals were seen to have secret lives much like spies or foreign agents. Shortly after his inauguration as president in 1953, Dwight Eisenhower issued an executive order barring gay men and lesbians from Federal employment.[34]

The link between anticommunism and homophobia was not merely psychological or metaphorical; in the atomic age, reproducing the nuclear family was understood to be the key to national survival. In the 1950s and early 1960s, seeking to take advantage of America's advantage in nuclear weapons, strategic planners stressed survivability in nuclear war. This strategic doctrine relied on a program of civil defense, the mass mobilization and education of the civilian population regarding their duties during nuclear war. At the heart of civil defense was the belief that the nuclear family was the primary social unit through which the American way of life could be preserved or resurrected.[35] Talcott Parsons, perhaps the most influential American sociologist between 1940 and the 1960s, argued that the middle-class family, with its "natural" division of labor between the sexes, was the most efficient and implicitly the highest form of social organization. In the absence of a state apparatus that might be obliterated or cut off from its people by nuclear war, the nuclear family was a natural social unit that would reproduce America.

NOTES

1. Frank Chin et al., eds., *Aiiieeeee! An Anthology of Asian-American Writers* (Washington, D.C.: Howard University Press, 1974).
2. In this case, the goal was not to meet a real threat to national security but to ease anxieties about the government's preparedness and to mobilize support for policies of austerity and sacrifice. See, for example, Michi Weglyn, *Years of Infamy: The Untold Story of America's Concentration Camps* (New York: William Morrow & Co., 1976); and Peter H. Irons, *Justice at War: The Story of the Japanese American Internment Cases* (Oxford: Oxford University Press, 1983).
3. "How to Tell Japs from the Chinese," *Life*, December 19, 1941, 14; "How to Tell Your Friends from the Japs," *Time*, December 22, 1941, 33.
4. "How to Tell Japs from the Chinese," 14.
5. Ibid., 14.
6. *Korematsu v. United States* in Hyung-chan Kim, ed., *Asian Americans and the Supreme Court* (New York: Greenwood Press, 1992), 833–867. Under "strict scrutiny," discrimination by the state on the basis of race is held to be illegitimate unless the state can show an overriding national interest. This ruling, that race is a "suspect category," became a much-cited justification of subsequent rulings against racial discrimination. Under *coram nobis*, Korematsu, Hirabayashi, and Yasui were granted a new trial in 1984. In 1986, Hirabayashi was vindicated, and the government decided not to contest the other cases. See Yasuko I. Takezawa, *Breaking the Silence: Redress and Japanese American Ethnicity* (Ithaca, N.Y.: Cornell University Press, 1995).
7. Fred Warren Riggs, *Pressures on Congress: A Study of the Repeal of Chinese Exclusion* (New York: King's Crown Press, 1950).
8. Reference to Asiatic Barred Zone of 1917. Asian immigration was "normalized" under the provisions of the Immigration Act of 1924, which had established a system of national quotas. Each country was assigned a quota of visas equivalent to 5 percent of the total number of immigrants from that country of origin who resided in the United States in 1905. The resulting quota for Chinese visas was a mere 105 per year, and Indian and Filipino visas were limited to 100 for each country.
9. William Peterson, "Success Story: Japanese-American Style," *New York Times Magazine* (January 9, 1966), 38; "Success Story of One Minority in the U.S.," *U.S. News and World Report* (December 26, 1966), 73.

10. Lee Rainwater and William Yancey, *The Moynihan Report and the Politics of Controversy* (Cambridge: Massachusetts Institute of Technology Press, 1967), 79.

11. Ibid., 124.

12. Ibid., 49. The likelihood that Moynihan also drafted Johnson's speech does not negate the point that the speech and the report reflect two quite different ideological tendencies.

13. "Success Story of One Minority in the U.S.," 73–78.

14. Yasuko I. Takezawa, *Breaking the Silence: Redress and Japanese American Ethnicity* (Ithaca, N.Y.: Cornell University Press, 1995).

15. See H. Mark Lai, "The Chinese Marxist Left in America to the 1960s," in *Chinese America: History and Perspectives* (San Francisco: Chinese Historical Association of America, 1992), 3–82.

16. See Bill Ong Hing, *Making and Remaking of Asian America through Immigration Policy, 1850–1990* (Stanford, Calif.: Stanford University Press, 1993); Robert G. Lee, "The Hidden World of Asian Immigrant Radicalism," in *The Immigrant Left in the United States*, ed. Paul Buhle and Dan Georgakas (Albany: SUNY Press, 1996), 256–288.

17. George Lipsitz, *Rainbow at Midnight: Labor and Culture in the 1940s* (Urbana and Chicago: University of Illinois Press, 1994).

18. David M. Gordon, Richard Edwards, and Michael Reich, *Segmented Work, Divided Workers: The Historical Transformation of Labor in the United States* (New York: Cambridge University Press, 1982), 170.

19. Claudia Goldin, *Understanding the Gender Gap* (New York: Oxford University Press, 1990), 152.

20. George Lipsitz, *Rainbow at Midnight*, 69–95.

21. Laurence H. Shoup and William Minter, *Imperial Brain Trust: The Council on Foreign Relations and United States Foreign Policy* (New York: Monthly Review Press, 1977).

22. In 1960, the United States still enjoyed a favorable balance of trade of six billion dollars.

23. Cited in Noel J. Kent, *Hawaii: Islands under the Influence* (New York: Monthly Review Press, 1983), 95.

24. Noel Kent claims that in this period the United States' direct investment abroad grew by approximately 10 percent annually, or twice as fast as the U.S. economy as a whole. Ibid., 97.

25. Gunnar Myrdal, *An American Dilemma: The Negro Problem and Modern Democracy* (New York: Harper & Brothers, 1944), lxxii.

26. See, for example, Franz Schurmann, *The Logic of World Power: An Inquiry Into the Origins, Currents, and Contradictions of World Politics* (New York: Pantheon Books, 1974), 16–19, 91–114, and *passim.*

27. Mary L. Dudziak, "Desegregation as a Cold War Imperative," *Stanford Law Review* 41 (November 1988): 105.

28. Ibid., 110.

29. Rainwater and Yancey, *The Moynihan Report*, 79.

30. Ibid., 47; the full text of Glazer's essay is in Nathan Glazer, *Affirmative Discrimination: Ethnic Inequality and Public Policy* (New York: Basic Books, 1975).

31. E. Franklin Frazier, *The Negro in the United States*, rev. ed. (New York: Macmillan, 1957), 681.

32. Milton Gordon, *Assimilation in American Life* (New York: Oxford University Press, 1964), 249.

33. John D'Emilio and Estelle B. Freedman, *Intimate Matters* (New York: Harper and Row, 1988), 282.

34. Ibid., 292–293.

35. Elaine Tyler May, *Homeward Bound: American Families in the Cold War Era* (New York: Basic Books, 1988), 102–104. See also Guy Oakes, *The Imaginary War: Civil Defense and American Cold War Culture* (New York: Oxford University Press, 1994).

Why China?

Identifying Histories of Transnational Adoption

Sara Dorow

We should not conflate a haunted history with nonspecificity; on the contrary, haunted history alerts us to context.

—Anne Anlin Cheng (2001: 28)

Contemporary poststructural and psychoanalytic theorists define *identification* as a process that occurs where individual lives meet the haunting of social relationships—a process that "names the entry of history and culture into the subject" (Fuss 1995: 3; see also Cheng 2001).[1] In this sense, there are several overlapping histories that "identify" Chinese adopted children: trans-Pacific migration, the social and legal contexts of domestic and international adoption, and the unfolding dynamics of China/U.S. adoption itself. I see the traces of these histories in the stories American parents tell about how they decided to adopt a child or children from China. As prospective adoptive parents sift through their options, the ways in which they imagine the child that might become "our own" conjure elements of these histories. The title of this chapter, "Why China?" thus refers to two things at once: (1) parents' reasons for choosing to adopt from China and (2) the historical forces that might explain the popularity and growth of the China adoption program.[2]

The histories that are invoked when parents choose *transnational* adoption tell us about racialized and gendered citizenship in the *domestic* nation and family. Yet my focus on parents is not meant to put them on the spot. Rather, parents' expressions of transnational family building should lead us to interrogate the historical weight of dominant social discourses and practices that reach beyond—and inform—individual beliefs and everyday interactions in contemporary American social life more generally (Anagnost 2000; Eng 2003). For the adoption process itself, this means we should try to understand how parents' choices are shaped within institutionalized practices in state and social service agencies. So while parent motivations for adopting are portrayed in the literature as notoriously difficult to pin down (Kirton 2000: 43–44), this becomes a problem for "knowledge about adoption" only when motivations are assumed to spring from inside the bounded individual decision maker, rather than from the juncture of individual and collective practices. I take the messiness of parents' decisions as evidence of the circulating forces of history that shape the possible horizons of identification for them and their children.

Throughout the following pages, I focus in particular on moments in my ethnographic data when adoptive choices meet racialized exclusions—those places where histories of color blindness, salvation, and universal humanism meet their dialectical partners of white privilege, marginalization, and particularity. My intention is not to attempt any kind of exhaustive history, nor to permanently hitch contemporary China/U.S. adoption to specific historical sign posts, but rather to suggest resonances of a discursive and practical nature. When it comes to racial formations, for example, I am more interested in how adoption decisions might play off of the shifting topography of imagined black-white-Asian relationships than I am in reinforcing the imprint of a racial hierarchy on American culture.

I begin with the story of just one adoptive parent to suggest what historical traces I mean, and what I intend to argue in this chapter on "why China." When we spoke in 1998, Jackie Kovich was a single white woman who had only recently adopted a daughter from China. Like most adoptive mothers and fathers I interviewed, Jackie began her adoption story with an explanation of her decision to adopt at all. She drew on humanitarianism and nonbiological parenting as naturally linked in a tacitly white embrace of a "different" child:

> I've always had the feeling that adoption was what people ought to do, from a political perspective, and from a, from a social justice perspective also. And I've never had the need to reproduce, to see a child that looks like me. . . . And I've always worked with underserved people and in the Third World.

This expressed commitment to and familiarity with global political and social inequities recalls a long-standing but selectively invoked thread of adoption discourse in the United States: fulfilling national and familial discourses of generous humanitarian outreach (Briggs 2003; Modell 2002). But it also laid the narrative groundwork for Jackie's choice to adopt from China in particular:

> [A]bout three months after I came back from a business trip to China, I went to see my sister. And she said, "Oh, did you see the thing on TV about the Chinese orphanages?" And I said, "Yeah, and you know, those children are so beautiful. There are no ugly Asian children." And my sister said, "Why don't you adopt one?" Okay? And I'd never mentioned anything to her [about wanting to adopt]!

In Jackie's account, a prescient remark by her sister seals her destiny with China, but only because overdetermined by the dual desirability of Chinese children as both needy and beautiful. "The thing on TV" refers to a 1995 media exposé of poor conditions in Chinese orphanages, beginning with a documentary titled *The Dying Rooms*, that ended up influencing a number of parents in their decision to adopt from China. At the same time, "there are no ugly Asian children" resonates with a history of American and European fascination with aestheticized, feminized Oriental others (Said 1994 [1978]; R. G. Lee 1999; Register 1991).

Taken together, these transnational expressions of need and desire figure through yet a third lens of domestic racialized history. A bit later in our discussion, Jackie had just finished telling me how important she thought it was to teach her daughter about Chinese culture, when she continued, "I mean, look at the black community. If they truly had pride in who they were, the community wouldn't be disintegrating. . . . I think the reason why the Asian communities have excelled in our society is that they *do* have pride in who they are." Simultaneously referencing discourses of the culture of poverty (associated with blacks), the model minority (associated with Asians), and globalized humanism (associated with whites), Jackie imagines what her daughter is and can be against what she is not and will not be. A racially and culturally proud, desirable, redeemable Asian child is distinguished from the racially and culturally abject, marginalized, and possibly irredeemable black (collective) body. As Cheng (2001) asserts, the "strain of Asian euphoria" that marks the model minority discourse "serves to contain the history of Asian abjection, as well as to discipline other racialized groups in America" (23). Explanations for transnational family building sometimes expose not only the historical blinders of American multiculturalism invoked by Cheng and others (Okihiro 2001; Omi 1996; Prashad 2003) but also its unspoken whiteness (which has little need to be culturally proud). Jackie's story of choosing or being fatefully chosen for China—while more overt in its racial constructions than was the case in most of my interviews—brings to the surface several histories that reproduce/transform white middle-class subjectivity at the juncture of domestic and transnational practices and through the migrating adoptee.

FLEXIBLE DIFFERENCE: ADOPTION AS A CHAPTER IN TRANS-PACIFIC MIGRATION HISTORY

China/U.S. adoption came along at the right time, or perhaps more accurately, because the times were right—that is, a confluence of historical processes made it both possible and attractive. It is toward this claim that my argument in this chapter is aimed, organized around three kinds of history that weave through Jackie's story. In subsequent sections I deal with adoption histories themselves, but I begin with the migration of people, cultural imaginaries, and material objects between China and the United States, a history that is in some ways the least recognized of contextual histories of adoption, yet which leaves a certain imprint on the reasons people give for adopting from China. Parents imagine their and their children's relationships to China through the traces of a long history of "trans-Pacific flights" of people, ideas, and sentiments. In other words, the reasons parents give for adopting from China are inseparable from the images and sociopolitical relationships that characterize the history of China/U.S. migration (Shiu 2001).

I do not want to suggest a direct and continuous link from century-old images and constructions of China to the present, but as Gungwu Wang (2001) has argued,

> [A]ny study of Chinese today must take account of the historical experiences of those who left China in the 19th and early 20th centuries, whose descendants form the majority of those abroad who are still identified as Chinese in some ways. Those experiences provide an important background to what it has meant for Chinese to live among different kinds of non-Chinese during the last hundred years or so. (119–20)

China/U.S. adoption fits Wang's general description of migration yet reworks the relationship between contemporary and past experiences of Chinese migration. Because Chinese adoptees enter at a young age into the legal and social embrace of (usually) white American homes, adoption migration abruptly raises the question of what it means to "live among" non-Chinese and at the same time suggests a path free of some of the usual obstacles to doing so. Chinese adopted children leapfrog into the national interior across boundaries of kinship, class, nation, and race. And it is for that very reason that their presence compels explanation.

Adoption migration thus turns our gaze to non-Chinese and, more specifically, white American imaginaries of the immigrant past. It forces us to consider the Chinese experience of migration as it both shapes and is shaped by Western images of China—those familiar and contradictory historical traces that "have designated China in a range of ways, as worthy of admiration, sympathy, curiosity, fear, ridicule, hostility, conversion to Christianity, or as a means of profit" (Mackerras 1989: 11). One kind of American discourse of China has placed it at the center of an increasingly transnational and "borderless" world, for instance, as invoked in the notion of the open economy of the Pacific Rim (Palumbo-Liu 1999). At the same time, however, representations of the Pacific Rim tend to recover East/West binaries; its Orientalized others, as Said's (1994 [1978]) pivotal work demonstrated, "recuperate a specific western individual at the core of reality" (Palumbo-Liu 1999: 339). These different but simultaneous imaginaries of China have developed through migration in both directions across the Pacific, for example, missionaries to China and railway workers to California. The cultural economy of adoption similarly occurs through the movement of people, ideas, and resources both from and to China.

The question of trans-Pacific migration must address the different historical contexts of the two areas in which I conducted research in the United States: the San Francisco Bay Area and the Minneapolis–St. Paul metropolitan area. The former has a 150-year history of Asian and especially Chinese immigration. Starting in the mid–nineteenth century, American westward expansion included the idea of developing East Asia (Dirlik 1993, referenced in Palumbo-Liu 1999), with San Francisco as its gateway to trade with China (Takaki 1989) and as the gatekeeper of Chinese immigrants who would provide labor for American nation building (E. Lee 2003; Takaki 1989). This means that in the contemporary Bay Area, where 30 percent of the population reports being Asian, Chinese American people and cultural representations are more pervasive as well as more variable than in the Twin Cities, where significant Chinese immigration is one or two generations old and only about 8 percent of the population is Asian.[3] Thus, the Asian America of the Twin Cities is an instance of the more recent expansion of Chinese and other East Asian student, business, and family immigration to North America. Also significant is that in San Francisco, an estimated one-fourth to one-third of families adopting from China include at least one Asian or Asian American parent (mostly Chinese American but also some who identify as Japanese American and Filipina American, for example)[4]—a proportion substantially higher than Minneapolis–St. Paul and probably most any other location in the United States. For these reasons, the question of "why China" begs consideration of geographic location. Of course, location must always be considered alongside other social factors. Jackie Kovich, for example, contrasted her child's identity to that of adoptive families living just over the hill from her in the Bay Area; she drew on the "free" cultural resources of her multiethnic working-class neighborhood, while wealthier white adoptive parents a few miles away could afford to send their children to private schools offering formal programs in Mandarin language and Chinese cultural arts.

Whether in San Francisco or the Twin Cities, parents' narratives of "choosing China" both echo and challenge a central theme of the history of China/U.S. migration: the American construction of the Asian Other as both strange and familiar, as insider and outsider, and as variably suited to incorporation into national projects of citizenship (Lee 2003; Palumbo-Liu 1999; Lowe 1996). Since the nineteenth century, immigration policies and practices have sometimes invited, sometimes forced, and sometimes barred the migration of Chinese workers and students and the relatives (including "paper sons")[5] who have joined them. From the Chinese Exclusion Act of 1882, to the 1965 reforms abolishing official race-based immigration, to the grounding of the *Golden Venture* that stranded hundreds of illegal Chinese immigrants in New York Harbor in 1993, China/U.S. migration has been shaped by universal discourses of transnational capital as well as particularizing notions of the uncivilized or exotic Asian, or more recently, the virtuous model minority (Palumbo-Liu 1999; Lowe 1996). The *flexibility* of Asian difference—strange but adaptable—has thus enabled contradictory positions of expansionary transnationalism, nativist exclusion, and assimilationist embrace.

The liminal space occupied by Asian America is and has been accomplished on cultural and racial territory, and in response to material realities. The reaction to increasing labor pressures in California that catalyzed the late-nineteenth- and early-twentieth-century exclusion period, for example, was as much a manifestation of Orientalist discourses of the untrustworthy and uncivilized Chinaman (E. Lee 2003) as it was a class issue. Brought back by American missionaries and traders, these racialized discourses were reproduced "at home" in various ways; one exemplary case is provided in Nayan Shah's (2001) study of political and social responses to Chinatown's "contagion" in turn-of-the-century San Francisco. But then, even as the 1906 establishment of the Angel Island immigration station ensured increasingly standardized practices of keeping out unwanted Asian people (E. Lee 2003), the importation of "Oriental-style" decorative arts and consumer products reached heights previously unprecedented in middle-class white American culture (R. G. Lee 1999).

This dialectic of danger and exoticism has echoed again since the 1960s in the seemingly more benign "model minority" discourse, which Lowe (1996) argues is yet another instance of the projection of American national anxieties onto the site of Asian American immigration. While purporting admiration of "traditional values," the model minority discourse tends also to depoliticize the material realities of racism and to deny histories of labor exploitation by promising "deliverance of minority subjects from collective history to a reified individualism" (Palumbo-Liu 1999: 415). But even so, there is regular confirmation that such transformation is not fully possible, as the case of Wen Ho Lee demonstrated.[6] R. G. Lee (1999) points out that in the late capitalist national American imaginary, Asian Americans have become both model minority and potential enemy within. In discourse echoing some of the nativist tone of the late nineteenth century, Asians are in and to America "economically productive but culturally inauthentic" (191). A more recent surge of "Asian cool"—hip but respectable popular Asian American culture—is perhaps the latest reinvention of America's flirtation with the exotic potential of such inauthenticity (see Galang 2003).

Reasons parents give for adopting from China at times reflect this contradictory history of Asian America, sitting uneasily on the impossible binary of rejecting/embracing images and ideologies of flexible Asian difference. Some of the multicultural promise of adopting children from China hinges on cultural-racial desirability and accessibility. But Asianness may still threaten to exceed the bounds of consumable difference. I argue below that such excess is at least partly kept in check through the construction of black difference as less assimilable difference. As suggested in Jackie's narrative, motifs of model Asian America play off the construction of abject black America and failed black-white relations (Gotanda 2000; Palumbo-Liu 1999), allegedly manifest in welfare dependence, criminality, and ingratitude.

For a select group of parents, feelings of connection to China and Chinese culture come from histories of trans-Pacific migration in their own families. Some Chinese American adoptive parents I interviewed cited a "natural" connection based on cultural heritage, even as they were sometimes quick to distinguish their second-, third-, or fourth-generation Chinese American experience from the Chinese heritage their children seemed more directly to embody. A number of white adoptive parents also cited a direct connection to China because they had relatives who had been missionary, diplomatic, or academic sojourners there or had themselves lived in or frequently visited China as businesspeople or teachers. But most white parents expressed an affinity with Chinese culture that bore more indirect traces of the cultural and political histories of migration discussed above. It was not uncommon, for example, for white adoptive parents to indicate a preexisting or growing interest in "ancient Chinese culture." Some named such an interest as a circumstantial bonus, while others indicated they thought it was a mistake for people to adopt from China if they did not have such an interest. Cultural knowledge and interest on the part of adoptive parents is encouraged by Beijing as well. The China Center of Adoption Affairs has long asked prospective foreign adopters to indicate in writing that they will teach their children about Chinese culture.

White parents usually construed Chinese culture as admirably different but accessible, lending itself to some form of celebration or incorporation into their family lives. Adoptive father John Padding said, "We obviously wanted to adopt for *us,* but maybe another reason it makes it okay is that it's also a good thing, for our daughter, for the world, for multiculturalism"; he later added, "We like Chinese people and food and things and culture, so it was an easy thing to connect to." In the middle of my interview with the Cook family, adoptive mother Nancy stopped mid-sentence to muse, "You know, I was just thinking as we're sitting here, looking at our house . . . we have a lot of Asian influence, and most of this was before we adopted her. This was just our *taste,* I guess." In the San Francisco Bay Area in particular, the accessibility of "things Chinese" contributed to justifications for adopting from China. As Jason Bradley discussed his and his wife's decision to adopt from China, for example, he noted that having lived on the West Coast for so long, "we had had Asian American friends, and had had exposure to that culture." On a number of occasions parents in the Bay Area contrasted its multicultural and especially Asian population to some town in the Midwest that represented a problematic lack of the same.[7] While white parents in Minnesota did not as often or as confidently claim to have been primed for adoption from China through "exposure" to Asian cultures and peoples, their reasons for being attracted to the China program also sometimes referenced the accessible difference of Chinese culture itself, and thus the imagined adaptability of their children.

Accessibility—naming the appeal of Chinese food and art objects or naming Asian American friends—was in turn made possible by the *definability* and *longevity* of Chinese culture. As Mackerras (1989) argues, late-twentieth-century images of China remained focused "on the past, and the strength of its role in present-day China" (217). Parents fairly consistently used words such as *strong, rich,* and *ancient* to describe Chinese culture, suggesting a reliable and contained kind of difference with which children (and parents) could proudly identify and be identified. Lila Noonan said it was important in her and her husband's decision to adopt that "Chinese history is so advanced, so developed. . . . I'm Hungarian American, and growing up with the traditions, the history, the values—it's made me who I am."

The point is not that parents thought they could fully adopt Chinese culture along with the children they brought home; for some, in fact, part of the attraction was that an authentic China remained just out of reach, even as it could be celebrated, admired, and accessed. China itself—"actual" China—was sometimes even narrated as intimidating. Cindy Coombs noted, "At the beginning, it was still a mystery. The idea that China might actually be a place that we could feel comfortable didn't even occur to us." Jennifer Bartz made clear that she knew her daughter's understanding of China through *Mulan* and picture books was an "abstraction from the real thing." This was true as well for a couple of Chinese American parents in the Bay Area who had chosen to adopt from China so they could have a child "like us," yet who laughed ironically at feeling "inauthentic" in relation to the China from which their grandparents or great-grandparents, and now their children, had directly come.

The flexible racialization of Asian subjects in the American imaginary is crucial to understanding the dialectic of strangeness and familiarity that contributed to "why China." This is especially so for white adoptive parents, who sometimes saw their own amorphous racial identities—what Frankenberg (1993: 205) calls the "unadorned, basic, essential" feeling of whiteness—potentially enlivened through transracial adoption. Deena Houston sheepishly admitted she had been somewhat disappointed that her daughter "was so white"; she had imagined one of those darker, rosy-cheeked country girls you saw in *National Geographic*, an outcome that might have made their whole family more interesting. Jennifer Bartz described her experience of the "difference" of China, which was also the experience of her own difference, as a kind of rush:

> I was overwhelmed by being in China. I had never been any place like China. There were times when I would just have to stop on the street and let it wash over me. And I would be standing on the street watching the tidal wave of bicycles go by, at sundown, and the sunlight would be filtered through the dust in the air, and you'd hear the sound of bicycle bells, and I would just stand and take it in, and people would be staring at me. You know, people from the country would be staring at me. Or their heads would swivel. And I had never had an experience like that. I liked it. I liked being—I liked having the experience of being Other. Because so rarely in my life have I been Other, except maybe as a lesbian. And even then, it's not like you could pick me out of a lineup. . . . I grew up the majority in a Midwestern suburb. So whatever hardwiring and life experience came to be that allowed me to enjoy feeling, most of the time, like Other, that felt good to me.

In Jennifer's description, the experience of being Other exposes the "hardwiring" of whiteness but then just as quickly welcomes relief from its bland normalcy. The transracial, transnational adoptive journey can be a dangerous pleasure, promising mutually beneficial Asian-white relations both through and for the child.

The potential to make whiteness more colorful depends in turn on the racial and cultural flexibility of Chinese children themselves. With particular attention to the commoditization of this process, Eng (2003) explores how the transnationally adopted child is both object and subject, performing the ideological labor of reproducing the white heterosexual nuclear family. He asks, "What does it mean that, in our present age, full and robust citizenship is *socially* effected from child to parent and, in many cases, through the position of the adoptee, its visible possession and spectacular display?" (8; emphasis in original). In this formulation, the American family and nation reproduce whiteness and weak multiculturalism[8] through the embrace of the transnational, transracial adoptee's cultural and racial difference (see also Shiu 2001; Ortiz and Briggs 2003). We are reminded that the history of struggles over the citizenship of Asian immigrants in America was also always about national citizenship in its dominant white patriarchal form (Palumbo-Liu 1999; Lowe 1996). But in the age of multiculturalism, and under the condition of unquestioned legal citizenship for the immigrant adoptee, social citizenship is not so much about making clear distinctions between "us" and "them" as it is about the extent to which "us" and "them" are reconstructed through the uneven exchange of difference.

Model minority discourses are part of the flexible racialization that facilitates the double act of making child and family for each other. While the assimilability of Chinese immigrants was largely questioned and denied up until the mid–twentieth century, the invention of the model minority and changes to immigration law have since allowed for a limited transformation from alien to citizen (Lowe 1996). While many parents saw model minority stereotypes as both a blessing and a curse, reasons for adopting from China found some justification in them. As an adoptive father I met in China put it, his Midwestern hometown was pretty homogeneously white, but he didn't think it would be a problem for his daughter because Asians had a "different kind of stereotype."

Of further importance is that, in some parents' narratives, this "different kind of stereotype" relied on the more weighty abjection of blackness. Discourses of enfranchisement and national identity in the nineteenth century may have relied on black/white binaries to repudiate the uncivilized "Oriental," but by the 1960s the model minority discourse had redeemed Asians as "not black" (R. G. Lee 1999)—a social topography of abjection that echoed in adoptive parent narratives of choosing China. "Real" race and racism were sometimes reserved for blacks, not Asians, whose appreciable cultural characteristics can be read off their bodies. Social worker Rita Jasper described one kind of encounter she has with prospective parents:

> People come in here and they say, "Okay, I'm open to adopting a child from anywhere." I'll say, "Okay, great. So how about doing a domestic adoption, African American child?" "Ooooohhh, no." "Okay, well why?" "Well really, it would be so hard for the child." "Okay, so why would it not be so hard for the child coming from China?" [Here Rita lowers her voice to mimic a parent talking to her in a knowing whisper.] "Well, you know, Rita . . ." [She laughs.] And they're afraid to say it. And what I end up saying is yeah, in this country there is definitely a hierarchy, and the darker color your skin, the more prejudice there is. . . . [She becomes the voice of the rationalizing parent again.] "Oh well, I'm not thinking about us, I'm thinking about the child."

Teresa, a white woman married to a Chinese American, told me, "It seems in the overall scheme of things that as far as stereotypes go, the Asian stereotype tends to be a little more 'favorable' than say the black or Hispanic stereotype." Patty expressed a similar sentiment: "It's really not that harsh for Asians. There's a little bit of, you know, 'they're smarter,' but there's not really the same kind of racism there is against blacks, unfortunate as that is." Aaron Kretz, a Jewish father living in California, owned that racism toward African Americans was embedded in and around him in part because race itself was conflated with black:

> To be honest, with me it was a racial thing. I didn't want a black child, and it was pretty much China or South America, and in South America you could get kids of color, and I didn't want to do that. You can't ask. And I just don't have any biases about Asians, so

for me it was an easier fit. . . . I mean, black is still, uh, not only a minority to me in this country, but a minority that doesn't, you know, fit in, as well as some other minorities. And like Jews, the minority of Jews, have chosen to fit in, or do fit in, or whatever, pretty much. There's other minorities that kind of get blended in. . . . I mean, it goes back to why I wanted to do Chinese. For me, [race] doesn't come up. I've gotta admit that if I had a black child, I'd probably think of us as more biracial.

Chinese children were in some instances desirable because they could be imagined as neither white nor black—interesting without being so different that they would not "fit in." We have here the suggestion of a racial "passing" in which the recognition of difference is key to the reproduction of whiteness and kinship. Indeed, the model minority discourse promises to scale down the Asian threat precisely by writing particularized cultural admiration onto racial difference—a far cry from the anxieties of the mid–nineteenth to mid–twentieth centuries that prompted Chinese immigrants to try to "pass" as respectable middle-class non-Chinese, or that produced a series of laws about marriages between Chinese and whites (E. Lee 2003). This does not mean that adoptive parents did not express anxieties about the interracial intimacy of their families, including explaining it to relatives and friends. But where and how parents found ways to explain it points to an aesthetics of racial passing that not only references a broad racial topography but also intersects with gendered and class productions of identity.

In a context in which 95 percent of adoptees are girls, it is important to address questions of how racialized desire might intersect with the construction of Asian *female* bodies. Cheung (2000), for example, argues that in American cultural history Asian women have been endowed with an "excess" of womanhood (alongside the full manhood denied Asian men). And in China/U.S. adoption, mothers Deena Houston and Jackie Kovich were not alone in conjuring the image of beautiful, enthralling Chinese girls. Adoption agencies consistently use photos of cute, dolled-up Asian girls in their advertising; some use phrases such as "From China with Love" to attract would-be parents. Some of those prospective parents said they had become enchanted with their friends' or neighbors' Chinese girls. Margaret Jennings said she saw a photo of a Chinese adopted girl in the paper and "knew I wanted to adopt from China right then." Some expressed embarrassment at what they suspected hinted at "racist love"—embrace of the "acceptable model" of the racial minority (Chan 1972, quoted in Cheung 2000: 309). Just days after she had met her daughter, Barbara and I were discussing what seemed among some new adoptive mothers an obsession with dolling up their daughters, when Barbara stopped to say in a low tone, "I hate to ask this, but are all the children beautiful? It seems like they're all beautiful."

Such raced and gendered aesthetics have bearing on social and legal citizenship, especially when considered along with the class conditions of belonging. Historically, Chinese women and children in particular gained legitimacy through formal kinship ties with respectable citizens (e.g., the War Brides Act that allowed Chinese Americans in the armed forces to bring spouses to the United States) and through other associations with whiteness (e.g., having white witnesses who could attest to nativity at citizenship hearings) (E. Lee 2003: 106–7).

Class and capital further differentiated racialized and gendered citizens, and continue to do so. In her work on late-twentieth-century Asian immigrant experiences in the United States, Aihwa Ong (1996) argues that class interacts with race and gender such that "money whitens"; transnational practices and exchanges of capital afford some transnational immigrant subjects more flexibility than others (Ong 1998). And while the model minority discourse in particular has underwritten a successful Asian class position over and above that of African Americans (Gotanda 2000), at the same time there lurks in the recent American imaginary the threat of both cheap Chinese labor and Chinese economic power (E. Lee 2000; Palumbo-Liu 1999).

Yet, as discussed above, China/U.S. adoption simultaneously creates kinship for both citizen parent and immigrant child. And here we must consider issues of class and capital from an angle somewhat different from what the history of immigration might usually suggest: it is the material and social capital of white middle-class citizen families that catalyzes the flexible belonging of Chinese adoptee migrants, who in turn reproduce and transform the family. The class (and race) position of adoptive parents is signified in a series of "choices"—the choice to adopt, the choice to adopt internationally, the choice to adopt from China—which then enable both parents and children to gain fuller social recognition. The point is underscored by cases in which parents' choice to adopt from China is marked by an excess of difference. Even as adoption might help fulfill middle-class family values for gay and lesbian parents (Eng 2003), for example, many choose China because it is one of few options available to them.[9] For Lisa and Gerry, a lesbian couple who are respectively white and Asian American, this choice was overdetermined by historical intersections of race, gender, and class. While they initially considered adopting a white child domestically, one crucial factor that led them to China was the painful awareness that with a white child in her arms, Gerry would be more likely to be read as the child's nanny than her mother. Their story demonstrates that the adoptive family is one of those sites of social formation that reflect, govern, and potentially challenge racialized and gendered social relationships, at the intersection of the national and transnational (Lowe 1996: 172).

Redeeming Acts: China/U.S. Adoption as a Chapter in Domestic and International Adoption Histories

While parents' narrations of "why China" both reiterate and contest the racialized, gendered, and classed relations of power that have marked China/U.S. immigration history, they must equally be understood within the history of adoption in the United States. This history, when domestic and international adoptions are considered together, especially foregrounds the dialectical relationship between acts of rescue and acts of market exchange. In my interviews, "saving" Chinese children was usually not first among reasons parents gave for adopting from China, but it often served as a complementary justification. Humanitarian rescue discourses helped distinguish international adoption from domestic adoption options. But as a number of researchers have pointed out, the idea of "rescuing a child" does not always sit comfortably with cultures of choice, value, and upward mobility (Melosh 2002; Modell 2002; Anagnost 2000; Zelizer 1985). Domestic family and nation can be imagined only by distinguishing themselves from but also imagining influence on "the global," through a prism of differentiating who can be saved and how. As I argue in this section, racialized projections of the nation shape China/U.S. adoption as fulfilling the needs of both humanitarian outreach as well as increasingly commodified formations of kinship and citizenship.

The story of adoption in the United States over the last century reflects a cultural struggle over the commodification and sacralization of children (Berebitsky 2000; Melosh 2002). In *Pricing the Priceless Child*, Viviana Zelizer (1985) traces in the period 1870–1930 a transition in the kind of value assigned to children, from economic usefulness to sentimental fulfillment. At the confluence of several broad social trends—differentiation between economic production and home life, the specialization of women into expert full-time motherhood, and the growing sacralization of the child—domestic adoption began to emphasize the "best interest of the child" and the emotional fulfillment the child would bring to adoptive parents. By the 1930s, legal adoption of "strangers" was much more common, and more focused on middle- and upper-class families looking for an infant to love. But this growing sentimentalization also meant a growing adoption business, both unofficial and official. "An apparently profound contradiction was thereby created, between a cultural system that declared children priceless emotional assets, and a social arrangement that treated them as 'cash commodities'" (Zelizer 1985: 201). As Berebitsky (2000) makes clear in her study of the "Child-Rescue Campaign" run by the magazine *The Delineator* from 1907 to 1911, commodification of children went hand in hand with their rescue, fulfilling the destiny of the nation. Urban orphans could be rescued from poor and backward Eastern European immigrants and transformed into valuable citizens in the hands of white middle-class mothers. Market exchanges thus facilitated the rescue of children but also the redemption of those upright citizens in whose care they would thrive.

This seeming contradiction between rescue and desire, care and market, continued to haunt adoption practices and narratives in various ways, and adoption professionals and adoptive families in turn sought ways to resolve it. The Child-Rescue Campaign promulgated the notion that "the rescued always paid back the rescuer" (59), anticipating subsequent official and unofficial discourses of adoption that emphasized "parity of need" and "matching" between parents and children. Families (meaning, for the most part, infertile white couples) and children who needed each other could be matched up for the mutual fulfillment of individual, familial, and national identities. Indeed, as adoption was professionalized under the management of state and social service agencies in the first half of the twentieth century, it constructed itself over and against markets, substituting the language of proper placement and matching for that of direct rescue and crass exchange. Parents thus learned to narrate adoption as raising children "like our very own," mirroring biological kinship. At the same time, however, the growth of consumer society meant that professional matching could ensure a child "had the ability to achieve the class position and status aspirations of its parents" (3). The matching criteria seen as most important to doing so have changed over time, but they have continually been crosscut by supply and demand as well as cultural and racial politics.[10]

The post–World War II era ushered in several decades of increasing acceptance of adoption, accompanied by charged discourses of race and rescue and complicated by the growth of international adoption and its relationship to the American imaginary of itself. It began with the placement of war orphans from Europe and Japan; then, in 1949, Pearl S. Buck established her Welcome House program of placing Amerasian orphans. This was followed by adoptions from Korea and Vietnam in the 1950s–70s, the former in numbers that now total more than 150,000.[11] As Lovelock (2000) and others have noted, intercountry adoption programs have often come in the wake of war and strife; "its history maps the global suffering wrought by war, hatred, hunger, and political oppression" (Melosh 2002: 195). The history of intercountry adoption is thus one immediately steeped in notions of rescue and humanitarian outreach. But that is not the whole story, as transnational adoption also sheds light on the valuation of children in relation to race and national origin (Modell 2002: 145). Adoption of war orphans, as Briggs (2003) so well argues, enacted Cold War emphases on the necessity of American intervention, the conflation of family and national security, and the color-blind universalisms that underwrote whiteness. Race and ethnic difference were subsumed under (and perhaps enabled) an ideology of rescuing poor Third World children for a "better life" in the bosom of American households (Lovelock 2000: 922). Gailey (1999) argues that "the adoption of Korean infants seemed at least in some way a laboratory for assimilationist beliefs in the redemptive qualities of capitalist culture. These children were going to become 'real' American Asians, because they would be reared by 'real,' that is, middle class, conservative and patriotic (i.e. military), white Americans" (60).

While rescue and color blindness (or, alternatively, multiculturalism) became impetuses for intercountry adoptions into the United States, especially from an underdeveloped Third World understood to *need* adoption, this history cannot be divorced from the politics of race at home. As many historical accounts of adoption suggest, the expansion of international adoption starting in the 1970s was entangled with at least two important developments in domestic adoption: an increasing demand for infants[12] and protests by the National Association of Black Social Workers (NABSW) against transracial placements, especially of black children with white parents (Lovelock 2000; Modell 2002; Melosh 2002; Patton 2000). Lovelock (2000) has suggested that a double standard emerged that made race an issue in domestic placements but not in international placements. But she goes on to suggest that this double standard was in fact a complementary set of racializations that served the needs of the proper national family and its prospective adoptive parents (922); in other words, the NABSW's cries of cultural genocide may have simultaneously resonated with white segregationist sentiments and fueled white humanitarianism outreach abroad.

Race has thus served as fulcrum for playing international and domestic adoptions off each other, shaping them as respectively "good" and "bad" adoptions

(Modell 2002).[13] How so, and to what end? International adoption became increasingly desirable over the last two decades (from eight thousand children in 1989 to more than twenty thousand children in 2004)[14] to prospective adopters who experienced infertility, did not think they met the requirements (age, health, sexual orientation, marital status) for domestic adoption, and sometimes harbored fears of domestic birth parents with questionable backgrounds and the power to reclaim children (Modell 2002)—all motivations that shape parents' decisions to adopt from China. As adoptive mother Lila Noonan put it, she was "afraid of contact" with birth families, and besides, she just knew "how traumatic children's life is in the States before they finally get in the system." In addition, domestic adoption of "nonsystem" children, i.e., healthy white infants, also looked increasingly marketized to some parents, as they competed for and even solicited birth mothers; adoptive father Jason Bradley cited the "sort of buy-a-baby tone" to domestic adoption as one motivation for going to China. Ironically, international adoption can be just as and often more expensive than domestic adoption,[15] and there are increasing concerns of trafficking in some international adoption programs, but it is here that multiple racializations help construct international adoption as meeting the needs of both children and parents—the former rescuable from poverty and abandonment, the latter able to fulfill their desire for family. Such discourses bring to the surface the racialized relationship between commodified and sacralized childhoods—between consumption and rescue—that makes some children more adoptable than others. This kind of humanism tends to bind people into sameness through various kinds of conscious or unconscious exclusion (Shiu 2001; Goldberg 1993; Balibar 1988a).

By the mid-1990s, vocal opposition to transracial placements in the United States—meaning, by default, African American and, to some extent, Native American children in white homes—had waned considerably and had even been replaced by a new official color blindness in adoption.[16] But in practice, as Patton (2000) has convincingly argued, this shift killed at least two birds with one stone, favoring the consumptive choices of white heterosexual families while vilifying single black (read "welfare") mothers. The former could be kept safe from the latter through a popular pathologizing of unreliable welfare mothers who gave birth to "crack babies." Despite official race parity, such children could be understandably labeled as unadoptable, while orphans abroad remained rescuable—what Ortiz and Briggs (2003) call "resilient (overseas) and toxic (U.S.) childhoods" (40). Ortiz and Briggs argue that even though domestic transracial adoption is promoted, it is promoted in ways that reproduce proper white families and barely redeemable black children, fixed on the interior as biologically and culturally tainted. Transnational adoption, in contrast, conjures children whose difference makes them both rescuable and valuable.[17] Instead of being fixed to abject mothers and cultures, they are innocent victims of "unpromising infrastructural soil" (Ortiz and Briggs 2003: 43). A complex interplay of interior and exterior racial categories joins family and nation in what Briggs (2003) calls "a coherent cultural logic that invest[s] the foreign in the domestic and the domestic in the foreign" (181).

We have already seen how the racial and cultural flexibility of Asianness may contribute to the desire for Chinese children, but it also contributes to notions of rescuability. One adoptive mother suggested that helping needy children provided some balance for the loss of physical sameness that would have been produced had infertility treatments been successful:

> I mean, there was that, there was the fantasy. We would have had, you know, a red-haired baby or something. You know, because we both had red hair. But for me it was a lot more important to be a parent, and to have a baby . . . for there to be a baby that *needed* to have a family. And there were real ones there, in that orphanage [in China], waiting!

Jackie Kovich told me she had briefly been tempted to adopt from Lithuania so she would not have to deal with issues of racial difference. "But then," she said, "I quickly went back to why I was attracted—why I wanted to do this in the first place," that is, to help a child in need. While Jackie had indicated she found Chinese children desirable for their looks, her reference to Lithuania—where there are children who might just as easily be seen as needing homes—indicates that Chinese children are also desirable for being "more" needy. Ortiz and Briggs (2003) suggest that being Third World and nonwhite makes for more rescuable subjects.

So then, we might also consider how the backwardness that produces marginalized Chinese children compares through racialized discourses to the backwardness that produces marginalized American children. For some parents, for example, a 1995 exposé of poor conditions in Chinese orphanages affirmed that China and its orphan children were in need; a few felt, out of religious conviction, that China was a society short on morals; and many referred to a China struggling to develop and modernize, burdened by a large population, low education, and a communist legacy. The American imaginary of such comparisons is, at times, arguably racialized. One white father who had originally looked into domestic adoption told me that when the possibility of adopting a biracial (meaning "black and white") child arose, some family members balked. "Yeah," he said, "we brought back a communist baby from a communist country and that was okay, but not a biracial child in our own country!" The rescuability of Chinese children—from the backwardness of communism and poverty—is contrasted to the abjectness of domestic black children. An adoption social worker was blunt about how this worked in some parents' adoption decisions: "I think there's a romanticism about saving a starving child on the other side of the planet. I'm often amazed that people would take an older child from the other side of the world but won't consider an older child here. I think it's racism." It must be noted, too, that the professional adoption world of which she is a part gives mixed messages about the rescuability of domestic and international children, and of what kinds of parents are right for what kinds of children.

The rescuability of Chinese children is intertwined with several dimensions of imagined racial flexibility. As indicated above, some parents felt they had to give up on the competition and long wait for healthy white infants. Parents also expressed nagging fears regarding the more accessible but less palatable route of domestic public adoption, which usually meant special-needs and/or non-white children. Lila Noonan said of the forces that pulled her away from domestic transracial adoption and toward international adoption, "I just knew too much; if I didn't, I would have been more open." Chinese children become flexibly rescuable, then, *in contrast to* a continuity of abject (black, older, special-needs) and unattainable (white, young, healthy) children at home. And just as important, they are seemingly less burdened by a volatile history of intractable black-white relations, read as a cautionary tale by some adoptive parents. African Americans could even be seen as recalcitrant for not making their children available for adoption. June, a white adoptive mother, told me that the newspapers in her hometown of Detroit were full of horror stories about children in foster care who were abused or even returned to abusive homes. She became indignant, then, that "the black community is so against placing black children in white families." Both Chinese and black children needed to be rescued, but it was easier to imagine the former being absorbed into white kinship.

Race and gender thus contribute to making orphans from abroad desirable as citizen-subjects; as some parents see it, children can be not only rescued *from* their unfortunate conditions abroad but also absorbed *into* a new life at home. They are at once strange and familiar, different yet knowable (Yngvesson 2000; Shiu 2001). On the one hand, people may be attracted to Chinese children for the differences of origin that make them both culturally/racially interesting and economically in need of rescue. On the other hand, they may be attracted to the change the children will undergo and enact in their parents. One reason parents gave for choosing China was that while not receiving the best possible orphanage or foster care, the available children seemed to "catch up" quickly. (A number of social workers and parents have lamented that Chinese children in particular are surrounded by a mythology of resilience that sometimes precludes attention to attachment or developmental problems.) As I argue in the next section, the history of the China/U.S. adoption program in particular neatly turns rescue into transformation of both children and parents, through a mutual "matching" of needs.

LIGHT BAGGAGE: HISTORY OF THE CHINA/U.S. ADOPTION PROGRAM

International adoptions have moved from a dominant discourse of rescue and humanitarian outreach for children who need families to one that just as emphatically endorses the needs and desires of prospective adoptive parents (Lovelock 2000; Solinger 2001). Adoption professionals prefer this as a more "honest" acknowledgment that prospective adoptive parents adopt for themselves as much as for children. Parents' expressed reasons for adopting from China are, in fact, dominated by how the characteristics of the program and of available children meet those of their own situation. Chinese children need rescue, and China is underdeveloped, but not so much as to threaten the desire for healthy, young infants whom parents can claim as their own. This symbiotic relationship between choice and rescue, consumption and care, is a necessary backdrop to the history of the China adoption program. "Why China"—why the formal inception and growing popularity of the program in the 1990s—must be understood as a mixture of material conditions of choice in China and the United States through which circulate imagined ways of belonging. We have seen how cultural intrigue, racial mapping, gendered images, and humanitarian national outreach have historically shaped the desirability of Chinese adoptions, but they are so important precisely because they animate the mundane matter of the policies and demographics that institutionalize the "fit" between Chinese parents and their prospective American parents. Fitting and belonging, as I argue in this section, are in large part a matter of smooth dislocations and desirable transformations.

Why the international adoption of Chinese children was implemented when it was and why it developed so quickly are separate but interrelated questions that must take into account perceived needs in both China and the United States. Research to date has not fully traced the developments that led Beijing to draft China's first adoption law in 1991 and increasingly to formalize international adoption in the succeeding few years; the details of this history are murky enough that Melosh (2002) simply assigns it to "unknown reasons" (193). But Kay Johnson's (2004) invaluable work foregrounds a social welfare system underfunded and overwhelmed by abandoned babies, many of them girls.[18] The crisis came to a head in the late 1980s and early 1990s, in part because of crackdowns in the enforcement of the family-planning policy. The resulting upsurge of abandoned children increased the burden on the cash-strapped social welfare system in China, where facilities were quite basic; per-child allowances for food, clothing, and medical care were minimal; and caregivers' salaries even in the year 2000 were rarely more than 400 RMB (U.S. $50) per month.[19] Even though a broadened acceptance of domestic adoption had grown in China, for the state to promote domestic adoption would mean the risk of pointing a finger right back at the sensitive family-planning policy and its drastic gendered effects; besides, argues Johnson, the adoption law was itself meant to combat those who "cheated" on the family-planning policy by adopting children over quota (145–46). In fact, early versions of China's international adoption policy mirrored its domestic regulations, restricting overseas adopters to childless people.

It is here that the question of why China opened to international adoption and the question of why China was so popular for American adopters become closely linked. By the early 1990s, the demand for international adoption in the United States was on the rise, especially as the Korea program decreased in size and domestic adoption became in some ways less attractive, for reasons discussed above (competition for "high-demand" children; age, health, and race of children available; fears of open adoption). Romania and Russia opened up, but by the late 1990s, the rapid increase in placements of Chinese children was matching that of Russia. There is little doubt that the rise in Russian adoptions in the 1990s was due in some measure to the availability of white children, meeting the "as-if-begotten" criterion Modell (2002) argues is still a strong strain in adoption. At the same time, however, "the claim of diversity in being a parent is equally powerful" (Modell 2002: 146), and the flexible racialization of Chinese children as "different, but not too different" made it an attractive adoption option for some.

But there are equally significant explanations that have to do with the matching of supply and demand. The Chinese adoption program offered relatively healthy young infants, free of ties to birth families. As one parent put it to me, she had been attracted to China in part because the children "wouldn't come with a lot of baggage." Things that bind children to a preadoptive identity—such as older age and birth-family contact—can appear especially burdensome to prospective parents who have come to adoption by way of a road strewn with the obstacles of infertility, their own older age, or their partnership status. From the perspective of the "demand" side, then, the less-restrictive requirements and fairly straightforward process of the China adoption program matched the experiences and demographics of an array of people eager to become parents.

In narrating their reasons for adopting at all, most parents, whether married or single, straight or queer, indicated that they had "reached a point" of some kind. Most of the forty families I interviewed had been through brief or extended infertility treatment, had explored various other reproductive alternatives, or had "given up" on looking for the right partner with whom to have a child. As one woman put it, "You reach an age in your life where you know you want to have at least one child. You know, you do not appear to be on the road to producing one of your own, so. . . ." For those who had opted for adoption after exhausting medical reproductive alternatives, their narratives often reflected the mantra of professionals that counsel this transition: "we decided it was more important to be a parent than to have a child that shared our DNA." Others—some in their late forties and early fifties—had decided they wanted to be parents at a point in their life course when biological parenting was a risky or missing option. There are both personal and systemic fragilities in "reaching this point." Many domestic and international adoption programs carry restrictions that preclude certain prospective parents[20] or seem risky from the perspective of parents searching for an adoption option. Jason Bradley told me, "It would have been more difficult and a lot more time-consuming for people our age to adopt an infant in the U.S." The China Center of Adoption Affairs in Beijing had and continues to have a fairly generous upper age limit, has been open to single and married applicants, and until the late 1990s seemed to turn a blind eye to placing children with gay and lesbian parents. And apart from quite early in the program, its bureaucratic but uniform process and reasonable timetable seemed to offer reliability and transparency to parents tired of obstacles. As Lila Noonan put it, "I wanted a guarantee. I wanted my baby."

That "guarantee" and "baby" are parallel constructions is significant; it is also significant that Lila went on to say that she badly wanted a daughter. Not only did China seem to want these parents, these parents wanted—and adoption agencies promoted—the healthy young infant girls that seemed to fill Chinese orphanages. Infants are desirable for a number of reasons, but often because their kinship and cultural attachments are seen as not fully formed; this translates into a child ready for a fresh start in her new family and nation.

Being able to make Chinese children "one's own" is a function of the child's age but also of (lack of) kinship ties. This was apparent in the comfort many parents expressed at not having to deal with birth parents who might reclaim children or want to be part of their children's lives. Peggy Peterson put it this way: "We felt more comfortable with China or Vietnam because they pretty much are not going to want to have the child back in a year." While media stories of domestic child reclamations loomed large, so did fears of having to share a child beyond the confines of the nuclear, adoptive family. One new adoptive mother told me she did not want a twenty-year-old dropping in six times a year with presents. "What kind of mother is that?" she asked, adding that one reason she liked Chinese adoption was that it was "clean, pure." Indeed, Chinese adoptions fit well with the "clean break" policies and practices of transnational adoption, whereby a child's adoptability is predicated on being legally and socially "free" of ties to family and place of birth (Yngvesson 2000; Ouellette and Belleau 2001; Gailey 2000).[21] Agencies variously join in promoting clean breaks. In an unusually stark example of this, one adoption agency stated on their Web site: "Adopting a Chinese child is very simple. There will be no birth mother knocking on your door. In China, it is a crime to abandon a child. If a birth mother changes her mind and comes back to a welfare home for the child, she will be put in prison."[22]

It is in statements like these that Chinese birth mothers, safely entangled in social and legal proscriptions, become a racialized medium for the baggage-free child. They are not only the right kind of mother because, as marginalized "Third World" women, they cannot touch their children but also because, in contrast to some other countries and to the United States, women in China can be constructed as giving up babies for reasons other than being young, unfit, and unhealthy social deviants. When Ian, a white father, said that he and his wife, Amy, adopted from China because they knew the children "were very, very healthy," Amy added, "You know, we knew that some of them were small and maybe not as well-nourished . . . but we knew that Chinese women didn't typically drink and smoke, culturally? Isn't that right?" Rather than being made villains in the story, Chinese birth mothers can be made into unfortunate but healthy victims. One adoptive mother pointed out that children in China were abandoned "just because they are girls"; to her and her husband, this meant they would not have to worry about the poor prenatal care, drugs, and alcohol that characterized the birth mothers—implicitly black and/or poor—whose children were in the American public welfare system. Why prospective American adopters prefer girls is complicated, but that Chinese children were abandoned ostensibly *because* they were girls made them unattached to birth family, and for reasons other than (in many cases) poor health.

The choices that make adoption an act of clean breaks and fresh starts, of detaching and reattaching, are enabled by class distinctions. Of increasing concern to critical observers is that "light baggage"—racial flexibility, good health, young age, distanced birth mothers—comes with a price tag through a stratified system that literally values some children more than others (Solinger 2001; Mansnerus 1998).[23] Most parents who adopt from China make this choice in part because they can—because they have or can find the means to pay the U.S.

$20,000-plus that it costs. The material means that drive this choice must be linked not only to the delimited choices of Chinese birth parents but also to the delimited desirability of other children. As I have argued, factors of race, gender, age, and health play into the narratives of choice that imagine the possible relocation of some children, and not others, into adoptive homes; but the imagined transformation of the child in her new adoptive family rests in part on the ability of such a family to enact it through material means.

It should not be surprising, however, that the material means that enable adoption choices remain mostly an arena of silence and indirect reference. The consumptive overtones that haunt adoption exchanges and exclusions (Yngvesson 2000; Modell 2002; Anagnost 2000) are coded in the meeting of needs and the giving of gifts, or narrated in terms of "how much we have to offer" a child. As adoptive mother Wanda Jones put it, "You know, if you were born here, or even being able to come here young, you have so many opportunities. And to be able to give those opportunities to somebody else is really important." Material choices were also tacitly expressed in the photos of nice homes sent in parents' applications to Beijing (and expected by Beijing) and mitigated by allusions to rescue. Barbara, for example, told me that she and her husband had initially considered adopting a white child from Russia. Given "all the problems" the children seemed to have, she and her husband had decided instead to go to China for a healthy infant girl. But for acquaintances who did not otherwise understand why the couple would adopt a child from another country, and especially one that did not look like them, Barbara found "saving a child" a quick and acceptable explanation. When orphaned Chinese children were "saved" by American church groups in the late nineteenth and early twentieth centuries,[24] civilizing benevolence was the guiding principle; in contemporary China/U.S. adoption, rescue discourses are corollary to professionally managed choices, and immigration laws and adoption policies smooth rather than block the way for well-off American citizens adopting Chinese children.

Consumptive choices haunt adoption in a dialectical pair of anxieties: that adoption will be seen as a market and that as a market it will take a downturn. One particular event in the history of China/U.S. adoption exemplifies this tension and highlights the nexus of benevolent desires and material resources in which it is embedded. In 1995, less than two years after international adoptions from China had started to take off, reports of poor conditions, high mortality rates, and intentional neglect in Chinese welfare homes reached a high level of exposure in the Western media, in the form of a Human Rights Watch report and a BBC documentary titled *The Dying Rooms*.[25] The reports had several significant effects: major U.S. media outlets covered the story as a sensational scoop but also covered the counterresponses of agencies and adoptive families; the Chinese government, issuing defensive and propagandistic retorts, shut down Chinese orphanages to foreign and many Chinese visitors;[26] and adoption agencies and adoptive families organized to tone down or discredit the reports through media releases, appeals to Washington, D.C., and letters and faxes to Beijing that claimed conditions were improving, many orphanages were doing their best, and there was no evidence of a national policy of relieving an overburdened orphanage system through deliberate starvation (Johnson 2004).[27] I am most interested in the last response, since it was in part born of a fear that China would shut down adoptions, or at least make the process more difficult, and that it would appear that only very malnourished, poorly cared-for children waited in Chinese orphanages. The human rights exposés had the effect of inspiring some prospective parents to save Chinese orphans through adoption. But adoption organizations cannot let rescue be the dominant motivation for international adoption. It not only portends an unequal parent-child relationship but also suggests children with more "baggage" than the current political economy of adoption choices can sustain. In the ensuing years, a strange equilibrium has resulted from the 1995 reports: China kept open its adoption doors and has increased numbers ever since; Beijing could be seen as struggling but sincere in its efforts for abandoned Chinese children; and those children could be seen as needy, but not too needy.

CONCLUSION: THE RETURN OF THE "WHYS" OF CHINESE ADOPTION

Jeff D. Opdyke, adoptive parent of a Chinese child and personal finance reporter for the *Wall Street Journal*, titled his "Love and Money" column on September 21, 2003 (p. D6): "Why We Decided to Adopt from China." In many ways, it summed up the impetuses for adopting from China I have covered in this chapter: providing hope to a child in the Third World, the ease of a fairly efficient process, availability of healthy infants, and reliable birth mothers. Opdyke set this in the framework of a kind of cost-benefit analysis that made China "worth it," putting in writing the considerations many parents weigh in their decisions but would probably express in less economic terms: "So in the end, an international adoption may not save us much money. But at least we would be assured of getting what we want—an infant." And given all the other factors that entered the equation, China came out on top: "At the end of the day, of course, it all comes down to personal choice for each family . . . and in dealing with those choices, Amy and I came to a unified conclusion: The road to our daughter runs through China."

Of course, individual choices do not occur in a vacuum—they drip with the residue of social relationships and of imaginaries of the identities of self and other. The sketch art that accompanied Opdyke's article showed a simple, stark scene of exchange: a woman handing a swaddled baby across the Great Wall, into the outstretched arms of a man whose female partner stands waiting beside him. Actually, given the particular poses of the characters, the piece could conceivably work the other way: the man *could* be handing the child to the lone woman. But this goes against the grain of what we imagine makes Chinese children and American parents a good match, why China "works": birth *mothers* (enclosed behind the Great Wall) reluctantly but necessarily give up children who can be rescued into the arms of middle-class, white, heterosexual couples who have calculated "the financial components of our decision because we want the limited dollars we have now and in the future to go as far as they possibly can." Opdyke unwittingly provides the first clue to why this calculation of desires and guarantees is a compromised prospect from the outset. His road runs *through* China and presumably back to him, making China one part of an ongoing circulation of resources and ideas that reproduce the family, and the adoption system. But this also means that the child and her new parents, as they move away from the Great Wall, carry with them not just the meanings of that moment of exchange but all the conditions that made it possible.

A Korean adoptee and friend has wryly suggested to me that perhaps all the factors that make adoption from China desirable make children from China the model minorities of adoption, or "model adoptees." But as with the Asian model minority rubric, this is a myth. And like all myths, it is powerful and revelatory, but it begs to be unpacked. Chinese children are not as easily rescuable/consumable, flexible, or baggage-free as dominant discourses of adoption would suggest—and not only because they individually come with their own quirks and needs or because the process does not always go smoothly. I have considered both senses of "why China" in this chapter—why parents choose to adopt from China and why, more generally, the practice has thrived—in order to open up the historical contexts that particularize it. I have looked especially at the racialized histories that impose themselves on adoptive choices. Imaginaries of flexible, rescuable identities take us *through* China and back to the exclusive desires of an American culture haunted by the fixations of race and market.

NOTES

1. I see this definition of identification as an updated version of C. Wright Mills's (1959) proverbial call to "understand what is happening in selves as minute points in the intersections of biography and history" (7). Nancy Riley (1997) also invokes Mills in her study of the sociopolitical matrices in which individual abandonment and adoption decisions are made in both China and the United States.
2. Portions of this chapter appear also in Sara Dorow, "Racialized Choices: Chinese Adoption and the 'White Noise' of Blackness," in a 2006 issue of *Critical Sociology*.
3. The implications of the differences between the two metropolitan areas are discussed further in chapter 7 of *Transnational Adoption* by Sara Dorow (2006), as are comparisons of the experiences and practices of Asian American and white adoptive parents. Statistics on the ethnic makeup of cities come from factfinder.census.gov, accessed February 2005.
4. While the kind of research necessary to get an accurate count of the racial and ethnic identities of adoptive parents is beyond the scope of this project, my description of San Francisco is based on informal fact-finding among adoptive parent support groups and my own interactions with a variety of adoptive parents and adoption agencies. It should also be noted that the proportion of Asian American adoptive parents varies quite significantly in different parts of the Bay Area.
5. Paper sons and daughters were Chinese individuals who, after the 1906 fire in San Francisco that destroyed most immigration and citizenship paperwork, immigrated to the United States under manufactured paperwork that claimed they were the children of American citizens of Chinese descent who had returned to China.
6. Dr. Wen Ho Lee was a physicist from Los Alamos National Laboratories, accused by the government in 1999 of violating the Atomic Energy Act. He allegedly mishandled material containing restricted nuclear weapons data, with the intent of unlawfully providing it to China. He was released in 2000 under a plea bargain. The handling of the story in the media and by the government invited accusations of racial profiling and anti-Asian sentiment.

7. In her popular book *The Lost Daughters of China: Abandoned Girls, Their Journey to America, and the Search for a Missing Past*, Karin Evans (2000) remarks on this as well: "In the San Francisco Bay Area or other places with substantial Chinese populations, it's relatively easy to offer children exposure to the Chinese community and the culture into which they were born, even if they have no recollections of it and their parents have to learn from scratch. But introducing children to the dragon dance or Mandarin in a small town in the South or deep in the heart of Amish country, say, may be somewhat challenging" (181).

8. Weak multiculturalism, sometimes associated with the work of Charles Taylor, maintains that differences among people are superseded by certain central values such as tolerance and respect for individual rights. As Steven Yates (1992) puts it, weak multiculturalism asserts that "peoples are different in some respects but alike in others, and can therefore learn by communicating openly with one another" (440); it rejects what it sees as "the naïve view that all cultures are epistemological and moral equals" (451). ("Multiculturalism and Epistemology," *Public Affairs Quarterly* 6: 435–56.)

9. Despite Chinese adoptions being officially closed to gay and lesbian parents, a kind of "don't ask, don't tell" policy characterized much of China/U.S. adoption practice until the CCAA formally instituted guidelines curtailing child placements with gay and lesbian parents in 2000 and 2001.

10. See Linda Gordon's (1999) *The Great Arizona Orphan Abduction* for a fascinating history of a 1905 case in which the courts upheld the "rescue" of white Catholic children from New York originally placed with Mexican families in a town in Arizona. And see Melosh (2002), especially the chapter "Families by Design," on changing and diverse "matching" criteria in the middle decades of the twentieth century.

11. Two things are noteworthy here. First, the largest number of Korean adoptees is found in California and Minnesota, the two states in which I conducted my U.S. fieldwork. Second, parents adopting from China have looked to this large, older cohort of Korean adoptees—online, at adoption seminars, in writings and films—for both affirmation of their own white-Asian adoptive families and advice on how to handle issues of racial and cultural difference.

12. Berebitsky (2000) argues that demand has always exceeded supply. By the 1970s and 1980s, panic over a shortage of infants reflected new kinds of demands from infertile couples and a new focus on meeting their needs. An increased demand for (healthy white) infants also came from newly empowered groups of adopters, namely, gays and lesbians and single straight people. Solinger (2001) has argued that this expansion of the choice to parent must be linked to the choices that contributed to a decreased "supply" of babies: abortion and single parenthood.

13. Only 5 to 10 percent of domestic adoptions in the United States are transracial (Freundlich 2000), but as is the case with China/U.S. adoptions, the cultural impact of the accompanying narratives and imagery are more powerful than the numbers might suggest.

14. Statistics on numbers of international adoption visas issued are from the U.S. State Department: http://travel.state.gov/orphan_numbers.html.

15. This includes a scale of adoptions in the United States ranging from "less adoptable" children that are available not only without fees but also possibly subsidized, to very costly private adoptions of healthy white infants. International adoptions do not vary quite as much but can vary from several thousand dollars to over thirty thousand.

16. See Patton (2000) and Ortiz and Briggs (2003) for more detailed commentary on the Adoption Promotion Act and Personal Responsibility Act of 1996.

17. Rescue serves to resolve distinctions not only between domestic and international adoption but also between adoption and other forms of migration from China. Anagnost (2000) offers a compelling argument regarding rescue discourse as a way privately to manage the political effects of adoption as an exceptional form of migration; to recognize its distinction among migrating bodies is to bring again to the surface the problem of privilege.

18. While most children in orphanages are girls, there are also a large number of special-needs children of both sexes and some healthy boys. It must be noted that the unbalanced sex ratio cannot be straightforwardly attributed to families not wanting girls. As

Greenhalgh and Li (1995) argue, the ideal family in China is "one of each," but under family-planning policies and social expectations of care and labor, girls are more likely to be abandoned than boys.

19. The dismantling of China's state-run work system means a growing demand for social welfare provisions, even as the state tries to put the burden of care back on families. Public institutions of all kinds have been encouraged to start profit-making enterprises or to seek other funding sources.

20. A 1991 report from the U.S. Senate Committee on Intercountry Adoption cited a survey in which parents said they were seeking adoption abroad because they did not meet requirements for domestic adoption (Modell 2002: 193).

21. The importance of a clean break to the attractiveness of adoption reveals the social importance placed on singularity of origin—of the difficulty of belonging to two places and families and mothers at once. See Eng (2003) for a smart discussion of the political and social reasons for a lack of psychic space that can accommodate two mothers.

22. From the Great Wall China Adoption agency (http://www.gwcadopt.org/facts.html), accessed in August 2000. While abandonment is indeed a crime in China, it is difficult to say how often or to what degree the laws against it are enforced.

23. "Hard-to-place" children in the United States, for example, can often be placed for free or with subsidies, while private adoptions of white infants and international adoptions are often U.S. $20,000 or more. It is important to note that from the perspective of adoption professionals, this is understood as a necessary strategy: minimizing costs is a way to attract families for children who might otherwise have little chance of finding homes, perhaps even subsidized by the higher fees paid for "more adoptable" children.

24. Jane Hunter (1984) has documented, for example, that American missionary women to China in this period adopted or fostered local children, even as racial proscriptions from missionary boards warned of such closeness going against "disinterested benevolence." At the same time, Presbyterian organizations in San Francisco established a shelter to "save" orphaned Chinese babies from a Chinatown characterized as unhealthy and uncivilized (even as local protests to the presence of so many Oriental children prompted regulations that would keep them contained) (Shah 2001).

25. For a more detailed explanation of and response to *The Dying Rooms* and the Human Rights Watch report, see Johnson (2004).

26. This was a predictable response, given that the BBC filmmakers, who won a Peabody Award, had apparently received access to Chinese orphanages by posing as social workers and had gathered footage with hidden cameras. In ensuing years, Beijing has opened an increasing number of orphanages to foreigners, starting with "showcase" institutions that have updated facilities, grounds, and equipment. For the most extensive example of Beijing's official (and propagandistic) rebuttal, see The Situation of Children in China (*Zhongguo de Ertong Zhuangkuang*) (April 1996), Beijing: Information Office of the State Council of the People's Republic of China.

27. I am indebted to Dan Kelliher, professor of political science at the University of Minnesota, for his careful, insightful study of the construction of childhood innocence in these events ("The Politics of Childhood Innocence," unpublished manuscript, 2000).

REFERENCES

Anagnost, Ann. 2000. "Scenes of Misrecognition: Maternal Citizenship in the Age of Transnational Adoption." *positions: east asia cultures critique* 8 (2): 390–421.

Balibar, Etienne. 1988. "The Nation Form: History and Ideology." In *Race, Nation, Class: Ambiguous Identities*, edited by E. Balibar and I. Wallerstein. London: Verso.

Berebitsky, Julie. 2000. *Like Our Very Own: Adoption and the Changing Culture of Motherhood, 1851–1950*. Lawrence: University Press of Kansas.

Briggs, Laura. 2003. "Mother, Child, Race, Nation: The Visual Iconography of Rescue and the Politics of Transnational and Transracial Adoption." *Gender & History* 15 (2): 179–200.

Cheng, Anne Anlin. 2001. *The Melancholy of Race: Psychoanalysis, Assimilation, and Hidden Grief.* New York: Oxford University Press.

Cheung, King-Kok. 2000. "The Woman Warrior versus the Chinaman Pacific: Must a Chinese American Critic Choose between Feminism and Heroism?" In *Asian American Studies: A Reader*, edited by J. Yu-wen Shen Wu and M. Song. New Brunswick, N.J.: Rutgers University Press.

Dorow, Sara. 2006. *Transnational Adoption: A Cultural Economy of Race, Gender, and Kinship.* New York: NYU Press.

———. 2006. "Racialized Choices: Chinese Adoption and the 'White Noise' of Blackness." *Critical Sociology* 32 (2–3): 357–379.

Eng, David L. 2003. "Transnational Adoption and Queer Diasporas." *Social Text* 21 (3): 1–37.

Evans, Karin. 2000. *The Lost Daughters of China: Abandoned Girls, Their Journey to America, and the Search for a Missing Past.* New York: Tracher/Putnam.

Frankenberg, Ruth. 1993. *White Women, Race Matters: The Social Construction of Whiteness.* Minneapolis: University of Minnesota Press.

Freundlich, Madelyn. 2000. *Adoption and Ethics.* The Role of Race, Culture, and National Origin in Adoption 10. Washington, D.C.: Child Welfare League of America, The Evan B. Donaldson Institute.

Fuss, Diana. 1995. *Identification Papers.* New York: Routledge.

Gailey, Christine Ward. 2000. "Ideologies of Motherhood and Kinship in US Adoption." In *Ideologies and Technologies of Motherhood*, edited by H. Ragoné and F. Winddance Twine. New York: Routledge.

———. 1999. "Seeking 'Baby Right': Race, Class, and Gender in US International Adoption." In *Mine, Yours, Ours . . . and Theirs: Adoption, Changing Kinship and Family Patterns*, edited by A. Rygvold, M. Dale, and B. Saetersdal. Oslo: University of Oslo.

Galang, M. Evelina. 2003. *Screaming Monkeys: Critiques of Asian American Images.* Minneapolis: Coffee House Press.

Goldberg, David Theo. 1997. *Racial Subjects: Writing on Race in America.* New York: Routledge.

Gordon, Linda. 1999. *The Great Arizona Orphan Abduction.* Cambridge, Mass.: Harvard University Press.

Gotanda, Neil. 2000. "Multiculturalism and Racial Stratification." In *Asian American Studies: A Reader*, edited by J. Yu-wen Shen Wu and m. Song. New Brunswick, N.J.: Rutgers University Press.

Greenhalgh, Susan, and Jiali Li. 1995. "Engendering Reproductive Policy and Practice in Peasant China: For a Feminist Demography of Reproduction." *Signs: Journal of Women in Culture and Society* 20 (31): 601–41.

Hunter, Jane. 1984. *The Gospel of Gentility: American Women Missionaries in Turn-of-the-Century China.* New Haven, Conn.: Yale University Press.

Johnson, Kay Ana. 2004. *Wanting a Daughter, Needing a Son: Abandonment, Adoption, and Orphanage Care in China.* St. Paul, Minn.: Yeong & Yeong Book Company.

Kirton, Derek. 2000. *'Race,' Ethnicity and Adoption.* Buckingham: Open University Press.

Lee, Erika. 2003. *At America's Gates: Chinese Immigration during the Exclusion Era, 1882–1943.* Chapel Hill: University of North Carolina Press.

Lee, Robert G. 1999. *Orientals: Asian Americans in Popular Culture.* Philadelphia: Temple University Press.

Lowe, Lisa. 1996. *Immigrant Acts: On Asian American Cultural Politics.* Durham, N.C.: Duke University Press.

Lovelock, Kirsten. 2000. "Intercountry Adoption as a Migratory Practice: A Comparative Analysis of Intercountry Adoption and Immigration Policy and Practice in the United States, Canada and New Zealand in the Post W.W.II Period." *International Migration Review* 34 (3): 907–49.

Mackerras, Colin. 1989. *Western Images of China.* New York: Oxford University Press.

Mansnerus, Laura. 1998. "Market Puts Price Tags on the Priceless." *New York Times*, October 26, p. A1.

Melosh, Barbara. 2002. *Strangers and Kin: The American Way of Adoption.* Cambridge, Mass.: Harvard University Press.

Mills, C. Wright. 1999 [1959].*The Sociological Imagination.* New York: Oxford University Press.

Modell, Judith S. 2002. *A Sealed and Secret Kinship: The Culture of Policies and Practices in American Adoption.* New York: Berghahn Books.

Okihiro, Gary Y. 2001. *Common Ground: Reimagining American History.* Princeton, N.J.: Princeton University Press.

Omi, Michael. 1996. "Racialization in the Post-Civil Rights Era." In *Mapping Multiculturalism,* edited by A. F. Gordon and C. Newfield. Minneapolis: University of Minnesota Press.

Ong, Aihwa. 1998. *Flexible Citizenship: The Cultural Logics of Transnationality.* Durham, N.C.: Duke University Press.

———. 1996. "Cultural Citizenship as Subject-Making." *Current Anthropology* 37 (5): 737–51.

Ortiz, Ana Teresa, and Laura Briggs. 2003. "The Culture of Poverty, Crack Babies, and Welfare Cheats: The Making of the 'Healthy White Baby Crisis.'" *Social Text* 21 (3): 39–57.

Ouellette, Françoise-Romaine, and Hélène Belleau, with the collaboration of Caroline Patenaude. 2001. *Family and Social Integration of Children Adopted Internationally: A Review of the Literature.* Montreal: INRS-Urbanisation, Culture et Société.

Palumbo-Liu, David. 1999. *Asian/American: Historical Crossings of a Racial Frontier.* Stanford, Calif.: Stanford University Press.

Patton, Sandra L. 2000. *BirthMarks: Transracial Adoption in Contemporary America.* New York: New York University Press.

Prashad, Vijay. 2003. "Bruce Lee and the Anti-Imperialism of Kung Fu: A Polycultural Adventure." *positions: east asia cultures critique* 11 (1): 51–82.

Register, Cheri. 1991. *"Are Those Kids Yours?" American Families with Children Adopted from Other Countries.* New York: Free Press.

Riley, Nancy E. 1997. "American Adoptions of Chinese Girls: The Socio-Political Matrices of Individual Decisions." *Women's Studies International Forum* 20 (1): 87–102.

Said, Edward. 1994 [1978]. *Orientalism.* New York: Vintage Books.

Shah, Nayan. 2001. *Contagious Divides: Epidemics and Race in San Francisco's Chinatown.* Berkeley: University of California Press.

Shiu, Anthony. 2001. "Flexible Production: International Adoption, Race, Whiteness." *Jouvert: A Journal of Postcolonial Studies* 6 (1–2). At http://social.chass.ncsu.edu/jourvert/v6i1–2/shiu.htm.

Solinger, Rickie. 2001. *Beggars and Choosers: How the Politics of Choice Shapes Adoption, Abortion, and Welfare in the United States.* New York: Hill and Wang.

Takaki, Ronald T. 1989. *Strangers from a Different Shore: A History of Asian Americans.* Boston: Little, Brown.

Wang, Gungwu. 2001. *Don't Leave Home: Migration and the Chinese.* Singapore: Times Academic Press.

Yngvesson, Barbara. 2000. "'Un Niño de Cualquier Color': Race and Nation in Intercountry Adoption." In *Globalizing Institutions: Case Studies in Regulation and Innovation,* edited by J. Jenson and Boaventura De Sousa Santos. Burlington, Vt.: Ashgate.

Zelizer, Viviana A. 1985. *Pricing the Priceless Child: The Changing Social Value of Children.* New York: Basic Books.

The "Four Prisons" and the Movements of Liberation

Asian American Activism from the 1960s to the 1990s

Glenn Omatsu

According to Ali Shariati, an Iranian philosopher, each of us exists within four prisons.[1] First is the prison imposed on us by history and geography; from this confinement, we can escape only by gaining a knowledge of science and technology. Second is the prison of history; our freedom comes when we understand how historical forces operate. The third prison is our society's social and class structure; from this prison, only a revolutionary ideology can provide the way to liberation. The final prison is the self. Each of us is composed of good and evil elements, and we must each choose between them.

The analysis of our four prisons provides a way of understanding the movements that swept across America in the 1960s and molded the consciousness of one generation of Asian Americans. The movements were struggles for liberation from many prisons. They were struggles that confronted the historical forces of racism, poverty, war, and exploitation. They were struggles that generated new ideologies, based mainly on the teachings and actions of Third World leaders. And they were struggles that redefined human values—the values that shape how people live their daily lives and interact with each other. Above all, they were struggles that transformed the lives of "ordinary" people as they confronted the prisons around them.

For Asian Americans, these struggles profoundly changed our communities. They spawned numerous grassroots organizations. They created an extensive network of student organizations and Asian American Studies classes. They recovered buried cultural traditions and produced a new generation of writers, poets, and artists. But most importantly, the struggles deeply affected Asian American consciousness. They redefined racial and ethnic identity, promoted new ways of thinking about communities, and challenged prevailing notions of power and authority.

Yet, in the two decades that have followed, scholars have reinterpreted the movements in narrower ways. I learned about this reinterpretation when I attended a class recently in Asian American Studies at UCLA. The professor described the period from the late 1950s to the early 1970s as a single epoch involving the persistent efforts of racial minorities and their white supporters to secure civil rights. Young Asian Americans, the professor stated, were swept into this campaign and by later anti-war protests to assert their own racial identity. The most important influence on Asian Americans during this period was Dr. Martin Luther King Jr., who inspired them to demand access to policy makers and initiate advocacy programs for their own communities. Meanwhile, students and professors fought to legitimize Asian American Studies in college curricula and for representation of Asians in American society. The lecture was cogent, tightly organized, and well received by the audience of students—many of them new immigrants or the children of new immigrants. There was only one problem: the reinterpretation was wrong on every aspect.

Those who took part in the mass struggles of the 1960s and early 1970s will know that the birth of the Asian American movement coincided not with the initial campaign for civil rights but with the later demand for black liberation; that the leading influence was not Martin Luther King Jr., but Malcolm X; that the focus of a generation of Asian American activists was not on asserting racial pride but on reclaiming a tradition of militant struggle by earlier generations; that the movement was not centered on the aura of racial identity but embraced fundamental questions of oppression and power; that the movement consisted of not only college students but large numbers of community forces, including the elderly, workers, and high school youth; and that the main thrust was not one of seeking legitimacy and representation within American society but the larger goal of liberation.

It may be difficult for a new generation—raised on the Asian American code words of the 1980s stressing "advocacy," "access," "legitimacy," "empowerment," and "assertiveness"—to understand the urgency of Malcolm X's demand for freedom "by any means necessary," Mao's challenge to "serve the people," the slogans of "power to the people" and "self-determination," the principles of "mass line" organizing and "united front" work, or the conviction that people—not elites—make history. But these ideas galvanized thousands of Asian Americans and reshaped our communities. And it is these concepts that we must grasp to understand the scope and intensity of our movement and what it created.

But are these concepts relevant to Asian Americans today? In our community—where new immigrants and refugees constitute the majority of Asian Americans—can we find a legacy from the struggles of two decades ago? Are the ideas of the movement alive today, or have they atrophied into relics—the curiosities of a bygone era of youthful and excessive idealism?

By asking these questions, we, as Asian Americans, participate in a larger national debate: the reevaluation of the impact of the 1960s on American society today. This debate is occurring all around us: in sharp exchanges over "family values" and the status of women and gays in American society; in clashes in schools over curricular reform and multiculturalism; in differences among policy makers over the urban crisis and approaches to rebuilding Los Angeles and other inner cities after the 1992 uprisings; and continuing reexaminations of U.S. involvement in Indochina more than two decades ago and the relevance of that war to U.S. military intervention in Iraq, Somalia, and Bosnia.

What happened in the 1960s that made such an impact on America? Why do discussions about that decade provoke so much emotion today? And do the movements of the 1960s serve as the same controversial reference point for Asian Americans?

THE UNITED STATES DURING THE 1960S

In recent years, the movements of the 1960s have come under intense attack. One national bestseller, Allan Bloom's *Closing of the American Mind*, criticizes the movements for undermining the bedrock of Western thought.[2] According to Bloom, nothing positive resulted from the mass upheavals of the 1960s. He singles out black studies and affirmative action programs and calls for eliminating them from universities.

Activists who have continued political work provide contrasting assessments. Their books include Todd Gitlin's *The Sixties: Years of Hope, Days of Rage*; James Miller's *"Democracy Is in the Streets": From Port Huron to the Siege of Chicago*; Ronald Fraser's *1968: A Student Generation in Revolt*; Tom Hayden's *Reunion: A Memoir*; Tariq Ali's *Street Fighting Years*; George Katsiaficas's *The Imagination of the New Left: A Global Analysis of 1968*; and special issues of various journals, including *Witness, Socialist Review,* and *Radical America*.

However, as Winifred Breines states in an interesting review essay titled "Whose New Left?" most of the retrospectives have been written by white male activists from elite backgrounds, and reproduce their relationship to these movements.[3] Their accounts tend to divide the period into two phases: the "good" phase of the early 1960s, characterized by participatory democracy; followed by the post-1968 phase, when movement politics "degenerated" into violence and sectarianism.

"Almost all books about the New Left note a turning point or an ending in 1968 when the leadership of the movement turned toward militancy and violence and SDS [Students for a Democratic Society] as an organization was collapsing," Breines observes. The retrospectives commonly identify the key weaknesses of the movements as the absence of effective organization, the lack of discipline, and utopian thinking. Breines disagrees with these interpretations:

> The movement was not simply unruly and undisciplined; it was experimenting with
> antihierarchical organizational forms. . . . There were many centers of action in the

movement, many actions, many interpretations, many visions, many experiences. There was no [organizational] unity because each group, region, campus, commune, collective, and demonstration developed differently, but all shared in a spontaneous opposition to racism and inequality, the war in Vietnam, and the repressiveness of American social norms and culture, including centralization and hierarchy.[4]

Breines believes that the most important contributions of activists were their moral urgency, their emphasis on direct action, their focus on community building, and their commitment to mass democracy.

Similarly, Sheila Collins in *The Rainbow Challenge*, a book focusing on the Jesse Jackson presidential campaign of 1984 and the formation of the National Rainbow Coalition, assesses the movements of the sixties very positively.[5] She contends that the Jackson campaign was built on the grassroots organizing experience of activists who emerged from the struggles for civil rights, women's liberation, peace and social justice, and community building during the sixties. Moreover, activists' participation in these movements shaped their vision of America, which, in turn, became the basis for the platform of the Rainbow Coalition twenty years later.

According to Collins, the movements that occurred in the United States in the sixties were also part of a worldwide trend, a trend Latin American theologians call the era of the "eruption of the poor" into history. In America, the revolt of the "politically submerged" and "economically marginalized" posed a major ideological challenge to ruling elites:

> The civil rights and black power movement exploded several dominant assumptions about the nature of American society, thus challenging the cultural hegemony of the white ruling elite and causing everyone else in the society to redefine their relationship to centers of power, creating a groundswell of support for radical democratic participation in every aspect of institutional life.[6]

Collins contends that the mass movements created a "crisis of legitimation" for ruling circles. This crisis, she believes, was "far more serious than most historians—even those of the left—have credited it with being."

Ronald Fraser also emphasizes the ideological challenge raised by the movements due to their mass, democratic character and their "disrespect for arbitrary and exploitative authority." In *1968: A Student Generation in Revolt*, Fraser explains how these concepts influenced one generation of activists:

> [T]he anti-authoritarianism challenged almost every shibboleth of Western society. Parliamentary democracy, the authority of presidents . . . and [the policies of] governments to further racism, conduct imperialist wars or oppress sectors of the population at home, the rule of capital and the fiats of factory bosses, the dictates of university administrators, the sacredness of the family, sexuality, bourgeois culture—nothing was in principle sacrosanct. . . . Overall . . . [there was] a lack of deference toward institutions and values that demean[ed] people and a concomitant awareness of peoples' rights.[7]

THE SAN FRANCISCO STATE STRIKE'S LEGACY

The retrospectives about the sixties produced so far have ignored Asian Americans. Yet, the books cited above—plus the review essay by Winifred Breines—provide us with some interesting points to compare and contrast. For example, 1968 represented a turning point for Asian Americans and other sectors of American society. But while white male leaders saw the year as marking the decline of the movement, 1968 for Asian Americans was a year of birth. It marked the beginning of the San Francisco State strike and all that followed.

The strike, the longest student strike in U.S. history, was the first campus uprising involving Asian Americans as a collective force.[8] Under the Third World Liberation Front—a coalition of African American, Latino, American Indian, and Asian American campus groups—students "seized the time" to demand ethnic studies, open admissions, and a redefinition of the education system. Although their five-month strike was brutally repressed and resulted in only partial victories, students won the nation's first School of Ethnic Studies.

Yet, we cannot measure the legacy of the strike for Asian Americans only in the tangible items it achieved, such as new classes and new faculty; the strike also critically transformed the consciousness of its participants, who in turn profoundly altered their communities' political landscape. Through their participation, a generation of Asian American student activists reclaimed a heritage of struggle—linking their lives to the tradition of militancy of earlier generations of Pilipino farm workers, Chinese immigrant garment and restaurant workers, and Japanese American concentration camp resisters. Moreover, these Asian American students—and their community supporters—liberated themselves from the prisons surrounding their lives and forged a new vision for their communities, creating numerous grassroots projects and empowering previously ignored and disenfranchised sectors of society. The statement of goals and principles of one campus organization, Philippine-American Collegiate Endeavor (PACE), during the strike captures this new vision:

> We seek . . . simply to function as human beings, to control our own lives. Initially, following the myth of the American Dream, we worked to attend predominantly white colleges, but we have learned through direct analysis that it is impossible for our people, so-called minorities, to function as human beings, in a racist society in which white always comes first. . . . So we have decided to fuse ourselves with the masses of Third World people, which are the majority of the world's peoples, to create, through struggle, a new humanity, a new humanism, a New World Consciousness, and within that context collectively control our own destinies.[9]

The San Francisco State strike is important not only as a beginning point for the Asian American movement, but also because it crystallizes several themes that would characterize Asian American struggles in the next decade. First, the strike occurred at a working-class campus and involved a coalition of Third World students linked to their communities. Second, students rooted their strike in the tradition of resistance by past generations of minority peoples in America. Third, strike leaders drew inspiration—as well as new ideology—from international Third World leaders and revolutions occurring in Asia, Africa, Latin America, and the Middle East. Fourth, in its demands for open admissions, community control of education, ethnic studies, and self-determination, the strike confronted basic questions of power and oppression in America. Finally, strike participants raised their demands through a strategy of mass mobilizations and militant, direct action.

In the decade following the strike, several themes would reverberate in the struggles in Asian American communities across the nation. These included housing and anti-eviction campaigns, efforts to defend education rights, union organizing drives, campaigns for jobs and social services, and demands for democratic rights, equality, and justice. Mo Nishida, an organizer in Los Angeles, recalls the broad scope of movement activities in his city:

> Our movement flowered. At one time, we had active student organizations on every campus around Los Angeles, fought for ethnic studies, equal opportunity programs, high potential programs at UCLA, and for students doing community work in "Serve the People" programs. In the community, we had, besides [Asian American] Hard Core, four area youth-oriented groups working against drugs (on the Westside, Eastside, Gardena, and the Virgil district). There were also parents' groups, which worked with parents of the youth and more.[10]

In Asian American communities in Los Angeles, San Francisco, Sacramento, Stockton, San Jose, Seattle, New York, and Honolulu, activists created "serve the people" organizations—mass networks built on the principles of "mass line" organizing. Youth initiated many of these organizations—some from college campuses and others from high schools and the streets—but other members of the community, including small-business people, workers, senior citizens, and new immigrants, soon joined.

The *mass* character of community struggles is the least appreciated aspect of our movement today. It is commonly believed that the movement involved only college students. In fact, a range of people, including high-school youth, tenants, small-business people, former prison inmates, former addicts, the elderly, and workers embraced the struggles. But exactly who were these people, and what did their participation mean to the movement?

Historian George Lipsitz has studied similar, largely "anonymous" participants in civil rights campaigns in African American communities. He describes one such man, Ivory Perry of St. Louis:

> Ivory Perry led no important organizations, delivered no important speeches, and received no significant recognition or reward for his social activism. But for more than 30 years, he had passed out leaflets, carried the picket signs, and planned the flamboyant confrontations that made the civil rights movements effective in St. Louis and across the nation. His continuous commitment at the local level had goaded others into action, kept alive hopes of eventual victory in the face of short-term defeats, and provided a relatively powerless community with an effective lever for social change. The anonymity of his activism suggests layers of social protest activity missing from

most scholarly accounts, while the persistence of his involvement undermines prevailing academic judgments about mass protests as outbursts of immediate anger and spasmodic manifestations of hysteria.[11]

Those active in Asian American communities during the late 1960s and early 1970s know there were many Ivory Perrys. They were the people who demonstrated at eviction sites, packed City Hall hearing rooms, volunteered to staff health fairs, and helped with day-to-day operations of the first community drop-in centers, legal defense offices, and senior citizen projects. They were the women and men who took the concept of "serve the people" and turned it into a material force, transforming the political face of our communities.

THE "CULTURAL REVOLUTION" IN ASIAN AMERICAN COMMUNITIES

But we would be wrong to describe this transformation of our communities as solely "political"—at least as our society narrowly defines the term today. The transformation also involved a cultural vitality that opened new ways of viewing the world. Unlike today—where Asian American communities categorize "culture" and "politics" into different spheres of professional activity—in the late 1960s they did not divide them so rigidly or hierarchically. Writers, artists, and musicians were "cultural workers," usually closely associated with communities, and saw their work as "serving the people." Like other community activists, cultural workers defined the period as a "decisive moment" for Asian Americans—a time for reclaiming the past and changing the future.

The "decisive moment" was also a time for questioning and transforming moral values. Through their political and cultural work, activists challenged systems of rank and privilege, structures of hierarchy and bureaucracy, forms of exploitation and inequality, and notions of selfishness and individualism. Through their activism in mass organizations, they promoted a new moral vision centered on democratic participation, cooperative work styles, and collective decision making. Pioneer poet Russell C. Leong describes the affinity between this new generation of cultural workers and their communities, focusing on the work of the Asian American Writers Workshop, located in the basement of the International Hotel in San Francisco Chinatown/Manilatown:

> We were a post–World War II generation mostly in our twenties and thirties; in or out of local schools and colleges. . . . [We] gravitated toward cities—San Francisco, Los Angeles, New York—where movements for ethnic studies and inner city blocks of Asian communities coincided. . . . We read as we wrote—not in isolation—but in the company of our neighbors in Manilatown pool halls, barrio parks, Chinatown basements. . . . Above all, we poets were a tribe of storytellers. . . . Storytellers live in communities where they write for family and friends. The relationship between the teller and listener is neighborly, because the teller of stories must also listen.[12]

But as storytellers, cultural workers did more than simply describe events around them. By witnessing and participating in the movement, they helped to shape community consciousness. San Francisco poet Al Robles focuses on this process of vision making:

> While living and working in our little, tiny communities, in the midst of towering high-rises, we fought the oppressor, the landlord, the developer, the banks, City Hall. But most of all, we celebrated through our culture; music, dance, song and poetry—not only the best we knew but the best we had. The poets were and always have been an integral part of the community. It was through poetry—through a poetical vision to live out the ritual in dignity as human beings.[13]

The transformation of poets, writers, and artists into cultural workers and vision makers reflected larger changes occurring in every sector of the Asian American community. In education, teachers and students redefined the learning process, discovering new ways of sharing knowledge different from traditional, authoritarian, top-down approaches. In the social-service sector, social workers and other professionals became "community workers," and under the slogan "serve the people" redefined the traditional counselor/client relationship by stressing interaction, dialogue, and community building. Within community organizations, members experimented with new organizational structures and collective leadership styles, discarding hierarchical and bureaucratic forms where a handful of commanders made all the decisions. Everywhere, activists and ordinary people grappled with change.

Overall, this "cultural revolution" in the Asian American community echoes themes we have encountered earlier: Third World consciousness, participatory democracy, community building, historical rooting, liberation, and transformation. Why were these concepts so important to a generation of activists? What did they mean? And do they still have relevance for Asian American communities today?

Political analyst Raymond Williams and historian Warren Susman have suggested the use of "keywords" to study historical periods, especially times of great social change.[14] Keywords are terms, concepts, and ideas that emerge as themes of a period, reflecting vital concerns and changing values. For Asian Americans in the 1980s and 1990s, the keywords are "advocacy," "access," "legitimacy," "empowerment," and "assertiveness." These keywords tell us much about the shape of our community today, especially the growing role of young professionals and their aspirations in U.S. society. In contrast, the keywords of the late 1960s and early 1970s—"consciousness," "theory," "ideology," "participatory democracy," "community," and "liberation"—point to different concerns and values.

The keywords of two decades ago point to an approach to political work that activists widely shared, especially those working in grassroots struggles in Asian American neighborhoods, such as the Chinatowns, Little Tokyos, Manilatowns, and International Districts around the nation. This political approach focused on the relationship between political consciousness and social change, and can be best summarized in a popular slogan of the period: "Theory becomes a material force when it is grasped by the masses." Asian American activists believed that they could promote political change through direct action and mass education that raised political consciousness in the community, especially among the unorganized—low-income workers, tenants, small-business people, high-school youth, and so on. Thus, activists saw political consciousness as rising not from study groups, but from involving people in the process of social change—through their confronting the institutions of power around them and creating new visions of community life based on these struggles.

Generally, academics studying the movements of the 1960s—including academics in Asian American Studies—have dismissed the political theory of that time as murky and eclectic, characterized by ultra-leftism, shallow class analysis, and simplistic notions of Marxism and capitalism.[15] To a large extent, the thinking was eclectic; Asian American activists drew from Marx, Lenin, Stalin, and Mao—and also from Frantz Fanon, Malcolm X, Che Guevara, Kim Il-sung, and Amilcar Cabral, as well as Korean revolutionary Kim San, W.E.B. Du Bois, Frederick Douglass, Paulo Freire, the Black Panther Party, the Young Lords, the women's liberation movement, and many other resistance struggles. But in their obsessive search for theoretical clarity and consistency, these academics miss the bigger picture. What is significant is not the *content* of ideas activists adopted, but what activists *did* with the ideas. What Asian American activists *did* was use the ideas drawn from many different movements to redefine the Asian American experience.

Central to this redefinition was a slogan that appeared at nearly every Asian American rally during that period: "The people, and the people alone, are the motive force in the making of world history." Asian American activists adapted the slogan, which originated in the Chinese revolution, to the tasks of community building, historical rooting, and creating new values. Thus, the slogan came to capture six new ways of thinking about Asian Americans:

- Asian Americans became active participants in the making of history, reversing standard accounts that had treated Asian Americans as marginal objects.
- Activists saw history as created by large numbers of people acting together, not by elites.
- This view of history provided a new way of looking at our communities. Activists believed that ordinary people could make their own history by learning how historical forces operated and by transforming this knowledge into a material force to change their lives.
- This realization defined a political strategy: political power came from grassroots organizing, from the bottom up.
- This strategy required activists to develop a broad analysis of the Asian American condition—to uncover the interconnections in seemingly separate events, such as the war in Indochina, corporate redevelopment of Asian American communities, and the exploitation of Asian immigrants in garment shops. In their political analyses, activists linked the day-to-day struggles of Asian Americans to larger events and issues. The anti-eviction campaign of tenants in Chinatown and the International District against powerful corporations became one with the resistance movements of peasants in Vietnam,

the Philippines, and Latin America—or, as summarized in a popular slogan of the period, there was "one struggle, [but] many fronts."

• This new understanding challenged activists to build mass, democratic organizations, especially within unorganized sectors of the community. Through these new organizations, Asian Americans expanded democracy for all sectors of the community and gained the power to participate in the broader movement for political change taking place throughout the world.

The redefinition of the Asian American experience stands as the most important legacy from this period. As described above, this legacy represents far more than an ethnic awakening. The redefinition began with an analysis of power and domination in American society. It provided a way of understanding the historical forces surrounding us. And most importantly, it presented a strategy and challenge for changing our future. This challenge, I believe, still confronts us today.

THE LATE 1970s: REVERSING DIRECTION

As we continue to delve into the vitality of the movements of the 1960s, one question becomes more and more persistent: Why did these movements, possessing so much vigor and urgency, seem to disintegrate in the late 1970s and early 1980s? Why did a society in motion toward progressive change seem suddenly to reverse direction?

As in the larger Left movement, Asian American activists heatedly debate this question.[16] Some mention the strategy of repression—including assassinations—U.S. ruling circles launched in response to the mass rebellions. Others cite the accompanying programs of cooptation that elites designed to channel mass discontent into traditional political arenas. Some focus on the New Right's rise, culminating in the Reagan presidency. Still others emphasize the sectarianism among political forces within the movement, or target the inability of the movement as a whole to base itself more broadly within communities.

Each of these analyses provides a partial answer. But missing in most analyses by Asian American activists is the most critical factor: the devastating corporate offensive of the mid-1970s. We will remember the 1970s as a time of economic crisis and staggering inflation. Eventually, historians may more accurately describe it as the years of "one-sided class war." Transnational corporations based in the United States launched a broad attack on the American people, especially African American communities. Several books provide an excellent analysis of the corporate offensive. One of the best, most accessible accounts is *What's Wrong with the U.S. Economy?*, written in 1982 by the Institute for Labor Education and Research.[17] My analysis draws from that source.

Corporate executives based their offensive on two conclusions: first, the economic crisis in the early 1970s—marked by declining corporate profits—occurred because American working people were earning too much; and second, the mass struggles of the previous decades had created "too much democracy" in America. The Trilateral Commission—headed by David Rockefeller and composed of corporate executives and politicians from the United States, Europe, and

Japan—posed the problem starkly: either people would have to accept less, or corporations would have to accept less. An article in *Business Week* identified the solution: "Some people will obviously have to do with less. . . . Yet it will be a hard pill for many Americans to swallow—the idea of doing with less so that big business can have more."

But in order for corporations to "have more," U.S. ruling circles had to deal with the widespread discontent that had erupted throughout America. We sometimes forget today that in the mid-1970s a large number of Americans had grown cynical about U.S. business and political leaders. People routinely called politicians—including President Nixon and Vice President Agnew—crooks, liars, and criminals. Increasingly, they began to blame the largest corporations for their economic problems. One poll showed that half the population believed that "big business is the source of most of what's wrong in this country today." A series of Harris polls found that those expressing "a great deal of confidence" in the heads of corporations had fallen from 55 percent in 1966 to only 15 percent in 1975. By the fall of 1975, public opinion analysts testifying before a congressional committee reported, according to the *New York Times*, "that public confidence in the government and in the country's economic future is probably lower than it has ever been since they began to measure such things scientifically." These developments stunned many corporate leaders. "How did we let the educational system fail the free-enterprise system?" one executive asked.

U.S. ruling elites realized that restoring faith in free enterprise could only be achieved through an intensive ideological assault on those challenging the system. The ideological campaign was combined with a political offensive, aimed at the broad gains in democratic rights that Americans, especially African Americans, had achieved through the mass struggles of previous decades. According to corporate leaders, there was "too much democracy" in America, which meant too little "governability." In a 1975 Trilateral Commission report, Harvard political scientist Samuel Huntington analyzed the problem caused by "previously passive or unorganized groups in the population [which were] now engaged in concerted efforts to establish their claims to opportunities, positions, rewards, and privileges which they had not considered themselves entitled to before." According to Huntington, this upsurge in "democratic fervor" coincided with "markedly higher levels of self-consciousness on the part of blacks, Indians, Chicanos, white ethnic groups, students and women, all of whom became mobilized and organized in new ways." Huntington saw these developments as creating a crisis for those in power:

> The essence of the democratic surge of the 1960s was a general challenge to existing systems of authority, public and private. In one form or another, the challenge manifested itself in the family, the university, business, public and private associations, politics, the government bureaucracy, and the military service. People no longer felt the same obligation to obey those whom they had previously considered superior to themselves in age, rank, status, expertise, character, or talents.[18]

The mass pressures, Huntington contended, had "produced problems for the governability of democracy in the 1970s." The government, he concluded, must find a way to exercise more control. And that meant curtailing the rights of "major economic groups."

The ensuing corporate campaign was a "one-sided class war": plant closures in U.S. industries and transfer of production overseas, massive layoffs in remaining industries, shifts of capital investment from one region of the country to other regions and to other parts of the globe, and demands by corporations for concessions in wages and benefits from workers in nearly every sector of the economy.

The Reagan presidency culminated and institutionalized this offensive. The Reagan platform called for restoring "traditional" American values, especially faith in the system of free enterprise. Reaganomics promoted economic recovery by getting government "off the backs" of business people, reducing taxation of the rich, and cutting social programs for the poor. Meanwhile, racism and exploitation became respectable under the new mantle of patriotism and economic recovery.

THE WINTER OF CIVIL RIGHTS

The corporate assault ravaged many American neighborhoods, but African American communities absorbed its harshest impact. A study by the Center on Budget and Policy Priorities measures the national impact:

- Between 1970 and 1980, the number of poor African Americans rose by 24 percent from 1.4 million to 1.8 million.
- In the 1980s, the overall African American median income was 57 percent that of whites, a decline of nearly four percentage points from the early 1970s.
- In 1986, females headed 42 percent of all African American families, the majority of which lived below the poverty line.
- In 1978, 8.4 percent of African American families had incomes under $5,000 a year. By 1987, that figure had grown to 13.5 percent. In that year, a third of all African Americans were poor.[19]
- By 1990, nearly half of all African American children grew up in poverty.[20]

Manning Marable provides a stark assessment of this devastation in *How Capitalism Underdeveloped Black America:*

What is qualitatively *new* about the current period is that the racist/capitalist state under Reagan has proceeded down a public policy road which could inevitably involve the complete obliteration of the entire Black reserve army of labor and sections of the Black working class. The decision to save capitalism at all costs, to provide adequate capital for restructuring of the private sector, fundamentally conflicts with the survival of millions of people who are now permanently outside the workplace. Reaganomics must, if it intends to succeed, place the onerous burden of unemployment on the shoulders of the poor (Blacks, Latinos and even whites) so securely that middle to upper income Americans will not protest in the vicious suppression of this stratum.[21]

The corporate offensive, combined with widespread government repression, brutally destroyed grassroots groups in the African American community. This war against the poor ripped apart the social fabric of neighborhoods across America, leaving them vulnerable to drugs and gang violence. The inner cities became the home of the "underclass" and a new politics of inner-directed violence and despair.

Historian Vincent Harding, in *The Other American Revolution*, summarizes the 1970s as the "winter" of civil rights, a period in which there was "a dangerous loss of hope among black people, hope in ourselves, hope in the possibility of any real change, hope in any moral, creative force beyond the flatness of our lives."[22]

In summary, the corporate offensive—especially its devastation of the African American community—provides the necessary backdrop for understanding why the mass movements of the 1960s seemed to disintegrate. Liberation movements, especially in the African American community, did not disappear, but a major focus of their activity shifted to issues of day-to-day survival.

THE 1980s: AN AMBIGUOUS PERIOD FOR ASIAN AMERICAN EMPOWERMENT

For African Americans and many other people of color, the period from the mid-1970s through the Reagan and Bush presidencies became a winter of civil rights, a time of corporate assault on their livelihoods and an erosion of hard-won rights. But for Asian Americans, the meaning of this period is much more ambiguous. On the one hand, great suffering marked the period: growing poverty for increasing numbers of Asian Americans, especially refugees from Southeast Asia; a rising trend of racist hate crimes directed toward Asian Americans of all ethnicities and income levels; and sharpening class polarization within our communities—with a widening gap between the very rich and the very poor. But advances also characterized the period. With the reform of U.S. immigration laws in 1965, the Asian American population grew dramatically, creating new enclaves—including suburban settlements—and revitalizing more established communities, such as Chinatowns, around the nation. Some recent immigrant business people, with small capital holdings, found economic opportunities in inner city neighborhoods. Meanwhile, Asian American youth enrolled in record numbers in colleges and universities across the United States. Asian American families moved into suburbs, crashing previously lily-white neighborhoods. And a small but significant group of Asian American politicians, such as Mike Woo and Warren Furutani, scored important electoral victories in the mainstream political arena, taking the concept of political empowerment to a new level of achievement.

During the winter of civil rights, Asian American activists also launched several impressive political campaigns at the grassroots level. Japanese Americans joined together to win redress and reparations. Pilipino Americans rallied in solidarity with the "People's Power" movement in the Philippines to topple the powerful Marcos dictatorship. Chinese Americans created new political alignments and mobilized community support for the pro-democracy struggle in China. Korean Americans responded to the massacre of civilians by the South Korean dictatorship in Kwangju with massive demonstrations and relief efforts, and established an important network of organizations in America, including Young Koreans United. Samoan Americans rose up against police abuse in Los Angeles; Pacific Islanders demanded removal of nuclear weapons and wastes from their homelands; and Hawai'ians fought for the right of self-determination and recovery of their lands. And large numbers of Asian Americans and Pacific Islanders worked actively in the 1984 and 1988 presidential campaigns of Jesse Jackson, helping to build the Rainbow Coalition.

Significantly, these accomplishments occurred in the midst of the Reagan presidency and U.S. politics' turn to the right. How did certain sectors of the Asian American community achieve these gains in the midst of this burgeoning conservatism?

There is no simple answer. Mainstream analysts and some Asian Americans have stressed the "model minority" concept. According to this analysis, Asian Americans—in contrast to other people of color in America—have survived adversity and advanced because of their emphasis on education and family values, their community cohesion, and other aspects of their cultural heritage. Other scholars have severely criticized this viewpoint, stressing instead structural changes in the global economy and shifts in U.S. government policy since the 1960s. According to their analysis, the reform of U.S. immigration laws and sweeping economic changes in advanced capitalist nations, such as deindustrialization and the development of new technologies, brought an influx of highly educated new Asian immigrants to America. The characteristics of these new immigrants stand in sharp contrast to those of past generations, and provide a broader social and economic base for developing our communities. Still other political thinkers have emphasized the key role played by political expatriates—both right-wing and left-wing—in various communities, but most especially in the Vietnamese, Pilipino, and Korean communities. These expatriates brought political resources from their homelands—e.g., political networks, organizing experience, and, in a few cases, access to large amounts of funds—and have used these resources to change the political landscape of ethnic enclaves. Still other analysts have examined the growing economic and political power of nations of the Asian Pacific and its impact on Asians in America. According to these analysts, we can link the advances of Asian Americans during this period to the rising influence of their former homelands and the dawning of what some call "the Pacific Century." Finally, some academics have focused on the significance of small-business activities of new Asian immigrants, arguing that this sector is most responsible for the changing status of Asian Americans in the 1980s. According to their analysis, Asian immigrant entrepreneurs secured an economic niche in inner city neighborhoods because they had access to start-up capital (through rotating credit associations or from family members) and they filled a vacuum created when white businesses fled.[23]

Thus, we have multiple interpretations for why some sectors of the Asian American community advanced economically and politically during the winter of civil rights. But two critical factors missing from the analyses can help us better understand the peculiar shape of our community in the 1980s and its ambiguous character when compared to other communities of color. First is the legacy of grassroots organizing from the Asian American movement, and second is the dramatic rise of young professionals as a significant force in the community.

A stereotype about the movements of the 1960s is that they produced nothing enduring—they flared brightly for an instant and then quickly died. However, evidence from the Asian American movement contradicts this commonly held belief. Through meticulous organizing campaigns, Asian American activists created an extensive network of grassroots formations. Unlike similar groups in African American communities—which government repression targeted and brutally destroyed—a significant number of Asian American groups survived the 1980s. Thus far, no researcher has analyzed the impact of the corporate offensive and government repression on grassroots organizations in different communities of color during the late 1970s. When this research is done, I think it will show that U.S. ruling elites viewed the movement in the African American community as a major threat due to its power and influence over other communities. In contrast, the movement in the Asian American community received much less attention due to its much smaller size and influence. As a result, Asian American grassroots formations during the 1970s escaped decimation and gained the time and space to survive, grow, and adapt to changing politics.

The survival of grassroots organizations is significant because it helped to cushion the impact of the war against the poor in Asian American communities. More important, the grassroots formations provided the foundation for many of the successful empowerment campaigns occurring in the 1980s. For example, Japanese Americans built their national effort to win reparations for their internment during World War II on the experiences of grassroots neighborhood organizations' housing and anti-eviction struggles of the early 1970s. Movement activists learned from their confrontations with systems of power and applied these lessons to the more difficult political fights of the 1980s. Thus, a direct link exists between the mass struggles of activists in the late 1960s and the "empowerment" approach of Asian Americans in the 1980s and 1990s.

But while similarities exist in political organizing of the late 1960s and the 1980s, there is one crucial difference: who is being empowered? In the late 1960s and 1970s, activists focused on bringing "power to the people"—the most disenfranchised of the community, such as low-income workers, youth, former prisoners and addicts, senior citizens, tenants, and small-business people. In contrast, the "empowerment" of young professionals in Asian American communities marks the decade of the 1980s. The professionals—children of the civil rights struggles of the 1950s and 1960s—directly benefited from the campaigns for desegregation, especially in the suburbs; the removal of quotas in colleges and professional schools; and the expansion of job opportunities for middle-class people of color in fields such as law, medicine, and education.

During the 1980s, young professionals altered the political terrain in our communities.[24] They created countless new groups in nearly every profession: law, medicine, social work, psychology, education, journalism, business, and arts and culture. They initiated new political advocacy groups, leadership training projects, and various national coalitions and consortiums. They organized political caucuses in the Democratic and Republican parties. And they joined the governing boards of many community agencies. Thus, young professionals—through their sheer numbers, their penchant for self-organization, and their high level of activity—defined the Asian American community of the 1980s, shaping it in ways very different from other communities of color.

The emergence of young professionals as community leaders also aided mass political mobilizations. By combining with grassroots forces from the Asian American movement, young professionals advanced struggles against racism and discrimination. In fact, many of the successful Asian American battles of the past decade resulted from this strategic alignment.

The growing power of young professionals has also brought a diversification of political viewpoints to our communities. While many professionals embrace concerns originally raised by movement activists, a surprisingly large number have moved toward neoconservatism. The emergence of neoconservatism in our community is a fascinating phenomenon, one we should analyze and appreciate. Perhaps more than any other phenomenon, it helps to explain the political ambiguity of Asian American empowerment in the 1980s.

STRANGE AND NEW POLITICAL ANIMALS: ASIAN AMERICAN NEO-CONSERVATIVES

Item: At many universities in recent years, some of the harshest opponents of affirmative action have been Chinese Americans and Korean Americans who define themselves as political conservatives. This, in and of itself, is not new or significant. We have always had Asian American conservatives who have spoken out against affirmative action. But what is new is their affiliation. Many participate actively in Asian American student organizations traditionally associated with campus activism.

Item: In the San Francisco newspaper *Asian Week*, one of the most interesting columnists is Arthur Hu, who writes about anti-Asian quotas in universities, political empowerment, and other issues relating to our communities. He also regularly chastises those he terms "liberals, progressives, Marxists, and activists." In a recent column, he wrote: "The left today has the nerve to blame AIDS, drugs, the dissolution of the family, welfare dependency, gang violence, and educational failure on Ronald Reagan's conservatism." Hu, in turn, criticizes the Left for "tearing down religion, family, structure, and authority; promoting drugs, promiscuity, and abdication of personal responsibility."[25]

Item: During the militant, three-year campaign to win tenure for UCLA Professor Don Nakanishi, one of the key student leaders was a Japanese American Republican, Matthew J. Endo. Aside from joining the campus-community steering committee, he also mobilized support from fraternities, something that progressive activists could not do. Matt prides himself on being a Republican and a life member of the National Rifle Association. He aspires to become a CEO in a corporation but worries about the upsurge in racism against Asian Pacific peoples and the failure of both Republicans and Democrats to address this issue.

The Asian American neoconservatives are a new and interesting political phenomenon. They are new because they are creatures born from the Reagan-Bush era of supply-side economics, class and racial polarization, and the emphasis on elitism and individual advancement. And they are interesting because they also represent a legacy from the civil rights struggles, especially the Asian American movement. The neoconservatives embody these seemingly contradictory origins.

- They are proud to be Asian American. But they denounce the Asian American movement of the late 1960s and early 1970s as destructive.
- They speak out against racism against Asian Americans. But they believe that only by ending affirmative action programs and breaking with prevailing civil rights thinking of the past four decades can we end racism.
- They express concern for Asian American community issues. But they contend that the agenda set by the "liberal Asian American establishment" ignores community needs.
- They vehemently oppose quotas blocking admissions of Asian Americans at colleges and universities. But they link anti-Asian quotas to affirmative action programs for "less qualified" African Americans, Latinos, and American Indians.
- They acknowledge the continuing discrimination against African Americans, Latinos, and American Indians in U.S. society. But they believe that the main barrier blocking advancement for other people of color is "cultural"—that unlike Asians, these groups supposedly come from cultures that do not sufficiently emphasize education, family cohesion, and traditional values.

Where did these neoconservatives come from? What do they represent? And why is it important for progressive people to understand their presence?

Progressives cannot dismiss Asian American neoconservatives as simple-minded Republicans. Although they hold views similar at times to Patrick Buchanan and William Buckley, they are not clones of white conservatives. Nor are they racists, fellow travelers of the Ku Klux Klan, or ideologues attached to Reagan and Bush. Perhaps the group they most resemble are the African American neoconservatives: the Shelby Steeles, Clarence Thomases, and Tony Browns of this period. Like these men, they are professionals and feel little kinship for people of lower classes. Like these men, they oppose prevailing civil rights thinking, emphasizing reliance on government intervention and social programs. And like these men, they have gained from affirmative action, but they now believe that America has somehow become a society where other people of color can advance through their own "qualifications."

Neoconservative people of color have embraced thinkers such as the late Martin Luther King Jr., but have appropriated his message to fit their own ideology. In his speeches and writings, King dreamed of the day when racism would be eliminated—when African Americans would be recognized in U.S. society for the "content of our character, not the color of our skin." He called upon all in America to wage militant struggle to achieve this dream. Today, neoconservatives have subverted his message. They believe that racism in U.S. society has declined in significance, and that people of color can now abandon mass militancy and advance individually by cultivating the content of their character through self-help programs and educational attainment, and retrieving traditional family values. They criticize prevailing "civil rights thinking" as overemphasizing the barriers of racism and relying on "external forces" (i.e., government intervention through social programs) to address the problem.

Asian American neoconservatives closely resemble their African American counterparts in their criticism of government "entitlement" programs and their defense of traditional culture and family values. But Asian American neoconservatives are not exactly the same as their African American counterparts. The growth of neoconservative thinking among Asian Americans during the past 25 years reflects the peculiar conditions in our community, notably the emerging power of young professionals. Thus, to truly understand Asian American neoconservatives, we need to look at their evolution through the prism of Asian American politics from the late 1960s to the early 1990s.

Twenty-five years ago, Asian American neoconservatives did not exist. Our community then had only traditional conservatives—those who opposed ethnic studies, the antiwar movement, and other militant grassroots struggles. The traditional conservatives denounced Asian American concerns as "special interest politics" and labeled the assertion of Asian American ethnic identity as "separatist" thinking. For the traditional conservative, a basic contradiction existed in identifying oneself as Asian American and conservative.

Ironically, the liberation struggles of the 1960s—and the accompanying Asian American movement—spawned a new conservative thinker. The movement partially transformed the educational curriculum through ethnic studies, enabling all Asian Americans to assert pride in their ethnic heritage. The movement accelerated the desegregation of suburbs, enabling middle-class Asian Americans to move into all-white neighborhoods. Today, the neoconservatives are mostly young, middle-class professionals who grew up in white suburbs apart from the poor and people of color. As students, they attended the elite universities. Their only experience with racism is name-calling or "glass ceilings" blocking personal career advancement—and not poverty and violence.

It is due to their professional status and their roots in the Asian American movement that the neoconservatives exist in uneasy alliance with traditional conservatives in our community. Neoconservatives are appalled by the violence and rabid anticommunism of reactionary sectors of the Vietnamese community, Chinese from Taiwan tied to the oppressive ruling Kuomintang party, and Korean expatriates attached to the Korean Central Intelligence Agency. They are also uncomfortable with older conservatives, those coming from small-business backgrounds who eye the neoconservatives warily, considering them political opportunists.

Neoconservatives differ from traditional conservatives not only because of their youth and their professional status but most important of all, their political coming of age in the Reagan era. Like their African American counterparts, they are children of the corporate offensive against workers, the massive transfer of resources from the poor to the rich, and the rebirth of so-called "traditional values."

It is their schooling in Reaganomics and their willingness to defend the current structure of power and privilege in America that gives neoconservative people of color value in today's political landscape. Thus, Manning Marable describes the key role played by African American neoconservatives:

> The singular service that [they] . . . provide is a new and more accurate understanding of what exactly constitutes conservatism within the Black experience. . . . Black conservatives are traditionally hostile to Black participation in trade unions, and urge a close cooperation with white business leaders. Hostile to the welfare state, they call for increased "self-help" programs run by Blacks at local and community levels. Conservatives often accept the institutionalized forms of patriarchy, acknowledging a secondary role for Black women within economics, political life and intellectual work. They usually have a pronounced bias toward organizational authoritarianism and theoretical rigidity.[26]

Marable's analysis points to the basic contradiction for African American neoconservatives. They are unable to address fundamental problems facing their community: racist violence, grinding poverty, and the unwillingness of corporate and government policymakers to deal with these issues.

Asian American neoconservatives face similar difficulties when confronted by the stark realities of the post-Reagan period:

- The neoconservatives acknowledge continuing discrimination in U.S. society but deny the existence of institutional racism and structural inequality. For them, racism lies in the realm of attitudes and "culture" and not institutions of power. Thus, they emphasize individual advancement as the way to overcome racism. They believe that people of color can rise through merit, which they contend can be measured objectively through tests, grades, and educational attainment.
- The neoconservatives ignore questions of wealth and privilege in American society. In their obsession with "merit," "qualifications," and "objective" criteria, they lose sight of power and oppression in America. Their focus is on dismantling affirmative action programs and "government entitlements" from the civil rights era. But poverty and racism existed long before the civil rights movement. They are embedded in the system of inequality that has long characterized U.S. society.
- The neoconservatives are essentially elitists who fear expansion of democracy at the grassroots level. They speak a language of individual advancement, not mass empowerment. They propose a strategy of alignment with existing centers of power and not the creation of new power bases among the disenfranchised sectors of society. Their message is directed to professionals, much like themselves. They have nothing to offer to immigrant workers in sweatshops, the homeless, Cambodian youth in street gangs, or community college youth.
- As relative newcomers to Asian American issues, the neoconservatives lack understanding of history, especially how concerns in the community have

developed over time. Although they aggressively speak out about issues, they lack experience in organizing around these issues. The neoconservatives function best in the realm of ideas; they have difficulty dealing with concrete situations.

However, by stimulating discussion of how Asian Americans define community problems, the neoconservatives bring a vibrancy to community issues by contributing a different viewpoint. Thus, the debate between Asian American neoconservatives and progressives is positive because it clarifies issues and enables both groups to reach constituencies that each could not otherwise reach.

Unfortunately, this debate is also occurring in a larger and more dangerous context: the campaign by mainstream conservatives to redefine civil rights in America. As part of their strategy, conservatives in the national political arena have targeted our communities. There are high stakes here, and conservatives regard the Asian American neoconservatives as small players to be sacrificed.

The high stakes are evident in an article by William McGurn entitled "The Silent Minority" appearing in the conservative digest *National Review*.[27] In his essay, he urges Republicans to actively recruit and incorporate Asian Americans into party activities. According to McGurn, a basic affinity exists between Republican values and Asian American values: many Asian immigrants own small businesses; they oppose communism; they are fiercely pro-defense; they boast strong families; they value freedom; and in their approach to civil rights, they stress opportunities not government "set-asides." McGurn then chastises fellow Republicans for their "crushing indifference" to Asian American issues. He laments how Republicans have lost opportunities by not speaking out on key issues such as the conflict between Korean immigrant merchants and African Americans, the controversy over anti-Asian quotas in universities, and the upsurge in anti-Asian violence.

McGurn sees Republican intervention on these issues strategically—as a way of redefining the race question in American society and shifting the debate on civil rights away from reliance on "an increasingly narrow band of black and liberal interest groups." According to McGurn:

> Precisely because Asian Americans are making it in their adoptive land, they hold the potential not only to add to Republican rolls but to define a bona-fide American language of civil rights. Today we have only one language of civil rights, and it is inextricably linked to government intervention, from racial quotas to set-aside government contracts. It is also an exclusively black-establishment language, where America's myriad other minorities are relegated to second-class citizenship.[28]

McGurn's article presages a period of intense and unprecedented conservative interest in Asian American issues. We can expect conservative commentaries to intensify black-Asian conflicts in inner cities, the controversy over affirmative action, and the internal community debate over designating Asian Americans as a "model minority."

Thus, in the coming period, Asian American communities are likely to become crowded places. Unlike the late 1960s, issues affecting our communities will no longer be the domain of progressive forces only. Increasingly, we will hear viewpoints from Asian American neoconservatives as well as mainstream conservatives. How well will activists meet this new challenge?

GRASSROOTS ORGANIZING IN THE 1990s: THE CHALLENGE OF EXPANDING DEMOCRACY

> *Time would pass, old empires would fall and new ones take their place, the relations of countries and the relations of classes had to change, before I discovered that it is not quality of goods and utility which matter, but movement; not where you are or what you have, but where you have come from, where you are going and the rate at which you are getting there.*[29]
> —C.L.R. JAMES

On the eve of the twenty-first century, the Asian American community is vastly different from that of the late 1960s. The community has grown dramatically. In 1970, there were only 1.5 million Asian Americans, almost entirely concentrated in Hawai'i and California. By 1980, there were 3.7 million, and in 1990, 7.9 million—with major Asian communities in New York, Minnesota, Pennsylvania, and Texas. According to census projections, the Asian American population should exceed 10 million by the year 2000, and will reach 20 million by the year 2020.[30]

Moreover, in contrast to the late 1960s—when Chinese and Japanese Americans made up the majority of Asian Americans—today's community is ethnically diverse, consisting of nearly thirty major ethnic groups, each with a distinct culture. Today's community is also economically different from the 1960s. Compared to other sectors of the U.S. population, there are higher proportions of Asian Americans who are very rich and very poor. This gap between wealth and poverty has created a sharp class polarization in our community, a phenomenon yet to be studied.

But the changes for Asian Americans during the past twenty-five years have not been simply demographic. The political landscape has also changed due to new immigrants and refugees, the polarization between rich and poor, and the emergence of young professionals as a vital new force. Following the approach of C.L.R. James, we have traced the origins of these changes. We now need to analyze where these changes will take us in the decade ahead.

Ideologically and politically, activists confront a new and interesting paradox in the Asian American community of the 1990s. On the one hand, there is a great upsurge of interest in the community and all things Asian American. Almost daily, we hear about new groups forming across the country. In contrast to twenty-five years ago, when interest in the community was minimal and when only progressive activists joined Asian American organizations, we now find a situation where many different groups—including conservatives and neoconservatives, bankers and business executives, and young professionals in all fields—have taken up the banner of Asian American identity.

On the other hand, we have not seen a corresponding growth in consciousness—of what it means to be Asian American as we approach the twenty-first century. Unlike African Americans, most Asian Americans today have yet to articulate the "particularities" of issues affecting our community, whether these

be the debate over affirmative action, the controversy regarding multiculturalism, or the very definition of empowerment. We have an ideological vacuum,
and activists will compete with neoconservatives, mainstream conservatives, and
others to fill it.

We have a political vacuum as well. In recent years, growing numbers of Asian
Americans have become involved in community issues. But almost all have come
from middle-class and professional backgrounds. Meanwhile, vast segments of
our community are not coming forward. In fact, during the past decade the fundamental weakness for activists has been the lack of grassroots organizing among
the disenfranchised sectors of our community: youth outside of colleges and universities, the poor, and new immigrant workers. Twenty-five years ago, the greatest strength of the Asian American movement was the ability of activists to
organize the unorganized and to bring new political players into community politics. Activists targeted high school youth, tenants, small-business people, former
prison inmates, gang members, the elderly, and workers. Activists helped them
build new grassroots organizations, expanding power and democracy in our
communities. Can a new generation of activists do the same?

To respond to this challenge, activists will need both a political strategy and
a new ideological vision. Politically, activists must find ways to expand democracy by creating new grassroots formations, activating new political players, and
building new coalitions. Ideologically, activists must forge a new moral vision,
reclaiming the militancy and moral urgency of past generations and reaffirming
the commitment to participatory democracy, community building, and collective styles of leadership.

Where will this political strategy and new consciousness come from? More
than fifty years ago, revolutionary leader Mao Zedong asked a similar question:

> Where do correct ideas come from? Do they drop from the skies? No. Are they innate
> in the mind? No. They come from social practice, and from it alone. . . . In their social
> practice, people engage in various kinds of struggle and gain rich experience, both
> from their successes and their failures.[31]

In the current "social practice" of Asian American activists across the nation,
several grassroots organizing projects can serve as the basis for a political strategy and new moral vision for the 1990s. I will focus on three projects that are
concentrating on the growing numbers of poor and working poor in our community. Through their grassroots efforts, these three groups are demonstrating
how collective power can expand democracy, and how, in the process, activists
can forge a new moral vision.

The three groups—the Chinese Progressive Association (CPA) Workers
Center in Boston, Asian Immigrant Women Advocates (AIWA) in Oakland, and
Korean Immigrant Worker Advocates (KIWA) in Los Angeles—address local
needs. Although each organization works with different ethnic groups, their history of organizing has remarkable similarities. Each organization is composed
of low-income immigrant workers. Each has taken up more than "labor" issues.
And each group has fashioned very effective "united front" campaigns involving

other sectors of the community. Thus, although each project is relatively small, collectively their accomplishments illustrate the power of grassroots organizing, the creativity and talents of "ordinary" people in taking up difficult issues, and the ability of grassroots forces to alter the political landscape of their community. Significantly, the focus of each group is working people in the Asian American community—a sector that is numerically large and growing larger. However, despite their numbers, workers in the Asian American community during the past decade have become voiceless and silent. Today, in discussions about community issues, no one places garment workers, nurses' aides, waiters, and secretaries at the forefront of the debate to define priorities. And no one thinks about the working class as the cutting edge of the Asian American experience. Yet, if we begin to list the basic questions now confronting Asian Americans—racism and sexism, economic justice and human rights, coalition building, and community empowerment—we would find that it is the working class, of all sectors in our community, that is making the most interesting breakthroughs on these questions. They are doing this through groups such as KIWA, AIWA, and the CPA Workers Center. Why, then, are the voices of workers submerged in our community? Why has the working class become silent?

Three trends have pushed labor issues in our community into the background during the past two decades: the rising power of young professionals in our community; the influx of new immigrants and refugees, and the fascination of social scientists and policy institutes with the phenomenon of immigrant entrepreneurship; and the lack of grassroots organizing by activists among new immigrant workers.

Thus, although the majority of Asian Americans work for a living, we have relatively little understanding about the central place of work in the lives of Asian Americans, especially in low-income industries such as garment work, restaurant work, clerical and office work, and other service occupations. Moreover, we are ignorant about the role labor struggles have played in shaping our history.[32] This labor history is part of the legacy that activists must reclaim.

In contrast to the lack of knowledge about Asian American workers, we have a much greater understanding about the role of young professionals, students, and, most of all, small-business people. In fact, immigrant entrepreneurs, especially Korean immigrants, are perhaps the most studied people of our community. However, as sociologist Edna Bonacich notes, the profile of most Asian immigrant entrepreneurs closely resembles that of workers, due to their low earning power, their long work hours, and their lack of job-related benefits. Thus, Bonacich suggests that while the world outlook of Asian immigrant entrepreneurs may be petit bourgeoisie, their life conditions are those of the working class and might better be studied as a "labor" question. Asian immigrant small businesses, she contends, play the role of "cheap labor in American capitalism."[33]

Other researchers have only begun to investigate the extent of poverty among Asian Americans and the meaning of poverty for our community. In California, the rate of poverty for Asian Americans rose from about 10 percent in 1980 to 18 percent in 1990. But more important, researchers found that there are higher numbers of "working poor" (as opposed to "jobless poor") in the Asian American community than for other ethnic groups. Thus, in contrast to other Americans, Asian Americans are poor not because they lack jobs but because the jobs they have pay very low wages. According to researchers Dean Toji and James Johnson Jr., "Perhaps contrary to common belief, about half of the poor work—including about a quarter of poor adults who work full-time and year-round. Poverty, then, is a labor question."[34]

Activists in groups such as KIWA, AIWA, and the CPA Workers Center are strategically focusing on the "working poor" in the Asian American community. KIWA—which was founded in 1992—is working with low-income Korean immigrants in Los Angeles Koreatown, including garment workers and employees in small businesses. AIWA—founded in 1983—organizes Chinese garment workers, Vietnamese garment and electronics workers, and Korean hotel maids and electronics assemblers. And the CPA Workers Center—which traces its roots to the landmark struggle of Chinese garment workers in Boston in 1985—is composed primarily of Chinese immigrant women. Although their main focus is on workers, each group has also mobilized students and social service providers to support their campaigns. Through these alliances, each group has carried out successful community organizing strategies.

The focus of the three groups on community-based organizing distinguishes them from traditional unions. Miriam Ching Louie of AIWA explains this distinction:

> AIWA's base is simultaneously worker, female, Asian, and immigrant, and the organization has developed by blending together several different organizing techniques. As compared to the traditional union organizing strategy, AIWA's approach focuses on the needs of its constituency. *Popular literacy / conscientization / transformation* [based on the teachings of Paulo Freire] is a learning and teaching method which taps into people's life experiences as part of a broader reality, source of knowledge, and guide to action. *Community-based organizing* takes a holistic view of racial/ethnic people and organizes for social change, not only so that the people can win immediate improvements in their lives, but so that they can also develop their own power in the course of waging the fight.[35]

AIWA's focus on grassroots organizing is illustrated by its "Garment Workers' Justice Campaign," launched in late 1992 to assist Chinese immigrant women who were denied pay by a garment contractor. AIWA organizers shaped the campaign to respond to the peculiar features of the garment industry. The industry in the San Francisco Bay Area is the nation's third largest—behind New York and Los Angeles—and employs some 20,000 seamstresses, 85 percent of them Asian immigrant women. The structure of the industry is a pyramid with retailers and manufacturers at the top, contractors in the middle, and immigrant women working at the bottom. Manufacturers make the main share of profits in the industry; they set the price for contractors. Meanwhile, immigrant women work under sweatshop conditions.

In their campaign, AIWA and the workers initially confronted the contractor for the workers' back pay. When they discovered that the contractor owed a number of creditors, they took the unusual step of holding the garment manufacturer, Jessica McClintock, accountable for the unpaid wages. McClintock operates ten boutiques and sells dresses through department stores. The dresses—which garment workers are paid $5 to make—retail in stores for $175. AIWA and the workers conducted their campaign through a series of high-profile demonstrations at McClintock boutiques, including picket lines and rallies in ten cities by supporters. AIWA designed these demonstrations not only to put pressure on McClintock and educate others in the community about inequities in the structure of the garment industry, but also to serve as vehicles for empowerment for the immigrant women participating in the campaign. Through this campaign, the women workers learned how to confront institutional power, how to forge alliances with other groups in the community, and how to carry out effective tactics based on their collective power.[36]

Thus, through its activities promoting immigrant women's rights, AIWA is expanding democracy in the community. It is bringing labor issues to the forefront of community discussions. It is creating new grassroots caucuses among previously unorganized sectors of the community, and forming new political alignments with supporters, such as students, young professionals, labor unions, and social service providers. Finally, AIWA is developing a cadre of politically sophisticated immigrant women and promoting a new leadership style based on popular literacy, community building, and collective power.

Similarly, in Boston, the CPA Workers Center is expanding democracy through its grassroots efforts around worker rights. The Center emerged out of the Chinese immigrant women's campaign to deal with the closing of a large garment factory in Boston in 1985.[37] The shutdown displaced 350 workers and had a severe impact on the local Chinese community due to the community's high concentration of jobs in the garment industry. However, with the assistance of the Chinese Progressive Alliance, the workers formed a labor-community-student coalition and waged an 18-month campaign to win job retraining and job replacement. Lydia Lowe, director of the CPA Workers Center, describes how the victory of Chinese immigrant women led to creation of the Workers Center, which, in turn, has helped other workplace campaigns in the Chinese community:

> This core of women activated through the campaign joined with community supporters from the CPA to found a community-based workers' mutual aid and resource center, based at CPA. . . . Through the Workers Center, immigrant workers share their experience, collectively sum up lessons learned, find out about their rights, and develop mutual support and organizing strategies. Today, the Workers Center involves immigrant workers from each of its successive organizing efforts, and is a unique place in the community where ordinary workers can walk in and participate as activists and decision-makers.[38]

Moreover, forming the Workers Center reshaped politics in the local Chinese community, turning garment workers and other immigrant laborers into active political players. "Previously the silent majority, immigrant workers are gaining increasing respect as a force to be reckoned with in the local Chinese community," states Lowe.

In Los Angeles, the formation of KIWA in March 1992—only a month before the uprisings—has had a similar impact. Through its programs, KIWA is bringing labor issues to the forefront of the Asian American community, educating labor unions about the needs of Asian American workers, and forming coalitions with other grassroots forces in the city to deal with interethnic tensions. KIWA is uniquely positioned to take up these tasks. Out of the multitude of Asian American organizations in Los Angeles, KIWA distinguishes itself as the only organization governed by a board of directors of mainly workers.

KIWA's key role in the labor movement and community politics is evident in the recent controversy involving the Koreana Wilshire Hotel.[39] The controversy began in late 1991 when Koreana Hotel Co. Ltd., a South Korean corporation, bought the Wilshire Hyatt in Los Angeles. The change in ownership meant that 175 unionized members, predominantly Latino immigrants, were out of jobs. Meanwhile, the new hotel management hired a new work force, paying them an average of $1.50 per hour less than the former unionized work force. The former workers, represented by Hotel Employees and Restaurant Employees (HERE) Local 11, called upon labor unions and groups from the Asian American, African American, and Latino communities to protest Koreana's union-busting efforts. Local 11 defined the dispute as not only a labor issue, but a civil rights issue. With the help of groups such as KIWA and the Asian Pacific American Labor Alliance, Local 11 initiated a letter-writing campaign against Koreana, began a community boycott of the hotel, and organized militant actions outside the hotel, including rallies, marches, and a picket line, as well as civil disobedience at the nearby Korean consulate. In each of these actions, Local 11 worked closely with KIWA and members of the Asian American community. Due to the mass pressure, in late 1992 the Koreana management agreed to negotiate with Local 11 to end the controversy and rehire the union members.

Throughout the campaign, KIWA played a pivotal role by helping Local 11 build alliances with the Asian American community. In addition, KIWA members promoted labor consciousness in the Korean community by urging the community to boycott the hotel. KIWA members also spoke at Local 11 rallies, mobilized for picket lines, and worked with the union in its efforts to put pressure on the South Korean government. By taking these steps, KIWA prevented the controversy from pitting the Korean community against Latinos and further inflaming interethnic tensions in Los Angeles.

Also, through campaigns such as this one, KIWA is educating Asian immigrants about unions; training workers around the tasks of political leadership; and creating new centers of power in the community by combining the resources of workers, young professionals, and social service providers.

Thus, through grassroots organizing, KIWA—like AIWA and the CPA Workers Center—is expanding democracy in the Asian American community. Moreover, the three groups collectively are reshaping community consciousness. They are sharpening debate and dialogue around issues and redefining such important concepts as empowerment. What is their vision of empowerment, and how does it differ from prevailing definitions?

THE TWENTY-FIRST CENTURY: BUILDING AN ASIAN AMERICAN MOVEMENT

[A] movement is an idea, a philosophy. . . . Leadership, I feel, is only incidental to the movement. The movement should be the most important thing. The movement must go beyond its leaders. It must be something that is continuous, with goals and ideas that the leadership can then build on.[40]

—PHILIP VERA CRUZ

In the late 1960s, Asian American activists sought to forge a new approach to leadership that would not replicate traditional Eurocentric models—i.e., rigid hierarchies with a single executive at the top, invariably a white male, who commanded an endless chain of assistants. In their search for alternatives, activists experimented with various ideas borrowed from other movements, but most of all, activists benefited from the advice and guidance of "elders" within the Asian American community—women and men with years of grassroots organizing experience in the community, the workplace, and the progressive political movement. One such "elder" was Pilipino immigrant labor leader Philip Vera Cruz, then in his sixties. Vera Cruz represented the *manong* generation—the first wave of Pilipinos who came to the United States in the early twentieth century and worked in agricultural fields, canneries, hotels, and restaurants.

Now eighty-eight years old, Vera Cruz continues to educate a new generation of activists. His lifetime of experience in grassroots organizing embodies the historic themes of Asian American activism: devotion to the rights of working people, commitment to democracy and liberation, steadfast solidarity with all who face oppression throughout the world, and the courage to challenge existing institutions of power and to create new institutions as the need arises. These themes have defined his life and shaped his approach to the question of empowerment—an approach that is different from standard definitions in our community today.

Vera Cruz is best known for his role in building the United Farm Workers (UFW), a culmination of his many years of organizing in agricultural fields. In 1965, he was working with the Agricultural Workers Organizing Committee, AFLCIO, when Pilipino farmworkers sat down in the Coachella vineyards of central California. This sit-down launched the famous grape strike and boycott, eventually leading to the formation of the UFW. Many books and articles have told the story of the UFW and its leader, Cesar Chavez. But until recently, no one has focused on the historic role of Pilipinos in building this movement. Craig Scharlin and Lilia Villanueva have filled that vacuum with their new publication about Vera Cruz's life.

Following the successful grape boycott, Vera Cruz became a UFW vice president and remained with the union until 1977, when he left due to political differences with the leadership. He was critical of the lack of rank-and-file democracy in the union, and of the leadership's embrace of the Marcos dictatorship in the Philippines. Since 1979, Vera Cruz has lived in Bakersfield, California, and has continued to devote his life to unionism and social justice, and to the education of a new generation of Asian American youth.

Vera Cruz's life experiences have shaped a broad view of empowerment. For Vera Cruz, empowerment is grassroots power: the expansion of democracy for the many. Becoming empowered means gaining the capacity to advocate not only for one's own concerns but for the liberation of all oppressed peoples. Becoming empowered means being able to change fundamentally the relationship of power and oppression in society. Thus, Vera Cruz's vision is very different from that of today's young professionals. For them, empowerment is leadership development for an elite. Becoming empowered means gaining the skills to advocate for the community by gaining access to decision makers. Thus, for young professionals, the key leadership quality to develop is assertiveness. Through assertiveness, leaders gain access to policy makers as well as the power to mobilize their followers. In contrast, Vera Cruz stresses the leadership trait of humility. For him, leaders are "only incidental to the movement"—the movement is "the most important thing." For Vera Cruz, empowerment is a process where people join to develop goals and ideas to create a larger movement—a movement "that the leadership can then build on."

Vera Cruz's understanding of empowerment has evolved from his own social practice. Through his experiences in the UFW and the AFL-CIO, Vera Cruz learned about the empty democracy of bureaucratic unions and the limitations of the charismatic leadership style of Cesar Chavez. Through his years of toil as a farmworker, he recognized the importance of worker solidarity and militancy and the capacity of common people to create alternative institutions of grassroots power. Through his work with Pilipino and Mexican immigrants, he saw the necessity of coalition-building and worker unity that crossed ethnic and racial boundaries. He has shared these lessons with several generations of Asian American activists.

But aside from sharing a concept of empowerment, Vera Cruz has also promoted a larger moral vision, placing his lifetime of political struggle in the framework of the movement for liberation. Three keywords distinguish his moral vision: "compassion," "solidarity," and "commitment." Vera Cruz's lifetime of action represents compassion for all victims of oppression, solidarity with all fighting for liberation, and commitment to the ideals of democracy and social justice.

Activists today need to learn from Vera Cruz's compassion, solidarity, commitment, and humility to create a new moral vision for our community. In our grassroots organizing, we need a vision that can redefine empowerment—that can bring questions of power, domination, and liberation to the forefront of our work. We need a vision that can help us respond to the challenge of conservatives and neoconservatives, and sharpen dialogue with young professionals. We need a new moral vision that can help fill the ideological vacuum in today's community.

Nowhere is this ideological challenge greater than in the current debate over the model minority stereotype. This stereotype has become the dominant image of Asian Americans for mainstream society, and has generated intense debate among all sectors of our community. This debate provides an opportunity for activists to expand political awareness and, in the process, redefine the Asian American experience for the 1990s.

In the current controversy, however, activists criticize the model minority stereotype politically but not ideologically. Activists correctly target how the concept fails to deal with Asian American realities: the growing population of poor and working poor, the large numbers of youth who are not excelling in school, and the hardships and family problems of small-business people who are not "making it" in U.S. society. Activists also correctly point out the political ramifications of the model minority stereotype: the pitting of minority groups against each other, and growing interethnic tensions in U.S. society. In contrast, conservative and neoconservative proponents of the model minority concept argue from the standpoint of both political realities and a larger moral vision. They highlight Asian American accomplishments: "whiz kids" in elementary schools; growing numbers of Asian Americans in business, politics, and the professions; and the record enrollment of youth in colleges and universities. Conservatives and neoconservatives attribute these accomplishments to Asian culture and tradition, respect for authority, family cohesion, sacrifice and toil, rugged individualism, and self-reliance—moral values they root in conservative thinking. Conservatives and neoconservatives recognize that "facts" gain power from attachment to ideologies. As a result, they appropriate Asian culture and values to promote their arguments.

But is Asian culture inherently conservative—or does it also have a tradition of militancy and liberation? Do sacrifice, toil, and family values fit with a conservative moral vision only—or do these qualities also constitute the core of radical and revolutionary thinking? By asking these questions, activists can push the debate over the model minority concept to a new, ideological level. Moreover, by focusing on ideology, activists can delve into the stereotype's deeper meaning. They can help others understand the stereotype's origins and why it has become the dominant image for Asian Americans today.

Historically, the model minority stereotype first arose in the late 1950s—the creation of sociologists attempting to explain low levels of juvenile delinquency among Chinese and Japanese Americans.[41] The stereotype remained a social-science construct until the 1960s when a few conservative political commentators began to use it to contrast Asian Americans' "respect for law and order" with African Americans' involvement in civil rights marches, rallies, and sit-ins. By the late 1970s, the stereotype moved into the political mainstream, coinciding with the influx of new Asian immigrants into all parts of the United States. But the widespread acceptance of the stereotype was not simply due to the increase in the Asian American population or the new attention focused on our community from mainstream institutions. More importantly, it coincided with the rise of the New Right and the corporate offensive against the poor. As discussed earlier, this offensive economically devastated poor communities and stripped away hard-won political gains. It also included an ideological campaign designed to restore trust in capitalism and values associated with free enterprise. Meanwhile, conservatives and neoconservatives fought to redefine the language of civil rights by attacking federal government "entitlement" programs while criticizing the African American "liberal establishment."

In this political climate, the model minority stereotype flourished. It symbolized the moral vision of capitalism in the 1980s: a celebration of traditional values, an emphasis on hard work and self-reliance, a respect for authority, and an attack on prevailing civil rights thinking associated with the African American community. Thus, the stereotype took on an ideological importance above and beyond the Asian American community. The hard-working immigrant merchant and the refugee student winning the local spelling bee have become the symbols for the resurrection of capitalist values in the last part of the twentieth century.

Yet, we know a gap exists between symbol and reality. Today, capitalism in America is not about small-business activities; it is about powerful transnational corporations and their intricate links to nation-states and the world capitalist system. Capitalist values no longer revolve around hard work and self-reliance; they deal with wealth and assets, and the capacity of the rich to invest, speculate, and obtain government contracts. And the fruits of capitalism in the last part of the twentieth century are not immigrant entrepreneurship and the revival of urban areas; they are more likely to be low-paying jobs, unemployment, bankruptcies, and homelessness.

However, as corporations, banks, and other institutions abandon the inner city, the immigrant merchant—especially the Korean small-business person—emerges as the main symbol of capitalism in these neighborhoods. For inner city residents, the Asian immigrant becomes the target for their wrath against corporate devastation of their neighborhoods. Moreover, as this symbol merges with other historical stereotypes of Asians, the result is highly charged imagery, which perhaps underlies the ferocity of anti-Asian violence in this period, such as the destruction of Korean small businesses during the Los Angeles uprisings. The Asian immigrant becomes a symbol of wealth—and also greed; a symbol of hard work—and also materialism; a symbol of intelligence—and also arrogance; a symbol of self-reliance—and also selfishness and lack of community concern. Thus, today the model minority stereotype has become a complex symbol through the confluence of many images imposed on us by social scientists, the New Right, and the urban policies of corporate and political elites.

Pioneer Korean immigrant journalist K. W. Lee—another of our Asian American "elders"—worries about how the melding of symbols, images, and stereotypes is shaping the perception of our community, especially among other people of color. "We are not seen as a compassionate people," states Lee. "Others see us as smart, hard-working, and good at making money—but not as sharing with others. We are not seen as a people who march at the forefront of the struggle for civil rights or the campaign to end poverty."[42] Like Philip Vera Cruz, Lee believes that Asian Americans must retrieve a heritage of compassion and solidarity from our past and use these values to construct a new moral vision for our future. Asian Americans must cast off the images imposed on us by others.

Thus, as we approach the end of the twentieth century, activists are confronted with a task similar to that confronting activists in the late 1960s: the need to redefine the Asian American experience. And as an earlier generation discovered, redefining means more than ethnic awakening. It means confronting the fundamental questions of power and domination in U.S. society. It means expanding democracy and community consciousness. It means liberating ourselves from the prisons still surrounding our lives.

In our efforts to redefine the Asian American experience, activists will have the guidance and help of elders like K. W. Lee and Philip Vera Cruz. And we can also draw from the rich legacy of struggle of other liberation movements.

In closing this chapter, I want to quote from two great teachers from the 1960s: Malcolm X and Martin Luther King Jr. Their words and actions galvanized the consciousness of one generation of youth, and their message of compassion continues to speak to a new generation in the 1990s.

Since their assassinations in the mid-1960s, however, mainstream commentators have stereotyped the two men and often pitted one against the other. They portray Malcolm X as the angry black separatist who advocated violence and hatred against white people. Meanwhile, they make Martin Luther King Jr. the messenger of love and nonviolence. In the minds of most Americans, both men—in the words of historian Manning Marable—are "frozen in time."[43]

But as Marable and other African American historians note, both King and Malcolm evolved, and became very different men in the years before their assassinations. Both men came to see the African American struggle in the United States in a worldwide context, as part of the revolutionary stirrings and mass uprisings happening across the globe. Both men became internationalists, strongly condemning U.S. exploitation of Third World nations and urging solidarity among all oppressed peoples. Finally, both men called for a redefinition of human values; they believed that people in the United States, especially, needed to move away from materialism and embrace a more compassionate worldview.

If we, too, as Asian Americans, are to evolve in our political and ideological understanding, we need to learn from the wisdom of both men. As we work for our own empowerment, we must ask ourselves a series of questions. Will we fight only for ourselves, or will we embrace the concerns of all oppressed peoples? Will we overcome our own oppression and help to create a new society, or will we become a new exploiter group in the present American hierarchy of inequality? Will we define our goal of empowerment solely in terms of individual advancement for a few, or as the collective liberation for all peoples?

> *These are revolutionary times. All over the globe men are revolting against old systems of exploitation and oppression, and out of the wombs of a frail world, new systems of justice and equality are being born. The shirtless and barefoot people of the land are rising up as never before. "The people who sat in the darkness have seen a great light." We in the West must support these revolutions. It is a sad fact that, because of comfort, complacency, a morbid fear of communism, and our proneness to adjust to injustice, the Western nations that initiated so much of the revolutionary spirit of the modern world have now become the arch anti-revolutionaries. . . . Our only hope today lies in our ability to recapture the revolutionary spirit and go out into a sometimes hostile world declaring eternal hostility to poverty, racism, and militarism.*
>
> —MARTIN LUTHER KING JR.[44]

I believe that there will ultimately be a clash between the oppressed and those who do the oppressing. I believe that there will be a clash between those who want freedom, justice and equality for everyone and those who want to continue the system of exploitation. I believe that there will be that kind of clash, but I don't think it will be based on the color of the skin.

—MALCOLM X[45]

NOTES

1. Iranian philosopher Ali Shariati's four prisons analysis was shared with me by a member of the Iranian Students Union, Confederation of Iranian Students, San Francisco, 1977.

2. Allan Bloom, *The Closing of the American Mind* (New York: Simon & Schuster, 1987).

3. Winifred Breines, "Whose New Left?" *Journal of American History* 75, no. 2 (September 1988).

4. Ibid., 543.

5. Sheila D. Collins, *The Rainbow Challenge: The Jackson Campaign and the Future of U.S. Politics* (New York: Monthly Review Press, 1986).

6. Ibid., 16.

7. Ronald Fraser, *1968: A Student Generation in Revolt* (New York: Pantheon Books, 1988), 354–355.

8. Karen Umemoto, " 'On Strike!' San Francisco State College Strike, 1968–69: The Role of Asian American Students," *Amerasia Journal* 15, no. 1 (1989).

9. "Statement of the Philippine-American Collegiate Endeavor (PACE) Philosophy and Goals," mimeograph; quoted in Umemoto, " 'On Strike!' " 15.

10. Mo Nishida, "A Revolutionary Nationalist Perspective of the San Francisco State Strike," *Amerasia Journal* 15, no. 1 (1989): 75.

11. George Lipsitz, "Grassroots Activists and Social Change: The Story of Ivory Perry," *CAAS Newsletter*, UCLA Center for Afro-American Studies, 1986. See also George Lipsitz, *A Life in the Struggle. Ivory Perry and the Culture of Opposition* (Philadelphia: Temple University Press, 1988).

12. Russell C. Leong, "Poetry Within Earshot: Notes of an Asian American Generation, 1968–1978," *Amerasia Journal* 15, no. 1 (1989): 166–167.

13. Al Robles, "Hanging On to the Carabao's Tail," *Amerasia Journal* 15, no. 1 (1989): 205.

14. Warren J. Susman, *Culture as History: The Transformation of American Society in the Twentieth Century* (New York: Pantheon Books, 1973); and Raymond Williams, *Keywords: A Vocabulary of Culture and Society*, revised edition (New York: Oxford University Press, 1976).

15. John M. Liu and Lucie Cheng, "A Dialogue on Race and Class: Asian American Studies and Marxism," in *The Left Academy*, vol. 3, ed. Bertell Ollman and Edward Vernoff (Westport, Conn.: Praeger, 1986).

16. See Mary Kao, compiler, "Public Record, 1989: What Have We Learned from the 60s and 70s?" *Amerasia Journal* 15, no. 1 (1989): 95–158.

17. Institute for Labor Education and Research, *What's Wrong with the U.S. Economy? A Popular Guide for the Rest of Us* (Boston: South End Press, 1982). See especially chapters 1 and 19.

18. Samuel Huntington, "The United States," in *The Crisis of Democracy: Report on the Governability of Democracies to the Trilateral Commission*, ed. Michel Crozier (New York: New York University Press, 1975).

19. Center on Budget and Policy Priorities, *Still Far from the Dream: Recent Developments in Black Income, Employment and Poverty* (Washington, D.C., 1988).

20. Center for the Study of Social Policy, *Kids Count: State Profiles of Child Well-Being* (Washington, D.C., 1992).

21. Manning Marable, *How Capitalism Underdeveloped Black America* (Boston: South End Press, 1983), 252–253.

22. Vincent Harding, *The Other American Revolution* (Los Angeles: UCLA Center for Afro-American Studies, and Atlanta: Institute of the Black World, 1980), 224.

23. For analyses of the changing status of Asian Americans, see Lucie Cheng and Edna Bonacich, eds., *Labor Immigration Under Capitalism: Asian Workers in the United States Before*

World War II (Berkeley: University of California Press, 1984); Paul Ong, Edna Bonacich, and Lucie Cheng, eds., *Struggles for a Place: The New Asian Immigrants in the Restructuring Political Economy* (Philadelphia: Temple University Press, 1993); and Sucheng Chan, *Asian Americans: An Interpretive History* (Boston: Twayne Publishers, 1991).

24. For an analysis of the growing power of Asian American young professionals, see Yen Espiritu and Paul Ong, "Class Constraints on Racial Solidarity among Asian Americans," in *Struggles for a Place* (Philadelphia: Temple University Press, 1993).

25. Arthur Hu, "AIDS and Race," *Asian Week*, 13 December 1991.

26. Marable, *How Capitalism Underdeveloped Black America*, 182.

27. William McGurn, "The Silent Minority," *National Review*, 24 June 1991.

28. Ibid., 19.

29. C.L.R. James, *Beyond a Boundary* (New York: Pantheon Books, 1983), 116–117.

30. LEAP Asian Pacific American Public Policy Institute and UCLA Asian American Studies Center, *The State of Asian Pacific America: Policy Issues to the Year 2020* (Los Angeles: LEAP and UCLA Asian American Studies Center, 1993).

31. Mao Zedong, "Where Do Correct Ideas Come From?" in *Four Essays on Philosophy* (Beijing: Foreign Languages Press, 1966), 134.

32. See "Asian Pacific American Workers: Contemporary Issues in the Labor Movement," ed. Glenn Omatsu and Edna Bonacich, *Amerasia Journal* 18, no. 1 (1992).

33. Edna Bonacich, "The Social Costs of Immigrant Entrepreneurship," *Amerasia Journal* 14, no. 1 (1988).

34. Dean S. Toji and James H. Johnson Jr., "Asian and Pacific Islander American Poverty: The Working Poor and the Jobless Poor," *Amerasia Journal* 18, no. 1 (1992): 85.

35. Miriam Ching Louie, "Immigrant Asian Women in Bay Area Garment Sweatshops: 'After Sewing, Laundry, Cleaning and Cooking, I Have No Breath Left to Sing,'" *Amerasia Journal* 18, no. 1 (1992): 12.

36. Miriam Ching Louie, "Asian and Latina Women Take On the Garment Giants," *Cross-Roads*, March 1993.

37. Peter N. Kiang and Man Chak Ng, "Through Strength and Struggle: Boston's Asian American Student/Community/Labor Solidarity," *Amerasia Journal* 15, no. 1 (1989).

38. Lydia Lowe, "Paving the Way: Chinese Immigrant Workers and Community-based Labor Organizing in Boston," *Amerasia Journal* 18, no. 1 (1992): 41.

39. Namju Cho, "Check Out, Not In: Koreana Wilshire/Hyatt Take-over and the Los Angeles Korean Community," *Amerasia Journal*, 18, no. 1 (1992).

40. Craig Scharlin and Lilia V. Villanueva, *Philip Vera Cruz: A Personal History of Filipino Immigrants and the Farmworkers Movement* (Los Angeles: UCLA Labor Center and UCLA Asian American Studies Center, 1992), 104.

41. For an overview of the evolution of the "model minority" stereotype in the social sciences, see Shirley Hune, *Pacific Migration to the United States: Trends and Themes in Historical and Sociological Literature* (New York: Research Institute on Immigration and Ethnic Studies of the Smithsonian Institution, 1977), reprinted in *Asian American Studies: An Annotated Bibliography and Research Guide*, ed. Hyung-chan Kim (Westport, Conn.: Greenwood Press, 1989). For comparisons of the "model minority" stereotype in two different decades, see "Success Story of One Minority Group in U.S.," *U.S. News and World Report*, 26 December 1966, reprinted in *Roots: An Asian American Reader*, ed. Amy Tachiki et al. (Los Angeles: UCLA Asian American Studies Center, 1971) and in the present volume, chapter 13; and the essay by William McGurn, "The Silent Minority," *National Review*, 24 June 1991.

42. Author's interview with K. W. Lee, Los Angeles, California, October 1991.

43. Manning Marable, "On Malcolm X: His Message & Meaning" (Westfield, N.J.: Open Magazine Pamphlet Series, 1992).

44. Martin Luther King Jr., "Beyond Vietnam," speech delivered at Riverside Church, New York, April 1967.

45. Malcolm X, interview on Pierre Breton Show, 19 January 1965, in *Malcolm X Speaks*, ed. George Breitman (New York: Grove Press, 1966), 216.

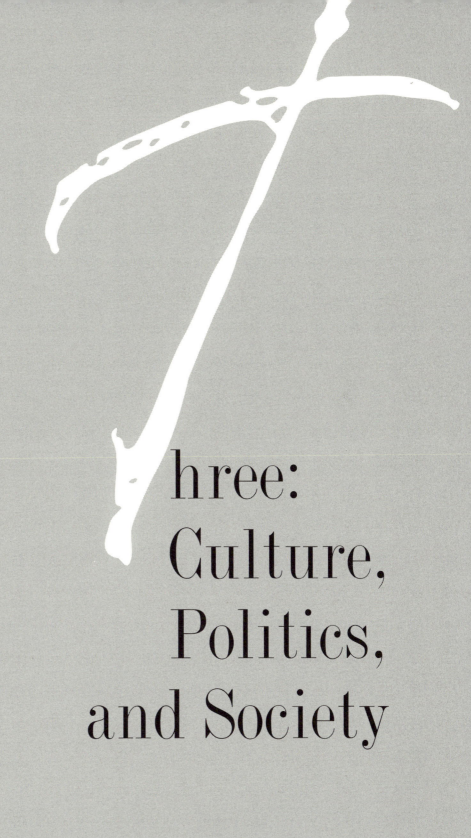

hree:
Culture,
Politics,
and Society

Youth Culture, Citizenship, and Globalization

South Asian Muslim Youth in the United States after September 11th

Sunaina Maira

Introduction: A State of Siege[1]

In the wake of the September 11, 2001 attacks, questions of citizenship and racialization have taken on new, urgent meanings for South Asian immigrant youth. Many South Asian Americans, Arab Americans, and Muslim Americans, or individuals who appeared "Muslim," have been victims of physical assaults and racial profiling as part of the renewed anti-Muslim backlash and demonization of Arabs in the U.S.[2] This is not a new form of racism, of course, for it has been experienced by Arab Americans and Muslim Americans for many years,[3] but South Asian Americans suddenly found themselves the objects of intensified suspicion and surveillance. There has been a shift, if only temporary, in U.S. race politics after 9/11 where the fault lines are no longer just between those racialized as white Americans/people of color, or even black/white Americans, but between those categorized as Muslim/non-Muslim, American/"foreign," or citizen/non-citizen.

Within six weeks of September 11, Congress passed the USA-PATRIOT Act of 2001 (which conveniently stands for United and Strengthening America by Providing Appropriate Tools Required to Intercept and Obstruct Terrorism Act) under considerable pressure from Attorney General John Ashcroft, who threatened Congress that "Those who scare peace-loving people with phantoms of lost liberties . . . only aid terrorists."[4] Not so conveniently for Muslim, Arab, and South Asian Americans, the new laws gave the United States government sweeping new powers of investigation and surveillance—powers in many cases that had been circumscribed after the Church Committee brought to light the excesses of the FBI's COINTELPRO operation that investigated and infiltrated civil rights groups in the 1960s.[5]

The Patriot Act has violated basic constitutional rights of due process and free speech, and, in effect, sacrificed the liberties of specific minority groups in exchange for a presumed sense of "safety" of the larger majority by creating an ambiguously defined category of "domestic terrorism"; by granting the government enhanced surveillance powers; and by taking away due process rights from non-citizens who can be placed in mandatory (and in actuality, indefinite and secret) detention and deported because of participation in broadly defined "terrorist activity" (often for minor immigration violations and also in secret).[6] Before 9/11, about eighty percent of the American public thought it was wrong for law enforcement to use racial profiling, popularly used to refer to the disproportionate targeting of African American drivers by police for the offense of "driving while black." However, after the shock of the 9/11 attacks, sixty percent favored racial profiling, "at least as long as it was directed at Arabs and Muslims."[7]

After the terrorist attacks, popular feeling was that "somebody had to pay" domestically, as well as internationally, to restore the illusion of national security for Americans. The groups whose civil rights were considered expendable were two populations who historically have had little power to combat infringement on their civil rights: immigrants and Arab Americans. Surveillance of Arab American communities is not new in the U.S. It is closely tied to U.S. support of the Israeli occupation of Palestine and clampdowns on those who have protested U.S. policy in the Middle East at various times since the 1967 Israeli-Arab war— from the FBI's monitoring of the General Union of Palestinian Students in the 1980s, to the attempted deportation of the pro-Palestinian activists known as the "L.A. 8," to the nationwide monitoring and interviews of Arab American individuals and organizations before and during the first Gulf War.[8]

However, South Asians in this country have generally had a different relationship than Arab Americans to the policies of the national security state. Since the early twentieth century, the anti-colonial activities of Indian immigrants who mobilized in the U.S. and published radical pamphlets such as "Ghadar" [Mutiny] have been targeted.[9] The primary influx of immigrants from South Asia actually came to the United States beginning in the late 1960s as part of an effort by the U.S. to shore up its scientific and military technology expertise during the Cold War. Graduate students, scientists, and professionals who emigrated after the Immigration Act of 1965 generally did not engage in challenges to their adopted home state's policies, and despite economically strategic lobbying for minority status in the 1970s to obtain civil rights benefits, the first wave of South Asians has, for the most part, tried hard to live up to the mythic "model minority" image.[10] However, the second wave of South Asian immigrants, who began coming to the U.S. in the 1980s through the family reunification provisions of the 1965 Act, was less affluent and credentialed than their predecessors, more likely to come from small towns or even villages, and to have had a very different exposure to U.S. race politics and the welfare state than those earlier immigrants. In addition, while immigrants from the first wave typically reside in middle- and upper-middle-class, predominantly white suburbs in the U.S., these more recent immigrants generally live in urban areas, often in multi-ethnic communities, and work in service-sector jobs or in small businesses. The civil rights crisis after 9/11 thus not only affected South Asian, Arab, and Muslim African Americans differentially due to their varied histories of arrival and residence in the U.S., and the different relationships of the U.S. with their home nation-states. It also affected various South Asian American communities differentially, based on their class status and previous understandings of U.S. racism. Unfortunately, it seems that so far there has been no nationally based, collectively organized response to the post-9/11 civil rights crisis.

This lack of coordinated national response by South Asian Americans is disturbing but not surprising. The relative absence of civil rights organizations established by the first wave of South Asian immigrants and the class schism in the community means that there is no organized national South Asian civil rights infrastructure, akin to the American Arab Anti-Discrimination Committee, to respond to the crisis affecting the South Asian American community.[11] The crisis of civil rights for South Asian Americans after 9/11 is the most virulent example of large-scale scapegoating of and violence against South Asians in the U.S. since the anti-Indian riots on the West Coast in the early twentieth century. As part of the domestic "War on Terror," at least 1,200 and up to 3,000 Muslim immigrant men were rounded up and detained in the aftermath of 9/11, without any criminal charges, some in high-security prisons. Nearly forty percent of the detainees are thought to be Pakistani nationals, though virtually none of the detainees has been identified publicly and the locations where many have been held remain secret, still true of the ongoing detentions in 2004.[12] After 9/11, Muslim families began experiencing the "disappearances" of their husbands, brothers, and sons, and many families ended up leaving the country after indefinite separations and loss of the means of family support.[13] Although unreported in the mainstream media, there have been mass deportations of Pakistani nationals leaving on chartered planes, some leaving in the middle of the night from New York State.[14]

In June 2002, the National Security Entry-Exit Registration System (NSEERS) was established; this grossly discriminatory system requires all male nationals over sixteen years of age from twenty-four Muslim-majority countries, including Pakistan and Bangladesh as well as North Korea, to submit to photographing and fingerprinting at federal immigration facilities.[15] After news broke of mass arrests of Iranians complying with special registration in southern California in December 2002, some undocumented immigrants and those with pending immigration applications, worried about registering and not being released, tried to flee to Canada. By 12 March 2003, the Canadian immigration service reported 2,111 refugee claims by Pakistanis just since 1 January of that year.[16] The irony of Pakistanis leaving the U.S. to try to get political asylum in another country is hidden, rather than lost, for most Americans. The earlier fear and anxiety surrounding the detentions in the first year following 9/11 seem to have largely diminished in the public sphere, and within South Asian American communities, seem to be borne ever more by Muslim and Sikh Americans to the exclusion of those who feel they are not "targets" of the war on terror. My own work on issues of immigrant rights with South Asian Americans in the Boston area reveals that there is, understandably, a heightened sense of fear and vulnerability in Muslim immigrant communities, particularly among working-class immigrants who cannot as easily afford legal counsel to help them if they are harassed or detained.

It would not be too dramatic to say that many in these communities feel under siege. The profiling and hysteria depicted in the eerily prescient 1998 film *The Siege*—in which Muslim and Arab Americans in New York are rounded up behind barbed wire in response to a terrorist threat—resembles truth more than fiction. The profiling of Muslim and Arab immigrants affects the composition of communities and the nature of relationships within them. This is particularly prominent in areas with large concentrations of these populations that have seen an exodus of immigrants seeking to avoid arrest or deportation, such as Brooklyn's "Little Pakistan" on Coney Island Avenue.[17] More than 15,000 undocumented Pakistanis had reportedly left the country for Canada, Europe, and Pakistan by June 2003, according to the Pakistani Embassy in Washington.[18] Perhaps more alarming, "an unknowable number of immigrants have burrowed deeper underground," creating an even more subliminal and precarious world of individuals who cannot fully admit they exist, who cannot safely live their lives in the U.S. for fear of deportation and so live in the shadows, as well as under siege.[19]

SOUTH ASIAN MUSLIM IMMIGRANT YOUTH IN CAMBRIDGE

These events in the aftermath of 9/11, now called the "war at home," raise questions about what the racial profiling and anti-Muslim backlash mean for South Asian and Muslim immigrant youth coming of age in the U.S. at a moment when their "right to belong" in the nation is suspect. How do U.S. immigration and "homeland security" policies targeting Muslim immigrants affect the understandings of race, nationalism, and citizenship of South Asian Muslim immigrant youth? This paper is based on an ethnographic study that I began in fall 2001, focused on working-class, Indian, Pakistani, and Bangladeshi immigrant students in the public high school in Cambridge, Massachusetts, and on their notions of cultural citizenship. As part of my research, I also interviewed immigrant parents, school staff, community and religious leaders, city officials, and community activists. I argue here that young Muslim immigrants' understandings of citizenship shed light on the ways in which nationalism in the U.S. is defined in relation to transnationalism and globalization, multiculturalism and polyculturalism, and increasingly overtly, to the links between domestic and foreign policy that underlie U.S. imperial power. Not all the immigrant youth in this study have been directly targeted by the War on Terror, but I found that all of them in some way had to grapple with the scapegoating of Muslims, the demonization of Islam, and the fear of surveillance and deportation after 9/11. I also found that some youth, rather than accepting uncritically the premises of the state's domestic and international War on Terror, were critical of U.S. responses to 9/11 from the perspective of global human rights, thus reframing the basis of citizenship, as my analysis will demonstrate.

Cambridge, Massachusetts is an interesting site for this research, for, while media attention and community discussions of racial profiling were primarily focused on South Asians in the New York/New Jersey area, there were hundreds of incidents around the country in places where South Asians have not been as visible in the public sphere or as organized, including incidents in the Boston area. It is also useful to focus on communities such as Cambridge, known to be more politically liberal, to understand what kinds of responses such a setting allows and does not allow, particularly for youth. The Cambridge Public High School has an extremely diverse student body that reflects the city's changing population, with students from Latin America, the Caribbean, Africa, and Asia. Students from India, Pakistan, Bangladesh, and Afghanistan constitute the largest Muslim population in the school, followed by youth from Ethiopia, Somalia, and Morocco. There are about sixty students of South Asian origin, including a few Nepali and Tibetan youth, who are almost evenly split between immigrant students and second-generation youth.[20]

The South Asian immigrant student population is predominantly working- to lower-middle class, recently arrived (within the last five to seven years), and with minimal to moderate fluency in English. As such, these youth generally seem to socialize predominantly with other South Asian immigrant youth and with other immigrant students in the bilingual education program. The majority of Indian immigrant youth are from Sunni Muslim families, most from small towns or villages in Gujarat in western India. Several of the South Asian students are actually related to one another as their families have sponsored relatives as part of an ongoing chain migration. Whole families have migrated from the same village in Gujarat, recreating their extended family networks in the same apartment building in Cambridge. The immigrant parents of these adolescents generally work in low-income jobs in the service sector, and they themselves work after school, up to thirty hours a week, in fast food restaurants, gas stations, retail stores, and as security guards.

At least half of the South Asian immigrant youth in the school live in public and/or private high-rise apartment complexes in North Cambridge. The remainder live in the Central Square area, an ethnically and racially diverse neighborhood that is undergoing gentrification. The families of these South Asian (Sunni) Muslim youth are not very involved in local Muslim organizations or mosques that draw a diverse Arab, North African, Asian, and African American population. They tend to socialize mainly with people from their own ethnic community, but neither do they seem to affiliate with the Indian American or Pakistani American community organizations in the Boston area, which tend to involve mainly middle- to upper-middle class, suburban families.[21] Thus the responses of these immigrant youth are rooted in the specificities of their urban, working-class experience, an experience that is often completely unknown to their more privileged South Asian American counterparts in the area.

CULTURAL CITIZENSHIP

I found that in nearly all my conversations with South Asian immigrant youth, as well as with their parents, the discussion would inevitably turn to citizenship, for this was an issue that had profoundly shaped their lives and driven their experiences of migration. Research on youth and citizenship is meager and generally tends to come out of traditions of developmental psychology or functionalist socialization theory, both of which assume a limited definition of what constitutes the "political." More recent work challenges these assumptions and pays attention to young people's own understandings of politics, and the ways they negotiate relationships of power in different realms of their everyday life.[22]

Citizenship has traditionally been thought of in political, economic, and civic terms, but increasingly, analysis focuses on the notion of cultural citizenship, for the rights and obligations of civic citizenship are mediated by race, ethnicity, gender, and sexuality, as well as religion, as apparent in the post-9/11 backlash.[23] Cultural citizenship, according to anthropologist Lok Siu, is comprised of the "behaviors, discourses, and practices that give meaning to citizenship as lived experience" in the context of "an uneven and complex field of structural inequalities and webs of power relations," the "quotidian practices of inclusion and exclusion."[24] Cultural citizenship becomes an important construct to examine because legal citizenship is clearly no longer enough to guarantee protection under the law with the state's War on Terror, as is clear from the profiling, surveillance, and detention of Muslim Americans who are U.S. citizens.

The concept of cultural citizenship has been developed by persons such as Latino studies scholars Renato Rosaldo and William Flores and Rina Benmayor, who take a new social movement–based approach to immigrant and civil rights. Their use of cultural citizenship analyzes how "Cultural phenomena—from practices that organize the daily life of individuals, families, and the community, to linguistic and artistic expression—cross the political realm and contribute to the process of affirming and building an emerging Latino identity and political and social consciousness."[25] The notion of cultural citizenship has also been developed, from a Foucauldian perspective, by cultural theorists such as Aihwa Ong, who are concerned with citizenship as a regulatory process, and who define cultural citizenship as "A dual process of self-making and being-made within webs of power linked to the nation-state and civil society."[26] Some writers in this vein, such as Toby Miller, have been skeptical about the possibility for using citizenship as the collective basis for political transformation—given its increasingly individualized, privatized definition—but are still open to its potential. My work, in a sense, bridges these two approaches. I am interested in the critical possibilities of cultural citizenship to galvanize the struggle for civil and immigrant rights, particularly for young immigrants, as suggested by the work of Latino Studies scholars. At the same time, I view citizenship as being a limited basis for social transformation, given that it is state-sponsored and also increasingly privatized.[27] Cultural citizenship brings with it all the contradictions of liberal multiculturalism and the inequities of global capital in which it is embedded, and so it is necessarily politically ambiguous in its emancipatory possibilities.[28]

In my research, I am finding that issues of economic or legal citizenship spill over into cultural citizenship. These categories are more blurred than some theorists of cultural citizenship have traditionally acknowledged, so it not always possible to cleanly distinguish between the economic, legal, and cultural bases of citizenship.[29] At this early stage in my analysis, I think there are three ways in which South Asian immigrant youth understand and practice cultural citizenship: flexible citizenship, multicultural or polycultural citizenship, and dissenting citizenship. These terms, drawn from the ways in which the young immigrants in my study expressed and practiced cultural citizenship, build on existing theories of flexible and multicultural citizenship, extending them but also suggesting new, critical forms (polycultural and dissenting), all of which, however, have their own contradictions and ambiguities. These three categories point to the ways in which the questions facing these youth go beyond debates about cultural rights to questions of economic, civil, and human rights, but, at the same time, point to the limitations of rights-based discourses, as the experiences of these youth demonstrate.

The forms of citizenship that emerged from this study—flexible, multicultural and polycultural, and dissenting citizenship—are responses produced by these immigrant youth simultaneously to the condition of living a transnational adolescence. They are not exclusive of one another, nor do they exist in some kind of hierarchy of political or personal efficacy. I view these modes of citizenship not as static categories in a typology but as processes that are dynamic, and crossing different spheres: social, economic, and political. These citizenship practices are performed by adults as well, but it is clear that young people have to negotiate particular concerns due to their positioning in the family and social structure, as well as their participation in education. While immigrant youth have to deal with the migration choices of their parents and the demands of being both students and workers, it is clear that their lives are profoundly shaped by the state and economic policies that drive their parents to cross national borders. Young people, too, grapple with the meaning of the state's role in their lives and with the implications of war, violence, and racism for an ethics of belonging.

FLEXIBLE CITIZENSHIP

"Flexible citizenship" is a concept that emerged to describe the experience of migrants who use transnational links to provide political or material resources not available to them within a single nation-state,[30] as has been argued for affluent Chinese migrants by Aihwa Ong. It is different from traditional notions of dual citizenship, which imply an actual legal status as citizen of two nation-states, for it leaves open questions of national loyalty or strategic uses of citizenship status. The Muslim immigrant youth in my study understand citizenship in relation to the U.S. as well as one or more nations in South Asia. For them, national affiliations (such as "Indian" or "Bangladeshi") as well as linguistic-regional identities (such as Gujarati or Pathan) were very important, and they viewed all these identifications as compatible with U.S. citizenship. Most of these young immigrants desired and had applied for U.S. citizenship since they came to the U.S.

sponsored by relatives who are permanent residents or citizens, in some cases fathers who migrated alone many years earlier. At least two boys had been separated from their fathers for about fifteen years. Faisal said his father had left Pakistan for the U.S. right after he was born, and had in effect missed his son's childhood while he was working in the U.S. to support him and the rest of his family until they could be reunited. By the time Faisal came to the U.S., however, his older brother was too old to enroll in high school and had to struggle to get a GED and find a job with limited English skills.

About half of these South Asian Muslim immigrant youth have green cards already; the rest are a mix of citizens and undocumented immigrants. They desired a U.S. passport because of what they perceived as its civic and also economic benefits. A few stated that they wanted to be able to vote, and several said that they wanted to be able to travel freely between the U.S. and South Asia, to be mobile in work and family life. After 9/11, of course, citizenship seemed to become less a matter of choice for immigrants, particularly Muslims and South Asian/Arab Americans, than a hoped-for shield against the abuses of civil rights. In fact, a few were surprised that I myself had not yet obtained citizenship in the fall of 2001, and were in some cases concerned that I seemed to have taken so long to obtain this vital document!

Citizenship for these immigrant youth is part of a carefully planned, long-term, family-based strategy of migration in response to economic pressures on those living in, or at the edge of, the middle class in South Asia. Some of these youth in Cambridge imagine their lives spanning national borders and speak of returning to South Asia, at least temporarily, once they have become U.S. citizens and perhaps when their parents have retired there. Transnational marriages and social ties are common in their families. For example, Sohail, who worked as a computer assistant after school, wanted to set up a transnational hi-tech business so that he could live part-time in Gujarat and part-time in Boston while supporting his parents. He saw this as a development strategy for Non-Resident Indians (or NRIs, a term used by the Indian government) to fulfill their obligations to the home nation-state, using the benefits of U.S. citizenship. It seems to me that these young immigrants' notions of flexible citizenship are based on at least two linked processes of "self-making" and "being-made" as citizens in relation to the various nation-states with which they affiliate.[31] First, their identification with India or Pakistan is based largely on transnational popular culture, on Bollywood films, South Asian television serials, and Hindi music that they access through video, DVD, satellite TV, and the Internet. In the interest of space, I cannot delve here into an analysis of transnational popular culture, but it is clearly an important arena for the expression of cultural citizenship by immigrant youth.[32]

Second, flexible citizenship is necessarily intertwined with labor and education, issues that are interrelated for working-class, immigrant youth. These youth have come to the U.S. with their families, in some sense, as migrant workers. They work in low-wage, part-time jobs in retail and fast food restaurants and struggle in school to get credentials for class mobility. These are the same jobs that are generally also occupied by young people of diverse ethnic backgrounds in the U.S.[33] However, unlike non-immigrants who provide this cheap and flexible labor, immigrant youth can perform the economic citizenship required of neoliberal citizenship, which is predicated on individual productivity in the capitalist state, but cannot win cultural citizenship because they are non-white, immigrant youth—and currently, because they are identified as Muslim. Their participation in U.S. public culture, in fact, is largely through work. Their relations outside the school and community are mainly with other immigrant or young workers and with employers. Waheed, for example, lamented that he could never go out into the city with his friends because they all worked on different schedules and it was almost impossible for them to have a night off together, since he worked night shifts at his weekend job as a security guard.

Compared to more affluent or highly credentialed South Asian immigrants, these working-class youth are more ambiguously positioned in relation to what Ong calls the U.S. neoliberal ideology of productivity and consumption that emphasizes "freedom, progress, and individualism."[34] They see the limits of this model of the self-reliant consumer-citizen—and of the "American Dream"—in their own lives and that of their families. Soman, who works in his family's Bengali restaurant in Central Square after school and who often waits on South Asian students from MIT, says, "Here, you live in a golden cage, but it's still a cage. . . . My life is so limited. I go to school, come to work, study, go to sleep." The idea of productive citizenship is necessarily predicated on legal-juridical regulations of citizens and workers, and on the need for a low-wage, undocumented/non-citizen labor pool by employers who wish to depress wages and keep labor compliant. The work of citizenship as a disciplining technology of the state that keeps labor and immigrants vulnerable to exploitation and suppresses dissent is very evident after 9/11 with the ongoing arrests and deportations of immigrant workers for visa violations.[35] There is a greater fear among non-citizens who have transnational ties, political or familial, that they are increasingly suspect when the "threat" to national security is attributed to specific foreign nations.

Yet, in the face of such regulations of citizenship and its cultural boundaries, it became apparent to me that these young Muslim immigrants thought about citizenship in ways that were themselves flexible, shifting, and contextual. In some cases, it seems that religious identity actually prompts youth to think of themselves as belonging to the U.S., or at least identifying with its concerns, if not identifying as "American." Sohail said to me in fall 2001, "Islam teaches [us that] whatever country you live in, you should support them. . . . See, if I live in America, I have to support America; I cannot go to India." This, of course, is the same boy who said that he ultimately wanted to return to India and support its development. But these statements are not as contradictory as they first appear. Sohail is able to frame his relationship to Islam in a way that will help him think through questions of loyalty at a moment in the U.S. when Muslims are being framed as non-citizens *because* of a particular construction of Islam. Instead, Sohail uses Islam to counter this technology of exclusion of Muslims from the nation-state, both officially and unofficially, and to support a flexible definition of citizenship.

At a Boston rally in November 2001, protesting the imminent war in Iraq, Imam Talal Eid of the Islamic Center of New England used rhetoric of Muslim citizenship that has been increasingly adopted by Muslim clerics and commentators after 9/11. He said that he spoke for peace as a U.S. citizen of many years who believed that Muslim Americans could contribute to the "civilizing" of America (an interesting turn on Samuel Huntington's phrase). Sohail's strategy is part of a rather sophisticated understanding of citizenship as necessarily mobile, as drawing on different ideological resources to respond to the exigencies of diverse moments and places. Flexible citizenship is clearly an economic/ family strategy for these youth but also part of a cultural strategy that allows them to manage diverse national affiliations.

MULTICULTURAL OR POLYCULTURAL CITIZENSHIP

Not surprisingly, some of these immigrant youth talked about ideas of "cultural difference" and relationships with others in terms of multicultural citizenship, even if only implicitly, since multiculturalism is such a pervasive discourse of cultural belonging in the U.S., particularly in the arena of education. Their vernacular understandings of multicultural citizenship are not just in Will Kymlicka's sense of minority cultural rights, but of everyday understandings of pluralism embedded in the social fabric of their relationships. For most of these youth, it is important to emphasize that they have friendships that cross ethnic and racial boundaries. In their daily lives, they do, in fact, hang out with Latino, Caribbean, African American, and Asian students, and with Muslim African youth from Somalia, Ethiopia, or Egypt, potentially forming an incipient pan-Islamic identity. Yet it is also apparent that students in the school, as in most American high schools and colleges, tend to cluster by ethnic group. Sohail comments that his friendships with non-South Asian students are sometimes questioned by other "desi" (South Asian) youth, but he defends himself by arguing for a more expansive conception of community:

> I hang out with different kids but even I heard it from a lot of desis who say, "Why you go with them?" They don't like it, but I say if you want to live in a different world, you have to exist with them. . . . Sometimes you have to go outside [your group] and say, "Yeah, alright, we are friends too, we are not going to discriminate [against] you, because you are white, we don't look like you." . . . Your relationship is gonna be bigger, right. But if you're gonna live in the desi community, you're only going to know desi people, not the other people.

Sohail seems to trace the value he places on multiculturalist co-existence to an idealized notion of India as a multi-ethnic nation, at least before the horrific massacre of Muslim Indians during the Gujarat riots in India in spring 2002. He said: "India is a really good place to live in . . . because they've got a lot of religions, different languages, different people."

It is also true that there are moments of tension among these different groups of youth, as there are in any school or community. After September 11, some of the South Asian immigrant youth, particularly the Muslim boys, felt targeted by other high school youth. Accusations of "You're a terrorist" or "You're a bin Laden" enter into what might otherwise be just an outbreak of youthful aggression among boys, but which is now a part of a national discourse about Islam in the U.S. The South Asian Muslim boys, and girls, feel this acutely: does this mean *they* are the enemy, and how can they live as such?

One anti-Muslim incident in Cambridge occurred in the high school when an African American girl accused two Pakistani boys, Amir and Wahab, of "killing people" and reportedly called them "Muslim niggers." The girl was eventually suspended, but Amir was, in fact, a friend of the girl's brother and said he tried to intervene to soften her punishment. Both boys emphatically refused to portray the incident as a Black/South Asian or Black/Muslim conflict. They insisted that this was the case of a lone individual who, Waheed half-jokingly said, must have been "drunk" or "high." Amir, in fact, said that he thought African Americans were less likely to have an uncritically nationalist response to the events of 9/11 than white Americans, even though he was hesitant to extend this generalization to their responses to the military campaign in Afghanistan.

For Waheed and Amir, 9/11 prompted a heightened self-consciousness about racialization that seemed, if anything, to reinforce the black/white racial polarization. Waheed felt that African Americans were not as shattered by the attacks on the U.S. because, in his view, black Americans feel alienated from the nation-state due to the legacy of slavery. While this racialized difference after 9/11 is more complex than Waheed suggests, what is important is that he *believes* that African Americans share his experience of marginalization within the nation. But Waheed does not completely dismiss the renewed nationalism of Americans after 9/11, saying, "The first thing is they're born here in the USA, so that's their country. . . . We are immigrants. . . . If something happens back home, like 9/11, and someone else did it, we're gonna be angry too, right?" Yet it is also apparent that 9/11 seems to have drawn him into an understanding of citizenship that is based on racialized fissures in claims to national identity and affiliation with other youth of color.

For Waheed and others, the response of African Americans seems more significant than that of Latinos or even of Arab Americans because, on the one hand, they are the largest group of students of color in the school, and on the other hand, they stand for a particular manifestation of contested U.S. citizenship to these youth, even if not all are actually U.S.-born. The responses of these young Pakistani males suggests to me a potential *polycultural citizenship*, based not on the reification of cultural difference that multiculturalism implies, but on a complex set of political affiliations and social boundary-crossings, as Robin Kelley's notion of polyculturalism suggests.[36] This nascent polycultural citizenship is embedded in the messiness and nuance of relationships of different groups with one another and with the state, and allows for political, not just cultural resonance, based on particular historical and material conjunctures.

Polycultural citizenship is not an idealization, however, of the complexities of race politics. I do not want to suggest that polyculturalism exists in the absence of anti-black racism in this community, or that racialized antagonisms and suspicion in the school are not taken in at all by immigrant youth. In getting to know these youth over a period of time, I have found that these tensions do indeed exist. Rather, I would like to argue that there is room in my notion of polycultural citizenship to acknowledge the resentment and competition bred by daily struggles for turf or resources. Given that polyculturalism critiques the idea of "pure" culture, or even "pure" hybridity, it would therefore not envision a "pure" politics of multiculturalist tolerance without any tension or negotiation. These young immigrants simultaneously invoke a multiculturalist discourse of pluralist co-existence and a polyculturalist notion of boundary-crossing and affiliation, embedded in political experience but also in popular culture practices shared with youth of color.

Muslim immigrant youth sense a connection with other youth of color and with African Muslim youth in the city, even as they struggle with the challenges that Muslim identity has posed to liberal multiculturalism. Syed Khan, an Indian immigrant who is on the Board of Religious Directors of the Islamic Center of Sharon, Massachusetts, is the founder of Muslim Community Support Services, an organization that is holding forums on issues of civil rights and cultural citizenship for Muslim Americans. He argues that the post-9/11 backlash has shown the limits of U.S. multiculturalism, in its inability to absorb Islam as a marker of difference within the nation, in a cultural if not religious sense. Khan said to me in fall 2002, "If this had happened to some other religious or ethnic group, which professors would speak out? How many rallies have you seen? How many protests? None of those traditional forms of response have happened. . . . Everybody is scared to speak up about basic values that are enshrined in the U.S. constitution or psyche." Like other Muslim Americans, Khan is grappling with the ambiguities of secularism and civil rights at a moment when the state uses religion, in addition to national origin, as the basis of its profiling.

DISSENTING CITIZENSHIP

Muslim Americans and Arab Americans are defined, particularly after 9/11 but also at other moments (such as the Iran hostage crisis and the Gulf War), as political scapegoats and therefore cultural aliens.[37] Their presumed cultural difference is highlighted as part of the Bush administration's political and cultural doctrine that defines U.S. interests and national identity in opposition to a "foreign enemy" and an "enemy within." In fall 2002, when referring to the White House's public embrace and then neglect of Muslim American leaders after 9/11, Khan commented, in a conversation with me: "Initially leaders, including Bush, had spoken up [against racial profiling], but afterwards, when it wasn't as critical, outreach to Muslim Americans has stopped completely. Now, it's bashing time."

Other South Asian Muslims living in the Boston area were quick to point out to me the outpouring of support offered by neighbors and friends after 9/11. The two perspectives are, of course, both true. Individual acts of solidarity have co-existed with acts of discrimination, private and state-sponsored, on a mass scale.[38] The two processes actually work together in racial profiling, which works on these multiple levels and through these contradictions of rhetoric and policy.[39] Legal scholar Leti Volpp argues that the post-9/11 moment has "facilitated the consolidation of a new identity category" that conflates "Arab/Muslim/Middle Eastern" with "terrorist" and "non-citizen." This identity category is obviously not new, but Volpp is right to point out that a "National identity has consolidated that is both strongly patriotic and multiracial."[40] This national identity both excludes and racializes Muslim identity, even if it is not racial at all, in the slippery sense of race in the U.S. The paradoxical racialization of Muslim identity is what Moustafa Bayoumi calls the "tragic irony" of "racial profiling" after 9/11.[41]

Khan worries that Muslim American communities have not been speaking up enough against the prospect of social and political, if not physical, internment. However, it seems to me that some immigrant youth are willing to voice political views, even publicly, that most South Asian middle-class community leaders have not been expressing. The Muslim immigrant youth I spoke with had an analysis of 9/11 and the U.S. war in Afghanistan that drew on a notion of international human rights and resisted the nationalization of the Twin Towers tragedy. Amir said to me in December 2001: "You have to look at it in two ways. It's not right that ordinary people over there [in Afghanistan], like you and me, just doing their work, get killed. They don't have anything to do with . . . the attacks in New York, but they're getting killed. And also the people in New York who got killed, that's not right either."

Jamila, a Bangladeshi girl, said, "I felt bad for those people [in Afghanistan] . . . because they don't have no proof that they actually did it, but they were all killing all these innocent people who had nothing to do with it." Aliyah, who could very easily pass for Latina, chose to write the words "INDIA + MUSLIM" on her bag after 9/11. For her, this was a gesture of defiance responding to the casting of Muslims as potentially disloyal citizens. She said, "Just because one Muslim did it in New York, you can't involve everybody in there, you know what I'm sayin'?" This critique of the anti-Muslim backlash was pervasive amongst the South Asian Muslim youth. Karina said, "After September 11, they [Americans] hate the Muslims. . . . I think they want the government to hate the Muslims, like, all Muslims are same."

After the anti-Muslim incident at Cambridge High School, the International Student Center organized a student assembly featuring two Arab American speakers who criticized the War on Terrorism and the attack on civil liberties. Amir, Waheed, and a Gujarati Muslim girl, Samiyah, delivered eloquent speeches condemning racism to an auditorium filled with their peers. Amir said that when he was threatened by some young men in Boston, "I could have done the same thing, but I don't think it's the right thing to do." Amir is a muscular young man and his call for non-violent response was a powerful one at that assembly—one that could also be taken to be an implicitly political statement about the U.S. bombing of Afghanistan in response to the attacks. Samiyah stood up in her salwar kameez and said, "We have to respect each other if we want to change society. You have to stand up for your rights." Muslim immigrant youth are being visibly drawn into race politics and civil rights debates in the local community, although it is not clear yet what the impact of this politicization will be over time. But a year later on the anniversary of September 11, when the International Student Center organized another student assembly in 2002, Samiyah's younger sister and another Gujarati Muslim girl voluntarily made similar speeches that were reported in the local press.

Even though these working-class youth do not have the support of or time to participate in community or political organizations, they have become spokespersons in the public sphere, willing to voice a dissenting view. Other Muslim American youth have been forced to play the role of educators as well, giving speeches at their schools and in community forums about Islam, though a coordinator of a Muslim youth group at the Central Square mosque says that it is a role not without pressure or fatigue for young Muslim Americans. Understandably, some of them are also hesitant to speak publicly about political issues given that even legal citizens are worried about expressing political critique or dissent, as the state has acquired sweeping powers of surveillance with the USA-Patriot Act. Repression works on two levels to silence dissent, as Corey Robin points out: on a state level, but also on the level of civil society, where individuals internalize repression and censor themselves.[42] Robin astutely observes that there is a "division of labor" between the state and civil society for "fear does the work—or enhances the work—of repression." Robin argues that the "effects of 'Fear, American Style' are most evident today in immigrant, Middle Eastern, and South Asian communities, as well as in the workplace where 'suppression of dissent' is evident since 9/11."[43]

In the face of such repression, I have found the Muslim immigrant youth with whom I spoke to be engaged in a practice of dissenting citizenship. Their expression of dissenting citizenship is based on a critique and affirmation of human rights that means they stand apart at some moments, even as they stand together with others outside the borders of the nation. Dissenting citizenship is not coeval with cosmopolitanism, at least in this instance, for it seems to me that even notions of cosmopolitanism that account for its particularity (as opposed to universalism), plurality of form, and imbrications with nationalism do not quite capture the specific political critique being waged here.[44] The critique of these Muslim immigrant youth is both far more attached to regional and religious identity, and far more critical in its appraisal of U.S. nationalism and state powers than some liberal theorists of cosmopolitanism allow.[45] The perspective of Muslim immigrant youth is very much rooted in their identities as Muslims who are targeted as such by the state, and also sheds light on the links between U.S. policies at home and abroad. In this critique of the U.S. state, I argue, dissenting citizenship goes beyond the debate between liberal and conservative appraisals of possibilities of cosmopolitanism because it raises an issue that is not emphasized enough by these critics:[46] that of cosmopolitanism, and relatedly of globalization, as an *imperial feeling*. I use the term "imperial feeling" to capture an emerging acknowledgment, by media commentators on both the right and the left, that U.S. policy on the global stage is linked to economic and military dominance. This view is generally expressed not as a full-blown critique in the U.S. mass media, but as an emerging sentiment in the public sphere, a growing "feeling" (often an anxiety) that the U.S. is occupying the role of a new *empire*.[47]

The dissenting views of Muslim immigrant youth implicitly critique this imperial feeling of U.S. nationalism after 9/11 through their linking of warfare *within* the state to international war. It is this link between the domestic and imperial that makes their perspective an important mode of dissent because the imperial project of the new "Cold War," as in earlier times, works by obscuring the links between domestic and foreign policies. Legal studies scholar Kathleen Moore points out that even before the post-9/11 curtailment of civil liberties, the Anti-Terrorism and Effective Death Penalty Act and the Illegal Immigration Reform and Immigrant Responsibility Act narrowed the definition of "civil community" in response to the "heightened sense of insecurity required to maintain a restructured, wartime regulatory state after the primary security target disappears."[48]

Moore emphasizes that the distinction between citizens/non-citizens is used in political discourse to support foreign policy and justify the military campaigns and domestic priorities of the U.S. state, such as the battles over "welfare, affirmative action, and immigration reform."[49] This is even more true when the illusion of a "peacetime economy" is discarded for a nation at war as in the present moment. Furthermore, the War on Terror is an extension of the "war on immigrants" waged since the late 1980s, for it has stripped civil rights from non-citizens and led to sweeps and mass deportations of undocumented immigrants, extending the assault on immigrant rights begun with the anti-immigrant Proposition 187 passed in California in 1994, the heightened policing of U.S. borders, and the 1996 immigrant acts.[50]

The dissent of Muslim immigrant youth is not vanguardist because it does not need to be. These young immigrants are simply—but not merely—subjects of both the "war on terror" *and* the "war on immigrants." Their exclusion from processes of "being-made" as citizens, legally and culturally, and their emergent political "self-making" highlight the ways in which civic consent to state policy is secured by imperial power. The targeting of a population demonized as "other," and the absorption of previously targeted communities into a unifying nationalism and climate of fear, shift attention away from the ways in which the war at home and the war abroad actually work in tandem, at the expense of ordinary people everywhere.[51] It is the links *between* legal, economic, and cultural citizenship that are so important for U.S. empire. Anthropologists Jean and John Comaroff argue that the neoliberal mode of "millennial capitalism" increasingly obscures the workings of labor and highlights instead processes of consumption, so that citizenship is recreated as consumer identity.[52] The immigrant youth in this study are not outside this process of consumer-citizenship. They too understand themselves as consumers of, among other things, a lifestyle or education that compelled their parents to migrate from South Asia.

The process of dissenting citizenship is not without its wrinkles, for it seems that these young immigrants implicitly understand the limits of a state-based notion of citizenship, in its economic, cultural, and political senses. As "transmigrants,"[53] they strategically use citizenship even as they manage the failures of both home and host states to guarantee protection and equal rights to Muslim subjects. The anti-Muslim massacres in Gujarat in 2002 and the military standoff between India and Pakistan reinforce a sense that South Asian Muslim youth are in an ambiguous zone between religious and national identification, between an Islamic state and a secular state turned Hindu nationalist. Although so far not many of the Indian immigrant youth seem ready or willing to speak about this, it is possible that the state-condoned anti-Muslim massacres in Gujarat have raised questions about their belonging and their rights for equal protection under the law in India. This is understandably a difficult subject even for their parents to speak about, but one Indian Muslim immigrant told me that in "private spaces" there are expressions of the vulnerability that Muslim immigrants have felt, both in the U.S. and at "home." At the least, perhaps, there is a sense that their cultural citizenship and loyalties are in question in both nations. When India and Pakistan were on the brink of war in 2002, one teenage Indian male said to me: "In India . . . they were asking Indian Muslims what we should do, right, that should we kill them because they are Muslims too," but he also said, "Pakistan is getting stupid right now . . . they don't think that all Muslims who live in India are Muslim, they think they are Hindu."

And yet, ironically, at the same moment, Indian Muslims in the U.S. were being targeted if they were identifiably Muslim and the allegiance of South Asian Muslims and Arab Americans, in general, was suspect. The post-9/11 moment has highlighted the gap between what the state can presumably guarantee, through citizenship or constitutional rights, and what a specific political project such as the War on Terror actually puts into effect, overriding the rights of citizens in order to secure a new Cold War agenda.

CONCLUSION

This moment of *empire* underscores that notions of citizenship developed by youth, some of which I have explored here, are constructed in a dynamic relationship with various institutions, including the state, which are themselves, of course, mutable and multi-faceted. The flexibility of capital evokes strategies of flexible citizenship by young immigrants and their families, but the state is also flexible in its implementation of regimes of governmentality. After 9/11, for example, immigrants and Muslim/Arab/South Asian Americans have been forced to respond to new and constantly shifting measures to limit their civil rights, some of which are not widely publicized, creating more uncertainty and terror. The loss of immigrant rights makes non-citizens vulnerable to hyper-exploitation by employers after 9/11, and to fear of simply living their lives. For instance, in Cambridge, I heard several such stories, from an undocumented immigrant girl unable to enroll in a community college and continue her education, to another high school graduate confused about whether she could marry an undocumented immigrant for fear that he would be deported.

Yet it is important to remember that there are important continuities, before and after 9/11, that are often not acknowledged enough. My use of "post-9/11" is not meant to signify a radical historical or political rupture, but rather a moment of renewed contestation over ongoing issues of citizenship and transnationalism, religion and nationalism, civil rights, and immigrant rights. This state of emergency, this crisis of civil rights and its concomitant mode of dissenting citizenship, is, in fact, not exceptional in the U.S.,[54] for the post-9/11 moment builds on measures and forms of power already in place. This is a state of everyday life in *empire*.

Contrary to Michael Hardt and Antonio Negri's amorphous theory of de-centered "*empire*,"[55] I argue that it is, in fact, *imperialist* power that is at work, even if it has been clearly transformed by the new logic of global capital and the weakened link between the state and the economy. It is clear that the relations among nation, state, and capital have been transformed since earlier eras of imperialism,[56] not to mention the fact that the state's power itself is in decline.[57] However, imperial power does not necessarily require direct governance of colonized states; thus, the model of "imperialism without colonies"[58]—or of neo-colonial occupation, as in Iraq. The current moment of *empire* is situated in a long history of what some call "informal" U.S. *empire* that has used the framework of "universal rights" to cloak a project of reconstituting social and economic relations into a global capitalist order.[59]

The conceptualization of U.S. empire is a project that has drawn renewed attention now that the term *empire* has come out of the closet in the academy and mass media. The power of the U.S. state to exercise the globality of violence and of economy characterizes this new mode of *empire*.[60] U.S. *empire* has become increasingly "covert," if not more formal, as U.S. economic and military power is visibly tied to unilateral foreign policy and national interests, particularly after the demise of Soviet communism and especially after the events of 9/11, which have led to an increasingly authoritarian exercise of U.S. state power both at home and abroad.[61] Although I share the skepticism of new theorists of *empire* and globalization about a state-bound notion of citizenship, I am interested in developing an ethnography of the new *empire* to understand the everyday struggles of those, such as immigrant youth, whose lives have been transformed by this ongoing crisis.

NOTES

1. The research on which this paper is based was funded by the Russell Sage Foundation and supported by my research assistants, Palav Babaria and Sarah Khan. Thanks to Louise Cainkar for her editorial feedback.

2. There were 700 reported hate crimes against South Asian Americans, Arab Americans, and Muslim Americans, including four homicides (two involving South Asian American victims), in the three weeks following 9/11/01. Jeff Coen, "Hate crime reports reach record level," *Chicago Tribune* (October 9, 2001). At least 200 hate crimes were reported against Sikh Americans alone. Jane Lampan, "Under attack, Sikhs defend their religious liberties," *Christian Science Monitor* (October 31, 2001). The Council on American-Islamic Relations (CAIR) reported that it had documented 960 incidents of racial profiling in the five weeks after 9/11/01, with hate crimes declining and incidents of airport profiling and workplace discrimination on the increase. Associated Press, San Jose, Calif/, "Hate crime reports down, civil rights complaints up" (October 25, 2001). The trend only continued to intensify; the CAIR report, *The Status of Muslim Civil Rights in the United States, 2004*, documented that in 2003 there was a nearly seventy percent increase in

"reports of harassment, violence and discriminatory treatment" against Muslim Americans since the previous year. <http://www.cairnet.org/asp/execsumm2004.asp> (August 1, 2004).

3. CAIR, 1998. *The Status of Muslim Civil Rights in the United States: Patterns of Discrimination* (Washington, D.C.: Council on American-Islamic Relations Research Center, 1998); Jack G. Shaheen, "Hollywood's Reel Arabs and Muslims," in *Muslims and Islamization in North America: Problems and Prospects*, ed. Ambreen Haque (Beltsville, Maryland: Amana Publications, 1999), 179–202.

4. Nancy Chang, *Silencing Political Dissent: How Post-September 11 Anti-Terrorism Measures Threaten Our Civil Liberties* (New York: Seven Stories/Open Media, 2002), 94.

5. Chang, *Silencing*, 29–32.

6. Chang, *Silencing*, 43–66s.

7. David Cole and James Dempsey, *Terrorism and the Constitution: Sacrificing Civil Liberties in the Name of National Security* (New York: The New Press, 2002), 168.

8. Cole and Dempsey, *Terrorism and the Constitution*, 35–48; Louise Cainkar, "No Longer Invisible: Arab and Muslim Exclusion After September 11," *Middle East Report* 224 (Fall 2002): pages. Accessed through website: <http://www.merip.org/mer/mer224/224_cainkar.html> (August 1, 2004); Jordan Green, "Silencing Dissent," *ColorLines* 6:2 (2003): 17–20.

9. Joan Jensen, *Passage from India: Asian Indian Immigrants in North America* (New Haven: Yale University Press, 1988), 163–193.

10. Vijay Prashad, *The Karma of Brown Folk* (Minneapolis: University of Minnesota Press, 2000), 69–82.

11. There have been impressive efforts by local groups such as Desis Rising Up and Moving (DRUM) in New York City, that has been organizing around the detentions, South Asian American Leaders of Tomorrow (SAALT) in Washington, D.C., South Asian Network in L.A., and Alliance of South Asians Taking Action (ASATA) in the Bay Area, among others. In addition, several progressive, community-based South Asian American organizations shifted their focus to address the impact of 9/11 on their constituents. South Asian Muslims have also worked within Muslim civil rights organization, such as the American Muslim Alliance, Muslim Public Affairs Council, Muslim American Society, and Council on American-Islamic Relations.

12. Stephen J. Schulhofer, *The Enemy Within: Intelligence Gathering, Law Enforcement, and Civil Liberties in the Wake of September 11* (New York: Century Foundation Press, 2002), 11.

13. Chang, *Silencing*, 69–87.

14. Oliver Ryan, "Empty Shops, Empty Promises for Coney Island Pakistanis," *ColorLines* 6:2 (2003): 14–16; 16.

15. The re-registration component of the program was officially ended by the Department of Homeland Security in December 2003, after protests by immigrant/civil rights and grass-roots community organizations, while other aspects of the program remained in place, and the detentions and deportations put in place by the program continue.

16. Ryan, "Empty Shops," 16.

17. Ryan, "Empty Shops," 16.

18. Rachel L. Swarns, "More Than 13,000 May Face Deportation," *New York Times* (7 June 2003).

19. Swarns, "More Than 13,000."

20. The high school has approximately 2,000 students, of which about forty per cent are white and the remaining sixty per cent are students of color. African Americans are the largest group of students of color (about twenty-five per cent), followed by Latino(a)s (fifteen per cent), and Asian Americans (about seven per cent). In 2000–2002, thirty-three per cent of students had a first language other than English and fourteen per cent were in the bilingual program, which suggests that the immigrant student population in the school is somewhere between these figures.

21. The 2000 Census reported 2,720 Indian immigrants (2.7 per cent of the population), 125 Pakistanis, and 120 Bangladeshis in Cambridge, a city that is 68.1 per cent white

American, 11.9 per cent African American, 11.9 per cent Asian American, and 7.4 per cent Latino (U S. Census Bureau, 2000: <http://factfinder.census. gov/bf._lang=en _2000_SF3_U_D_P2_geo_ID> (November 13, 2002). This, of course, does not include undocumented immigrants. The "native" population is 74.1 per cent, and foreign-born is 25.9 per cent; 17.7 per cent are not citizens and 31.2 per cent speak a language other than English. Cambridge is of course skewed by the presence of the academic community; while 8.2 per cent (3,108) of those enrolled in schools are in high school, fully 70.5 per cent are in college or graduate school, and 38.5 per cent of the population over twenty-five years old has a graduate or professional degree.

22. Kum-Kum Bhavnani, *Talking Politics: A Psychological Framing for Views from Youth in Britain* (Cambridge: Cambridge University Press, 1991); David Buckingham, *The Making of Citizens: Young People, News, and Politics* (London and New York: Routledge, 2000).

23. Lauren Berlant, *The Queen of America goes to Washington City: Essays on Sex and Citizenship* (Durham, N.C.: Duke University Press, 1997); Kathleen Coll, "Problemas y necesidades: Latina Vernaculars of Citizenship and Coalition-Building in Chinatown, San Francisco" (paper presented at Racial (Trans)Formations: Latinos and Asians Remaking the United States, Center for the Study of Ethnicity and Race, Columbia University, New York, March 2002); Toby Miller, *The Well-Tempered Subject: Citizenship, Culture, and the Postmodern Subject* (Baltimore: The Johns Hopkins University Press, 1993); Renato Rosaldo, "Cultural Citizenship, Inequality, and Multiculturalism," in *Latino Cultural Citizenship: Claiming Identity, Space, and Rights*, eds. William. F. Flores and Rina Benmayor (Boston: Beacon Press, 1997), 27–38.

24. Lok Siu, "Diasporic Cultural Citizenship: Chineseness and Belonging in Central America and Panama," *Social Text* 69 19:4 (2001): 7–28; see 9.

25. William V. Flores and Rina Benmayor, eds., *Latino Cultural Citizenship: Claiming Identity, Space, and Rights* (Boston: Beacon Press, 1997), 6.

26. Aihwa Ong, "Cultural Citizenship as Subject-Making," *Current Anthropology* 37:5 (December 1996): 738.

27. Gill Jones and Claire Wallace, *Youth, Family, and Citizenship*, (Buckingham, England and Philadelphia: Open University Press, 1992).

28. Will Kymlicka, *Multicultural Citizenship* (Oxford, UK: Oxford University Press, 1995); John Hutnyk, Stephen Corry & Tris Jean-Klein vs. Richard Wilson & John Hutnyk, in *The Right to Difference is a Fundamental Human right*, ed. Peter Wade (GDAT debate no. 10) (Manchester: Group for Debates in Anthropological Theory, University of Manchester, 2000), 40–52.

29. T. H. Marshall, *Citizenship and Social Class* (Cambridge: Cambridge University Press, 1950).

30. Linda Basch, Nina Glick Schiller, and Cristina Szanton Blanc, eds., *Nations Unbound: Transnational Projects, Postcolonial Predicaments, and Deterritorialized Nation-States* (Amsterdam: Gordon and Breach, 1994).

31. Aihwa Ong, "Cultural Citizenship," 737; Aihwa Ong, *Flexible Citizenship: The Cultural Logics of Transnationality* (Durham, N.C.: Duke University Press, 1999).

32. See Maira, forthcoming.

33. Katherine S. Newman, *No Shame in My Game: The Working Poor in the Inner City* (New York: Alfred A. Knopf and the Russell Sage Foundation, 1999); Stuart Tannock, *Youth at Work: The Unionized Fast-Food and Grocery Workplace* (Philadelphia: Temple University Press, 2001).

34. Ong, "Cultural Citizenship," 739.

35. Manu Vimalassery, "Passports and Pink Slips," *SAMAR (South Asian Magazine for Action and Reflection)* 15 (2002): 7–8, 20; see Ong, "Cultural Citizenship," for a fuller discussion.

36. Robin D. Kelley, *Yo' Mama's Disfunktional! Fighting the Culture Wars in Urban America* (Boston: Beacon Press, 1997).

37. Cole and Dempsey, *Terrorism*; Fereydoun Safizadeh, "Children of the Revolution: Transnational Identity Among Young Iranians in Northern California," in *A World*

Between: Poems, Short Stories, and Essays by Iranian-Americans, ed. Persis Karim and Mohammad M. Khorrami (New York: George Braziller, 1999), 255–276.

38. See Karen Barkey and Mark von Hagen, *After Empire: Multiethnic Societies and Nation-Building—The Soviet Union and the Russian, Ottoman, and Habsburg Empires* (Boulder, Colo.: Westview Press, 1997).

39. Bill O. Hing, "Vigilante Racism: The De-Americanization of Immigrant America," *Michigan Journal of Race and Law* 7:2 (2002): 441–456; Vijay Prashad, "The Green Menace: McCarthyism After 9/11," *The Subcontinental: A Journal of South Asian American Political Identity* 1:1 (2003): 65–75; Corey Robin, "Fear, American Style: Civil Liberty After 9/11," in *Implicating Empire: Globalization and Resistance in the 21st Century World Order,* ed. Stanley Aronowitz and Heather Gautney (New York: Basic Books, 2003), 47–64.

40. Leti Volpp, "The citizen and the terrorist," *UCLA Law Review* 49 (2002): 1575–1600; see 1584.

41. Moustafa Bayoumi, "How Does It Feel To Be a Problem?" *Amerasia Journal* 27:3/28:1 (2001/2002): 69–77; see 73.

42. Corey Robin, "Fear, American Style," 48.

43. Robin, "Fear," 48, 53.

44. James Clifford, "Mixed Feelings," in *Cosmopolitics: Thinking and Feeling Beyond the Nation,* ed. Pheng Cheah and Bruce Robbins (Minneapolis: University of Minnesota, 1998), 362–370. Bruce Robbins, "Introduction, Part I: Actually Existing Cosmopolitanism," in *Cosmopolitics: Thinking and Feeling Beyond the Nation,* ed. Pheng Cheah and Bruce Robbins (Minneapolis: University of Minnesota, 1998), 1–19.

45. Martha C. Nussbaum, "Patriotism and Cosmopolitanism," in *For Love of Country,* ed. Martha C. Nussbaum and Joshua Cohen (Boston: Beacon Press, 2002), 3–17.

46. Martha C. Nussbaum and Joshua Cohen, eds., *For Love of Country* (Boston: Beacon Press, 2002).

47. For example, Michael Ignatieff's cover article, "The Burden," *New York Times Magazine* (5 January 2003), <http://www.nytimes.com/2003/01/05/magazine/05EMPIRE.html> (August 3, 2004), and the pro-empire historian Niall Ferguson's "The Empire Slinks Back," *New York Times Magazine* (27 April 2003), 52–57. See also the cover story of a recent issue of *Harper's Magazine,* titled "The Economic of Empire," by William Finnegan (May 2003), 41–54.

48. Kathleen Moore, "A Closer Look at Anti-Terrorism Law: American Arab Anti-Discrimination Committee v. Reno and the Construction of Aliens' Rights," in *Arabs in America: Building a New Future,* ed. Michael Suleiman (Philadelphia: Temple University Press, 1999), 84–99; see 95. The 1996 Anti-Terrorism Act "Reintroduced to federal law the principle of 'guilt by association' that had defined the McCarthy era," reintroducing "guilt by association" with groups defined by the state as "terrorist" and thus reviving the ideological exclusion of the Cold War–era McCarran-Walter Act, and giving the authority to deport non-citizens on the basis of secret evidence (Cole and Dempsey, *Terrorism,* 117–126). From 1996 to 2000, the government sought to use secret evidence to detain and deport two dozen immigrants, almost all of them Muslims, but ultimately the government evidence was thrown out and the accused were released (see Cole and Dempsey, *Terrorism,* 127).

49. Moore, "A Closer Look," 87.

50. Bill O. Hing, "No Place for Angels: In Reaction to Kevin Johnson." *University of Illinois Law Review* 2 (2000): 559–601; Bill O. Hing, "The Dark Side of Operation Gatekeeper," *UC Davis Journal of International Law & Policy* 7:2 (2001): 123–167.

51. See Prashad, "Green Menace," 65–75.

52. Jean Comaroff and John Comaroff, "Millennial Capitalism: First Thoughts on a Second Coming," in Jean and John L. Comaroff, eds., *Millennial Capitalism and the Culture of Neoliberalism* (Durham, N.C.: Duke University Press, 2001), 1–56.

53. Nina Glick Schiller and Georges Fouron, *Georges Woke Up Laughing: Long-Distance Nationalism and the Search for Home* (Durham, N.C.: Duke University Press, 2001), 3.

54. Keya Ganguly, *States of Exception: Everyday Life and Postcolonial Identity* (Minneapolis: University of Minnesota Press, 2001).

55. Michael Hardt and Antonio Negri, *Empire* (Cambridge, Mass.: Harvard University Press, 2001).

56. Stanley Aronowitz and Heather Gautney, "The Debate about Globalization: An Introduction," in *Implicating Empire: Globalization and Resistance in the 21st Century World Order*, ed. Stanley Aronowitz and Heather Gautney (New York: Basic Books, 2003), xi–xxx; Karen Barkey and Mark von Hagen, eds., *After Empire: Multiethnic Societies and Nation Building—The Soviet Union and the Russian, Ottoman, and Habsburg Empires* (Boulder, Colo.: Westview Press, 1997); Leo Panitch and Sam Gindin, "Global Capitalism and American Empire," in Leo Panitch and Colin Leys, eds., *The New Imperial Challenge* (London: Merlin Press, 2003), 1–42.

57. Glick Schiller and Fouron, *Georges Woke Up*, 208–214.

58. Harry Magdoff, *Imperialism Without Colonies* (New York: Monthly Review Press, 2003).

59. Panitch and Gindin, 10–13.

60. Alain Joxe, *Empire of Disorder* (Los Angeles and New York: Semiotext(e), 2002).

61. Manning Marable, "9/11: Racism in a Time of Terror," in Stanley Aronowitz and Heather Gautney, eds., *Implicating Empire: Globalization and Resistance in the 21st Century World Order* (New York: Basic Books, 2003), 3–14; see 6.

ASIAN IMMIGRANT WOMEN AND GLOBAL RESTRUCTURING, 1970s–1990s

Rhacel Salazar Parreñas

Genny O'Connor, a Filipina domestic worker in Los Angeles, left her office job in the Philippines in hopes of seeking a much higher paying job in the United States. In the Philippines, her salary could barely cover her day-to-day expenses and, needless to say, did not leave her with many resources to provide her family with the financial support expected of her as a single daughter. Having attained a bachelor's degree in the Philippines, Genny had not anticipated that without documents in the United States she would find a job only in the low-wage informal sector. Even after years in domestic work, she is still trying to adjust to her experience of underemployment. She states:

> I was crying all the time. (Laughs.) When my employer gave me the bucket for cleaning, I did not know where I had to start. Of course we are not so rich in the Philippines, but we had maids. I did not know how to start cleaning and my feelings were of self-pity. I kept on thinking that I just came to the U.S. to be a maid. So that was that. I would just cry and I wanted to go home. I did not imagine that this was the kind of work that I would end up doing.[1]

Like many other immigrant women, Genny O' Connor faces severe underemployment. Her participation in the U.S. labor market entails a sharp decline in occupational and social status.

Ever since she was a young girl in the Philippines, Beth Orozo had dreamed of working as a nurse in the United States. Growing up in a not-so-well-to-do family, Beth aspired to leave the Philippines in order to provide financial support to her parents. Since arriving in 1992, Beth has worked as a registered nurse in a convalescent hospital, which is the easiest avenue available for

Philippine nursing graduates to enter the United States. Now earning much more than the average nurse, Beth works as a supervisor at a skilled nursing facility. On average, she works one hundred hours every two weeks, logging in overtime hours to increase her pay. Overall, she likes her life in the United States and feels proud that she can provide for her parents in the Philippines. However, her path to the United States was not an easy one. For one thing, it was made difficult by various examinations, the first being the Commission on Graduates of Foreign Nursing Schools, which she had to take two times, and the second being the State Nursing Board Examination of California. Having overcome these obstacles, Beth has been able to put to use the education she earned in the Philippines and describes her migratory experience as one of "success."[2]

The stories of Genny O' Connor and Beth Orozo are but two of the many different experiences of Asian immigrant women in the U.S. labor market. Post-1965 Asian women migrants to the United States include professionals who correct the labor shortage in certain skilled professions, immigrant entrepreneurs who fill abandoned labor markets in declining urban economies, and workers who provide low-wage labor in service and decentralized manufacturing employment in global cities.

The recent labor migration of Asian Pacific American women takes place in the context of global economic restructuring.[3] This macrostructural process refers to the integration of national economies into a single global labor market. From advanced capitalist nations such as the United States to developing nations such as the Philippines, countries trade goods and services, export products to achieve a viable economy, and depend on multinational corporations and foreign direct investments to increase domestic production.[4] This chapter situates the labor market experiences of recent Asian immigrant women in the globalization of the market economy.

It examines three categories of workers—unskilled laborers, entrepreneurs, and professionals. In this chapter, I show that, each in their own way, these three groups of workers provide "cheap labor" to the U.S. economy—meaning, the costs of their labor are cheap acquisitions for U.S. society and/or the conditions of their employment are below prevailing labor standards. The shared experience of providing cheap labor should be underscored because it is a platform for coalition among diverse classes of immigrant Asian women.

GLOBAL RESTRUCTURING

As the development of a single global market economy contributes to the formation of a decentered global labor market—that is, multiple consumer markets in different regions of the world—it also results in the relocation of production. Under globalization, manufacturing activities have moved from advanced capitalist countries such as the United States to developing countries such as the Philippines and newly industrialized nations such as Korea; for as an intratrade industry develops in globalization (i.e., countries trade similar goods), domestic producers must compete with foreign producers and businesses more than ever to find low-cost resources (e.g., labor and materials) to reduce production costs and maximize profits. Consequently, 25 percent of U.S. manufacturing is done outside the country's national borders.[5]

A new global division of labor is forming from the relocation of manufacturing production. As manufacturing has declined significantly in advanced capitalist nations, export-oriented economies have emerged across the globe. There is a difference between the growth potential of nations that export primary goods and those that export more highly demanded manufactured goods. As shown by the economic boom of the newly industrialized countries in East Asia, the latter are more likely to achieve rapid economic growth.

Globalization does not bode as well for export-based nations without highly demanded goods. Nations such as Sri Lanka and the Philippines not only seek investments of transnational corporations and export products or goods manufactured in free-trade zones; they also export the bodies of their citizens to introduce foreign currency into their economies. The Philippines is doing so to a growing extent, as the number of emigrants (who send remittances) has increased steadily since the 1970s. Numbering fewer than 50,000 in the early to mid-1970s, the number of overseas contract workers annually deployed jumped to 266,243 in 1981 and to more than 700,000 workers in 1994. Of these workers, roughly 60 percent are women.[6]

Globalization induces labor migration from export-oriented developing countries to both newly industrialized nations such as Singapore and Malaysia and advanced capitalist nations in North America and Europe. In the case of newly industrialized nations, the traditional proletariat female workforce, who would otherwise perform low-wage service jobs, now seek higher-paying manufacturing positions. This shift in labor market concentration generates a need for the lower wage labor of women, prompting emigration from neighboring countries such as the Philippines.

In advanced capitalist countries, secondary tiers of manufacturing and service industries have expanded under globalization. To compete with low production costs in developing countries, corporations now increasingly rely on post-Fordist modes of production, decentralized and deregulated forms of manufacturing such as those reflected in assembly lines and sweatshops. Low-wage service jobs have also increased because of the emergence of global cities, where multinational corporations with production facilities across the globe maintain their central operations. Specialized professional services (e.g., legal, financial, accounting, and consulting services) in these new economic centers (e.g., New York and Los Angeles) generate a need for low-wage services to maintain the lifestyles of professionals.[7] The vulnerability of Asian immigrant women, who face social, political, and cultural barriers (e.g., language), makes them a target group to fill various low-wage positions.

Globalization also spurs the migration of skilled workers. Both newly industrialized nations and advanced capitalist nations fill labor shortages by recruiting professionals from developing countries. In a stratified global economy, such workers are attracted by the higher wages offered in more developed nations. Moreover, they seek the knowledge brought about by the greater technological advances in these nations. However, sending nations usually lose, as skills are transferred out of their country. Migration consequently results in the shortage of certain skilled labor in export-oriented nations. In contrast, receiving nations benefit from the skills of immigrant professionals without having to invest in the costs of the education and training needed to reproduce their skilled workforce.

Not surprisingly, the Immigration Act of 1990 put into effect legislation that responded to the economic need for the U.S. workforce to have a supply of highly skilled professionals and technicians. At the same time, this law acknowledged the existing need for the U.S. economy to maintain a supply of low-wage workers. Under this act, the United States raised the number of occupational preference visas from 534,000 to 738,000 by 1995.[8] Preference was given to migrants with "extraordinary ability," for example, those with advanced degrees, or professionals. Eligibility was also given to ten thousand "other workers," including the unskilled.

AN OVERVIEW OF THE LABOR MARKET ACTIVITIES OF ASIAN IMMIGRANT WOMEN

Since the 1930s, women have for the most part outnumbered male migrants in the United States.[9] The shift from a male- to a female-dominated flow of immigrants took place with the prioritization of family reunification as an immigration criterion, beginning most critically with the War Brides Act of 1945.[10] This trend continued with the Hart-Cellar Act, or 1965 Immigration Act, which ended four decades of Asian immigration restrictions and increased the immigration quota to twenty thousand for each country. This law radically changed the composition of the Asian population by gender and level of educational attainment with the direct recruitment of skilled workers. Taking advantage of the priority given to family-based migration, these workers, in turn, have sponsored the migration of their relatives. In fact, most Asian immigrants, including the Chinese, Asian Indians, and Filipinos, enter the United States via family-preference categories.[11]

Due to the large inflow of migrants, the Asian American population grew exponentially, from 1.5 million in 1970 to 3.7 million in 1980 and to 7.3 million in 1990. The majority of Asians (65.6 percent) in the United States in 1990 were foreign-born.[12] This flow is also women-dominated. Between 1975 and 1980, working-age women immigrants from China, the Philippines, Taiwan, Korea, Burma, Indonesia, Japan, and Thailand outnumbered men.[13] The notable exception has been India, where men constitute a greater number of working-age migrants, likely due to the high demand for their skills in science and technology.

Most Asian women migrate as part of a family unit. Approximately 75 percent of professional Asian immigrants who entered the United States between 1988 and 1990 migrated with their families. Moreover, Southeast Asian refugees usually enter the United States with their families.[14] While many Asian women enter the United States as "secondary migrants," to create or reunite a family, they also enter as primary migrants who sponsor the migration of families. This is especially true of Filipinos. The heavy recruitment of nurses spurred the primary migration of women in this community.

Regardless of their mode of entry into the United States, Asian immigrant women actively participate in the labor market. They contribute to the family income and maintain dual-wage-earning households so as to make up for their husband's earnings, which are generally lower than those of native-born men. Income pooling is the primary reason for the high median family income of Asian Americans.[15] Of the general female population age sixteen years and over, 56.8 percent are in the paid labor force.[16] As Table 1 indicates, the percentage of labor market participation of Asian immigrant women compared to immigrant men varies by ethnic group.

TABLE 1

Labor Market Participation of Asian American and Asian Immigrant Women (by percentage), 1990

	All	*Foreign-born*
Japanese	47.5	40.8
Chinese	65.4	57.8
Filipina	77.7	73.1
Korean	61.0	55.5
Indian	56.9	59.6
Vietnamese	56.9	55.8

Source: U.S. Census, *1990 Census of the Population, Asians and Pacific Islanders in the United States.* Washington, D.C.: U.S. Government Printing Office, 1993.

Notably, the rate of labor force participation among Filipina immigrant women far exceeds that of the general population and of other Asian groups and is much higher than in the Philippines, where women's labor force participation was 33.7 percent in 1992.[17] Their higher labor force participation has various reasons, including their better command of the English language and concentration in wage labor. Filipinos have the lowest rate of self-employment in the United States, at thirty-two per thousand. In contrast, the rate of self-employment for the general U.S. population stands at 69.74 per 1,000 and is even higher for other Asian ethnic groups: 180.46 per 1,000 for the Koreans and 72.77 per 1,000 for the Chinese.[18] Thus, it is likely that the rate of labor market participation for other Asian immigrant women is undercounted because the assistance they offer as wives in family businesses is not officially recognized as paid labor activity.

For Asian immigrant women, their generally high levels but also diverse range of educational attainment within and across ethnic groups have implications for their employment. In 1990, 20.3 percent of the U.S. general population had completed four years of college.[19] In contrast, the level of educational attainment of foreign-born Asian women in the five largest ethnic groups is significantly higher (Table 2). Only Southeast Asian refugees have a much lower percentage than the general population.

TABLE 2

Educational Attainment of Bachelor's Degree or Higher of Asian American and Asian Immigrant Women, 1990

	All	*Foreign-born*
Chinese	35.0	32.4
Filipina	41.6	44.5
Japanese	28.2	22.2
Asian Indian	48.7	49.0
Korean	25.9	25.5
Vietnamese	12.2	12.7
Cambodian	3.2	3.1
Hmong	3.0	3.0
Laotian	3.5	3.4
Thai	24.9	24.9

Source: U.S. Census, *1990 Census of the Population, Asians and Pacific Islanders in the United States.* Washington, D.C.: U.S. Government Printing Office, 1993.

Filipina and Chinese women occupy a wide variety of jobs in the labor market, while other Asian ethnic groups are more highly concentrated in particular occupational categories, for instance, Koreans in self-employment and Vietnamese in low-wage employment. In some ethnic groups, the labor market incorporation of women is bifurcated. For example, 24.6 percent of employed Chinese female migrants are in managerial and professional occupations and 29.7 percent are in service and manufacturing production employment.[20] This contradicts the common description of immigrant women as mostly disadvantaged low-paid workers in dead-end jobs, with limited financial security and upward mobility.[21]

Although the generally high level of educational attainment among Asian immigrant women has allowed them to seek a wider range of occupations than their Latina and Caribbean counterparts, the educational capital of Asian immigrant women does not necessarily mirror the characteristics of their labor market incorporation. Skilled Asian immigrant women have turned to lower-skilled occupations because of restrictive measures against foreign-trained professionals as well as language barriers.[22] For instance, in 1990, 23.7 percent of Asian Indian women migrants held professional and managerial occupations, even though 49 percent of them had completed four or more years of college.[23]

Underemployment is a quintessential way that Asian immigrant women provide "cheap labor" for the skills that they bring into the U.S. labor market. An example is the case of migrant Filipina domestic workers. In my study of Filipina domestic workers in Los Angeles, I found that seventeen of twenty-six interviewees have achieved some years of college.[24] Ten had education degrees and worked as teachers prior to migration. As domestic workers, they enhance the low-cost services that they provide employers by offering free tutoring and other educational services to their wards.

To summarize, Asian immigrant women have a high rate of labor market participation and a diverse range of levels of educational attainment. Unlike other immigrant women, they hold a wide variety of occupations in the U.S. labor market and actively participate in the labor force in myriad ways.

ASIAN IMMIGRANT WOMEN AND GLOBAL RESTRUCTURING

How are the labor market activities of contemporary Asian immigrant women situated in global restructuring and linked together? Addressing a similar question, Lisa Lowe illustrates the material links that tie the activities of low-wage manufacturing Asian women migrant workers to those in Asia by situating them in global restructuring. As she describes:

> Women migrate from countries of origin formerly colonized by the United States, or currently neocolonized by U.S. corporate capital and come to labor here as racialized women of color. In this sense, despite the obstacles of national, cultural, and linguistic differences, there are material continuities between the conditions of Chicanas and Latinas working in the United States and the women working in maquiladoras and low-cost manufacturing zones in Latin America, on the one hand, and Asian women working both within the United States and in Asian zones of assembly and manufacturing, on the other.[25]

The material continuities that Lowe draws between low-wage women workers across advanced capitalist and developing nations should be extended to include other groups of Asian migrant workers, as they are also part of the singular socioeconomic process of globalization and in various ways provide low-cost labor for the benefit of the U.S. economy.

Low-Wage Workers

Asian immigrant women fill the labor market need for low-wage manufacturing and service workers in urban centers of the United States. They are in decentralized industries, particularly in the garment industry, performing low-wage assembly jobs, and they provide services, including affordable manicures, to middle- and upper-class professionals.

With the offshore relocation of manufacturing, the production that does remain in the United States (e.g., garment, electronics, and furniture production) is decentralized and informal. For instance, the garment industry is structured like a pyramid. Manufacturers cut the costs of production by subcontracting to garment shops and awarding contracts to the lowest bidders. Consequently, they do not leave contractors with much capital to pay seamstresses wages that meet prevailing labor standards. As a result, native women usually shun this work. Without the same opportunities and human capital (e.g., language proficiency) as their native counterparts, immigrant women, including Asian women, fill this existing demand in the labor market.

Garment shops tend to be located in ethnic enclaves such as Chinatown, where the access of potential immigrant entrepreneurs to a pool of co-ethnics as a cheap labor force makes them more attractive and lucrative. Immigrant entrepreneurs are also attracted to sewing shops because they require less investment and lower overhead costs than other businesses. For instance, in Oakland, newspaper ads indicated that "$25,000 is sufficient to start a ten to fifteen person shop."[26]

By using immigrant labor, small-business operators facilitate the process of global restructuring. In the garment industry, they give manufacturers direct access to the low human capital of immigrant women. In this way, manufacturers can remain flexible to the constant turnover in fashion trends and at the same time remain competitive against production in the Third World. Overworked and underpaid, immigrant seamstresses are usually paid by piece rate and often lack overtime pay, as well as health insurance and other work compensations.[27]

In the global cities of New York, San Francisco, and Los Angeles, sewing jobs have pulled a large number of Chinese female immigrants into the bottom rungs of the garment industry and made them "the garment workers par excellence." In New York City, over half of Chinese immigrant women workers are in the garment industry, with most of them working as sewing-machine operators.[28] In the San Francisco Bay Area, 90 percent of garment workers are women, with over 80 percent of them Chinese-speaking.[29] In Los Angeles, approximately 10 percent of the estimated 120,000 garment workers are Asians.[30]

Streamlining production is another way that U.S. manufacturers reduce overhead costs. For the most part, low-level manufacturing employment has been divided into simpler and simpler tasks and is therefore low-paying. These jobs are often unsafe (e.g., they expose workers to hazardous materials), are monotonous, and require few skills.[31] In the Midwest, meatpacking plants increasingly rely on the low-wage labor provided by Southeast Asian refugees. For Vietnamese and Laotian women, packing plants are often their best option for employment, as the work requires few skills (e.g., jobs are set up as mechanized assembly work), provides better pay than other available low-skill employment, and is now shunned by the Anglo-American men who traditionally dominated the industry.[32] In Silicon Valley, one study indicates that in the late 1980s women made up approximately 80 percent of production workers, with most being members of minority groups and with Filipina women as the largest group of recent migrants entering assembly-line manufacturing.[33]

Low-wage service work is another way that Asian immigrant women provide cheap labor to the U.S. economy. Many of the available low-wage service jobs are considered women's work, as they have been relegated to women historically in a sex-segmented labor market. These personal and industrial services are provided in different economic sectors, including the informal sector (e.g., domestic workers), the formal industry sector (e.g., hotel housekeepers, restaurant workers, and certified nurse's aides), and ethnic economies (e.g., manicurists and restaurant workers).[34]

Providing low-wage service is difficult work. Domestic work such as elder care may require twenty-four hours of labor.[35] Trinidad Borromeo, a sixty-eight-year-old woman whom I interviewed in Rome, describes a daily work routine that generally reflects those of her counterparts in Los Angeles.[36]

> I begin at seven in the morning. I change her, feed her, give her all of her injections and medication. Then I clean the apartment. When you take care of an elder, the first thing you have to have is patience. If you don't have it, you won't last. For example, when you feed her, it can take up to an hour. It gets hard when they don't want to open their mouth or swallow the food. But taking care of an elder like this one is better than a mobile one. Those ones are demanding. You wipe them already then they want you to wipe them again. They have no shame. These types are better . . . you just move them around from the bed to the chair. You have to just clean her bed everyday because it will smell like pee around the house if you don't. . . . I wake up at four in the morning just to check that the woman is still alive. Then if there is no problem, I sleep until a little bit before seven and I am done with her by nine. I just serve her coffee and biscuits. I sleep around midnight or one in the morning.

Despite their nonstop labor, elder caregivers seldom take a day off because of the tremendous emotional dependence of their elderly patients.[37]

Along with their Caribbean and Latina counterparts, contemporary Asian immigrant women respond to the demand for low-wage service labor in various global cities in the United States, but they do so to a much lesser degree. Yet they are more heavily concentrated in this labor market sector in certain cities. For example, according to the Pilipino Worker's Center, immigrant Filipina workers dominate elder caregiving in Los Angeles, in both personal (e.g., private home) and industrial (e.g., nursing home) services.[38] In the Filipino immigrant community, recent women migrants frequently turn to domestic work because of their limited options in the labor market.[39] In a study of undocumented women in the San Francisco Bay Area, Chris Hogeland and Karen Rosen found that 41 percent of fifty-seven survey participants from the Philippines are elder care or childcare workers and an additional 23 percent are employed as housekeepers.[40]

Other groups of Asian immigrant women provide low-paid services through ethnic economies. For instance, ethnic entrepreneurs have taken up running nail salons to take advantage of the concentration of service professionals in global cities.[41] In this way, Asian immigrant women provide cheap labor by making this luxury affordable to a wider range of consumers. Any visitor to New York or Los Angeles will notice the abundance of nail salons operated by Korean and Vietnamese women who provide low-cost services to compete with each other. One study found that Koreans operate up to 80 percent of nail salons in New York City.[42]

Small-Business Entrepreneurs

Contemporary Asian immigrant workers contribute to the economic development of global cities in another crucial way. They spur economic growth with the operation of small businesses. For example, they provide convenient services such as dry cleaning to the growing professional class and run contracting shops that are part of the informal manufacturing economy.

Immigrant Koreans have entered the deteriorating urban centers of the United States in full force; more than 50 percent of them operate small businesses.[43] Many of these businesses are not enclosed in ethnic enclave economies (e.g., Koreatown) but instead cater to a larger urban clientele. These types of urban businesses include greengrocers, dry cleaners, liquor stores, and retail shops of Asian manufactured goods (e.g., wigs, clothing). Opening a business in an urban area is more affordable for prospective entrepreneurs than in, for example, the safer area of the suburbs. High levels of crime and poverty have made urban neighborhoods—ghettos and barrios—what Jennifer Lee calls "vacant niches," as local economies have been abandoned by large corporations such as gasoline companies and supermarkets.[44] Taking advantage of these abandoned neighborhoods, Koreans have franchised gasoline stations and opened groceries and liquor stores in these "high-risk" markets. In doing so, they give big businesses access to these once-deserted markets but at the same time absorb the risks that the big businesses choose to avoid.

Immigrants are often disadvantaged to compete against the native-born in the primary labor market because they are unable to put to use their educational and occupational capital, face language difficulties and discrimination, and are unfamiliar with American cultural practices.[45] To avoid low-wage jobs like those performed by Chinese garment workers or Filipino hotel housekeepers in San Francisco, immigrants with class and ethnic resources may choose to operate small businesses to better negotiate the segmented U.S. labor market. In doing so, they take advantage of the business know-how brought by their human capital (e.g., high levels of educational attainment) and the ethnic resources (e.g., rotating credit associations) that make available financial capital required to open a business.[46]

Although they have more resources and advantages than contemporary Asian immigrant women in low-wage manufacturing and service employment, small-business entrepreneurs provide cheap labor as well.[47] First, the maintenance of such businesses requires long hours. As Kyeyoung Park describes, "Korean men and women involved in small business often work more than twelve hours daily and six or seven days a week. According to an August 1987 survey by the Korean American Small Business Service Center of New York, 85 percent of Korean proprietors kept their stores open more than ten hours per day. Some 70 percent used family labor."[48] Second, businesses also rely on the unpaid labor of wives and children. How do long hours and family work translate to cheap labor? Edna Bonacich explains, "If one adds up the hours of work put into many immigrant enterprises and divides that number by the money taken out of business to live on, the result is not infrequently a very low rate of earnings."[49]

In general, small ethnic businesses could not possibly survive without family labor, most importantly the often unrecognized labor of women. While unrecognized, the work of women in small businesses also suffers from a gendered hierarchy that relegates the "less skilled" and thus more monotonous work to them. For instance, men often take over the managerial tasks (e.g., accounting) that are required in the daily operation of small Korean businesses. Similarly, in Chinese take-away shops in England, Miri Song observed that mothers often performed the more labor-intensive and unskilled labor in the kitchen.[50] By relegating the less-skilled and seemingly less important work to women, men are able to justify their own lower contributions to housework. As a result, the "double day" plagues women in small businesses as well as in low-wage work. Women are not only expected to keep long hours in small businesses but are also relied upon to perform the bulk of domestic chores in the household.[51]

Professional Women

The global labor market also needs to attract the highly skilled professionals to their global cities. In this way, advanced capitalist countries such as the United States economically benefit from immigrants' know-how while amending the shortages in certain skilled professions that have been created by cutbacks in social spending.

The growth of capitalism in the United States has led to the greater reduction of social, health, and education benefits to society.[52] As such, the labor shortage of professionals in the United States, which is an acute problem in the fields of science, engineering, and health, is an institutionalized structural problem that has been mended in part by the recruitment of Asian professionals. These workers provide cheap labor in that their educational training did not cost the United States any money. By facilitating their entry, the U.S. government can avoid the consequences of its failure to invest in the reproductive costs of the country's labor force. The highly skilled labor of Asian immigrants, particularly women, is also arguably cheaper than that provided by their native-born counterparts. One study found that Asian women who are employed in core industries earn $2,179.06 less than white female scientists and engineers.[53]

Recent Asian immigrants have helped fill the professional labor force shortage. From 1988 to 1990, more than half of the 150,000 highly skilled migrants who entered the United States originated in Asia.[54] That they have done so more than any other group is a legacy of U.S. colonialism.[55] In particular, the modeling of the educational infrastructure in Asia after that in the United States has homogenized educational standards and objectives to create an expanded international labor pool of professionals who constitute an available resource for the U.S. labor market.[56]

Due to the direct recruitment of Asian professionals into the United States, the percentage of Asian American scientists and engineers increased from 2 percent in 1970 to 7 percent in 1990. Moreover, the numbers of scientists and engineers escalated from just 21,000 to 150,000 in two decades.[57] While the majority of professional immigrants are men, 42 percent of the highly skilled Asian migrants who entered the United States from 1988 to 1990 were women.[58]

A high percentage (68 percent) of highly skilled women from the Philippines entered the United States during this time. As the Philippines is the largest source of foreign-trained health professionals in the United States, many entered as nurses, for which the labor shortage is estimated at 370,000.[59] The reluctance of the United States to invest in the reproductive costs of its labor force is much to blame for this shortage. As Paul Ong, Edna Bonacich, and Lucie Cheng describe:

> The United States has been reluctant to spend money on the training of health personnel, such as nurses, in a general effort at cost containment for health care. The ultimate goal is to reduce health care costs for capitalist employers by lowering the costs of their benefits packages. This policy creates a shortage of nurses in the United States and a demand for immigrant nurses.[60]

Yet the process of labor migration is neither easy nor convenient. In most cases, Filipina nurses first enter as temporary workers. During this time, they are ineligible to sponsor the migration of their families, whom they are forced to leave behind in the Philippines. Foreign-trained nurses also relieve the sponsoring medical facility of the costs of their recruitment and bear most of the costs of their labor placement. On average, migration to the United States costs Filipino nurses $7,000, which is usually deducted from their pay.[61] This debt binds them and consequently leaves them vulnerable to the sponsoring facility. Once in the United States, they also find themselves with the most demanding and stressful jobs. In the mid-1980s, one survey found that 82 percent of Filipino nurses work in hospitals, versus 53 percent of non-Filipinos.[62] Often these hospitals are concentrated in inner cities and are more congested and busier than other health facilities.

At the same time that the "cheapening of labor" in the United States has forced employers to turn to the recruitment of professional Asian workers, it has also deepened the cheap labor pool and limited the opportunities of underprivileged members of society. As Ong, Bonacich, and Cheng describe:

> In general, the cheap labor approach to restructuring has the impact of curbing the development of local professionals by limiting the opportunities of the local working class. People who work for minimum wage can hardly afford to send their children to college. Attacks on the working class thus have the consequence of undermining the strategy of reorganization and innovation by limiting the growth of the class that can implement it. This contradiction sets the stage for the immigration of professionals and managers.[63]

Thus, while the entrance of professionals into receiving nations such as the United States helps deepen the cheap labor pool, global restructuring also generates the need for their recruitment.

CONCLUSION

The labor market activities of recent Asian immigrant women indicate that their economic adaptation is unlike that of other groups of immigrant women. They can be found in a wide variety of occupations in the U.S. labor market, both cross-ethnically and within ethnic groups. As such, it is difficult categorically to address their labor market incorporation in a singular framework that is inclusive of the diverse range of their labor market activities. The high rate of labor market participation of Asian immigrant women as well as the diversity of their labor market activities attest to the feminization of the wage labor force under globalization. However, the conditions of their labor market incorporation and their low standards of employment suggest that women still hold a fairly low status in the labor market.

By surveying the labor market activities of recent Asian immigrant women and by viewing these activities as processes embedded in global restructuring, I argued that they provide cheap labor in the U.S. economy in myriad ways. The concept of cheap labor is one that I loosely describe to mean that in some way the costs of their labor are "cheap" acquisitions for U.S. society and/or the conditions of their employment are below prevailing labor standards. This definition applies to unskilled workers, ethnic entrepreneurs, and professionals. For instance, it is applicable to the experiences of migrant Filipina nurses whose training did not come with any financial costs to the United States, to the Korean women who operate small businesses for long hours, and to the Chinese immigrant women who dominate the needle trade in various global cities in the United States.

 The women workers in the three categories I have surveyed have unequal levels of mobility. They face different opportunities and constraints. While they may share the opportunity to earn more than they would in their countries of origin, a nurse such as Beth Orozo and a domestic worker such as Genny O'Connor cannot be considered equally displaced by the capitalist system in the United States. For one, Beth has been able to transfer her educational capital, while Genny clearly has not. Thus, our understanding of their labor market activities should not disregard their differences.

So as not to ignore the diversity of the labor market participation of Asian immigrant women, my analysis emphasizes the specificities in the location of three groups of workers in the larger schema of global restructuring. My analytical approach accounts for the specific contexts of each of these groups' labor market incorporation. Employing such an approach shows that the material realities of their labor are quite different. At the same time, it shows that from their specific location in global restructuring, Asian immigrant women contribute some form of "cheap labor" to the United States.

NOTES

1. Rhacel Salazar Parreñas, *Servants of Globalization: Woman, Migration, and Domestic Work* (Stanford, CA: Stanford University Press, 2001), 150.
2. Personal interview with author, Iloilo City, Philippines, May 2001.
3. By recent immigrants, I refer to those who entered after 1965, which is when the United States eliminated discriminatory racial barriers and established an open-door policy based on the criteria of occupational skills and family reunification.
4. David Held, David Goldblatt McGrew, and Jonathan Perraton, *Global Transformations: Politics, Economics, and Culture* (Stanford, CA: Stanford University Press, 1999), chaps. 3–5.
5. Harold Perkin, *The Third Revolution: Professional Elites in the Modern World* (London and New York: Routledge, 1996), 19.

6. Parreñas, *Servants of Globalization*, chap. 2.

7. Saskia Sassen-Koob, "Notes on the Incorporation of Third World Women into Wage Labor through Immigration and Offshore Production," *International Migration Review* 18:4 (1984): 1144–67.

8. Kitty Calavita, "Gaps and Contradictions in U.S. Immigration Policy: An Analysis of Recent Reform Effects," in David Jacobson, ed., *The Immigration Reader: America in a Multidisciplinary Perspective* (Maiden, MA: Blackwell, 1998), 105.

9. Marion F. Houstoun, Roger G. Kramer, and Joan Mackin Barrett, "Female Predominance of Immigration to the United States since 1930: A First Look," *International Migration Review* 28:4 (1984): 908–63.

10. This law facilitated the entrance of more than two hundred thousand Asian war brides, fiancées, and children into the United States. See Judy Yung, "Appendix: A Chronology of Asian American History," in Asian Women United of California, eds., *Making Waves: An Anthology of Writings by and about Asian American Women* (Boston: Beacon Press, 1989), 423–31.

11. See Bill Ong Hing, "Asian Immigrants: Social Forces Unleashed after 1965," in Jacobson, ed., *The Immigration Reader*, 144–82; and Pyong Gap Min, "An Overview of Asian Americans," in Pyong Gap Min, ed., *Asian Americans: Contemporary Trends and Issues* (Thousand Oaks, CA: Sage Publications, 1995), 10–37.

12. U.S. Census, *1990 Census of the Population, Asians and Pacific Islanders in the United States* (Washington, D.C.: U.S. Government Printing Office, 1993).

13. Yen Le Espiritu, *Asian American Women and Men* (Thousand Oaks, CA: Sage Publications, 1997), 63.

14. Ibid., 62.

15. Alejandro Portes and Rubén Rumbaut, *Immigrant America*, 2d ed. (Berkeley: University of California Press, 1998).

16. U.S. Census, *Census of Population and Housing, 1990 PUMS* (Washington, D.C.: U.S. Government Printing Office, 1993).

17. Sylvia Chant, *Women-headed Households: Diversity and Dynamics in the Developing World* (New York: St. Martin's Press, 1997).

18. Portes and Rumbaut, *Immigrant America*, 72.

19. U.S. Census, *Census of Population and Housing 1990 PUMS*.

20. U.S. Census, *1990 Census of the Population, Asians and Pacific Islanders in the United States*.

21. According to Linda Miller Matthei, half of immigrant women enter low-wage employment in operations and services, because they lack educational credentials and have few employment skills. See "Gender and International Labor Migration: A Networks Approach," in Susanne Jonas and Suzie Dod Thomas, eds., *Immigration: A Civil Rights Issue for the Americas* (Wilmington, DE: Scholarly Resources Inc, 1999), 77.

22. Examples are provided by Esther Chow, "Asian American Women at Work," in Maxine Baca Zinn and Bonnie Thornton Dill, eds., *Women of Color in U.S. Society* (Philadelphia: Temple University Press, 1994), 203–27.

23. Keiko Yamanaka and Kent McClelland, "Earning the Model Minority Image: Diverse Strategies of Economic Adaptation by Asian American Women," *Ethnic and Racial Studies* 17:1 (January 1994): 79–114.

24. Parreñas, *Servants of Globalization*, introduction.

25. Lisa Lowe, *Immigrant Acts: On Asian American Cultural Politics* (Durham, NC and London: Duke University Press, 1996), 165.

26. Miriam Ching Louie, "Immigrant Asian Women in Bay Area Garment Shops: 'After Sewing, Laundry, Cleaning and Cooking, I Have No Breath Left to Sing,'" *Amerasia Journal* 18:1 (1992): 1–26.

27. See also Xiaolin Bao, chapter 17, in Shirley Hane and Gail Nomura, eds., *Asian/Pacific Islander American Women: A Historical Anthology* (New York: New York University Press, 2003).

28. Nancy Foner, "Benefits and Burdens: Immigrant Women and Work in New York City," *Gender Issues* 16:4 (1998): 8.

29. Louie, "Immigrant Asian Women," 2.

30. Richard Kim, Kane K. Nakamura, and Giselle Fong, with Ron Cabarloc, Barbara Jung, and Sung Lee, "Asian Immigrant Women Garment Workers in Los Angeles," *Amerasia Journal* 18:1 (1992): 69.

31. Karen Hossfeld, "Hiring Immigrant Women: Silicon Valley's 'Simple Formula,'" in Zinn and Dill, eds., *Women of Color*, 765–93.

32. Janet E. Benson, "The Effects of Packinghouse Work on Southeast Asian Refugee Families," in L. Lamphere, A. Stepick, and G. Grenier, eds., *Newcomers in the Workplace: Immigrants and the Restructuring of the U.S. Economy* (Philadelphia: Temple University Press, 1994), 109.

33. Rebecca Villones, "Women in the Silicon Valley," in Asian Women United of California, eds., *Making Waves*, 172.

34. See Ivan Light, Georges Sabagh, Mehdi Bozorgmehr, and Claudia Der-Martirosian, "Beyond the Ethnic Enclave Economy," *Social Problems* 41:1 (1994): 65–79. By definition, *ethnic economy* refers to the self-employed with co-ethnic employees.

35. Charlene Tung, "The Cost of Caring: The Social Reproductive Labor of Filipina Live-in Home Health Caregivers," *Frontiers* 21:1/2 (2000): 72.

36. Parreñas, *Servants of Globalization*, 159.

37. Tung, "The Cost of Caring," 76.

38. Informational brochure provided by Pilipino Worker's Center, 1996.

39. This is caused by a combination of their undocumented status, their inability to put to use their training and work experience from the Philippines, and the ethnic niche in caregiving that has developed in the Filipino migrant community from the large flow of nurses into the United States.

40. Chris Hogeland and Karen Rosen, *Dreams Lost, Dreams Found: Undocumented Women in the Land of Opportunity* (San Francisco: San Francisco Coalition for Immigrant Rights and Services, 1990).

41. Millian Kang, "Manicuring Race, Gender, and Class: Service Interactions in New York City Korean-owned Nail Salons," *Race, Gender, and Class* 4:3 (1997): 143–64.

42. Kyeyoung Park, *The Korean American Dream* (Ithaca, NY: Cornell University Press, 1997), 117.

43. Pyong Gap Min, "Korean Americans," in Min, ed., *Asian Americans*, 199–231.

44. Jennifer Lee, "Striving for the American Dream: Struggle, Success, and Intergroup Conflict among Korean Immigrant Entrepreneurs," in Min Zhou and James Gatewood, eds., *Contemporary Asian America: A Multidisciplinary Reader* (New York: New York University Press, 1999), 284.

45. Ibid., 280.

46. Ivan Light and Edna Bonacich, *Immigrant Entrepreneurs: Koreans in Los Angeles, 1965–1982* (Berkeley: University of California Press, 1988).

47. Edna Bonacich, "The Social Costs of immigrant Entrepreneurship," *Amerasia Journal* 14:1 (1988): 119–28.

48. Kyeyoung Park, "Impact of New Productive Activities on the Organization of Domestic Life: A Case Study of the Korean American Community," in Gail M. Nomura, Russell Endo, Stephen H. Sumida, and Russell C. Leong, eds., *Frontiers of Asian American Studies* (Pullman: Washington State University Press, 1989), 147.

49. Bonacich, "Secret Costs," 120.

50. Miri Song, *Helping Out: Children's Labor in Ethnic Businesses* (Philadelphia: Temple University Press, 1999), 55.

51. Park, "Impact of New Productive Activities," 140–50.

52. Paul Ong, Edna Bonacich, and Lucie Cheng, "The Political Economy of Capitalist Restructuring and the New Asian Immigration," in P. Ong, E. Bonacich, and L. Cheng, eds., *The New Asian Immigration in Los Angeles and Global Restructuring* (Philadelphia: Temple University Press, 1994), 3–35.

53. Shang-Luan Yan, "The Status of Asian American Women Scientists and Engineers in the Labor Force," *Race, Gender, and Class* 6:3 (1999): 119.

54. William Kanjanapan, "The Immigration of Asian Professionals to the United States: 1988–1990," *International Migration Review* 291 (1995): 15.

55. John Liu and Lucie Cheng, "Duality of Post-1965 Asian Immigration," in Ong, Bonacich, and Cheng, eds., *New Asian Immigration*, 80.

56. Ong, Bonacich, and Cheng, "Political Economy of Capitalist Restructuring," 3–35.

57. Paul Ong and Evelyn Blumenberg, "Scientists and Engineers," in Darrell Y. Hamamoto and Rodolfo D. Torres, eds., *New American Destinies: A Reader in Contemporary Asian and Latino Immigration* (New York: Routledge, 1997), 166.

58. Kanjanapan, "Immigration of Asian Professionals," 20.

59. See Paul Ong and Tania Azores, "The Migration and Incorporation of Filipino Nurses," in Ong, Bonacich, and Cheng, eds., *New Asian Immigration*, 164–95.

60. Ong, Bonacich, and Cheng, "Political Economy of Capitalist Restructuring," 25.

61. Information obtained from informal interviews I conducted with recruitment agencies and prospective migrants in the Philippines between January and July 2000.

62. Ong and Azores, "Migration and Incorporation," 164. See also Catherine Ceniza Choy, chapter 20 in Shirley Hune and Gail M. Nomura, eds., *Asian/Pacific Islander American Women A History Anthology* (New York: New York University Press, 2003).

63. Ong, Bonacich, and Cheng, "Political Economy of Capitalist Restructuring," 25–26.

MEDICAL, RACIST, AND COLONIAL CONSTRUCTIONS OF POWER IN ANNE FADIMAN'S *THE SPIRIT CATCHES YOU AND YOU FALL DOWN*

Monica Chiu

INTRODUCTION

This essay is about medical, racist, and colonial constructions of power. It incorporates the following seemingly disparate, but what I will prove to be inextricably connected, discourses: those surrounding the Vietnam War and its subsequent stateside refugee management; current medical care for Southeast Asian patients; and so-called authorial (medical, textual, cultural) constructions of Hmong representation. My critique is based on a reading of literary journalist Anne Fadiman's *The Spirit Catches You and You Fall Down: A Hmong Child, Her American Doctors, and the Collision of Two Cultures,*[1] her re-presentation of the actual case of epileptic Hmong American child Lia Lee. Her book raises thorny questions concerning why Lia's "proper" care remains a contentious debate between medical knowledge and Hmong cultural practice; how the historical construction of Asian American identity contributes to present and continued Hmong mythologization and feminization and to the Lees' identity as deviant parents; and how Fadiman's often ethnographic, and not always critical, text often contributes to reinscribing her subjects into the very colonial parameters from which she attempts to extract them. My work offers new readings of the book's stated "cultural collisions" in which cross-cultural healing is both accomplished and simultaneously denied via practices that Fadiman interrogates and employs.

Briefly, Lia Lee was born in July of 1982, in Merced County, California, to first-generation Hmong[2] refugees Fuoa Lee (her mother) and Nao Kao Lee (her father) as their fourteenth child. Delivered naturally and in good health, she suffered from her first epileptic seizure at three months of age. While the physicians conclude that Lia has suffered from an "electromagnetic storm inside her head," the more eloquent, iatric articulation of an epileptic seizure, they are unaware that the Lees have attributed Lia's symptoms to *qaug dab peg*, or "the spirit catches you and you fall down." Her family blames her condition on the departure of one of Lia's many spirits—the one responsible for health and happiness—which occurred at the moment her elder sister Yer accidentally slammed the door with such ferocity that she frightened a *dab*, a spirit, away (10, 20). The Lees intend to retrieve the lost *dab* through a shaman. The Hmong view those experiencing *qaug dab peg* as shamanistic, their seizures mimicking the trance-like states of shamans in the throes of contacting other-world spirits. Hmong medical and spiritual practices are steeped in animism—wherein spirits are ascribed to beings and objects and can be frightened away, causing disease and death—and shamans represent a necessary and positive link between the body and the lost spirit, between the world of the living and the dead. They are the designated arbiters between the corporeal and the spirit world, recalling lost spirits and relaying augurs of ill or good fortune through trance and animal sacrifice.[3]

At Merced County Medical Center (MCMC), however, such cultural explanations carry little weight in effecting a cure, even though the hospital had treated numerous Hmong patients since the late 1970s who made so-called unusual medical requests. Throughout Lia's subsequent, numerous, and severe seizures, MCMC legitimizes its own narrative, here the brain's "electromagnetic storm" and the appropriate use of drugs to quell them, despite frequent consternation exhibited by the Lees. Yet the family continues to transport her to the emergency room, placing some faith in Western biomedicine. Much to MCMC's and the Lees' anguish, Lia is eventually pronounced brain dead at five years of age but continues to live a vegetative existence disconnected from any life support system. That both MCMC and the Lees hoped for another outcome is the sole narrative uniting the two fraught parties throughout the ordeal. I therefore probe the limits of medical, colonial, and authorial knowledge and their attendant (often racist) power within this complicated case; my work investigates the value strategically attributed or denied to "culture" (whether medical culture or history) in order to refine the interconnecting parameters within and to respect the intermittent gaps between Lia's illness and health as they are inextricably bound up in a constant negotiation of Asian American cultural citizenship.

My reading of *Spirit* involves an assessment, mediated by Fadiman, of what counts as knowledge for MCMC, for the nation, for the Lees, and for Fadiman herself, and how such competing knowledge constructs the involved actors and the medical establishment; how such knowledge is shaped by the politics of U.S. colonialism vis-à-vis Southeast Asian refugees and Asian American identity construction, broadly. I map Fadiman's motive to illuminate the Lees' healing beliefs against those of MCMC. Fadiman intends to unpack—yet often inadvertently problematizes—the utility of MCMC's diagnostic praxis in the face of the

Lees' mytho-cultural perceptions shaping the life-and-death assumptions of Lia, its central, Asian American patient. Intertwined within this medical case is an historical narrative of the fraught acceptance and rejection of Asian Americans in general, and Hmong acceptance in particular, that exacerbate conditions surrounding the treatment of Lia's parents and therefore their growing consternation over Lia's declining condition and their escalating frustration with the MCMC staff. Because the Hmong threaten accepted, routine operations of not only this California County, but of MCMC's health care practices, both Fadiman and I necessarily contextualize the figure of Lia and the cross-cultural difficulties surrounding her care. I keep my summaries of necessary historical information—necessary both to understanding Fadiman's argument and to grasping mine—to what I consider a bare minimum. My discussion, unlike Fadiman's, considers how Asian American disruptions to the nation have resulted in Asian Americans' pathologization and internal colonization. That is, Southeast Asian refugees and immigrants (from Laos, Vietnam, Thailand, and Cambodia) are the most recent targets in a national, racist trajectory that has systematically vilified Asian American immigrants as "alien" and "polluting" threats to the health and welfare of the nation despite a seeming vindication as model minorities.[4] As such, Lia is doubly de-humanized: first by her illness and then by her classification as Asian, which evokes an historical pathologization and feminization of Asian subjects, which I will discuss later.

The frictions animated through Lia about the diagnosis and treatment of her epilepsy occur not only between MCMC's so-called paradigmatic Western (read: masculine) biomedicine[5] and the Lees' Asian, feminine, mytho-cultural beliefs about the relevance and conception of the body; but the frictions also vex Fadiman's representation of the case in which she criticizes the colonizing practices of MCMC only to replicate them in her portrayal of the Lees.

In this interpolated tale, written by a literary journalist who is neither a medical anthropologist nor an ethnographer, the narrative itself raises puzzling questions about her intent, her authorial method, and her audience. She finds "how hard it was to lay blame at anyone's door"—either with the Lees or Lia's medical staff—for the child's eventual, vegetative state at five years of age (x). Rather, she blames "crosscultural misunderstanding" for this particularly tragic case deemed "preventable" by Lia's physicians (262, 55). Despite such attempts at neutrality, Fadiman leans heavily toward sympathizing with the Lees, thus obligating the reader to untangle the various unspoken assumptions and strains that inflect the text and from which one gleans an understanding of Lia, her parents, and her physicians. Within the essay, I offer answers to the following complicated questions: How are Lia's parents being read (or even managed) by Fadiman? Is Fadiman's text a dialogic bridge between medical authority and cultural adherence? If the Lees' words and actions are Fadiman's interpretations of translations—given that her knowledge of the Hmong is circumscribed by her Western ways of thinking and given the Lees' inability to speak English—how do readers responsibly interpret *Spirit*, especially if the Hmong are known to strategically deliver only "acceptable" cultural information to their Western counterparts?[6] For whom, then, is the book written? Even if the Lees had spoken for themselves, would we understand their voices as partially constructed fictions accorded to Fadiman's purpose? And most pressing, whom does *Spirit* serve: did the Lees solicit Fadiman in order to make their story known or did Fadiman pursue this cultural drama? In the third section of the essay, such an analysis of the book's ur-narrative—Fadiman's contextualization through an ethnographic gaze that often renders the Lao Hmong exotic—complicates and contributes to *Spirit*'s complexity and therefore to the urgency of negotiating cross-cultural solutions in an increasingly multicultural nation that, unfortunately, practices varying types of subtle but powerful and devastating colonization.

THE EFFECT OF MEDICAL AND COLONIAL NARRATIVES ON LIA'S CASE

Power, both colonial and medical, remains the driving, critical force behind the results of Lia's case, a conclusion that Fadiman herself suggests throughout *Spirit* and one to which I agree. This section will serve as a necessary overview of Hmong/Southeast Asian history,[7] the contested acceptance of Asian Americans and their feminization, which redoubles the pathologization of this female, Hmong patient. Lia's case bears out the personal, national, and political cost of knowledge: who possesses what constitutes as knowledge, to what and to whose advantage or detriment?

In the particular arena of Hmong medical care in the United States since the late 1970s, cross-cultural conflict has proven an impasse in diagnosing and treating the intriguing and perplexing phenomenon of Sudden Unexpected Death Syndrome (SUNDS), in which otherwise healthy Hmong men have been dying from medically unexplained nighttime heart attacks, usually following a nightmare or a bad dream.[8] Western medical practitioners are adamant about locating a reasoned, scientific (or proof-based) rationale for these deaths, a medical narrative at odds with a Hmong animist-based explanation in which "death attack" survivors recall the presence of "an incubuslike *dab* [spirit] who sits on the victim's chest and presses the breath out of him" (Fadiman 188). Yet in the medical model of patient pathography, in which the patient "presents" her personal *story* of pathology (or illness narrative)[9] to the physician, it is then duly translated and legitimized (via specialized medical terminology and nosology) for diagnosis, treatment, and, hopefully, cure.[10] Unfortunately, Katherine Montgomery Hunter argues, such a process retells and reorders the patient's initial narrative in a manner and context that may very well be conducive to medical epistemology, but one that also effectively erases the patient as subject to render her an object: "a case, the narrative of her malady."[11] In overlooking cultural narratives of illness, such as those Hmong explanations circumscribing SUNDS, patients' and medical practitioners' "logical" explanations compete, often prompting some Hmong patients to forgo medical treatment.

Meanwhile, resistance to biomedicine's socializing/colonizing aspect of Southeast Asian patients has erupted in their manipulation of their own bodies and illnesses in order to "circumvent" the medical system, outlines Aiwha Ong in her study of San Francisco–based Cambodian refugees. By mimicking ills, these refugees continue to receive the social (often financial) support they need; by attending prenatal discussions or keeping doctors' appointments, they "maintain official connections that do not threaten their family security" in their host country, but once at home, they continue to "follow their own desires about having babies" or treating their own ills.[12] In other words, individual cases can alter standard practice as in the creation of Southeast Asian Mental Health. Unfortunately, such attempts have resulted, in part, in further entrenched views of "passive, obedient" and "noncompliant" refugee patients in a health care model whose "constructs are universally applicable, while ignoring the complex micropolitics and consequences of encounters with the health profession,"[13] and thus they clearly bear out Julia Epstein's observation that "[I]f medical 'cases' are socially as well as biologically constructed, then case histories participate in producing as well as recording what they observe."[14] Furthermore, in a type of medical and corporeal colonialism, constant revisions of what constitutes acceptable modes of being sick or healthy (a topic pursued later in the essay) demonstrate how patient management can be negotiated to the detriment of the ill and to the advantage of the health care system.

Using such a broad reading of Southeast Asian diseases and the consequences of how they are diagnosed helps to locate the Lee's treatment in the multiethnic, but often racist, matrix of the United States, where internal colonialism constructs these subjects in a manner that often exposes or conceals elements of their history and culture depending on the political outcome desired by the dominant population. Because the Lees, along with Lia's persistent, unmedicatable seizures, threaten MCMC's routine practices and its physicians' medical training, they become symptomatic of a history in which "unassimilable" and "inscrutable" Asian Americans have been posed as perils to national health and welfare, demanding forms of domestication and management. The quintessential strand of such Asian American race abjection is the Yellow Peril, a sociohistoric categorization, emerging in the 1880s, of Asians as the harbingers of illness and the progenitors of pollution deeply rooted in American rhetoric. From fictions created about so-called diseased and dirty Chinese immigrants[15] evolved spurious medical "facts" and eventually political acts prohibiting the legal and civil actions and internal migrations of not only Chinese but other Asian immigrants as well.[16] Their "cleaning up" involved not necessarily instructions in bathing habits, but socialization and domestication embodying racist, Western norms. An etiology of Asian American pathology has left a linguistic, semiotic, political, and symbolically bitter trace within American culture. This played out recently in the 1990s when high incidences of tuberculosis and HIV diagnosed in New York's Chinatown re-pathologized the community.[17] Such narratives rest on biocultural foundations that are derivative of the discursive intersections between fact and fiction and that have plagued social reaction and attendant legislative (colonialist) action against Asian Americans, resulting in the symbolic institutionalization of the Asian American corporeal within this peril/(para)lyzing paradigm even as the attribution of dirty and diseased to the Chinese speaks more to the nation's own preoccupation with moral and medical self-hygiene than to any Other's.[18]

The Lees of Fadiman's book are interpolated by such cultural constructions, becoming part of an historical trajectory illuminating a politically convenient method by which "good" and "bad" Asian Americans have been constructed according to U.S. need. I begin by noting that Lia's pediatricians Neil Ernst and Peggy Philip learn what they can about the Lees' ethnicity by reading "old *National Geographic* articles about the Hmong," a well-intentioned gesture illuminating a certain dedication to their patient (57). *National Geographic*, however, represents the epitome of Western anthropological accounting of the "other," a simplified, layperson's introduction to what is often an exoticization—especially photographically—of other cultures and places.[19] Hardly a self-conscious publication, it is prone to solidifying others through so-called grand narratives of Western anthropology, "othering" "natives" for readers via an "us-and-them" hierarchy, highlighting bodily differences based on color, cultural practice, hygiene, and nutrition. My ideas about what is generalized as Western anthropology are informed by Trinh T. Minh-ha, who categorizes such anthropology as conversations among white men about "others," conversations that conveniently overlook the latter's intellectual input about themselves and therefore such Western study offers views reflecting only white values and judgment.[20] For Neil and Peggy, the publication serves as a catalyst, not a deterrent, to accepted, fixed narratives about the Hmong, emphasizing the devious effects of constructions of knowledge and types of representation of others.

And yet such "fixity" becomes pliable when the stakes for re-interpretation benefit American politics, especially war politics. I consider here the "Secret Wars," a name that describes the silence surrounding Hmong contributions, on behalf of the United States, to the Vietnam "conflict" (as it has unfortunately come to be called).[21] Many of the West's most successful war efforts in the Laotian jungle were possible only after the CIA's recruitment of Hmong soldiers who had knowledge of and physical agility in their native environment. But their historical value for the West has been fleeting—their representation more fluid than fixed—based exclusively on their contributions toward Western victory over Eastern/Vietcong communist foes, delineating this essay's critique of a narrow adherence to certain narrative strands at the expense of others: the French occupiers enlisted Hmong men who "were 'magnifique' in the jungle" only to abandon them as the Indochinese empire fell; the Americans later trained them on "CIA stockpiled World War II weapons" and depended on their extensive knowledge of the jungle to reach downed U.S. pilots before the Communist forces of the Pathet Lao took them as POWs or killed them.[22] Thus, while the military is without a doubt one of the most regimented, ordered, and hierarchized of all American political bodies, it warranted the seemingly unorganized and primitive Hmong soldiers to successfully navigate impressive victories amid the equally irrational and dense jungles of Laos, elucidating the West's inability to navigate outside of its ordered ranks, beyond its national boundaries. The deal outlined in what capacity the U.S. would aid the Hmong, in return for their military expertise, in resisting North Vietnamese forces, and the U.S. promised to secure them "a new place" to live and farm if they were defeated by the Pathet Lao.[23] The U.S., unfortunately, did not readily honor either of these promises. Thus, the Lees' skepticism toward biomedicine, bound up in a larger Hmong wariness toward Western solutions to disease, represents their broad-based leeriness toward many American broken promises in which Hmong were deserted and forced to face the murderous Pathet Lao from whom the Americans so quickly fled. Such racist power cannot help but influence refugee distrust.[24] This conveniently allows the dominant population, viewing the "deviant" behavior of its Southeast Asian constituents, to lay blame on these seemingly problematic citizens. To add injury to insult, some Americans who regard Hmong immigration as increased tax burdens—yet ignorant of their U.S.-backed maneuvers in Vietnam—chafe at hearing that, as Jane Hamilton-Merritt documents, "the Hmong are unique in that they may be the only refugees in the world that do *not* want to resettle in the U.S.," but would have preferred to return to Laos if that were possible.[25]

These Hmong narratives and their reinscriptions via ignorant American resentment complicate the already convoluted misinformation passing between Americans and Hmong. Because MCMC had witnessed an extensive population of Hmong refugees moving into their county, they were familiar with journalists' often sensationalist representations of the Hmong as "primitive," "low-caste" and "Stone Age" "tribe[s]" (188), and disseminated reports of how community tempers flare over the religious sacrifice of chickens and pigs in Hmong urban living rooms; others, unaware of significant Hmong contribution and devastating personal losses in fighting against Communism with American aid, begrudged their right, as political refugees, to governmental funding through welfare, Medicare, or California's Medi-Cal. For example, the Lees—who became "enemies of the state [of Laos]" for either supporting the U.S. or "attempt[ing] to remain neutral"— survived two arduous journeys: first to Thai refugee camps, losing three children en route; once in the states, they moved from Portland, Oregon, to Merced, California, enduring racism and ignorance.[26] Only when the Hmong's culturally incompatible narratives clash with those of their U.S. neighbors—that is, when Hmong war refugees, along with those from Vietnam and Cambodia, began arriving to the U.S. in significant numbers—do they become highly visible, highly charged community members.[27] For MCMC, the necessity to know about the formerly invisible, unknown Hmong is prompted only from emergencies in Lia's care, replicating the manner (via crisis, as in war) by which the Hmong were introduced (made visible as expendable soldiers) to the United States.[28] While biomedicine makes a concerted, necessary attempt to operate in tandem with other narratives, unfortunately for MCMC, such narratives are bolstered by a type of colonial epistemology. Fadiman references Kleinman's warning that "traditional ethnic stereotypes . . . may exert a mischievous influence on care."[29] In allowing unsubstantiated information to influence MCMC's medical knowledge, and in forgetting how medicine itself contextualizes and attributes value to knowledge, Lia's medical staff overlooks how the particular must be contextualized in the Lees' personal historical and cultural narratives.

That medicine itself adheres to militaristic metaphors exacerbates the negotiation between war-ravaged refugees and refugee medicine, the latter a convenient colonization of victims to suit American notions of health and welfare.

Consider the defense-infused language of medicine evident in phrases such as "fighting cancer" or "battling AIDS," "fortifying the immune system" or "building immunological defenses."[30] While American military powers benefited from the battling, fortifying, and fighting exhibited by Hmong soldiers on behalf of the U.S., these Southeast Asian soldiers' eventual status as refugees, subject to Western medicine's narratives of disease and diagnosis, relegate what is an acceptable or unacceptable fight-as-resistance narrative within internal colonialism, a point I will return to in the third section of the essay.

This resonates with refugee management, the socialization of refugees in order to reinscribe limitations that eventually necessitate the civilizing care of a "first nation."[31] U.S. Hmong refugee "dispersal" occurred among "53 cities in 25 different states," in which they were "spread like a thin layer of butter through the country so they'd disappear."[32] When Southeast Asian families pack up and move from designated refugee locales in order to be closer to relatives, often in cities boasting large Southeast Asian populations, they work against their stereotype as the model minority. Furthermore, their strategies at finding and creating critical mass in national locations prove a "masculine" gesture on a now passive nation that is unable to stop their internal migration, toppling an expected Asian American feminization, an expected obedience and passivity.[33] The image of the domesticated Asian arises, again, from a history of so-called emasculated Chinese immigrant "bachelors'" who were tethered to so-called feminine forms of employment—such as busing tables, washing and pressing laundry, cooking food—when their application to other jobs only fueled the fire of White antagonism over scarce employment.[34] More recently, the Vietnamese "enemy" during the War acquired the appellation "gook" that highlights wild, untamed feminine representations and proved invaluable in promoting American soldiers' military mentality of assumed dominance over an inferior, effeminate Asian enemy.[35] The designation of Asians as the model minority since the 1960s—what I view as a continuation of the feminized, passive, obedient subject—becomes a disjunction between their "enjoyment" of model minority status and the fact that Asian American intellect has never eclipsed historical stereotypes surrounding their bodily presence as a threat.[36]

The Lees' noncompliance grates against such a history of expected Asian American/feminized obedience. While non-Asian patients certainly express noncompliance more often than not, the book interrogates which patient's noncompliant behavior is accepted and which is berated. What occurs is a medical construction of deviance that accords itself with a contrived Asian American feminization and passivity. As Aihwa Ong pointed out, some Southeast Asian patients practice noncompliance as a form of resistance to expected, medical behavior, to which the Lees' noncompliance fits. Briefly, in the early years of Lia's epilepsy, the Lees exhibit a certain ambivalent faith in Western biomedicine by rushing their daughter to the emergency room each time she has a seizure. But Lia's primary pediatricians become increasingly frustrated at their patient's confounding responses to tried and tested epileptic medications. That the Lees resisted MCMC's medical authority to embrace a so-called lesser-valued mytho-cultural authority; and that Lia's seizures remained uncontrollable through usually effective medical routes, contribute to the Lees' categorization as "difficult" and "noncompliant." The Lees struggle with all aspects of their daughter's care, hardly complacent in a cross-cultural context that befuddles them. Unable to speak or read English or Arabic numerals, they are overwhelmed with verbal and written hospital interaction and with the diagnostic directions of Lia's "confounding" and ever-changing drug regimen.[37] They do not understand measurement concepts such as "one teaspoon," and their notion of time is dictated not by a clock, but rather by the crowing of the cock. Finally, as the Lees witness hyperactivity as side effects of the drug Tegretol or the subduing effects of phenobarbital, they create a drug regimen in accordance with what they believe is best for their daughter, but a regimen antithetical to what her physicians deem best for Lia.[38] The Lees' defiance marks their deviance. The more the Lees resisted via this avenue of drug (mis)compliance, the more adamantly the medical staff attempted to socialize them into the parameters of "proper" patient behavior.

Physician Neil Ernst's solution amid this economy of power and knowledge both reifies and questions his medical authority. Although the "doctors only saw her [Lia] when she was sick and never in her [loving] home environment," states Effie Bunch, a visiting public health nurse, Neil finally removes Lia from her loving home arena, accusing the Lees of child endangerment, "a form of child abuse" (55, 79). Lia is first lodged with two Mennonite sisters who strap her to an infant car seat in their living room during bouts of hyperactivity, a feasible drug side effect (as her parents have noted already, with chagrin, about the drug Depakene), and not the antics of a naughty child as their particularly cruel solution seems to suggest. The sisters' reaction begs the question, why should (and how can) a sick child be strapped into submission? Or even into health? Later, with the Korda foster family, Lia cries for days (up to 10 until sedated), and urinates and defecates on the floor, unusual behavior for this toilet trained child. Even though Lia receives the prescribed doses of medicine during her stint in foster care, she has seizures more often here than when in the custody of her biological parents who do not follow her medical regime in the painstaking details of the foster care givers (81, 87, 88). I question, then, if Neil's unsubstantiated assessments about drug noncompliance contributed to the corporeal abuse meted out upon Lia's body through continued seizures. In Lia's case, what type of substandard care, if any, becomes the fallout from Neil's misunderstandings over the Lees' so-called defiance and disrespect? Physician Dan Murphy, whom Fadiman interviews, says that "[p]eople in the early years of their medical careers have invested *an incredible amount of time and energy and pain* in their training, and they have been taught that what they've learned in medical school is the only legitimate way to approach health problems" (76, emphasis mine). And he admits, in a statement so fitting to an essay critiquing power, that "They [Hmong] won't do something just because somebody more powerful says do it" (71). Why does Murphy assume that he is inherently "more powerful"—however that might be defined—than his patients? How does one incorporate into these terms of empowerment the "incredible amount of time, energy, and pain" expended by Hmong refugees not only in their contributions to the American war effort in Vietnam, but also in their flight from Laos to the United States?

In November of 1986, Lia suffers a seizure that effectively shuts down her brain, rendering her "Comatose. Brain Damage[d]. Vegetable." She is "quadriplegic, spastic, incontinent, and incapable of purposeful movement" (151, 210). Much to the hospital's surprise, Lia lives far beyond the hours and days the hospital staff expects. By the book's conclusion, Lia is still alive at seven years of age—two years after her doctors expected her to die—continuing to baffle medical-rational authority. Lia's family lovingly accepts her as the person she still is. Once at home, Nao Kao and Fuoa care for her around the clock, first in those days where death was "imminent," then for years thereafter, feeding, changing, carrying, sleeping with, and loving a child in "a persistent vegetative state" (210). Fadiman's text, and I believe Fadiman herself, begs the question, "Why not?" According to MCMC staff, the Lees' loving and protective behavior, consistent throughout Lia's life, only now "miraculously [transforms them] from child abusers to model caregivers" (214), exemplifying that "deviant" others are acceptable only when their actions are deemed appropriate to Western ideals. Indeed, as long as Asian Americans remain compliant, they are easily accepted into the American fold.

That many of Lia's seizures were recorded as idiopathic (30)[39]; and that other Hmong complaints like SUNDS rest in no organic cause becomes a mirror to an attendant inability to make rational sense of, and therefore incorporate, the Hmong and their beliefs except as members of an ironically described "celebratory" multiculturalism, a footnote in a continuously evolving and contested American culture. If the Lees envision that "the crisis was the *treatment*, not epilepsy," then Fadiman's work suggests that it is both Hmong and biomedical belief structures themselves, and how we understand them, that demand change (53). Fadiman does not advocate a total investment in shamanism over medical solutions, but rather observes that Lia's MCMC health care providers should have dignified the Lees' beliefs—asked them for explanations, listened thoughtfully, acknowledged their validity in Hmong belief, even encouraged shaman use (what harm could it do?)—in light of the urgency exacerbated by existing cross-cultural tensions. While biomedicine works effectively in the Western social context from which it has arisen, so, too, has shamanism proven effective in certain historical and social conditions, providing comforting explanations of terrifying behavior and offering community-based mechanisms for healing. In no uncertain terms, the Asian/American body is assigned and or denied value according to American cultural and political convenience, clearly unmasking that "foreign" others and the cultural narratives they embody continue to be accepted or rejected on a negotiated basis.[40] Lia's case therefore raises intriguing questions about how the Hmong have been marked indelibly by U.S. contact; and in turn, how the U.S. has been forced to accommodate them in ways whose initial frictions have been resolved by attempting to pathologize, socialize, and colonize them. Lia's treatment highlights how Asian American bodies are a reminder of how abstract political concerns play themselves out on concrete, somatic selves.

READING A READING

In an interview by Ron Hogan, Fadiman explains how her encounter with the Lees happened by chance, and how her motivation to pursue the family's story arose from the excitement of looking at one case via two views: " . . . if I could take one case and look at it from both points of view—the doctor's and the patient's—I might have something really interesting."[41] Her results conclude in an honest and publicly accepted attempt—exemplified in the numerous awards that Fadiman garnered for her work[42]—to understand and record the difficulties involved on both sides. The book's complexity serves many purposes: as an introduction to Hmong culture and history; as a cautionary tale—for the casual reader as well as the first-year medical or nursing student—of the limits of medical knowledge; as a primer on expected and accepted immigrant behavior and the consequences of expecting assimilationist practices in a nation often promoting their resistant actions.

And yet, Fadiman cannot help but write from her own Western cultural context, even as she seeks to see both sides. Her underlying investigative motivation relentlessly pursues *why* Lia's care was so fraught with conflict and anger on the part of Fuoa, Nao Kao, and Lia's hospital staff. In order to answer her own questions, she contextualizes Hmong history, culture, and Hmong refugee circumstances—new to Fadiman herself (she admits)—and, as she suspects, to her readers as well, thus coding her readers as non-Hmong. To a lesser degree, Fadiman also outlines the pre-refugee Merced County community and makes brief reference to the backgrounds and medical training of Lia's primary pediatricians, Neil and Peggy. Fadiman's sympathies list toward the Lees, and she is more critical of the MCMC staff, an opinion garnered when she quotes Arthur Kleinman (260–261). She seems to find an answer to how Lia's case should have been handled through Kleinman's "model of mediation," one dedicated to compromise, and not coercion, between patient and physician (261), one legitimizing not only the physician's version of the pathography, but also that of the patient and her culture. But her weighty emphasis on Hmong people and culture vis-à-vis a dearth of information about the equally mysterious and relatively unknown culture of medicine—at least to the lay person—resonates uncomfortably with assumptions about "others" created in "our" own naïve understandings of ourselves. In many ways, Fadiman's text assumes that her readers understand *why* Lia's physicians tried so hard to indoctrinate her parents into the medical model; it simultaneously assumes that readers need a "logical" explanation for the Lees' "abnormal" resistance, thus necessitating Fadiman's contextualization of the Hmong in general, and the Lees in particular. The text therefore raises troubling assumptions about literary intent (to inform the "West" about the "East"/Hmong) in a book whose aim is to bridge, not contribute to, cross-cultural misunderstandings. Such discursive frictions destabilize any simple categorization of authorial or textual intent and their resultant readings.

To be fair, however, Fadiman's captivating read presents what could be dry and unpalatable historical reporting as pedagogical work without dogmatism. She consults sources—those more reputable than a dependence on *National*

Geographic—and interviews all of the case's participants in order to hear first-hand versions of each narrative. In fact, according to one of *Spirit*'s reviewers, Fadiman succeeds in "intimately reveal[ing] the Hmong to the reader."[43] On the whole, Fadiman remains sensitive to her subjects, but at times, her narrative risks reestablishing the pitfalls of cultural typing she so vehemently guards against. Fadiman herself does not heed the limits of cultural knowing, however, for she privileges Westerncentric logic in many instances. Fadiman, who has exhibited an enormous measure of self-consciousness concerning MCMC's medical practices, at times becomes unself-conscious about her own culturally confined representations. The book, for example, is framed by what Fadiman represents as a "typical" Hmong birth and a Hmong shaman healing ceremony, both of which subtly inform (even direct) how we view the Lees: with a certain awe and fascination at their "exotic" ways. In the opening pages, a laboring Hmong woman silently delivers her child, into her own hands, in her dirt-floored home in Laos. The event is ritualistic in that all of her children have been born in such a manner, and only the newborn's cries disturb the assembled group of sleeping children (a subtle comment on the high birthrate among Lao Hmong). The view establishes a dichotomy between Hmong and "American" births. It becomes a seemingly neutral reporting of the facts that retain narrative suasion by rendering the American side—and all of its own idiosyncrasies—invisibly acceptable vis-à-vis a "third world" delivery.[44] Thus, one might ask if Fadiman is re-naturalizing the always and already naturalized contours of "alien" thought and practice, as in the "third world" woman seemingly more tolerant of pain (it is the newborn who cries out and not the laboring mother). What reassurances about "us" and "them" does *Spirit* offer a naïve reader?

Fadiman's representations of the Hmong contextualize the Lees' beliefs, practices, fears, and reactions to make them graspable, palatable, more easily acceptable to her reading audience. According to several of *Spirit*'s reviewers, themselves Hmong, the book "romanticizes," exaggerates, or misrepresents Hmong culture. According to Mai Na M. Lee, Fadiman falsely attributes the Lees' fighting spirit to a history of Hmong persecution, thus endowing all Hmong, in the U.S. and Laos alike, with an admirable stereotype-as-trait.[45] This American designation is, in fact, a domestication of resistance or deviance. For an ethnic group to be endowed with a fighting spirit renders admirable the use of that spirit against a common enemy—the Vietcong, for example—while simultaneously denying, even vilifying its potential to overturn racist U.S.-based practices as in refugee management. If, for example, the Lees' so-called fighting spirit contributes to their medical deviance, it is no longer constructive nor is it admirable. The basic tenet of a celebratory Asian American fighting spirit has an analogue in the trajectory of Asian Americans as model minorities as long as the spirit is employed in and contained to practices deemed acceptable to the nation's political objectives of containing Asian Americans. As such, culture's and medicine's colonialist containment of the Hmong does, indeed, work toward the common purpose of constant ethnic reconstruction. Ellen Wiewel, reviewing the book for *Medical Anthropology*, regards Fadiman's attempts to historicize and contextualize the Hmong as "sincere"—as a legitimation of Fadiman as a source of knowledge—yet she worries over her "zealousness . . . at coming up with a definitive Hmong culture. . . . She uses knowledge garnered from Hmong leaders to forward her thesis about the nature of the clash between the Lees and California health care" when it "is impossible to judge the weight of the figures that Fadiman interviewed as representatives of Hmong organizations."[46]

According to Fadiman, the negative, medical categorization of epilepsy runs counter to that of the Lees' simple acceptance of Lia's condition, which angered the MCMC hospital staff witnessing or hearing of the 17 devastating seizures she endures, between the ages of eight months and four-and-a-half years, some bouts continuing for up to 20 minutes (depriving her brain of oxygen and contributing to her mental retardation) (38–39). When commenting on Fadiman's observation that the Hmong place epileptics in high regard, reviewer Lee, who is Hmong herself and grew up in a Hmong community, only remembers "the stigma attached to the disease. Aside from leprosy, Hmong people fear epilepsy the most, and the fact that the Hmong attribute its causes to spirit possession makes it even more frightening to them."[47] The "highly idealistic" representation that Fadiman attributes to Lia's epilepsy has a heavy hand in crafting readerly response toward the Lees.

On the one hand, Fadiman creates a valuable narrative answering many questions about Hmong culture; on the other, the text's drive to produce reasonable answers for what we may deem unusual or irrational actions points to the narrative's inability to acknowledge that some aspects of Hmong culture, for the Western reader, are unknowable. It is just this tension between complimenting Fadiman and chastising her that offers a reading of *Spirit* by which one can view how the author often succumbs to the very ethnic pitfalls she initially exposes and condemns.

Contrary to a need to understand everything that one writes about or all that one reads about concerning ethnic subjects, there exists a certain efficacy in textual lacunae—whether ideas that cannot be translated or those which the author's subject refuses to translate. And filling those gaps as an authorial, editorial, or readerly obligation often results in romanticization and stereotype, as *Spirit*'s reviewers have outlined. Doris Sommer reveals the efficacy of making readers "worry" as they read, a tenet of many minority works. She advises her readers to "proceed with caution," the title of her book, allowing that sometimes, for example, "a trauma story wisely refuses to satisfy impertinent curiosity" (xii). "Worry should be part of the work, if we learn to read the distance written into some ethnically marked literature" (xi).[48] She continues, "The lessons in listening for surprises and pausing before they are neutralized; the training to stretch our expectations of difference and to recoil from quests for mastery—these may be universal markers of literature worth discussing" (xi–xii). My point is that amid Fadiman's predominantly culturally sensitive approaches to her various "texts" lurks the urge, sometimes satisfied, to overcompensate for the unknown, whether by overlooking Western medicine itself as a mysterious entity for the layperson in order to highlight the "mysterious" Hmong; or whether privileging Western logic. It is true that Fadiman resists taking sides. Yet within *Spirit* two narratives are sublated: on the one hand, her sympathies often lie with the Lees and thus she critiques Western biomedicine; but in her propensity to unconsciously fall back upon her Westerncentric presuppositions, her observations stereotype her subjects in a manner reestablishing the caveats she desires to dismantle.

As a non-medical practitioner, Fadiman's, and other lay readers', familiarity with Western medicine arises from the historical and social conditions that privilege and endorse it, rendering practices that fall outside biomedical models less easily admired or accepted. In fact, like the Hmong who believe in and seek out shamanism (detrimental to successful care), much of biomedical narrative (and even cure) relies on patients' acceptance of medical explanation and diagnosis. Indeed, we seek it out. Such narrative expectations themselves contribute to shaping health care workers' attitudes and practices, including "deviant" ones. That the medical profession is its own cultural laboratory, producing physicians, is witnessed in a profusion of autobiographical books that chart—or rather demystify—the process of medical acculturation from "raw" student to polished physician. Such books become a "politics of representations" in their "reproduction of medical domains"[49]: Melvin J. Konner's *Becoming a Doctor: A Journey of Initiation in Medical School*; Michelle Harrison's *A Woman In Residence;* Kenyon J. Rainer's *First Do No Harm: Reflections on Becoming a Brain Surgeon*; Howard S. Becker, ed., et al., *Boys in White: Student Culture in Medical School*; Ellen Lerner Rothman's *White Coat: Becoming a Doctor at Harvard Medical School*; Perri Klass's *A Not Entirely Benign Procedure: Four Years as a Medical Student*; Sayantani DasGupta's *Her Own Medicine: A Woman's Journey from Student to Doctor*; Steve Giergerich's *Body of Knowledge: One Semester of Gross Anatomy, the Gateway to Becoming a Doctor.* Tellingly, the books are published by non-university or crossover presses such as Ballantine, Scribner, Penguin, or Quill, suggesting that an interest in the cultural construction of medicine is hardly relegated to a strict academic audience. It bolsters the notion that a nonmedical reading public acknowledges the existence of a medical culture, one so complicated it warrants a passel of explanatory texts. David B. Morris, for example, states that "Western medicine for over a century has worked to perfect a dominant scientific discourse based on viewing disease as the product of biological and chemical mechanisms within the body—a view for which the biomedical model provides a convenient shorthand—and this traditional biomedical model remains, despite resistance, slippage, and some outright defections, entrenched as the ruling paradigm of contemporary Western medicine."[50] Therefore, this constructed medical arena is no less influential to the larger understanding of Lia's case than an introduction to, say, how the construction of "primitive" Hmong religious beliefs influence Hmong attitudes toward biomedicine. Such a foray insists on questions of audience. We can accept that the majority of Fadiman's readers are non-Hmong, hence justifying her trajectories into Hmong culture and history. But in that same vein, we can safely assume that many, but not all, of her readers are unaffiliated with the medical profession. Thus her elision of medicine's culture and history suggests its "universal" acceptance and understanding.

Fadiman's assumptions about what is accepted (MCMC's biomedical model) and what demands explanation (the Hmong) resonate with an economy of knowledge and power: who possesses knowledge and how is power-knowledge put to cultural use? For example, Fadiman takes great lengths in preparing for her initial meeting with the Lees, not only locating a necessary translator, but also educating herself in Hmong etiquette, hoping not to offend, threaten, or seem critical. "Meeting a Hmong is like getting into a speakeasy: everything depends on who sent you" (97). Fadiman describes no similar preparations before meeting Lia's physicians most evidently because she has acculturated the proper American etiquette of the deference that is expected of her in the clinical setting. Fadiman's physical descriptions work similarly toward rendering invisible the manner in which cultural stereotyping is bound up in our own entrenched cultural knowledge. This is attributed, in part, to our (and my) acceptance of Western anthropological narratives: explanations of an "other" cannot but be contextualized against our own, accepted, cultural norms. Fadiman describes the Lees as "good-looking," Fuoa with "glossy black hair" and Nao Kao who looks "intellectual and a little nerdy" in a pair of thick, black glasses. As well, both are "short, and although neither were fat, they looked well-rooted, as if it would take a gale force wind, or maybe even an earthquake, to knock them over" (97–98). In contrast, physical descriptions of Neil and Peggy are taken from their pre-med days: they are "tall, good-looking, athletic . . . students." For the rest, their personalities and intelligence are emphasized *as* description: they were "a combination of idealism and workaholism that had simultaneously contributed to their successes"; "Neil's curriculum vitae . . . [was] flush with academic and professional honors" (41). Whereas Nao Kao "looks intelligent," one might question if Neil's medical successes reify that "looking" is not "being" intelligent. What is the referent for "intelligence"—intelligent in what?—and how is the term defined? Furthermore, the Lees' determination is metaphorized through references to natural forces—gale winds and earthquakes cannot shake their resolve—and thus primitivizes them by unnaturally naturalizing a relationship between the former agrarians and their so-called connection to the earth. While Neil and Peggy possess a strong self-determination that seems equally unshakable, their physical/intellectual references remain free of a kind of coded *National Geographic* language. And what could be more successful, even intelligent, than escaping the murderous bent of the Pathet Lao, surviving Thai transit camps, and starting one's life over in a cultural realm that views, to their surprise, *qaug dab peg* (the spirit catches you) as "an electromagnetic storm" in the brain?

Furthermore, Fadiman's own failure to comment about curious MCMC staff utterances begs interpretation. An MCMC nurse, for example, witnesses Lia's decline from a headstrong but demonstrative and very active toddler to one who increasingly exhibits mental retardation, stumbles "drunkenly" on medication, or has uncontrollable seizures "when the spirit catches her." The nurse quickly describes her as a "blowfly flitting about, just totally out of control and wild and unsocialized but—well, absolutely adorable" (113). The quote provokes no textual musings from Fadiman, the text's cultural arbiter, who might have demanded, here, if "Asian" were being coded as "wild"? Is Lia completely adorable because she is Asian, a trait that demands taming? Or is Lia wild and unsocialized because she is "high" on drugs? To *what* should Lia be socialized—into *whose* society? As well, Fadiman's impressions of institutionalized children become a reference by which to read Lia's loving home care: institutionalized children, Fadiman observes, are "pasty-skinned carcasses with slack mouths" (216). Even though she intends to compliment the Lees on their tender, parental care of a daughter now in a vegetative state—Lia's hair is always neatly combed, shiny and black; she is "cuddled" and "rocked" and "sang to," played with by her siblings, she even "smelled delicious" (216)—her harsh words reveal disturbing biases about "clean" and "dirty" children. Thus, what meanings does Fadiman's text create about illness and about health? Or, as the Lees themselves already question, how might institutions render their patients sicker?

The process by which Fadiman and her readers are acculturated into beliefs and accepted behaviors informs one's reading of Fadiman's text. However, such seemingly invisible narratives adopt very visible parameters wherein the Lees' "mysterious" Hmongness figures as importantly in—or figures *as*—the "cultural collisions" of Lia's experiences. The type of so-called negative *worry* prompted from such a reading arises out of the necessity to mitigate the positive *worry* (or unexplained but necessary gaps) that Sommer finds so valuable in reading texts by and about Others.

NARRATIVE, WOUND CLOSURE, AND MAINTAINING RESPECTFUL GAPS

In an essay about colonizing narratives, I conclude with the impulses that narrative invites. I consider three narrative stances whose strands are both related and divergent. The tension created among such stratified theories of reading, applied to Lia's case along medical, political, authorial, and interpretive avenues, contributes to its fraught results while offering a few, final thoughts to my reading of the book's "cultural collisions."

According to Robert Leigh Davis, narrative's natural propensity to connect parts to the whole is useful in reading medicine's driving narrative force. Examining the written work of surgeon-writer Richard Selzer, Davis finds a "restorative impulse" in both surgery and Selzer's prose, "the conservative impulse to close off disruption and 'make whole what is sick or injured.'" Likewise, a surgeon such as Selzer needs to "stabilize and control the experience of illness—[in relation to] the writer's need to construct 'a beginning, a middle and an end.'"[51] Western medicine seeks to logically explain illnesses and subsequently prescribe a course of action (whether medication, exercise, rest, physical or psychological therapy, altered diet, surgery, radiation, etc.) to bring about expected results. Yet every day, physicians also accept that not all ills can be cured and that while death is not the hoped-for final paragraph, it represents both a literal and figurative ending point.

A Hmong oral narrative often begins with the phrase *hais cuaj txub kaum txub*, or "to speak of all kinds of things." It is "a way of reminding the listeners," states Anne Fadiman, "that the world is full of things that may not seem to be connected but actually are; that no event occurs in isolation; that you can miss a lot by sticking to the point; and the storyteller is likely to be rather long-winded" (Fadiman 12–13). Yet, Sommer, referenced earlier in her advice about readers' worry, warns us to be careful of certain texts, for "[t]hey can sting readers who feel entitled to know everything as they approach a text, practically any text, with the conspiratorial intimacy of a potential partner." She suggests cautionary reading strategies in order to respectfully mark "cultural distance" when approaching works by (and about) minorities (ix).

The three reading strategies suggest mutual exclusivity. Medical narratives drive toward conclusion. Hmong narratives implore listeners to forge connections. Sommer excoriates readers to respect textual lacunae. Consider, furthermore, that Western narratives, medical or not, thrive on linearity, the beginning-middle-end of story to which Davis refers. To leave a reader in suspense is to cheat him/her of a reader's satisfaction. We prefer neatly wrapped-up stories, concluded whether for good or bad. In *Spirit*, Fadiman as researcher and narrator knows the story's outcome or conclusion—Lia's final, vegetative state, and the anger and chagrin expressed on both sides of the case's cultural divide. Thus the text's structure is a reflection of authorial crafting toward that end in order to captivate, inform, and question. Or, the end becomes the means for the rest of the book. But as with any re-told tale, meaning is shaped, as I have already discussed. Its crafting questions whether Fadiman's text is a palimpsest (and of what)? A revelation (of what)? A moral tale (concluding in what lessons)?

But I am too hasty in assigning *Spirit*'s conclusion. The Lees' invitation of yet another shaman at book's end "concludes" in an inconclusive manner. In "believ[ing] that her [Lia's] condition was probably beyond the reach of spiritual healing . . . there was still this faintest flicker of a chance [in the Lees], not altogether extinguished even after years of failed [animal] sacrifices" (283). The possible reunification of body and soul through shamanism opens the text to possibility, to answers, and to endings that Fadiman, the Lees, and the MCMC staff cannot know. This is evident in Lia's defiance of her physicians' predictions: she continues to live after all of her life support systems are disconnected and despite predictions of her pending death. In ceding control to the shaman, the Lees willingly resign control to another, to the unknown, and live with their decisions. Meanwhile, MCMC continues to agonize over vexing questions: Neil wonders "in retrospect whether the course of her life might have been different if his hospital had offered her optimal medical care from the beginning" (41). I detect a certain anxiety in Neil's comment: is he worried that substandard care might invoke inquiries into MCMC's (and his) subtle discrimination? The uncertainty of what causes Lia's eventual demise creates consternation for physicians and many others who would prefer answers to uncertainty. Whereas the Lees' stance between hoping for the *dab*'s return and accepting Lia as she is represents a narrative motion from uncertainty to uncertainty.

Folklore or narrative "is the foundation on which the entire Hmong culture is based," states Dawn L. Remsing, especially because the Hmong had no written language until the 1950s and thus an oral tradition has buoyed the transfer of cultural, familial, and historical narratives.[52] Hmong embroidery contributes to a narrative thematic of remembering: many first-generation Hmong women create traditional story cloths, *paj ntaub*, that document agricultural life in the mountains of Laos, catalogue highland animals, or depict their flight from the Pathet Lao; furthermore, through narrative videos, some Hmong Americans teach their American-born children recent Lao political history via dramas that re-enact harrowing escapes across the Mekong River into Thailand.[53] Likewise, the *txiv neeb*, or shaman, offers a story about Lia's condition and cure which rests in locating her frightened spirit and enticing it to return. The shaman, who links body to lost spirit and the living to the dead, becomes a copula of sorts between a beginning and an ending. The shaman's failure to link Lia's lost *dab* to her body represents a narrative lacking a conclusion.

While Southeast Asian refugees and immigrants themselves have impacted the nature of biomedical health care—that now increasingly provides necessary interpreters and will defer to certain cultural paradigms and practices—Fadiman's conclusionless text not only mimics the open-endedness of the Hmong narrative, but also suggests that much cross-cultural work remains to be done.

My critique itself is problematic and reveals new gaps and new questions about how, as well as if, such gaps *should* be closed. I return to and appreciate Sommer's advancement of a necessary and respectful cultural distance—the inability, and the efficacy in that inability, to know (and retain power over) everything about another. Yet, according to Fadiman, if MCMC's biomedical practices must change, knowledge becomes that crux for alteration. Is it possible to have it both ways—to know as well as to resist an entitlement to knowing? Subsequently we might ask, is that which is unknowable crucial for healing? And who decides? If we adopt what Kleinman calls a model of mediation, and attend to a "local cultural system,"[54] in what ways have the Lees—and not solely MCMC—resisted compromise? Does Fadiman's critique of MCMC's biomedical model overlook ways in which the Lees (and the Hmong living within Merced County) also necessitate changes to their cultural adherence?[55] Finally, such an understanding and appreciation of cultural gaps *as* distances that cannot be closed re-opens the quagmire over responsibility for cultural healing: who are the victims, who the perpetrators, and who is responsible for resolution? Answers are circumscribed by the privileging of context, as *Spirit* bears out. But at text's "end," Fadiman responsibly returns Lia's pathography to her and to the Lees. In the final pages, she illustrates how the Lees' hope for finding Lia's lost *dab* is directed toward yet another sacrifice and the invitation of another shaman. And we, the readers, are left pondering the gap between and among beliefs whose incommensurability now seems a little less daunting.

NOTES

1. Anne Fadiman, *The Spirit Catches You and You Fall Down: A Hmong Child, Her American Doctors, and the Collision of Two Cultures* (New York: Farrar, Straus, and Giroux, 1997).
2. The term Hmong refers to an ethnic group, predominantly from Laos, whom the Chinese, Thai and Lao have derogatorily named "Miao" or "Meo," which can mean "barbarians," or "bumpkins," "people who sound like cats," or "wild uncultivated grasses" (Fadiman 14).

3. According to Hmong beliefs, humans are endowed with more than one soul, often up to three, but more are never disputed. See Keith Quincy's *Hmong: History of a People* (Cheney, Washington: Eastern Washington University Press, 1988, 1995), 88–89. Also see his chapter "The Spirit World" for a history and explanation of Hmong shamanism.

4. From Robert. G. Lees' *Orientals: Asian Americans in Popular Culture* (Philadelphia: Temple University Press, 1999), 2.

5. Arthur Kleinman, for example, speaks of a "biomedical system [that] replaces [an] allegedly 'soft,' therefore devalued, psychosocial concern with meanings with the scientifically 'hard,' therefore overvalued, technical quest for the control of symptoms." See his *The Illness Narratives: Suffering, Healing, and the Human Condition* (New York: Basic Books, 1988), 9. Yet Western medicine is hardly monolithic as explored by Marc Berg and Annemarie Mol, eds., *Differences in Medicine: Unraveling Practices, Techniques, and Bodies* (Durham, N.C.: Duke University Press, 1998). But critics of Western medicine's overwhelming hegemonic practices have influenced my own use and criticism of the term "biomedicine." They recognize a wide variance in biomedical practice, including resistance to its strict parameters by biomedical practitioners themselves. Julia Epstein, for example, states, "The notion that Active and clinical narratives might bear relation to one another has begun to seem less radical and more conceptually useful for an understanding of clinical thinking and the social functions of medicalization" in her *Altered Conditions: Disease, Medicine, and Storytelling* (New York: Routledge, 1995), 26.

6. According to Jo Ann Koltyk, Hmong refugees negotiate their public images in order to avoid disapproval from the American society in a practice called "collective impression management" (14). See her *New Pioneers in the Heartland: Hmong in Wisconsin* (New York: Allyn and Bacon, 1995), 14.

7. For historical sources other than those used in this essay, see for example Sucheng Chan's *Hmong Means Free: Life in Laos and America* (Philadelphia: Temple University Press, 1994); and Nancy D. Donelly's *Changing Lives of Refugee Hmong Women* (Seattle: University of Washington, 1994).

8. "The rate of death from SUNDS among Laotian-Hmong men has reached alarming proportions, being equivalent to the sum of the rates of the leading five causes of natural death among United States males." Shelley R. Adler, "Sudden Unexpected Nocturnal Death Syndrome among Hmong Immigrants: Examining the Role of the 'Nightmare,'" *Journal of American Folklore* 104 (1991): 54–71 (54). Medical theories have tentatively attributed these deaths to "potassium deficiency, thiamin deficiency, sleep apnea, depression, culture shock, and survivor guilt [following the Vietnam War]," says Fadiman (*Spirit*, from the asterisked footnote on page 188), but have not been able to find any direct cause.

9. Those who address medicine and narrative in interdisciplinary fashion by forging connections to anthropology, literary theory, sociology, and psychiatry are, most notably: Cheryl Mattingly and Linda C. Garro, *Narrative and the Cultural Construction of Illness and Healing* (Berkeley: University of California Press, 2000); Kleinman, *Illness Narratives*; Julia Epstein, *Altered Conditions*; Howard Brody, *Stories of Sickness* (New Haven: Yale University Press, 1987); Arthur Frank, *The Wounded Storyteller: Body, Illness, and Ethics* (Chicago: University of Chicago Press, 1995); Anatole Broyard, *Intoxicated by My Illness* (New York: Potter, 1992); Oliver Sacks, *The Man Who Mistook His Wife for a Hat and Other Clinical Tales* (New York: Perennial Library, 1987); as well as the journal *Literature and Medicine*'s special volumes on "The Art of the Case History" 11.1 (1992) and that on "Narrative and Medical Knowledge" 13.1 (April 1994); and the extensive work of Byron J. Good and Mary-Jo DelVechhio Good, here, their "'Fiction' and 'Historicity' in Doctors' Stories: Social and Narrative Dimensions of Learning Medicine" in Mattingly and Garro's *Narrative*. Also see David B. Morris, *Illness and Culture in the Postmodern Age* (Berkeley: University of California, 1998): "X rays and CT scans, it is well worth remembering, are not self-explanatory, not facts, but visual representations of the body, images that are often deeply ambiguous and that demand interpretation, creating the occasions for complex and not wholly scientific narratives" (273).

10. The physician participates in a patient's pathography by legitimizing it through medical terminology and nosology, thus yoking "epistemology and storytelling," says Katherine Montgomery Hunter (21). Unfortunately, according to Hunter, such a process retells and reorders the patient's initial narrative. The physician decides which presented information is important and applicable to cure and what information is extraneous (62). Hence, two narratives have been created: the pathography (a patient's subjective account of "illness") and its translation (even alteration, according to Hunter) into a medical case—referred to as the "disease"—by its "medical narrator" (63). See Hunter's *Doctors' Stories: The Narrative Structure of Medical Knowledge* (Princeton: Princeton University Press, 1991), 13. Howard Brody also recognizes that the physician is trapped between "the uniqueness of the individual patient" and the necessity to reframe the illness "by means of generally applicable laws" in his *Stories of Sickness* (17).

11. Hunter, *Doctors' Stories*, 135.

12. Ong, "Making the Biopolitical Subject," 105, 102.

13. Ibid., 91.

14. Epstein, *Altered Conditions*, 29.

15. See Alan M. Kraut, *Silent Travelers: Germs, Genes, and the "Immigrant Menace"* (New York: Basic Books, 1994); John Kuo Wei Tchen, "Believing Is Seeing: Transforming Orientalism and the Occidental Gaze," in *Asia/America: Identities in Contemporary Asian American Art*, ed. Pacita Abad, et al. (New York: New York University Press, 1994).

16. "[R]acial stereotypes have been linked with images of pathology, especially psychopathology," from the mid nineteenth century, says Sander L. Gilman in *Difference and Pathology: Stereotypes of Sexuality, Race, and Madness* (Ithaca, N.Y.: Cornell University Press, 1985), 129.

17. Nayan Shah's *Contagious Divides: Epidemics and Race in San Francisco's Chinatown* (Berkeley: University of California Press, 2001) is an apt example of a recent, scholarly revisitation of the Yellow Peril in order to excavate how Chinese American activists, up to the mid-twentieth century, rallied against their communities' constricting pathological designations and for their full, civic inclusion within American society.

18. For Gina Marchetti, the medical scare coupling Chinese immigrants with the bubonic plague resulted in "the notion that all nonwhite people are by nature physically and intellectually inferior, morally suspect, heathen, licentious, disease-ridden, feral, violent, uncivilized, infantile, and in need of the guidance of white, Anglo-Saxon Protestants." See her *Romance and the "Yellow Peril": Race, Sex, and Discursive Strategies in Hollywood Fiction* (Berkeley: University of California Press, 1993), 2–3. Therefore, what we now call Yellow Peril narratives—depicting "the sinister and evil character of the quarter [Chinatown] and most of its inhabitants"—are described as "Anglo-American literature [that] does not tell us about Asians . . . but tells us about Anglos' opinions of themselves, in relation to their opinions of Asians," according to Elaine H. Kim in *Asian American Literature: An Introduction to the Writings and Their Social Context* (Philadelphia: Temple University Press, 1982), 20.

19. *National Geographic* "is continually drawn to people in brightly colored, 'different' dress, engaged in initially strange-seeming rituals or inexplicable behavior," state Catherine A. Lutz and Jane L. Collins in their thorough study of the magazine. "This view . . . [is] a world of happy, classless people outside of history but evolving into it, edged with exoticism and sexuality, but knowable to some degree as individuals." How, then, the authors ask, do such images "change or reinforce" or even influence readers' practices? See their *Reading National Geographic* (Chicago: University of Chicago Press, 1993), 89, 116, 117.

20. See Trinh's "The Language of Nativism: Anthropology as a Scientific Conversation of Man with Man" in her *Woman, Native, Other* (Bloomington: Indiana University Press, 1989): 47–76.

21. Renny Christopher deems this an "ongoing meta-war, which attempts to erase the Vietnamese from their own reality and make them part of American reality." The U.S. "may have lost the shooting war," she writes, but rectifies such a blow by winning a homeland meta-war that "abstracts 'Vietnam' the war from 'Viet Nam' the country." She exemplifies how the correct spelling of the country—Viet Nam, which includes a space

between the two syllables—evolved into "Vietnam" in American newspapers and finally within the American imagination. Not only did the U.S. misspell the nation, but any mention of "Vietnam" tends to conjure up the "conflict," as the war is euphemistically deemed, and not the country or its people. See her work *The Viet Nam War, The American War: Images and Representations in Euro-American and Vietnamese Exile Narratives* (Amherst: University of Massachusetts Press, 1995), 4, 7.

22. Jane Hamilton-Merritt, *Tragic Mountains: The Hmong, the Americans, and the Secret Wars for Laos, 1942–1992* (Bloomington: Indiana University Press, 1993), 55, 87.

23. Fadiman says of this verbal agreement between an American CIA agent, known only as "Colonel Billy," and Vang Pao, the most well-known Hmong military leader: "Every Hmong has a different version of what is commonly called the 'Promise,' wondering what went wrong and why they are chastised in the country for which they offered their own lives." See Fadiman's "Heroes' Welcome," *Civilization: The Magazine of the Library of Congress* 4.4 (August–September, 1997): 53–61 (59).

24. Americans, for example, often vociferously complain that Southeast Asian refugees are community tax burdens while the protestors remain grossly ignorant of their participation during the Vietnam War, during which the Hmong lost one-third of its Laotian-based population "including half of all the males over fifteen," states Lillian Faderman in *I Begin My Life All Over: The Hmong and the American Immigrant Experience* (Boston: Beacon, 1998), 7. President Johnson's comment that "virtually no American casualties" occurred in Laos during the war demonstrates the value attributed to some human lives and tragically denied to others (Fadiman, "Heroes' Welcome," 55).

25. Hamilton-Merritt, 519, emphasis in text.

26. The Lees twice tried escaping to Thailand, the first attempt ending in capture by Vietnamese soldiers and the death of one child; they spent three years guarded by armed soldiers—witnessing the starvation of another child—until their second escape attempt with a group of about 400 other Hmong. Vietnamese soldiers attempted to burn them out of the jungle while some children (not those of the Lees) were shot over and over until "their heads were squashed." The dangerous journey, on foot, to the Thai border lasted 26 days, after which they spent two years in a Thai transit camp, losing one daughter there (Fadiman, *Spirit*, 155–157).

27. If at one time Hmong soldiers were an invisible body, they become highly and visibly corporeal, as refugees, in all their rumored idiosyncrasies, often those that conflict with accepted Western beliefs (eating skunks and cat food, rinsing rice in the toilet, washing clothes in public pools, picking their ears and noses in public). See *Spirit*, 186–188.

28. MCMC staff, for example, are stupefied and angered over Fuoa's fifteenth pregnancy. However, they remained ignorant of a former Hmong agrarian existence that necessitated large families; as well, frequent deaths, including the massacre of Hmong during the Vietnam War, now drives their strong desires to reproduce; and the practice of marrying at a very young age facilitates a long period of active fertility, which is coupled with Hmong intense love of children, "the most treasured possession[s] a person can have" (Fadiman 21–22). Fadiman quotes ethnographer Hugo Adolf Bernatzik who lived with the Hmong in Thailand during the 1930s. See *Spirit* for Hmong "reasons for prizing fecundity" (specifically page 72).

29. Kleinman, *Illness Narratives*, 25.

30. See Susan Sontag's *Illness as Metaphor and AIDS and Its Metaphors* (New York: Anchor, 1978, 1989), 57. Also see Scott L. Montgomery's "Of Codes and Combat: Images of Disease in Biomedical Discourse," *Science as Culture* 12 (1991): 55–73.

31. Jeremy Hein, *From Vietnam, Laos, and Cambodia: A Refugee Experience in the United States* (New York: Twayne, 1995), 24.

32. Fadiman, "Heroes' Welcome," 56.

33. For an astute presentation of how the "feminized" East dupes the so-called masculine West, reversing the stereotyped roles, see David Henry Hwang's *M. Butterfly* (New York: Penguin, 1988, 1989).

34. Given the Chinese men's social exclusion as an unclean peril, it is ironic that Chinese immigrant men found their employment limited to food service and cleaning underclothes, arenas that traditionally demand employees' overt cleanliness and good health in their covert connection to consumers' intimate personal hygiene (gastronomy and underwear).

35. See Jacqueline E. Lawson, " 'She's a Pretty Woman . . . for a Gook.' The Misogyny of the Vietnam War" in *Fourteen Landing Zones: Approaches to Vietnam War Literature*, ed. Philip K. Jason (Iowa City: University of Iowa Press, 1991), 23. Lawson illustrates how the language of combat itself is riddled with sexual innuendoes and domination in words such as pacification, engagement, escalation, de-escalation, withdrawal, humping the boonies, and cherry (a soldier without battle experience) (24).

36. This is evident in recent controversies over Asian Americans' abundant presence on campuses in California and Texas; accusations over campaign financing during Clinton's run for the presidency; and the spying allegations against Wen Ho Lee, to name a few.

37. Fadiman writes, "Over time, her drug regimen became so complicated and underwent so many revisions that keeping track of it would have been a monumental task even for a family that could read English. For the Lees, it proved to be utterly confounding" (45).

38. A public health nurse notes, "Father had become more and more reluctant to give medications at all because he feels that the medicines are causing seizure and also the fever" (50). During one of Fadiman's interviews with Nao Kao, he angrily states, "I am very disappointed at the hospital. I am mad. Is this a hospital that fixes people or makes them die?" (177).

39. More specifically, while the attribution of Lia's affliction to a spirit is unscientifically based, Fadiman reports, it is no more or less enlightening than those gaps in Western medicine's knowledge which reference seven epileptic cases out of ten that are idiopathic or untraceable to any known cause (Fadiman 28–29).

40. See Christopher's *The Viet Nam War* (cited earlier) in which she discusses, specifically, Euro-American images of Asians in popular culture as a "result of U.S. wars in Asia," and how these images contributed to "the lens through which most Euro-American works representing the war in Viet Nam view Vietnamese" (21). She speaks of how "many U.S. narratives complain of the supposed 'impossibility' of telling the enemy from the civilians" (6), a concept whose stateside translation is the outbreak of American anger and frustration toward Southeast Asian refugees whose help was necessary and valuable "over there" but whose present cry for help is now perceived as a governmental drain.

41. Ron Hogan, "Beatrice Interview," http://www.beatrice.com/interviews/fadiman/.

42. Winner of the National Book Critics Circle Award for General Nonfiction; Los Angeles Times Book Prize for Current Interest; A Salon Book Award Winner; Boston Book Review 1997; Ann Rea Jewell Non-Fiction Prize; A New York Times Notable Book; A Best Book of the Year (*People, Newsday, Glamour,* and the *Detroit Free Press*); Finalist PEN / Martha Albrand Award for First Nonfiction. From http://www.spiritcatchesyou.com/pressroom.htm.

43. Mai Na M. Lee, http://www.hmongnet.org/publications/spirit-review.html.

44. In Mai Lee's review, she states that it is highly "improbable" and "unbelievable" that any Hmong woman birthed twelve children by herself, as village female elders would have been in assistance and that such a birthing tale was most likely "to metaphorically convey the general hardship of Hmong women and should not be taken seriously."

45. Ellen Wiewel states, "I found her application of the cultural description [that the Hmong are 'strong-willed'] to be burdensome, because she occasionally used it to stereotype Hmong behavior. . . . Fadiman derived the fight or flight reaction of individual Hmong in America, from the entire group's response when their Laotian highland territory was challenged." Wiewel's "Review and Assessment of *The Spirit Catches You and You Fall Down,*" *Medical Anthropology* (Fall 1999): http://www.imsa.edu/~elbel/spirit.html.com.

46. Wiewel says that Fadiman "treats Hmong culture idealistically and stereotypically at times."

47. Reviewer Mai Lee takes issue with the following paragraph from *Spirit:* "The history of the Hmong yields several lessons that anyone who deals with them might do well to remember.

Among the most obvious of these are that the Hmong do not like to take orders; that they do not like to lose; that they would rather flee, fight, or die than surrender; that they are not intimidated by being outnumbered; that they are rarely persuaded that the customs of other cultures, even those more powerful than their own, are superior, and that they are capable of getting very angry." Lee deems it Fadiman's romanticization that unfortunately guides many of her Hmong representations.

48. Doris Sommer, *Proceed with Caution, When Engaged by Minority Writing in the Americas* (Cambridge: Harvard University Press, 1999).

49. Donald Pollack, "Physician Autobiography: Narrative and the Social History of Medicine," in Mattingly and Garro, *Narrative* (110, 109). Pollack addresses the "genre" of the "training tale" and accounts of "gender in medicine," most of which begin with the "end" of medical school or residency as a point by which graduated medical students and board-certified physicians reflect on who they have become and how.

50. Morris, *Illness and Culture*, 72. He conclusively states, "*Postmodern illness is fundamentally biocultural—always biological and always cultural—situated at the crossroads of biology and culture*" (71, emphasis in text). And Miriam E. Warner and Marilyn Mochel state that "Western biomedicine *is* a culture" (quoted in "The Hmong and Health Care in Merced, California," *Hmong Studies Journal* 2.2 [Spring 1998]: http://www.como.stpaul.k12.mn.us/Ve-Benson/HSJ-v2n2.html).

51. Robert Leigh Davis, "The Art of Suture: Richard Selzer and Medical Narrative," *Literature and Medicine* 12.2 (Fall 1993): 178–193 (179, 181).

52. Dawn L. Remsing, *Hmong Folklore: The Art of Storytelling* (M.A. Thesis, University of Wisconsin–Eau Claire, August 1996), 1.

53. See Sally Peterson's "Translating Experience and the Reading of a Story Cloth," *Journal of American Folklore* 101 (1988): 6–22; and Jo Ann Koltyk's "Telling Narratives through Home Videos: Hmong Refugees and Self-Documentation of Life in the Old and New Country," *Journal of American Folklore* 106.422 (1933): 435–449.

54. Kleinman, *Illness Narratives*, 27.

55. This is *Spirit* reviewer Weiwel's contention as well: "Fadiman did not offer any suggestions for the Hmong to show more interest in working with the doctors. . . . She briefly mentioned the Hmong National Development organization's efforts (page 198), but she vastly portrayed Lia's family's situation as a travesty on the part of the biomedical system. We know we want to change the biomedical establishment, because it failed Lia on cultural grounds. But for biomedicine to successfully meet the needs of specific groups such as the Hmong, it needs input from the Hmong themselves" (no page numbers in the online article).

Searching for Community

Filipino Gay Men in New York City

Martin F. Manalansan IV

Introduction

In 1987, a Filipino gay man named Exotica was crowned Miss Fire Island. The Miss Fire Island beauty contest is an annual drag event in Fire Island (located off the coast of Long Island) and is considered to be the premier gay summer mecca in America. It was interesting to note that a considerable number of the contestants who were not Caucasian were Filipinos. Furthermore, Exotica was not the first Filipino recipient of the crown; another Filipino was crowned earlier in the seventies. In 1992, a Filipino gay and lesbian group called *Kambal sa Lusog* marched in two parades in New York City, Gay Pride Day and Philippine Independence Day. These iconic events suggest the strong presence of Filipinos in the American gay scene, particularly in New York City.

This chapter delineates this presence by analyzing the issues of identity and community among fifty gay Filipino men in the city in their attempts to institutionalize or organize themselves. Through excerpts from life history interviews and field observations, I explore the ways in which being "gay" and being "Filipino" are continually being shaped by historical events.

I use the term "community" not as a static, closed, and unified system. Rather, I use the term strategically and conceptualize it as a fluid movement between subjectivity/identity and collective action.[1] Therefore, intrinsic to this use of the term "community" is a sense of dissent and contestation along with a sense of belonging to a group or cause. I also use Benedict Anderson's[2] notion of community as "imagined," which means symbols, language and other cultural practices and products from songs to books are sites where people articulate their sense of belonging. The concept of identity is not a series or stages of development or as a given category, but a dynamic package of meanings contingent upon practices that are both individually and collectively reconfigured.[3]

The first section briefly explores the cleavages that gave rise to a diversity of voices and outlines differences such as class, attitudes toward various homosexual practices, and ethnic/racial identity. In the next two sections, two pivotal moments, the *Miss Saigon* controversy and the AIDS pandemic, are discussed in terms of the patterns of cultural actions and counteractions. I focus on new or reconfigured collective discourses, specifically language and ritual. I also emphasize the organizing efforts of Filipinos to create a gay and lesbian group (*Kambal sa Lusog*) and an AIDS advocacy group. A specific activity called the *Santacruzan* by *Kambal sa Lusog* incorporates symbols from different national traditions and provides an example of the collective representation of community.

DIVERGENT VOICES

> Ang sabi nila, iba't iba daw ang bakla, mayroon cheap, may pa-class, nandito yoong malandi at saka ang mayumi—kuno!
>
> [*They say there are different kinds of bakla, those who are tacky, those who pretend they have class, then there are the whorish and the virginal—not!*]
>
> We are all gay. We are all Filipinos. We need to empower ourselves as a group.
>
> Tigilan ako ng mga tsismosang bakla, wiz ko type maki-beso-beso sa mga baklang Pilipino—puro mga intrigera!
>
> [*Get me away from those gossipy* bakla, *I don't want to socialize with those Filipino* bakla, *they are all gossip mongers!*]

If we take these voices as indices of the opinions and stances of Filipino gay men, we will find a spectrum of similarities and divergences. Most Filipino gay men consider place of birth as an important gauge of the attitudes and ideas of a gay individual. The dichotomy between U.S.–born versus Philippine or native-born Filipino gay men is actually used by many informants I have interviewed. This simplistic dichotomy is inadequate and erroneous. It does not begin to address the diversity among Filipino gay men.

ATTITUDES TOWARD HOMOSEXUAL PRACTICES

In a group discussion I lead with a group of Filipino gay men and lesbians, one gay man pointed out that the culture in which one was raised in and more importantly where one was socialized into a particular homosexual tradition mattered more than place of birth. This is particularly true in many of my informants who immigrated as young children or in their early teens. Many of them explored their sexual identities under the symbols and practices of American culture. Many of them were not exposed to the *bakla* traditions[4] and more frequently followed the idioms and practices of American gay culture. These men were usually concerned with issues of coming out and identified more with a hypermasculine gay culture.

While almost all of my informants identified as gay, many of those who immigrated as adults and had some encounters in *bakla* practices and traditions were emphatic in delineating major difference between American gay and Philippine *bakla* culture. Most of these differences centered on the issue of cross-dressing and effeminacy.

However, there were some informants, including two American-born Filipinos, who through frequent visits to the Philippines as well as extended stays as students in Philippine schools, were exposed to and involved in the *bakla* tradition. This group of men were more familiar with the cross-dressing traditions of homosexuality in the Philippines and usually spoke versions of Filipino sward-speak (a kind of gay argot).[5]

A case illustrates this point. One informant who was born and raised in California said that a turning point in his life was when he went to the Philippines at the age of sixteen and his uncle introduced him to cross-dressing and other practices among homosexuals. That brief (month and a half) visit was to become an important element in the way he now socialized in the gay community. He seeks cross-dressing opportunities not only with other transvestites but with other Filipinos. He said that Filipino gay men did not cross-dress for shock value but for realness. He further mentioned that he was unlike those gay men who were into queer androgyny consciously looking midway between male and female. He and other gay men who cross-dressed attempted to look like real women. More important, despite the fact that he was raised speaking English at home, his friendships with other Philippine-born gay men have encouraged him to attempt to speak at least some smattering of the Filipino gay argot.

Some informants felt that Filipino cross-dressers had illusions (*ilusyonada*) and were internally homophobic or self-hating. These same informants were the ones who reported that they were part of the mainstream gay community. Some of them go to gyms and assume masculine ("straight-acting") mannerisms. They saw the cross-dressing practices of other Filipinos to be either low-class, archaic/anachronous (meaning cross-dressing belonged in the Philippines and not here in America).

On the other hand, the cross-dressers would call these guys *pamacho* (acting macho) or *pa-min* (acting like men). Filipino gay cross-dressers accused these "masculine" men of mimicking white Americans and of having illusions of being "real" men. Exotica,[6] one of my informants, said that cross-dressing for him was a way of getting men. He liked assuming more exotic identities and *noms de plume* such as "Suzie Wong" or "Nancy Kwan." In the Philippines, he said he was able to get men for sex, but he had to pay them. In America, he said there was a "market" for his cross-dressing talent and exotic beauty. He said that he could not compete in the hypermasculine, gym-oriented world of mainstream gay life in New York. He said, "With my slight build, who would even give me a second look if I was wearing a T-shirt?" However, he said that there were men, particularly those who were not gay-identified who were attracted to "beautiful," "oriental" cross-dressers. He said that here in America, he did not have to pay the man to have sex with him, it was the other way around. He said, "Sometimes I feel so cheap because the man will insist on paying for everything including the pleasure of having sex with you. It is like everything goes on an opposite current here in America. I like it."

Conflicts between Filipino gay cross-dressers and non-cross-dressers are not dramatically played out in violent confrontations, but rather in avoidance. Furthermore, the differences are usually played down with a "live and let live" or *"yun ang type niya"* (that is his/her choice) attitude.

SOCIAL CLASS

Class is a more implicit boundary marker among gay Filipinos. Many of my informants denied noting any difference between themselves and other gay Filipinos. However, upon further probing, several of them (mostly those who were born and raised in the Philippines) will say, "Well, there are those who gossip a lot and just make bitchy remarks," or "Other Filipino gays are so tacky." Some Filipino gay men actually used such terms as *baklang talipapa* (the *bakla* of the wet market), *baklang cheap* (tacky *bakla*), and *baklang kalye* (*bakla* of the streets), to designate gay Filipinos who they think are of a lower class standing or of lower "breeding." The indices of "low breeding" are myriad, but some informants agree on fluency in the English language, styles of dress, schools attended and "bearing" or how a gay Filipino carries himself.

Family roots are said to be another marker of class. *De buena familia* (from a good family) is a term used by gay men to portray how someone has class and social standing. Another word used to describe somebody who has a lot of money is *datungera* (*datung* is swardspeak for money and the noun is given the feminine form). In most conversations between Filipinos that I have heard and observed, the typical insults hurled at other gay men apart from physical traits were the idioms derived from class or the lack thereof.

Despite these occurrences, many still assert that America has leveled off some of these distinctions. An informant said, "There are some Filipinos I would normally not have contact with back home in the Philippines, but here in America we are thrown together in the bars, in the streets, some neighborhoods . . . you know."

The case of David, a gay Filipino in his forties, is particularly instructive. He was very proud of his aristocratic background in the Philippines. He said America was very funny because he was able to maintain relationships with people who were not of his class. Coming from a landed family in the Philippines, he said that he tried to create some distance from people who were not his equal. But this was not true in America. For a long time, his lover was a telephone linesman with a high school degree. He said there were times when the class disparity showed. For example, conflicts occurred in situations when their tastes for particular leisure activities were divided into, in his mind, the classy and the tasteless, between a concert and bowling.

He further reported that his first ten years of living in America were spent as an illegal alien. Despite having money and a good education, he started as a janitor or a busboy due to lack of legal papers. He said, "I guess living during those years and doing those kinds of jobs were exciting in a way . . . a different way of experiencing America." Indeed, David's own class-conscious ways have been tempered to a large extent by the immigration experience. He now has contacts with several Filipino gay men many of whom were of lower-class origins.

Most of those who were born in America did not report any class distinctions among Filipinos. They were, however, more up front about their class origins. Two of my informants who were born and raised in California prefaced their stories about childhood by stating that they were from working-class families in the U.S. army.

ETHNIC/RACIAL IDENTITY

Most articles on Asian American gay men regard identity as a static given and construct ethnic identity as a polar opposite of gay identity.[7] Among the questions I asked my fifty Filipino informants was how they identified ethnically or racially. All but one said that they identified as Filipino or Filipino American. When I asked about the category Asian/Pacific Islander, most of them said that while they assumed this category in official papers and functions, they perceived Asia or Asian only in geographic terms. When I asked the Filipino gay men how they differed from Asian gay men, many Filipino informants said that they did not have the same kind of issues such as coming out and homophobia.

A majority of informants, mostly immigrants, felt that Philippine society was relatively tolerant of homosexuality. Some informants reported very good responses from families when they did "come out." Others felt that they didn't have to come out about being gay because they thought that their families knew about their identity without their having to verbally acknowledge it. Filipino informants felt that other Asian men, particularly those who had just immigrated to America, did not speak English as well as they did. Important cultural differences, such as religion, were cited by informants as significant. Many felt that they had a closer cultural affinity with Latinos.

Among those who were born in the Philippines, regional ethno-linguistic differences became apparent in relation to other Filipinos. Some of the informants did not speak Pilipino or Tagalog and instead spoke a regional language such as Bisaya or Ilongo. However, differences in languages and region were usually displaced by the use of English or Filipino swardspeak, a gay argot used by many of the informants.

What I have presented above is a broad outline of the differences and similarities among Filipino gay men. This is to provide a kind of foundation in which to situate the succeeding discussions of Filipino men coming together and acting in a more collective manner. This section has shown how there are pivotal points that act as markers of difference such as class, cultural traditions and practices on homosexuality.

THE *MISS SAIGON* INTERLUDE: IRONY OF A DIFFERENT KIND

In the first full-length article on Asian gays and lesbians in the now-defunct magazine *Outweek*,[8] Nina Reyes (a Filipino American lesbian) wrote how the controversy surrounding the Broadway show *Miss Saigon* acted as a catalyst in bringing together many Asian gay and straight political activists in the forefront. According to Reyes, apart from the controversy around hiring (specifically, the use of a Caucasian, Jonathan Price, to play a Eurasian pimp) and the allegedly racist Madame Butterfly–inspired storyline, the opening night of *Miss Saigon* was the venue of protests by Asian gay and lesbian groups.

It is ironic that in the same article, Miss Reyes quoted a Filipino gay man who pointed out that not all Filipinos agreed with the protests since after all, the star of the show, Lea Salonga, was a Filipina. Indeed, many of my informants have seen the show and have reported how relatives and Filipino friends (both gay and straight), particularly those from other states and the Philippines, would include seeing the show as the highlight of their visits to the Big Apple. The issue here was not just a matter of taste but had important political underpinnings. Many Filipinos felt that their sentiments and thoughts about the show were not represented in the mass media.

This was not to be the end of this controversy. The Gay Asian Pacific Islander Men of New York (GAPIMNY), one of the most vociferous groups in the *Miss Saigon* protest, celebrated its anniversary with a variety show and dance at the Lesbian and Gay Community Center in Manhattan in the summer of 1992. One of the drag performers, a Filipino gay man, decided to participate with a lip-sync performance of one of Lea Salonga's songs in *Miss Saigon*. This caused a lot of ruckus. Before the performance, attempts were made by certain non-Filipinos to dissuade the drag performer from going though his intended repertoire even while the emcee was reading a disclaimer by GAPIMNY that stated that the group disavows any connection with the Broadway show. Furthermore, the disclaimer also stated that the audience should enjoy the performance and at the same time remember the racist underpinnings of the show's storyline and production practices.

It is important to note not only the effects of the *Miss Saigon* controversy on Asian American gay politics, but also how the representations and characters of this Broadway show have become icons of Filipino gay men. After each show, many Filipinos gathered backstage to talk to the actors and actresses (many of whom are Filipino or Filipino American). A good number of these fans are gay men.

Filipino gay men have appropriated many of the symbols and figures of this Broadway play. For Halloween in 1991, Leilani, a Filipino cross-dresser, bought a *cheongsam* in Chinatown, had a friend pull his hair back into a bun and paraded around Greenwich Village with just a small woolen scarf to protect him from the blustery cold weather. He was extremely delighted to hear people scream "Miss Saigon" at him.

Several cross-dressing Filipinos I interviewed have admitted to using either Kim (the main character in *Miss Saigon*) or Lea Salonga as drag names. In fact, they said that when they talk about another gay Filipino who is either in a moody sad state or is extremely despondent, they say that he is doing a *Miss Saigon* or he is playing the role of Kim (*nagmi—Miss Saigon* or *Kim ang drama niya ngayon*).

The issues surrounding the controversy and the reaction of Filipinos, particularly gay men, have to do with several factors. The first is that of immigration and the American dream. For many of these gay Filipinos, Lea Salonga represented their own aspirations regarding America. She initially had to be certified by Actor's Equity to enable her to work on Broadway since she was neither an American citizen/resident nor a member of the group. Her success in winning the Tony Award and her receiving the green card (permanent resident status) was very much seen as a collective triumph. An informant pointed to Miss Salonga's Tony acceptance speech as particularly meaningful. After receiving the award, she said, "Your dreams can come true."

Indeed for many Filipinos, gay or straight, these words seemed to be directed at them. Since a large number of my informants are immigrants, some of whom are illegal, the play provided an alternative narrative to the frustrations of daily life as a foreigner trying to attain the American dream. As one informant said, "*Mahirap dito sa Amerika pero kaunting tiyaga . . . byuti ka na*" [It is hard here in America, but with a little perseverance, you will succeed (beauty here is used as part of swardspeak, and connotes good luck or fate)].

Race and racism, which were the central issues of the controversy, were less significant for many of my informants. Those who saw the play talked about the singing abilities of the actors and the magnificent stage design. When queried about the themes of the show, they said that the bar scenes reminded them of Olongapo and Angeles, cities in the Philippines. These cities were sites of the two biggest U.S. military installations outside America. In these places, bars, prostitutes and American servicemen were everyday scenes.

The discourse of race was not particularly meaningful for many of my informants, a majority of whom had immigrated in their twenties. Out of the fifty informants, four reported an incident of racial discrimination. Most reported never encountering it. This was not entirely fortuitous. These men may have encountered some kind of discriminatory practices, but interpreted it as part of the hardships of being an immigrant in America.

While many of them did not pick up on the Orientalist symbolisms of *Miss Saigon*, this should not be interpreted as a case of false consciousness; rather, this kind of reaction is symptomatic in immigrant cultures. Immigrants constantly negotiate both dominant/hegemonic and subordinate (minority) cultural products and practices into meaningful arrangements that inform their lives.[9] In the case of *Miss Saigon* the racial stereotypes are subsumed, and instead the play is interpreted as a symbolic and literal vehicle for attaining success in America. Many of my informants felt that the crucial element of the play was that of getting to America and attaining the American dream.

In sum, with the *Miss Saigon* controversy, we have a historical moment which provided Filipinos in the U.S. a pool of collective symbols from which they could create discursive practices from cross-dressing to swardspeak. For many gay Filipino men in New York City, *Miss Saigon* was the impetus for the generation of camp symbols and discourses about some kind of national/ethnic and immigrant identities and aspirations.

AIDS: OR THE AUNT THAT PULLED US TOGETHER

> *I remember that around 1986, I began to hear about some Filipino* bakla *dying of AIDS in the West Coast. Then soon after that I heard about a Filipino who died in New York City. Then, I heard about this famous Filipino hairdresser who died. Afterwards the first of my friends came down with pneumonia. It was of course, Tita Aida. She struck again and again.*

Tita Aida or Auntie/Aunt Aida is the name Filipino gay men have coined for AIDS. I have explored this unique construction of AIDS by this group of men in an earlier paper,[10] but it is necessary to note that this construction is not idiosyncratic. It emanates from Philippine concepts of illness, gender and sexuality. The personification of the disease by gay Filipinos reflects the growing number of AIDS cases among Filipino gay men in America.[11] During the period from 1986 to 1988, the rise of AIDS cases among Asians in San Francisco was first documented.[12]

It was the same period of time when many of my informants started to become aware of the devastation of the disease. Most of them thought that the disease only affected white men. One informant said, "I thought that only white men, *yung mga byuti* (the beautiful ones) who were having sex constantly, were the only ones getting it." Before 1986, there were rumors as well as some published articles both in Filipino publications here and back in the Philippines which talked about the natural immunity of Filipinos against the disease. Some articles talked about the diet (such as eating *bagoong* or salted shrimp paste) as the reason why there were no Filipinos with AIDS.

This was soon dispelled by the sudden onslaught of Filipino cases during the late eighties. An informant remembered how he took care of about five friends. He said,

> *Ang hirap . . . manash* [it was hard sister] I had to massage, clean, shop and do so many things. It was a horror watching them die slowly and painfully. And when they died. . . . My friends and I realized that there was no money for a burial or to send the bodies back to the Philippines. That was when we had some fundraising dinners. We just had dinner not the *siyam-siyam* (traditional Filipino prayer ritual held several days after a burial) but just a simple get-together at somebody's place and a hat is passed to get some money to defray some expenses.

Many of the informants who have had friends die of AIDS reported similar themes and situations. Many of their friends were alone and without family because they were the first in their families to settle here or because their families refused to have anything to do with them after the truth came out. Some families took these ailing gay Filipinos back and refused to acknowledge both these men's disease and sexual orientation. However, there were also a number of families who accepted them, their gay friends and lovers. In cases where there was a lover (usually Caucasian), it was he who oftentimes took care of the ailing Filipino.

In cases when the Filipino was alone, going back home to the Philippines was not seen as a viable option. First, because there were no adequate medical facilities that could take care of a patient with AIDS. Second, there were horror stories going around about how some Filipinos with AIDS were deported from the Philippines. Third, coming down with the disease was seen by some as a failure on their part of attaining the American dream, particularly those who found out as part of their naturalization (citizenship) process. American immigration laws prohibit (despite high hopes for changes in the new Clinton administration) the immigration of people who either have AIDS or are HIV seropositive.

AIDS has created a common experience from which gay Filipinos in New York build and create new discourses and practices. *Abuloy* or alms for the dead have become institutionalized and have acquired a new dimension. Gay Filipinos put up fashion shows and drag parties to help defray the burial or medical expenses of friends who have died. These collective efforts have become a regular occurrence.

Other collective efforts (most of which are by gays and lesbians) include symposia about AIDS in the Filipino community in New York. A group of gay Filipino men was formed to institutionalize efforts to help Filipinos with AIDS. This group, the Advocacy Group, got Filipinos with HIV/AIDS, and formed to provide support services. There are still problems. Some Filipino gay men with AIDS are wary of other Filipino gay men helping them because of the interlocking network of gay Filipinos. There is a real possibility coming into contact with other Filipinos whom one knows. Other problems include Filipinos' inadequate access to services due to fear and lack of information.

Notwithstanding these difficulties, AIDS has provided a way of pulling Filipinos into some kind of collective action. While there are still sporadic attempts at solving some of the issues and problems many Filipino gay men face in the pandemic, there is a growing systematization of efforts.

Coming Together: Some Voices and (Re)Visions

In March 1991, an organization of Filipino gay men and lesbians called *Kambal sa Lusog* (which literally means "twins in health," but is interpreted to be "comrades in the struggle") was formed. Some informants who were members of this organization said that one of the impetuses for the formation of this group was the *Miss Saigon* controversy. However, after talking to one of the founders of the group, he said that there has been talk about such a group even before the *Miss Saigon* controversy. A large factor was that many Filipinos do not relate to other Asians or to an Asian identity.

This statement had been confirmed by my interviews with Filipino gay men. Many perceived Asia only in terms of geography; significant differences existed between other Asians and themselves. Furthermore, there was also a perception that Asian meant East Asians such as Japanese and Chinese. Due to these views, many felt that their interests as gay men would not be served by a group like GAPIMNY.

Kambal sa Lusog is a unique group because it includes gay men, lesbians, and bisexuals. It has a newsletter that usually comes out monthly. The group meets almost every month at the Lesbian and Gay Community Center in Manhattan. They have had numerous fundraisers and other group activities.

Among such fundraising activities was the *Santacruzan*. It was not only successful in attracting other Filipino gay men who were not members but more importantly, this particular production of the traditional Filipino ritual is perhaps the most evocative example of the kind of community and identity-formation that Filipino gay men in New York are struggling to achieve.

The *Santacruzan* is an important traditional Catholic celebration in the Philippines held every May. It is a street procession that begins and ends in the church. The procession is essentially a symbolic reenactment of the finding of the cross of Christ by Queen Helena or Reyna Elena, the mother of Emperor Constantine of the Holy Roman Empire. The procession usually includes female personages, both mythical and historical. Among the usual figures are: *Reyna Sentenciada* (Justice), the three Virtues (*Fe, Esperanza,* and *Caridad* or Faith, Hope and Charity), *Reina Banderada* or Motherland (Queen of the Flag), Reina Elena, Rosa Mistica, Constantino (the young Emperor Constantine), and biblical characters such as Judith and Mary Magdalene.

In the Philippines, the important figures in the processions are usually portrayed by women with male escorts. Constantino is the only named male figure and is usually played by a child. However, in some areas, there have been cases when cross-dressing men have participated in these processions. In fact one of these kinds of *Santacruzans* in Pasay City (one of the cities in the metropolitan Manila area) is famous for its cross-dressing procession.

Kambal sa Lusog's Santacruzan is significant not only for its cross-dressing personages, but because of the re-configuration of the whole structure of the ritual. By describing the procession staged at the Lesbian and Gay Community Center in Manhattan in August, 1992, I am presenting what can be interpreted as a collective representation of identity and community. It is in this ritual where idioms of American and Philippine social symbolisms are selectively fused to provide structure to an implicit and subtle narrative of a community as well as a common cache of meanings and sentiments. This specific event locates the efforts of the organization at establishing a sense of collectivity.

First of all, this *Santacruzan* was not presented as a procession, but as a fashion show. The focal point of the show was the stage with a fashion runway. In the center of the stage, before the runway began, was a floral arch which is reminiscent of the mobile arches of flowers that are carried in the procession for each mythical or historical personage.

The personages or figures were a combination of traditional *Santacruzan* figures as well as configurations of traditional figures and personages together with the creation of new ones. For example, while *Reyna Sentenciada* is usually portrayed as the figure of Justice, carrying scales and in a blindfold, the "gay" *Reyna Sentenciada* is dressed in leather (S & M) dominatrix garb. During the presentation, before he left the stage, *Reyna Sentenciada* lifted his wig to show his bald pate. *Reyna Libertad* or Liberty was dressed also in dominatrix garb complete with a whip. Liberty in this instance was construed to be sexual freedom. The three Virtues were the only figures who were portrayed by women (lesbians) dressed in denim shorts, combat boots and *barong tagalog* (the traditional Filipino male formal attire). Constantino, who is usually portrayed by a child, was a muscular Filipino in brief swimming trunks.

Other bolder representations were *Reyna Banderada,* who usually carried the Philippine flag and who in this case incorporated the symbols of the flag, such as the stars and the red and blue stripes, in a slinky outfit. The three stars of the flag were strategically placed on each nipple and in the crotch area. A mask of the sun was carried by this new version of the motherland. Infanta Judith came out as a Greek goddess and instead of the head of Holofernes, the gay Judith revealed the head of George Bush. A new kind of queen was created for this presentation, *Reyna Chismosa* or Queen of Gossip. This queen came out in a tacky dressing gown and hair curlers, screaming into a cordless phone.

However, the finale was a return to tradition as *Reyna Elena* and the Emperatriz were dressed in traditional gowns and tiaras. The *Reyna Elena* carried an antique cross and flowers as all *Reyna Elenas* have done in the past.

The combination of secular/profane and religious imagery as well as Filipino and American gay icons provided an arena where symbols from the two countries were contested, dismantled and reassembled in a dazzling series of statements. This *Santacruzan* therefore was built on shared experiences that juxtaposed such practices as S & M and cross-dressing with androgyny (the pulling off of the wig) with traditional Filipino ones like the *bakla* notion of drag.

Filipino gay men who participated in this presentation operated within the contours of the *Santacruzan* ritual while at the same time transgressing long-held beliefs and practices by injecting the culture and politics of the adopted country (i.e., George Bush's head). The *Santacruzan* can be seen as "a style of imagining" a community. In other words, the presentation can be seen as an attempt by Filipino gay men to negotiate and represent their collectivity to themselves and to others.

THE FUTURE OF A FILIPINO GAY COMMUNITY

The edges or borders of a Filipino gay community cannot be clearly demarcated as they traverse the edges of other communities of this diasporic world. However, despite the cleavages that run across individuals and group interests, Filipino gay men, as I have shown, respond to various historical instances, such as the AIDS pandemic, anchored to shared cultural traditions that are continually renewed and reassembled. This kind of anchoring is never complete or final. There will always be oscillations between attachments or allegiances to particular groups, be it the Filipino gay community, the Asian gay community or even the so-called "American" gay community.

While many observers and theorists of Asian American political movements see both the political necessity and the historical inevitability of pan-Asian ethnic groupings, I argue that the path of the political evolution of Filipino gay men in America will not be unilinear. Filipinos as a group will not "mature" into a monolithic pan-Asian stage of development. Rather, there will emerge a multiplicity of identities and groupings.[13] Sentiments and allegiances to cultural traditions are continually strengthened and reshaped by the circular pattern of diasporas and migrations. The Filipino diaspora is continually replenished and altered by the sentiments and allegiances of its migrants and exiles.

Such responses are reflected nationally in Filipino gay men's reactions to the *Miss Saigon* controversy and the AIDS pandemic. Especially with the *Santacruzan*, we find a vigorous and continued creation and reconstitution of cultural symbols and practices that go hand in hand with the revivification of a sense of belonging. These discourses will pave the way for a stronger future for the Filipino gay community in New York.

Notes

1. Terralee Bensinger, "Lesbian Pornography: The Re/Making of (a) Community," *Discourse* 15:1 (1992):69–93.
2. Benedict Anderson, *Imagined Communities: Reflections on the Origin and Spread of Nationalism* (London: Verso, 1983).
3. See Gillian Bottomley, *From Another Place: Migration and the Politics of Culture* (Melbourne: Cambridge University Press, 1992).
4. See William Whitam and Robin Mathy, *Homosexuality in Four Societies* (New York: Praeger, 1986), as well as my paper "Tolerance or Struggle: Male Homosexuality in the Philippines," which explored the tolerant and seemingly benign attitude of Filipinos as well as the cultural practices toward that *bakla*.

    I do not use the term *bakla* as the equivalent of gay. Rather I juxtapose the native term for homosexual/faggot as a way of portraying the different homosexual traditions, U.S. and Philippines. *Bakla* is socially constructed as a transvestic and/or effeminized being that occupies an interstitial position between men and women. In this paper, therefore, I use the term "gay" only as a provisional term and do not imply a totally gay-identified population. I also do not want to portray *bakla* traditions as static and unchanging, but rather as specifically demarcated practices continually being shaped and reshaped by both local and global influences and processes.
5. See Donn Hart and Harriet Hart, "Visayan Swardspeak: The Language of a Gay Community in the Philippines," *Crossroads* 5:2 (1990):27–49; and Manalansan, "Speaking of AIDS: Language and the Filipino Gay Experience in America" (in press).
6. All names of informants and other identifying statements have been changed to protect their identities.
7. Examples include Connie S. Chan, "Issues of Identity Development among Asian-American Lesbians and Gay Men," *Journal of Counseling & Development* 68 (1989):16–20; and Terry Gock "Asian Pacific Islander Identity Issues: Identity Integration and Pride," in Betty Berzon, ed., *Positively Gay* (Los Angeles: Mediamix Association, 1984).
8. Nina Reyes, "Common Ground: Asians and Pacific Islanders Look for Unity in a Queer World," *Outweek* 99 (1990).
9. See Bottomley, chapter 6.
10. Manalansan, *ibid.*
11. While more than 85 percent of Filipino AIDS cases in America are gay and bisexual men, the opposite is true in the Philippines, where more than half of the cases are women.
12. Woo, Jean M., George W. Rutherford, Susan F. Payne, J. Lowell Barnhardt and George F. Lemp, "The Epidemiology of AIDS in Asian and Pacific Islander Population in San Francisco," *AIDS* 2 (1988):473–475.
13. See Yen Le Espiritu, *Asian American Panethnicity* (Philadelphia: Temple University Press, 1992), chapter 7.

How to Rehabilitate a Mulatto

The Iconography of Tiger Woods

Hiram Perez

"A Real American Story"

Tiger Woods's tongue-in-cheek identification as "Cablinasian" on the *Oprah Winfrey Show* in April 1997 resulted in such contentiousness within the black community that Winfrey followed up later that same month with a program devoted to the "Tiger Woods Race Controversy."[1] Woods's identification as Cablinasian during that interview has more often than not been taken out of context. He relates arriving at that category ("Ca, Caucasian; bl, black; in, Indian; Asian—Cablinasian")[2] during his childhood as a survival strategy against racist taunting and violence, including an incident after the first day of kindergarten when he was tied to a tree and called a monkey and a nigger. However, that moment on *Oprah* when he pronounced the word "Cablinasian" constituted for the multiracial category movement an Amalgamation Proclamation of sorts. Following the program, he was soundly blasted by black media and intellectuals, among them Manning Marable,[3] but such criticism has only deepened the resolve of the multiracial category movement that its ranks are misunderstood and victimized not only by a dominant culture but by other racial minorities, particularly what they regard as a militant, uniracial old guard.

The white parents of biracial (in this case, usually black and white) children constitute the majority of the proponents for the addition of a multiracial category to the census.[4] These parents are attempting to protect their children from what they perceive as the hardships that ensue from identification as black. As Tanya Katerí Hernández explains, "White parents will seize opportunities to extend their privilege of whiteness to non-White persons they care about."[5] Their naiveté lies in the belief that evading the legal classification "black" or "African American" will entirely spare a child from the socioeconomic and psychic hardships common to black people. An examination of the history of passing confirms that the legacy of hypodescent is never eradicated by the act of passing. Part of the insidiousness of racial classification in the Americas, which relies on notions of racial contamination and purity, is the manner in which that one drop of tainted blood assumes a ghostly life, not just in terms of its symbolic quality (by which the threat of invisibility is managed) but by its perpetual return either across generations or, for the subject who passes, at that inevitable moment of confession or betrayal.[6]

I argue that the celebrity of a figure such as Tiger Woods functions to rehabilitate the mulatto in order to announce the arrival of a new colorblind era in U.S. history. Woods's multiracial identity is recuperated as a kind of testimonial to racial progress that simultaneously celebrates diversity in the form of Cablinasianness and the multiplicity that category suggests while erasing the histories of black disenfranchisement, racial-sexual violence, and U.S. imperialism that generate, result from, and entrench the legal, scientific, and popular definitions of race, including each racial component of Cablinasianness and their various amalgamations. The word Tiger Woods chooses to describe his racial makeup effects, ironically, his racial unmaking. As I demonstrate in this essay, Nike advertising, with the exception of the company's very first television advertisement featuring Woods, obliquely references race only to register its insignificance (within the discourse of constitutional color-blindness) or to capitalize (just as obliquely) on racial fantasies about the black body and the Asian body. The Tiger Woods iconography shuttles seamlessly between race consciousness and racial elision. That seamlessness is facilitated by the unlikely union in recent years between the ostensibly incompatible ideologies of multiculturalism and color-blindness. Although multiculturalism and the rhetoric of color-blindness appear to espouse contradictory positions, these philosophies ultimately advance very similar ideologies, as various critical race theorists and cultural critics have already argued. Diversity, as a central goal of multiculturalism, does not transform the economic, legal, and cultural institutions that secure white privilege.[7] Both multiculturalism and color-blindness conceive of racial difference as independent of institutionalized racism. The inconsistencies implicit in the iconography of Tiger Woods (i.e., a celebration of multiraciality that simultaneously heralds color-blindness) become transparent at this intersection of multiculturalism and color-blindness; consequently, the celebrity of Tiger Woods functions ideologically to preserve the status quo, an inviolable institutionalized racism.

In the iconography of Tiger Woods the mulatto becomes a proud product (*sans* irony) of American democracy. In fact, according to this logic, Woods (not just his celebrity, but his very existence) is possible only because of American democracy, hence Oprah Winfrey's reference to Woods as "America's son."[8] Sigrid Nunez's narrator in the novel *A Feather on the Breath of God*, the product of a Chinese Panamanian father and German mother, observes for example that "when I talked about my mother and father people often said things like, 'Only in America.' People called their story 'a real American story.' "[9] A figure such as Tiger Woods hails the success of American democracy and the advent of a multicultural *and* colorblind society. I want to clarify here that I am not attempting with this analysis to address Tiger Woods's personal accountability—or at least that is not my principal concern. By speaking to Woods's transformation into "America's son," I shift the focus of my analysis from an independently acting Tiger Woods to the conglomerate interests informing his iconography. I use the word "conglomerate" to reference both corporate and public interests in Woods as well as the convergence of those interests in the construction of Woods the icon.

For the historian Eric Foner, the period of Radical Reconstruction constitutes an "unfinished revolution": "From the enforcement of the rights of citizens to the stubborn problems of economic and racial justice, the issues central to Reconstruction are as old as the American republic, and as contemporary as the inequalities that still afflict our society."[10] Tiger Woods confirms for Americans that the revolution effected by Radical Reconstruction has indeed been consummated. He is the proof that the inequalities that Foner speaks of no longer hinder racial progress. That he is the product of a black father and an Asian mother provides testament to that progress. Again I want to clarify that I am referring here not to the personal relationship between Earl and Kultida Woods but to the significance symbolically of that relationship in the production of Tiger Woods's celebrity. According to the fictions of color-blind ideology, Earl Woods's access to the Asian woman's body (the body of a woman who is not black) symbolizes his fully actualized citizenship. How that access to the Asian woman's body for the black man is secured by U.S. military occupation and neo-colonialism in Asia remains uninterrogated. Woods's celebrity depends on a eugenical fantasy that stages a disciplining of the black, male body through an infusion of Asian blood and an imagined Confucian upbringing. The way that Tiger Woods represents racial progress and the fulfillment of American democracy is contingent upon both the specific formula of his fractional identity and the institutions of forgetting.

In his book, *Training a Tiger: A Father's Guide to Raising a Winner in Both Golf and Life* (1997), Earl Woods describes the circumstances that made possible his marriage to Kultida Woods: "I also saw the world and, in two tours of Vietnam as a Green Beret, stared death in the face more than once. I also met and fought side by side with a Vietnamese officer and Tiger's namesake, Lieutenant Colonel Nguyen T. Phong. I had become an information officer years earlier, and it was on one of those information assignments that I met Tiger's mother, Kultida."[11] Earl Woods's access to an Asian wife confirms that a last obstacle to black citizenship has been eradicated. The notion of women as property underlies much of the antipathy toward interracial unions in both black and white communities. The white woman, as a form of property protected from black male acquisition, becomes representative of a two-tiered citizenship. For the white male citizenry, dominion over her body remains a guarantor of white superiority against the encroaching demands of a free, black population. The tenacity with which the fantasy of the black rapist loosed upon the nation has embedded itself in the imagination of the dominant culture underscores this anxiety about black male designs on white womanhood. As a product of a black man and a woman who is not black, Woods confirms that a final vestige of two-tiered citizenship has been eliminated. That his mother is Asian and not white makes the interracial relationship between his parents less objectionable and secures for Woods this symbolic status. Tiger Woods would not mean the same thing for America if he were the product of a black man and a white woman. Images of Mariah Carey, Lenny Kravitz, Halle Berry, Jason Kidd, or Derek Jeter, for example, have not been mobilized toward the same ends as those of Woods. While the ancestry of all five of these celebrities has received some media attention, in none of their cases has miscegenation been imagined to represent the final actualization of the nation's founding ideals of freedom and equality.

The representation of Woods's multiracial ancestry exploits the stereotype of the black man's superior (suprahuman) athleticism as well as the stereotype of the Asian American "model minority." The idea of the model minority has historically been used to blame African American and Latino/a communities for their own disenfranchisement. The December 1966 *U.S. News and World Report* article, "Success Story of One Minority in the U.S.," provides one of the earliest articulations of the model minority stereotype: "At a time when it is being proposed that hundreds of billions be spent on uplifting Negroes and other minorities, the nation's 300,000 Chinese Americans are moving ahead on their own with no help from anyone else."[12] Just as model minority rhetoric functions to discipline the unruly black bodies threatening national stability during the post–civil rights era, the infusion of Asian blood together with his imagined Confucian upbringing corrals and tames Tiger's otherwise brute physicality. Some variation of *his father trained the body and his mother trained the mind* is a recurring motif for sports commentators diagnosing Woods's success at golf. Earl Woods has encouraged this fantasy:

> Her teaching methods weren't always orthodox, but they were effective. When Tiger was just a toddler, she wrote the addition and multiplication tables out for him on 3-by-5-inch cards, and he would practice them over and over every day. He started with addition and later advanced to multiplication as he got older. His reward was an afternoon on the range with me. Tida established irrevocably that education had a priority over golf. (Woods 9)

The qualities of Woods's model minority mother compensate for the black man's cognitive deficiencies. In fact, since the stereotype of the model minority secures the normalcy of whiteness by attributing Asian American successes (the evidence for which is often exaggerated and overly generalized) to a biological predisposition toward *over*achievement, the contributions of the Asian mother actually exceed the capacity for white blood and a Protestant work ethic to compensate for black degeneracy. Woods's success at golf, traditionally a sport reserved for the white elite, is in part explained by the logic of eugenics.

The celebration of Tiger Woods as the embodiment of American multiculturalism and racial democracy institutes an instance of "organized forgetting."[13] Oprah Winfrey's celebratory vision of Tiger Woods as "America's son" displaces, for example, historical memories of the bastardized children of white slave owners or U.S. soldiers overseas. Miscegenation as a legacy of slavery is forgotten, as is the miscegenation that has resulted from the various U.S. military occupations in Asia dating back to the late nineteenth century.

Being Tiger / Wanting to Be Like Mike

In one of its first television ads using Tiger Woods's image, Nike presents a montage of children of different races, each proclaiming, "I am Tiger Woods." Nike very astutely capitalizes on Woods's mixed racial heritage in creating a picture of inclusiveness and color-blindness. As Robert Goldman and Stephen Papson argue in their study of Nike culture, "Nike . . . has chosen to foreground race as a category, first in order to draw attention to their association with Tiger Woods, and then doing a 180 degree turn to demonstrate the declining relevance of race as a category."[14] The shots of children of different races located in various geopolitical spaces (in some shots clearly suggesting urban poverty), interspersed with the image of Tiger Woods, documents the democratizing process that Woods symbolizes. Particularly because Woods has succeeded in a traditionally white, upper-crust sport, the advertisement's identification of each of these children as Tiger Woods delivers the children from poverty and racial oppression. Woods's conquest of golf signifies a final frontier of racism. That barrier now vanquished, black, Latino, and Asian children are unshackled from the tyranny of systemic oppression; racial categories become not only obsolete but also retrogressive and dangerous. Goldman and Papson observe, "Remember how *Nike* constructed Barkley in its 'I'm not a role model' ad. Now, *Nike* positions Woods as the ultimate role model. The ad's children don't chant 'I want to be like Tiger Woods,' rather, they state total identification: 'I am Tiger Woods'" (Goldman and Papson 114). This tendency of Nike's marketing of Tiger Woods to reference race primarily as a means for endorsing a color-blind ideology has made Tiger Woods more serviceable to the rhetoric of the multiracial movement than any other mixed-race celebrity.

Tom Petri, a Republican Representative from Fond du Lac, Wisconsin, who served on the congressional subcommittee in charge of the census, tried for several years to enact legislation to introduce a "multiracial" category to the census. Following Tiger Woods's victory at the Masters golf tournament in 1997, Petri renamed the legislation "the Tiger Woods bill."[15] It is not too cynical to suggest that Petri's apparent sensitivity to issues of racial identity is somewhat suspicious. Concerning the general perception of the census by members of Congress, Lawrence Wright clarifies, "the attitude of most elected officials in Washington toward the census is polite loathing, because it is the census, as much as any other force in the country, that determines their political futures. Congressional districts rise and fall with the shifting demography of the country" (46). The introduction of a "multiracial" category undermines governmental structures established to safeguard the equal representation of minorities within a democracy.

Petri's embrace of the multiracial category movement demands closer scrutiny of that movement's ideological underpinnings. The proponents for the addition of a multiracial category on the census and other federal, state, and local government forms base their arguments on four principles: (1) the value of individualism; (2) the elimination of racism; (3) the need for group recognition; and (4) the value of diversity. The claim, very often heard among promoters of a multiracial category, that people should have the right to define themselves, is rooted in notions of American individualism. However, the quality of individualism in the United States is entrenched in notions of property and particularly self-ownership and acquisitiveness. When on June 7, 1892, Homer Plessy challenged both segregation and Louisiana race codes by sitting in a section of a railway car reserved for whites, he discovered that the qualities of self-ownership and acquisitiveness were restricted along race lines. The U.S. Supreme Court agreed with Plessy that "belonging to the dominant race, in this instance the white race, is *property*, in the same sense that a right of action, or of inheritance, is property."[16] Yet, the court was "unable to see" how Homer Plessy, as an octoroon (a person of one-eighth black ancestry), had been deprived of such property.

Nearly ninety years later, under very different circumstances, Susie Guillory Phipps learned the same lesson. Phipps, in the process of applying for a passport, learned that she was classified on her birth certificate as "colored." She sued the state of Louisiana to change her racial status from "colored" to "white" and lost. The U.S. Supreme Court refused in 1986 to hear her appeal. While Plessy's challenge to Louisiana racial codes constituted part of a larger, organized protest against Louisiana's "Jim Crow Car Laws," Phipps's challenge was quite unapologetically an attempt to protect her own property interests in whiteness.[17] According to Neil Gotanda, Phipps reported being "sick for three days" upon discovering that she was classified at birth as "colored."[18] Whiteness functions as a form of property. The tradition of American individualism is very much ingrained in this notion of property. As john a. powell observes, "[g]iven the normative structure of whiteness in the United States, the claim of individualism is often a thinly veiled effort to claim the privileges of whiteness."[19] The multiracial category movement's appeal to American individualism is no exception.

When children of every race can proclaim, "I am Tiger Woods," race becomes insignificant. Woods represents the culmination of the principles of American democracy and the end of racism. The decidedly multicultural flavor of this Nike ad follows on the heels of Woods's first ad for Nike, which portrayed him as an outsider in the predominantly white world of golf. Superimposed over footage of Woods's victory at the U.S. Amateur tournament, the text reads: "Hello world. I am the only man to win three consecutive U.S. Amateur titles. There are still courses in the U.S. I am not allowed to play because of the color of my skin. Are you ready for me?" As Goldman and Papson point out, critics of the ad not only accused Nike of exploiting race consciousness for profit but charged as well that the ad was dishonest since, as Bob Garfield of *Advertising Age* argued, "Tiger Woods was not a victim of racism" (Goldman and Papson 113). Garfield's objection presumes both that Woods's status as an elite athlete and celebrity exempts him from racism and that Woods's success in itself confirms that Jim Crow has irrevocably been laid to rest.

While this first ad emphasized a history of officially sanctioned racial discrimination, the succeeding "I am Tiger Woods" ad ushers in a new era of egalitarianism. James Small, a Nike publicist, responded to the criticism against the first ad by explaining that there are no courses in the United States that would bar Woods from play. The advertisement, according to Small, means to "raise awareness that golf is not an inclusive sport";[20] he explains that we are not to read the ad literally. It turns out that the Tiger Woods represented in the ad whom we mistook for a black man is only a metaphor for the black man. As Goldman and Papson recount, *"Nike's* public relations director maintained that the ad was not to be taken literally, but as 'a metaphor,' with Woods representing other black golfers" (113). Nike learned from its mistake in this first advertisement and immediately distanced itself from any material, social commentary. Instead Nike executives chose to embrace the richer possibilities embodied in Tiger Woods the metaphor, forsaking the much more disquieting figure of an angry and historically disenfranchised black man.[21]

This backpedaling by Nike executives would be much more amusing if not for the violent forgetting enacted by the "I am Tiger Woods" advertisement, clearly offered up by Nike as a kind of restitution for the race consciousness of the first ad. The refrain of the ad recalls Spike Lee's 1992 film *Malcolm X,* which concludes with black schoolchildren rising from their desks, both in the United States and in South Africa, and pronouncing, "I am Malcolm X." However, the original moment of this spontaneous, black, communal identification appropriated by both Nike and Spike Lee occurs during a mass for Fred Hampton, the twenty-one-year-old head of the Chicago chapter of the Black Panther Party, assassinated during a police raid on December 4, 1969. The mass was conducted by Father George Clements of the Holy Angels Church, who describes the response of Chicago's black schoolchildren to the murder of Hampton:

> I had a mass for Fred, and I was just shattered. I was devastated. And in the midst of this mass I was trying to explain to our children—we had the school children there, all thirteen hundred—and I was trying to explain to them the importance of Fred, and I wasn't getting through—at least I felt like I wasn't getting through. And in the midst of my explanation I just burst into tears, and the next thing I knew here was one of our eighth grade boys—he jumped up and he said "I am Fred Hampton." And then a girl in the sixth grade, she jumps up: "I am Fred Hampton." Another kid in first grade, "I'm Fred Hampton." And before you knew it the whole church, kids were all shouting, "I am Fred Hampton!" And wow! I just felt so wonderful. I felt like, gee-whiz, this death was not in vain at all, because these kids are saying that they are willing to get up here and speak out for liberation, for first class citizenship.[22]

Hampton was slain by local Chicago police using information gathered by J. Edgar Hoover's F.B.I. COINTELPRO program targeting black liberation groups. According to historian Winston A. Grady-Willis, Hoover's counterintelligence program was directed at groups such as the Black Panther Party, the Nation of Islam, and the Student Nonviolent Coordinating Committee and it sought to prevent

1. the formation of a Black political front, 2. "rise of a messiah," 3. violence directed at the state, 4. the gaining of movement credibility, 5. and long-range growth of organizations, especially among young people.[23]

The irony here is appalling. In attempting to remedy its commercial misstep (suggesting that racism still exists in America), Nike invokes the communal reaction to the state-authorized murder of Fred Hampton (no doubt one of the rising messiahs Hoover feared) but perverts it into a slogan for color-blind ideology. Nike's "I am Tiger Woods" advertisement yields its own messianic son, who can deliver the nation from its messy and violent past—announcing the arrival of a fantasied color-blind democracy and obliterating in the process any evidence to the contrary.

This scene described by Father Clements undoubtedly inspires the conclusion of Lee's filmic account of the life of Malcolm X. Lee's appropriation of "I am Fred Hampton" is in itself troubling as evidence of the filmmaker's propensity for finessing black political resistance into successful mass marketing. Lee, comparing the major Hollywood studios to "plantations," justifies his marketing strategy as means to an end for the black filmmaker:

> While we were shooting *Jungle Fever* in late 1990, I made up an initial design for the "X" cap. I'd already decided I had to do *Malcolm X*, and marketing is an integral part of my filmmaking. So the X was planned all the way out. I came up with a simple design—silver X on black baseball cap. The colors could be changed later on as the campaign advanced. It looked good. I started wearing it, and we began selling it in our store, Spike's Joint, and in other places. I gave them away strategically. I asked Michael Jordan to wear it, and he has. Then I asked some other stars to wear it and, what can I say, it just caught on. Then the knock-offs started appearing. These X caps are coming from everywhere now. It's raining X caps, X this, X that, *sometimes without the wearers knowing the story behind the X. The word of mouth is beginning to pick up on this already.*[24] [emphasis added]

Lee's candor is astonishing. His proprietary attitude toward Malcolm X's name (after all, "X" becomes a Spike Lee Joint, infringed upon by "knockoffs") contradicts the anticapitalist politics of both Malcolm X and Fred Hampton. More significantly, the value of "X" to Lee as a commodity clearly supersedes the story of Malcolm X and his message. The fact of "word of mouth," insuring box-office success for his film, is more important than "the story behind the X." It is unclear how much irony Lee intended when he entitled his account of the making of *Malcolm X, By Any Means Necessary.* Lee not only contributes to the vacuous sloganization of Malcolm X's call for black liberation but also transforms those words into an endorsement of black capitalism. Spike Lee's long-standing corporate relationship with Nike is well known and difficult to overlook. However, the question of his collaboration with Nike is not necessarily pertinent here. In regard to his choices as a filmmaker, he is already complicit in stylizing and diluting black protest into a form digestible by a mass audience.

Spike Lee's determination to prioritize marketability over questions of ethics and responsibility vis-à-vis the very complicated politics of memorialization opens the door for Nike's corporate assimilation of black resistance and race consciousness. The spontaneous invocation of Fred Hampton by Chicago's black schoolchildren, as described by Father George Clements, is likely inspired by

Hampton's own words: "when I leave, you remember I said, with the last words on my lips, I am a revolutionary, and you gonna have to keep on saying that. You gonna have to say that I am a proletariat. I am the people. I'm not the pig." It is an unthinkable perversion of Fred Hampton's legacy that the response of Chicago's black community to his death should be manipulated by a multinational corporation to sell the fiction of America's color-blindness as well as golf shoes.

The "multiracial" figure invoked by Woods's celebrity must be shorn of any historical and material significance in order to consolidate a national fiction of color-blindness. The deracialization of this symbolic mulatto or "multiracial" figure is fulfilled by the identification, "I am Tiger Woods." Woods's service to the fantasy of color-blindness requires a slippage from the material to the metaphorical and a sanctioned forgetting of the legacies of U.S. imperialism and racial oppression. The designation "America's son," although it bears great irony for minority audiences, does not identify a history of racial and sexual violence but rather the availability of Tiger Woods's body for universal consumption. In other words, his celebrity belongs to all of us, but only some of us get to decide what that celebrity can signify. As Lisa Jones protests, "[t]he doors of opportunity that Tiger himself once walked through are shutting, while the nation gloats over him."[25]

The marketing of Michael Jordan also sought to universalize his appeal. As Michael Eric Dyson explains, Jordan has been marketed as "an icon of race-transcending American athletic and moral excellence."[26] The accessibility of the Jordan icon for transracial identification has been encapsulated in the chant, "I want to be like Mike," popularized in the Gatorade advertising campaign. However, this commodification of Jordan for global consumption has not foreclosed race-conscious black identifications. As Dyson observes, "[t]here is also the creative use of desire and fantasy by young blacks to counter, and capitulate to, the forces of cultural dominance that attempt to reduce the black body to a commodity and text that is employed for entertainment, titillation, or financial gain" (Dyson 70). Forms of black cultural expression survive (and adapt to) the commodification of the black body and black culture. These forms of expression remain recognizable to black audiences despite the universalization of the Jordan icon within consumer culture.[27]

The resilience of black cultural expression does not necessarily designate an uncomplicated moment of resistance against the dominant culture. Jordan's articulation of black cultural style has also been successfully exploited by Nike in order to expand its market to the poorest and most marginalized communities in the United States. Dyson condemns not only Nike but also Jordan for his complicity in this project:

> Moreover, while sneaker companies have exploited black cultural expressions of cool, hip, chic, and style, they rarely benefit the people who both consume the largest quantity of products and whose culture redefined the sneaker companies' raison d'être. This situation is more severely compounded by the presence of spokespeople like Jordan, Spike Lee, and Bo Jackson, who are either ineffectual or defensive about or indifferent

to the lethal consequences (especially in urban black-on-black violence over sneaker company products) of black juvenile acquisition of products that these figures have helped make culturally desirable and economically marketable. (Dyson 73)

As golf does not possess the same cachet in urban black communities as basketball, Tiger Woods will never be as marketable as Jordan in black urban centers. The Jordan iconography combines both race consciousness and universalism. The race consciousness is necessary to appeal not only to black urban youth but also to a dominant culture that has redefined its relationship to the spectacle of black athleticism. White men and black men "want to be like Mike" in very different ways. The identification with Michael Jordan by the dominant culture does not circumvent racial difference; instead, it requires and reinforces a fantasy of black masculinity that reduces the black man to a physicality that in the case of Jordan and other black celebrity athletes is simultaneously both superhuman and not quite human. The white spectator desires the superior athleticism essentialized in the black body and remains both attracted to and repelled by that body. Advertising featuring black celebrity athletes typically resists humanizing those athletes. As opposed to representations of white celebrity athletes, advertising images of black athletes such as the Williams sisters, Michael Johnson, Marion Jones, Bo Jackson, and Shaquille O'Neal typically use special effects to emphasize their fantasied superhuman/not quite human capacities.

The manner in which Tiger Woods's celebrity references his racial ancestry functions simultaneously to elide the significance of that ancestry. The cast of multicultural faces pronouncing "I am Tiger Woods" tropes his multiracial heritage while performing an incorporation of that racial heritage that renders it insignificant except as a hallmark of the success of color-blind ideology. The difference between *wanting to be like Mike* and *being Tiger Woods* corresponds to the specific racialized constructions of their celebrity. Jordan's marketing relies persistently on his raced embodiment, while the marketing of Woods references race obliquely only to divest the image of Woods ultimately of any race specificity. Nike's initial campaign, promoting race consciousness, was indeed a misstep. The dominant culture embraces Woods as long as he remains serviceable to a colorblind ideology.

Tiger Woods's celebrity rehabilitates the mulatto to announce the arrival of an era in U.S. history when race will no longer matter. This rehabilitated, amnesic mulatto functions to consolidate a national identity and a national forgetting. Woods's anxious embodiment of a national symbol tellingly represses any Asian constituency. Although Tiger Woods's mother is Thai, she has not figured prominently in the commodification of his image. Commercial interests in Tiger Woods's media image have seized instead on his relationship to his African American father. However, as I have argued in this essay, Kultida Woods's imagined biological contribution to the construction of "America's son" satisfies more subliminally a eugenical fantasy. The black, male body in this case is disciplined by the influence of a Confucian ethic fetishized as essentially and generically Asian. Tiger Woods is not the model minority but rather the remodel(ed) minority. Nike advertising has of course appreciably shaped the Tiger Woods icon. Hence, while Woods's transcendent celebrity heralds an era of color-blindness, it is still his racialized body being bought and sold.

But America's son is eager to forget. The invisible labor exploited by Nike in Asia materially sustains Tiger Woods's iconic embodiment of racial democracy. Far from being color-blind, the transnational labor of export manufacture is by design both racialized and feminized.[28] It turns out that America's son, ironically a guarantor of American multiculturalism, recalls the classic passing figure; he cannot publicly acknowledge his mother's body—the body of feminized, Third World labor—without compromising his own mobility.

CONCLUSION: CITIZENSHIP AS A FORM OF PROPERTY

One of the ironies of Tiger Woods's status as "America's son" and his imagined embodiment of the ideals of American democracy is that, of course, there exists a large Amerasian population sharing a racial heritage very similar to Woods. Yet, far from being celebrated as America's sons and daughters, most of those children of U.S. servicemen and Asian women are in actuality denied U.S. citizenship. I conclude with a discussion of Tuan Ahn Nguyen's legal challenge to section 1409 of the Immigration and Nationality Act because of the way this particular statute reinscribes a tradition of state-enforced, racialized bastardy dating back to slavery, a legacy of miscegenation that the Tiger Woods iconography works to forget.

Nguyen v. INS (2001) challenges section 1409 of the Immigration and Nationality Act which stipulates for a child born abroad to one U.S. citizen and one alien parent different criteria for citizenship depending on the status of the mother. If the mother is a U.S. citizen, citizenship is conferred automatically on the child; if the mother is an alien, the child must meet strict criteria in order to successfully apply for citizenship. I also want to return briefly to the *Plessy v. Ferguson* decision in order to complicate the understanding of whiteness as a form of property introduced by Homer Plessy's legal counsel in 1896 and subsequently expounded upon by the legal scholar Cheryl I. Harris in her influential essay "Whiteness as Property" (1993).[29]

As the subtitle to Kimberlé Crenshaw's anthology of Critical Race scholarship suggests, Harris's article is one of the "key writings that formed the movement." Originally published in the June 1993 *Harvard Law Review*, Harris's essay examines how the legal protection of property rights in the United States has historically secured personhood and citizenship while simultaneously maintaining racial oppression. Returning to the *Plessy v. Ferguson* decision, especially Homer Plessy's assertion (corroborated by the Supreme Court) that whiteness constitutes a form of property, Harris delineates the "property functions of whiteness," including "rights of disposition," "right to use and enjoyment," and "the absolute right to exclude."[30] I rely on and agree with Harris's theorization of the property functions of whiteness. My concern is that the centrality of this theory to the critical study of race inadvertently impedes an analysis of race relations that fall outside the (often unspoken) black-white model for racial difference in the United States. Harris's essay provides an example of just such an oversight.

Although she provides a close analysis of the language of *Plessy*, she does not extend that analysis to Justice John Marshall Harlan's discussion in his dissenting opinion of the Chinese vis-à-vis white and black citizens.[31] Her examination of the link between whiteness and citizenship extends only to a consideration of the exclusion of blacks and Native Americans from the constitutional guarantees of citizenship: "Race and property were thus conflated by establishing a form of property contingent on race: only blacks were subjugated as slaves and treated as property. Similarly, the conquest, removal, and extermination of Native American life and culture were ratified by conferring and acknowledging the property rights of whites in Native American land" (Harris 278). In order to argue for black enfranchisement, however, Harlan situated the Chinese as duly ineligible for citizenship in opposition to the "citizens of the black race":

> There is a race so different from our own that we do not permit those belonging to it to become citizens of the United States. . . . I allude to the Chinese race. But by the statute in question, a Chinaman can ride in the same passenger coach with white citizens of the United States, while citizens of the black race in Louisiana, many of whom, perhaps, risked their lives for the preservation of the Union . . . are yet declared to be criminals, liable to imprisonment, if they ride in a public coach occupied by citizens of the white race.[32]

Significantly, Harlan's appeal for the guarantees of citizenship on behalf of the black race required that he define the quality of black personhood in contradistinction to that of the Chinese race *and* a propos of black military service. These criteria are relevant then to any historical understanding of U.S. racial formation, especially regarding the role of the Asian body in mediating a perennially compromised black citizenship. This is true not only in regard to Harlan's opposition of Chinese to black and white but also in regard to the foregrounding of the black soldier in his argument. However vexed the history of African American military service—and the disproportionate number of blacks in the U.S. military speaks precisely to a compromised black citizenship—the black soldier nonetheless embodies a hostile, occupying force in the various East and Southeast Asian nations subject to U.S. imperialism. In order to more fully understand, for example, how U.S. imperialism complicates racial dynamics both domestically and internationally, it is necessary to shift the terms of Harris's formulation so that we can evaluate not only the property of whiteness but also the property of citizenship. As *Nguyen v. INS* (2001) demonstrates, citizenship also functions as a form of property that must be protected from ever-encroaching alien hands.

In his work on history and memory, *Lost Narratives: Popular Fictions, Politics, and Recent History*, Roger Bromley asserts, "forgetting is as important as remembering" (12). The symbolic embodiment of Tiger Woods as "America's son" facilitates the kind of "organized forgetting" that Bromley characterizes as a struggle over cultural power. Tiger Woods's iconography revisits a contest over the official narrative memory of miscegenation in the Americas also staged in *Nguyen v. INS* and *Plessy v. Ferguson*. At stake is not only the history of miscegenation but also how we in the present recognize and grapple with its more difficult legacies, including bastardy, shame, forgetting, sexual violence, and the race secret.

The recent Supreme Court decision in the case of *Tuan Anh Nguyen and Joseph Boulais v. Immigration and Naturalization Service* (2001) revives, for example, the tradition instituted by American slavery whereby the child assumes the status of the mother.[33] The ruling is also consistent with the traditions of state-enforced, racialized bastardy variously realized through slavery, antimiscegenation statutes, and U.S. military occupations in Asia. Tuan Anh Nguyen, the son of an American citizen (Joseph Boulais, the copetitioner) and a Vietnamese citizen, was born in Vietnam. In 1975, when he was five years old, Nguyen came to the United States with his father and became a permanent resident. Following his arrest and imprisonment for sexual assault on a child, the Immigration and Naturalization Service began deportation hearings against Nguyen. Although he is the child of a U.S. citizen (Boulais obtained DNA evidence to confirm his paternity), an immigration judge found Nguyen deportable.[34] The Immigration and Nationality Act that governs the acquisition of citizenship requires different criteria, depending on the gender of the citizen parent, for children born abroad to unwed citizen and alien parents.[35] Had Nguyen's mother been a U.S. citizen and his father Vietnamese, he would automatically have qualified for citizenship. Nguyen and Boulais appealed the INS decision on the grounds that the gender-based classification of the statute in question (Title 8 U.S.C. section 1409) violates the constitutional guarantee of equal protection. The U.S. Supreme Court ruled against Nguyen on June 11, 2001, finding that the statutory gender-based distinction withstood equal protection scrutiny, serving "important governmental objectives" (7).

The circumstances leading to Nguyen's deportation—convictions on two counts of sexual assault against a child—threaten to obscure the historical significance of this case. Because the most immediate result of the Supreme Court decision is the deportation of a child molester, the case has not garnered much outrage. Criticism of the decision has also stumbled on this obstacle. For example, while Steve Rissing, writing for the *Columbus Dispatch*, criticizes the ruling as both bad law and bad science, he cannot overcome the hurdle of Nguyen's criminal conviction: "The legal result: deportation. Frankly, I think the punishment should have been more severe."[36] It is perhaps Nguyen's history as a sex offender that allows the Court to seize upon this case in order to uphold the constitutionality of statute 1409. Justice Kennedy, in his majority opinion, notes that the same statute had been challenged three years earlier without resolution in *Miller v. Albright* (1998).[37] Kennedy also cites various conflicting lower court rulings on the constitutionality of the statute. Although Kennedy argues that the presence of the father (Boulais) before the Court singularly distinguishes *Nguyen* from *Miller*, Nguyen's criminal history, even if it did not in fact influence the opinion, impinges on how effectively resistance to this ruling might be mobilized.[38] It is imperative that we look beyond Tuan Anh Nguyen's criminal history in order to assess the implications of this case.

Kennedy's majority opinion in *Nguyen* essentializes maternity while recognizing that paternal ties are necessarily contingent. According to the Court, the Immigration and Nationality Act protects natural ties of the child to the nation conferred biologically by the mater citizen to her offspring. According to Kennedy, the mother's situation is "unique":

> In the case of a citizen mother and a child born overseas, the opportunity for a "meaningful relationship between citizen parent and child inheres in the very event of birth, an event so often critical to our constitutional and statutory understandings of citizenship. The mother knows that the child is in being and is hers and has an initial point of contact with him. There is at least an opportunity for mother and child to develop a real, meaningful relationship. (10)

The father's relationship to the child is much less remarkable. Kennedy observes in fact that it is not always clear that "the mother will be sure of the father's identity," a situation that for him merits particular concern in the case of children born overseas. In the context of this decision, the indiscriminate mother who worries him is not the "citizen mother" suckling the potential citizen but rather the alien mother (in the cases of Tuan Anh Nguyen and Lorelyn Penero Miller, respectively a Vietnamese national and a Filipina national). Section 1409 protects national interests:

> Congress is well within its authority in refusing, absent proof of at least the opportunity for the development of a relationship between citizen parent and child, to commit this country to embracing a child as a citizen entitled as of birth to the full protection of the United States, to the absolute right to enter its borders, and to full participation in the political process. If citizenship is to be conferred by the unwitting means petitioners urge, so that its acquisition abroad bears little relation to the realities of the child's own ties and allegiances, it is for Congress, not this Court, to make that determination. Congress has not taken that path but has instead chosen, by means of §1409, to ensure in the case of father and child the opportunity for a relationship to develop, an opportunity which the event of birth itself provides for the mother and child. (12)

By this reasoning, the mother confers naturally upon the child cultural and national identity. The "event of birth" in itself sufficiently establishes the citizen mother's role in mediating national "ties and allegiances." The female citizen is charged with reproducing the nation. Although Tuan Anh Nguyen has resided as a legal resident in the United States since the age of five, his birth to an alien mother renders his national allegiance suspect.

As with the amnesic celebration of miscegenation common to both the multiracial category movement and the iconization of Tiger Woods, the decision in *Nguyen* effaces any history of miscegenation that contradicts constitutional guarantees of justice, welfare, and equality. The miscegenous unions that produce Tuan Anh Nguyen and Lorelyn Penero Miller are made possible by U.S. imperialism. The Court refuses to recognize the state's obligation toward a population of Amerasian children whose existence results from U.S. military occupations in Asia. Without acknowledging any legal or moral obligation by the United States to Nguyen and similarly situated individuals, Justice Kennedy reports, "the year in which Nguyen was born, there were 3,458,072 active duty military personnel,

39,506 of whom were female" (10). Kennedy identifies "the unique relationship of the mother to the event of birth" (9) as the justification for the gender-specific distinctions of section 1409. But the statute is in fact less concerned with extending and validating (in the form of national citizenship) the natural ties between the citizen mother and child than it is in excluding from citizenship the Amerasian children of military personnel. Kennedy admits, "[o]ne concern in this context has always been with young people, men for the most part, who are on duty with the Armed Forces in foreign countries" (10). He characterizes these men as "young people" in order to absolve them (and the state) of any responsibility toward their children born overseas out of wedlock.

These men apparently do not exercise any racial, patriarchal, or colonial privilege in relation to the women residing in the territories that they forcibly occupy. The Asian mother in this instance bears the burden and the shame for miscegenation and its legacy of illegitimacy. She figures as the seductress. The "young men" serving their nation overseas cannot reasonably be held accountable for their seduction by indiscriminate foreign women who, after all, regarding their illegitimate claim, cannot even "be sure of the father's identity." With respect to the increased border-crossing resulting from globalization, the *Nguyen* decision also seeks to safeguard the indiscretions of the American tourist and international capitalist. The gender-specific conditions of statute 1409 become a practical consideration when one considers, as Kennedy indicates, that "the average American overseas traveler spent 15.1 nights out of the United States in 1999" (11).

This essay seeks to disrupt the amnesic contemporary representations of miscegenation. The case of *Nguyen v. INS* (2001), consistent with the legal treatment of miscegenation dating back to slavery, enforces the condition of bastardy on miscegenous subjects in order to exclude similar constituencies (specifically Amerasian children of U.S. soldiers overseas) from the rights and privileges of citizenship. The state-sanctioned bastardy implemented by the Immigration and Nationality Act not only delegitimizes the child's relationship to the father but also invalidates the child's political membership in the public sphere. *Nguyen* traces how the more difficult legacies of miscegenation, such as state-sanctioned bastardy and sexual exploitation, have not only endured (despite the promise embodied by "America's son") but also evolved, protecting national, patriarchal, and dominant white cultural interests beyond the local onto a global field. An interrogation of the Tiger Woods iconography reveals an unlikely convergence of discourses (including American individualism, consumerism, multiculturalism, color-blindness, and eugenics) working likewise to protect the property interests of both whiteness and citizenship and to preserve the structural transparency of institutionalized racism. I raise the *Nguyen* case to disturb the "organized forgetting" of the nation advanced by Tiger Woods's celebrity.

NOTES

1. "Tiger Woods Race Controversy," *Oprah: The Oprah Winfrey Show*, Harpo Productions, April 29, 1997.
2. "Tiger Woods," *Oprah: The Oprah Winfrey Show*, Harpo Productions, April 24, 1997.

3. Marable criticized Woods as well as Mariah Carey and Paula Abdul for minimizing their blackness: "The litmus test for American democracy has been around the issue of blackness. Tiger's statements are troubling because they seem to minimize his black identity, something that has long been done, in part, to escape racism. Tiger apparently does not understand or minimizes what blackness means and that's what blacks are picking up on." See Denene Millner, "In Creating a Word to Describe His Racial Make-Up, Golfer Tiger Woods Has Also Stirred Up a Round of Controversy among Blacks," *Daily News* (New York), June 8, 1997: 2.

4. See Trina Grillo, "Anti-Essentialism and Intersectionality: Tools to Dismantle the Master's House," 10 *Berkeley Women's Law Journal* 16 (1995). Grillo, a legal scholar, describes her experience at a conference on multiraciality:

> The multiracial movement is not helped by the fact that some of those pressing most vigorously for a multiracial category are the white mothers of children whose fathers are Black. I went to a conference on multiraciality a few years ago that included time for discussion in small groups. There were a number of white mothers of biracial children in my group. The refrain I heard from these mothers was this: "My child is not Black. My child is *golden.*" So it is not simply paranoia that some members of the multiracial movement are perceived as wanting to dissociate from Blacks. (Grillo 26)

5. Tanya Katerí Hernández, " 'Multiracial' Discourse: Racial Classifications in an Era of Color-Blind Jurisprudence," *Maryland Law Review* 57:1 (1998): 119.

6. Narratives of passing in literature, film, and popular culture, for example, often pathologize the race confession, building on the pseudoscientific biology of hypodescent. Consider for example the following moment of self-examination by the anonymous narrator of James Weldon Johnson's *Autobiography of an Ex-Colored Man* (1912): "I feel that I am led by the same impulse which forces the unfound-out criminal to take somebody into his confidence, although he knows that the act is likely, even almost certain, to lead to his undoing" (1). James Weldon Johnson, *Autobiography of an Ex-Colored Man* (New York: Penguin Books, 1990). The internalization of the logic of the one-drop rule by mixed-race subjects functions similarly to compel confession (or guard continuously against the imagined inevitability of self-betrayal).

7. As the legal theorist Neil Gotanda argues, "The assumption that it is possible to identify racial classifications of black and white, to consider them apart from their social setting, and then to make those same racial categories the basis for positive social practice is unfounded. Without a clear social commitment to rethink the nature of racial categories and abolish their underlying structure of subordination, the politics for diversity will remain incomplete." Neil Gotanda, "A Critique of 'Our Constitution Is Color-Blind,'" in *Critical Race Theory: The Key Writings That Formed the Movement*, ed. Kimberlé Crenshaw, Neil Gotanda, Gary Peiler, and Kendall Thomas (New York: New Press, 1995), 271.

8. "Tiger Woods," *Oprah*, April 24, 1997.

9. Sigrid Nunez, *A Feather on the Breath of God* (New York: HarperPerennial, 1995), 87.

10. Eric Foner, *Reconstruction: America's Unfinished Revolution 1863–1877* (New York: Harper & Row, 1988), xxvii.

11. Earl Woods, with Peter McDaniel, *Training a Tiger: A Father's Guide to Raising a Winner in Both Golf and Life* (New York: HarperCollins, 1997), xv–xvi.

12. "Success Story of One Minority in the U.S.," *U.S. News and World Report* (December 26, 1966), 73.

13. I borrow the term "organized forgetting" from Roger Bromley. He elaborates on the relationship between history and memory: "Forgetting is as important as remembering. Part of the struggle against cultural power is the challenge to forgetting posed by memory. What is 'forgotten' may represent more threatening aspects of popular 'memory' and have been carefully and consciously, not casually and unconsciously, omitted from the narrative economy of remembering." Roger Bromley, *Lost Narratives: Popular Fictions, Politics, and Recent History* (New York: Routledge, 1988), 12.

14. Robert Goldman and Stephen Papson, *Nike Culture: The Sign of the Swoosh* (London: Sage, 1998), 113.

15. Frank A. Aukofer, "Petri Still Seeking Multiracial Category," *Milwaukee Journal Sentinel,* May 18, 1997:16.

16. *Plessy v. Ferguson,* 163 U.S. 537, 549 (1896). For a discussion of the relationship between race and property, see Cheryl I. Harris, "Whiteness as Property," in *Critical Race Theory,* eds. Kimberlé Crenshaw et al., 276–291.

17. *Jane Doe v. State of Louisiana,* 479 So. 2d 369 (La. App. 1985).

18. Gotanda, 262.

19. john a. powell, "The Colorblind Multiracial Dilemma: Racial Categories Reconsidered," 31 *U. of San Francisco Law Review* 789, 799 (Summer 1997).

20. Goldman and Papson, *Nike Culture,* 113.

21. I do not assume from the content of this ad that Woods is himself committed to eliminating discrimination, at least not at private clubs. He made his attitude quite clear during the 2002 Masters, when he defended the right of Augusta National to exclude women as members: "They're entitled to set up their own rules the way they want them. . . . There is nothing you can do about it." See Michael D'Antonio, "Tiger Shoots a Bogey in Social Consciousness," *Los Angeles Times,* July 23, 2002.

22. See *Eyes On the Prize II: America at the Crossroads—1965 to 1985; A Nation of Law? (1968–1971),* pt. 6 (Boston: Blackside, 1989).

23. From U.S. Congress, Senate, *Book III: Final Report of the Select Committee to Study Government Operations with Respect to Intelligence Activities* (Washington, D.C.: S.R. No. 94–755, 94th Congress, 2d. Sess., 1976), 187. Quoted in Winston A. Grady-Willis, "The Black Panther Party: State Repression and Political Prisoners," in *The Black Panther Party Reconsidered,* ed. Charles E. Jones (Baltimore: Black Classic Press, 1998), 363–389.

24. Spike Lee, with Ralph Wiley, *By Any Means Necessary: The Trials and Tribulations of the Making of* Malcolm X (New York: Hyperion, 1992), 21–22.

25. Lisa Jones, "Are We Tiger Woods Yet?" in *Step into a World: A Global Anthology of the New Black Literature,* ed. Kevin Powell (New York: John Wiley, 2000), 50. Jones elaborates, "Lurking behind Woods's coronation in Image America, and the wrangling over his identity, is the nagging truth that black America, circa 1997, is not Tiger Woods. Every day we see federal and state governments chipping away at what Tiger's life really represents: access for those long denied" (50).

26. Michael Eric Dyson, "Be Like Mike? Michael Jordan and the Pedagogy of Desire," in *Reflecting Black: African-American Cultural Criticism* (Minneapolis: University of Minnesota Press, 1993), 64.

27. Dyson identifies three characteristics of "black cultural style" personified by Jordan: "the *will to spontaneity" (67); "stylization of the performed self"* (68); and "the subversion of perceived limits through the use of *edifying deception"* (68) [emphasis in the original].

28. For a discussion of the global feminization of wage labor, see Saskia Sassen, *Globalization and Its Discontents: Essays on the New Mobility of People and Money* (New York: New Press, 1998). "The most obvious reason for the intensive recruitment of women is firms' desire to reduce costs, but there are other considerations as well: young women in patriarchal societies are seen by foreign employers as obedient and disciplined workers, willing to do tedious, high-precision work and to submit themselves to work conditions that would not be tolerated in the highly developed countries" (42).

29. The essay is reprinted in Kimberlé Crenshaw's *Critical Race Theory: The Key Writings That Formed the Movement* (1995). See supra n. 7.

30. While Justice Henry Billings Brown, writing for the majority, agrees with Plessy that whiteness is a form of property, he cannot "see" how Homer Plessy, an octoroon, has been deprived of such property.

31. Neil Gotanda's essay "A Critique of 'Our Constitution is Color-Blind,' " also included in Crenshaw's collection and previously cited here, likewise neglects this aspect of Harlan's argument.

32. *Plessy*, 561.

33. An antimiscegenation statute passed in colonial Virginia in 1662 was the first departure from English common law practice regarding the status of the child in relation to the father: "1662. Act XII. Children got by an Englishman upon a Negro woman shall be bond or free according to the condition of the mother, and if any Christian shall commit fornication with a Negro man or woman, he shall pay double the fines of a former act." Cited in A. Leon Higginbotham, Jr., *In the Matter of Color: Race and the American Legal Process* (New York: Oxford University Press, 1978), 43.

34. *Tuan Anh Nguyen v. INS*, 533 U.S. 99–2071 (2001). Text available on the Internet at www.supremecourtus.gov/opinions/oopdf/99-2071.pdf.

35. According to Title 8 U.S.C. section 1409, the applicant for citizenship must meet the following requirements if the applicant's parents are unwed and the father is a U.S. citizen and the mother an alien: "(1) a blood relation between the person and the father is established by clear and convincing evidence; (2) the father had the nationality of the United States at the time of the person's birth; (3) the father (unless deceased) has agreed in writing to provide financial support for the person until the person reaches the age of 18 years, and (4) while the person is under the age of 18 years—(A) the person is legitimated under the law of the person's residence or domicile, (B) the father acknowledges paternity of the person in writing under oath, or (C) the paternity of the person is established by adjudication of a competent court." On the other hand, if the citizen parent of a child born abroad is the mother and not the father, the citizenship of that child is guaranteed as long as "the mother had the nationality of the United States at the time of such person's birth, and if the mother had previously been physically present in the United States or one of its outlying possessions for a continuous period of one year." Cited in *Nguyen v. INS*, 4–5.

36. Steve Rissing, "Court's Citizenship Ruling Flunks Basic Biology Test," *Columbus Dispatch* (June 24, 2001), 5C.

37. Lorelyn Penero Miller, the daughter of a Filipina-national mother and a U.S. citizen who served in the Philippines as a member of the U.S. Air Force, filed suit against the Secretary of State (Madeleine K. Albright) following the denial in 1992 of her application for citizenship. Because she was born out of wedlock and did not establish by the age of eighteen paternity by a U.S. citizen, she was ineligible for citizenship according to the Immigration and Nationality Act. The U.S. Court of Appeals for the District of Columbia Circuit determined that "the requirements imposed on the child of a citizen father but not on the child of a citizen mother were justified by the interest in fostering the child's ties with the United States." The U.S. Supreme Court, unable to arrive at a majority opinion concerning the constitutionality of section 1409, also determined nonetheless that Miller was not entitled to relief. See *Miller v. Albright*, 523 U.S. 420 (1998).

38. In *Nguyen*, Kennedy actually reverses the view on section 1409 that he had expressed in *Miller v. Albright*. Kennedy originally concurred with Justice Sandra Day O'Connor's judgment that although the daughter (Lorelyn Penero Miller) did not have standing to seek relief on the basis of her father's gender discrimination claim, the statute in question could not ultimately withstand heightened scrutiny. Justice O'Connor, who writes the dissenting opinion in *Nguyen*, argued in *Miller* that section 1409 violated equal protection regarding its differential treatment of male and female parents:

> Although petitioner may still assert her own rights, she cannot invoke a gender discrimination claim that would trigger heightened scrutiny. Section 1409 draws a distinction based on the gender of the parent, not the child, and any claim of discrimination based on differential treatment of illegitimate versus legitimate children is not presented in the question on which certiorari was granted. Thus, petitioner's own constitutional challenge is subject only to rational basis scrutiny. *Even though § 1409 could not withstand heightened scrutiny*, it is sustainable under the lower standard. [emphasis added]

Occult Racism

The Masking of Race in
the Hmong Hunter Incident

*A Dialogue between Anthropologist Louisa Schein
and Filmmaker / Activist Va-Megn Thoj*

When the fatal shooting of six hunters by a Hmong man in the woods of Wisconsin received sensationalized national coverage in 2004, Hmong Americans struggled with an intensification of the hostile typing that had haunted their arrival in the United States since 1975. Mainstream accounts all the way through the trial in fall 2005 asserted that the incident, whether from the point of view of the white hunters or that of the Hmong man, could not be interpreted as primarily racial, but more probably centered on misunderstandings of property. The Hmong shooter, Chai Soua Vang, was convicted by an all-white jury of six counts of first-degree intentional homicide and three other counts of attempted homicide against other hunters present. Prosecuted by Wisconsin's attorney general herself, Vang was sentenced to six consecutive life terms, guaranteeing that he would never be released from prison. In May 2007, Vang's request for a new "minority counsel" on the grounds that he had been the victim of a racially biased court system was rejected by the Third District Court of Appeals in Wisconsin. Vang was framed as a depraved murderer, with emphasis placed on his multiple intentional shots, including four shots to hunters' backs, with the effect that no argument of self-defense under racial threat could even be considered.[1] Simultaneously, the Hmong people and their culture were, by many accounts of Hmong in Minnesota and Wisconsin, likewise convicted through one sweeping judicial act.

Meanwhile, in eerie anticipation of the gruesome incident, Hmong filmmaker Va-Megn Thoj had in 2001 penned a screenplay, *Die By Night*, that conjured a contrapuntal image to that of dominant representations regarding the air of racial danger in the northern woods. Written a full three years before the actual shooting incident, the dark script echoes *The Blair Witch Project*, portraying the terror of a group of Hmong campers who are methodically hunted, maimed, and murdered by what they think is a Hmong demon that has followed them from Laos. Daybreak, however, reveals to the sole survivor that it is white hunters in ski masks who have ruthlessly pursued the party, gored them, and strung them up as prey over the course of the night.

Die By Night plays as a macabre thriller that commingles hard-edged racial politics with the fantastical world of Hmong spirit beliefs. Working from the many actual hunting confrontations he already knew of, and evoking the racial tension that had long saturated the everyday lives of Hmong in the Midwest, Thoj infused the script with a political subtext. Unaware at the time of writing of how uncannily the script anticipated the horrific events that were to come, he rendered it a tale of harsh interactions between Hmong and whites, rather than a thriller based on Hmong and the supernatural. The screenplay, yet to be made into a film, represents an intriguing amalgam of Hmong immigrant themes and slasher horror. In the process, Thoj fashioned a work that inadvertently makes the case that Chai Soua Vang, hunting alone and vastly outnumbered by eight hostile white hunters, could not but have perceived grave threat.

The story begins with three young men, a young woman, and a middle-aged uncle—all Hmong—heading out into the Minnesota forest for a camping trip. From the beginning, there is tension in the SUV: tension among the Hmong young men, two of whom have served prison terms and increasingly reveal their scars from having done time; tension between Hmong and the various whites, including cops, that they encounter on their way; and sexual tension between the young woman, Evie, and Rock, who turns out to be her clan cousin, and therefore subject to a Hmong incest taboo. One of the ex-cons, Snake, has brought a handgun on the excursion, and this quickly becomes a problem when he threatens one of his own and shoots at a gas station because he is threatened by the abusive white hunters he has met inside.

Eventually, the party settles around the fire at a campsite deep in the forest. Rock and Evie play at violating incest prohibitions, Snake is getting drunk, and uncle Goodman is becoming edgy because of a demon he remembers from Laos that preys on wayward souls in the forest by tearing their guts out. After one of the men, Clown, disappears, having gone to relieve himself in the woods, Snake and Rock go to look for him and the horror begins. Clown reemerges into the clearing, nearly dead and with his intestines hanging out, but Snake and Rock do not. After a time both Goodman and Snake are drawn screaming from the clearing by "a creature" that makes much rustling in the scrub brush. Rock and Evie are left to attempt escape, dragging injured Clown on a makeshift stretcher through the dark woods. Eventually Rock is also plucked off by the "creature," and Evie, having left Clown dead, faces the dawn with near relief. Within minutes, however, she confronts the strung-up bodies of all her companions, and the "creature" is revealed to be the group of four hunters in ski masks with blood-encrusted scythes. They proceed to methodically rape her one by one, but she ultimately escapes to the vehicle, and wreaks revenge on her attackers by running them all over. Just as we think she is to emerge as a victorious survivor, she swerves the car into a tree to avoid a state trooper on the road and dies on impact.

In what follows, we explore the potential for the occult demon feared in *Die By Night* to illuminate the active and ongoing *occulting* of race in Hmong-white relations. Keeping artistic vision and social analysis tightly articulated, we draw out the figurative effects of a supernatural being conjuring the palpable but hidden threat of racial hatred that lurks in and beyond the American woods. We proceed through the logics of *Die By Night*, histories of racial dynamics in the Midwest, the politics of media representation, and notions of turf and property, in order to ask: What accounts for the masking of race in so much discourse on Hmong over the decades, those same decades in which racialized interactions have been so salient to Hmong resettlement in the United States? Our dialogue, abridged and edited for readability, is intercut with portions of Thoj's script and Schein's critical commentary, as well as excerpts from the trial proceedings and the print and broadcast media.[2]

ABOUT THOJ

LS: Say a little bit about who you are and what kinds of work you've done.

VMT: I left Laos in 1978 and came to the United States in 1980 at the age of ten. I grew up in Indianapolis in the eighties and early nineties. At that time, Indianapolis didn't have a community of Hmong refugees or, for that matter, Asians. So as an Asian you kind of stuck out. I went through the public school system, where desegregation was the policy. I was bused into a suburb to go to school, but I identified more with the poor blacks because we came from the same neighborhoods.

LS: Were you coded or treated as new immigrants, or were you just being recognized as people of color?

VMT: When we first went to school we were seen differently even from the African Americans who had been there. At that time, no one ever heard of a Hmong person. If you were from Southeast Asia, they thought you were one of the boat people—Vietnamese or Cambodian refugees. The failure to differentiate between the different refugee groups at that time definitely had an effect on how I saw race. Coming from Laos it was really easy to distinguish one minority group, one ethnic group, from another, to know this group is Hmong, this group is Lao, or Vietnamese, or whatever. But when you go to a country where all Asians are grouped together, it's a different perspective on race, culture, and ethnicity. It's like: Wait—how can people mistake you for someone else?

And then the other issue was that you were pointed out as a refugee. Because the state is so involved with refugees, as a refugee you're kind of put through the system, processed, because you're on public assistance. It singles you out as an outsider, because maybe if you were normal you wouldn't have to go through the welfare system that the government set up to subsidize refugees from Southeast Asia.

LS: There's an interesting continuity between being invisible as Hmong among generic refugees and race being occulted in the hunter incident. In both cases there's an invisibilization.

VMT: The point I wanted to make was that I was always conscious of race early on. And then when I went to college there was this Asian American identity that I didn't know and I confronted for the first time being the other Asian American. That furthered the awareness of racial politics.

And then after college I had this idea of becoming a filmmaker. I remember seeing Charlie Chaplin's silent movie *City Lights* when I was in grade school. That's one of the first movies I saw. A friend of the family took us to see *City Lights* and, y'know, it's a silent film, there was no dialogue or anything, but you could still follow the story.

I wanted to tell stories through writing . . . at that time I was more familiar with writing than film. . . . It wasn't until I took some film classes that I remembered Charlie Chaplin and how you could tell stories visually. And at this point I knew a little bit more about the Hmong community and how the Hmong people didn't really have a tradition of literature, but we *did* have a tradition of storytelling, oral storytelling, that to me was very visual. I realized that if I became a writer, no Hmong person would be able to read my stories, so the next best thing, or the *best* thing, was to tell it through the visual medium.

My school [Indiana University] didn't have any film production courses. So my major ended up being comparative literature with an emphasis on film studies. By the middle of my college career I decided "OK, I am going to try to make films." But at that point I didn't know how to go about that. I contacted Third World Newsreel [in New York] and they accepted me into their film production workshop. All of the people in the class were in their twenties. Everyone had a purpose for being a filmmaker—they had an idea that film was a political tool to advance certain political or social issues. I didn't have that yet.

INVISIBILITY—DOUBLED

LS: In [your early short film] *Borne in War* that you made at Third World Newsreel there's a kind of anger about not being knowable as Hmong, as from Laos[3]

VMT: Basically *Borne in War* did have a lot of rage, and it was autobiographical, and what you're talking about had a lot to do with the fact that Asian American history in the United States was centered around Japanese American and Chinese American identities and histories. It goes back to my experience in college, where everything Asian was either Chinese or Japanese American. And the point you brought up about "nobody knew who a Hmong person was" I think has a lot to do with it. You're with people who you kind of identify with, but they can't identify with you because you're not Chinese or Japanese; you're a Hmong person—I'm just talking about the Asian American community. You would expect them to include you in that definition of Asian American.[4] So that was part of it, and then a large part of it, of course, is that mainstream America had no idea who Hmong people were at that point.

LS: All these experiences of not being knowable as Hmong—that kind of flip flops by the time of the hunter incident, where it's kind of the hypervisibility of Hmong as new immigrants that underlies some of the tensions, right?

VMT: The notoriety of Hmong people arose out of a lot of high-profile criminal cases, whether it was "bride stealing" or gang violence or the hunting incident. That's just one aspect of the community. The other thing is that what you would call the Asian American community—with the hunting incident especially—appropriated that and made it an Asian American issue.

LS: During the Chai Vang trial, Fred Graham on Court TV, when he, as an anchor, is interviewing a guest, Lauren Lake, a black woman lawyer, denies race head on.

COURT TV, SEPTEMBER 10, 2005

Fred Graham: Now Lauren, should race properly be any issue in this case? We saw that story that showed about the feelings in the Hmong community. Why? He killed six people—why does race have any part in the case?

Lauren Lake: I think it's a very important part. This is something that is going to be so tough for the defense attorney to get across to this jury. Unfortunately they didn't get a good cultural mix in the jury, it's just an all-white jury, but the defense attorney's got to explain how a person of a minority culture in this country can feel that the majority culture doesn't value their life. The way that they are perceived in that culture is that they're not as important, as valued. Therefore I think in the Hmong community there were serious racial tensions between hunters and the Hmong people. . . . That's why when this defendant became, as he felt, under siege, attacked, the way that he reacted was based upon probably his opinion that "these people don't value me as a person."

LS: I think it's very telling that a black guest on Court TV has to explain these most elemental basics of racial dynamics to the white anchor in a way that you can also imagine needed to be explained to a Madison, Wisconsin, white jury.

It's like—in society at large the burden of proof that racial dynamics are present is always on the minority.

VMT: Last week I went to the University of Minnesota and screened my short film *Slaughtered in Hugo.*[5] This was a class for the master's program. The audience was mostly white; the students were professionals. Afterward there was a Q and A and one of the students said, "I was offended at the accusation of racism in the film." For a while I wasn't sure how to respond to her, but in the end I basically said that between the accuser and the person who is accused of being racist, as a third party you can't really judge the legitimacy of the accuser's accusation unless you have the perspective of a minority.

LS: And I think the burden of proof for Asians is redoubled because of Asian race being put under erasure by the black-white binary. So in much of the United States, with the exception of some of the West Coast, Asians are at pains not only to show racial dynamics, but to show that specificity of racial dynamics that's not just subsumable to blackness.[6]

VMT: Right.

LS: Because what always mitigates that for Asians is this other trope of, say, model minority, or economic success, that purportedly whitens Asians so that it's easy for the mainstream to say "racial prejudice doesn't apply here."

VMT: Yup. The question a lot of people raised was—it would have been easier, or the burden of proof would not have been on the defense if Vang was black. There wouldn't be erasure or suppression if he was a black person.

LS: And one of the ways that that erasure is policed discursively is precisely by something like the prosecutor Lautenschlager accusing the defense of "playing the race card" as if it's a rupture in what should otherwise be a color-blind proceeding.

VMT: Right.

> HAYWARD, WISCONSIN, *SAWYER COUNTY RECORD*, SEPTEMBER 21, 2005, A18
> [Defense Attorney] Kohn said that the white hunters had a "mind set of racial preju-dice" when they confronted Vang. "That shows why they were so angry" with him and used the term "mud duck" as a racial epithet, he said . . .
>
> In her rebuttal, Lautenschlager said Vang didn't walk in the direction he was told to and testified he did not hear the term "mud duck" used by Willers. She suggested that Vang "is playing the race card" by claiming that Willers told him "You people shoot too many does". . . .
>
> Vang "was mad," Lautenschlager said. "He wanted to get back at these guys for giving him grief."

ABOUT SCHEIN

VMT: Talk a little bit about your background and how you came to work with the Hmong.

LS: I grew up in New England and went to a liberal school in Cambridge which was pretty white and where race was pretty much under erasure. There were a few black kids from the inner city attending and we were well trained not to rec-ognize their difference. Even though it was the civil rights era, we pretty much denied connections to anything happening in our own northeastern commu-nity. I think we unconsciously assumed race was reserved for the South.

My paternal grandfather was Jewish and left Europe for Chicago just before the Holocaust. He died when I was three. I was basically raised as a nonpractic-ing Protestant. Only when I started looking at the Chai Vang case did I learn from my father how haunted my grandfather had been when they drove to vaca-tion in the Wisconsin woods and there were anti-Semitic signs posted on various businesses saying things like "No Jews allowed."

Meanwhile, it was also the Vietnam era and my school was progressive enough that they actually organized field trips to antiwar demonstrations. My coming of age took place in the context of the peace movement.

I first encountered Hmong immigrants during college in Providence, Rhode Island. It was the late seventies, the early years of Hmong arrival, and I got involved in a co-op that was helping women to market their handicrafts for supplementary income. Eventually I took time off school and moved over to the Hmong neighborhood. I was teaching Hmong women English out of my apartment and I also got involved in making a documentary film, *The Best Place to Live*, with a Rhode Island School of Design filmmaker.[7] It was a personal account of the first years of resettlement of several Hmong families.

VMT: And after that?

LS: When I eventually graduated, I had a fellowship to go overseas for a year to trace Hmong roots back to China. I was so surprised by the complexity of the contemporary China situation—it was nothing I could have imagined based on the way Hmong in the United States represented their land of origin. There was a similar dynamic to what I'd seen within the United States: Americans insisted on freezing Hmong newcomers in the traditional culture of the land they came from; likewise, Hmong in the diaspora insisted on remembering China—the land they *originally* came from—as fixed and unchanging. So I went into grad school in anthropology with the motivation to bring the current reality of the Hmong in China to visibility in the West.

VMT: How does media representation of Hmong in China compare to representation of Hmong here?

LS: When I got into my China research, I started writing on "internal orientalism"—the dynamic in which Chinese state, media, tourism and other representational regimes exoticized minority cultures. I argued that in effect these regimes were stigmatizing, condemning minorities to always being less modern than the Han.

VMT: You've been researching Hmong media for years. What drew you to it?

LS: My current work is a book on Hmong media called *Rewind to Home*. I got drawn to this topic because I started charting what Hmong Americans were doing in video representations of their homelands. It was the 1990s and a lot of refugees had gotten their citizenship and were traveling back to Asia. They would shoot videos and sell them to the Hmong American community. What sold well at that time was images of culture back home. So Hmong Americans were into consuming nostalgic memories of their own people frozen as emblems of the past in Asia.

VMT: In that project, were you interested in race and representation of Hmong? Or is this the first time you're dealing with race and media?

LS: Since I was looking at media productions by and about and then consumed within the Hmong community, race issues were not as salient. But this is what interested me in some of your work, as work that was much more engaged with larger social relations. And then after the Chai Vang news broke, I found that I was always talking about *Die By Night* as a way of contextualizing the incident in terms of race conflict. It was a cruel irony that after decades of virtual invisibility for Hmong, now I was constantly meeting people who were stereotyping Hmong in terms of this incident.[8]

EXPOSING RACE IN *DIE BY NIGHT*

LS (writing on *Die By Night*): From the outset, *Die By Night* crafts characters who have had their share of urban tribulations. The seething anger that the young men have conjured in the crucible of American minoritization generates all manner of conflict. On the first page of the script, Snake has already jostled hostilely for street space with a black man who had called him "gook." Rock and Snake then reminisce with irony about the "good old days" when they were "fresh off the boat" and "lived in fear," "until we fought back," growls Snake smugly, implying gang activity. "After that, they left us alone." But Rock and Uncle Goodman are not convinced: "Is that how you get respect, violence and fear?" Rock challenges. And Goodman adds in Hmong: "Violence begets violence." Thus is posed the immigrant dilemma that weaves through Thoj's anguished script. As newcomers, is there an alternative to swallowing one humiliation after another, merely to gain a toehold on life in American society?

> *DIE BY NIGHT*, P. 10
> Snake, Goodman, and Rock get pulled over by cops in St. Paul. When Officer 2 pulls the lever to open and search the trunk:
>
> *Snake:* You can't search the car. I know my rights.
> *Officer 2:* You don't have any rights. Not on my watch.
>
> Officer 2 pulls Rock's and Snake's wallets from their back pockets and checks their IDs. He tosses them into the car. Officer 1 goes to the trunk, and looks through the contents.
>
> *Officer 1:* You boys going camping?
> *Goodman:* Yes, sir.
> *Officer 2:* You think you own this town, don't you? Your kind belongs in jail.
> *Rock* (In Hmong): I'll see you in hell first.
> *Officer 2:* Speak fucking English!

LS (writing on *Die By Night*): Unfairly stopped and persecuted by the police on an Asian gang watch, the men are forced to relinquish their dignity. Spread-eagled, insulted, and searched, they are constrained to curse the police only in Hmong. Already wound tight from this encounter, Snake loses it when the evil hunters condescend to Clown at a nearby gas station. Snake is agitated because Clown is taking too long playing a video game in the gas station.

> *DIE BY NIGHT*, P. 28
> Snake pulls the plug on the video game.
>
> *Clown:* Dude, whatchoo do that for? I almost won.
> *Snake:* Shut up, let's go.
> *Clown:* Fuck you, dude. You wasted my quarters.
>
> One of the hunters throws a quarter at Snake.
>
> *Hunter 1:* Here's a quarter for ya.
> *Snake:* Go fuck yourself, you redneck, white nigger.

Hunter 1 stands up, punches Snake in the stomach. Snake groans in pain, falls to his knees in front of him.

Clown: Oh, shit!

Clown throws a wild punch, knocking out Hunter 1. Hunter 2, seeing what happened, rushes Clown. Clown kicks him in the groin and he curls over in excruciating pain. Hunter 3 fumbles to open his rifle case.

Clown: He's got a gun! Get up!

Clown pulls Snake off the floor. They run as fast as they can out the door.

LS (writing on *Die By Night*): Knowing from his urban street smarts just how to affront a middle American white man, Snake has deployed a strong racial slur and Clown has thrown punches, but once again, the Hmong are forced to flee for their lives. Thoj animates a conundrum that, for Hmong, has become a time-honored structure of feeling, one that extends back far beyond their immigration to the West. It is the story of their being vanquished at the hands of the Chinese empire, and then again in Laos, upon U.S. withdrawal from the Vietnam war.

Racial Persecutions

VMT: Die By Night is based on incidents that I knew of. I have friends who told me stories about how they went hunting and were harassed by white hunters. I'd even heard of stories involving gunfights. But up until then it was secondhand experience.

LS: When did you have your own experience [with white hunters]?

VMT: About a year and a half after my coming to Minnesota I went hunting with my friends and met some white hunters where we went to park our truck. Not much happened actually. As we got there, they were leaving and we exchanged, well, *our* party anyway, exchanged greetings, or *we* said greetings to *them* and they just looked at us, like—well my interpretation anyway—was like, "what are you doing here?" As a Hmong person in the United States, when you go to some place where you stand out, in the back of your mind, you're always conscious of race and difference. So I don't know if it was my imagining or if it actually took place, but the hunters were not really friendly in their encounter with us. What happened eventually was that once they left us they called a park ranger.

LS: And you were in a public park?

VMT: Right, we were in the public park and all of a sudden the park ranger came up and told us that we were under observation. I think what the white hunters did was probably report, "There's a bunch of Asians here and they're breaking the law, or trespassing," whatever.

VA-MEGN THOJ, OP ED PIECE, *ST. PAUL PIONEER PRESS*, DECEMBER 29, 2004

I went deer hunting once. And I never went back because of the racial tension I encountered. My experience in southern Minnesota was relatively benign, involving two condescending white hunters calling the Department of Natural Resources to check up on my group, which was Hmong, even though we had done nothing wrong.

The experience reaffirmed my stereotype that small midwestern towns are bigoted toward people of color.

It also confirmed what I had heard about white hunters' threats and intimidations against Hmong hunters. I put these experiences into a short film, *Flight*, about a violent encounter between Hmong and white hunters.[9]

White hunters have a set of stereotypes for Hmong hunters: don't know the law, don't understand private property rights, can't speak English, and can't be understood. In short, they see Hmong hunters as ignorant and not to be trusted. Yet, Hmong are allowed guns to go around and hunt just like they are. This represents an unacceptable threat and just galls some white hunters and landowners to no end.

EXCERPTS FROM E-MAIL RESPONSES TO THOJ EDITORIAL

"Just like blacks and other minorities instead of taking responsibility for lawless behavior you blame the victims. Many of your people come to this country welcomed with open arms and shit on our citizens. You demand the rights of what our ancestors fought for but want to wright your own rules when you get here. Private property is one of those rights, yet you come here and act like it is all yours. You damn lucky to be here much less hollering about bigotry."

"Now we have groups that come and don't want to be a part of American culture (yes, we have one). They want to continue as they did in their old country, which is puzzling as if you loved it so much, why did you leave? Why come here if you dislike us so much?"

"I really liked your column on Dec. 29th, you hit the nail on the head. The people that live and hunt in the rural areas of our state have the idea that it is only for them, all others stay out. I wrote a letter to the editor on the tragic event in northern Wisconsin, about how if I, a person of European immigrants, were the shooter, would they mention that? Of course we both know the answer to that question, NO!!! It is absolute ignorance of other races that keep the whites in the dark ages."

". . . how arrogant can you be to write 'to me racism was the spark that caused Chai Soua Vang to allegedly kill six white hunters.' Well TO ME Chai Soua Vang is just common thug criminal. Not white, not Hmong just a criminal that should have kept himself under control (like most of us white hunters do)."

"I'm from Western Wisconsin and work in the Twin Cities now. After reading your rant about 'white racism' in Wis., I must say that you people should take a good look at yourselves in the mirror. After all, since your arrival to this country, we have something we've never had before in the Twin Cities . . . Asian gangs that are in to drugs, prostitution, etc. . . . all doing quite well since then. You said you didn't feel 'welcome' when you went out hunting and that your buddies said the white hunters think they own everything. . . .' Well, let me tell you that all that nice property you see in Wis. and Minn. IS owned by these 'white racist' people who pay high taxes on that property, and much of those taxes go to pay for freeloading parasites from foreign lands who couldn't care less about land management or good land stewardship . . . or other peoples constitutional rights for that matter."[10]

"I agree with everything you say in your article especially the part about the media drowning out the fact that there is a racial tone to Vang's story. But I disagree with your statement that if he (Vang) was black this would not have happened. Don't you know that what Hmong people are going through with hunting we also have been there. We are the very ones who understand exactly what you are talking about."

"Vang is an asshole. Violence is his tool to get what he wants. A racial word set him off? That is ok in your mind to rationalize blame back on the whites? Lets try something here. Fuck you you slant eyed fucking gook!!!

Now that being said as an experiment. Now that that was said to you, does that make it ok to hunt me and 5 others down and shoot us?"

ACTIVISM AGAINST MEDIA RACISM

LS: So, in your short film, *Flight,* you have this Tom Barnard character on the radio.

FLIGHT (2004)

Tom Barnard's Voice, a shock-jock in the Twin Cities, comes on the car radio, ripping racist jokes about Hmong people.

Tom Barnard (from the radio): . . . more Hmong refugees just got off the boat yesterday and guess where their new homes are people? You guessed it! The Twin Cities, folks. So get out your chopsticks and your checkbooks cause we're all gonna be puttin' out some major cash flow.

Don't you think if you're gonna come to this country these people should at least speak the language? It's *English!*

I went over to St. Paul the other day—can someone tell me where the hell all the white people went? I asked for some directions over there the other day and all I got was "ching chong ding dong." "No," I said. "I'm not ordering chicken." What do you think we oughta do with these people—ship them back to the rice fields and caves where they came from? If the Hmong don't like it here, they should go back where they came from. Assimilate or hit the goddamn road!

Snake: Tom Barnard is a dumb fucking idiot.

Rock: Change the station.

VMT: I wanted to make explicit connection to an event in 1998. Tom Barnard is the real name of the shock jock.

LS: Talk more about what happened with that incident.

VMT: It occurred in 1998 when a young girl in Wisconsin had a baby in a public school bathroom and killed the baby in the bathroom. That was reported in the local newspaper here and a local radio show picked up that story. It's like a talk show in the morning. They had this shock jock as their host, and he basically mocked the tragedy and the Hmong culture and told the Hmong community to leave the country if they didn't know how to assimilate to American society. There were a lot of racial comments made.

LS: Racial comments like what?

VMT: There were a lot of stereotypes used, and the show had this Asian charac-ter with a stereotypical Asian accent, and a lot of Hmong people found it very offensive that he would, first of all, use a tragic story involving a teenage woman killing a baby. And then denigrating the Hmong community and the Hmong culture and having this racist caricature on the show. This wasn't the first time that the show had done something like that. The host was very anti-immigrant. So I decided to gather some people together and we started organizing a boycott campaign. Within a few weeks of our decision we had formed a coalition of young students and professionals and our parents. As the organizing went along it became a multiethnic racial coalition.

I think at that point the Chinese and Japanese Americans had been the lead if there was any Asian American activism in the Twin Cities. When I came [from New York] I saw that there was no response from the Hmong community, and I kind of took that on. We refocused it on the Hmong community and made it a Hmong issue, whereas before it was more like a pan-Asian, Asian American issue, and it was successful because of that strategy.

In the past the only kind of activism that came out of the Hmong community had been around social services and government services. Whenever there was a cut in government services to the Hmong immigrant community, you would have established organizations, nonprofits involved in social justice, organize Hmong immigrants to do a campaign to protest. This campaign around the media racism issue was the first non-social service campaign.

We not only called for boycotts. We had several demands. We wanted the radio station to apologize on the air, to get rid of their racist Asian caricature, and to place ads in local papers with the apology.

Because it was a very popular radio show, they refused to do any of these. So we had several public demonstrations. Each one drew a few hundred people. We drew a lot of media attention. The station didn't want to give in to our demands. They were the number-one show in the Twin Cities, owned by ABC, which is part of Disney Corporation, so they didn't want to succumb to community pressure. But eventually we did pressure them to meet all our demands. Because of our organizing, the local news were turning against them. At the beginning they were like "oh no, this is not a racist show," but eventually we were able to turn that conversation in the media around.

LS: What do you think turned it?

VMT: First of all, we framed it as a media racism issue. A big part of it was that the media that were reporting *on* the issue also looked at themselves and said, "We have this very diverse community and are we doing a good job of covering this community?" The standard that they'd used in the past was not high enough. The demographics had changed—their audience was more than just a middle-class white audience.

LS: The media that turned against the radio show included print and broadcast?

VMT: Yeah, the local media are all connected, and some of them are owned by the same parent company, so they're reluctant to say anything bad about each other. I remember going on a news show on the local PBS station with this media columnist for the *Pioneer Press* local newspaper and he basically said, "You guys have no case against this radio show. You can't substantiate racism against them. You guys are just silly." But as our campaign went on, that same media columnist turned around and said, "This radio station has to apologize for what they said." All of them—they started with "that's silly," and at the end it was like: "we have higher standards"—so it was a total turnaround. They ended up apologizing on their show, placing ads in two major papers and in the small ethnic papers.

LS: What did they say in their apology?

> KQRS and the Morning Show Staff recognize that comments made on our June 9, 1998, broadcast were insensitive to the Hmong community. We apologize for these comments. It was not our intention to offend the Hmong community.
>
> We are sorry for making offensive remarks about the Hmong culture on the Morning Show and for stating that Hmong should "either assimilate or hit the g-damn road." Many Hmong fought bravely and died as soldiers for the United States during the Vietnam war in Laos. Hmong are deserving of our fullest respect. Like all Americans, Hmong have the right to free speech, life, liberty, and the pursuit of happiness under the protection of the U.S. Constitution. All people, regardless of their culture, ethnicity, or the color of their skin should be free from discrimination.

VMT: Other demands were that they get rid of that racist caricature, which they did. They published their nondiscriminatory on-air policy along with the apology. They gave free air time for us to do a PSA.

LS: You think those lessons have held?

VMT: I noticed a big change in the news reporting after that. They became more "sensitive," as they say. They say less of the wrong thing. Before that if there was a crime that involved an Asian gang, they would say "these Hmong kids"—they would always mention the ethnicity of the perpetrator. They stopped doing that. Their reporting became more neutral and more about the facts and less about the race or ethnicity of the people they were reporting about.

LS: So there was a deliberate connection in *Flight?*

VMT: Even the dialogue I wrote: some of the words I used were the exact words he used on the radio back in 1998. Like "assimilate or hit the goddamn road"— that was the incendiary phrase that we used in our protest.

LS: So is Barnard still on the radio?

VMT: Oh yeah, he's on every morning.

LS: And is he still talking that way?

VMT: He didn't for years. Not about the Hmong people. He was afraid of another big protest.

CULTURAL CONVICTION

LS: Getting back to bad reporting. When you were talking about the initial incident with the girl who killed her baby and Hmong culture being derided in the discussions of it, there's an implication that there's less of a valuing of life in

Hmong culture. It reminded me of the Court TV anchor, Fred Graham, who, during the Vang trial, basically put Hmong culture on trial.

COURT TV, SEPTEMBER 10, 2005

Fred Graham: You know it's very interesting: there's a lot of reasons to regret what the U.S. did in the Vietnam War but as the years go by we see additions to these reasons. Here you have the Hmongs, who were sought out by the CIA because they were fierce fighters and they could shoot and they *would* shoot and they didn't have perhaps the same regard for human life that our culture has, who knows?

VMT: I don't know where that came from. I heard of the Viet Cong having no value for human life but not the Hmong people. I never heard that before.

LS: It becomes a theme that goes to the teenage mother killing her kid, goes to Chai Vang, goes to this characterization of Hmong during war. And I think it's so telling that at the same time this black woman is telling the Court TV anchor that the situation of being minority in the United States is that you feel that *your* life is not as valued as others. It's this kind of reciprocal discourse.

VMT: It's a good justification, or explanation, for Chai Vang, for his killing of white hunters.

LS: It's a *cultural* one.

VMT: Right, and that's how the whole case was framed, culture versus culture.

LS: Which allows for the *Hmong people* to be convicted, not just Chai Vang.[11] So that really exposes the way in which, even though racial hatred was masked, racism encoded in culture becomes the metacontent of what's going on. So it can't ever only be about convicting Chai Vang; it's about indicting the Hmong as a people.

VMT: Right.

LS: In the gas station scene, is this what's going on with the white guy?

DIE BY NIGHT, P. 25

PAN UP to Snake staring at a WHITE MAN, in a shirt, tie and sweater, who stares back at him from the next pump.

Snake (In Hmong): What are you looking at, Mr. Rogers?

White Man: You are Hmong, right?

Snake: You the man. I be whatever you want me to be.

White Man: You're the preliterate mountain tribe from the Golden Triangle. You were opium traffickers and mercenaries.

VMT: The white guy is what I call the "naive white guy." You know, he thinks he knows who the Hmong people are.[12]

NEW YORK TIMES, NOVEMBER 28, 2004, 1

A HUNT TURNS TRAGIC, AND TWO CULTURES COLLIDE

In three decades, St. Paul has drawn at least 25,000 Hmong immigrants, transforming it into what they call the Hmong capital of America. Even there, it has not always been an easy fit, with so many Hmong refugees arriving so rapidly, often with no English and little education or urban job skills.

LS: Did you feel, reading the press, that the local press was better than elsewhere in the way they covered the case?

VMT: I did feel that reading both local coverage and national coverage, that the local coverage was way better. I read some of the AP articles and it seemed like I was reading articles from the 1980s or early 1990s. Every story would have a preface like "the Hmong people, refugees from Laos, fought in the war, recruited by the CIA"—you don't get that anymore in the Twin Cities. But in the national press they are still repeating this stuff. Does it matter? It really doesn't describe the community anymore. There's such a disconnect there.

LS: And it's not only a disconnect. If you think about media as having discursive effects, then it's also about freezing Hmong in that stereotype.

VMT: Right, exactly. This is something that the Fadiman book, *The Spirit Catches You and You Fall Down*, is also implicated in.[13]

LS: Yes, which underscores that even when the portrayal is ostensibly sympathetic—like in Fadiman's sensitive description of a family that strives for their daughter's health through deploying their own culture's healing repertoire—the metamessage is that Hmong immigrants can never do anything but hold on to traditional culture.

VMT: Similarly, TV has an especially sensationalist slant to a lot of the things that they report about Hmong. They resort to stereotypes of the kind that we heard on Court TV.

LS: There is a sort of counterpart of the stereotype: Nancy Grace is sitting in the Court TV headquarters and she is talking about Chai Vang with a local reporter who's on the scene, Jean Casarez:

COURT TV, SEPTEMBER 8, 2005

JC: I think that he believed that to protect the honor of the Hmong culture that he had to shoot these people that he believed were yelling racial slurs at him.

NG: To protect what culture?

JC: I'm sorry?

NG (sneeringly): To protect *what*?

JC: His own culture. The Hmong culture.

LS: This whole thing of staging the complete unintelligibility of Hmong culture—even the word *Hmong*—is another instance of the remoteness of TV from the local scene and of it being OK to even stage that as where the audience would be at. It's basically the inverse of using stereotypes. It's using the inscrutability of Hmong people as another way of negating the race content by substituting this unreadable culture.

Can you talk a little bit about what happened after the incident but before the trial in terms of Hmong-white relations?

VMT: After the incident, when the story broke in the media, there was some backlash against the Hmong community. In the Twin Cities there was some literature distributed by the KKK. In Mankato there was an incident of this convenience store selling these bumper stickers that said "Save a deer; kill a

Hmong." In Wisconsin there were a few incidences of vandalism—Hmong houses were vandalized. Even after the trial, Vang's house was burned down. His family sold the house after the trial and the new owners, who were also Asian, moved in, and one night it was just burned down and the investigation showed that it was arson. Then in April 2006, Vang had to be moved out of his prison in Wisconsin to one in Iowa. The prison officials said the primary reason was "racial concerns."

LS: What was it about the way the incident was reported that allowed for those kinds of fallout?

VMT: It was how the media highlighted his race without discussing the role race played in the incident. It was technically irrelevant, but reported in a way that implied that his ethnicity was a cause for him to shoot and kill. The media would basically say, "Here's a person; he killed these white people because he was Hmong."

PROPERTY AND TURF

MINNEAPOLIS STAR TRIBUNE, NOVEMBER 28, 2004, A8

Late Sunday morning, Vang's deer hunt led him to the land owned by Willers and Crotteau. Wearing a blaze orange vest, he climbed up eight wooden planks to an empty deer stand. He was violating a sacred creed of the woods: Do not tread on another person's land. Hunters, said Fleischauer, the local bar owner, are very protective of their turf. "This is their domain," he said.

LS: So were you thinking about property issues in any of your conceptualization of *Die By Night?*

VMT: I did. When [the campers] were in the forest, I thought about whether I should make that forest public land or private land. In the end I decided that *it didn't matter* whether it was private or public because the killings would happen anyway. In the case of the killing in Wisconsin, territory and property became a really big issue. . . . To me it wasn't an issue. Because I think it's more about the interaction and the dynamics of the relationship between the hunters than anything else.

LS: So this is another way that race gets masked. If it's about property then it's deracialized.

MINNEAPOLIS STAR TRIBUNE, SEPTEMBER 8, 2005, 18

Many arguments concerning this case have involved race. In a letter to a *Chicago Tribune* reporter, Vang wrote from jail that he acted to "defend myself and my race." Haus bristles at the suggestion that the slain hunters may have made racially insensitive comments to trigger Vang's alleged onslaught.

"It's trespassing that started this, not race," he said.

VMT: Right, the concentration is on the property issue, which is one of the ways that the media or the court or the prosecutor avoided the issue of race.

LS: Can you talk a little bit about your perspective, given all the media treatment about Hmong not understanding private property?

VMT: My perspective is that Hmong hunters *do* understand property—an American concept of property ownership. You know—you're not supposed to trespass, you're not supposed to encroach on private property. I think Hmong hunters understand that. Unless they are new hunters or just arrived in this country—anybody would not understand property law if they'd just arrived in this country.

CHAI SOUA VANG IN LETTER TO *CHICAGO TRIBUNE* REPORTER
COLLEEN MASTONY, MARCH 8, 2005
Some of us Hmong people got lost into other property. Is not because we didn't respect their land. Some of us are new to the area or got lost. Go into other property are everybody. Including Caucasian as well not just minority only. We didn't hunt anywhere we felt like it. The question is "Are you doing enough to protect your property or family?"

VMT: My point is that even though there's a difference in the concept of property, the hunters would understand what the American concept is.

I think that the traditional Hmong concept of property is that you don't really own land unless you build a house on it or you use it for farming. Land is not something that you can own. You can use it. When you're not using it, someone else can use it. Even if you're using it, someone could walk across it. There's no sense of trespassing.

Throughout the history of the Hmong people they've been migratory. They've really never settled in one place. They tend to go to where there's land to farm and settle on that piece of land and once that land can't produce more crops they move on to the next piece of land.

ASSOCIATED PRESS WORLDSTREAM, NOVEMBER 30, 2004[14]
At the upper edge of the nation, in the thick woods of northern Minnesota and Wisconsin, there are rules. Rules about property. Rules about deer hunting and the generations-old traditions that surround it. Rules about how people treat each other when they come upon armed strangers among the trees.

Most of these rules are not written down. So when different kinds of hunters—people with different backgrounds, different traditions—come together in the North Woods, anything can happen. . . .

With the arrest of Chai Soua Vang . . . a member of the Hmong ethnic group . . . questions are being asked, suspicions whispered: Was this the doing of an untethered individual or a cultural clash? . . .

"Your hunting area, if you own the land, is kind of sacred," said Rob Petersen, who owns land a few miles (kilometers) from where the shooting happened. "It's such a touchy thing."

VMT: So, what was actually very apparent in the media coverage and what came out of that case was that that notion of private property is superior to any other notion. For example, the constant accusation was that Hmong hunters don't understand the concept of private ownership of property. My interpretation of that is: "Your concept of property is primitive and you should leave that behind and learn our concept of private property. If you don't learn to live by that then you will remain forever un-American or foreign or inferior, primitive."

LS: So it's a mark of a lack of meriting Americanness.

VMT: Yeah, or respect . . . therefore you *deserve* to be discriminated against or oppressed or killed, or shot at when you go hunting.

> TRIAL TRANSCRIPT, CHAI SOUA VANG UNDER DIRECT EXAMINATION
>
> *A:* He [landowner Robert Crotteau] told me (witness using loud voice): Do you know you are on, do you know you are trespassing on 400 acres of land, you damn gook?
>
> Then I say, No, 'cause I don't see any sign, I don't see fence anywhere.
>
> And he said (witness using loud voice): I don't have to put a fucking sign up, you fucking chink. . . .
>
> *Q:* Then what happened after that?
>
> *A:* And then he told me (witness using loud voice): I'm sick of you fucking Asians coming to my land.
>
> Then Mr. Crotteau also say: If you fucking Asians keep coming to my land I'm going to kick your fucking Asian ass. . . .
>
> Then I start moving south to my left. And I started, as I start to walk away, and Mr. Joe Crotteaus come behind the Rhino ATV, come and block in front of me just in front of the Honda ATV. And then when he, when he come and block in front of me, then Lauren Hesebeck, Mr. Lauren Hesebeck come in close to my right a little bit and then two persons, Mr. Mark Roidt and Mr. Dennis Drew jump out from the ATV one step to Mr. Crotteau right, it's on my left, and then once behind, one guy's behind him. So when, at that time I thought they were going to beat me or something.
>
> So they said, What the hell you think you going, dang gook?[15]

VMT: Hmong Americans *have* adopted the concept of private property ownership—legal as well as economic. Evidence of that is the number of people buying homes, buying land as an investment asset. I saw some numbers recently from a study that was done by the Asian American Justice Center, and they have several indicators of how Hmong Americans are doing in the Twin Cities. As far as home ownership and property ownership, the Hmong people are doing quite well compared to indicators such as educational attainment and literacy and English proficiency. The percentage is close to 50 percent home ownership. As Hmong people acculturate themselves to American society, land ownership is one of the biggest things that they have adopted and it's an indicator of their success in this country.

LS: OK. How does that interface with what you were saying about the more traditional concept of property? Are both present in Hmong American subjectivity?

VMT: I think [the traditional concept] is still there, but there's a different value attached to it. Now there's monetary value; it's an investment. But the concept of trespassing in traditional Hmong value is foreign, or it's not as stringent. Trespassing has such a legal implication to it.

LS: At the same time, it has an almost spiritual quality to it. So many of the media accounts talk about private land as "sacred" during hunting season. What they seem to mean by sacred is that it shouldn't be trespassed upon by nonowners. I've wondered about the relation between this notion of sacredness and the supernatural in *Die By Night*. Could we say that the hostile demon signifies the inviolability of sacred white turf in the midwestern woods?

VMT: In my script, when the characters describe what the creature is, they imply that one of the qualities of the creature is to keep people out of the woods, which is its natural habitat. The creature therefore embodies a place that humans, in this case Hmong people, should not venture into. So you could say that the creature is about place, or turf, that should not be encroached upon because it is connected with an otherworldly or supernatural realm.

In my script, I have a coincidental scene where a shaman performs a ritual before the group of campers leaves the city for the woods. I subtly hint through the ominous look on his face that the shaman gained knowledge of what will happen to the Hmong campers while he was in his trance on his journey to the afterworld. Of course, what the Hmong campers believe to be a supernatural creature turns out to be the white hunters in the daylight. So the shaman, the supernatural, turf, and race all connect together.

LS: In the case of Chai Vang, the war history, which he did not experience as an adult, also factors into his sense of the forbiddingness of the jungle.

> CHAI SOUA VANG LETTER TO *CHICAGO TRIBUNE* REPORTER COLLEEN MASTONY
> On Sunday morning just before Thai woke me up about 5:00 AM I have a dream: that we're soldier in the jungle of Laos and I encounter with several Vietnam soldier in the wood, so I shot most of them (we shot each other) and some escape to get help, then later I ran into a lake, there I was surround by Vietnam soldier, tank and armor so they take me as a prisoner, then Thai woke me up. I almost didn't want to go hunt that day because I never have that kind of dream in my life, but I thought that it's just another bad dream.

LS: Significantly, the premonition he recounts is not about a supernatural threat but is materialized in the specter of the predatory Vietnamese who outnumber him. The war context and the figuring of the armed enemy make it unquestionable that, for him, his life would have felt threatened. We could speculate about what the dream meant from the perspective of his shaman's subjectivity as a quite literal scripting of what was to come.

BLACK, WHITE, AND ASIAN TURF

LS: What about other issues of turf, in urban spaces for instance?

VMT: In the past there's been very visible conflict between the African American community and the Hmong immigrant community. Historically, St. Paul's University Avenue is a black community neighborhood that goes back to the early part of the twentieth century. There's a lot of tension about the identity of this neighborhood. Is it black, is it Asian, is it multiethnic?

DIE BY NIGHT, P. 1

Two Hmong American men are in an old car driving through the residential streets of Frogtown. . . .

The car approaches a BLACK MAN walking in the middle of the street going in the same direction.

Snake HONKS the horn at him.

Snake (shouting): Get your ass out of the street!

Snake drives alongside the man.

Black Man: What's your problem, gook? I was here first.

LS: There is scholarship on immigrant populations that posits a kind of black-white continuum, black-white being the paradigmatic racial formation in the United States, in which new immigrants have to negotiate their positioning, in the space between blackness and whiteness. The argument is that, to the extent that you are economically self-sufficient or successful, you whiten yourself.[16]
VMT: If you look at all the Asian businesses here, they fall neither into the black end nor the white end of that continuum.
LS: So there is a triangular relationship. It's not simply about who can get whiter faster, but the kinds of obstacles to legitimacy presented by the people who were here first.

What about the emulation of black culture among Hmong youth?
VMT: It's kind of ironic in a way, when a lot of lip service is being paid to the economic power of the Asian and Hmong community. Meanwhile, a large part of the Hmong community has adopted what they see as legitimate, and that is urban black culture. In the script I make a point of that. To a character like Clown it's not about being black at all; it's an insider's view. It's a view of someone who's gained that urban competency.[17] Being street smart, getting that street credibility with the people they live with.

DIE BY NIGHT, P. 42

The campers, settled in the woods, look at the stars under the night sky:

Clown: Someday I'm gonna be a star, just like that bright one there.
(rapping)

"Check it. They call me the one and only Clown,
Cuz I was born on the wrong side of town.
I ain't black, I ain't white.
I'm the Yellow kid that never run from a fight."

RACE AS UNMARKED PRESENCE

VMT: In my script, the three male characters, Rock, Snake, and Clown, had these experiences that were deeply ingrained in their psyche, this racial experience, and that determines to a large extent the events that happened in the woods that night. I didn't want to explicitly make it racial. I would be underestimating the intelligence of the audience.

LS: The question is, if it's whites killing Hmong, is that more easily readable as racial than Hmong killing whites? Socially we have a repertoire for reading it as a racial killing—so when we get to that point in *Die By Night* we don't have any trouble seeing these as racial killings even though you leave them completely unmarked. I think that's also very freighted—with the history of white persecution, lynching etc. of blacks in U.S. history.

VMT: I think, depending on who's watching it, they could come away with different interpretations. They can ask, "Why were the white hunters killing the Hmong campers? It makes no sense."

ST. PAUL PIONEER PRESS, NOVEMBER 23, 2004
"It makes no sense," the sheriff said. The suspect, he said, "speaks fluent English. He's educated. He's an American citizen."

LS: And when it works the other way around, especially maybe with an Asian, not a black, there are some barriers to perceiving that as a racial killing, and the barrier is that the racism that he's experienced that prompted the killing is made invisible.

VMT: So in the Chai Vang case, it made no sense for Chai Vang to kill the hunters: "He's just crazy!"

Wisconsin Attorney General Peggy Lautenschlager, in the sentencing memorandum, used the following characterizations to make the case for maximum, consecutive sentences:

VANG
- "intentionally and systematically turned the Willers-Crotteau hunting property into a killing field" (p. 7)
- had a "calculating and depraved character" (p. 10)
- had "utter disregard for human life" (p. 11)

LS: So race was ignored, or suppressed.

VMT: Right, it was intentionally suppressed.

LS: There's this line on Court TV where [anchor] Nancy Grace says: "What a tragedy! So many deaths and we still don't have the *real* motive. . . ." There's this kind of incredulity to the way she says it; it's just unthinkable that the motive would be about retaliating or having experienced racial hatred and therefore needing to fight back or defend oneself.

VMT: Well yeah, it's hard to accept, as I was thinking: ambiguity in the script would play into some of that—it's hard to accept that the white hunters would kill these Hmong campers based on some racial motivation. The encounter in the woods is not overtly racial. So the audience might have the same reaction: "No, it can't be race."

LS: So what it does is create a circumstance where the *contexts* of racial hatred and persecution are, as we say in court, inadmissible to popular understandings.

They're extraneous and, because they can be omitted from consideration of that incident, the only defense he had—which was self-defense—falls apart.
VMT: Right.

CHICAGO TRIBUNE, SEPTEMBER 8, 2005, A19
Lauren Hesebeck, who found his friends' bodies and made the first desperate calls for help . . . says he can't remember whether the men called Vang names. "To me, it wasn't a race issue. It was about someone trespassing," Hesebeck said. Hesebeck admits that the men cursed at Vang. But, he says, "I don't know how he would be fearful of his life."

ST. PAUL PIONEER PRESS, NOVEMBER 3, 2005, 6B
Kelly Kennedy, a spokesman for Wisconsin Attorney General Peg Lautenschlager, defended the composition of the jury, noting it was drawn from more diverse Dane County instead of rural Sawyer County. Kennedy also dismissed concerns that the case was about race. "I think what this case showed was it was an individual who had an anger problem. He reacted violently and the race issue really isn't there."

LS: What about the way in which *Die By Night* conjures the atmosphere in the woods?
VMT: The film focuses on the dynamics of the relationship between the Hmong campers and the white hunters. It makes the dynamics more the flashpoint of the conflict. My sense is that in reality whenever there's a conflict between a Hmong hunter and white hunter it has a lot more to do with the way people perceive each other and how they interact.
LS: So you're saying there wouldn't have needed to be any kind of direct provocation or even speech, necessarily, or racialized speech? It could have been a more subtle interaction but understood as racially tense?
VMT: Yeah, it could be something that normally is very insignificant. What happened could have been a glance between the hunters, or a gesture, or a comment that one hunter thought was really innocuous but interpreted by the other hunter as offensive or disrespectful.
LS: This thing about the disrespect being palpable but not spoken or communicated through specific acts—this gets us back to what the supernatural is evoking in the script. You are suggesting something that is felt, in an inchoate way, but very acutely. So much discussion in the case focused on acts and words: Who shot first, whether racial epithets were used, etc. But you're talking about bodily sensations of threat, and of affective awareness that is outside of language and probably outside of cognition. It comes from things like the relentless accretion of racial incidents in the life course of the subject, and from the bodily experiences of things like a look, a posture of the antagonist, a sense of being outnumbered.
VMT: The affective awareness and experience of racism being outside cognition is why what hunts the Hmong campers has to be supernatural. It's not just any supernatural; it's important that it's occulted, can't be seen or grasped. So it provokes fear and all kinds of affective responses.[18]
LS: Interestingly, though, what is represented as the unseen in your script might be the unsaid for Chai in the woods. Hmong I've talked to who followed the

case suggested how important it was that Vang might have been not only out-numbered, but surrounded. And that these men were much, much taller and bigger in build than he was. And that they spoke, or yelled, with a certain tone of voice. These were all bodily sensations that tripped off a kind of deep affective response because of embodied memories, including that of the feeling of his life being threatened in the dream he had that morning.

VMT: And these experiences are not isolated. They're the result of a whole edifice of systemic racism. I guess I'm saying something about systemic racism through the supernatural too. It doesn't really reveal itself in explicit words or acts. It just works below the surface, doing damage methodically and invisibly.

LS: Its occulting is crucial to how it works.

VMT. Yeah. And when you look at the two sides of the story, the Hmong hunter was saying, "I was disrespected," and what did the white hunters say? They were saying that "no, we didn't disrespect him. We said what needed to be said at that moment." So just in that interaction, you could learn a lot. It really had very little to do with property or trespassing; it had more to do with each party's interpretation of the other's action.

LS: Or it *could* have. Because I think part of the import of what you're saying is that we don't necessarily need to know what happened in terms of what was said, or what was gestured or whatever, because it's conceivable that it was a subtle thing that wouldn't even be reported afterward, wouldn't even necessarily be remembered. But that doesn't mean it wasn't there.

MINNEAPOLIS STAR TRIBUNE, NOVEMBER 28, 2004, A1
Two cultures, two traditions, at peace in the outdoors. Until they met. . . .

LS: So what happens in the script is that when we get to the final encounter with the hunters, we see that they are the same hunters [as in the hostile gas station encounter] and we know that they are white, but there's nothing that racializes the encounter, that gives us an explicit notion that they are hunting Hmong people for racial reasons. So talk about why you left it unmarked that way.

VMT: Y'know, when I was writing the script I was thinking of another movie— *Night of the Living Dead.* It's about these people who are trapped in this house when these dead people start rising from their graves. One of these people who went into this house to hide out was a black man, so there were a lot of racial overtones in the movie. The whites seemed as afraid of the black man trapped in the house as they were afraid of the living dead that were breaking the windows trying to enter. And it turned out that the black man was the last surviving character. I thought it was ingenious how they put race into the movie like that.

LS: And it's inserted subtly, without being marked in the dialogue. So the viewer needs to be conversant in previous semiotics of racial tension to be able to read the interactions between the characters as racialized.

What do you think is the meaning of or the white motivation for wearing ski masks in *Die By Night?*

VMT: My interpretation of what I wrote as far as that masking device of the hunters is that this kind of violence is inexplicable. The masking of it means there's no way to explain it. Racism does have a certain—

LS: Hiddenness, lurkingness?

VMT:—lurking aspect to it. You're not always aware of it. You only come to know that they are wearing masks in the daytime; so even in the daylight, still masked. Racism is, if you want to interpret it that way, ominous, systemic.

LS: It depersonalizes it too. It makes it sort of a force rather than a few guys. It refuses exceptionalizing it by saying "this is a few crazy people" and makes it more of a solid wall of something unknown.

VMT: Yeah, definitely. That was a big part of it: the intent of the hunters was to hide their individual identities.

LS: What is the importance of the demon being figured as supernatural for so much of the script?

VMT: What I had in mind when I made it supernatural was that the Hmong characters, when it comes to this kind of enemy, are up against something that they can't really fight—the enemy being racism.

LS: The enemy has supernormal powers.

VMT: Right. And they are not going to prevail. They are powerless against it.

LS: Is it supernatural in the sense of being ghostlike and invisible, or if they could actually come face to face with it they could see it?

VMT: Well, when they couldn't see it, it was supernatural, but in the daylight, when it was revealed that they were white hunters, the Evie character was able to escape and kill them.

LS: In the lore that creates the demon, is it imagined as ghostlike and invisible, or as concrete, like a hairy beast or whatever?

VMT: In the myth it can be invisible if it wants to be. And if it wants to be seen you can see it, but most of the time it wants to be invisible so it can attack you by surprise.

LS: It's also consistent with what you are trying to say about the white hunters ultimately. Maybe they can become embodied figures. But in their perpetrating this in the course of the night, they can't be envisioned as what they are. Just as race can't be envisioned as what it is in the hunter incident.

VMT: Right.

LS: Why does Evie have to get raped? What function does that have? If I was to suggest that the rape as an intimate act produced a transfer, or an inversion, in which the monster was humanized as the hunters while Evie became monstrous as a killer, how would you react?

VMT: Yeah, you could say that. It is a transforming for Evie from being the victim, the pursued, to being the pursuer.

LS: We could also say that it produces masculine power in her.

VMT: Yeah, you could say that if you want to equate her power as killer with masculinity. I'd rather say she is killing them as woman. She backs up the car trying to escape and runs over the first two hunters. Up to the point where she kills them, she is still a victim. The situation calls for her to kill, not as a masculinized subject, but as woman warrior, in order to escape death.[19]

LS: There's a book by Linda Williams called *Playing the Race Card* in which she argues that in the American pop culture treatment of race there have been only two modes of interaction that are what she calls "racially legible"—the black man being beaten by the white man, and the black man threatening the white woman. She uses Rodney King and O. J. Simpson as examples of these two.[20] I'm wondering if some of the hyperattention to the Vang case is precisely because it is racially illegible—it doesn't fit either of these configurations. In fact, I'm wondering if part of the public outrage around Vang's act is that it in effect feminized the white hunters since—in the dominant regime of racial legibility—men of color menace *women.* Your screenplay pushes the inversion even farther, because it is a *woman* of color who aggresses against white men.

VMT: She aggresses and she also figuratively unmasks them. She is the one who recognizes them for what they are.

LS: Yes, which brings me to the scene in which the last hunter is wounded on the ground. Evie goes up to him and begins to roll back the ski mask on his face. But before she reveals his whole face, she rolls the mask back down. Then she slices him through the groin and abdomen, splitting him in half. Why does she replace the mask before she kills him?

VMT: I guess unmasking him would personalize him. Evie doesn't want revenge against one guy. What she wants to strike against is the whole edifice of hate.

ON DEFENSE

MINNEAPOLIS STAR TRIBUNE, JUNE 10, 2005, A1

Chai Vang told a reporter in a phone call from jail that he felt sorry about shooting some of the hunters he is accused of killing but that others deserved to be shot, because they called him racist names and threatened him, according to a transcript of the conversation.

In a letter sent from the Sawyer County jail to the same *Chicago Tribune* reporter, Vang sought to justify the six killings: . . . "I feel that this incident is happen because people are not able to [treat] others with respect like they wanted to be treated, and [because of] hatred toward other people or race," Vang, 36, of St Paul, wrote in a letter dated March 8.

Vang has claimed that . . . one of the hunters fired a shot his way, prompting him to open fire on them.

VMT: In *Die By Night*, the hunter pulls out his gun first—that's why Snake pulls out his gun to shoot. Snake could supposedly justify shooting first by saying it's self-defense.

LS: And later, Rock and Snake are arguing, and Clown says, "We can tell the cops those guys started it. It was self-defense."

VMT: Right, Rock and Clown say self-defense, but Snake says, no, that's not going to work. That's why he says "keep going, don't stop." He feels that the police are not going to believe him. If they stop, what happens is that he just goes to jail.

LS: And how prescient that all turned out to be.

VMT: In the case, Chai Vang said he was shot at first, and that's why he shot them, but his defense didn't work, he went to jail, he's in prison for life.

LS: So Snake turns out to have been the canny one.

VMT: Again, it's based on true stories that I've heard. A lot of Hmong hunters go out into the woods and they're harassed and threatened, but they don't want to report it because they feel that the authorities would not believe them or take their side, so they just let it go.

> *NEW YORK TIMES*, DECEMBER 1, 2004
>
> The authorities have quoted Mr. Vang as telling investigators that the hunters who were shot had first fired at him and cursed him with racial epithets.
>
> Racial insults while hunting in Wisconsin, some Hmong say, are nothing new. And Tou Vang, who is not related to the accused, said a hunter fired several shots in his direction when they argued over hunting rights three years ago near the Wisconsin town of Ladysmith.
>
> "I left right away," Mr. Vang said. "I didn't report it, because even if you do, the authorities might not take any action. But I know that every year there are racial problems in the woods up there."[21]

VMT: For a Hmong person anyway, you can't see the incident in Wisconsin without looking at the history of the relationship between Hmong hunters and white hunters during hunting season. If you ask a Hmong person, they'll just say, "Yeah, it's happened before and the reason why he snapped in the woods is because of his experience with white hunters in the past."

LS: So you've said that racism is this force they cannot fight, but Evie does fight. What is your point here? Is it ultimately about the outcome—that Evie dies? In that case, the screenplay once again strangely anticipates the Chai Vang case in suggesting that a person of color can never kill whites and get away with it . . . is this the logic of why Evie has to die?

VMT: Evie fights only to die. The result for her is no different from the results for her friends, or Chai Vang.

LS: How do you relate this point to Chai Vang's comment that he did something to "defend myself and my race"? Is there a larger symbolic significance to fighting back, even if the fighter loses in the short term? One Hmong Minnesotan I spoke to suggested that what Vang was doing—in his shooting and in recounting it during the trial—was putting *all* hunters on notice that they should think twice about messing with Hmong people.

VMT: My script doesn't deal with deterrence as a solution. Maybe the message that Chai Vang wanted to send was: "In defending myself, I defended my race." Vang not only wanted to defend his race and bring balance to race relations, but he wanted to gain power over future actions of whites. But what my script is asking is, "What good is that going to do?" It doesn't eliminate the problem of racism that we experience daily growing up in America.

LS: And a big part of that problem is precisely how racism lurks, is that what you're saying? How racism haunts so many interracial encounters without naming itself? It insidiously makes itself known to people of color while maintaining its deniability in official mainstream discourse. That's why its appearance can be called ghostly, like a supernatural being that you know is there but cannot see. Which gets me back to why I think the notion of "occult" works to evoke this dynamic. By virtue of being hidden, or masked, racism manifests itself—instead— as something otherworldly, maybe outside language, outside rationality, and not objectively knowable.

VMT: Yeah, so fighting back in violent encounters only accomplishes so much, and at a cost. As long as race remains occulted, then the person of color will get dismissed, or imprisoned, and labeled as depraved and overly angry.[22]

LS: So some other kind of action is called for. What would that be?

VMT: It comes back to unmasking, right?

LS: Yes, maybe in the form of naming, exposing. Could we say that that is what your campaign against the radio station was doing? And your editorial on Chai Vang?

VMT: Maybe, yeah. It's interesting that during the campaign Tom Barnard went on the air calling us a bunch of "goddamned liars." He tried to pull it back to his word against ours. But by then it wasn't only about words. Our actions were already having effects.

LS: Right—you could say that people were *seeing* the issue differently.

VMT: Or they were seeing the issue, period. They were seeing that talking that way on the air was racist, which they hadn't seen before.

LS: Something was coming into visibility.

VMT: Something more systemic than a ghostly apparition.

CODA

Since the dialogue recorded in this piece, the prescience of Thoj's screenplay has become even more uncanny. In January 2007, a Hmong man was brutally killed by a white hunter, once again in the woods of Wisconsin. Almost from the moment the case was reported, there was little mystery about who had shot and stabbed the Hmong father of five, rammed a stick down his throat, and attempted to conceal his lifeless body: The murderer, twenty-eight-year-old James Nichols, not only confessed to having done it, but told the police that the "Hmong group are bad," that the Hmong "are mean and kill everything" and "go for anything that moves." Although some saw this attack as a direct retalia-tion for the Chai Vang murders two years earlier, there are more systemic pos-sibilities, intimated by the fact that Nichols had been convicted of breaking into an African American hunting cabin and spray-painting "KKK." And the Klan had recently been reported to be turning its attention to anti-immigrant mobi-lization. There is also the role of Vietnam-era imaginary in that part of the country. Just as Chinese American Vincent Chin was misrecognized a quarter-century ago as a Japanese who could somehow be perversely blamed and bludg-eoned to death for the Japanese auto industry's dislocation of Michigan workers, so Hmong who had fought in the employ of the CIA may be elided, through popular amnesia, with that paradigmatic Vietnamese enemy they were hired to war against. Hmong court observers recall that during Chai Vang's trial, a white man paced outside in camouflage fatigues with a placard sneering: "Killer Vang Send Back to Vietnam."

Ironically, the racial dimension of the more recent murder came in for *hyper-*visibility since now the configuration was "legible" as a man of color being assaulted by a white man. Newspaper headlines screamed: "Some suspect racial issues exist in the outdoors."

AGENCE FRANCE PRESS, JANUARY 12, 2007
Slaying of Hmong hunter reignites racial tensions in Wisconsin.[23]

Members of the Hmong community have called for adding "hate crime" to Nichols's charges, but the district attorney has been reluctant to add the charge. The trial has been set for a small town in Wisconsin, where it is likely that the jury will be all white and will be invested in not acknowledging the larger racial agonism at play here. It is quite conceivable that some kind of "reasonable doubt" will allow for a self-defense argument to hold and Nichols will walk. The murder may be exceptionalized as almost random, the act of a reckless and hot-headed individual, and collectively purged, rather than seen as of a piece with a larger pattern that is as orchestrated about occulting its racial agenda as it is about pursuing it.

What this case reveals is that occulting can work on either racial axis, that exceptionalization of either the white man or the man of color as "crazy" or "depraved" effectively masks the systemic workings of race. With the culture alibi in the mix, anti-Asian racial conflict can be recoded as simply the latest incarnation of new immigrant culture clash. In turn, if Nichols *was* holding his Hmong victim responsible for Chai Vang's deeds, it would imply the opposite of exceptionalization—that, tarred by the same brush, all Hmong have been made to bear the guilt for Chai Vang's actions.

With the recent Virginia Tech mass murder we saw, just as with Chai Vang, the press inclination to fetishize shooter Seung-Hui Cho's Koreanness, along with much deliberation over the possibility of racial backlash. If Cho becomes linked in a signifying chain to Chai Vang as well as to the longstanding urban American imaginary of gun-toting Asian gangs, we may witness—alongside the prevailing images of Asians as feminized model minorities—an intensification of the figure of the hyperviolent, ruthless Asian male. This discursive shift toward the hyperviolent, if it plays out that way, would render *Die By Night's* nearly gunless Hmong campers an especially strategic counterpoint in the politics of visibility.

N OTES

For help with materials used in developing this piece, we thank Tzianeng Vang at the Hmong Nationality Archives, the New York University Asian/Pacific/American Institute Archives, and the Coalition for Community Relations. We are extremely grateful for the critical engagement of the following readers: Carlos Decena, David Eng, Lindsey French, Jeremy Glick, Laurel Kendall, Josephine Lee, Martin Manalansan, Fran Mascia-Lees, Andrea Louie, Mitchell Ogden, Mary Louise Pratt, Ana Yolanda Ramos Zayas, Ed Schein, Lok Siu, Karen Shimakawa, Ted Swedenburg, Bo Thao, Ma Vang, Zoua Vang, Ann Waltner, Ken Wissoker, the students in Schein's Anthropology and Cultural Studies seminar, Curtis Marez and members of the editorial board, as well as two anonymous readers for *American Quarterly*, and especially Edgar Rivera Colon, who contributed to this work as our invaluable third interlocutor from its inception. We remain solely responsible for the final product, which may not reflect opinions or suggestions of our readers.

1. The incident took place on November 21, 2004. Chai Soua Vang was confronted by hunters for having climbed into their deer stand. Vang alleged, and the surviving hunters denied, that racial epithets were directed at him and that the one armed hunter fired a shot first. The hunters had ATVs, surrounded Vang with them, and would have been able to pursue Vang. But only one had a gun. Vang then started to leave, but turned around and fired many shots, ultimately killing six hunters and wounding two others. Four were shot in the back. The conviction rested on the credibility of the surviving hunters' denying any use of *racial* epithets and of having shot first, thus undercutting any self-defense argument for Vang. The actual use of slurs, and which ones, remains murky in the trial transcripts (*State of Wisconsin v. Chai S. Vang*, Circuit Court, Sawyer County, Wisconsin [2005]). Whereas Vang maintained that the words "gook," "chink," and "fucking Asian" were directed at him (1237–39), one of the white witnesses maintained that the only relevant statement made was "You fucking assholes . . . are always on my property" (623), while the other denied hearing any such language (507–8). In her closing statement, Attorney General Lautenschlager referred to a written statement by one of the whites that "acknowledged some language was said. It acknowledged that the language likely contained ethnic slurs, but these remarks came and he was honest about them" (1420–21). Yet, even though the prosecutor herself alluded to the slurs, they were purged from relevance in the course of most of the trial; instead, it was Vang's "depraved character" that was foregrounded.
2. Subsequent citations were added to endnotes by Schein during the editing process.
3. *Borne in War: A Real Personal Story*, VHS, directed by Va-Megn Thoj (New York: Third World Newsreel, 1996).
4. Aihwa Ong makes a similar point. See *Buddha Is Hiding: Refugees, Citizenship, the New America* (Berkeley: University of California Press, 2003), 259.
5. *Slaughtered in Hugo*, DVD, directed by Va-Megn Thoj (St. Paul, Minn.: Frogtown Media Productions, 2002).
6. Among the many commentaries in Asian American studies on the tyranny of the black-white binary, one of the most foundational has been Gary Y. Okihiro, *Margins and Mainstreams: Asians in American History and Culture* (Seattle: University of Washington Press, 1994).
7. *The Best Place to Live: A Personal Story of the Hmong Refugees from Laos*, VHS, directed by Peter O'Neill and Ralph Rugoff (Providence, R.I.: Skylight Films, 1982).
8. For example, the fact that Vang had been trained as a sharpshooter in the National Guard for six years, instead of working to stress how American he was, could also be used to make him out to be an especially deadly killer. In this light, it is tempting to read Vang's acts—from domestic violence to sharpshooting to the murders—as strivings at remasculinization in an American cultural context in which Asian Americans are historically feminized. But see David L. Eng, *Racial Castration: Managing Masculinity in Asian America* (Durham, N.C.: Duke University Press, 2001), who cautions against the potential complicity with patriarchal and heteronormative ideals that such a reading of gender would imply.
9. *Flight*, DVD, directed by Va-Megn Thoj (St. Paul, Minn.: Frogtown Media Productions, 2004).
10. See George Lipsitz, *The Possessive Investment in Whiteness: How White People Profit from Identity Politics* (Philadelphia: Temple University Press, 2006), 17–18, which exposes the means by which land ownership and accumulated wealth of whites has been protected by tax codes and many other structural factors.

11. The notion of "cultural conviction" is a play on the legal notion of the "cultural defense," which has been much commented upon in the past in relation to some high-profile Hmong cases. See Malek-Mithra Shebanyi, "Cultural Defense: One Person's Culture Is Another's Crime," *Loyola of Los Angeles International and Comparative Law Journals* 9.3 (1987): 751–83, for a legal discussion, and Kristin Koptiuch, " 'Cultural Defense' and Criminological Displacements: Gender, Race, and (Trans)Nation in the Legal Surveillance of U.S. Diaspora Asians," in *Displacement, Diaspora, and Geographies of Identity*, ed. Smadar Lavie and Ted Swedenburg (Durham, N.C.: Duke University Press, 1996), 215–33, for a critical discussion of the disciplinary ramifications of the cultural defense. See also Leti Volpp, "(Mis)Identifying Culture: Asian Women and 'The Cultural Defense,' " *Harvard Women's Law Journal* 17 (Spring 1994): 57–80.

12. On the repeated framing of all Asian immigrants in terms of alien culture aligned with the past, see Lisa Lowe, *Immigrant Acts: On Asian American Cultural Politics* (Durham, N.C.: Duke University Press, 1996).

13. Ann Fadiman, *The Spirit Catches You and You Fall Down: A Hmong Child, Her American Doctors, and the Collision of Two Cultures* (New York: Farrar, Straus and Giroux, 1997). Indeed, much Hmong studies scholarship to date has replayed the culture clash and the fraught assimilation/acculturation paradigms in describing Hmong challenges in the United States. Such an approach to scholarship risks complicity with the more popular perception of Hmong as misfits in American society. For some recent exceptions to this approach, see Chia Youyee Vang, "Reconstructing Community in Diaspora: Narratives of Hmong American/Refugee Resistance and Human Agency" (Ph.D. diss., University of Minnesota, December 2006); Stacey J. Lee, *Up Against Whiteness: Race, School, and Immigrant Youth* (New York: Teacher's College Press, 2005); Mitch Ogden, "Magnetic Diaspora: Medi(t)ation of Hmong Diasporic Homeland through Audio Cassette Letters and Videographic Documentaries" (paper presented at the Association for Asian American Studies meetings, April 7, 2007); Gary Y. Lee, "Dreaming across Oceans: Globalization and Cultural Reinvention in the Hmong Diaspora," *Hmong Studies Journal* 7 (2006): 1–33; Louisa Schein, "Homeland Beauty: Transnational Longing and Hmong American Video," *Journal of Asian Studies* 63.2 (May 2004): 433–63. See critiques of Fadiman's book in Monica Chiu, "Medical, Racist, and Colonial Constructions of Power: Creating the Asian American Patient and the Cultural Citizen in Anne Fadiman's *The Spirit Catches You and You Fall Down*," *Hmong Studies Journal* 5 (2004–5); Mai Na M. Lee, "Book Review: *The Spirit Catches You and You Fall Down*," http://www.hmongnet.org/publications/spirit_review.html (accessed September 10, 2007); Janelle Taylor, "The Story Catches You and You Fall Down: Tragedy, Ethnography, and 'Cultural Competence,' " *Medical Anthropology Quarterly* 17.2 (June 2003): 159–81; and Ma Vang, "Nation, Citizenship, and Identity: Re-imagining Hmong Transnationalism in *The Spirit Catches You and You Fall Down*" (honors thesis, University of Oregon, 2005). For collections in which Hmong tell their own stories through oral narratives, see Sucheng Chan, *Hmong Means Free: Life in Laos and America* (Philadelphia: Temple University Press, 1994); and Lillian Faderman with Ghia Xiong, *I Begin My Life All Over: The Hmong and the American Immigrant Experience* (Boston: Beacon Press, 1998).

14. See online at http://web.lexis-nexis.com.proxy.libraries.rutgers.edu/universe/document?_m=b10ffbb722a4e87fbf3ee389bb045809&_docnum=15&wchp=dGLbVtb-zSkVA&_md5=1bb5531708e657d329c4cf666d066e8b (accessed August 16, 2006).

15. Excerpt from trial transcript (p. 1238) of Chai Soua Vang under direct examination by Defense Attorney Steven Kohn.

16. See Aihwa Ong, "Cultural Citizenship as Subject-Making," *Current Anthropology* 37.5 (December 1996): 737–62.

17. On the notion of black youth culture as signifying urban competency, see Ana Yolanda Ramos Zayas, "Becoming American, Becoming Black: Urban Competency, Racialized Spaces, and the Politics of Citizenship Among Brazilian and Puerto Rican Youth in Newark," *Identities* 14.1–2 (January 2007): 85–109; see also Sunaina Marr Maira, *Desis in*

the House: Indian American Youth Culture in New York City (Philadelphia: Temple University Press, 2002).

18. See by comparison Avery F. Gordon, *Ghostly Matters: Haunting and the Sociological Imagination* (Minneapolis: University of Minnesota Press, 1997), 8: "If haunting describes how that which appears to be not there is often a seething presence, acting on and often meddling with taken-for-granted realities, the ghost is just the sign . . . that tells you a haunting is taking place." Building on Gordon, Grace Kyungwon Hong affirms that "race . . . is a kind of ghost: almost inarticulable, always slipping away" ("The Ghosts of Transnational American Studies: A Response to the Presidential Address," *American Quarterly* 59.1 [March 2007]: 33–39).

19. Thoj, interestingly, devised this plot/gender structure with no knowledge of the "final girl" analysis developed in Carol J. Clover's *Men, Women, and Chainsaws: Gender in the Modern Horror Film* (Princeton, N.J.: Princeton University Press, 1992).

20. Linda Williams, *Playing the Race Card: Melodramas of Black and White from Uncle Tom to O. J. Simpson* (Princeton, N.J.: Princeton University Press, 2001).

21. Excerpt from an article in the *New York Times*, December 1, 2004, online at http://web.lexis-nexis.com.proxy.libraries.rutgers.edu/universe/document?_m= 4315288b7d7e9793e990955a7924dac5&_docnum=1 &wchp=dGLbVzz-zSkVA&_md5= 37211ef633599f60d20ea8a694c1bf66 (accessed May 20, 2006).

22. Notably, much was made—from initial coverage through the trial and even in the sentencing—of Vang's reported history of domestic violence, while a similar purported history on the part of one of the victims was muted.

23. Excerpt from a newspaper article, *Agence France Press*, January 12, 2007, online at http://web.lexis-nexis.com.proxy.libraries.rutgers.edu/universe/document?_m= e3c4586d48eff4766e26696664d12d06&_docnum=19&wchp=dGLbVtbzSkVb&_md5= d2128571391ee40d439de03763978cd7 (accessed August 18, 2006).

COLLATERAL DAMAGE

SOUTHEAST ASIAN POVERTY
IN THE UNITED STATES

Eric Tang

On 22 August 1996, President Bill Clinton signed into law the Personal Responsibility and Work Opportunity Reconciliation Act (PRWORA). Once fully implemented, this act has the potential to destroy the means of subsistence of millions of working and jobless poor who will be removed from all federal assistance programs granted under the Social Security Act by the year 2002.[1] Yet the damaging effects of PRWORA have already been felt. Those who were targeted to suffer the most immediate and life-threatening cuts to the welfare state were "legal," green-card-holding immigrants receiving federal aid through the Social Security Administration (SSA). In September 1997, states began implementing their specific plans to remove immigrants from SSA-administered Supplemental Security Income (SSI) for the disabled and elderly, and food stamps for dependent, immigrant children. Following this initial immigrant removal, federal cash assistance programs, namely Aid to Families with Dependent Children (AFDC), will be drastically reduced and eventually eliminated for both citizens and immigrants within five years of the signing of PRWORA.[2]

Southeast Asians in the United States—primarily Vietnamese, Lao, Hmong, and Cambodian immigrants—represent the largest per capita race or ethnic group in the country receiving public assistance.[3] Originally placed on federal welfare rolls as a temporary and "adaptive" measure under the Indochina Migration and Refugee Assistance Act of 1975, a large segment of Southeast Asian refugees who fled their homelands in the aftermath of the U.S. invasion of Vietnam and the subsequent bombing of Cambodia by the United States are now entering a third consecutive decade of welfare dependency, contrary to government officials' predictions of a seamless transition into American labor markets. Stripped of their refugee status in the post–Cold War era, virtually all Southeast Asians have now been reclassified as permanent residents (or "legal" immigrants) and are therefore fully subject to the impending cuts under PRWORA. The consequences of the new law's "immigrant removal" campaign are sweeping and disastrous for Southeast Asian communities that, in California alone, have shown poverty and welfare-dependency rates of nearly 80 percent for the state's entire Southeast Asian population.[4]

For many of its critics, PRWORA represents a post–civil rights, neoconservative backlash against the poor and nonwhite sectors of the United States, particularly against the black urban poor who have been labeled the new "underclass"—a damaging term that encompasses a range of racist imagery including the sexually deviant "welfare queen," the "dysfunctional" black family, and the uncontrollably violent black male. These distorted and dehumanizing constructions are reproduced in mainstream periodicals, popular literature, and even liberal-leaning policy reports.[5] Yet, despite its wide circulation, the term *underclass* evades a precise and agreed-on definition. According to historian Robin Kelley, this lack of precision stems from the fact that *underclass* has never actually referred to a class of people but rather to a set of behaviors. "What makes the 'underclass' a class," suggests Kelley, "is members' common behavior—not their income, their poverty level, or the kind of work they do. . . . It's a definition of class driven more by social panic than by systemic analysis."[6] The common behaviors that comprise the underclass are wide-ranging and arbitrary; they can include criminal mischief, sexual promiscuity, shiftlessness, dependency, nihilism, immorality, and deviance. In an attempt to offer some coherence to these random sets of behaviors, underclass proponents have conveniently drawn on the term *culture*. Indeed, underclass behaviors are often grouped together to represent a so-called culture of poverty. Here, the new underclass literature is appropriating and distorting the work of Oscar Lewis, who, in the early 1960s, first introduced the phrase *subculture of poverty*. Lewis, however, did not evoke *culture* to describe a set of immutable behaviors, but rather to describe the daily practices that poor people engaged in, in an effort to both survive and resist systemic inequality and class polarization.[7] For contemporary culture of poverty theorists, the addition of *culture* still fails to yield a more precise definition of the term. However, its evocation is nonetheless powerful, for it designates an ethnographic field, an "area of difference" wherein the aforementioned behaviors are confined to a particular group—the black urban poor. Moreover, as Michael Katz suggests, once *culture* is used to conveniently identify the underclass, it functions as a "euphemism for the pathology of the undeserving poor, an explanation for their condition [and] an excuse . . . for both inaction and punitive public policy."[8]

Certainly, we can read PRWORA as part of an ongoing punishment of this constructed black culture of poverty. However, as we currently witness the first phase of PRWORA's implementation, we find its most immediate and vulnerable targets among welfare-dependent immigrants from the Third World. Considering PRWORA as a *racial project*—to borrow the term from Michael Omi and Howard

Winant—we may interpret it as a simultaneous assault on poor blacks and Third World immigrants.[9] While we have witnessed numerous legislative attacks against both groups over the past decade—from the congressional Family Security Act (FSA) of 1988 to California's anti-immigrant Proposition 187—such attacks have operated as rather discrete racial initiatives. Indeed, FSA was clearly aimed at disciplining the black welfare recipient by forcing her to participate in highly exploitative "workfare" programs in exchange for welfare benefits, as well as by policing her with new measures aimed at curbing welfare fraud.[10] Undergirding the support for FSA was the racist image of a black single mother who augmented her welfare benefits by giving birth to numerous children. Meanwhile, Proposition 187, an act that sought to deny immigrants (both documented and undocumented) access to virtually all public benefits in California, was promoted with an equally compelling yet definitively immigrant imagery—that of the Mexican "hordes" making a mad dash for the U.S. border, or Asian immigrant families overcrowding California cities and suburbs. Although both legislative acts were aimed at dismantling the welfare state, their successful passage was made possible by two distinct sets of racial rhetoric and imagery. Yet by implementing anti-immigrant measures as its first step in a broader push to deny welfare to both immigrants and nonimmigrants, PRWORA was unique in that it momentarily abandoned the racial logic that guided preceding legislation. Indeed, PRWORA, as a racial project, did not separate "native" blacks from Third World immigrants. On the contrary, the two groups were taken as a combined coordinate, a rare and perhaps unwitting disclosure of their common location vis-à-vis the nation's conservative welfare policy.

Allowing our optimism to get the best of us, we may view any resistance to the implementation of PRWORA as an opportunity to assert common interests and political alliances, to make those very crucial connections across poor and racialized communities. Yet the first two years has failed to yield such a united front. Although opposition to PRWORA has emerged from numerous political sectors—ranging from grassroots organizations, to the civil rights establishment, to independent policy groups—very few of these challenges openly acknowledge what is commonly at stake between the black working class and the Third World migrant. Indeed, from across the political spectrum, community advocates, welfare pundits, and ethnic journalism insist that Asian American poverty resides in a sphere quite distinct, if not contradistinctive, to that of the black culture of poverty.[11] So too, on the scholarly front, social scientists have produced numerous studies whose organizing questions presuppose the mutual exclusion between "native" blacks on the one hand and Third World immigrants on the other. At the vanguard of this body of scholarly work is the sociological subfield known as the "economic sociology of immigration." The core assumptions of this subfield suggest that immigrants are inclined to engage in a set of social and cultural practices—namely, tight kinship networks—which save them from underclass status. Here, we are confronted with the rudiments for what I consider a discourse of the immigrant as the "deserving poor." Much like the theory of an undeserving poor, the location of the deserving poor is determined by a set of sedimented behaviors that constitute a culture of poverty. Yet the behaviors that form this "immigrant culture of poverty" are organized in such a way that they guarantee a teleology of arrival and survival, as opposed to the devolution of a decidedly black underclass.

In this essay, I explore the makings of an Asian immigrant culture of poverty through the core assumptions and theories of the economic sociology of immigration, analyzing the ways in which this sociological imagination casts Asian immigrant life as a cultural, political, and economic negation of a black culture of poverty. In this sense, both of these imagined cultures serve to reinforce each other; they are not only simultaneous discourses but interactive ones. Such interaction plays itself out in the form of policy reports, urban planning, and mainstream ethnic journalism, all of which are deeply influenced by the core assumptions of the underclass scholarship and the economic sociology of immigration.

Following my discussion of the formation of an immigrant culture of poverty, I discuss the contradictions involved in applying such a culture to particular Asian communities. Here, Southeast Asian refugees figure centrally in my argument. Perhaps more than any other racial or ethnic group in the United States, Southeast Asians in the postindustrial setting defy definitions set out by the immigrant culture of poverty thesis. Southeast Asians are at once located within the welfare state *and* the sweatshop firm, they are both the unemployed "slum dweller" *and* the overworked, and their youth embody neoliberalism's nihilistic fantasy of the "menace to society" as well as its promise for a brighter, multicultural future.

Yet, in much of the academic and popular writings on Southeast Asians, these contradictions are viewed as mere aberrations. Rather than accept the full heterogeneity of Southeast Asian life, these writings, influenced by the economic sociology of immigration, have cast it aside as a set of rare, if not intriguing, exceptions—attributed, no doubt, to the "exceptional circumstances" of refugee flight and resettlement. In this essay, I explore how these theories of refugee exceptionalism serve to consolidate a homogeneous black culture of poverty. Here Southeast Asian poverty can be metaphorically thought of as the "collateral damage" in the war against the underclass. "Collateral damage" is a military euphemism that was made popular during the Vietnam War, as it both described and justified the "unintentional" killing of Vietnamese civilians who resided on the periphery of targeted bombing sites. In today's full-scale war against the black urban poor, Southeast Asian refugees have been called on by culture of poverty theorists to once again serve as unintended targets. But much like the real war, the metaphorical war—when fully exposed—reveals that there is no such thing as the unintended.

In my conclusion, I seek an alternative to both the underclass culture of poverty and immigrant culture of poverty theses. My intention, however, is not to "prove" the existence of immigrant cultural practices within black communities, or vice versa. Such a move only reinforces the legitimacy of these cultures of poverty theories. Rendering an alternative requires that we change the terms on which cultures of the poor are constructed and read. To illustrate this alternative, I draw on examples from the daily lives of Southeast Asian residents of the northwest Bronx.

"MAKING IT": ASIAN IMMIGRANTS AND THE ECONOMIC SOCIOLOGY OF IMMIGRATION

How has the economic sociology of immigration come to dominate the discussion of today's Asian immigrant working class? And how do we begin to complicate the seemingly homogeneous sociological imagery through which Asian immigrant poverty in America's postindustrial city is invariably located and narrated? According to Mark Grannovetter, part of the answer lies in the history of disciplinary formation itself. The origins of economic sociology can be traced to the innovative work of Max Weber and Emile Durkheim, both of whom challenged the disciplinary segregation of economics and sociology.[12] Yet it was not until the "renegade" economist Talcott Parsons introduced his structural functional theory that a fuller integration between the micro-operations of the market and its social preconditions would emerge. For several decades, the Parsonian school maintained relative prominence in the subfield of economic sociology, advancing the claim that "social systems" influenced economic outcomes, and not vice versa. But by the 1950s the Parsonians were victims of a backlash led by neoclassical economists who demanded more empirical evidence for this claim.

The mid-1970s, however, brought about a revival for economic sociology as leftist economists, influenced by Marxism, were paying closer attention to the ways in which both labor and capital failed to meet predicted, rational outcomes. For these emerging scholars (Grannovetter among them), the expectations, desires, values, and moral considerations of people mattered when considering the rules of the economy. Indeed, these factors were *embedded* in all economic systems, and it would be impossible to comprehend them separately. The theory of embeddedness posed an exciting new challenge to neoclassical theory. Yet the problem of scant empirical evidence still remained. How were sociologists going to scientifically identify and distill desires and moral consideration—erratic variables that resided outside the rationalist science of the economist?

Enter here the watershed event of post-1965 immigration to the United States. Economic sociologists searching for the ideal laboratory to test their theory of embeddedness encountered the work of immigration sociologists who were enthusiastically searching for a theory with which to analyze the adaptation and acculturation of the new "foreign wave." Among those dominating this wave were, of course, Asian immigrants from a variety of nations and of multiple class/caste backgrounds.

For decades, the sociology of immigration had been asking how and why the immigrant was capable of sustaining forms of "ethnic" capitalism—small-scale and slightly disorganized enterprises—thus evading the Weberian and Marxist prediction that such "traditional" economies would eventually be swallowed up by the highly centralized, universalistic, profit-driven system.[13] As the 1970s wore on, living-wage jobs in the manufacturing sector were becoming increasingly scarce, and the state's war on poverty was dismantled before it had begun to have a real impact. But the new immigrant arrivals were somehow able to circumvent the pitfalls of postindustrialism by once again creating these ethnically discrete commercial livelihoods. From the Cuban migrant of the Mariel exodus, to the Korean grocer, to the Dominican bodega owner—each had "made it" in America at a time when economic forecasts pointed to the contrary.

In an attempt to account for this phenomenon, immigration sociologists drew quite heavily on the heuristic models provided by embeddedness. Embedded in immigrant life were kinship solidarity, primordial ties, and an ineluctable sense of loyalty and trust that transcended class difference. These peculiar behaviors of the Asian working class could be scientifically measured by reading them within social networks. The strength or density of these networks, which hold the embedded relationship, are determined by the number and cluster of "enforceable ties," "normative expectations," and "reciprocity obligations" that can be counted in a given field.

In his essay "Economic Sociology and the Sociology of Immigration: A Conceptual Overview," Alejandro Portes documents this important synthesis, calling into existence a new school of thought that would be aptly titled the "economic sociology of immigration." According to Portes:

> Sociological studies of immigration and ethnicity bear directly on theoretical develop-
> ments in economic sociology because they provide a distinct set of empirical materials
> to draw on for the generation and refinement of general concepts and hypotheses.
> Seldom are the sociological underpinnings of economic action laid bare with such clar-
> ity as in the process that gives rise to immigration and determines its outcomes. . . . In
> the current climate of revived interest in what sociology has to say about economic life,
> the field of immigration represents . . . a "strategic research site" (SRS)—an area where
> processes of more general import are manifested with unusual clarity.[14]

If earlier attempts at economic sociology collapsed owing to a lack of empirical evidence, this newer endeavor will suffer no such fate so long as the ongoing "event" of new immigration continues to fuel it.

THE ASIAN IMMIGRANT CULTURE OF POVERTY

The Asian immigrant culture of poverty is perhaps best described by Alejandro Portes and Min Zhou in their 1992 essay, "Gaining the Upper Hand: Economic Mobility among Immigrants and Domestic Minorities," which explores the ways in which newly arrived immigrants from Latin America, the Caribbean, and Asia have defied the odds and found employment and economic stability in the postindustrial city. According to Portes and Zhou, these immigrants have avoided poverty neither by assimilating into the American mainstream and increasing their human capital (marketable skills, knowledge of English) nor by matching their skills with the high-tech industries of the postindustrial city. Rather, these immigrants have succeeded by creating their own labor-market match through self-employment and the building of the ethnic enterprise. This self-generated match, according to the authors, is the result of the embeddedness of bounded solidarity and enforceable trust, which are *particular* to the immigrant experience. *Bounded solidarity* refers to the process whereby immigrants, realizing that they are phenotypically and culturally different, develop a greater sense of solidarity with coethnics within the U.S. nation-state. For Portes and Zhou, this heightened nationalism has direct consequences for the success of the ethnic enterprise: "As consumers, immigrants manifest a consistent preference for items associated with the country of origin. . . . As workers, they often prefer to work among 'their own,' interacting in their native language even if it means sacrificing some material benefit."[15] Bounded solidarity is in turn accompanied by an enforceable trust whereby the immigrant, fearing expulsion from the psychologically safe and materially beneficial circle of (national) solidarity, engages in self-regulating acts that preclude double-dealing and that ensure the carrying out of one's word. Enforceable trust may therefore be used to explain why immigrants so readily entrust their savings in informal "rotating credit associations," which allow them to bypass the highly selective bank loan, or why the immigrant finds the "spoken agreement" to be greater insurance than the legal contract.

Portes and Zhou acknowledge that a theory of immigrant solidarity and enforceable trust begs the inevitable question: "Why don't blacks and other 'domestic minorities' develop similar economic and social practices?" Indeed, how is it that the immigrant avoids dead-end jobs in the primary labor market while the "domestic minorities"—namely blacks, Mexican Americans, and Puerto Ricans—continue to languish in unemployment and concentrated ghetto poverty? To answer this question, the authors abandon all empiricism and engage in a sweeping set of cultural and pathological assumptions about the behaviors of the "acculturated" minority, particularly the black urban poor. According to Portes and Zhou, a "thorough process of acculturation among U.S.-born members [of the black community] . . . has led to a gradual weakening of their sense of community and to a re-orientation toward their values, expectations, and preferences." In the post-segregation period, the black middle class has fled the ghetto, leading to a loss of "vivid memories of a common past," and leaving behind concentrations of poor black areas that are economically disorganized and often self-loathing. Portes and Zhou claim that the absence of strong community ties among blacks leads to an "identification with mainstream values, including a disparaging evaluation of their own group."[16] To illustrate their point, the authors quote from an anonymous yet "noted" black community leader who draws on black-community self-loathing to explain the enigma of why black consumers refuse to buy from black business owners, why black children have low self-esteem, and, of course, why "black-on-black" violence persists.

Yet the full ideological power of this all too familiar discussion on the behaviors of the black urban poor is best illuminated when juxtaposed to the equal yet opposite behavior exhibited by the working-poor Asian immigrant. Take, for instance, Portes and Zhou's assertion that newly arrived Chinese immigrants who labor in Chinese-owned industries often subject themselves to low wages, long hours, and harsh conditions as part of their bounded solidarity:

> From the point of view of the workers . . . Chinese-owned businesses offer material and symbolic compensations that escape a gross account of benefits based exclusively on wages. . . . For many newly arrived immigrants, a tour of duty in low-paid menial work is part of the time-honored path toward family advancement and economic independence.[17]

The suggestion here is that the Chinese immigrant worker purposely engages in her own self-subjection and exploitation—a pathological claim in its own right. Yet this pathology somehow results in economic mobility as opposed to the deepening of poverty, violence, and hopelessness.

Here, then, are all the ingredients of a narrative about Asian America's own culture of poverty, a crucial piece of the broader postindustrial narrative. The ever-expanding segment of working-poor Asian immigrants is now thoroughly explained through a cultural discussion involving primordial kinship ties, sacrificing one's own economic interest for a broader capitalist ethic, and an almost insatiable desire to labor.

In the next section, I explore how the Asian immigrant culture of poverty has dominated our contemporary understanding of Southeast Asian immigrant life. Despite statistical evidence that draws striking parallels between Southeast Asian poverty and the type of poverty typically used to describe the underclass, I note how the Asian culture of poverty thesis works to quickly remove Southeast Asians from this decidedly black underclass status. Such a move not only renders Southeast Asians as the deserving poor, but simultaneously posits a theory of exceptionalism in an effort to neatly explain refugee poverty.

Southeast Asian Exceptionalism

In 1975, over 145,000 refugees were airlifted out of Vietnam, marking the beginning of nearly two decades of refugee flight from Vietnam, Cambodia, and Laos. Of those initial Vietnamese refugees, approximately 86,000 were sent directly to the United States, the majority of them being placed in makeshift camps at the notorious Camp Pendleton military base in southern California. Awaiting their arrival at Camp Pendleton was a team of researchers led by sociologist William T. Lui. Lui had been commissioned by the Asian American Mental Health Research Center to conduct interviews with refugees, documenting their recent flight and assessing their ability to adapt to a new society under such mental and physical duress.

Lui's study—which was eventually converted into a book titled *Transition to Nowhere: Vietnamese Refugees in America*—was the first in what would be a string of sociological and anthropological studies of refugee life that utilize the refugee's "own voice," in an attempt not to relate a historically situated and complex narrative of violent uprooting but to convey an ahistorical tale of American national recovery in the post-Vietnam era. Indeed, as one reads through *Transition to Nowhere*, what emerges is a nationalistic tale of American pluralism, packaged into a narrative of refugee arrival, adaptation, and assimilation.[18]

That the refugee ethnography has been used to tell a story of U.S. nationalist coherence during the last decade of the Cold War is not entirely surprising. Yet, in the post–Cold War era, the cultural significance of the refugee is not what it once was. With the rapid globalization of capitalism, particularly the establishment of U.S. corporate outposts in Vietnam, the Southeast Asian refugee no longer serves as a symbol of national reconciliation and the eventual "return" of Western-capitalist hegemony in Southeast Asia. This changing role of the refugee is made evident by recent state policies toward refugee assistance; over the past several years, virtually all Southeast Asian refugee relief and adaptation programs have been liquidated by state and federal legislatures. Meanwhile, unemployment and poverty figures continue to skyrocket in many Southeast Asian enclaves throughout the nation. A recent study conducted in the northwest Bronx—home to over 85 percent of New York City's Southeast Asian community—reveals a 65 percent unemployment rate in this community.[19] In California, newspaper headlines announce a new wave of Southeast Asian gang violence, as well as a rapid increase in the number of Southeast Asian prison inmates.[20] Finally, Southeast Asian women on welfare—along with hundreds of thousands of African Americans and Latinas—have been removed from welfare rolls and placed on indefinite workfare assignments.

How does the economic sociology of immigration deal with this particular form of Asian poverty, which seemingly cuts across the grain of the immigrant "culture of poverty" thesis? Indeed, here it would seem that Southeast Asian postindustrial life falls squarely under the sociological category of the underclass—indistinguishable from a black culture of poverty. It is here that the full rhetorical power of the "deserving poor" comes into play, rendering the closing of refugee exceptionalism irrelevant, and rescuing the Southeast Asian from the gate of the underclass.

READING SOUTHEAST ASIAN CRIME AND SEXUAL DEVIANCE

Rescuing Southeast Asian poverty has long been the project of sociologist Rubén Rumbaut, who, throughout the 1980s, published numerous studies on the adaptation of refugees. Rumbaut's work is particularly interesting for the ways in which it renders impossible an "Asian underclass" by engaging the very issues through which the black culture of poverty is constructed: juvenile crime, female sexuality and reproduction, and women in the welfare state.

In 1987, as director of the Indochinese Health and Adaptation Research Project (IHARP), Rumbaut and colleague Kenji Ima conducted a study of the development patterns of Southeast Asian youth titled *The Adaptation of Southeast Asian Refugee Youth: A Comparative Study*. From the onset, they had organized their research questions by presupposing the teleology of arrival, adaptation, and incorporation of these refugee youth in American society, coding or "scoring" this process by drawing on some key variables from the economic sociology of immigration, such as the number of enforceable kinship ties, the density of networks, the time of arrival in the United States, and the accumulation of human and social capital to match the primary labor market.[21] Rumbaut and Ima's promotion of this inevitable outcome has much to do with the context within which the authors conducted their study. Indeed, the authors were researching and writing during a time of heightened discussion of the jobless and welfare-dependent black underclass.[22] Recognizing that their own study would reveal Southeast Asian unemployment, welfare, and crime statistics that parallel, if not exceed, the statistical evidence found in the black underclass literature, Rumbaut and Ima begin their report by removing the discussion of Southeast Asian poverty from the underclass debate. In the introduction to their report, the authors offer the following prediction:

> While some may raise questions about the creation of a second generation of [Southeast Asian] welfare dependent populations, resembling some of the American underclass families with histories of two or more generations of welfare dependency, it is our feeling, shared with many social service providers, that most children of Southeast Asian refugees will enter gainful employment and avoid the welfare dependency syndrome. Assuming the validity of this projection, we wonder what kind of policies will not only insure this transition out of welfare but also create measures that will shorten the time from dependency to independence.[23]

As underclass proponents were writing of the decline of black youth (who were contracting the "welfare dependency syndrome" as if it were some kind of virus), Rumbaut and Ima were insisting on a different inevitability, one based on a "continuum of adaptive processes and outcomes." This early prediction would guide many of the study's later conclusions.

Some of the more interesting conclusions drawn from Rumbaut and Ima's report stem from their analysis of Southeast Asian juvenile crime. During the mid- to late 1980s, a wave of violent crime among Southeast Asian youth (both intra- and interracial) had peaked as Vietnamese gangs were spreading outward from their hub in Orange County, California, and as Khmer and Lao youth were creating new "Third World fronts" in the ongoing Bloods and Crips saga. All of this was taking place in a time when southern California gangsterism had reached new heights in the popular imagination, inspiring the public demand for more prisons, as well as fomenting what Mike Davis has termed a "blacklash" from the civil rights establishment.[24] Within this context, Southeast Asian youth would be rescued from the fire by quick enlistment into the immigrant culture of poverty. According to Rumbaut and Ima, Southeast Asian gang violence was merely a result of the occasional breakdown in the otherwise resilient networks that characterize Southeast Asian communities. Relying on an argument of refugee exceptionalism, the authors suggest that this rare breakdown in social and familial organization can be attributed to the psychological trauma that stems from war and refugee flight. Yet, the claim that Southeast Asian crime is the result of an *absence* of support networks and tightly knit extended family organizations is later contradicted by Rumbaut and Ima's assertion on the general importance of networks in the carrying-out of crime. According to the authors, Southeast Asian crime reflects a "more collective nature of . . . delinquency than that of other youths." "Refugee youth are more likely to be associated with gangs than are white or other minority serious offenders . . . reveal[ing] a striking 'compulsion' to associate with peers beyond what one expects of other youths."[25] Here, the immigrant culture of poverty is hardly absent; on the contrary, it remains a central element in the functioning of Asian crime. This paradox is especially pronounced within the Vietnamese community; at one point, Rumbaut and Ima go so far as to suggest that the social network pressures and expectations that push Vietnamese youth to excel in school are the very pressures and expectations that compel them to join gang networks. In the years following their study, Rumbaut and Ima's "paradox" would become a popular trope in the discussion of Southeast Asian gang life, prompting the *Los Angeles Times* to report on the unusual profile of Vietnamese gangsters who are at once "exceptionally intelligent and violent."[26]

Sociological discussions of Southeast Asian gang life focus almost exclusively on male juveniles, with virtually no mention of Southeast Asian women's participation in this paradoxical culture. Yet, as underclass discourses have made plainly clear, young women of color figure quite centrally in any culture of poverty thesis, particularly at the intersection of sexual deviance, fertility, and the welfare state. This fact is best illustrated by the introduction of workfare programs under the Family Security Act of 1988. While much has been written on the ways in which workfare serves the postindustrial logic of flexible accumulation—by forcing mothers on welfare to work part-time, below the minimum wage, and with no benefits at formerly unionized jobs—there is little discussion of workfare as a means of policing and punishing the "sexually deviant welfare queen." During the late 1980s, the debate surrounding FSA centered largely on the racist myth of the young, single black mother whose high fertility rate was attributed to her desire to extract more funds from the welfare state. Workfare, it was reasoned, would act as a deterrent to such criminal mischief.[27]

In the context of this prevailing discussion (and legislative implications) of the deviant sexuality and fertility of black women in the welfare state, Rumbaut and John Weeks, another IHARP colleague, set out to explain the extremely high fertility rates among Southeast Asian women on welfare. Much like Rumbaut's treatment of Southeast Asian juvenile crime, his discussion of Southeast Asian fertility attempts to distance the refugee from the underclass welfare recipient.

In their 1988 essay, "Fertility and Adaptation: Indochinese Refugees in the United States," Rumbaut and Weeks advance a number of explanations for the high fertility rate among Southeast Asian refugee women on welfare. Primary among these explanations is the desire for Southeast Asian families to "make up" for the children they lost during the course of civil war and refugee flight, particularly from Pol Pot's regime in Cambodia. With little ethnographic evidence to support this claim, however, Rumbaut and Weeks turn to the more accessible culturalisms provided by the economic sociology of immigration. They stress the ways in which childbearing is a means of strengthening and extending networks of labor and capital for the refugee family. But this explanation does not match statistical evidence that reveals that many Southeast Asians do not participate in small enterprises of the ethnic economy that require an extended network of labor.[28] Finally, Rumbaut and Weeks claim that high levels of Southeast Asian fertility are merely the result of rural culturalisms that have yet to go away.[29] Here again they present us with another exceptional circumstance, one that the refugee will no doubt overcome through economic adaptation to the capitalist democracy and through closer ties to Anglocultural family norms. In short, a lower fertility rate is only a matter of time.

Rumbaut and Weeks's theory of high fertility as "cultural retention," as well as their assurance of eventual "behavioral changes" through assimilation, serves to disengage the Southeast Asian immigrant from the pathologies that characterize the black underclass. Indeed, they ignore the fact that many of the Southeast Asian women on welfare are not members of the first generation who came of age in rural Asia. Rather, they are younger women who, much like their black and Latina counterparts, have been "acculturated" into capitalist democracy by way of violent state policies and postindustrial joblessness. By removing the young Southeast Asian welfare recipient from this particular setting, the sociological images of immigrant life work to consolidate the racial project of welfare reform, which demands that the color of sexual deviance remain unequivocally black.

Finally, by reducing Asian immigrant poverty to a narrative of developmental phases in refugee adjustment, Rumbaut's work ignores the role that the state and private capital play in the expansion of low-wage labor and, consequently, the creation of urban poverty. As I shall later explore, Southeast Asians living in the Bronx are today, nearly twenty years after their arrival in the United States, entering into low-wage factory work; this shift is a direct consequence of the state's failure to protect the minimum wage, labor standards, and health and safety provisions in the broader labor market. It has little, if anything, to do with phases of immigration.

READING WELFARE

In the aftermath of the Los Angeles insurrection of 1992, virtually every sector of the nation had some theory to offer on the question of race, poverty, and the postindustrial city. Solutions ranged from the corporate-driven "Rebuild L.A." (RLA) to the resurrection of the Black Panther Party platform for self-determi- nation (reissued by the Los Angeles Crips). Notwithstanding this range of opin- ions, most commentators acknowledged that the core issue at hand was black and brown joblessness. For political thinkers and policy makers within the Asian American community, the exclusive focus on the jobless poor posed quite a challenge; indeed, to discuss Asian American poverty in the post-insurrection period, one needed to delve into the world of the *working*-poor immigrant— the overworked garment sweatshop laborer, the restaurant worker, the impov- erished small entrepreneur.

Taking up this task was an emerging Los Angeles–based policy group known as Leadership Education among Asian Pacifics (LEAP). Working in partnership with the UCLA Asian American Studies Center, LEAP published several studies on a growing Asian immigrant poverty—a poverty bounded by the social net- works and self-disciplining order of the ethnic enclave.[30] Incorporating many of the key formulations of the economic sociology of immigration, these studies sought to provide an Asian "cut" on the question of race and postindustrial poverty: the story of working-poor immigrants who, despite their seeming self- reliance and full-time employment, were nonetheless languishing in a state of poverty. But this explanatory model for the new Asian poverty could not ignore the ever-growing segment of jobless poor Asian immigrants, particularly among Southeast Asians who subsisted on the welfare state. Certainly, this segment posed quite a dilemma to the report's core thesis of the working poor.

Here Rumbaut's evacuation of the Southeast Asian from the gate of the black underclass would prove quite useful. According to Rumbaut and Ima, "in assessing the prospects for economic self-sufficiency even of those [who] remain dependent on public assistance, we would ask the question 'when' not 'if' they will leave the welfare system."[31] This prediction is reinforced by LEAP contributors Paul Ong and Evelyn Blumenberg in their important essay, "Welfare and Work among Southeast Asians." According to Ong and Blumenberg, Southeast Asians on welfare are unlike "other groups." The authors mark these differences by making note of the way in which Southeast Asians maintain nuclear family structures despite their welfare status, and by pointing to their uncanny work ethic—even in a state of joblessness.[32] For Ong and Blumenberg, evidence that the Southeast Asian welfare recipient will evade underclass life can be found in their desire to maintain two-parent nuclear families. In an age when most women on welfare remain single in an effort to subsist in the welfare state for an indefinite period, maintenance of the Southeast Asian nuclear family structure points to the desire of refugees to eventually leave welfare and become self-sufficient, as nuclear families are conducive to the economic success of the small ethnic enterprise. In addition, Ong and Blumenberg point to the extremely high percentage of Southeast Asians who actively seek work while living on welfare. Citing California statewide statistics, the authors shows that 68 percent of Asians on welfare actively applied for work over a one-year period; this figure stands in sharp distinction to the 53 percent shown by Latinos and 30 percent for blacks.

Ong and Blumenberg's predicted outcomes for Southeast Asian welfare usage can be misleading for several reasons. First, the marital status of virtually all Southeast Asians in the United States who entered the country as refugees is already documented by federal refugee programs and the Immigration and Naturalization Service. Because refugee programs prioritized the resettlement of nuclear families, Southeast Asians reported two-parent households in an effort to survive the welfare system—an equal yet opposite strategy used by the single mother. If nuclear families point to the uniqueness of Southeast Asian welfare life, then we must attribute this rarity to the pressures exerted by state regulations on refugee resettlement. This is supported by the fact that those refugees who have either been reclassified as permanent residents or granted citizenship are now attempting to report single-parent homes. In a similar vein, the authors overlook the fact that local refugee assistance agencies, in accordance with federal funding guidelines, are often *required* to process job applications for refugees. Oftentimes, this is a matter of caseworkers submitting a quota number of job applications for Southeast Asian clients. Rarely are these applications responded to by employers; as Ong and Blumenberg themselves note, "refugees who used the service were employed at approximately the same level as those who did not."[33]

But Ong and Blumenberg's analysis is most problematic because it implicitly reinforces the culture of poverty discourse that pathologizes the behaviors and desires of the black urban poor. Their argument promotes the unique potential for Southeast Asian economic adaptation by implying that the desire to develop nuclear families and to find work while receiving welfare is greater among Southeast Asians than among blacks (and, with some variation, Latinos). In their effort to promote Southeast Asians as the deserving poor, they overlook the myriad and complex ways in which poor blacks, particularly black women, "work" the welfare state. As sociologist Kathryn Edin points out, black women who receive welfare are constantly laboring both within and outside the welfare system in an effort to maintain their families. Contradicting the popular belief that welfare makes recipients lazy and unmotivated, Edin reveals how it actually compels women to find additional work by failing to provide enough funding for basic survival. In her interviews with over fifty welfare recipients, Edin found that each of her informants was either working in "off-the-book" jobs, negotiating income from absentee fathers and boyfriends, or soliciting donations from churches and community agencies. Some recipients engaged in the underground economy; this work ranged from doing a neighbor's laundry, to selling small amounts of drugs, to selling sex.[34] In the process of demonstrating how welfare-state policies and practices create work for the urban poor, Edin's study also challenges dominant culture of poverty theories. Indeed, by implicating the state, she refuses to reduce the social practices of black women to a set of individualized behaviors or culturalisms; from here an alternative rendering of the cultures of the poor might emerge.

THE CULTURE OF POVERTY TRANSFORMED

Challenging the "behavior-as-culture" model should not discourage us from engaging *culture* entirely, nor should it lead us to a counteranalysis where the preferences, pleasures, and desires of the poor are cast aside as arbitrary, relative, and, hence, irrelevant. Indeed, rendering an alternative to the culture of poverty scholarship discussed throughout this essay is not a matter of avoiding the pitfalls of a cultural discussion; to the contrary, it involves a fuller engagement with cultural practices and the ways in which they are read and interpreted.

The cultural alternatives in Edin's study can be found in her interviews with women on welfare who "sell" sex in order to secure supplemental income. Prostitution can easily function as the incontrovertible evidence of a "damaged" black urban culture, as well as justification for extending a long history of policing black women's sexuality.[35] Yet this obvious conclusion is challenged by one of Edin's informants, who suggests an alternative meaning to the practice of exchanging sex for material resources. According to this informant:

> I also think a lot of people have affairs with guys who will pay some of their bills. It's like a more legitimate prostitution. There is not really an exchange of money for services. It's more a social thing. You are sleeping with this person, and in return he is taking care of a few things for you.[36]

While the sociological narratives discussed in this essay would characterize this informant as either the typical sexual deviant or the ultimate victim of poverty driven to desperation, Edin reveals a subject who speaks at once about self-identification, economic needs, pleasure, and social networking. While Edin's informant is indeed exchanging sex for material resources, and while another informant claimed that she would only engage the trade when all other resources have been exhausted, rendering an *alternative* cultural discussion of her actions requires that we read beyond the obvious economic motives. At stake for Edin's informant is the construction of an identity that does not adhere to dominant notions of legitimate and illegitimate sex; that collapses the boundaries between choosing a safe community network and a safe sexual partner; and that signifies that sex is never void of materiality. Finally, we must take into account the informant's sexual desire. Here, I return to Robin Kelley, who asserts the importance of sexual desire in his discussion of the aesthetics and pleasures derived from the income-generating activities of "jobless" black urban youth. According to Kelley, discussions of heterosexual prostitution invariably neglect female desire—in effect, the sexual act itself. While Kelley acknowledges the violent, exploitative, and power-laden dynamics that often accompany prostitution, he nonetheless cautions against "stripping women of any agency or removing . . . the issue of female desire":

> While prostitution offers women a means of income, we must consider the extent to which anonymous sex is a source of pleasure. Furthermore, in light of the ways in which black women's sexual expression has been constrained historically, black women's involvement in the pleasure industry might be seen as both typical and transgressive. Typical in that black women's bodies have historically been exploited as sites of male pleasure and embodiments of lasciviousness; transgressive in that women were able to break with the straightjacket of what historian Evelyn Brooks Higgenbotham calls the "politics of respectability" in exchange for the politics of pleasure.[37]

There is indeed a "culture of poverty" to be read here. Yet this culture is not a set of pathological behaviors passed from generation to generation, nor is it merely a response to economic hardship or the denial of opportunity.

This alternative reading of culture provides an opportunity to challenge the immigrant culture of poverty thesis and, in the process, to reinterpret the daily practices of the Southeast Asian poor. In an effort to render such an alternative reading, I rely on examples drawn from my shared experiences and conversations with Vietnamese and Cambodian community members of the northwest Bronx. The northwest Bronx is home to over 20,000 Vietnamese and Cambodian immigrants who were resettled to the area either under state programs (often administered through religious organizations) or through the act of "secondary migration"—when immigrant families take it upon themselves to relocate from original areas of resettlement.[38] At first glance, however, secondary migration to the Bronx may seem a rather puzzling phenomenon. Unlike Lowell, Massachusetts, home to the second-largest Cambodian community in the country (90 percent of whom are secondary migrants), the Bronx has never offered the promise of living-wage industrial jobs. Nor does the Bronx even slightly resemble rural cities, such as Stockton, California, or the gulf cities of Texas, where refugees have a minimal chance of applying their agricultural and fishing skills, respectively.[39] In contrast to these other areas of opportunity, the Bronx maintains some of New York's highest unemployment and welfare-dependency rates while suffering from a complete absence of a formal manufacturing base. Yet, within this context, the Southeast Asian community of the Bronx expanded.

Approximately 75 percent of the Southeast Asian community of the Bronx is receiving some form of public assistance. However, much like the subjects of Edin's study, the vast majority of these welfare recipients engage in informal trades to supplement welfare benefits that invariably fall far short of meeting basic needs. Some of the more popular informal trades include food vending in local parks, small-stakes gambling, and finding off-the-books work in the downgraded manufacturing firms of New Jersey.

Apsara, a Cambodian mother of three, earns approximately $300 per week selling food in Devoe Park, a popular hangout for Southeast Asian families. Food sales have been the primary source of her family's income, especially since her public assistance benefits were severely reduced under PRWORA. "Without the park, it would be very bad for us," Apsara remarks. "We can't do anything with the welfare, so we come to the park." The food is set up on several straw mats located at the northern corner of the lawn. Because the women who sell food in the park do not have city-issued vendor licenses, they are vulnerable to police raids and confiscation. As such, they try their best to make the vending spots appear like large picnic areas. As one woman recalled, "Last year the police came [into] the park and took everything. . . . They kicked [around] all our supplies and threw [some supplies] in the truck . . . and then they took all our money." Following this police raid, vending activities were temporarily halted. Before long, however, the women vendors slowly reconquered the northern lawn; today they carry on with their food sales—albeit, with greater discretion.

Under prevailing culture of poverty theories, the persistence exhibited by these women would be analyzed through one of two behavioral assumptions: either the underclass's propensity to make a profit through petty vice, or the Asian immigrant's uncanny ability to turn any situation into a small business. But according to Chhaya, a twenty-year-old Cambodian woman, the illicit selling of food in Devoe Park fulfills a range of needs and desires that culture of poverty theories cannot account for:

> The women are here to make some money, but I don't think it's just about that. When you think about it, there's no other place where they can go to support each other. I know that a lot of the women come here to talk about what's going on with them. Some women will talk about abusive husbands and other trouble they're having. Selling food gives them a chance to just come outside.

The parks function as one of the few locations where Southeast Asian women can create a space of their own. Although economic needs are certainly being met, the significance of the park lies in its ability to serve as an alternative to confining and often abusive private spheres. For one woman, the park functions as a space for women to build community consensus against shiftless husbands: "He likes [that I] make money . . . but he's afraid that I will talk . . . so he never comes here to show his face." In the process of challenging patriarchal domination, the women vendors have also found opportunities to overcome divisive nationalisms. Indeed, Devoe Park is one of the few areas where Vietnamese and Cambodian residents openly socialize. As Chhaya notes, "At the [apartment] buildings, most of these people won't even look at each other . . . but in the park it's a different story. They even learn each other's language in the park. They learn a couple of important words, and they can have a long conversation."

In addition to food sales, Devoe Park provides another form of economic opportunity: small-stakes gambling. To be sure, those who purchase food from the women vendors invariably stick around to try their luck at a number of gambling mats set up around the park. Gambling has functioned as a long-standing trope in the ethnographic study of the male-dominated Asian immigrant ghetto, particularly the Chinatown "bachelor society." Indeed, if studies on the Chinese immigrant community have ever come close to resembling the underclass literature, it has been through the discussion of gambling and its accompanying social problems: addiction, desperation, broken families, and gangs. But the gambling scene at Devoe Park tells quite a different story. According to Phalla, a young factory worker, gambling sessions at the park involve a wide range of community members: "I see everybody here . . . the old ladies, the young guys, the people with money, and the people who don't have a dime." For each of these participants, gambling fulfills a number of needs and desires. In Phalla's case, gambling represents his time away from the long months at the factory:

> When I gamble . . . that's all that I'm doing. I'll take turns. For three months I'll be at the factory and save money. And then I'll quit the factory, and for the next three months, I'll just use my gambling skills. You can't "O.D." [overdose] on just one thing.

Here gambling functions not only as a coping strategy in the face of hard factory labor but also as an opportunity to demonstrate and take pride in a set of skills. This desire is quite distinct from the narratives of escapism, desperation, and hopelessness that emerge in contemporary studies of Chinatown and the effects of gambling on the Chinese working class.[40]

Phalla's desire to showcase gambling skills while dropping factory work entirely can be interpreted as a desire to create an alternative identity when confronted with limited options. For many young Southeast Asian men, factory work in downgraded manufacturing firms is the only option for those looking to supplement the family welfare check.[41] According to Samlath, another young factory worker, Southeast Asians have two choices: going to school or going to the factory.

> You can't do "nothing" with yourself. The community expects you to go to school or go to New Jersey [where the factories are located]. Nobody likes to work at the factory. . . . a lot of these guys won't come back after the first try. But if they're not in school, they need to work. Otherwise the community thinks you're worthless. It's important for them to just say to people, "I've been to the factory."

Samlath's utterance of a "need to work" does not register as a purely economic need, nor does it reflect the mythology of a time-honored tradition of hard work among Asians—as the immigrant culture of poverty literature would suggest. Rather, this need refers to a desire for social affirmation and identity in a community suffering the impact of postindustrial joblessness. This identity is not so much about hard work as it is about merely going to work. Indeed, once arriving at the job site, the degree to which one actually engages in hard work is questionable. According to Phalla, "There are a lot of hard workers. Asians are hard workers. But a lot of times I won't do the things they ask me to do. Like if a box is too heavy, I won't touch it. And sometimes I'll just walk around all day, talking to people [and] looking like I'm busy. Or maybe I'll just hide behind a wall of boxes and fall asleep." For Phalla, any proletarian identity is far too limiting; therefore, gambling is viewed as an opportunity to render an alternative identity, one with its own set of rules and codes of behavior:

> Yeah, you can make some money . . . and sometimes you win enough to pay the whole rent. But winning money is not everything to us. It's about proving something to yourself and to the other gamblers. You have to prove that win or lose you can walk away happy—that you got a thrill. And that's what this is about. People are here to have fun. If it becomes more than that, then you really can't show your face around here.

Among the Southeast Asians who frequent Devoe Park, there is indeed a culture of the poor. This culture, however, is not based on sedimented behaviors, traditions, or purely economic strategies of survival. Rather, Devoe Park presents us with a wide range of needs and desires: the need to communicate, the desire to create alternative identities, the desire for a mere "thrill." These elements provide the raw materials for a fuller understanding of the cultural and social practices of the poor in postindustrial America. As Chandra Mohanty suggests in her study of Third World women workers, the basis of action among the poor and disenfranchised cannot be reduced to "common interests" in formal economic terms; rather, it must be based on the "deeper, more fundamental question of understanding and organizing around needs, desires, and choices"; indeed, they provide a "transformative dimension" that is lacking in "common interests."[42] Thus, if we are to seriously consider a broad, counterhegemonic challenge to the war against the poor—exemplified by the collapse of the welfare state—then we must begin by taking into account the way in which these needs and desires are constructed and played out.

NOTES

Many thanks to Jane Bai and Andrew Ross for their careful editing and critical commentary. Cathy Cohen, Michael Omi, and George Lipsitz provided much needed criticism to keep the thought process going. Finally, special thanks to Aijen Poo, Hyun Lee, Johnn Tan, and all the youth organizers at CAAAV for their inspirational leadership.

1. For a full reading of PRWORA see Public Law 104–193, 104th Cong., 2d sess. (22 August 1996).

2. Most AFDC recipients have already been switched to a downgraded program called Temporary Aid to Needy Families (TANF). Under PRWORA, TANF eligibility cannot exceed a total of five years for the rest of the recipient's life, beginning on 22 August 1997.

3. Paul Ong and Evelyn Blumenberg, "Welfare and Work among Southeast Asians," in *The State of Asian Pacific America: Policy Issues to the Year 2020,* ed. Don Nakanishi (Los Angeles: Leadership Education for Asian Pacifies [LEAP] and UCLA Asian American Studies Center, 1993), 113.

4. Ngoan Le, "Policy for a Community 'At-Risk,'" in *The State of Asian Pacific America,* 177.

5. For the range of underclass depictions see Ken Auletta's inaugurating study, *The Underclass* (New York: Random House, 1982); Dinesh D'Souza's neoconservative culturalist account, *The End of Racism: Principles for a Multiracial Society* (New York: Free Press, 1995); and William Julius Wilson's liberal-structuralist study, *The Truly Disadvantaged: The Inner City, the Underclass, and Public Policy* (Chicago: University of Chicago Press, 1987).

6. Robin D. G. Kelley, *Yo' Mama's Dysfunktional! Fighting the Culture Wars in Urban America* (Boston: Beacon, 1997), 18.

7. See Oscar Lewis, *The Children of Sanchez* (New York: Random House, 1961); *La Vida: A Puerto Rican Family in the Culture of Poverty, San Juan and New York* (New York: Random House, 1966).

8. Michael B. Katz, "The Urban Underclass as a Metaphor of Social Transformation," in *The Underclass Debate: Views from History,* ed. Michael B. Katz (Princeton, N.J.: Princeton University Press, 1993), 13.

9. Michael Omi and Howard Winant, *Racial Formation in the United States* (New York: Routledge, 1994).

10. Introduced by Senator Daniel Patrick Moynihan, FSA was the first congressional bill requiring that welfare recipients participate in welfare-to-work programs in exchange for the monthly benefits. These programs, also known as "workfare," force the welfare recipient to work for wages far below the minimum wage. The new policing measures introduced by FSA include fingerprinting and random home inspections.

11. For example, see the following articles from several popular ethnic periodicals: Karen Narasaki, "Welfare and Wedge Politics," *Asia Week,* 24 November 1995, 7; "A Contract with Asian America," *A Magazine,* 31 March 1995, 14; Elenor Tataem, "Welfare Cuts Seen as Repressive and Detrimental to Poor Women and Children," *Amsterdam News,* 18 February 1995, 5. While all these articles take a stand against PRWORA, they do so without acknowledging the bill's broader impact against all racial groups. For the Asian American periodicals in particular, opposition to PRWORA and the defense of the immigrant poor is ensconced in a language of eventual immigrant adaptation and incorporation. In other words, providing immigrants with public assistance is a matter of long-term economic investment on behalf of policy makers. Scripting this immigrant defense requires that Asian American political advocates decouple immigrant assistance from the "more wasteful" programs—namely, those that fund nonimmigrant groups for more than one generation. As such, these Asian American critiques of PRWORA fail to give any mention of the bill's long-term impact on African Americans, who comprised over 35 percent of all AFDC recipients.

12. Mark Grannovetter, "The Old and the New Economic Sociology: A History and an Agenda," in *Beyond Marketplace: Rethinking Economy and Sociology* (New York: Aldine de Gruyter, 1990), 89.

13. See Ivan Light and Stavros Karageorgis, "The Ethnic Economy," in *The Handbook of Economic Sociology,* ed. Neil J. Smesler and Richard Swedberg (Princeton, N.J.: Princeton University Press, 1994), 647.

14. Alejandro Portes, "Economic Sociology and the Sociology of Immigration: A Conceptual Overview," in *The Economic Sociology of Immigration: Essays on Networks, Ethnicity, and Entrepreneurship,* ed. Alejandro Portes (New York: Russell Sage Foundation, 1995), 2.

15. Alejandro Portes and Min Zhou, "Gaining the Upper Hand: Economic Mobility among Immigrants and Domestic Minorities," *Ethnic and Racial Studies* 15 (fall 1992): 514.

16. Ibid., 516.

17. Ibid., 510.

18. William T. Lui, *Transition to Nowhere: Vietnamese Refugees in America* (Nashville, Tenn.: Charter House, 1979). So influential was Lui's narrative that it became, in Monique Troung's account, an origin text for Southeast Asian literature. See Monique Thuy-Dung Troung, "The Emergence of Voices: Vietnamese American Literature, 1975–1990," *Amerasia Journal* 19, no. 3 (1993): 30. Key ethnographic works that replicated the narrative form of Lui's book include James Freeman, *Hearts of Sorrow: Vietnamese American Lives* (Stanford, Calif.: Stanford University Press, 1989); and Usha Welaratna, *Beyond the Killing Fields: Voices of Nine Cambodian Survivors in America* (Stanford, Calif.: Stanford University Press, 1993).

19. This Southeast Asian Community Survey was conducted by the Committee against Anti-Asian Violence (CAAAV) from December 1997 through June 1998. It involved a random sample of approximately two hundred Southeast Asian families living in the Fordham-Bedford section of the Bronx. In addition to this extremely high unemployment rate, the survey also revealed that nearly 70 percent of the Southeast Asian residents were receiving some form of public assistance. Ninety percent of those receiving public assistance had their benefits either reduced or completely stripped with the passage of PRWORA.

20. See Duke Hefland, "A Tenuous Peace Moves into Some Gang Areas," *Los Angeles Times,* 21 October 1994.

21. Rubén Rumbaut and Kenji Ima, *The Adaptation of Southeast Asian Refugee Youth: A Comparative Study* (San Diego, Calif.: Department of Sociology, San Diego State University, 1987), 5. Rumbaut's numerous other studies of Southeast Asian refugee adaptation include "Portraits, Patterns, and Predictors of the Refugee Adaptation Process," in *Southeast Asian Refugees in the United States,* ed. David Haines (Totowa, N.J.: Rowman and Littlefield, 1988); "Mental Health and the Refugee Experience: A Comparative Study," in *Southeast Asian Mental Health,* ed. Tom C. Owan (Rockville, Md.: National Institute of Mental Health, 1985), 433–86; and with John R. Weeks, "Fertility and Adaptation: Indochinese Refugees in the United States," *International Migration Review* 20 (summer 1986): 428–66.

22. A good deal of the contemporary underclass canon was published during the mid- to late 1980s. They include the following texts already cited: Auletta, *The Underclass,* and Wilson, *The Truly Disadvantaged.* Other canonical texts include Charles Murray, *Losing Ground: American Social Policy: 1950–1980* (New York: Basic, 1984); and Nicholas Lemann, "The Origins of the Underclass: Part I," *Atlantic Monthly,* June 1986, 31–61; and "The Origins of the Underclass: Part II," *Atlantic Monthly,* July 1986, 54–68.

23. Rumbaut and Ima, *The Adaptation of Southeast Asian Refugee Youth,* 4.

24. See Mike Davis, *City of Quartz: Excavating the Future in Los Angeles* (New York: Vintage, 1990), 269–300.

25. Rumbaut and Ima, *The Adaptation of Southeast Asian Refugee Youth,* 65.

26. See K. Connie Kang, "Asian Gang Rise Strikes a Paradox," *Los Angeles Times,* 25 January 1996.

27. See Teresa Amott, "Black Women and AFDC: Making Entitlement Out of Necessity," in *Women, the State, and Welfare,* ed. Linda Gordon (Madison: University of Wisconsin Press, 1990), 280–94.

28. See David Haines, "Patterns in Southeast Asian Refugee Employment," *Ethnic Groups* 7 (1987): 39–63.

29. Rumbaut and Weeks, "Fertility and Adaptation," 455.

30. These studies include *The State of Asian Pacific America: Reframing the Immigration Debate* (Los Angeles: UCLA Asian American Studies Center, 1996); and *Beyond Asian American Poverty* (Los Angeles: LEAP Asian Pacific American Policy Institute, 1993).

31. Rumbaut and Ima, *The Adaptation of Southeast Asian Refugee Youth,* 122.

32. Paul Ong and Evelyn Blumenberg, "Welfare and Work among Southeast Asians," in *The State of Asian Pacific America,* 123.

33. Ibid., 125.
34. Kathryn Edin, "Surviving the Welfare System: How AFDC Recipients Make Ends Meet in Chicago," *Social Problems* 38 (November 1991): 462–74.
35. See Hazel Carby, "Policing the Black Woman's Body in an Urban Context," *Critical Inquiry* 18 (summer 1992): 738–55.
36. Edin, "Surviving the Welfare System," 469.
37. Kelley, *Yo' Mama's Dysfunktional!* 73.
38. This latter strategy, while often driven by economic motives, is also a challenge to refugee resettlement programs that sought to prevent the formation of Southeast Asian enclaves by scattering refugee families throughout various regions of the county.
39. For a history of secondary migration to Lowell, Massachusetts, see Peter Kiang, "When Know-Nothings Speak English Only," in *The State of Asian America*, ed. Karin Aguilar-San Juan (Boston: South End, 1994), 125–45. Although Stockton, California, has provided some opportunities in agriculture for Southeast Asian secondary migrants, the vast majority of Southeast Asians in this city remain unemployed. See Shiori Ui, "Unlikely Heroes: The Evolution of Female Leadership in a Cambodian Ethnic Enclave," in *Ethnography Unbound*, ed. Michael Burawoy (Berkeley: University of California Press, 1991), 161–77.
40. See, for example, Peter Kwong, *The New Chinatown* (New York: Hill and Wang, 1987), 69.
41. According to Saskia Sassen, the rapid deindustrialization of U.S. cities and the concomitant rise of "global cities" such as New York should not lead us to conclude that manufacturing work has been completely vanquished. On the contrary, global cities—cities wherein the leading industries are those that serve as "command points" for global capitalism—actually feed the expansion of downgraded, informal, and flexible manufacturing. These leading industries cause greater income and class polarization within the broader labor market, thus shrinking the middle sectors of the economy that once functioned to stabilize manufacturing. But this polarization has not completely driven manufacturing out of the U.S. city; rather, it has driven it underground. Hundreds of nonstandardized manufacturing firms currently proliferate in the New York metropolitan area; these firms hire a predominantly immigrant workforce (including minors) that is paid entirely off the books, provided absolutely no benefits, and often compelled to work twelve-hour shifts. For several hundred Southeast Asian residents of the Bronx, the vast majority of whom receive welfare, these firms have become the primary source of supplemental income. See Saskia Sassen, *The Global City* (Princeton, N.J.: Princeton University Press, 1991), 245–317.
42. Chandra Mohanty, "Women Workers and Capitalist Scripts," in *Feminist Genealogies, Colonial Legacies, Democratic Futures,* ed. Chandra Mohanty and Jacqui Alexander (New York: Routledge, 1997), 23.

four:
Pedagogies
and Possibilities

WHITHER ASIAN AMERICAN STUDIES?

Sucheng Chan

Beginning in the late 1980s in the wake of a second round of student activism, new Asian American studies programs started appearing at colleges and universities around the country. By the 2000s, a number of old as well as new programs had become autonomous departments that enjoy the right to hire their own faculty, which means they no longer have to secure joint appointments in other departments for appointees. Once again, students who were determined to have Asian American studies by any means necessary were the motive force that enabled the field to grow.

Though administrators and faculty review committees still resisted setting up such programs, their resistance in the 1990s was milder compared to the intransigence that characterized the late 1960s to the late 1980s. By the 1990s, Asian American students had become a demographic force in many universities, so their concerns could not be ignored. Some administrators had also learned hard lessons about the consequences of turning down the students' requests out of hand.

This relatively more hospitable environment, however, does not mean that the field no longer has problems, because it does. In this chapter, I discuss two interrelated challenges that I believe the field must meet now and in years to come if it hopes to remain a distinctive enterprise on American campuses. First, there is still no graduate program anywhere in the country that systematically trains future faculty members to teach Asian American studies, although there are several Ph.D. programs in comparative ethnic studies. The professional pathways that incoming faculty have followed to date have been diverse—indeed, one might say, haphazard. Second, there are many disagreements over how the field should be conceptualized in this age of transnationalism and globalization and what its goals should be. In particular, should its political legacy be erased or discarded?

These issues are hard to deal with because they embody contradictions that revolve around struggles for power and dominance. That is why the answers to "Whither Asian American Studies?" will depend a great deal on how these differences are played out.

Although the existence of different viewpoints can lead to creative innovations, the underlying struggles for power can also, sadly, cause the field to self-destruct.

A superficial look at Asian American studies today indicates that we have made considerable progress. Since the early 1990s, professional associations in various disciplines have included panels on Asian American topics in their annual conferences. Scholars in the field have given talks all over the country. A few senior faculty members have played a power broker's role on campuses other than their own, helping to negotiate political settlements to student unrest. More faculty positions opened up in the 1990s than in the 1970s and 1980s combined. At least half a dozen academic presses now publish book series on Asian Americans. Hundreds of people attend the annual meetings of the Association for Asian American Studies, presenting papers on a wide range of topics, some of which espouse theoretical frameworks that the field's founders could never have imagined. However, even though these developments seem to indicate that the field has finally "arrived," we cannot rest on our laurels. Despite our new visibility and vigor, we continue to exist on contested terrain. And the contestation today is not only between us and the university but also among ourselves.

One urgent problem facing the field is the absence of graduate programs that specifically train future faculty members to teach Asian American studies. To gain some insight into the academic trajectories that the present faculty members in a great variety of institutional settings have followed, I conducted a survey on behalf of the Curriculum Committee of the Department of Asian American Studies at UC Santa Barbara in January 1999. I sent questionnaires to 304 faculty listed in the 1998 directory of the Association for Asian American Studies. Seventy-five responses drifted in over a six-month period. Even though the response rate was low (only 24.6 percent), still, the survey results offer a rough indication of what kind of people compose the Asian American studies professorate and how they got there.

The survey collected five kinds of information: the respondents' academic training and present institutional locations, the relative importance of various factors that entered into their decisions to teach Asian American studies, what activities have been most useful in preparing them to teach Asian American studies, what preparations did they *wish* they had but did not, and what kind of graduate degree program they thought most marketable in today's job market. The respondents included tenured and not-yet-tenured full-time faculty as well as part-time lecturers. Some of the latter had not yet completed their Ph.D.s at the time they responded to the survey.

Among the seventy-five respondents, the largest number, fourteen, are historians. They are followed by twelve sociologists, ten literary scholars, six scholars with Ph.D.s in ethnic studies, and five psychologists. The rest are in American studies, anthropology, art, economics, education, folklore, geography, law, mathematics, music, Pacific Islands studies, philosophy, political science, rhetoric, South Asian studies, and urban planning. This broad array of fields does not mean that all of them offer courses in programs or departments explicitly named Asian American studies. Rather, the individuals who now teach one or more courses on Asian

Americans, for one reason or another, developed a sufficient commitment to the field to offer courses with Asian American content regardless of their own educational backgrounds or institutional locations.

Forty-one of the respondents are affiliated with only one program or department. Of these, sixteen teach solely in an ethnic studies or an Asian American studies program or department. Twenty-nine individuals have joint appointments, but only twenty-two in this group have joint appointments in units named "Asian American studies." That means only thirty-eight of the respondents have a formal affiliation with units called ethnic studies or Asian American studies. The rest teach courses that focus on Asian American groups, issues, or topics within the disciplinary units housing them.

The survey asked respondents to indicate the relative importance of various factors that had influenced their decisions to teach Asian American studies. The eleven possible factors were 1) I had taken undergraduate courses in Asian American studies; 2) I had taken graduate courses in or related to Asian American studies; 3) I had written a B.A. honors thesis or an M.A. thesis on an Asian American topic; 4) I had written a Ph.D. dissertation on an Asian American topic; 5) I had read books by or about Asian Americans; 6) my graduate advisor urged me to apply for Asian American studies jobs; 7) I had been active in Asian American issues on campus or in the community; 8) I had worked in one or more Asian American community organizations; 9) the best jobs available when I went on the job market were in Asian American studies; 10) I am an Asian American, so I have a personal interest in the field; and 11) I was responding to student interest and demand for Asian American studies on my campus. For each factor, respondents could check "extremely important," "very important," "fairly important," "somewhat important," not important at all," or "not applicable."

The five most influential factors were self-directed reading, personal interest, writing a Ph.D. dissertation on an Asian American topic, involvement in Asian American issues, and responding to student interest and demand. Fifty-two percent of the respondents said reading books by and about Asian Americans on their own was "extremely important," while 18.6 percent said it was "very important," giving a combined 70.6 percent. Personal interest was "extremely important" to 38.6 percent and "very important" to 25.3 percent, yielding a combined 64.9 percent. For 38.6 percent of the respondents, writing a Ph.D. dissertation on an Asian American topic was "extremely important," while 10.6 percent said it was "very important," giving a combined 49.2 percent. Active involvement in Asian American issues was "extremely important" to 32 percent and "very important" to 14.6 percent, adding up to a total of 46.6 percent. Responding to student demand was "extremely important" to 21.3 percent and "very important" to 18.6 percent, making a combined score of 39.9 percent.

The factors deemed "somewhat important" and "not important at all" were writing a B.A. or M.A. thesis on an Asian American topic (combined 74.6 percent), taking undergraduate courses in Asian American studies (combined 61.3 percent), being advised by a graduate mentor to apply for jobs in Asian American studies (combined 49.3 percent), and taking graduate courses in Asian American studies (combined 48 percent).

Thus, formal course work in the field, especially at the undergraduate level, had relatively little to do with the respondents' decisions to teach Asian American studies. Very few had taken any undergraduate courses in Asian American studies, and only 29.2 percent had taken one or more graduate course, seminar, or directed reading in the field even though 49.2 had written Ph.D. dissertations on Asian American topics. That is to say, the choice of dissertation topic was not strongly linked to prior undergraduate or graduate course work and ranked only slightly higher than active involvement in Asian American issues. Although the questionnaire did not ask the respondents to indicate what "Asian American issues" they had been involved in, it can be surmised that one important issue was probably the struggle to establish Asian American studies on the campuses where they were located. Based on my own observations over the years, since the field's beginnings it has been individuals who became involved in Asian American studies while they were still in graduate school who eventually became its most dedicated faculty. Even though there are very few graduate courses about Asian Americans taught anywhere, graduate students in many fields with little relationship to Asian American studies have been exposed to it while they work(ed) as T.A.s (teaching assistants) in large Asian American studies undergraduate courses on campuses with such courses. Finding this experience meaningful, they made up their minds to pursue an academic career teaching Asian American studies.

The most disappointing finding, to me at least, is that even though dozens of colleges and universities now offer undergraduate courses in Asian American studies, very few of the undergraduates who take such courses end up teaching Asian American studies at the college or university level. When I talked to Asian American studies majors at UC Santa Barbara about their career plans, I discovered that relatively few of them aspire to a university career. "Why?" I asked. Their answers ranged from "I'm tired of going to school," "I want to earn money as soon as possible," and "I'd rather go to law school where I'll be done in three years," to "I've seen how hard you and the other faculty work—day, night, and weekends! I'd rather have a job that gives me time to have a life." "Well," I responded, "teaching and research are our lives." The usual retort was, "Maybe for you, but not for me!"

Another, and to me more disturbing, reason is that most of the Asian American studies majors who do want to go to graduate school want to major in Asian American studies *only*, but there are few graduate programs they can apply to. At present, those who do not wish to leave California can apply mainly to the M.A. degree program in Asian American studies at either UCLA or San Francisco State University or to the comparative ethnic studies Ph.D. program either at UC Berkeley or UC San Diego. The two institutions that grant ethnic studies Ph.D.s are highly competitive, and undergraduates with only average grade point averages (GPAs) are unlikely to get admitted. Graduate students at campuses such as UC Irvine may choose an "emphasis" in Asian American studies but they cannot yet get a Ph.D. in the field.

At UC Santa Barbara, many Asian American studies majors are very bright, but their cumulative GPAs are not high because they received low grades during their first two years of undergraduate study. In many instances they had initially chosen a science or engineering major, partly as a result of parental advice and/or pressure even though they themselves were not really interested in those subjects and had a difficult time doing well in them. In fact, some of them barely managed to stay in school during their freshmen and sophomore years. Fortunately for them, since UC Santa Barbara has a long list of General Education requirements, and Asian American studies courses fulfill some of those requirements, somewhere along the way these science and engineering students get exposed to Asian American studies. Loving our courses, they change majors and transfer to our department despite the opposition of some parents. "Does that mean you came to Asian American studies as refugees?" I asked wryly. "Yes!" they replied. "We love Asian American studies because it's a home away from home."

At the graduate level, some of the M.A. students aspiring to become college or university professors also strenuously resist the idea of getting Ph.D.s in any of the traditional disciplines. They said emphatically that they would feel alienated in such fields, so they did not even want to give them a try. Much as I understand and appreciate the existential imperatives that fuel such a sense of alienation, at the same time I am bothered by the anti-intellectualism this attitude reflects—that is, they want to study only subject matter that is of personal interest to them, but they do not wish to undergo training in any traditional discipline. The bottom line is, despite all the progress we have made, there is still no well-defined academic *ladder* that leads systematically from one rung up to the next within Asian American studies.

As a result, with the exception of those getting Ph.D.s in comparative ethnic studies at UC Berkeley and UC San Diego, and those getting Ph.D.s in disciplinary departments at UCLA and at other universities, where they manage to find graduate advisors who support their desire to write dissertations on Asian American topics, the Asian American studies professorate is largely self-trained. Thus, even though a significant number of jobs have opened up since the early 1990s, only a small proportion of the job applicants had become Asian American studies "specialists" before they started teaching. Due to the paucity of "already prepared" applicants, during the nine years I served as chairperson of Asian American studies at UC Santa Barbara I had no choice except to hire a number of faculty who had only a passing acquaintance with the scholarly literature (beyond their dissertation topic) in Asian American studies but who promised to learn it as quickly as possible. One historian to whom we had offered a position in the early 1990s and who had already published a well-researched book in Chinese American history resigned before he even made the move to California because he felt completely overwhelmed by a bibliography I sent him of books he might want to start reading during the summer before his move. He realized there was no way he could instantaneously transform himself into a historian of Asian America. As his wife pointed out, he told me apologetically, his life would be a lot more relaxed if he simply continued to teach the history of East Asia, in which he had been trained.

Since the challenge of mastering the ever-burgeoning literature in the field is so daunting and since some new faculty members, when they are first hired, are barely acquainted with the writings on Asian Americans in their own disciplines, much less with Asian American–related publications in other disciplines, the questionnaire asked the respondents to indicate what had helped them the most to prepare for a teaching career in Asian American studies. The eighteen possible factors listed on the questionnaire were 1) undergraduate courses I have taken; 2) graduate courses I have taken; 3) readings I had done on my own before I began teaching full-time; 4) readings I am currently doing on my own; 5) readings suggested by the professors who taught me in graduate school; 6) readings suggested by my current colleagues; 7) readings suggested by nonacademic friends; 8) research I did for my M.A. thesis; 9) research I did for my Ph.D. dissertation; 10) my current research; 11) formal faculty seminars I have attended; 12) informal exchanges with colleagues on my own campus; 13) informal exchanges with colleagues on other campuses; 14) Association for Asian American Studies annual meetings; 15) meetings of other professional organizations; 16) teaching experience while I was a teaching assistant; 17) teaching experience while I was a part-time faculty member; and 18) teaching experience while I was a tenure-track faculty member at another campus before I got my present job.

The critical significance of reading the existing literature is again highlighted in the responses to this set of questions. Fully 65.3 percent of the respondents indicated that the current readings they are doing on their own are "extremely useful" while 22.6 percent said they are "very useful," giving a combined 87.9 percent. As for readings done before teaching began, 61.3 percent deemed them "extremely useful" and 18.6 percent said they were "very useful," yielding a combined score of 79.9 percent. Next in importance is the respondents' current research: 60 percent said it is "extremely useful" and 18.6 percent checked "very useful" (a combined score of 78.6 percent). Readings suggested by colleagues were "extremely useful" to 29.3 percent and "very useful" to 30.6 percent (a combined 59.9 percent).

In comparison, only about a third of the respondents thought their prior teaching experience was useful. Experience as teaching assistants was "extremely useful" or "very useful" to a combined 33.3 percent of the respondents, while their experience as part-time faculty was "extremely useful" or "very useful" to a combined 36 percent. Exchanges with colleagues on other campuses (a combined 64 percent) are considerably more useful than exchanges with colleagues on their own campuses (a combined 49.3 percent)—figures that reflect the fact that with notable exceptions, most universities have only a handful of Asian Americanists and few colleagues in the traditional disciplines know enough about the histories, contemporary lives, and cultural expressions of Asian Americans to engage in meaningful conversations with them. Such person-to-person informal exchanges, however, are nevertheless considered more important than interactions at either the Association for Asian American studies annual meetings (a combined percentage of 40 percent) or those of other professional organizations (a combined percentage of 25.2 percent).

There was room in the questionnaire for respondents to write in the preparation they wish they had received but did not. The largest number, not surprisingly, said they wished they had been able to take courses in Asian American studies, especially at the graduate level, that address both substantive and theoretical issues. In addition, some individuals also wished they had received better training in theories of race and ethnicity; in cultural studies; the writings of

Marx, Althusser, Lacan, Foucault, and other theorists; "epistemological and political" issues related to Asian American studies; quantitative research methodologies; how to do interdisciplinary research; and Asian languages. Aside from substantive and theoretical knowledge, some respondents also wished they had known before they started teaching how to cope with "school politics"; to effectively teach students of different class, racial, and ethnic backgrounds all sitting in the same classrooms; to engage in collaborative teaching and research projects; to design courses in uncharted areas; and to combine academic and community work. One person wrote that having a graduate seminar on the professional, academic, and institutional issues that women faculty and faculty of color are likely to face would have been really helpful.

Finally, respondents were asked to rank the perceived marketability of various graduate degrees in light of the current job market. The possible choices were 1) a degree in a traditional discipline; 2) a degree in a traditional discipline but with an emphasis in ethnic studies or Asian American studies; 3) a degree in Asian American studies; 4) a degree in comparative ethnic studies; and 5) a degree in American studies. The answers indicate that the respondents considered a degree in a traditional discipline with an emphasis in ethnic or Asian American studies to be the most marketable in the prevailing job market: 46.7 percent chose "extremely marketable" and 30.7 percent chose "very marketable," giving a combined 77.4 percent. The percentages for a traditional discipline alone were 10.7 and 40 percent, respectively; comparative ethnic studies is thought to be "extremely marketable" by 17.3 and "very marketable" by 25.3 percent. Only 16 and 14.7 percent, respectively, thought a Ph.D. in Asian American studies (alone) would be "extremely marketable" and "very marketable." The scores for American studies were 4 and 28 percent, respectively.

Written comments illustrate the difficulties of finding workable ways to train new generations of Asian Americanists. Many commentators observed that while it may be wonderful to be able to get a Ph.D. in Asian American studies, a majority of the job openings are in existing disciplinary departments. So, a Ph.D. in Asian American studies is not particularly useful. As one person put it, "Given that traditional disciplines/departments still hold the power of hiring, Asian American Ph.D.s need to demonstrate a mastery of traditional fields. From what I've seen, candidates who can teach not only Asian American studies but also [courses in the] traditional disciplines appear to have the broadest appeal to schools, especially small liberal arts colleges." A second respondent wrote, "I'm not sure if a Ph.D. in Asian American studies would be productive at this point—up against too much opposition even from allies of Asian American studies. More effort should be spent *capturing* talented scholars who are still in 'traditional' disciplines in graduate school and converting them early." A third commentator noted how aspiring Asian American studies faculty get two conflicting messages:

One message emerges from the recent development of curricula and programs where student and community activism has led to the ultimate establishment of courses and instructors. The message points to the need for people who have a high level of commitment to program development, teaching, and community outreach. The second message, however, is connected to the traditional structure of the university since its scientific and corporate transformation over recent decades. That message is, "You must research and publish quality scholarship in sufficient amounts in order to receive merit increases, promotion, and tenure." The [second] message thoroughly conflicts with, and in many ways counters, the first. . . . Any program granting a doctorate in Asian American studies would need to be attentive to this dilemma.

Some respondents couched their comments in intellectual rather than pragmatic terms. One person wrote, "I am opposed to bounded ethnic studies units . . . [because of] identity politics [and because they] narrow intellectual and political growth. I would rather have interdisciplinary emphases across traditional departmental lines." In contrast, another faculty pointed out that the main advantage of having an Asian American studies program or department is that in such a setting, works can be presented with an "emphasis on how [particular writings] work as Asian American texts and [how they] differ in theoretical and/or methodological orientation from traditional disciplinary approaches. Candidates applying for Asian American studies positions appear to be increasingly well trained in their disciplines but know little about Asian American Studies." Yet another respondent cautioned that "mounting a Ph.D. program in Ethnic and/or Asian American studies is a daunting task. You need to have faculty who are not only willing but able to teach across disciplines and to train [incoming graduate] students who may be untutored/unmentored in the tools, pedagogies, and epistemologies of Asian American Studies. [Training graduate students] also takes a lot away from existing undergraduate teaching."

Though the above findings are only suggestive, it is clear that advocates of Asian American studies must constantly wrestle with the question of whether it would be preferable to pressure disciplinary departments to hire faculty with a teaching and research interest in Asian American studies or for campuses to establish autonomous Asian American studies programs or departments. This is a complex and vexed issue because there are advantages and disadvantages to each of the currently available institutional arrangements.

As I see it, faculty housed in departments in the disciplines in which they had received their graduate training are subjected simultaneously to both less and more pressures than those housed in Asian American or ethnic studies programs or departments. Less, because they can feel secure about their disciplinary grounding and need worry only about acquiring substantive knowledge about Asian Americans within the confines of their own disciplines. They are not compelled to learn and keep up with writing by scholars in disciplines other than their own. At the same time they may also experience more pressure because their departmental colleagues may not respect their specialization in Asian American studies or, worse, may resent the fact that they had been coerced by students and other supporters of the field to hire someone in Asian American studies. In such a situation, Asian Americanists are only grudgingly accepted and may always feel marginal and powerless.

In contrast, faculty who join autonomous Asian American studies programs or departments that can do their own hiring without input from other academic units experience different kinds of pressure. Since these programs or departments are, at least in theory, supposed to be multidisciplinary (or even interdisciplinary) and house faculty trained in a variety of disciplines, there is an implicit obligation to read, learn, and keep up with the pertinent writings related to Asian Americans in more than one discipline. As that body of literature grows, it is becoming well-nigh impossible for anyone to be truly multi- or interdisciplinary. Not surprisingly, as it exists today, Asian American studies is at best multidisciplinary; there has not been much intellectual cross-fertilization despite the fact that its practitioners have invoked interdisciplinarity as a goal for more than three decades. Having tried to be interdisciplinary in my own research and teaching, I know what a lot of effort that takes. I could spend an enormous amount of time acquainting myself with the literature in several disciplines only because I have no children and manage to function on very little sleep.

A second challenge confronting autonomous Asian American studies programs or departments is that not only does each discipline have its own theories and methodologies but different disciplines also measure "productivity" in different ways. A lack of understanding regarding such differences may lead to strong disagreements when departmental colleagues trained in disparate disciplines evaluate one another's work during promotion and tenure reviews. Since there is usually only one historian, or one sociologist, or one psychologist, or one literary scholar in a small Asian American studies program or department, colleagues may, in fact, not be fully qualified to judge the quality of one another's work, which is, in most instances, still grounded in the disciplinary training we received. To get around this problem, the Asian American Studies Department at UC Santa Barbara has often invited one or more senior colleagues from the discipline in which a reviewee was trained to advise us during such reviews. This is, however, at best a band-aid solution.

A more troubling problem in stand-alone programs or departments is that because Asian American studies faculty often feel so besieged, some expect their colleagues to evaluate their records in glowing terms, regardless of what they have or have not accomplished. Such individuals are easily offended by any kind of criticism, no matter how constructive. The implicit assumption is that, as coethnics, we are not supposed to evaluate one another in the same critical way that non-Asians judge us. The expectation that more senior faculty members should unquestioningly and unconditionally support more junior faculty members makes it difficult for the field to demonstrate that it *does* have "standards" even though they may not be a carbon copy of those that traditional disciplines claim to uphold. For example, a colleague of mine filed a formal grievance against me some years ago when I was department chair because he/she felt I had "discriminated" against him/her by not presenting his/her record in sufficiently laudatory terms. This individual objected to the fact that I had used the word "excellent" to characterize his/her teaching. "Excellent," he/she averred, "is such a banal word."

Two additional factors make it difficult for autonomous Asian American studies programs or departments to function with integrity: a new kind of racism and sexism that some administrators now seem to espouse and a grab-what-you-can attitude that some faculty members seem to exhibit. I first discovered the changing administrative attitude when an administrator told me that I better "go easy" on a new faculty member who had complained that I expected too much of him/her. Administrators at some "liberal" campuses had reason to "go easy" on women faculty and faculty of color in the mid-1990s. The UC Santa Barbara campus in particular lost a major lawsuit filed by a senior Chicano studies faculty who failed to get an offer from the campus—a lawsuit that cost the University of California several million dollars. Moreover, UC Santa Barbara's "faculty affirmative action statistics" did not look very good in those days because many traditional departments still resisted hiring female or nonwhite faculty. Therefore, the three ethnic studies departments at UC Santa Barbara performed a crucial function for the campus: the faculty we hired helped increase the number of "minorities" on the faculty. For that reason, instead of resisting the appointment of "minorities" and scrutinizing their records, as was done in the past, administrators increasingly treated the ones hired within ethnic studies units with kid gloves. They usually cannot treat the "minority" faculty hired by traditional departments in a similarly paternalistic or maternalistic way because the senior faculty members in those departments would object vehemently to "double standards."

Though seemingly supportive, I saw the soft touch as an insidious form of sexism and racism—the sexism/racism of low expectations. The unspoken subtext of the message to me was "Don't be so demanding on your faculty. We shouldn't expect too much from them because . . . well, you know . . . they come from 'disadvantaged' backgrounds, after all." I pointed out that not all women faculty members or faculty of color are "disadvantaged." No matter. In the administrators' eyes, they are "minorities," and their hiring improved the university's affirmative action statistics. And *that* was what counted during the years when affirmative action was still mandated by university policy.

Such thinking is diametrically opposite to my own. While I have done everything in my power to get competent faculty of color appointed, I also believe that once they join the faculty they should follow the same rules—in terms of work load and promotion criteria—as everybody else. It offends me deeply when we are treated simply as boosters of affirmative action statistics. While some faculty of color may welcome a lowering of the bar, I think it robs us of dignity and self-respect. It would be better that we be rewarded for our performances and not our phenotypical characteristics. Racism can take disparate forms, but all of them, including those that seem "supportive" of women and people of color, are ugly.

Another kind of faculty behavior can also undermine the integrity of Asian American studies. In my own department two faculty members hired at the full-professor level demanded accelerated promotions only a year after their arrival even though they had already "skipped" several steps when they joined our faculty. Full-time faculty in the UC system are called "ladder-rank faculty" because they are reviewed at fixed intervals as they advance up the faculty ranks, and the amount of salary increase between steps is also specified. While exceptions are possible, such exceptions are made only for those individuals whose accomplishments are truly extraordinary or who have competing offers (in writing) from other universities of equal stature. Because UC faculty members normally go up one step at a time each time they are reviewed, I could not in good conscience support demands for out-of-line promotions when the initial appointment levels were *already* much higher than warranted. One person sarcastically branded me a "gatekeeper" for the establishment. How ironic! Had I not worked so hard for so many years to pry open the gates of the university, these individuals probably would not have become UC faculty. Such self-serving behavior is so detrimental because it confirms the suspicions harbored by non-ethnic studies faculty members—that autonomous ethnic studies departments are incapable of acting "objectively" when it comes to faculty appointments, salary increases, or promotions.

I never anticipated these problems because I had been too single-mindedly focused on opening the gates of the university to "unconventional" applicants, but I failed to take into account who might apply for the jobs that became available as a result of the political pressures exerted by students and faculty in Asian American or ethnic studies in the 1990s. In other words, while I developed considerable insight into how universities are structured and how they function, I paid no attention to the larger changes in the world that are impinging upon faculty applicant pools in the United States.

I initially attributed the differences between me and some faculty members we hired to a generation gap. Because the field had remained stagnant in terms of faculty numbers from the mid-1970s to the late 1980s, the notion of "generation gap" seemed pertinent. It would be more accurate, however, to use the plural, "generations," because academic generations do not last very long. In that fifteen-year interval of virtually zero growth, three or four generational cohorts would have been formed had faculty positions been available. But they were not. Thus, on a superficial level one might attribute the differences between me and the new faculty members who entered the field decades after I had done so to a multigeneration gap.

Chalsa Loo, Don Mar, and Michael Omi first analyzed such a gap in three essays they contributed to *Reflections on Shattered Windows* (1988).[1] The titles of those essays reflect the authors' concerns: "The 'Middle-Aging' of Asian American Studies," "It Just Ain't the Sixties No More: The Contemporary Dilemmas of Asian American Studies," and "The Lost Second Generation of Asian American Scholars." In the fifteen years following the publication of those essays it seems that the gap has not only not narrowed but also mutated into new forms. After reflecting deeply upon my own experience, I concluded that if there is indeed a gap it is not one of age, generation, nativity, ethnicity, or class. In my own case, students and I continued to understand and appreciate one another, and my relationship with the two youngest faculty members, who joined the faculty while in their twenties, was friendly. What separated me from the three individuals who became very antagonistic toward me were fundamental differences in our subject positions and ideologies.

Faculty members who joined Asian American studies in the 1990s did so within a context quite different from those that had existed in earlier decades. Because I was quite ill with post-polio syndrome during the years when Asian American studies at UC Santa Barbara grew most rapidly, I did not pay much attention to the world outside of the university's narrow confines. It was not until I helped design a new major in global studies in the late 1990s that I became aware of the immense and multifaceted impacts that globalization is making on faculty applicant pools on American campuses. After the United States liberalized its immigration laws in 1965, mass immigration from Asia resumed after decades of exclusion or semi-exclusion.

Initially, many post-1965 immigrants were family members of individuals already here. By the mid-1970s, however, well-educated professionals from Asia (and other continents) also began making their way to America. Those who come for graduate studies arrive as adults with well-formed personalities, well-defined worldviews, and great personal ambition. As they complete their graduate education, some look for jobs in academia. Since they had not been "minorities" in their natal countries, some of them apparently feel uncomfortable about being placed into a "minority" slot in American society. One convenient way to avoid such a racialized identity is to insist that they are a part of various Asian diasporas and that they have diasporic or transnational identities. That is, they intentionally *dis*identify with the country in which they now live and earn a living. For example, a colleague in another department once snapped at me, "Don't ever call me an Asian American!" Taken aback by the annoyance this person, who had lived in the United States since he/she was a young teenager, expressed, I asked, "What should I call you, then?" "I'm an overseas Chinese" was the curt reply.

Unlike members of the diasporas of old—the classic diaspora being that of the Jews—who nursed a never forgotten yearning for the "home(s)" left behind, members of today's diasporas have little desire to return to their natal countries while they are still in their prime. Some say that when they are ready to retire they may return to their countries of origin—but only if political conditions there are stable, if the economies are prosperous, and if they can enjoy a social standing much higher than what they have managed to achieve in the countries where they currently live and work.

In my opinion, given their contingent attitude, "transnational" is a more accurate adjective than "diasporic" to describe such people. Transnational migrants (or transmigrants) maintain ongoing ties to people and developments in two or more countries without committing themselves, in terms of political allegiance, to any. They seem interested mainly in advancing the fortunes of themselves and their families. Some transmigrants from Asia have little desire to become "Americans" because becoming "Americans" means being incorporated into U.S. society as ethnic or racial "minorities." Even though Asian Americans may be perceived as "a model minority," they are members of a *minority* nonetheless. A "minority" status is not only disadvantageous but also psychologically uncomfortable. Some people resist any kind of deeper identification with American society even after they acquire U.S. citizenship. That is, they obtain US. citizenship only because it guarantees their right to remain, among other privileges, but they prefer to possess "hybrid identities"—identities that are constantly in flux and are "deterritorialized."

In light of these world-shaking transformations, ideological differences manifest themselves within Asian American studies in ways that are related only tangentially, if at all, to age, generation, ethnicity, or even nativity. What really divides faculty who teach in the field, I think, are, first, the intensity of one's concern for rapid career advancement and personal aggrandizement versus one's commitment to serving students and communities and engaging in "progressive" politics, and, second, how one perceives the integrationist U.S. civil rights movement and the later separatist Black Power movement and the value judgments one confers on them. Since the Asian American movement did not begin until the heyday of the civil rights movement was over, the Black Power movement had a greater influence on Asian American activists. The ramifications of that fact have not yet been completely explored and explicated.

While it may be possible in a few rare instances for Asian American studies faculty members to advance up the ladder *while* serving students and communities, in most instances the two goals pull in opposite directions. Every activity takes time, and there are only twenty-four hours in a day. As young faculty members form families, they must also spend time with their spouses and children. Given such multiple and conflicting pressures, over the years more and more Asian American studies faculty abandoned the goal of serving "the community." Only a handful of individuals have remained true to that vision. The rest of us, myself included, salve our conscience by saying that our students *are* the communities we serve. Some of us borrow Antonio Gramsci's concepts of "organic intellectuals" and "hegemony" to justify why our efforts are focused largely on what goes on within the academy. Consequently, the contrary pull between teaching and community service is no longer as vexatious as it used to be.

What remains as a powerful divide are differences in how Asian Americanists regard the civil rights and the Black Power movements. The first movement focused on gaining equality for African Americans, while the second aimed truly to empower them. Asian Americans who identified with either or both movements, therefore, at one level or another, supported the myriad forms of struggles that African Americans engaged in as well as our own battles. Many senior faculty in the field (some of whom, including myself, were not even born in the United States) take pride in having participated, however peripherally, in the social movements of the 1960s. There are also many younger scholars, regardless of where they were born, who likewise believe in the necessity of continuing the struggles for justice and equality, not only on campuses but in the world at large. That is to say, while we may have stopped trying to serve "the community," we have not given up "politics."

The above two groups of faculty differ from a third whose members see the social movements of the 1960s and 1970s, including the movement to establish the various branches of ethnic studies, as relics of the past that should be discarded. Possessing no emotive connection to those movements, such individuals do not think the "originary vision" of Asian American studies is worth upholding. They frame the issue as a contrast between doing "research" versus engaging in "politics." What they fail to understand is that the thinking of the older generation of scholars was never so simplistic. We long ago recognized the necessity of engaging in *both* scholarship and political action.[2]

The real contrast, I think, is between faculty who identify with and participate in "minority" issues and those who do not. The latter spent their childhood and formative years in countries—including those formerly colonized by Europeans and that now exist as postcolonial societies—in which they were members of the *majority* population, at least in terms of numbers if not power. After arriving in the United States, they think they can use their middle- or upper-class standing to evade "minority" status. When individuals who did not grow up as minorities teach Asian American studies they have a hard time comprehending why so many American-born or American-reared youth of Asian ancestry have to struggle so hard to develop self-esteem and self-respect; why Asian American studies is more than an academic field of inquiry; and why taking our courses can be a cathartic, life-transforming experience for some of our students.

Despite their aversion to being identified as racial/ethnic minorities, some Asian transmigrant scholars have applied for jobs in Asian American studies because many of the positions available during the 1990s and the 2000s were or are at "prestigious" universities. That is, they were/are "desirable" jobs to status-conscious individuals. Starting their careers at prestigious universities enables ambitious scholars to climb the career ladder as quickly as possible because the teaching load is lighter and research support is more available. Transmigrant scholars have been quite successful in their job searches because their academic credentials are usually good. More important, from the point of view of administrators and senior faculty members in the traditional departments doing the hiring, they offer the added (though unspoken) advantage of being "ethnic" but not "radical."

Ironically, the very name of our field—*Asian* American studies or *ethnic* studies—has put us in a bind. Just because job applicants belong to the same "ethnicity" as the faculty who first developed the field, it cannot be assumed they share the latter's vision. Being coethnics does not guarantee a shared consciousness. Not only do some faculty members who entered the field in the 1990s and thereafter have different worldviews, but a few have expressed considerable impatience with the old-timers. As Philip Q. Yang stated in 2000:

> To be sure, the mission of ethnic studies and the process of establishing and sustaining an ethnic studies program are political. Ethnic studies is a voice for progressive social change, humane treatment of ethnic groups, and improved intergroup relations. Each step forward entails hard-fought political battles. *However, the discipline and curriculum of ethnic studies should not be politicized.* As a discipline, ethnic studies is a systematic study of ethnicity, ethnic groups, and intergroup relations using interdisciplinary, multidisciplinary, and comparative methodologies. It is by no means synonymous with political activism. [emphasis added][3]

There is a contradiction in that passage that its author does not seem to recognize: the "hard-fought political battles" could not have been won without "political activism." "Progressive social change" and more "humane treatment" came about only as a result of political engagement.

Min Zhou, a sociologist and a prolific writer, analyzed the existing tensions this way:

> While the ongoing discussion of goals and methodologies is at once refreshing and evident of the field's continuing vitality, it also testifies to the degree to which intellectual

and organizational tensions are built into the field. On the one hand, the very language of the debate, often filled with jargon and trendy concepts, stands in conflict with the self-professed orientation toward the community and its needs. On the other hand, there is a certain nostalgia among veteran activists, now mainly tenured professors, for the spirit of the 1960s and, to some extent, that yearning for the past ironically threatens to produce a divide between U.S.-born (and/or U.S.-raised) scholars and some of their Asian-born counterparts, especially those whose education in the United States was more likely to begin at the college and graduate level, and who may not share the same connection to a history that they never experienced. Moreover, the ideological suppositions of the scholars oriented toward the Movement has the potential to create distance between them and the growing number of Asian American (often Asian-born) scholars who work on Asian American topics, but from the standpoint of the more traditional disciplines.[4]

What caught my eye was her assertion that the "distance" is being created by the "veteran activists." As I see it, that "distance" is *also* being forged by the newcomers' disdain for the allegedly outmoded goals of the earlier generations of Asian Americanists. The gulf, in short, is being mutually constituted.

While I recognize that aging scholars such as myself need to move aside and to relinquish whatever power we "mainly tenured professors" are seen to possess, the faculty members who entered the field in more recent years should realize that many of them have the jobs they hold today mainly because student activists, who have been consistently vocal and committed, and the first-generation faculty members, who have labored under the most adverse working conditions, collectively have kept the various components of ethnic studies alive. Regardless of whether or not these late-entering cohorts of faculty feel any connection to the "Movement," they owe it a special debt in terms of their personal career advancement. Therefore, however uncomfortable some of them may feel about the political history of Asian American studies, they should not denigrate, much less erase it.

As an increasing number of faculty members who have no use for the political legacy of Asian American studies enters the field we hear more and more talk about why Asian American studies needs to be transformed into something other than what it has been. Should Asian American studies merge with Asian studies? with American studies? with postcolonial studies? with cultural studies? As these questions become increasingly salient in the years to come we must be honest with ourselves and admit that such debates are not simply intellectual discussions; rather, they camouflage thinly disguised struggles for dominance within the Asian American professorate in terms of who gets to set the agenda for the field.

As I see it, the crux of the dilemma isn't theory but practice. I think the transnational, diasporic, globalization, cultural studies, poststructural, postmodernist, or postcolonial studies conceptual frameworks are *all* important as heuristic devices for analyzing key developments in the late twentieth and early twenty-first centuries. The extraordinary heterogeneity of the population of Asian ancestry now living in the United States (note that I am carefully not saying "Asian Americans" here because I do not want to offend those who do not consider themselves to be "Americans") *mandates* that multiple frameworks be used to guide our research. We must help our students as well as ourselves not only to understand the racialized (and still largely "minority") positions in American society to which we continue to be relegated but also to make sense of the ever more complex transnational linkages that now form webs encompassing virtually every aspect of our lives. We must ponder deeply not only what it means to be American citizens but also what it means to be "global citizens." At the same time, we need to realize that the various branches of ethnic studies will lose their critical edge if we forget why they were established and the political nature of the historical moment that gave them birth.

The tug between "scholarship" and "politics" is not unique to Asian American studies. In women's studies, feminist scholars Ellen Carol DuBois and her coauthors made a resounding declaration in 1987 that concisely captures the contradiction: "We believed—we still believe—that the connection to a political movement is the lifeblood of feminist scholarship, not its tragic flaw."[5]

In cultural studies, another multidisciplinary field with a "political" history, Stuart Hall posed the issue this way:

> The enormous explosion of cultural studies in the U.S., its rapid professionalization and institutionalization, is not a moment which any of us who tried to set up a marginalized Centre [for Contemporary Cultural Studies] in a university like Birmingham could, in any simple way, regret. And yet I have to say, in the strongest sense, that it reminds me of the ways in which, in Britain, we are always aware of institutionalization as a moment of profound danger. . . . Why? Well, it would be excessively vulgar to talk about such things as how many jobs there are, how much money there is around, and how much pressure that puts on people to do what they think of as critical political work and intellectual work of a critical kind, while also looking over their shoulders at the promotions stakes and the publication stakes, and so on.[6]

In American studies, another field in ferment, George Lipsitz recalled "the transformative power of public political action" during the 1960s and contrasted that era with today's conditions:

> Intellectuals and artists today often live disconnected from active social movements. . . . They work within hierarchical institutions and confront reward structures that privilege individual distinction over collective social change. . . . Artistic and intellectual work takes place today in a contradictory context, and it produces people with a contradictory consciousness. . . . they are . . . pressured to segregate themselves from aggrieved communities, and to work within the confines and ideological controls of institutions controlled by the wealthy and powerful. . . . The contradictory consciousness that pervades the lives of academic intellectuals, artists, and cultural workers present[s] specific impediments to progressive politics.[7]

The above statements all resonate with the issues being debated within Asian American studies at the dawn of the twenty-first century. Furthermore, the same tensions roil an Asian-ancestry population now demographically dominated by post-1965 immigrants. Looking at the political landscape outside the academy, Paul Ong and David Lee noted:

Although Asian immigrants are a part of a minority group that has been subjected to past acts of overt racism, they are not strongly aligned with the civil rights agenda. For many immigrants, Asian American history is not their history, so they have no sense of membership in a historically victimized population. Although Asian immigrants do experience discrimination, many attribute that discrimination to cultural and linguistic differences rather than race. As a consequence . . . most Asian immigrants do not readily support minority-oriented efforts and programs. . . . The emergence of an immigrant majority can have profound implications for Asian American politics. One impact is the threat it might pose to progressive activists.[8]

To those of us who still care about "progressive" politics—that is, struggles for racial equality, socioeconomic justice, and political empowerment—the historical legacy of Asian American studies must not be pushed aside because the political-cum-scholarly work that the first generation of Asian American, African American, Chicano/Latino, and Native American scholars tried to do still needs to be done. What undergirded the foundations of those fields was a critique of American society. Today, our critiques must be directed not only at the American nation-state but also at an entire world dominated by a form of capitalism that is flexible, dispersed, transnational, and robust.

But even as we supplant the older American-based antiracist critique in order to avoid becoming theoretically and substantively "outdated" we should keep in mind that while global forces are affecting all strata of the world's inhabitants, it is the upper stratum that benefits while the middle and lower strata get mired in ever more destitute forms of poverty. The current world order is characterized by a growing disparity between the rich and the poor. While many ethnic studies pioneer scholars also came from middle-class backgrounds, at least we (counting myself in this group) identified ideologically and politically with oppressed people, not just in the United States but around the globe. Teaching ethnic studies gave us a way to participate in the fight for equality, justice, and self-empowerment.

Even as a commodified, globalized, but American-dominated popular culture touting consumerism as the answer to all problems increasingly reigns supreme, we cannot allow that trend to camouflage the abject miseries that characterize an ever larger proportion of the world's inhabitants. Just because professionals of various hues are now accepted as members of the middle and even upper classes in the United States and in other "First World" countries or former "metropoles," that acceptance should not blind us to the fact that discrimination based on race, national or ethnic origins, class, gender, sexual orientation, and physical handicaps continues to structure social relations in the countries where many transnational professionals now live.

What I am arguing for is this: while we certainly should add the currently modish schools of thought to our intellectual pantheon, we must also be aware of at least three hidden dangers in using such academically chic theories as normative guides to *action*. First, while the repudiation of "master narratives" is indeed a needed corrective to the underlying assumptions and exclusions of the Enlightenment project, we should recognize that the fragmentation and the often radical relativism that such theories valorize make it more difficult to

develop solidarity as we attempt to form coalitions to counter the oppressive-
ness of the conditions under which the middle and lower strata of the population, including "minorities" of various kinds, still live. Members of the relatively
small, multiracial or multiethnic transnational elite can indeed easily travel to,
buy homes in, do business with, and find work any place they please, but the
privileges they enjoy are out of reach for the downtrodden majority among the
world's population. Should scholars in Asian American studies care about such
inequality? Some of us think so. That is why even though we may be a fast-
disappearing numerical minority within Asian American studies, our drumbeat
is still insistently loud. *There's* the rub for impatient colleagues who wish we
would disappear into the walls of old folks' homes.

Second, while the extraordinary emphasis on culture, especially culture read
textually, as a major arena of contestation is also a needed corrective to the economic determinism that structured the ways in which some of us used to think
about the world, I believe we must continue to monitor and analyze economic and
political changes that cannot be reduced to culture per se, regardless of how capa-
ciously "culture" may be understood. Cultural politics cannot be the only kind of
politics we engage in. The materialist foundations of human life are fundamental
sources of oppression; as such they must not only be studied alongside the miseries
we experience in the symbolic realm of the imagination but also combated in whatever limited ways may be possible in the material world.

Third, I do not think it is time yet to throw out every aspect of the
Enlightenment project. The students and young scholars who fought for the
establishment of the various branches of ethnic studies did so by arguing that
their right to a "relevant" education was a form of civil rights—that is, the rights
we should all enjoy as citizens and permanent residents of the United States. We
could make claims on the university because it is state-supported—supported,
that is, by taxpayers such as ourselves and our parents. We could make claims on
the United States because we insisted we are Americans, regardless of our skin
color. One strategy we used was to turn the rhetoric of a supposedly liberal state
upon itself. We were quite aware that during much of the nation's history there
was a huge gap between ideology and reality. But by embracing the liberal democratic state's professed norms of inclusiveness we exposed the hypocrisies in the
society in which we live. We called upon that society to reform itself so that it can
realize its true promise. No one could stop us from *invoking* the rights supposedly guaranteed by the U.S. constitution and by various laws because we claimed
those laws apply to us darker-hued Americans as well. Because the American
nation-state is a manifestation of the Enlightenment project, an "ethnic studies
project" that made its claims based upon the American creed was at once a critique and an affirmation of such Enlightenment values as progress, rationality,
freedom, equality, justice, and democracy. Just because so many scholars now
scoff at the Enlightenment, its metaphorical babies—the ideals it professed—
need not be thrown out with the bath water.

At least, not yet. Because some members of the U.S. power structure still pay lip
service to these liberal ideals, scholar-activists in ethnic studies and in other fields
have been able to carve out a tiny space—indeed, small *bases* of resistance—from

which we offered counter-hegemonic narratives to the prevailing national myths rooted in the Enlightenment vision. For that reason, the moral, legal, and political reasons we used to make our claims are not yet outmoded. So, why the rush to throw out the "minority" paradigm, even though it is indeed embedded in a still-unjust American society, when it has not yet outlived its utility?

To be sure, there are scholars who argue we can also make claims on the basis of "human rights"—a more universal form of rights not rooted in any nation-state. Unfortunately, the institutional structures for enforcing human rights are still in a nascent stage of development. While globalization is indeed eroding the power of nation-states, still, in terms of immigration and civil rights, the American state apparatus remains potent. Just ask the undocumented migrants who risk their lives daily to enter the United States, many of whom are caught, jailed, and deported, or worse, die in the attempt. Therefore, should we, in our rush to keep "up to date" theoretically, kick the "nationalist" moorings from under ourselves, as some transnationally oriented colleagues argue we should do, we will lose a truly useful tool that may yet ensure our continued survival in whatever hard times may lie ahead. And there will be hard times as neoconservatives, who have become smart enough to accept "diversity" as an imperative, develop more and more sophisticated methods to seduce some of us into joining their camp while simultaneously doing everything in their power to make the rich richer and the poor poorer.

It is not nostalgia, therefore, but a cold, clear-eyed realism that leads to the following exhortation: Let us not jettison the very tools we have used to get to where we are today.

NOTES

1. Gary Y. Okihiro et al., eds., *Reflections on Shattered Windows: Promises and Prospects for Asian American Studies* (Pullman: Washington State University Press, 1988).
2. See Part 1 of Sucheng Chan, *In Defense of Asian American Studies: The Politics of Teaching and Program Building* (Chicago: University of Illinois Press, 2005).
3. Philip Q. Yang, *Ethnic Studies: Issues and Approaches* (Albany: SUNY Press, 2000), 276.
4. Min Zhou and James V. Gatewood, eds., *Contemporary Asian America: A Multidisciplinary Reader* (New York: New York University Press, 2000), 7–8.
5. Ellen Carol DuBois et al., *Feminist Scholarship: Kindling in the Groves of Academia* (Urbana: University of Illinois Press, 1987), 8.
6. Stuart Hall, "Cultural Studies and Its Theoretical Legacies," in *Cultural Studies*, ed. and with an introduction by Lawrence Grossberg, Cary Nelson, and Paula Treichler (New York: Routledge, 1992), 85–86.
7. George Lipsitz, *American Studies in a Moment of Danger* (Minneapolis: University of Minnesota Press, 2001), 58, 277–78.
8. Paul M. Ong and David E. Lee, "Changing of the Guard? The Emerging Immigrant Majority in Asian American Politics," in *Asian Americans and Politics: Perspectives, Experiences, Prospects*, ed. Gordon H. Chang (Washington: Woodrow Wilson Center Press and Stanford, Calif.: Stanford University Press, 2001), 165–66.

FREEDOM SCHOOLING

RECONCEPTUALIZING ASIAN AMERICAN STUDIES FOR OUR COMMUNITIES

Glenn Omatsu

. . . new situations bring new contradictions, requiring new visions.[1]

—GRACE LEE BOGGS

The possible is richer than the real.[2]

—ILYA PRIGOGINE

"The educational system today is designed for failure."

I hear this statement often these days. I hear it often, and I say it myself. I hear it from K–12 activist teachers as they confront mandates for standardized testing and orders to "teach to the test." I hear it from college teachers who work with first-generation college students as they cope with stringent new policies limiting those who can come to the university and those who can stay. Yet, behind this indictment of the educational system is neither cynicism nor passivity. Based on a critique of today's educational system, activists are crafting a new paradigm. Currently, this paradigm exists only in its broadest outlines. We call this paradigm Freedom Schooling.

In an L.A. Koreatown public school, Tony Osumi is teaching third-grade students about the importance of teamwork, interethnic unity, and community-building. His classroom consists almost entirely of children of low-income, new immigrant families from Latin America and Asia. Tony's teaching approach draws heavily from his work as a community organizer and neighborhood artist, his past graduate work in Asian American Studies, and his appreciation of liberatory pedagogy from the Civil Rights Movement, Asian American Movement, and popular education. He calls his approach to teaching "Freedom Schooling."

Several thousand miles away in Philadelphia Chinatown, activists associated with Asian Americans United, including ESL high school teacher Debbie Wei, are launching a Chinatown Freedom School for inner-city youth long abandoned by the public school system. The plans are based on AAU's fifteen years of political organizing work with youth in Chinatown, including its summer Freedom Schools.

The efforts of Tony Osumi and AAU are emerging independently of each other; in fact, until recently, neither knew of the other's existence. Moreover, in this period of severe problems in the U.S. educational system, many other long-time activists are engaged in similar grassroots efforts aimed at not simply reforming educational practices but placing at the very center of their teaching approaches the goals of community-building, community organizing, and liberation. Like AAU, some envision actual independent schools, while others like Tony Osumi have begun to practice Freedom Schooling in day-to-day work in their classrooms.

The concept of Freedom Schooling itself goes back to the Civil Rights Movement where African American parents and community activists in the South created their own schools in response to segregation and the barring of their children from the public school system. According to long-time activist Grace Lee Boggs, the new schools did far more than teach traditional academic subject matter:

> In the 1960s Movement activists had to create Freedom Schools in the South because the existing school system had been organized to produce subjects, not citizens. People in the community, both children and adults, needed to be empowered to exercise their civil and voting rights. To bring about a kind of "mental revolution," reading, writing and speaking skills were taught through the discussion of black history, the power structure and building a Movement to struggle against it. Everyone took this basic "civics" course and then chose from more academic subjects, like algebra and chemistry. All over Mississippi, in church basements and parish halls, on shady lawns and in abandoned buildings, volunteer teachers empowered thousands of children and adults through this community curriculum.[3]

Today, Boggs is associated with Detroit Summer, a Freedom School for the new millennium that challenges young people to "rebuild, redefine and respirit" devastated inner-city neighborhoods. She and other seasoned activists interpret today's emerging Freedom Schooling movement as part of an overall revolutionary effort to create new institutions in society. Specifically, today's Freedom Schools not only overturn outdated teaching methods and curriculum but also are based on goals fundamentally different from current schools. According to Boggs:

> Just as we had to create a Movement in the 50s and 60s to challenge racism, we now need a movement to challenge the concept of schools as mainly training centers for jobs in the corporate structure or for individual upward mobility and replace it with the concept of schools as places where children learn firsthand the skills of democracy and the responsibilities of citizenship and self-government. This will require a profound change in our own thinking because we ourselves have bought into the idea that the main purpose of education should be to train personnel to fit into the corporate structure. What we need to do

now is to begin engaging our children in community-building activities with the same audacity with which the civil rights movement engaged them in desegregation activities thirty-five years ago. Classes of school children from K–12 should be taking responsibility for maintaining neighborhood streets, planting community gardens, recycling waste, rehabbing houses, creating healthier school lunches, visiting and doing errands for the elderly, organizing neighborhood festivals, painting murals. This is the fastest way to motivate all our children to learn and at the same time reverse the physical deterioration of our neighborhoods. . . . Learning will come from practice which has always been the best way to learn.[4]

The Freedom Schools described by Boggs and organized by AAU in Philadelphia are remarkably alike in purpose: they stress a constructivist approach to the education of children; they emphasize a curriculum that connects students to the needs of their immediate neighborhood; they move beyond the existing narrow definition of schools as places for training youth for jobs in the corporate economy; they are explicitly multicultural even though each school will focus on largely one ethnic group; and they are overtly political, i.e., they are based on an incisive critique of the current U.S. educational crisis and promote ways to organize students, parents, teachers, other school staff, and communities to change this system. In short, Freedom Schools promote and expand democracy by changing power relations in society. They do this by enabling students to practice democracy. But Freedom Schools are not simply for youth; they are community schools that reconceptualize education as an intergenerational process linked to solving community needs.

Also, the Boggs and Philadelphia schools share one other important commonality. In both cases, the activists envision a strategic connection between their schools and university Ethnic Studies programs—Asian American Studies, in particular—but thus far this connection has not materialized, largely due to indifference on the part of those at the university. What are the reasons for this indifference? My feeling is that most in Asian American Studies interpret the efforts of AAU in "small" terms—as "charter schools"—and place them in the narrow framework of the debate between public and charter schools. Most would also question why it is important to divert what they see as scarce university resources to small-scale neighborhood efforts, feeling that these same resources could be used to address larger policy questions related to educational reform at the national, state, and district levels.

In this essay I emphasize why the concept of Freedom Schooling is essential for Asian American Studies today. As will become apparent in my argument, I do not define the concept only in terms of actual independent schools—at least not at this time. I see Freedom Schooling as the necessary radical vision that we need in this period to transform our existing classrooms and our own world outlooks. I propose ways that all educational activists can begin practicing Freedom Schooling in their day-to-day work, whether in classrooms or in communities. Conceptualizing our work in this way will enable us to deal with both the new problems and the new opportunities facing us, especially in Asian American Studies. It will also promote greater dialogue among educational activists, especially about ways we can link our work across what we now see as separate levels of the educational system (i.e., preschool, K–12, special education, adult education, higher education, as well as the array of community education projects).

ASIAN AMERICAN STUDIES AND ITS ROOTS IN FREEDOM SCHOOLING

In previous writings I have critiqued the current state of Asian American Studies for its departure from its founding radical vision.[5] I have focused my critique on questions of curriculum, pedagogy, and guiding philosophy. In this essay I deepen and extend this analysis by framing my ideas around the concept of Freedom Schooling. Let me summarize the main points from my earlier writings:

1. Three decades ago, Asian American Studies emerged from the fire of student and community activism that was itself connected to larger social movements seeking to transform all aspects of society. Thus, the founding vision of Asian American Studies not only challenged the prevailing framework of education; it also served as the basis for creating vehicles to implement these ideas.

2. Based on this radical vision, activists saw schooling as not merely imparting information to students but as promoting critical awareness and encouraging political engagement. They linked classroom learning to the solving of community needs and asserted that students—as well as teachers—could learn best by doing, particularly through involvement in grassroots struggles.

3. Activists further asserted that knowledge gained from classrooms must be used to confront power in society. All students and teachers had the responsibility not only to study our communities but to change them.

4. Similarly, activists stressed the responsibility of students and teachers to share knowledge. They emphasized that every student taking a class in Asian American Studies had the obligation to share what they were learning with friends, parents, and others in our community and called upon teachers to build this responsibility into course objectives. Knowledge was too important to stay in the classroom.

5. Activists identified the key role that students taking classes in Asian American Studies could play in our communities. By arming themselves with knowledge from Asian American Studies and thinking strategically about ways to share this knowledge with others, students could become agents of social change—but only if they were willing to link themselves to community movements. In other words, knowledge and ideas could become material forces if grasped by large numbers of people. Students could help make this happen.

6. Activists envisioned Asian American Studies as beginning within institutions of higher education but rapidly spreading to sectors of the community that would never walk into a college classroom—e.g., prison inmates, high school dropouts, senior citizens, immigrant workers, tenants in inner-city housing projects, housewives, and small business people. To implement this mission, activists brought Asian American Studies to the community through

traditional academic activities such as community lectures and forums, as well as audacious experiments such as the creation of community classes, worker cooperatives, bookstores, newspapers, community drop-in centers, tenants unions, and arts collectives.

7. Finally, the founding vision of Asian American Studies stressed that changing society also meant transforming oneself—i.e., accepting the ideological challenge to remold one's own values and worldview. This remolding, activists emphasized, could not happen individually but only by participating with others in movements to serve the community.

8. Over the past three decades, Asian American Studies has retreated to a narrower definition of its mission based on the adoption of traditional academic criteria. Today, links to the community usually take place by offering student internships and field studies in social service agencies, training students in research methodology, encouraging professors and researchers to provide professional expertise in off-campus organizations, and defining students and teachers as advocates who can change public policy through their research. While these are all valuable activities, they represent a departure from the founding vision of the field.

9. During the past decade, Asian American Studies has expanded nationally to now include nearly forty full programs and probably as many as 25,000 students taking classes each year. Never before have our communities had such a large number of students and teachers educated around problems affecting Asian Americans. This new social base presents intriguing possibilities for Freedom Schooling in this period.

10. Nevertheless, the growth of Asian American Studies has been uneven, with a concentration of programs and classes in elite universities and its near absence outside higher education. Unlike the earlier period, when activists took Asian American Studies outside the college classroom and into high schools, adult schools, workplaces, housing projects, and community centers, most of today's practitioners limit Asian American Studies to higher education, especially in elite institutions.

Thus, today, activists face both new problems and opportunities in Asian American Studies. This challenges us to think in different ways about the connection between our long-term goals relating to education and our day-to-day work in classrooms and communities. I believe that the concept of Freedom Schooling provides us with the necessary radical vision to grapple with this question. First, Freedom Schooling enables us to retrieve the valuable founding mission of Asian American Studies, especially its emphasis on the key role that students can play in our communities. Second, Freedom Schooling provides a strategy for dealing with new conditions in Asian American Studies, in particular its concentration in elite institutions of higher education. Third, Freedom Schooling is the larger consciousness we need today—a paradigm shift—to enable us to recognize the significance of struggles in the educational arena and their relation to the overall transformation of society. In the remainder of this essay, I elaborate on these three important points.

Freedom Schooling Enables Activists to Reclaim the Radical Legacy of Asian American Studies

The roots of Asian American Studies lie in Freedom Schools and the spirit of bold experimentation that marked the movements of the late 1960s and early 1970s. Inspired by the liberatory vision of education emerging from the Civil Rights Movement, early activists defined the first classes in Asian American Studies as places for learning, organizing, and ultimately, collective empowerment.

Today, with the concentration of courses only in universities, it is probably difficult for young activists to picture a time when university classes were but one part of the learning environment of Asian American Studies. Yet, it is precisely this enlarged vision of schooling that we need for Asian American Studies today, a period marked by greater resources than at any previous time. Thus, it would be helpful to summarize how an earlier generation of students with limited resources brought Asian American Studies to the community. This understanding can serve as the inspiration for thinking about new ways that we can continue this legacy today in a period when we have much greater resources available to us through Asian American Studies.

Like the first Freedom Schools in the South that were held in church basements, early "classes" in Asian American Studies were conducted in community centers, homes, and at teach-ins at rallies and demonstrations. In these community settings the distinction between students and teachers was not rigidly defined, and participants easily switched roles, often many times in the course of intense discussions. Learning in these community settings was also intergenerational—much different from the traditional classroom where youth are isolated from older generations.

Like companion Freedom Schools in African American and Chicano communities, early classes in Asian American Studies mobilized students to respond to community needs through involvement in grassroots movements around labor issues, housing needs, immigrants rights, and youth and elderly problems. Participation in these movements schooled students in power relations in society and provided them training in valuable leadership skills. Through these struggles, students also learned the importance of redirecting university resources back to their neighborhoods. Through connections to community movements, students discovered firsthand the dual liberatory mission of education—to expand democracy in society and to transform oneself.

In several cities students and community activists launched educational projects based on this liberatory vision of education. One example is the summer "Asian American Community College" organized and coordinated by students associated with the UCLA Asian American Studies Center in the early 1970s. Here is the way student organizers described their project in *Gidra*, the Asian American Movement newspaper created by students from the first wave in Asian American Studies:

> Over the past several months concerned community members have developed a college to serve our people. It is being called the Asian American Community College. It arose from the assumption that education is not restricted to the ivory tower classroom,

but is an on-going process. The college belongs to the community. It can be molded to fit the needs of the community.

For this summer there are nine classes planned. The courses offered are: 1) Group Dynamics and Interpersonal Relations, 2) The Creative Culture—New Life Styles, 3) Asian American Movement Seminar, 4) Workshop in Film, 5) Asian Adult Awareness, 6) Asian American Women and the Movement, 7) Cantonese Language, 8) General Political Awareness Forum, and 9) Draft Counselor's Workshop and a class in First Aid and Legal Aid.

Of particular interest to adults is the Asian Adult Awareness which will discuss and analyze current social and political trends with a view to bridging the communication gap between the generations.

The classes are open to everyone and will be held on weekday evenings. Brochures are being distributed throughout the Los Angeles area.[6]

This summer college launched by student activists in the early 1970s is a good example of projects created by students with limited resources. Today, in a period when Asian American Studies has greater resources, what types of projects can students organize? To answer this question, we need to grapple with two new conditions distinguishing Asian American Studies today: the large number of students now taking Asian American Studies classes and the concentration of these classes in universities, especially elite institutions.

FREEDOM SCHOOLING PROVIDES US WITH A STRATEGY FOR DEALING WITH NEW CONDITIONS IN ASIAN AMERICAN STUDIES

In the old days of the Asian American Movement, activists frequently got together to discuss "what to do till the revolution comes." "What to do till the revolution comes" was a valuable outlook because it emphasized the urgency of always thinking about the connection between day-to-day activities and the larger goal of transforming society. "What to do till the revolution comes" goaded activists to overcome feelings of passivity and the tendency to rationalize inaction due to the lack of resources. Thus, rather than waiting for others to launch large-scale efforts, each activist recognized the responsibility to take the initiative in their own sphere of work and to always watch for new opportunities to expand political consciousness.

We can draw from these earlier insights to help us immediately implement a liberatory vision of education. Obviously, at the current time, only a handful of activists have the resources and power to open their own physical Freedom Schools. However, all activists have the capacity to immediately begin practicing Freedom Schooling in their day-to-day work. In a previous essay I described the creative ways that K–12 activists were profoundly changing teaching and learning in their classrooms.[7] Here, I focus on examples in higher education, where currently there is a concentration of resources in Asian American Studies. I use my own recent classes as examples. For this essay I focus on my upper-division classes, although in a future essay I will address how Freedom Schooling is also essential in lower-division classes, especially for first-generation college students.

For the past six years, I have had a chance to teach on a part-time basis at different levels of the California system of higher education: Pasadena City College; California State University, Northridge; and UCLA. Not only have I logged many miles as a "freeway flyer," I have also gained a deep appreciation for the unique strengths of each institution and the distinct needs of students at the different levels of higher education. I have also seen firsthand the growing numbers of students now taking classes in Asian American Studies, and I have begun to understand the special challenges in this period confronting both students and teachers at elite institutions such as UCLA.

In recent years at each of the three institutions, I have begun experimenting with the concept of Freedom Schooling in all of my classes. At first, my experiments were modest: a minor change in a syllabus, the addition of a new assignment, and the modification of a lecture or two during the course of the term. However, my experiments have grown bolder with my growing understanding of the rich possibilities embedded in our classrooms when we begin to engage students with a liberatory vision of education. Thus, in my most recent classes I have experimented with teaching a class without an assigned textbook or pre-assigned readings in order to open students to a new awareness of the importance of choosing reading materials and the relationship between reading, reflection, and practice. I have also experimented by conducting an entire course without giving a traditional lecture. For another course, I held sessions in a community setting to push students beyond their perception that learning requires the four walls of a college classroom. Finally, at resource-rich UCLA, I have experimented with web technology. With the help of webmasters Tarn Nguyen and Steven Masami Ropp, I have had students create largely text-based web magazines: first, in 1997, for a course on the Asian American Movement with Steve Louie, and in 1998 and 1999 for my Investigative Journalism and People of Color classes.[8] I now regard the creation of web magazines as an important tool for networking and communicating with other educational activists, and I have tried to include a web component in my classes whenever feasible, despite my own lack of knowledge about web technology.

From the very first Asian American Studies class I taught in 1975, I have always emphasized an approach to learning that connects students to grassroots community movements, promotes learning through practice, and highlights students' responsibilities to our communities. However, in recent years, I have further developed these core teaching practices to address more sharply the new conditions in Asian American Studies. In the examples that follow, I share ways I have taken up this challenge through five of my recent upper-division classes at UCLA and California State University, Northridge.

UCLA Fall Quarter 1999, "Asian American Social Movements: The Role of Students in Defining the Future of Asian American Studies"

Class Web Magazine: www.sscnet.ucla.edu/99F/asian197j-1/webmag99.html

For this class I had students examine the current state of Asian American Studies—and Ethnic Studies as a whole—focusing on the pivotal role they could play in expanding the field. The course syllabus identified four critical questions:

1. With UCLA now having a strong Asian American Studies program with nearly 3,000 students taking classes annually, what enlarged role can UCLA students play in bringing Asian American Studies into the community?

2. With the proliferation of Asian American Studies on college campuses but the near invisibility of Asian American Studies outside the college classroom (e.g., K–12 classrooms and other community settings), what new responsibilities face students taking these classes?

3. With the growing strength of Asian American Studies programs in elite institutions nationally, including UCLA, what dangers and opportunities does this new situation pose for students in these institutions?

4. In this critical period, what special challenges face student activists relating to the expansion of Asian American Studies?

For this class, rather than assigning a textbook or even a course reader, I provided students with an initial set of handouts and then, together as a class, we gathered other readings that could help us answer the questions facing us. Some reading materials are listed on the class web magazine.

One new assignment that I used in this class—and that I now regularly include in other classes—required students to participate in and/or lead two "political tours" of Los Angeles communities. In classroom discussions we distinguished "political tours" from the more common "community tours" as well as other "tourist tours" of ethnic and racial neighborhoods. In preparation for this assignment, students reviewed what they had learned in previous classes about specific neighborhoods, such as information relating to socioeconomic factors, political issues, and interethnic relations. Before, during, and after their tours, I asked students to envision an expanded role that students could play in these communities.

I also provided training for students as community educators by drawing from the latest insights from constructivism, brain-based research, and service-learning. Far too often, I have seen Asian American student activists at elite institutions such as UCLA grow in political arrogance as they have grown in knowledge and power. As a result, they begin to practice community education with a top-down approach, replicating the elitism of their institution. Counteracting this tendency requires an ideological approach stressing the quality of humility as well as militancy in community work, as well as providing concrete training in good teaching practices. For the latter, I combine learning through practice with methods adapted from cooperative learning, the use of inquiry method, and other brain-based educational practices. One helpful resource I have used in recent classes is *Helping Health Workers Learn: A Book of Methods, Aids, and Ideas for Instructors at the Village Level* by David Werner and Bill Bower. Influenced by Freire, their work advocates a teaching approach that "draws ideas out of people" rather than only "putting ideas into peoples' heads."[9]

For the final exam students decided to organize a half-day campus conference to share with other students what they learned and to mobilize others around an expanded vision of Asian American Studies. In an essay published in the campus newspaper, *Daily Bruin*, one student from the class, Rena Wong, described the purposes of this conference and her own insights from her political tour of the Los Angeles garment district:

> Here [at UCLA], we are trained to be the professionals of the future, to be the leaders of a country of people we do not really understand. Ethnic Studies courses encourage and offer opportunities for students to interact with groups within different communities. It is participation in the community and in movements for social change that form the key to understanding the differences between groups of people. . . . I hope the grassroots approach of this class will be a starting point for us to re-envision our obligations to the university, our communities and ourselves.[10]

UCLA Spring Quarter 2000, "Asian American Student Community Activism"

Class Web Magazine: www.sscnet.ucla.edu/aasc/classweb/spring00/webmag_197j/index.html

This student-initiated course emphasized community organizing in Los Angeles immigrant enclaves and the role of student activists in these struggles. This once-a-week class met off-campus in a Koreatown building housing Korean Immigrant Worker Advocates (KIWA), the Thai Community Development Center (TCDC), and Pilipino Worker Center (PWC). Originally, the goal of this class was to have students help with recruitment for the Summer Activist Training program sponsored by the three organizations along with Nikkei for Civil Rights and Redress (NCRR). However, at the beginning of the course, KIWA launched what would become a year-long boycott of Elephant Snack Corner, a Koreatown restaurant that had exploited its Latino immigrant workforce, and asked students to help with picketing and publicity. In addition, Thai CDC asked for student support for its campaign protecting the human rights of a young boy brought into the U.S. by smugglers connected to the global sex slavery trade.

Written assignments covered different dimensions of student and community activism, with a particular focus oh the need for student activists to transform themselves personally in order to be of service to communities. For example, students grappled with the challenge of Franz Fanon to discover the mission of their generation and to fulfill it and not betray it. They attempted to put into practice Grace Lee Boggs's perspective to make the community their curriculum. They reflected on the insight of Gandhi that education must be of "the head, the heart, and the hand." They studied and implemented the approach used by Freire to raise political consciousness in others by drawing ideas out of people and not simply putting ideas into them. They accepted the ideological challenge of Lu Xun to both militantly and humbly work in our communities and distinguish between those to defy and those to serve. In addition, they focused on three other dimensions of student activism: the need to link local activism with global concerns, the need for sustainable activism and to guard against burn-out, and the need to engage in personal transformation while taking part in movements for social change.

Diana Yi, one student from the class, reflected on the relationship between her work as an activist and educator:

> The three words [of Gandhi]—"the head, heart, and hand"—represent three crucial components of an activist. The head represents creativity and knowledge, the heart passion, and the hand putting into practice what you learn. . . . At UCLA, classes don't emphasize the three components equally. Most classes emphasize "brain knowledge" and involve reading and memorizing the professor's lecture material. . . . We don't really learn how to apply this "brain knowledge" to our daily lives. . . . How can I use this class to enhance my work as an activist and educator? Increasingly, I'm beginning to think an activist and educator are the same. But the distinction is that an activist should be an educator, but an educator is not always an activist. . . . As an activist, I need to work on my organizing and outreach skills. As an educator, I need to gain more knowledge and remain open-minded.[11]

UCLA Fall Quarter 2000, "Asian American Social Movements: Students and the Filipino Vets Movement for Justice and Equity"

CSUN Fall Semester 2000, "Asian American Studies Field Practicum: Students and the Filipino Veterans Movement for Justice and Equity"

Class Web Magazine: www.seas.ucla.edu/~hoangv/aas197j/

In fall 2000, I had the opportunity to coordinate student work in two classes—one at UCLA and the other at CSUN—on the campaign by Filipino veterans and their community supporters for justice and equity. Both classes focused on the pivotal role that students armed with Asian American Studies can play in social movements for justice and emphasized the historic mission of students taking classes in Asian American Studies—that of sharing knowledge they gain from the classroom with others. For both classes, I connected students to the Los Angeles–based organization, Justice for Filipino American Veterans (JFAV), led by Manong Peping Baclig, and their more than fifty-year-old campaign to gain veterans' benefits promised to them during World War II but rescinded by the U.S. Congress immediately after the war.

Working with students on this campaign at two different campuses enabled me to appreciate the strengths of students at each institution. At UCLA my students organized an end-of-the-term forum that educated other students about the significance of the veterans' campaign. Under the leadership of Asian American Studies graduate student Jessica Kim, students created an educational brochure called "Conquering Injustice" that analyzed the veterans' campaign from the larger framework of Asian American history and the ongoing struggle for rights and dignity. In this brochure the students wrote:

> Ethnic and racial minorities in the U.S. have historically struggled for legal, economic, and social equality. Placed within this context, the Filipino veterans' struggle for recognition and justice represents more than a fight for medical benefits, monthly stipends, and military burials. Their movement has an historical context that reveals a pattern of

legal, social, and economic repression of people of color in the United States. The Filipino vets' campaign is part of this struggle to test and extend the boundaries of American democracy. Placing the vets' campaign within an historical context reveals its significance as part of a long struggle to obtain legal, political, economic, and social justice for all marginalized groups in the United States.[12]

In addition, another UCLA student, Anouh Vang, a Hmong American, wrote an eloquent op-ed piece for the *Daily Bruin* coinciding with Veterans' Day:

> My father is a veteran of the CIA-sponsored secret war in Laos. When I see the Pilipino veterans living in decrepit rooms with three or four other fellow veterans, I see my father. I see him living his final days alone and distraught. Though broken, these veterans continue to struggle for justice and equity. . . .
>
> By becoming involved in this campaign, I've learned that Veterans Day is about history. . . . The surviving Pilipino veterans represent a point in history that should be addressed. These heroes are history, and today we must face this injustice.[13]

Meanwhile, at CSUN—where students do not have nearly as many resources as UCLA students—students from my class launched a grassroots educational campaign, taking this issue into other Asian American Studies classrooms and before student groups, their families, friends, and co-workers through presentations and a petition drive. Although my CSUN class was much smaller than my UCLA class, students from my CSUN class collected three times as many signatures on their petitions supporting benefits for the vets. I believe they were able to do this because of their willingness to take this campaign deep into the hearts of their communities rather than simply collecting signatures on campus.

My students at CSUN also contributed two additional educational resources to the veterans' campaign. A Korean American Business major, Sung Lee, was so greatly impressed by the sincerity and dedication of Manong Peping Baclig when he met him in downtown Los Angeles that our class brought him to campus to speak on the vets' campaign before a student group. Sung also used his background in technology to create a Powerpoint presentation for the campaign. Sung's Powerpoint presentation focuses on the ordeal of Filipino vets on the Bataan Death March and links photographic images with a poem by classmate Ismael Tumaru. Ismael's eloquent poem brought tears to Manong Peping Baclig's eyes, himself a Bataan Death March survivor. In the poem entitled "Bahala Na," Ismael traces the history of U.S. involvement in the Philippines, the promises made by the U.S. government to the Filipino vets during World War II, and their fifty-year effort to gain dignity and justice. Sung's Powerpoint presentation and Ismael's poem were eventually adapted into a "flash introduction" for a website created by UCLA student Vincent Hoang for the vets' campaign focusing on the pivotal role that students can play in the campaign.[14]

CSUN, 1995–Today, "Contemporary Issues in Asian American Communities"
It is one thing to emphasize the mission of students sharing knowledge with the community at an institution like UCLA but quite a different thing at a state

college like CSUN, where the average student works thirty hours each week. At CSUN one of the classes I have taught since 1995 is "Contemporary Issues in Asian American Communities." With Asian Americans accounting for roughly 15 percent of the student body at CSUN—in contrast to the 40 percent share of their counterparts at UCLA—there is little sense of Asian American student empowerment at CSUN at this time. On the one hand, this means that students are conditioned to accept more traditional teaching methods in their class-rooms—even when these methods hinder learning—and to respond with initial uneasiness to new methods. On the other hand, this also means that there is little of the arrogance associated with the trappings of university knowledge and power that is increasingly evident at UCLA.

My work at CSUN has enabled me to become a better teacher as I interact with a diverse population of students in my classrooms, such as non-Asian students from the university's teacher credential programs, older students (including a few who are older than me), and students from a range of skill levels. My understanding of teaching has also expanded due to my work with "high-risk" but high potential students specially admitted through the EOP Summer Bridge Program. Finally, my commitment to the goals of liberatory education have deepened due to association with fellow activist Warren Furumoto, who has encouraged me to incorporate into my teaching the valuable insights from con-structivism and brain-based learning.

My class on Asian American contemporary issues is a weekly, early evening, lecture-style class that attracts a large number of non-Asian students due to satis-fying one of the requirements in the university's teacher credential program. Over the years, I have come to appreciate these students as an important resource in my classroom. Many are already teaching in schools and take my course with the hope that they can learn something practical to help them work with Asian American children and other children of color. These teachers usually con-stitute a third to half of my class, with the remaining students being young Asian Americans. Because my class is only a once-a-week class with students who nor-mally would not interact closely under other circumstances, I spend the first part of the semester promoting good group dynamics in my classroom. I do this through small group discussions, activities linking subject matter with food, and homework assignments designed to unleash imagination and curiosity. I agree with brain-based researchers such as Renate Caine and Geoffrey Caine that a major responsibility of the teacher is community-building in the classroom.[15] I also share the insight of Margaret Wheatley in her valuable book *Leadership and the New Science* that the creation of good organizational culture—or, in my case, good classroom culture—is vital for healthy group functioning, learning, and growth. This group culture, according to Wheatley, functions like a "field" in physics, which, while invisible, is absolutely essential for enabling the transformation of particles into waves and vice versa.[16] Similarly, a classroom "field"—i.e., a good classroom culture—is also invisible but is essential for enabling students and teachers to transform into learners.

Almost all students enter my class with the expectation that I will teach them "content" relating to Asian American issues—or what I call "supplementary content," i.e., new knowledge to add on to their existing perspective of society. Instead, I focus on teaching an approach that seeks to overturn their perceptions of society. I call this approach an "alternative framework" for understanding issues. I describe Asian American Studies as arising from the necessity to create this alternative framework. Thus, for the first part of the semester, I help students construct an understanding of the approach underlying Asian American Studies by focusing on seven building blocks:

- Learning about history and understanding how history relates to the present
- Discovering how each person's life intersects with history and explaining why this discovery is both "terrible" and "magnificent"
- Identifying key characteristics of a community we are studying
- Uncovering stereotypes, especially the political use of stereotypes
- Analyzing the "mainstream" framework surrounding each issue
- Creating alternative frameworks, especially those that uncover the influence of larger social, political, and economic factors
- Identifying social and political movements that mobilize people to fight for justice

Like my other classes, I emphasize the responsibility of students taking my class to become sharers of knowledge. In my syllabus I describe the mission in this way:

> This course emphasizes the *special responsibility* of students in Asian American Studies to share what they are learning with others, such as parents and younger sisters and brothers. Students at universities such as CSUN are a relatively privileged group today because they remain the only sector in our community able to learn about Asian American history and contemporary issues. In contrast, most people in our community, especially new immigrants, will never have a chance in their lifetimes to learn what we are studying in this class. Students, thus, have a *special responsibility* to find ways to share their knowledge with others.

For the final paper, I require each student to carry out this mission by creating and implementing an educational strategy to share what they have learned in my class with others—whether in their own K–12 classrooms or with friends and family. I ask each student to focus on building better race relations in Los Angeles and promoting a greater understanding of the alternative framework underlying Asian American Studies. Thus, through their final papers, the thirty-five to forty students who take my class each semester at CSUN can share these ideas with several hundred additional people.

During Spring Semester 2000, Loc Nguyen, a Vietnamese immigrant student, created an exemplary educational strategy for his final paper targeting his uncle, an older refugee.[17] "It is so sad and depressing when I visit my uncle's family," Loc wrote. "There's always arguing between my uncle and his children. Out of five kids he had, two died when they tried to get out of Vietnam by boat. The remaining three were raised in the States. Although my cousins are not so bad, my uncle does not get along with them. He once told my Dad: 'I'm glad that two of my sons are dead. Otherwise, I couldn't stand five devils at the same time.'"

Loc analyzed tensions in his uncle's household as due to cultural conflict. "My uncle considers his kids as foreigners, and my cousins consider their father as an obsolete man. . . . His body is here [in the U.S.], but his soul is back in the homeland." Through his semester-long educational strategy, Loc wanted to help his uncle solve his family problems by changing his world outlook. "I want him to care more for himself, for the Vietnamese Americans here. I want him to understand our status is not the same as white Americans, and any changes in government policy that relate to minorities here can affect him a lot," stated Loc.

For the content of his educational strategy, Loc drew from the educational approach developed in our class, especially the importance of connecting each person's life to history. He also wanted to educate his uncle about immigration controversy in U.S. society and how it affected new immigrants and refugees, race relations involving Asian newcomers, and grassroots social movements, such as the community mobilization around the arrest of Wen Ho Lee.

To implement his educational strategy, Loc enlisted his own father as an assistant and mediator to help with discussions with his uncle. These discussions were often intense, as described in the following exchange:

> I tried to explain to my uncle about the behavior of his children that upset him. The thing that hurt him the most was their impolite attitude when my cousins expressed their opinions. They talked to my uncle just like two men with equal rank talking to each other. In Vietnamese culture, this is not the way. My uncle told me he could not handle that aspect of stupid American culture. But I explained to him that this is not stupid because in American culture, it is fair to talk that way and two persons, no matter who they are, should have equal rights and equal power when trying to express their opinions. I also pointed out the weakness of Asian cultures regarding the matters of respect and obedience. Absolute obedience could never lead a society toward a democratic path. If there are no equal rights in a family, a fraction of society, then there are no rights for the society as a whole. I also told him that my own passive character is a result of unequal rights in the family. I used to be afraid of my grandparents, my dad, and all of my teachers. I barely said a word or asked a question in any of my high school classes. I said this obedience was the reason why Asia had so many dictators and authoritarians.

Aside from discussions, Loc also brought his uncle on "field trips" to Asian American ethnic enclaves, Latino communities, and the Museum of Tolerance (a requirement in my class). Assessing the overall impact of his educational strategy, Loc felt that his efforts helped to bring his uncle and his cousins together and also to "create a chain reaction" of education in his community:

> My uncle gained a new view about American society and about his kids. . . . The outcome that I had not expected is when I saw my uncle talk to his friends. He was spreading the ideas that he had learned to his friends and his neighbors. And this would create a chain reaction in the community. Hopefully the gate to the outside world will be opened to other people like my uncle.

ASIAN AMERICAN STUDIES AND "THE END
OF THE WORLD AS WE KNOW IT"

In a provocative collection of essays, Immanuel Wallerstein asserts that "the world as we know it" is rapidly ending. According to Wallerstein, "the world as we know it" consists of the system of nation-states organized around corporate capitalism and the ideology of liberalism and its belief that social change can be managed by those in power through gradual reform. This world system has existed for several hundreds of years but is now disintegrating politically, economically, and ideologically and is not likely to exist in fifty years. According to Wallerstein, we do not know what will replace it but the period ahead is likely to be a "terrible time of trouble." However, as a social scientist, Wallerstein also identifies this transition period as a critical time for activists for "intensive, rigorous analysis of historical alternatives." He asserts that in this period of enormous uncertainties, "very small actions by groups here and there may shift the vectors and the institutional forms in radically different directions."[18]

It is interesting to compare Wallerstein's provocative analysis to a recent CIA report on the world in 2015. Like Wallerstein, the CIA report projects a world in turmoil, where due to environmental degradation, future wars will likely be fought over fresh water, and new epidemics of AIDS and tuberculosis will ravage nations in the developing world. But unlike Wallerstein, the CIA report—as a report written by those in power seeking to protect the interests of the U.S. nation-state and the corporate economy—ignores the social transformative forces at work in this period, focusing only on the ways that governments, the military, and corporations can best manage turmoil at this time.[19]

Taken together, Wallerstein's analysis and the CIA report raise three critical questions for activists in Asian American Studies today: How are we addressing the question of "the end of the world as we know it"? How are we developing within our communities new survival skills needed for this transition period? And, finally, what alternatives are we putting forward to replace the disintegrating institutions of the current world system? From my vantage point, these questions are not being asked in Asian American Studies, and it is the responsibility of activists to bring them to the forefront, especially with the vision of Freedom Schooling.

I agree with Wallerstein's assessment that in this period of historical transition, the small actions of activists can "shift the vectors and the institutional forms in radically different directions." But I add that in this transition each activist involved in "small actions" must find ways to share lessons with other activists to push forward the creative dialogue about "historical alternatives."

In her book *Leadership and the New Science,* Margaret Wheatley promotes a similar viewpoint, which is based on her critique of the pervasive impact of concepts from Newtonian physics on our social thinking today. According to Wheatley, scientific thinking over the past century has moved beyond a Newtonian conception of the world, but our social and organizational thinking—and I would add our thinking about social change—continues to lag behind, remaining influenced by Newtonian concepts of "critical mass," "inertia," and "entropy."

Drawing from quantum theory and studies of complex systems from the "new science," Wheatley emphasizes how new analytic frameworks like self-organizing systems can help us better understand the process of social development and change and our own role as activists in the process. Complex systems are characterized by not only stability but change and renewal, and behavior in these systems occurs in a "web of connectedness," where "local, small actions" can have great significance throughout the system:

> In a web, the potential impact of local actions bears no relationship to their size. When we choose to act locally, we may want to influence the entire system. But we work where we are, with the system that we know, the one we can get our arms around. From a Newtonian perspective, our efforts often seem too small, and we doubt that our actions will make a difference. Or perhaps we hope that our small efforts will contribute incrementally to large-scale change. Step by step, system by system, we aspire to develop enough mass or force to alter the larger system.
>
> But a quantum view explains the success of small efforts quite differently. Acting locally allows us to be inside the movement and flow of the system, participating in all those complex events occurring simultaneously. We are more likely to be sensitive to the dynamics of this system, and thus more effective. However, changes in small places also affect the global system, not through incrementalism, but because every small system participates in an unbroken wholeness. Activities in one part of the whole create effects that appear in distant places. Because of these unseen connections, there is potential value in working anywhere in the system. We never know how our small activities will affect others through the invisible fabric of our connectedness. I have learned that in this exquisitely connected world, it's never a question of "critical mass." It's always about "critical connections."[20]

Wheatley's emphasis on "critical connections" rather than "critical mass" highlights for educational activists the importance of sharing with others all of our experiments with Freedom Schooling, no matter how small. When we begin to see our local activities as part of a "web of connectedness," we can link our ideas together to engage in the necessary "intensive, rigorous analysis of historical alternatives" to transform our communities. We can envision new possibilities and organize to bring these into being.

Engaging in this process of critical and creative visioning is especially important for the development of the new survival skills that people at the grassroots level will need in this transition period of turmoil and upheaval. Brain-based educational researchers Renate Caine and Geoffrey Caine in their book *Education on the Edge of Possibility* define these new survival skills in terms of what they call "the possible human." They urge teachers to transform their classrooms and schools around a new set of goals for education in this period:

> Rather than discuss the knowledge that people should have, or the skills that they need to acquire, we would like to frame the purposes of education in terms of what sort of person one needs to be to develop sustainable communities and thrive within the new paradigm. If change really is taking place in the way that we have discussed, and if, as

Kauffman (1995) and others contend, the development of higher orders of complexity is natural, then what we are working toward is the development of more complex and integrated people.[21]

In a previous book—*Making Connections: Teaching and the Human Brain*—the Caines elaborate on the kinds of "new survival skills" that educators should be teaching in this period. They assert that teaching should help students "appreciate complex issues in order to make better choices." They identify the prefrontal cortex—the newest part of the brain in the evolutionary, scale—as the region where values such as compassion, altruism, concern for others, and empathy are located. Education, they assert, should focus on enhancing the cognitive skills of students by linking the expansion of intelligence to the development of new adaptive values. "This requires us to use our brains in ways that they have never been used before on a large scale," the Caines write.[22]

This emphasis on redefining our teaching to evoke new human possibilities provides us with a deeper understanding of the significance of Freedom Schooling and our tasks in this period. I have always intuitively felt that the purpose of education—and, for that matter, of activism—is for the expansion of democracy by changing power relations in society and promoting the necessary personal transformation in each individual to better serve society. Or, as much more eloquently expressed by long-time activists Yuri Kochiyama and Grace Lee Boggs, the goal of education and activism is one of "expanding our humanity."

Increasingly in my classes today, under the influence of Freedom Schooling, I find myself encouraging students to envision the rich possibilities embedded in our communities and within ourselves. Through Freedom Schooling, we can work with others to transcend the failing educational system, to envision new alternatives, and to act to bring these new possibilities into being. Through Freedom Schooling, we can expand our humanity.

NOTES

A version of this paper was presented at the Asian/Asian American Lecture Series of Scripps College, organized by the Asian/Asian American Student Union, Claremont, California, on April 10–11, 2001.

1. Grace Lee Boggs, *Living for Change: An Autobiography* (Minneapolis: University of Minnesota Press, 1998).
2. Ilya Prigogine, *The End of Certainty: Time, Chaos, and the New Laws of Nature* (New York: The Free Press, 1996). To the best of my knowledge, this quotation does not appear in this book, which is an English translation of the original work, *La fin des certitudes* (Paris: Odile Jacob, 1996), and is quoted in Immanuel Wallerstein, *The End of the World as We Know It: Social Science for the Twenty-First Century* (Minneapolis: University of Minnesota, 1999, 258, n6).
3. Grace Lee Boggs, "Freedom Schooling," Michigan Citizen, August 20, 2000, and James and Grace Lee Boggs Center website, http://boggscenter.org/freedomschool.htm.
4. Grace Lee Boggs, "'Children's Miracle' Needed to Solve School Crisis," Voices in Dialogue Series, Philadelphia School District, Philadelphia, March 23, 2000, and James and Grace Lee Boggs Center website, http://boggscenter.org/phi13–23–00.htm.
5. See Glenn Omatsu, "Defying a Thousand Pointing Fingers and Serving the Children: Re-envisioning the Mission of Asian American Studies in Our Communities," unpublished

paper, www.sscnet.ucla. edu/99F/asian197j–1/Omatsu.htm; "Filling the Hole in the Soul: New Otani Hotel Workers & Ethnic Studies," *Race File,* January–March 1998, 33–37; "Teaching for Social Change; Learning How to Afflict the Comfortable and Comfort the Afflicted," *Loyola of Los Angeles Law Review* 32:3 (April 1999), 791–797; "Feeding the Soul and Polishing the Mind: A Film Series for Asian American Studies Boot Camp," *ColorLines* (Winter 1999); and " 'The Four Prisons' and the Movements of Liberation: Asian American Activism from the 1960s to the 1990s," in Karin Aguilar-San Juan, ed., *The State of Asian America: Activism and Resistance in the 1990s* (Boston: South End Press, 1994), 19–69.

6. "Asian American Community School," *Gidra,* June–July 1970.

7. Omatsu, "Defying a Thousand Pointing Fingers."

8. Asian American Studies 197J, "Asian American Movement," co-taught by Steve Louie and Glenn Omatsu, Spring Quarter 1997, UCLA, www.sscnet.ucla.edu/aasc/mvmt/; Asian American Studies M163 & African American Studies M195, "Investigative Journalism & Communities of Color," Fall Quarter 1997, UCLA, www.sscnet.ucla.edu/aasc/classweb/fa1197/M163/; and Asian American Studies Ml63 and African American Studies M195, "Investigative Journalism & Communities of Color," Fall Quarter 1998, UCLA, www.sscnet.ucla.edu/aasc/classweb/fa1198/M163/webmag.html

9. David Werner and Bill Bower, *Helping Health Workers Learn: A Book of Methods, Aids, and Ideas for Instructors at the Village Level* (Palo Alto: Hesperian Foundation, 1982), 1–16.

10. Rena Wong, "Ethnic Studies Essential to Cultural 'World' Communities," *Daily Bruin,* December 3, 1999, www.dailybruin.ucla.edu/db/issues/99/12.03/view.wong.html.

11. Diana Yi, "The Head, the Heart, and the Hand," Asian American Studies 197N, "Asian American Student Activism," Spring Quarter 1999, UCLA, www.sscnet.ucla.edu/aasc/classweb/spring00/webmag_197j/dianayi1.html.

12. Asian American Studies 197J, "Asian American Social Movements: The Role of Students in the Filipino Vets' Campaign for Justice and Equity," "Conquering Injustice: Pilipino World War II Veterans," www.seas.ucla.edu/~hoangv/aas197j/pamphlet/thevets.htm.

13. Anouh Vang, "Holiday Excludes Pilipino Sacrifices: Student Help Would Energize Campaign to Repeal Rescission Act," *Daily Bruin,* November 9, 2000, www.dailybruin.ucla.edu/db/articles.asp?ID=1897.

14. Sung Lee and Vincent Hoang, "Conquering Injustice: Pilipino World War II Veterans," www.seas.ucla.edu/~hoangv/aas197j7.

15. Renate Nummela Caine and Geoffrey Caine, *Making Connections: Teaching and the Human Brain* (Menlo Park, California: Addison-Wesley Publishing Company, 1991), 115–133.

16. Margaret J. Wheatley, *Leadership and the New Science: Discovering Order in a Chaotic World* (San Francisco: Berret-Kohler Publishers, 1999).

17. Loc Nguyen, final exam, Asian American Studies 345, "Contemporary Issues in Asian American Communities," California State University, Northridge, Spring 2000.

18. Wallerstein, *The End of the World as We Know It,* 1, 3, 33, 132.

19. National Foreign Intelligence Board and Central Intelligence Agency, "Global Trends 2015: A Dialogue about the Future with Nongovernmental Experts," Washington, D.C., December 2000, www.odci. gov/cia/publications/globaltrends2015/.

20. Wheatley, *Leadership and the New Science,* 44–45. Grace Lee Boggs uses Wheatley's analysis to help activists understand the significance of localized protests in challenging the larger world order, such as demonstrations in Seattle in 2000 against WTO.

21. Renate Nummela Caine and Geoffrey Caine, *Education on the Edge of Possibility* (Menlo Park, California: Addison-Wesley Publishing Company, 1997), 97. The Caines cite the work of Stuart Kauffman on complex systems, *At Home in the Universe: The Search for the Laws of Self-Organization and Complexity* (New York: Oxford University Press, 1995).

22. Renate Nummela Caine and Geoffrey Caine, *Making Connections,* 66–68.

Asians on the Rim

Transnational Capital and Local Community in the Making of Contemporary Asian America

Arif Dirlik

pervades

An issue of *AsianWeek* in January 1996 contained two items that cogently illustrate the problem I would like to discuss in this chapter. One was an invited editorial by Matt Fong, California state treasurer and "one of the nation's highest elected Asian American officials." Entitled "From Gold Mountain to the Golden Door," Fong's editorial outlined his vision of making California into "the capital of the Pacific Rim." He wrote,

> California's strategic location, coupled with its huge and diverse economic base and available capital, make it an ideal gateway to the Pacific Rim to facilitate trade and capital flows between the Pacific and the rest of the world.
>
> California has the opportunity to lead the charge toward dramatically expanded global trade by developing its role as a financial services center to increase the sophistication, speed, volume, reliability, and cost-effectiveness of international commerce. Business, labor, government, and the academic community must aggressively work together to seize this opportunity and chart a new course for California. . . . As the global economy changes, we must provide a vision and take advantage of opportunities that will make California a better, more prosperous place in which to work, live and do business. California's Golden Door to the Future is the Gateway to the Pacific Rim.[1]

The other was a news item about the appointment to a post with the California Department of Education of Henry Der, who had served as the executive director of Chinese for Affirmative Action in San Francisco since 1974. The Superintendent of Education Delaine Eastin, who was able to appoint Der in spite of opposition from the office of Governor Pete Wilson, described Der as "progressive . . . dedicated to the community and to minorities . . . who's not afraid to speak for the community." Der himself stated that while his new job made it inappropriate for him to serve as a spokesperson for the Asian American community, "I'm so much rooted in this community that I'm not going to that new job to forget that I am an Asian American." His concerns, however, transcended his Asian Americanness: "I firmly believe we must do everything possible to close the gap between the haves and the have-nots in American society . . . I feel very, very strongly that education is one strategy."[2]

For *AsianWeek*, Fong and Der are equally illustrations of Asian American success, two of "50 Asian Americans who'll make a difference in the new year."[3] But the success story also conceals deep contradictions that bear directly on our understanding of Asian America, and its meaning in the contemporary world, which is the problem I would like to discuss here. I am not concerned about Fong's and Der's political affiliations or about their trajectories as individuals.[4] My concern, rather, is with their contrasting orientations, which are informed by quite different self-images as Asian Americans: the one looking out to the Pacific and the future, through the "Golden Door" of California; the other looking to communities rooted in California and their historical legacies, centered around but not restricted to Asian Americans. The difference is spatial, but not in an inert geographical sense (east-west), or even in the sense of spaces defined by national boundaries. The spaces in this case derive their meaning from associations that are quite contemporary in their implications, and the contradictions that they present: the global, and globalizing, spaces of transnational capital versus the local spaces of communities. Given the significant part that the ideal of community played in the formation of an Asian American consciousness historically, the spatial contradiction appears also as a temporal contradiction between a contemporary Asian American consciousness and the originary assumptions of Asian America.

The contrast between the two orientations, I would like to suggest, is paradigmatic of fundamental contradictions that are essential to grasping contemporary Asian America as social and ideological formation. The contradiction between the global and the local as structuring moments in contemporary society is not exclusive to Asian America, which is also a reminder that the Asian American experience is but one instance of what is increasingly a common phenomenon not just in the United States but worldwide; the problem of Asian America as I conceptualize it is not a cultural or a regional problem but a problem in global post-modernity.[5] What is specific to Asian America is its relationship to new centers of global economic power in Pacific and, to a lesser extent, South Asia, that have been responsible for bringing the Pacific to the forefront of global consciousness, in the process challenging Eurocentric conceptions of modernity that were themselves empowered by the apparently unchallengeable supremacy of Euro-American capitalism. What this challenge implies remains to be seen, but in an immediate sense, the emergence of Pacific Asian economies as key players in the global economy has had a transformative effect on the Asian American self-image, as well as on the perceptions of Asian Americans in the society at large.

While the most visible effect may be the elevation in Asian American status vis-à-vis other minority groups, the transformation has not put an end to earlier problems in the conceptualization of Asian America, which persist in reconfigured forms, has introduced new burdens on being Asian American, and has complicated the very notion of Asian America to the point where it may break apart under the force of its contradictions. Especially important, I will suggest, is the increasing ambiguity in the conceptualization of Asian America of Asian populations as members of grounded communities versus as diasporic Rimpeople.

I will argue that while earlier conceptualizations of Asian America seem irrelevant under current circumstances, and have come under criticism for being outdated, those conceptualizations may be more relevant than ever, if for different reasons than those which inspired them in the first place. We need to rethink earlier conceptualizations because they no longer seem to be capable of containing the changes either within Asian America or in its relationship to its local and global environments. On the other hand, "forgetting" the past is hardly a way to rethink it, which requires that we remember differently. Especially important in my view is the community ideal in Asian American consciousness, which has been all but swept away by the enthusiasm over Asian Americans as Rimpeople.

THE PACIFIC AND ASIAN AMERICAN ETHNICITY IN HISTORICAL PERSPECTIVE

A spatial contradiction has shaped the history of Asian America from the arrival of significant numbers of Asians on Pacific shores in the mid-nineteenth century. For the larger part of this history this contradiction was expressed in the language of a racist Orientalism. I have argued elsewhere that emigration from Asia from the beginning represented a Pacific component in U.S. national history that was suppressed, literally, by repression and eventual exclusion and, ideologically, by the ideology of a Western moving frontier.[6] Already by the mid-nineteenth century the Pacific appeared as an extension of an expanding Western frontier, which would not allow for any alternatives to the idea of "civilization" that propelled it, let alone a counter frontier emanating from across the Pacific. It was across the Pacific that a "Western civilization" destined to rule the world met once again its ancient nemesis, the "Orient."[7]

Gary Okihiro has argued at length the ways in which the Orientalist legacy shaped American views of those who obstructed this frontier, including Amerindians, but especially of the immigrants from Asia.[8] The very term *Asian* was an invention of this Orientalism. The people who immigrated from across the Pacific did not think of themselves in continental and, until the late nineteenth century, even in national terms, their primary identifications being with their origins in local societies. Asians were rendered into a racial and cultural formation in their construal as "Asians," "Orientals," or "Mongolians" by the hegemonic discourse.[9] This discourse also rendered Asians into permanent foreigners, incapable culturally and even genetically of becoming "real" Americans, which would serve as justification for their exclusion from 1882 through World War II. The exclusion did not extinguish memories of ties to native origins, or even involvement in the politics of nations of origin, but it rendered affirmation of such ties into a further liability. Even where consciousness of origins was weak, as with generations born in the United States, the very "Asianness" of Americans of Asian descent was deemed to preclude their becoming "real" Americans, as in the social scientific "dual personality" thesis, which assumed an Asian coding in the personalities of this group of Americans, regardless of their cultural orientations. The most tragic manifestation of this racist Orientalism was the incarceration in concentration camps of Americans of Japanese descent.

These Orientalist assumptions were to prevail against egregious evidence that Asians themselves did not have a sense of unity as Asians, or even the explicit recognition that different groups of Asians could be used against one another in perpetuating their exploitation and oppression, a tactic employed by white capital against Asian laborers. While they were able occasionally to unify in struggles against their oppression, there is little evidence that Asians of different nationalities had a sense of kinship for one another on account of being "Asian." On the contrary, to the extent that they identified with their national origins in Asia, conflicts within Asia pitted different groups of Asians against one another, resulting in "disidentification," whereby members of one group distanced themselves "from another group so as not to be mistaken and suffer the blame for the presumed misdeeds of that group."[10]

Grounded very much in U.S. soil, Americans of Asian descent were excluded from a U.S. national history for more than a century. It was the radical struggles of the 1960s that eventually rephrased the terms of the discourse on Asian America and also produced the idea of Asian Americanness as concept and vision. Once it had been coined, the term *Asian American* would acquire enormous power in shaping the discourse on the past, the present, and the future of Asian America. Yet its origins seem to have been fortuitous. According to the distinguished Japanese American historian Yuji Ichioka, who was to become one of the pioneers in Asian American studies, he coined the term in a meeting in Berkeley in 1968, out of analogy with other terms of ethnic identification, especially African American, which was at the source of much of the ethnic vocabulary of the time.[11] The term would be crucial in uncovering and reconstructing, to borrow the title of one of Ichioka's works, the "buried past" of Asian America. It would also have far-reaching political and intellectual consequences in mobilizing an "Asian American movement" as well as serious institutional consequences in official definitions of Asian America.

The term *Asian American* nevertheless bore upon it the imprint of its historical legacy. The *Asian* component was derivative of the hegemonic discourse on Asians rather than the actual experiences and self-images of the Asian peoples covered by it and by implication at least shared a commonality with the Orientalist reification of Asia in erasing the significant differences among these peoples. But this is where the similarity ended. Where the Orientalism of the hegemonic discourse had nourished off a culturalist denial of history to Asia and, by extension, to Asians in the United States, the discourse spawned by the reconceptualization of Asian as Asian

American was informed by a radical historicism that repudiated the fundamental assumptions of the hegemonic discourse. If it bore traces of an earlier hegemonic discourse, the new discourse was informed in its "rearticulation" of the problems of Asian America by the radical challenge to existing social relations of the radical thinking of the 1960s.[12]

The historicism of the new discourse was expressed at the most fundamental level in "claiming America" (in Maxine Hong Kingston's words) by rooting Asian Americanness in the ground of U.S. history. In his preface to *Roots: An Asian American Reader*, which was the first collection of its kind, Franklin Odo wrote that "this volume was written and edited with the intent of going to the 'roots' of the issues facing Asians in America. It may, therefore, strike the reader as 'radical'—a term which derives from the Latin *radix*, meaning, appropriately enough, roots." Tortured by questions of identity, he continued, "increasing numbers [of Asian Americans] . . . look to their 'roots.' The central section of this volume deals with the history of Asian Americans, from the emigration period to the present. This was another facet of the title's significance—our 'roots' go deep into the history of the United States and they can do much to explain who we are and how we became this way."[13]

Asian Americans, in other words, rather than being transplantations in the United States of racially and culturally marked Asian peoples without history, were the very products of the history of the United States in the making of which they had been participants from the beginning. What justified the inclusion of these different peoples in one category was also historical experience: "All Asians have much in common: the history of their exploitation. . . . But there are unique qualities to each of the ethnic groups which make united struggles difficult."[14]

If a common historical experience of oppression and exploitation justified speaking of an Asian America, this discourse also presupposed that Asian America was not to be taken for granted, as Odo's statement suggests, but was something that was to be created in the course of struggles against oppression and exploitation; Asian America, in other words, was not simply a product of past legacy, but a vision of the future. As John Liu was to write a decade later, in connection with the problems of Asian American studies:

These attempts at delineating a common culture should admonish Asian American studies instructors to focus on what Asian American meant at its inception: *a political choice.* Asian American studies arose from a *commitment* to build a common identity and a common culture. Most of the people who first worked toward building Asian American studies consciously tried to create a culture that challenged the cultural hegemony of the dominant society. Because many of the early people were political activists, they knew Asian Americans could only be successful in their struggles if they developed an alternative way of seeing and living along with their political demands. It was no accident that the counter culture movement developed during the student, civil rights, women and ethnic movements. The demand for political change was simultaneously a call to transform the ways in which people did and saw things—that is, a call for a different cultural nexus.[15]

The grounding of Asian America in U.S. history underlined the commonality of the Asian American experience with the experiences of other oppressed groups in American society, while it problematized the relationship of Asian Americans to distant origins in Asia. In the same essay cited previously that affirmed the Americanness of Asians, Odo phrased the latter problem in the form of questions: "What should be a 'proper' stance toward the inculcation or maintenance of a cultural heritage? How closely, if at all, and in what ways should Asian Americans relate to Asia? Responses vary from 'back to Asia' types to a strictly Americanist, localized point of view."[16]

The "localized point of view" by far had the greater weight in the originary conceptualization of Asian America. Paraphrasing a statement by Eugene Genovese that "all good Marxist writing leads to an explication of class," Gary Okihiro wrote that "all ethnic studies history may, from one point of view, be judged good or poor by the extent to which it contributes to our understanding of community."[17] What was at issue, however, was much more than an "understanding" of community in the usual academic sense; the fundamental issue was the political one of strengthening communities. A work such as Yuji Ichioka's *Issei: The World of the First Generation Japanese Immigrants, 1885–1924* carefully delineates in great detail the history of Japanese Americans of the first generation so as to preserve and promote memories of community.[18] The community concerns of the generation of scholars informed by the idea of Asian America, it needs to be emphasized, were not parochial concerns, but saw in the community ideal a concern that was common to all ethnic groups. Community represented for all such groups a basis for resistance to racial and cultural oppression as well as the source of alternative visions of social organization for the future.

Finally, the idea of community was very much tied in with the perception of ethnic communities as objects of an "internal colonialism" that gave them a commonality with colonialized societies worldwide. The Asian American movement, like other ethnic movements of the 1960s, identified externally not with Asia per se, but with other Third World societies that were the objects of colonial oppression. Within the context of the U.S. war in Vietnam, Asian Americans felt a special sense of kinship with the Vietnamese, which distinguished their responses to the war from others who protested against it, but their responses were couched in terms of Third World solidarity in general, as evidenced in the vocabulary of the Third World employed by political protesters in San Francisco State University and the University of California–Berkeley in 1968, which also produced the idea of Asian America.[19]

In her *Asian American Panethnicity*, Yen Le Espiritu has offered a thoughtful account of the successes and limitations of the Asian American movement. Rearticulating the dominant society's exclusionary idea of "Asian," the movement created a new ideological and institutional context for Asian America:

> Although the pan-Asian concept may have originated in the minds of non-Asians, it is today more than a reflection of this misperception. Asian Americans did not just adopt the concept but also transformed it to conform to their ideological and political needs . . . young Asian American activists rejected the stereotyped term "Oriental" and coined

their own term, "Asian American." Although both terms denote the consolidation of group boundaries, Asian American activists insisted on their term because they wanted to define their own image—one that would connote political activism rather than passivity. . . . Not only did Asian Americans consolidate, but they also politicized, using the very pan-Asian concept imposed from the outside as their political instrument.[20]

Initially consisting mostly of Chinese, Japanese, and (to a lesser extent) Filipino Americans, by the mid-1970s the movement made efforts to include other groups such as Koreans, South Asians, and even Pacific Islanders, spawning another term, *Asian Pacific Americans*.[21] Movement activity and publications gave Asian Americans visibility on the political scene and spawned institutions that gave their achievements permanence—Asian American studies programs on university campuses and social and political organizations of various kinds around which to unite Asian Americans and ensure their representation on government programs. Asian American scholarship was to reconstruct the history of Asians in the United States, putting an end to long-standing notions of Asians as temporary residents of the United States, as well as demonstrating Asian participation in and contributions to U.S. history. Asian American literature did much to reveal the complexities of the inner lives of Asians in their efforts to make homes for themselves against oppression and discrimination. And "Asian American" was quickly assimilated into official language in government programs and censuses.

The movement also faced critical problems almost immediately. In spite of conscious efforts to respect diversity, the rearticulation of Asianness in the language of radicalism did not eliminate the contradiction between the homogenizing implications of an Asian American panethnicity and nationally defined ethnic self-perceptions. Filipino Americans were uncomfortable from the beginning with their inclusion under categories of "yellow" or "Asian," their discomfort exacerbated by the Japanese and Chinese American domination of the movement.[22] Within the Chinese and Japanese American groups themselves, there was a disjuncture between the perceptions and aspirations of the young radical intellectuals who defined the movement and the ethnic and political identifications of the peoples for whom they spoke; the disjuncture implicit in the term also brought forward generational and class differences.

Other problems were products of the success of the movement. As with other radical movements at the time, the movement in its unfolding brought out significant gender differences, with women demanding that their multiple-layered oppression not be dissolved into categories of ethnic, racial, or class oppression. The institutionalization of the movement, which required also some assimilation to existing structures of power, quickly distanced activists further from the communities for which they spoke. By the early 1980s, Asian American scholars were already acutely aware of the ways in which academic demands distanced them from the radical, community-oriented scholarship that had given rise to Asian American studies programs in the first place. Espiritu has argued cogently that those involved in community programs faced this problem in even more critical ways: success in dealing with government programs required professionalization, which not only distanced community activists from the communities for which they worked, but also exacerbated class divisions between an emergent professional-managerial group and the communities at large.[23] Rather than being defined by the originary radical vision of the movement, the discourse on Asian America was shaped increasingly by the dialectics of state policy and the professional-managerial commitments of an Asian American elite—which, incidentally, further undermined panethnic unity, as the more established groups of Chinese and Japanese continued to dominate this new elite.

Still, it is important to underline here that these contradictions were informed by a new ideological and structural context that had been established by the Asian American movement, which continues to this day to serve as a frame of reference for understanding Asian America. The movement imbedded the problems of Asian America in U.S. soil. In doing so, it also endowed panethnic identification with normative status so that while ethnic "disidentification" is ever-present as an option (and perhaps also in everyday practice), it no longer seems "natural" but calls for explanation and justification against this new frame of reference. The new ideological and institutional framework, of course, also facilitates panethnic unity when needs and interests require it. Having started as political fiction, in other words, panethnicity has come to be a source of political legitimacy.

These contradictions may not be significantly different from those of other minority groups in the United States whose struggles likewise led to new unities but also to new divisions and conflicts. Asian America, however, was to experience another radical transformation that would lead to a break with the situation created by the struggles of the 1960s, which has called into question the possibility of thinking of the problems of Asian America in the language of those struggles. I am referring here to the already widely recognized demographic transformation of Asian America, itself bound up with radical changes in the relationship of the United States to Asia, as expressed in the new language of the Pacific. What may be less widely recognized is that this new transformation, the future of which is highly unpredictable, may be in the process of constructing new ethnicities that are no longer containable within the national framework that earlier bounded thinking about ethnicity and giving new meaning to older divisions as well.

The idea of Asian America faced a critical challenge from the outside almost as soon as it had come into existence—the challenge of the new immigration from Asia, made possible by the immigration law of 1965 that was to result in a dramatic increase in the number of Asian immigrants. On the surface, the new immigration boosted the power of Asian America by rapidly inflating the numbers of Asians in the United States: from a total of around 1,357,000 in 1970, the number of Asian American Pacific Islanders in the United States would increase to around 3,700,000 in 1980 to approximately 7,274,000 in 1990. Because of certain preferences in the immigration law, the new immigrants also included a high percentage of educated professionals who were less likely to keep silent in the face of discrimination and more likely to add their voices to calls for Asian American empowerment.[24]

Equally important, however, was the fact that the new immigration almost immediately made irrelevant the fundamental assumption that had guided the struggle for Asian America: the rootedness of Asian Americans in U.S. history. In 1970, U.S.-born and -educated Asians made up about two-thirds of the population of Asian America. By 1980, the percentage had been reversed, with the foreign-born constituting 73 percent of the population, up dramatically for all groups except Japanese Americans. The immigration also transformed the relative numerical strength of the various national ethnic groups, moving Chinese and Filipinos way ahead of Japanese Americans as well as adding immense numbers to formerly numerically marginal groups such as Koreans, South and Southeast Asians and Pacific Islanders. "Roots" for this new population was more likely to mean roots somewhere in Asia or the Pacific than in the United States or in U.S. history.

The new immigration to the United States coincided with crucial transformations within the Pacific. The United States was to play a crucial part in the new Pacific formation, and from a U.S.-based perspective, what is most striking is the flow across the Pacific of Asian peoples; indeed, the new immigration, with its economic and cultural implications, appears if not as a reversal of the nineteenth-century frontier, then at least as a revival of the eastern flow of Asian peoples that was aborted by the ideology of a Western-moving frontier. Nevertheless, it is important to remember that now, as then, the flow of Asian peoples to the United States is part of a larger process of motions of peoples that is at once a product and a constituent of a Pacific formation. The major difference between the present and the past is the economic and political emergence of Pacific Asian societies, which has resulted in a restructuring not only of the Pacific but of global economic, political, social, and cultural relations in general and endowed these motions of Asian peoples with a new meaning. The new Asian immigration to the United States partakes of this altered meaning and represents an unprecedented challenge to the very idea of an Asian America.

There is no space here to elaborate on the multiple dimensions of a contemporary Pacific formation, and little need to do so, since my concern is with the consequences of the new Pacific formation for people's motions, rather than for its inner workings per se. Suffice it to say here that past legacy and present circumstances have interacted in complex ways in shaping new patterns of immigration—and in blurring the differences between the present and the past, especially in the United States. For nearly two centuries, during which a Pacific formation coincided with the U.S. national formation, a Eurocentric racism excluded Asians from the United States, which was to become untenable after World War II. By the end of the war, the United States had achieved its goal of making the Pacific (including East Asia) into an American Lake, but policy by then was dictated by considerations of containing the spread of Communism in Asia, which called for a reconsideration of domestic policies that were informed by racism (in the same manner that the fight against Nazi racism had called forth a reconsideration of racism at home). Two tragic wars in Asia would help speed up the process whereby those people who were already part of the American Lake could become Americans as well. The 1965 immigration law made up for past injustices by allowing foreign relatives of American citizens to become American citizens. The same law allowed for the immigration of those who sought to escape under one guise or another circumstances of economic deprivation and political oppression. Filipinos, colonialized by U.S. aspirations to rendering the Pacific into an American Lake, but long denied their Americanness nevertheless, would benefit from these provisions; so would Chinese, released from control by a Communist regime opening up to capitalism and not knowing how to dispose of a "surplus" population. In these and other cases, immigration has followed an earlier push-pull model of motions of peoples from poor to rich countries in search of economic or political survival. The parallels with the past do not end there; people's motions across the Pacific once again have become an occasion for business, reviving earlier practices of indentured servitude, most notably in the case of Chinese migration to the United States, but with other groups as well.[25]

The burden of the past may weigh heavily on the poor, but the parallels with the past must not be exaggerated, for the new migrations take place in a Pacific restructured by contemporary economic forces. United States domination provided the context for the new Pacific formation, but it is clear in hindsight that the United States could not dictate the outcome of its own policies. The strengthening of the Western Rim economies to contain Communism was to end up creating economic powers that have come to challenge U.S. economic domination of the Pacific. The emergence of these powers has also created a Pacific formation that has brought societies of the rim much closer economically and culturally, has rendered their relations much more systemic, and has introduced a multidimensionality to the flows of capital, commodities, and people. Commodity chains, capital flows, and even transfers of people under the aegis of transnational corporations have bound Pacific economies together. Pacific Asian economies are active players in this economic activity. They are no longer the exporters of merely labor, but also of capital. And they are crucial to the productive activity of U.S. corporations, which have become major exporters of jobs across the Pacific.[26]

Two important consequences of this systemic integration of the Pacific are relevant to the discussion here. First is the generation of diasporic populations or, where such populations already existed, their transformation into transnational ethnicities. The term *diaspora* has become increasingly current over the past decade, in connection mainly with Chinese but also with Asian Indian and Filipino populations. In the case of the first two groups in particular, migration abroad is not a new phenomenon but goes back to the nineteenth century and even earlier. But they have acquired a new significance in light of global economic developments, and the localized identities that they had acquired in their settlements abroad have been overwhelmed in reassertions of cultural nationalism that stress their "essential" unity across global spaces.[27]

The other consequence is the emergence of a highly vocal and visible trans-Pacific professional-managerial class that is the product of the new Pacific formation. As Paul Ong, Edna Bonacich, and Lucie Cheng put it,

> as the Asian countries have emerged from their peripheral status within the world economy, their focus on scientific and technical innovation is luring back many of their professional expatriates from the United States. This phenomenon has three

consequences. For the developing Asian countries, the return of highly educated and experienced people helps relieve a significant shortage of professionals in selected fields. For the United States, the departure of these highly trained professionals with experience in the most advanced areas of research presents a potential threat. Finally, for the world system as a whole, the frequent movement back and forth of professionals contributes to the internationalization of the professional-managerial stratum.[28]

We need to remember that, in addition to family members, the 1965 immigration law gave preference to this group, whose immigration was to make a major impact on Asian American communities as well as on perceptions of Asian Americans. Their presence would do much to bolster the idea of Asian Americans as a "model minority." Their "movement back and forth"(which is not equally available to the poorer immigrants) has also contributed to the reshaping of Asian American ethnicity.

As it has come to include these groups that are no longer containable within national boundaries, Asian America is no longer just a location in the United States, but is at the same time a location on a metaphorical rim constituted by diasporas and motions of individuals. To understand Asian Americans it is no longer sufficient to comprehend their roots in U.S. history or, for that matter, in countries of origin, but a multiplicity of historical trajectories that converge in the locations we call Asian America that may diverge once again to disrupt the very idea of Asian Americanness. It is multiple location in the same physical space that has introduced a new fundamental contradiction to the idea of Asian America, overdetermining the inherited contradictions of panethnicity and nationally or more locally defined ethnicities. This multiplicity of location is evident in even a cursory examination of Asian American publications, which, unlike in an earlier day, include within their compass everything from local U.S. news and events to happenings in remote locations in Asia, and even elsewhere so long as they involve "Asians."[29] It also finds a counterpart in discussions of Asian American identity in the new positive value assigned to the idea of hybridity, which in its "dual personality" manifestation provided the occasion for rejecting the Americanness of Asians, and which Asians earlier struggled against in claiming their history as Americans.[30] While few would object to the openness implicit in cultural inclusiveness, or a hybridity that allows for individual or group "multiculturalism," the diffuseness of Asian American identity that they imply simultaneously may end up, against earlier efforts to construct such an identity, encouraging the ever-present possibility of ethnic insularity.

It seems clear that the idea of Asian America today requires a different mapping of the United States, Asia, the Pacific, and the world than that which produced the idea less than three decades ago. The old political and economic units, and spatial directionalities, that informed the older mapping are no longer sufficient to grasp the forces that are in the process of reshaping nationalities, racial affinities, and ethnicities.[31] Ironically, these same changes have revived some of the earlier problems in reconfigured forms. I have already referred to the significant class differences in the experience of the new trans-Pacific motions. Another important problem arises out of the closer relationships to societies of origin in Asia. To the extent that the contemporary Asian American populations identify with their societies of origin in Asia, they are once again vulnerable in their relationships to one another to replicating the divisions and conflicts that beset Asian societies. At the same time, closeness to Asia opens up the possibility of distancing themselves from their immediate environments in the United States, especially in their relations to other minority groups. Finally, a kind of Orientalism in reverse, or a self-Orientalization, has reappeared in discussions of Asian American populations. Gary Okihiro has argued that the idea of "model minority" is a product of just such an Orientalist stereotyping of Asian Americans:

> yellow peril and the model minority are not poles, denoting opposite representations along a single line, but in fact form a circular relationship that moves in either direction. . . . Moving in one direction along the circle, the model minority mitigates the alleged danger of the yellow peril, whereas reversing direction, the model minority, if taken too far, can become the yellow peril.[32]

Perhaps the most blatant example of a revived Orientalism is the dehistoricized culturalism that traces the economic success of Asian societies and, with them, of Asian Americans, to some vaguely defined "Asian" characteristic. In the case of Pacific Asian societies, this has taken the form of erasing crucial historical and structural differences under the rubric of "Confucian" values. The same kind of culturalism is visible, as I noted previously, in cultural nationalist homogenizations of diasporic populations.[33]

FROM JOHN HUANG TO BEIJING: THE PITFALLS OF DIASPORA DISCOURSE

The reconceptualization of Asian Americans in terms of diaspora or transnationality responds to a real situation: the reconfiguration of migrant societies and their political and cultural orientations. But diaspora and transnationality as concepts are also discursive; not only do they have normative implications, but they also articulate—in a very Foucauldian sense—relations of power within populations so depicted, as well as in their relationship to societies of origin and arrival. Diaspora discourse has an undeniable appeal in the critical possibilities it offers against assumptions of national cultural homogeneity, which historically has resulted in the denial of full cultural (and political) citizenship to those who resisted assimilation into the dominant conceptualizations of national culture, were refused entry into it, or whose cultural complexity could not be contained easily within a single conception of national culture. This critical appeal, however, also disguises the possibility that diasporic notions of culture, if employed without due regard to the social and political complexities of so-called diasporic populations, may issue in reifications of their own, opening the way to new forms of cultural domination, manipulation and commodification. The problems presented by diaspora discourse may be illustrated through the recent case of John Huang, the Chinese American fund-raiser for the Democratic National Committee. When Huang was charged with corruption on the grounds that he raised funds from foreign sources,

the Democratic National Committee proceeded immediately to canvas all contributors with Chinese names to ascertain whether or not they were foreigners,
turning a run-of-the-mill case of political corruption into a racial issue. The committee's action reactivated the long-standing assumption that anyone with a
Chinese name might in all probability be foreign, reaffirming implicitly that a
Chinese name was the marker of racial foreignness. What followed may not have
been entirely novel, but seemed quite logical nevertheless in terms of contemporary diasporic "networks" (perhaps, more appropriately in this case, "webs").
John Huang's connections to the Riady family in Indonesia, which surfaced
quickly, not only underlined the probable foreignness of Chinese contributors
but also suggested further connections between Chinese Americans and other
Chinese Overseas that seemed to be confirmed by revelations that several other
Chinese American fund-raisers, or contributors, had ties to Chinese in South
and Southeast Asia. As these overseas Chinese had business connections in the
People's Republic of China, before long a petty corruption case turned into a
case of possible conspiracy that extended from Beijing, through Chinese Overseas
to Chinese Americans.[34]

This linking of Chinese Americans to diasporic Chinese and the government in
Beijing has provoked charges of racism among Asian Americans and their many
sympathizers. Racism is there, to be sure. But is this racism simply an extension of
the historical racism against Asian Americans, or does it represent something
new? If so, is it possible that at least some Asian Americans have been complicit in
producing a new kind of racist discourse? The question is fraught with difficulties—chief among them shifting responsibility to the victim—but it must be raised
nevertheless.

The linking of John Huang, Chinese Overseas, and the Beijing government, I
would like to suggest here, has been facilitated by the new discourse on the
Chinese diaspora, which, in reifying Chineseness, has created fertile grounds for
nourishing a new racism. The idea of diaspora is responsible in the first place for
abolishing the difference between Chinese Americans and Chinese elsewhere
(including in China). In response to a legacy of discrimination against Chinese
Americans, which made them hesitant even to acknowledge their ties to China and
other Chinese, some Chinese Americans and their sympathizers have been all too
anxious to reaffirm such ties, in turn suppressing the cultural differences arising
from the different historical trajectories of different Chinese populations scattered
around the world. The antiassimilationist mood (expressed most fervently in liberal "multiculturalism") itself has contributed in no small measure to such cultural
reification. The question, moreover, is not merely that of culture. *Because* of the
fact that the very phenomenon of diaspora has produced a multiplicity of Chinese
cultures, the affirmation of "Chineseness" may be sustained only by recourse to a
common origin, or descent, that persists in spite of widely different historical trajectories, which results in the elevation of ethnicity and race over all the other
factors—often divisive—that have gone into the shaping of Chinese populations
and their cultures.

In its failure to specify its own location vis-à-vis the hegemonic, self-serving, and
often financially lucrative reification of "Chineseness" in the political economy of

transnationalism, critical diaspora discourse itself has fallen prey to the manipulation and commodification made possible by cultural reification and contributes to the foregrounding of ethnicity and race in contemporary political and cultural thinking. There has been a tendency in recent scholarship, publications industry, and arts and literature, for instance, to abolish the difference between Asians and Asian Americans. In scholarship, contrary to an earlier refusal of Asian studies specialists to have anything to do with Asian American studies, there have been calls recently to integrate Asian American studies into Asian studies, which partly reflects the increased prominence of trans-Pacific population flows, but also suggests the increasingly lucrative promise of reorienting Asian American studies in that direction. Publishers' catalogs, especially those devoted to "multiculturalism" and ethnic relations, freely blend Asian with Asian American themes, and it is not rare to see these days a catalog in which *Woman Warrior* is placed right next to *The Dream of the Red Chamber*. A film series on "Asian American film" mysteriously includes many more films from Asia than from Asian America.

Moreover, and more fundamentally, within the context of flourishing Pacific economies (at least until very recently), some Asian Americans—most notably Chinese Americans—have been assigned the role of "bridges" to Asia; which role they have assumed readily for its lucrative promises. I referred previously to the homogenization of Chinese populations in the recent Confucian revival, which attributes the economic success of Chinese, without regard to time or place, to the persistence of "Confucian values," which were viewed earlier as obstacles to capitalism but have been rendered now into the source of everything from economic development to the production of "model minorities."[35] Thus, one promoter of Pacific economies writes, "With their cultural, linguistic, and family ties to China, Chinese-American entrepreneurs like [Henry Y.] Hwang are proving to be America's secret weapon in recapturing a predominant economic role in the world's most populous nation."[36] It may not be very far from a portrayal of Chinese Americans as American economic moles in China to William Safire's depiction of John Huang as a Chinese political mole in Washington, D.C. Finally, widely different Chinese populations have in recent years been endowed with supposedly identical cultural characteristics that further erase their differences. Networked through *guanxi,* and driven by Confucianism, Chinese around the world in this representation have been rendered into a "tribe" (in the same Kotkin's description) in relentless search for wealth and power.[37]

The attitudes that lie at the root of these recent tendencies are not the less products of racism for being produced by or sympathetic to Chinese and other Asian populations. Chinese populations are no less divided by class, gender, and ethnic differences than other populations. Not the least among those differences are differences of place and history. If these differences are erased by the shifting of attention from these categories to a general category of diaspora, it is necessary to raise the question of whom such erasure serves. There is no reason to suppose that the government in Beijing (or, for that matter, Taiwan) is any more reluctant than the government in Washington or U.S. transnational corporations to use diasporic Chinese for its own purposes. On the other hand, both from a political and an economic perspective, some diasporic Chinese are obviously of greater use than others and in turn benefit from the erasure of differences among Chinese, which enables them to speak for all Chinese.[38] Reconceptualization of Chinese populations in terms of diasporas, in other words, serves economic and political class interests (it is not accidental that the Chinese American John Huang was connected with the Riady family, which made him useful in a number of ways).

In this context, it is also important to raise the question of the relationship between diaspora and national boundaries, for as the notion of diaspora erases differences among Chinese, it seeks also to question national boundaries. Here, too, there is a question of who stands to benefit the most from the erasure of national boundaries. Whatever its own colonizing tendencies, the nation-state is still capable, properly controlled from below, of offering protection to those within its boundaries. It is not very surprising, therefore, that those Chinese Americans devoted to social issues and community building (such as Henry Der) should be suspicious of the claims of diasporas or the questioning of national boundaries.[39]

What I am suggesting here is not a return to the nation with its colonial, homogenizing, and assimilationist ideology, but the qualification of diasporic with place consciousness. To raise the question of places is to raise the issue of difference on a whole range of fronts, including those of class, gender, and ethnicity. It is also to raise the question of history in identity. Identity is no less an identity for being historical (is there any other kind?). Contrary to a hegemonic cultural reification or a whimpering preoccupation with the location of "home," which seem to have acquired popularity as alternative expressions of diasporic consciousness, what is important is to enable people to feel at home where they live.[40] This does not require that people abandon their legacies, only that they recognize the historicity of their cultural identities and that those identities are subject to change in the course of historical encounters.

Diasporas are dispersals from some remembered homeland, from some concrete place, which after the fact is conceived in terms of the nation (at least over the past century), although concrete places of origin retain their visibility even in their incorporation into the language of the nation or of diaspora. The dispersed also land in concrete places in the host society, which, too, is captured in national terms, even if the very fact of diaspora if nothing else disturbs efforts to define nation and national culture. Ling-chi Wang tells us that one Chinese metaphor for the diasporic condition is "growing roots where landed" (*luodi shenggen*).[41] While a prejudice for the nation makes it possible to speak of "national soil" and demands assimilation to some "national culture," rootedness as a metaphor points inevitably to concrete places that belie easy assumptions of the homogeneity of national soil or culture. Kathleen Neil Conzen writes of German immigrants to the United States that,

> as change occurred, it could proceed without the kinds of qualitative shifts implied by the familiar notions of acculturation and assimilation. Culture was more strongly localized—naturalized in the literal botanical sense of the term—than it was ethnicized, and the structures of everyday life, rather than being assimilated to those of some broader

> element within American society, responded to the transforming pressures of modern
> life on a parallel trajectory of their own.[42]

The statement points to both the concrete place-basedness and the historicity of diasporic identity. James Clifford uses the metaphor of "routes" to capture the spatiotemporality of cultural identity; I will describe it simply as "historical trajectory through places."[43] Encounters in places traversed involve both forgetting and new acquisitions. The past is not erased, therefore, but rewritten. Similarly, the new acquisitions do not imply disappearance into the new environment, but rather the proliferation of future possibilities.

What attention to place suggests is the historicity of identity. The "assimilation theory" to which Conzen objects presupposed dehistoricized and placeless notions of culture; assimilation implied motion from one to the other. One could not be both Chinese and American, but had to move from being Chinese (whatever that might mean) to being American (whatever that might mean). Hence failure to become "fully American" could produce such notions as "dual personality," which precluded being American—as well as suggesting that such an identity represented the degeneration of the components out of which it was formed.

Such cultural assumptions in the end could only rest on the principle of descent, in other words, race. Ironically, contemporary critiques of assimilation theory, to the extent that they ignore place and history, end up with similar assumptions. A case in point is the currently fashionable idea of hybridity, which "multiculturalism" evaluates differently than monoculturalism permitted earlier, but which nevertheless retains similar culturalist assumptions (some notion of Chineseness conjoined to some notion of Americanness to produce a hybrid product). And since culturalism still runs against the evidence of difference, it may be sustained only by the reification of ethnicity and, ultimately, race. Diasporic identity in its reification does not overcome the racial prejudices of earlier assumptions of national cultural homogeneity, but in many ways follows a similar logic, now at the level not of nations but offground "transnations." The "children of the Yellow Emperor" may be all the more a racial category for having abandoned their ties to the political category of the nation.[44]

The insistence on places against diasporic reification has consequences that are not only analytical in an abstract sense. It draws attention, in the first place, to another, place-based kind of politics. One of the dangerous consequences of undue attention to diasporas is to distance the so-called diasporic populations from their immediate environments, to render them into foreigners in the context of everyday life. Given the pervasiveness of conflicts in U.S. society that pitch different diasporic populations against one another, rather than retreat behind reified identities that further promote mutual suspicion and racial division, it is necessary to engage others in political projects to create political alliances where differences may be "bridged," and common social and cultural bonds formed to enable different populations to learn to live with one another.[45] A Chinese living in Los Angeles has more of a stake in identifying with his/her African or Hispanic American neighbors than with some distant cousin in Hong Kong (without implying that the two kinds of relationships need to be understood in zero-sum terms). Following the logic of this argument, I suggest that place-based politics offers the most effective means to achieving such ends. Place-based politics does not presuppose communities that shut out the world, but refocuses attention on building society from the bottom up.

The other consequence is also political, but within the context of academic politics, for there is a pedagogic dimension to realizing such political goals. It is rather unfortunate that recent ideological formations, backed by the power of foundations, have encouraged the capturing of ethnicities in "diasporic" American or cultural studies. In the case of studies of Asian Americans in particular, the most favored choices these days would seem to be to recognize Asian American studies as a field of its own, to break it down into various national components (Chinese, Japanese, Filipino, etc.), or to absorb it into American or Asian studies. Each choice is informed by political premises and goals. Asian American studies as a field is under attack from the inside for its homogenizing implications as well as its domination by some groups over others. Breaking it down, however, does not offer any readily acceptable solution, as it merely replaces continental homogeneity with national homogeneities; why should there be a Chinese American rather than, say, a Fuzhounese American studies? And why stop at Fuzhou? On the other hand, absorbing Asian American studies into either Asian or American studies would seem to achieve little more than bringing it as a field under the hegemony of the study of societies of origin or arrival.

If education has anything to do with politics, and it does have everything to do with it, the wiser course to follow in overcoming ethnic divisions would be to reinforce programs in ethnic studies, which initially had the bridging of ethnic divisions and the pursuit of common projects (based in communities) to that end as fundamental goals. Ethnic studies since its inception has been viewed with suspicion by the political and educational establishments and suffered from internal divisions as well. Whether or not these legacies can be overcome is a big question, embedded as they are in the structures of U.S. society and academic institutions. The irony is that while ethnic studies might help ideologically in overcoming ethnic divisions, it is not likely to receive much support unless interethnic political cooperation has sufficient force to render it credible in the first place. The ideology of globalization, of which diasporic ideology is one constituent, further threatens to undermine its promise (and existence). Here, too, place-based politics may have something to offer in countering the ideologies of the age.

THE LOCAL AND THE GLOBAL IN ASIAN AMERICA

By way of conclusion, I would like to return to what I described in the introduction as a contradiction between the present and the past, the originary vision of community that defined the term *Asian American* when it first emerged in the 1960s and the contemporary understanding of Asian America, to which recalling that vision appears now as "the trope of nostalgic history."[46] The original vision of Asian America may no longer be able to contain the forces reshaping Asian America. But is it, therefore, irrelevant? The question is not an abstract question of ethnicity, it is a deeply political one. So is the answer.

As I noted previously, the forces that have restructured Asian America over the past three decades have boosted the power of Asian America, but also created new strains on an already problematic social formation. The new immigration was to create new problems in Asian American relations with other minority groups (the African/Korean American conflict comes readily to mind),[47] but also between different national ethnic groups within a Pan-Asian ethnicity as well as within individual groups. Karen Leonard has documented conflicts between settled Punjabi groups and new immigrants from South Asia, while Peter Kwong has shown the ways in which Chinatowns have been remapped by conflicts between the older residents from Guangdong and the new immigrants from Fujian.[48] The conflicts include basic economic and class issues but, ironically, are expressed in the language of cultural authenticity: "real Americans" versus "real Asians."

The discourse on Asian America has stayed clear of the language of authenticity, but has undergone noticeable changes in its efforts to accommodate the restructuring of Asian America. As early as the 1980s, Asian American scholars recognized the problems presented to the idea of Asian America by the new immigration and sought to find ways of incorporating the problems and orientations of the new immigrant population into ways of speaking about Asian America. New immigrants, and the need to include them in Asian American studies, was very much on the minds of the scholars (some of whom were themselves new immigrants) contributing to the volume *Reflections on Shattered Windows*, published in 1988. The title is itself indicative of their concerns (and an affirmation of the origins of the movement in windows shattered at San Francisco State College). Nevertheless, they were also wary of the consequences for Asian America of the Pacific connection ushered in by the same immigration. The volume was prefaced by a poem by Russell Leong titled "Disarmed/1968–1987: San Francisco State College," which included the lines

Those who understand
America today
hesitate
before crossing
the Pacific bridge
tomorrow.
Forty years ago
the tinge of our skin
wrongly imprisoned us
under the shadow of the rising sun
across the sea.
Yet today
we bargain our lives
for an inflated currency:
Human capital.
Transnational investment.
Economic migrants.
What does this mean—

Where does it end?
The "dominoes" of a defunct theory
reincarnated into building blocks
of the Pacific Century
As Asians, once again
form the bridge
toward a new manifest destiny.
But bridges have been burnt
whole villages napalmed before.[49]

Or, as Michael Omi put it in the same volume, less poetically but with equal passion:

Asian American studies should contribute to an understanding of, and perhaps help to define, the emergent political, economic, and cultural relations between the U.S. and Asia. With the demise of the "Atlantic era," Pacific Rim studies is "hot." The crucial task for Asian American studies will be to define an approach that avoids the exploitative developmental outlook endemic to international capital. If Asian American studies does not intervene, Pacific Rim studies will be monopolized by the wolves.[50]

The effort to draw a distinction between the new immigration and the Pacific idea that accompanied it was an important one, and one that has continued to inform the debate on Asian America. The effort seems in hindsight to have been quixotic in its urge to preserve the radical vision of communities rooted in an Asian *American* history for, in the interesting observation of Kent Ono, "The argument that Asian Americans try to make immigrants subjects of the state as quickly as possible may, in fact, work in reverse. In the process of normalizing immigrants, 'Asian Americans' may in fact be socialized to become more like those they serve, more migrant."[51] This is indeed what seems to have happened over the past decade, when Asian Americans have appeared increasingly, in the words of Edna Bonacich, as a "middleman minority." The strong affirmation of identity at the origins of the Asian American movement seems also to have retreated before a situation where the postmodern presents "the moment for the ethnic to be conjoined with the universal, as everything is now in a correlate condition of fragmentation and revision," or erases "at that very moment the specificity of ethnicity."[52]

What is interesting is that the questions raised about Asian American ethnicity currently, expressed now in the language of postmodernism and postcoloniality, still take as their frame of reference the ideological and institutional structures created by the Asian American imaginary of the 1960s. This is no doubt partially because of the persistence of organizational structures (including Asian American studies) that were products of the movement. I would like to venture here, however, that the continuing concern is also because of the persistence of structures of racial, class, and gender division, embedded in the capitalist organization of society, that perpetuate in reconfigured forms the problems that gave rise to the Asian American movement in the first place and necessitate the preservation of that frame of reference.[53]

The reconfiguring of the problems, nevertheless, calls for a reconfiguring of the answers, and this is what necessitates a new understanding, if not a new vision, of Asian America. In her contribution to the special issue of *Amerasia Journal*, "Thinking Theory in Asian American Studies,"[54] from which I have previously quoted generously, Sau-ling Wong offers a thoughtful appraisal of the problems of reconsidering Asian America that bears some comment. Wong's argument is similar to the argument I have offered previously in the necessity of drawing a distinction between what she calls *diasporic* and *domestic* perspectives in the understanding of contemporary Asian America; the one stressing the global dimensions of Asian America, the other focusing on the national context.[55] Arguing the ways in which these perspectives confound easy definitions of Asian American identity and undermine cultural nationalism, Wong nevertheless returns to a reaffirmation of identity as a necessity of meaningful political action. In this case, the meaningful political action implies not just a return to earlier notions of community, but the defense of the very notion of community against the developmentalist ideology of a transnational capitalism that is in the process of engulfing the local by the global (in the specific case of Asian Americans, by an ideology of the Pacific, which has become the most recent location for the legitimization of "developmentalism").[56]

Given the strategic importance that Asian America has been assigned in a Pacific economic formation, it may also have a very significant part to play in the reassertion of local welfare against the globalizing forces of transnational capitalism, which returns this discussion to where it started. As the contrasts between Matt Fong and Henry Der reveal, the question of a Pacific versus a community orientation is no longer simply a question of Asian America as expressed in the vision of the 1960s, or perpetuated in racially or nationally conceived notions of ethnicity. Those questions are themselves embedded in the confrontations between futures mortgaged to the promises of a utopianized transnational capitalism and the very concrete realities of everyday existence at the level of the local, in which there are few differences between old-timers and newcomers, between Asians and others. Where "bridges" are placed under such circumstances is a matter not of ethnic destiny, but of political choice. I will conclude here with a long quotation that I hope embodies in the concrete the many themes, and the complex history, of an idea that is Asian America:

Kathy Nishimoto Masaoka is standing in front of the twelve-foot-tall "Friendship Knot," a double helix of concrete anchored in the mall next to the New Otani. She is scowling at the bronze plaque that dedicates the sculpture to Morinosuke Kajima, the wartime boss of the Hanaoke slaves, but here described as an "international businessman, whose vision and generosity initiated the revitalization of Little Tokyo."

"This used to be the heart of the community," she explains, pointing toward a courtyard of glitzy tourist shops selling Armani suits and English hunting gear under the shadow of the New Otani. "Three old hotels provided affordable housing for elderly Issei [first-generation immigrants] as well as young Latino families. There were scores of traditional, family-run storefronts and cheap restaurants.

"But then, in 1973, Kajima created the East-West Development Corporation to oversee the redevelopment of this area. The residents wanted replacement senior housing and the preservation of existing business. The Downtown corporate leaders and the city's Community Redevelopment Agency (C.R.A.), on the other hand, pushed Kajima's plan for a luxury hotel and shopping center. They saw Little Tokyo as a conduit for Japanese corporate investment, not as a vibrant Japanese-American neighborhood. Kajima eventually selected the New Otani chain, headed by a wealthy Japanese family, to manage the hotel."[57]

According to Mike Davis, Little Tokyo activists, led by a female Salvadoran immigrant, were in touch with elderly Chinese men who had been victims of Kajima operations during World War II, to establish solidarity against Kajima, welcomed otherwise through the "Golden Doors" of the Pacific. That, too, may be trans-Pacific panethnicity, but one that is defined by a different kind of politics that grounds transnationalism in the welfare of local communities.

NOTES

This is a revised version of an essay that was commissioned by the Asia Society, but initially published in *Amerasia* 22(3) (1996). I would like to thank the Asia Society, especially Vishakha Desai, vice president in charge of cultural programs, for permission to publish the essay first in *Amerasia*. The views expressed in this chapter are strictly my own and implicitly or explicitly at odds with those of the Asia Society, which initially sponsored the "Bridges with Asia" project. I hope the differences are productive in consequence; institutions such as the Asia Society may make important contributions to the resolution of the problems I discuss in the chapter.

1. Matt Fong, "From Gold Mountain to the Golden Door," *AsianWeek* 17(12) (January 19, 1996): 7.
2. Alethea Yip, "APA [Asian Pacific American] Spokesman," *AsianWeek* 17(12) (January 19, 1996): 9. Governor Wilson's office objected to Der for the latter's views on "affirmative action, 'English-only' legislation, Proposition 187, and Wilson himself," which obviously differed from those of the governor.
3. See *AsianWeek* 17 (19) (January 5, 1996): 13–18, for the list.
4. It is noteworthy here that while many of the changes I discuss, especially the revitalized orientation to Asia and the Pacific, are associated with the post-1965 immigrant population, with its immediate ties to countries of origin. This is not the case with Matt Fong, who, according to *AsianWeek*, is a fourth-generation Chinese American. The question, in other words, is not one of being more or less American, conceived in generational or other terms.
5. For further discussion of this problem, see Arif Dirlik, "The Global in the Local," and the other essays in the collection *Global/Local: Cultural Production and the Transnational Imaginary*, ed. Rob Wilson and Wimal Dissayanake (Durham, N.C.: Duke University Press, in print). My interpretation here obviously places structural relationships ahead of culturalist arguments that promote an "Asian" exceptionalism, which is popular especially among non-Asian writers on Asian Americans and the contemporary Pacific.
6. Arif Dirlik, "Asia-Pacific in Asian-American Perspective," in *What Is in a Rim? Critical Perspectives on the Pacific Region Idea, Second Edition*, ed. Arif Dirlik (Lanham, Md.: Rowman & Littlefield, 1997), 283–308.
7. For a recent (and still unabashedly triumphalist) discussion, see Arrell Morgan Gibson, *Yankees in Paradise: The Pacific Basin Frontier* (Albuquerque: University of New Mexico Press, 1993), completed with the assistance of John S. Whitehead.
8. Gary Y. Okihiro, *Margins and Mainstreams: Asians in American History and Culture* (Seattle: University of Washington Press, 1994), chap. 1.
9. I owe the term *racial formation* to Michael Omi and Howard Winant, *Racial Formation in the United States: From the 1960s to the 1980s* (New York: Routledge, 1986). In the article

cited previously in endnote 6, I explain at some length why, given the legacy of Orientalism, culture is also an important element in considerations of Asian America.

10. Yen Le Espiritu, *Asian American Panethnicity: Bridging Institutions and Identities* (Philadelphia: Temple University Press, 1992), 20. Espiritu derived the idea from David M. Hayano, "Ethnic Identification and Disidentification: Japanese-American Views of Chinese Americans," *Ethnic Groups* 3(2) (1981): 157–71.

11. At a conference at Duke University, "Asia-Pacific Identities: Culture and Identity Formation in the Age of Global Capital," April 13–15, 1995. Other terms of identity available at the time included *yellow* and even *Oriental*.

12. Omi and Winant have usefully defined "rearticulation" as "the process of redefinition of political interests and identities, through a process of recombination of familiar ideas and values in hitherto unrecognized ways." Omi and Winant, *Racial Formation*, 146, fn 8.

13. Franklin Odo, "Preface," in *Roots: An Asian American Reader*, ed. Amy Tachiki, Eddie Wong, Franklin Odo, and Buck Wong (Los Angeles: UCLA Asian American Studies Center, 1971), vii, viii.

14. Odo, "Preface," in *Roots*, ix.

15. John M. Liu, "The Relationship of Migration Research to Asian American Studies: Unity and Diversity within the Curriculum," in *Reflections on Shattered Windows: Promises and Prospects for Asian American Studies*, ed. Gary Y Okihiro, Shirley Hune, Arthur A. Hansen, and John M. Liu (Pullman: Washington State University Press, 1988)), 117–25, here 123–4.

16. Odo, "Preface," in *Roots*, x–xi.

17. Gary Y. Okihiro, "The Idea of Community and a 'Particular Type of History,'" in *Reflections on Shattered Windows*, 175–83, here 181.

18. Yuji Ichioka, *Issei: The World of the First Generation Japanese Immigrants, 1885–1924* (New York: Free Press, 1988).

19. See Odo, "Preface," in *Roots*, x, for the Third World. For differences of Asian American responses to the war in Vietnam, see Espiritu, *Panethnicity*, 44. For the student movement in 1968, see the special issue of *Amerasia* 15(1) (1989).

20. Espiritu, *Panethnicity*, 162.

21. See Emma Gee, ed., *Counterpoint: Perspectives on Asian America* (Los Angeles: UCLA Asian American Studies Center, 1976), pref. I should note here that this inclusiveness has not always been welcomed by those so included. Native Hawaiians, for example, who identify with indigenous rather than ethnic causes, see Asian Americans in Hawaii as participants in the expropriation of Hawaiian lands and part of the structure of foreign domination. From this perspective, the idea of Asian Pacific American is another instance of the imperialistic erasure of Hawaiian indigenism. For an example, see the essays in Haunani Kay-Trask, *From a Native Daughter: Colonialism and Sovereignty in Hawaii* (Monroe, Maine: Common Courage, 1993). Other Pacific Islanders, too, often identify more closely with indigenism, and their relationship to Asians is shaped by local experiences with Asian populations that are direct rather than intermediated by what happens in the United States (e.g., Asian Indians in Fiji, or Japanese and, more recently, Taiwanese investments in the South Pacific).

22. Espiritu, *Panethnicity*, 104. Already in 1976 an examination of the movement by a Filipino writer challenged its panethnic assumptions. See Lemuel F. Ignacio, *Asian Americans and Pacific Islanders (Is There Such an Ethnic Group?)* (San Jose, Calif.: Pilipino Development Associates, 1976).

23. See, especially, chap. 4.

24. See, for example, Leland T. Saito and John Horton, "The New Chinese Immigration and the Rise of Asian American Politics in Monterey Park California," in *The New Asian Immigration in Los Angeles and Global Restructuring*, ed. Paul Ong, Edna Bonacich, and Lucie Cheng (Philadelphia: Temple University Press, 1994), 233–63, here 243.

25. Peter Kwong, "China's Human Traffickers," *The Nation* (October 17, 1994): 422–5. In other cases, as with Filipinas or women from Southeast Asia, indentured servitude would seem to be more gender specific.

26. In his testimony before an incredulous congressional committee in 1877, Henry George argued against Chinese immigration while at the same time defending "free trade" on the grounds that while the import of the products of cheap labor benefited the United States, the import of the labor itself did not. George nevertheless backed away from a suggestion that employers should "employ where they can the cheapest." More than a century later, the latter has become the common practice in the Pacific economy, which is what I mean here by the export of jobs. While there may not be much difference between the export of capital and the import of labor, as some of the congressmen suggested to George in 1877, labor immigration still meets with immediate opposition while the free mobility of capital usually goes unnoticed. See Philip S. Foner and Daniel Rosenberg, eds., *Racism, Dissent, and Asian Americans from 1850 to the Present: A Documentary History* (Westport, Conn.: Greenwood, 1993), 25–9.

27. For further discussion, see Arif Dirlik, "Critical Reflections on 'Chinese Capitalism' as Paradigm," *Identities* (forthcoming). Cultural nationalism is complicated, and contradicted, by simultaneous claims to an "Asian" legacy as an explanation of success that seeks to dislodge a Eurocentric conceptualization of capitalism. For a discussion of the complexities of diasporic identities, see Ling-chi Wang, "Roots and Changing Identity of the Chinese in the United States," *Daedalus* (Spring 1991): 181–206.

28. Paul Ong, Edna Bonacich, and Lucie Cheng, "The Political Economy of Capitalist Restructuring and the New Asian Immigration," in *New Asian Immigration*, 3–35, here 13.

29. This blurring of boundaries between Asia and Asian America may be typical of a phenomenon that pertains to ethnic studies in general. Young Mexican Americans, according to one source, "reject the 'Chicano' label, and, even more vociferously, 'Hispanic' and 'Latino.' 'We're Mexicans,' they say." Ana Castillo, "Impressions of a Xicana Dreamer," *The Bloomsbury Review* (November/December 1995), 5, 13, here 5. A 1995 Bantam Doubleday Dell catalog for "ethnic studies" is divided into sections that include "Asian studies" (the "core curriculum," which includes Chinese novels such as the *Dream of the Red Chamber* and *Wild Swans*), "Middle Eastern studies," "Native American Studies," and "Hispanic/ Latino/Chicano studies." With the exception of Native American studies, all the sections draw freely on literature from the "areas" from which the ethnicities presumably hail. In the case of Asian Americans, there have been calls in scholarly circles to bring Asian American studies closer to Asian studies. Asian American studies are much in demand these days, mostly in response to student protests. Very often, however, the impression given by these demands is that Asian American studies should be studies of Rimpeople, rather than Asian Americans within the context of ethnic relations within the United States. I have stressed the importance of the Pacific dimension of Asian America, but as an element that disturbs national histories on both sides of the ocean. There is something quite dangerous politically in overemphasizing the Asianness of Asian Americanness, which renders them "foreign," even if that "foreignness" may be more acceptable presently than in the nineteenth century, and may even be marketable under the rubric of "multiculturalism" (at least of a transnational corporate multiculturalism). It also distances ethnic groups in the United States from one another, by identifying them with their various areas of origin, rather than with the locations that they share, and provides the point of departure for any kind of common political action. There is a good case to be made here that the blurring of area boundaries plays into the hands of existing hegemonic constructions of globalism and "multiculturalism," rather than challenging them, which also reflects the needs of an Asian American elite in complicity with existing structures of power. Against this construction, the call for the original goals of "ethnic studies" seems radical indeed. For an example by a Korean American student activist who stresses the need for "ethnic studies," rather than "area studies," see Ronald Kim, "The Myth and Reality of Ethnic Studies," *AsianWeek* (February 16, 1996): 7.

30. For an example, see the influential essay by Lisa Lowe, "Heterogeneity, Hybridity, Multiplicity: Marking Asian American Differences," *Diaspora* 1(1) (Spring 1991): 24–44. For an early discussion of "hybridity" that stresses its disabling consequences for young

Asian Americans, see William Carlson Smith, *Americans in Process: A Study of Our Citizens of Oriental Ancestry* (New York: Arno and the *New York Times*, 1970), chap. xvii, "Cultural Hybridism." Originally published in 1937.

31. While different groups may experience this remapping differently, it is clear that the phenomenon itself is not exclusive to any one group, but a product of what I referred to as global postmodernity. A seminal work to address the question, this time in relation to the African diaspora, is Paul Gilroy's *The Black Atlantic: Modernity and Double Consciousness* (Cambridge, Mass.: Harvard University Press, 1993).

32. Okihiro, *Margins and Mainstreams*, 142. For an earlier critique that emphasizes the conservative implications of the model minority idea, see Keith Osajima, "Asian Americans as the Model Minority: An Analysis of the Popular Press Image in the 1960s and 1980s," in *Reflections on Shattered Windows*, 165–74.

33. For a more detailed discussion, see Arif Dirlik, "Confucius in the Borderlands: Global Capitalism and the Reinvention of Confucianism," *Boundary 2* 22(3) (Fall 1995): 229–73.

34. There is a great deal of material on the John Huang case, although no studies as yet. For a blatant example of the unscrupulous linking of John Huang with the Riadys and the PRC, see William Safire, "Listening to Hearings," *New York Times* (13 July 1997).

35. It is noteworthy that with the so-called meltdown of Asian economies in late 1997, "Asian Values," among them Confucianism, have once again lost their luster. It turns out once again that Asian values have been responsible for creating a corrupt "crony capitalism" that inevitably led to economic breakdown.

36. Joel Kotkin, "The New Yankee Traders," *INC* (March 1996): 25.

37. For critiques of these tendencies in connection with the John Huang case, see Ling-chi Wang, "Foreign Money Is No Friend of Ours," *AsianWeek* (November 8, 1996): 7, and Nick Cullather, "The Latest 'Peril' From Asia," *AsianWeek* (November 15, 1996): 7.

38. For an important discussion, see Peter Kwong, *Forbidden Workers: Illegal Chinese Immigrants and American Labor* (New York: New Press, 1997), especially chap. 5, "Manufacturing Ethnicity."

39. Such suspicion is not limited to Chinese Americans. In a recent conference in Singapore, one paper presentation that foregrounded diasporas and "transnations" was challenged by the well-known Singapore sociologist and activist Chua Beng-huat, who declared without qualification that he was a Singaporean, not a transnational or diasporic.

40. I am referring here to the title of a conference held in early November 1997 at New York University, "Where Is Home?" (previously the title of an exhibition on the Chinese in the United States). The preoccupation has its roots in a particularly narcissistic and manipulative offshoot of cultural studies.

41. Ling-chi Wang, "Roots and Changing Identity," 199–200.

42. Kathleen Neils Conzen, "Making Their Own America: Assimilation Theory and the German Peasant Pioneer," German Historical Institute, Washington, D.C., Annual Lecture Series, No. 3 (New York: Berg Publishers, 1990), 9.

43. See the collection of his essays in *Routes: Travel and Translation in the Late Twentieth Century* (Cambridge, Mass.: Harvard University Press, 1997).

44. For a recent trenchant critique of "hybridity," see Jonathan Friedman, "Global Crises, the Struggle for Cultural Identity and Intellectual Porkbarrelling: Cosmopolitans versus Locals, Ethnics and Nationals in an Era of De-hegemonisation," in *Debating Cultural Identity: Multi-Cultural Identities and the Politics of Anti-Racism*, ed. Pnina Werbner and Tariq Madood (London: ZED, 1997), 70–89. My critique here, needless to say, refers not to the intentions of those who employ the concept of hybridity, but rather to the logic of the metaphor.

45. The divisive effects of diasporic discourse as I approach it here are similar to the divisive effects of the idea of a "model minority."

46. Kent A. Ono, "Re/Signing 'Asian American': Rhetorical Problematics of Nation," *Amerasia Journal* 21(1 & 2) (1995): 67–78, here 77, fn. 20.

47. For a critical (and sensitive) discussion of the African/Korean American conflict, see Nancy Abelmann and John Lie, *Blue Dreams: Korean Americans and the Los Angeles Riots*

(Cambridge, Mass.: Harvard University Press, 1995). I am grateful to Mette Thunoe for bringing this work to my attention.

48. Karen I. Leonard, *Making Ethnic Choices: California's Punjabi Mexican Americans* (Philadelphia: Temple University Press, 1992); Peter Kwong, "The Wages of Fear," *The Village Voice* (April 26, 1994): 1–5. See also his more recent *Forbidden Workers*.

49. Okihiro et al., *Reflections on Shattered Windows*, xiv.

50. Michael Omi, "It Just Ain't the Sixties No More: The Contemporary Dilemmas of Asian American Studies," in Okihiro et al., *Reflections on Shattered Windows*, 31–6, here 35.

51. Ono, "Re/Signing," 75.

52. David Palumbo-Liu, "Theory and the Subject of Asian American Studies," *Amerasia Journal* 21(1 & 2) (1995): 55–65, here 58.

53. For a passionate reaffirmation of the movement's original goals, see Glenn Omatsu, "The 'Four Prisons' and the Movements of Liberation: Asian American Activism from the 1960s to the 1990s," in *The State of Asian America: Activism and Resistance in the 1990s*, ed. Karin Aguilar-San Juan (Boston: South End, 1994), 19–69.

54. This interesting collection contains contributions that range from near rejection of the idea of Asian America to an affirmation of "Asiacentrism." If I may rephrase the subtitle of Sau-ling Wong's essay, what the collection reveals is not that theory is at a crossroads, but that Asian America is. I would like to take note of the essay by Paul Wong, Meera Menvi, and Takeo Hirota Wong, "Asiacentrism and Asian American Studies?" (137–47), which argues for an Asiacentrism comparable to Afrocentrism. While the argument replicates some of the worst excesses of Orientalism in its reductionist argument for a spiritual Asia, it is important in the case it makes for an alternative development (as well as its suspicion of "theory" for its inevitably hegemonic premises), which was a goal of the Asian American movement in its radical phase. Interestingly, the idea of Asia proposed here is also radically different from the idea of Asia promoted by the likes of Lee Kuan Yew of Singapore, to whom the defining feature of the Asian spirit is its unquestioning commitment to capitalism.

55. Sau-ling C. Wong, "Denationalization Reconsidered: Asian American Cultural Criticism as a Theoretical Crossroads," *Amerasia Journal* 21(1 & 2) (1995): 1–27, here 2.

56. The vocabulary of the local and the global is mine, but I think it is consistent with what Professor Wong is arguing; I hope, at any rate, that my vocabulary does not distort her intentions. Unlike her, and others such as Lisa Lowe, I think also that "cultural nationalism" is more a product of contemporary developments than of the original aspirations of the Asian American movement, which, as I have argued, had a much more historicized notion of both nation and culture than seems to prevail currently. The polemics against cultural nationalism should be part of a present-day struggle against the homogenization of identities, rather than directed at straw targets in the past. Wong uses the example of Frank Chin and the *Big Aiiieeeee!* editors as the foremost examples of cultural nationalism. It is arguable that Frank Chin at any rate has moved from an earlier historicist representation of Asian America to a culturalist position; his essentialist culturalism in his introduction to the *Big Aiiieeeee!* contrasts sharply with the historicist representations in his fiction, but most importantly, with the 1971 essay that he and Jeffrey Chan coauthored, "Racist Love," published in the volume *Seeing through Shuck*, ed. Richard Kostelanetz (New York: Ballantine Books, 1972), 65–79. The shift may well have something to do with the resurgent Orientalism of the present, not least of all in the works of writers such as Amy Tan, against whom Chin positions himself.

57. Mike Davis, "Kajima's Throne of Blood," *The Nation* (February 12, 1996): 18–20, here 19. The contradiction between community and transnational capital affects all ethnicities and has become an inescapable issue of contemporary politics. For a recent discussion, see Thomas Friedman, "Balancing NAFTA and Neighborhood," *Rocky Mountain News* (from the *New York Times*) (Saturday, 13 April 1996): 44A.

CRAFTING SOLIDARITIES

Vijay Prashad

Azia, Red Star Youth Project, Leicester, 1980s: "We come from all kinds of families, but when it comes to our rights we are black."

—PNINA WERBNER AND MUHAMMAD ANWAR,
BLACK AND ETHNIC LEADERSHIPS IN BRITAIN

Asian Indian, New York City, 1970s: "I can't call myself white. But Caucasian, that's the blood, I think, as far as racial things go. . . . On forms, I put myself down as brown, I can't help it—I can't write myself down as white and I can't write myself as black."

—MAXINE FISHER, *THE INDIANS OF NEW YORK CITY*

Many people adhere to the idea that political interests must be based on a *single* conception of identity (whether of gender, race, class, or sexual orientation). This theory, which operates under the omnibus label "identity politics," wallows in parochialism and rejects any attempt to formulate universal categories (considered to be "totalitarian"). This tradition fails to acknowledge the dialectical relationship between parochialism and universality. I argue that the *process* of politics encourages the formation of parochial identities (which retain the tension of our contemporary inequalities) alongside those categories that offer the possibility of finding common ground that would allow us to abolish parochialism in favor of a complex universalism of the future. Such universal categories (of which "people of color" is one) might enable us to craft complex solidarities to struggle against the divisions among various communities.

The question of the position of South Asians within Asian America is not an abstract question posed for a Platonic solution. The question, in my opinion, is posed to allow us to tease out the contradictions within the question itself in order to bridge the "gap" through praxis. In order to open the contradictions of the question of the "gap," I want to explore the terms that are presumed to be sundered apart ("Asian America" and "South Asian America") and to see if these terms indeed belong to the same order of reality and can therefore be joined. This essay is then a meditation on categories as well as an argument for a particular category as the bridge between communities. In 1960, W.E.B. Du Bois heralded an acknowledgment of commonality between South Asians and blacks, which although premature in 1960, is important to repeat (and it is quoted below): the history of colonial oppression and the contemporary reality of capitalist exploitation links South Asians with other people of color and forces us to confront the question of linkages. The site of linkage, I argue, is already being mapped out by an urban youth culture that is notoriously radical and angry: in a revision of a Punjabi wedding song, Paaras sings the praises of "My Black Prince, My Black Sardar: Remove the Whites" (*Kala Shah Kala, Kala Shah Kala, mere kale hi Sardar, Gore aure dafa karo*). The lyrics' cultural roots provoke us to think about the antiracism of this youth statement as well as the ethnocentrism and masculinity of the Bhangra culture that it refers to (I will say more about the culture of Bhangra later, but for now it is enough to know it as the name that defines a cultural tradition originating in England among South Asians and heavily inflected by Punjabi and Caribbean traditions). The youth bear the hopes of the future, but they also carry with them avoidable components of our cultural history. This essay is an attempt to chart the structural location of South Asians in America as well as to argue that South Asians must craft a political category that is open to the formation of broad solidarities. In order to arrive at that point, I must first elaborate upon the central concept that governs the use of "South Asian American"—Asian American.

"ASIAN AMERICAN"

"Asian American" is a category with a series of meanings, each forged out of different political and historical contexts and projects. In his study of the Asian American Movement, William Wei offers us two dominant meanings: Asian American as a cultural identity, and Asian American as a sociopolitical movement.[1] In a remarkable oversight, Wei does not question the term "Asian American," which he uses in both senses simultaneously. In an important corrective to Wei's history of the movement and to his use of the term "Asian American," Glenn Omatsu historicizes the meaning of the term. Omatsu argues that the Asian American movement began as a sociopolitical movement that "embraced fundamental questions of oppression and power" only to be transformed in the 1980s into a movement "centered on the aura of racial identity" (Omatsu 21). The transformation of the category from a predominantly sociopolitical focus to a cultural (ethnic) focus occurred following a series of complex maneuvers exemplified by the rise of the New Right and the "new racism" that developed in the 1960s, but attained respectability two decades later.

"Asian American" emerged in the 1960s from a political movement provoked by a variety of issues, notably the autonomous control of institutions in ethnic enclaves (Chinatowns, Japantowns, Manilatowns) as well as in universities (Ethnic Studies). Activists fought for autonomy from the bureaucrats at city hall in order to fashion the space and texture of their own neighborhoods (which became the concrete manifestation of control over one's community). The political project around the term "Asian American" still endures among seasoned veterans of the movement and those who acknowledge its heritage. For historical reasons, the term Asian American largely refers to those who claim East Asian ancestry. West Asians (Iraqis, Israelis, Iranians, Syrians, etc.) operate under the rubric "Arab American" or "Jewish American," while there has not been a historically significant Central Asian migration (except Armenians, but their consciousness of "Asian" is rather limited). North Asians (Russians) are more likely to be seen as, and nominate themselves as, Slavic Americans or as European Americans. The only significant addition under the umbrella term "Asian American" has been from South Asians and that development begins in the late 1980s under pressure from South Asians in the academy. In the main, the term "Asian American" refers to East Asian Americans and this, I argue, has more to do with a racist ethnology than with the historical fact of the movement's origins.

The new racism of the 1960s, which fostered the ethnoracialization of terms such as "Asian American," has a simple logic: the Enlightenment's anthropology (written by Buffon, Cuvier, Gobineau, Maupertuis, et al.) is borrowed wholesale (particularly the typology of "races": Caucasoid, Mongoloid, Negroid) and transformed from a zoological classification to a statement about "culture." In one of the more confused gestures of modern logic, this transformation takes a theory saturated in blood and genetics and aims to make it tell us something of culture. The use of black (for Negroid) as an adjective is supposed to tell us something about the cultural system of blacks, for example. While "Asian American" becomes a "cultural" designation (from its origins as a political organizing category), it remains rooted in phenotypes (yellow skin and "slant" eyes). The liberal version of this racial hierarchy exists today in the guise of cultural or national differences, which rest on presumptions of racial division (European, Chinese, Indian, African, etc.). The new racism drew new boundaries for "Asian America" in terms of phenotypes. Culture and ethnicity, despite being understood as socially constructed, are grounded upon a zoological Chain of Being. That is, as a result of a historical homology between culture and race, cultural categories are based upon and governed by racial categories. The discourse of race, in other words, forms the bedrock upon which our categories of cultural groups rest.

Before moving ahead with a discussion of the new racism of the 1960s, I want to consider a formal problem with the term "Asian American." To hyphenate America with a place of origin prolongs the myth of America as a land of immigrants who each bring their continental ethnicity to enrich the new world: therefore, Europeans as European-Americans, Spanish-speakers as Hispanic-Americans, Africans as African-Americans, and Asians as Asian-Americans are given homologous histories and offered identical entry into the dialectic between assimilation and segregation (if we break these continental ethnicities into national ethnicities, such as Chinese-American or Italian-American, the point remains the same). The differences of power implied in the names are lost. The hyphen reinforces the celebration of ethnicity without a sharp political consciousness of the uneven development of the various peoples who are now under the American umbrella. Certainly, the continent of origin retains the *idea* of difference, but the *form* in which it is retained produces a tendency to assume a similarity in the experience of Americanization: that is, even though the content of different traditions is retained in the hyphenated names, the form of the practice serves to erase the differential histories of the various racialized communities. "Black," unlike "African-American," connotes the Black Power movement and symbolizes the history of structural disenfranchisement as well as the radical struggle for freedom; "Latino" and "Chicano," unlike "Hispanic-American," recall the invasion of the American Southwest, the Bracero program and the Chicano movement.

The erasure of differential histories and of relations of power implied by these terms reminds us of the shallow use of "equality" made by the New Right in order to revoke the gains of the civil rights, labor, and women's movements in this country. Equality, for a leftist agenda, cannot mean sameness, for then it loses its contradictory sense: as the need to produce an *equal* civilization from extant *inequality* that comes in myriad forms (Marx 9–10). To claim that all people are already equal obscures the inequalities that must be combated in order to produce equality. Equality is an instinct, and a simple gesture toward equalization of community names does not begin to address the structural gaps that divide people.

THE "NEW RACISM" OF THE 1960S

Alongside the efflorescence of the Asian American movement, the American state put forward its own agenda for "Asian America" in the form of the "model minority" stereotype. The stereotype emerges with special reference to East Asians, but its import is quickly grasped by new South Asian migrants who use the term to their own strategic advantage. When South Asians adopted the term from the 1970s onwards, they did so with a sense of pride and without an awareness of the racist history that produced that stereotype. The term "model minority" implies that Asians are a "model" for somebody and that the Asians are a "minority" in terms of a majority. These implications need to be elaborated. First, the issue of the "model." The "model minority" stereotype emerged in 1966 in the *New York Times Magazine* and in *US News & World Report*, which suggested that the Japanese and Chinese, respectively, are self-sufficient and their children are able to succeed because of family support. Why was it important to highlight these "successes," given that the Japanese and Chinese have historically been the victims of American racism? A statement by the *US News & World Report* makes the timing of these articles very clear: "At a time when it is being proposed that hundreds of billions be spent to uplift Negroes and other minorities, the nation's 300,000 Chinese-Americans are moving ahead on their own, with no help from anyone else" (quoted in Osajima 167). In the wake of the Black Liberation Movement launched in the 1950s, the ghetto rebellions of 1965, the Voting Rights Act of 1965 and the 1965 Moynihan Report on the "dysfunctionality" of the black family, the media created the stereotype as a weapon against blacks, as well as to ensure the growth of mutual suspicion between blacks and Asians. The Asians now represented all that the blacks were not and could not hope to be.

If the "Asian" was positioned as a "model" for blacks, in what sense was the "Asian" a "minority"? A "minority" of what? A "minority" must be counterposed to a "majority," but the history of attempts in the United States to find a legal definition for its natural citizens demonstrates its anxiety with regard to this question. The famous Ozawa-Thind cases in the early 1920s illustrate the depth of this racial anxiety. Unable to specify its tests for citizenship, the Supreme Court held that to be a U.S. citizen was to be white (skin color), which meant being European (culture). In the 1910 census, the state classified people from India as nonwhite because they represented "a civilization distinctly different from that of Europe" (Jensen 246–69). As Lavina Shankar's essay in this volume points out, "Asian Indians" have been confusedly named and renamed both as "whites" and as "minorities" throughout the twentieth century. Except for a period of three decades, the United States has seen the Asian Indians as non-white, hence their status as a minority. In real life, however, white Americans have been unable to decide how to identify Asian Indians in terms of race.[2]

The stereotype of the "model minority" had important effects within the East Asian community. Of course, it did not apply to *all* East Asians. In response to the Soviet launching of Sputnik in 1957, and other Cold War–related concerns, the United States revised the immigration laws (the 1965 Immigration and Naturalization Act) so that professional and technical workers could enter the country in large numbers. A large percentage of the South Asians who entered the United States after 1965 were professionals and graduate degree holders and established a demographically unusual community. Rather than attribute this unusualness to the nature of immigration law, American common sense and the South Asian migrant attributed it to a putative "Asian" culture of education. Asians, like Jews, are seen to have "family values" that encourage their children to study hard and succeed; others, it seems, do not share this heritage. An Asian who fails is a double failure—both as an Asian and as a human being. Working-class Asians (such as the Vietnamese and Hmong "boat-people," the Chinese American sweatshop workers, or the South Asian taxi drivers and kiosk workers) do not use the term "Asian American," which carries connotations of bourgeois status, to refer to themselves. The myth of Asian success excludes those outside the networks of cultural and mercantile capital from access to federal funding and special programs for the dispossessed (Crystal; Hu). Working-class Asians are marginalized from their "community" (which is unified only in the eyes of the American state). The emerging elites of the various Asian communities distance themselves from the working class, who are regarded as either failures or only potentially successful and only peripherally as members of the "community" (the "community" is not something one is born into, but something that one earns, much like the idea of "Society" in Victorian England).

The new racism of the 1960s is not a bipolar racism (black-white), but a racism that seeks to validate its zoological bipolarity on the basis of culture and "values" (in fact, on the intermediary "races" such as Asians). In the early decades of this century, Robert E. Park (who came to the University of Chicago after being Booker T. Washington's secretary) and the school of Franz Boas attacked the zoological notion of race: these arcadian Americans found the division by "race" contrary to the best instincts of humanity. Instead of a zoological understanding of "race," these sociologists and anthropologists argued that "races" are "ethnicities" that are socially formed. In the 1960s, such arguments supported the radical opposition to the naturalized notion of race. The American right used these arguments over the decades in a sinister manner to argue that Enlightenment racism is a paradigm superseded by that of capitalist merit (DeSouza). The right, in some versions, accepted the idea that race is a social construct and that cultures are real: once this was established, the hierarchy of races was simply transposed onto a hierarchy of cultures (which performed the functional role once accorded to race). This version of rightist discourse adheres to the belief that each culture (read race) has an indelible set of "cultural values" that are its own. Asians are all brain and no body; blacks are all body and no brain; and whites enjoy an Aristotelian medium of body and brain.[3] The cultural implications for this schema are that Asians are good at mental work and have tight family networks; blacks are good at sports and music and have no family networks; and whites enjoy a measured success in mental and manual work and have family networks that do not suffocate. The new racism allows Asians and whites to enjoy the privilege of some form of family network, although it is often said that the Asian family structure is too authoritarian (arranged marriages, etc.). This narrow construction of "values" underlies many stereotypes about Asian social life. For some upwardly mobile Asians, the stereotype is useful in supporting a new philosophy of mobility and empowerment. For professional South Asians, complicity with the new racism has short-term benefits, conferring a reputation as a hardworking and highly qualified group. Such racial typologies, however, also give rise to violence against Asians and the so-called glass ceiling; as such they are an obstacle to long-term gains.

Gary Okihiro has identified the powerful contradiction that strikes at the heart of the "model minority" stereotype. Alongside the notion of model minority, the idea of "yellow peril" sits, not "at apparent disjunction," but forming a "seamless continuum." "The very indices of Asian 'success' can imperil the good order of race relations when the margins lay claim to the privileges of the mainstream." As Asians begin to succeed in school and the professions, the media complain of an Asian takeover of America. Okihiro parses the stereotype accurately:

> "Model" Asians exhibit the same singleness of purpose, patience and endurance, cunning, fanaticism, and group loyalty characteristic of Marco Polo's Mongol soldiers, and Asian workers and students, maintaining themselves at little expense and almost robotlike, labor and study for hours on end without human needs for relaxation, fun, and pleasure, and M. I. T. becomes "Made in Taiwan," and "Stop the Yellow Hordes" appears as college campus graffiti, bumper stickers, and political slogans. (Okihiro 141)

The "model minority" image, therefore, embodies many contradictions whose elaboration encourages the proliferation of racism, elitism, and violence against succeeding generations, who are expected to measure up to the false standards set for and by the Asian community.

South Asians entered the United States in substantial numbers after the category "Asian American" had been narrowed from its political to its ethnoracial sense. Certain elements of the South Asian community, such as the Hindustani Ghadar Party, participated in the broad movement against racism and for internationalism in the 1960s and 1970s.[4] The bulk of the South Asian community, however, came to political consciousness as the "model minority," with no memory of the category's emergence and with no memory of the radical traditions offering contrary values. In our discussion of the South Asian community, this context is vital, or else we will fail to grasp the inconsistent use of the term "Asian American" among the various Asian groups in the United States.

SOUTH ASIAN AMERICA

> *A Bangladeshi domestic worker who is active in Sakhi, New York City: "Sometimes I sense a difference between people in the [South Asian] community with regard to those who can hire and those who are hired. I don't feel everyone is the same. I feel some people have become established, say as doctors. They don't help other people—those who are taxi drivers or those who do not know English. How can we all feel part of a community?" (SAMAR Collective 15)*

"South Asian American" is a very recent category, a rubric for a social movement that is still in its early stages. Social identities constructed outside social and political movements tend not to attract people, because they lack the historical traditions that elicit emotional loyalty from participants and beneficiaries of the social movement. Frustrated by the historical divisions between the peoples of the Subcontinent and anxious to forge a unity in this country, in the 1980s progressive activists began to deploy the term "South Asian" in the names of organizations in order to attract a diverse membership. These activists, united by the secular and democratic traditions of the anticolonial movements of South Asian history, are equally militant in the fight for justice and equality (not only among South Asians, but among all peoples). In the United States, progressive South Asian organizations evolved in the late 1980s after the realization that the Hindu Right (the Vishwa Hindu Parishad of America and the Overseas Friends of the BJP) finances much of its fascist work in India through front organizations in the United States (Mathew and Prashad).

Organizations committed to fighting religious bigotry, narrow regionalism, homophobia, and elitism used the term to unite progressive South Asians who share a common politics.[5] In a timely reminder, Naheed Islam has pointed out that in spite of the best of intentions, "the use of the term 'South Asia' has become interchangeable with the term 'India'" (Islam 244), but perhaps she draws the point too sharply. Although Indian activists and Indian concerns tend to overshadow South Asian organizations, many of the organizations are grappling with problems of definition and strategy, conscious of the pitfalls of tokenism. Recognizing that no category is flawless and no political project is without its limitations, there is a need to express the kinds of concerns put forward by Islam, just as there is a need to combat forces of oppression through political activism. We must pull together broad-based communities that are organizationally built on common ground. Race, for example, cannot be ignored; nor can it be the basis for an exclusionary politics.

Race, a social fact governing the way we interact in late imperial America, is not grounded in biology: as a social construction, the idea of "race" materialized into determinate practices and institutions that produced a dramatically racialized world. Recognizing race as a social principle, the state deploys race to shape social space and to reconfigure our various contested social compacts. This deployment is racist in two ways: first, in disseminating the ideology of race and, second, in the hierarchy of races (which promotes a form of white supremacy). Various activists mobilize race as a principle of organization against racism. When the organizational principle becomes a system of exclusion, "race" ceases to perform its progressive role. The Black Panther Party leader Fred Hampton (assassinated by the Chicago Police at the age of twenty-one on December 4, 1969), left a crowded Olivet Church in the days before his death with the following message:

> We've got to face the fact that some people say you fight fire best with fire, but we say you put fire out best with water. We say you don't fight racism with racism—we're gonna fight racism with solidarity. We say you don't fight capitalism with no black capitalism; you fight capitalism with socialism. (Hampton 9)[6]

An unalloyed notion of race (as a thing whose purity must be preserved) invariably falls prey to chauvinism and genocide. Politics on the basis of blood does not offer the potential for creating the benevolent community of the future. For this complex reason, I argue that there is a need to mobilize South Asians as South Asians (or as Indians, Pakistanis, Bangladeshis, et al.), and to organize according to a universal ethical agenda. Hence, begin with the narrow terms, but lead them dialectically to a broader community.

What are the parameters of this "community" called South Asian? South Asians are divided in three major ways: first, by religion, which is often but not always synonymous with nation (India/Hindu, Pakistan/Muslim, etc.); second, by language, which is often but not always synonymous with region and class (Tamil/Tamil Nadu, Hindi/Gangetic Plains, Gujarati/Gujarat, English/elites, etc.); and third, by class (professionals, taxi drivers, storekeepers, etc.). Given these internal fissures, what would a coherent South Asian agenda look like? Would many of the subcontinental folk refer to themselves as "Asian American" or even "South Asian American"? Subcontinental people meet in our respective homes, in religious buildings, on college campuses, and at local ethnic enclaves, and our discussions center on "homeland" issues, some divisive (Kashmir, BJP, "liberalization"), others nostalgic (memorable personal or social events). Our sense of community manifests itself in many ways in everyday life, but there has been almost no attempt to explore the roots of this desire for community, which cuts across class, nation, region, caste, language and religion. Progressive South Asians do not use the term "South Asian" without sensing a need for such a term. What is that sentimental longing for unity and what are its implications?

At the most sentimental level, South Asians seek each other out to share commonalities based on a shared culture, history, and politics, and the shared experience of tokenism and marginalization in the overdeveloped nations. United by colonial institutions (such as schools, colleges, law courts) and institutions of society (such as caste identities; iconic figures from religion, politics, and film; jokes from college classmates; family and social relationships), the South Asian overseas has certain characteristics that make the desire for community a realizable goal. "It is only when we came here that we realized how much we have in common," a professional in California told me. "We learnt that we all had a thing for Amitabh and for Rekha [emblematic Hindi film stars], but also that we like the game of cricket perhaps more than we support our various national teams" (Shaliendra). Such common cause can be sought across the narrowly defined region, since many South Asians find that those Africans and Caribbeans who are raised in the aftermath of the British Empire share a similar culture.

The desire for community draws subcontinentals to socialize with each other and to seek solace from the rigors of corporate America in such gatherings and to share a common vision—to make enough money and then return to their respective homelands. Retirement in the homeland is viewed as liberation. Implicit in this narrative is a fundamental critique of the work ethic of corporatist America.[7] Work, central to accumulation of capital, is the evil that must be escaped by the South Asian economic migrant. Even for a community integrated into the networks of professionalism, the very foundation of the system (work) is anathema. The rigors of work and the travails of society are deemed worthwhile in return for the reward of a pension and a foreign-returned status in the homeland. This strand in subcontinental culture needs to be developed further for it provides us with a way to bridge a number of gaps: the antiwork ethos (idealized into the future) is in lived contradiction with a workaholic ethos (lived in the present). The social form of the consciousness of the South Asian migrant is structured around this contradiction. Retirement, however, is not chosen as often as it is discussed; as savings are reduced by increased consumption, particularly on college tuition, few can afford to retire.[8] A few South Asian migrants succeed, and the ethnic media accord them the status of "role model," which itself is not a generalizable condition. Retirement in the homeland gradually ceases to be a goal and becomes a dream. The feeling of social detachment from American life justifies a withdrawal from the social and political life of America. The most common place where the South Asian migrants enter American political discourse is to complain about the lack of individual economic growth (which will enable them to realize their retirement utopia). Herein lie the roots of the political conservatism of the South Asian migrants, and we will have cause to reflect upon the dangers of this element in South Asian America.

The American state reassures itself of the vitality of the South Asian community because of its high number of professional degree-holders. In the late 1970s, Maxine Fisher found, however, that despite their impressive degrees, "many Indians are unable to obtain work commensurate with their qualifications" (Fisher 20). In March 1995, the Federal Glass Ceiling Commission reported that despite their high qualifications, the bulk of Asians found that they were being held in technocratic rather than managerial positions (too much brain, not enough good sense). Unable to accumulate sufficient money to retire (and still ensure the best education for their children), subcontinental folk are altering their vision—to own a small business, the measure of success in contemporary America. Rather than ensure their disenchantment with a system that uses their skills for minimum rewards, the subcontinentals long for economic stability at the very least. Representing the retooled subcontinental, one entrepreneur explained that "you have to wait five years to vote, but you can be a capitalist the first day. I became a capitalist because I called myself a capitalist." With a master's degree in physics and many years experience working in the European electronics industry, this man is the owner of Action Instruments, which produces industrial products (India News Network). For progressive South Asians, retooled subcontinentals are not reliable allies for a project committed to social justice.

Is it possible, then, to craft solidarities that might include an entrepreneur, a taxi-driver, a domestic worker and a political activist? Is the only thing that unites them, their "ancestry," enough to forge a "community"? What would be the values in such a "community"? Is it worthwhile to deploy categories that include people whose political goals are irreconcilable? I am of the opinion that such categories are politically worthless because they fail to clarify the political differences within social communities. The current use of such categories (including South Asian American) is not at the level of the South Asian migrant, but at the level of their children and those who migrated to the United States at a young age. For the youth, a racialized notion of "community" has been inescapable, given the social milieu in which we live ("my people" is the operative self-designation of American minorities, whether this is used to indicate the black community or the Raza of the Chicanos). It is the young people who deploy categories such as South Asian American in order to create a space for themselves within this racialized social world; we need to offer a critique of such labeling in order to emphasize the political dangers inherent in such usage. The underlying point I have been trying to make is that we need not confuse our social and cultural longing for tradition and belonging with the need to fashion political solidarities. Before we try to close political gaps, we might check the ground underfoot.

YOU CAN'T FOOL THE YOUTH, BUT THE YOUTH CAN SURE FOOL YOU

Young people, in this age of mass production, seek to mark their bodies and minds with icons of difference in order to resist the relentless pressure of sameness. Over the years, corporate America has been able to absorb this desire for difference into its own universalist and imperialist dynamic, but the desire for difference remains an obsession with the young, who form subcultures to signal their retreat from the values of an overly acquisitive society. Often these markers of difference tend toward ethno-racial exclusivity (a kind of hypernationalism) rather than toward the creation of complex spaces that allow for the cultivation of common political ground. The hypernationalism of the young requires strong criticism precisely because they are closest to the project of complex universalism as well as to the project of ethnoracial exclusionism. Rather than set the former against the latter, I will try to explore the means by which the young people resolve the blatant contradictions between the two projects.

South Asians in the overdeveloped, or postindustrial, world have fashioned their cultural politics around many of the icons of a black diaspora culture, which itself seeks a way to keep from being culturally normalized at the same time that blacks are economically disenfranchised. A South Asian diasporic culture is being fashioned in this youth activity, but thus far it is largely parasitic on the culture originating in England.[9] The Bhangra and deejay sounds of Birmingham and Southall fill the headphones and the parties of the youth: the music of XLNC, Apna Sangeet, Apache Indian, Safari Boys, and the sounds of Bindushri and Bally Sagoo. Bhangra is a form of Punjabi music based on the beat of the dholak (a double-faced drum). In England, young urban children of Punjabi migrants used the beat and the songs of Bhangra alongside the dance hall sounds of Caribbean music and New York hip-hop to produce a vibrant sound unique to the complexities of inner-city England. This musical fusion allowed for a certain amount of social fusion, but one must not mistake the two. While inner-city South Asian, Caribbean, and white Britons forge cultures to combat the disenfranchisement of their localities, they also create ethnoracial subcultures that both enrich their lives and pit them against each other. One social group cannot be seen as more natural than another; what tends to happen is that "racial" groups are articulated in such a way as to appear to be more natural than class or neighborhood groups. This naturalness is constructed in accordance with the ideology of modernity (and of the vocabulary of the modern state, which judges people by race more than by class).

Youth culture, in its many manifestations, tries to negotiate the gaps between communities in everyday life, gaps such as the difficulties of living up to parental and societal utopias (most immigrant kids know that they can never be president and many realize that they might never have access to full-time employment). One must be wary of the easy expectation that these new cultural products will create a creolized youth. In December 1994, for example, a South Asian boy was beaten up by a group of white youths in Providence, Rhode Island, for playing a Bhangra tape (Hudson).[10] The sounds of music are not a passport into the New World. The music and its attendant cultures find their sustenance in communities of color (in Toronto, San Jose, and Queens) where the crisis of capitalism is starkly visible. But music and other cultural products implore us to listen to the youth's disenchantment with the false utopias of the past. As various class fragments of the subcontinental community meet, there is an appreciation of the failure of the parental Utopia. When I write of various class fragments, I include the meeting of the Indo-Caribbeans and the subcontinentals in places such as Queens, New York, which has its own history of conflict and its own indices to show the shallowness of such myths as "model minority." With 42 percent of the taxi drivers in New York City being South Asian, the myth of Asian success is threatened and the Utopia is at risk (Shankar; Bhattacharjee).

It is the duty of the South Asian political activists to inform the young people of South Asian America about the new world they are entering; we need to prepare this generation for the crisis that began after 1989. The parents of this generation entered the United States when the nation was in the midst of a Cold War struggle for technological dominance and was therefore expanding its educational and research institutions. Since the fall of the Berlin Wall in 1989, education has become a low priority as the state shrinks its investment in training a workforce. Capital is keen to utilize the skills of those trained overseas, thereby transferring the work of nurturing and of the nursery, of training and of retirement, to countries with social-democratic welfare States (such as India, China, and Russia). During this extended crisis of capital, its managers use the profit-securing mechanism of contract labor in sweatshops, factories, and computer software firms (Prashad). Social costs are shifted overseas (where the value of labor is historically cheaper) or borne by the domestic working class itself (whose ill-developed traditions of proletarianism force it to focus on making ends meet rather than combating injustice). Steady at 4 percent in the 1950s, the official unemployment rate has moved to 11 percent in the 1990s. The nature of work has changed significantly:

> In the wake of the information revolution (now four decades old—the terms cybernetics and automation were coined in 1947), people are now working harder and longer (with compulsory overtime), under worsening working conditions with greater anxiety, stress and accidents, with less skills, less security, less autonomy, less power (individually and collectively), less benefits, less pay. Without question the technology has been developed and used to deskill and discipline the workforce in a global speed-up of unprecedented proportions. And those still working are the lucky ones. For the technology has been designed above all to displace. (Noble 50)

Weaned on dreams of a good life, our South Asian American brothers and sisters are going to be in for a major shock. The bedtime story used to be simple: go to college, study premed or engineering or prelaw or computer science, and success is ensured. Success, however, is no longer guaranteed. The burdens of the economic crisis are being laid at the door of working-class immigrants (particularly Mexican migrants). In order to differentiate between the "parasitic" migrant (the manual laborer) and the "productive" migrant (the professional), the South Asian migrant is inclined to support measures against working-class migration. This can be seen in the large South Asian support for Proposition 187 in California (to exclude all undocumented residents from state services, including education and medical care). The solidarities that must be crafted to combat our oppressive present must be alert to the desire among South Asian migrants to set themselves apart from the obvious targets of American racism (here the Latinos). The recent Welfare Reform Bill, which seeks to restrict the benefits to legal immigrants, demonstrates that the anti-immigrant dynamic knows no convenient boundaries, as is widely recognized even by South Asians within the Republican party (Potts). Asians cannot set themselves apart from other people of color in the United States, for at moments such as these, they are all lumped together by a powerful chauvinist movement (even when they join the movement as eager participants).

The story for the youth is slightly different. Much of their anxiety about the present is being organized into "gang" activity, whose radicalism is more than questionable. From Queens, New York (Malayali Hit Squad; Medina), to San Jose, California (Asian Indian Mob), to Toronto, Canada (Pangé Lane Wale), urban South Asian boys are forming "gangs" in order to protect their communities and to transmit the culture of the community to the next generation. As an "original gangsta" from the Asian Indian Mob put it, "we want to help the younger kids get involved in the community. We help them learn about their culture. They get to hang out with others like them" ("Gangsta,' Gangsta'" 16).

What is this "culture" that the "gangs" are transmitting and what is the notion of "protection" deployed by them with regard to the community? What kind of solidarity are these young gangs trying to craft?

To answer these questions, the experience of the Southall Youth Movement (SYM) and "gangs" such as Holy Smokes and Tooti Nung need to be shared on this side of the Atlantic. SYM was founded in memory of Gurinder Singh Chaggar, who was murdered in 1976, as a defensive mobilization against neofascist elements such as the National Front, the skinheads, and the British police. Tuku Mukherjee helps us understand the very specific context of SYM political activity: "The street has been appropriated by our youth and transformed into a political institution. It is for them at once the privileged space of confrontation with racism, and of a relative autonomy within their own community from which they can defend its existence" (Mukherjee 223). A convenient alliance was formed between the Asian commercial bourgeoisie (who did not want to lose control of their neighborhoods and marketplaces) and the local Asian lumpenproletariat; the alliance was not radical, but defensive in order to protect the bourgeois aspirations of the community (Bains 237).

The "gangs" and SYM are fraught with an internal contradiction; they accept a rigid and racist notion of "culture" and they seek to protect this culture and its community against all odds. Part of this protection must be from internal elements who wish to transform the cultural practices in line with principles of justice and freedom. SYM accepts multiculturalism's racist dictum that each "culture" has a discrete logic that must not be tampered with. "Culture," however, is not a fixed set of practices that are determined without history and power. "Culture" is a field upon which some of the most important political battles are fought, such as questions of gender relations, the status of faith and of religious practice, the question of education and questions of elitism and prejudice. To close off these discussions is to narrow the rhetoric of freedom mobilized by the youth (and drawn, it must be added, from a moral universalism whose roots are as much in the pasts of the subcontinent as they are in Europe) (Sahgal).

The "culture" upheld by these "gang" formations is a specific Jat masculine culture (represented by the massive hit song *Jat De Dushmani* or "Animosity of the Jats" by Dippa) which has very detrimental effects. For instance, women are seen as the repositories of culture and as the showcases of the culture. Just as culture is to be preserved, so too are women. This means that women are denied moral equivalence with men and the capacity to make autonomous decisions. Women are more often the physical and psychological targets than the beneficiaries of this culturalism. Writing from the standpoint of the Southall Black Sisters (SBS), Pragna Patel speaks of the need to channel the male youth into radical activity alongside their sisters to produce "a culture in which violence and degradation do not exist" (Patel 46). SBS provides us with a model that is replicable and necessary; an organization of Asian and Afro-Caribbean women, SBS was founded in 1979 and has struggled against domestic violence, fundamentalism, Thatcherism, sexism, and racism. In the United States, there are many groups that do the kinds of work done by SBS, groups that find their hub in the Center for Third World Organizing in Oakland, California.[11] There is a need to write more about these groups that are drawing in young South Asians and training them to fight for social justice and not for narrow identity interests (which as the "model minority" stereotype shows often leads to antiblack politics). There is a need to formulate a theory of political work that will allow us to leave the language of political expediency behind. In the remaining space, short of such an analysis, I want to make a preliminary case for the revival of the class category "people of color" for the politics of South Asians and others in America.

PEOPLE OF COLOR

Peculiar circumstances have kept Indians and American Negroes far apart. The Indians naturally recoiled from being mistaken for Negroes and having to share their disabilities. The Negroes thought of Indians as people ashamed of their race and color so that the two seldom meet. My meeting with Tagore [in 1929] helped to change this attitude and today Negroes and Indians realize that both are fighting the same great battle against the assumption of superiority made so often by the white race.

—W.E.B. DU BOIS, *AGAINST RACISM*

There can be no radical politics of South Asian America that does not deny the model minority stereotype and that does not ally itself with elements of the black and Latino Liberation Movement as well as with currents of American socialism. This is the minimum contribution that Asian communities must make to a political project against the racial formation that is embedded in capitalism. I propose that instead of trying to bridge the gap between South Asian America and Asian America, we put forward the call to renegotiate the category "people of color." The mobilizations around Jesse Jackson's candidacy for president in 1984 offer some indication of the widespread solidarities that can and must be crafted (Marable). In an age when the right is organized to destroy the last vestiges of the social democratic framework in America, the politics of identity plays firmly into its divisive hands. On the other hand, a voluntarist call like "Black and White Unite and Fight" will not provide the sorts of complex strategic and tactical analyses that will overcome the social divisions among those who are to continue the fight for social justice.

In the midst of identity politics, we are losing the politics of class. Identity politics is no more "natural" than class politics. Race, for instance, is a social construction of the eighteenth century. Class is a political construction of the nineteenth century that enables activists to forge solidarities against the political divisions of everyday life. Since "class," as a principle of self-conscious organization, is a place that welcomes people who share an opposition to the systematic exploitation of the proletariat and the oppression of women and racial minorities, the ruling class has sustained an attack on "class politics" by arguing that "class" is an unnatural bond. Saturated by racial sensibilities, American workers have been unable to adopt the language of class beyond its most economistic uses (Davis). When "people of color" was introduced to American politics, it provided a way for blacks to run a political campaign as a vanguard for the entire proletariat. That was the tenor of Jesse Jackson's campaign in 1984. In order to make a bid for power, the Rainbow Coalition fought to define the issues from the perspective of class (being very clear about inflections of race and gender). Such a socialist project enabled Asians to find room to struggle for social justice and equality alongside blacks, Latinos, and whites. To fight alongside another group politically is not to obliterate one's own community socially and culturally. The elision between the "cultural" and the "political" is the limitation of the political imagination of the votaries of identity politics and new social movements. To craft solidarity is not to undermine the basis for other forms of kinship and fellowship that often produce the means for us to live complex and rich lives. To craft solidarity is to negotiate across historically produced divides to combat congealed centers of power that benefit from political disunity.

The Jackson campaigns (in 1984 and 1988) did not grow from the vibrant political work being done by activists who were not organized on a national scale; the campaign simply brought these activists together for a momentary push for state power. Since these electoral campaigns, a wide array of political actors (labor unions, radical clergy and their congregations, community organizers, tenant rights activists, leftist intellectuals, left-wing political parties, and others) have attempted to negotiate a political future in opposition to the organized will of the right. Organizations such as the National Organizers Alliance (NOA, convened in 1991), the newly energized Young Communist League and the Communist Party, the newly militant AFL-CIO, the Labor Party, and the New Party are among the various groups engaged in crafting solidarities for a moral future.[12] Gihan Perera, trained by the AFL-CIO, at work in UNITE, offers a vision of the struggle:

> I desired to come together with all those great folks [in NOA] not only to affirm our commonalities, but also to be challenged by them, to challenge them, to venture toward the unfamiliar, to step on *un*common ground. I wanted to explore the gaps and contradictions in our own work, and take a bold leap into the unknown. (Perera 3)

Solidarity must be crafted on the basis of both commonalities and differences, on the basis of a theoretically aware translation of our mutual contradictions into political practice. Political struggle is the crucible of the future, and our political categories simply enable us to *enter* the crucible rather than telling us much about what will be produced in the process of the struggle. "Some things if you stretch it so far, it'll be another thing," Fred Hampton explains, "Did you ever cook something so long that it turns into something else? Ain't that right? That's what we're talking about with politics" (Hampton 10). In line with this definition of politics, we need to create spaces that allow for the discussion of contradictions just as we fight against the forces of reaction: Asian America (and South Asian America) are narrow spaces that, far from continuing a political dialogue across social divides, tend to perpetuate these divisions, along with the notion of the "model minority," which is the grain we must rub against.

NOTES

With thanks to Lisa Armstrong, Mark Tony, Sudhir Venkatesh, Nayan Shah, Biju Mathew, Naheed Islam, Rajini Srikanth, and Lavina Shankar.

1. As cultural identity: "The concept *Asian American* implies that there can be a communal consciousness and a unique culture that is neither Asian nor American, but Asian American" (Wei 1). On sociopolitical movement: "In bringing Asian American activists together to participate in a common cause that transcended college campuses and Asian ethnic communities, the anti-war movement helped transform previously isolated instances of political activism into a social movement that was national in scope—the Asian American movement" (Wei 41).

2. In 1978, NORC survey no. 4269 asked a sample of Americans for the "race" of Indians: 11 percent said White, 15 percent said Black, 23 percent said Brown, 38 percent said Other, and 13 percent did not know how to classify them (Xenus, 2–3).

3. We are in the land of what has been called "Goldilocks-and-the-three-bears theory of racial culture and identity" (Gilroy, 89). The Social Darwinian side of the thesis has been recently revised in the spurious book by Herrenstein and Murray (which is based on graphs without scatter diagrams).

4. I have copies of *Chingari*, the monthly journal of the group which was published from Toronto, Canada, from 1968.

5. Using a geopolitical term was convenient, but the use of the term had little to do with the geopolitical farce known as the South Asian Association of Regional Cooperation (SAARC formed in Colombo in April 1981). SAARC's attempt to build bridges of peace and mutual understanding across the boundaries is foiled by the fifty-year enmity between its constituent nations. There are, of course, some beneficial things done by the association, but by and large it fails its ultimate mission, which is to encourage its member nations to pay more interest to each other than for each of them to be transfixed and manipulated by the advanced industrial nations, who operate under the hegemony of the United States.

6. Certainly, "race" has been mobilized in political battles against the modern multiracist States (battles in the United States, for instance, joined by the Black Panthers on *race* lines in order to combat *racism*). The Black Panther Party was aware of the problems of their use of "race." On Aug. 26, 1970, Huey Newton called a press conference to announce that the "the Black Panther Party does not subscribe to 'Black Power' as such. Not the 'Black Power' that has been defined by Stokely Carmichael and Nixon. They seem to agree upon the stipulated definition of 'Black Power,' which is no more than Black capitalism, which is reactionary and certainly not a philosophy that would meet the interest of the people" (Major 102).

7. I am basing these speculations on extensive interviews with South Asian Americans and with extended journeys through discussion groups on the Internet. I will present the evidence more scientifically in a later publication.

8. Interest rates in India for savings are generally much higher than such rates in the United States. The utopia of savings and retirement is classically Indian, where pensioners are not put in such economic straits as they are in the United States. In America, retirement is not economically viable for the salariat and small shopkeepers.

9. This has much to do with the generous funding unleashed by the state (in Britain and Canada) as part of the favorable contradictions of multiculturalism. On this see Srinivas Krishna's film *Masala,* which was funded by the multicultural ministry and yet pokes fun at the concept of such a ministry. As far as Bhangra music is concerned, the explosion has been encouraged by the commodification of world music as a hip genre (Bauman).

10. The most useful flyer was prepared by the South Asian Students Association, "It *Was* Racism" which offers some correctives to Hudson's university-friendly article (in my possession).

11. CTWO can be reached at (510) 533-7583 for more information.

12. Contact numbers for these organizations: NOA [202-543-6603], YCL [212-741-2016], CPUSA [212-989-4994], AFL-CIO Organizing Institute [202-639-6200], Labor Party [202-986-8700] and the New Party [510-654-2309].

WORKS CITED

Bains, Harwant S. "Southall Youth: An Old Fashioned Story." In *Multi-Racist Britain,* edited by Philip Cohen and Harwant S. Bains. London: Macmillan, 1988, 226–43.

Bauman, Gerd. *Contesting Culture: Discourses of Identity in Multi-Ethnic London.* Cambridge: Cambridge University Press, 1996.

Bhattacharjee, Anannya. "Yellow Cabs, Brown People." *South Asian Magazine for Action and Reflection* (Summer 1993): 61–63.

Crystal, David. "Asian Americans and the Myth of the Model Minority." *Social Casework* 70.7 (1989): 405–13.

Davis, Mike. *Prisoners of the American Dream.* London: Verso, 1986.

DeSouza, Dinesh. *The End of Racism.* New York: Free Press, 1995.

Du Bois, W.E.B. *Against Racism: Unpublished Essays, Papers and Addresses, 1887–1981.* Edited by Herbert Aptheker. Amherst: University of Massachusetts Press, 1985.

Fisher, Maxine P. *The Indians of New York City.* Columbia, Mo.: South Asia Books, 1980.

"Gangsta,' Gangsta': an interview with South Asian gang members." *Hum* 1.2 (1994): 14–17.

Gilroy, Paul. *Small Acts.* London: Serpent's Tail Press, 1993.

Hampton, Fred. *You've Got to Make a Commitment!* Chicago: Black Panther Party, 1969.

Herrenstein, Richard J., and Charles Murray. *The Bell Curve: Intelligence and Class Structure in American Life.* New York: Free Press, 1994.

Hu, Arthur. "Asian Americans: Model Minority or Double Minority." *Amerasia* 15.1 (1989): 243–57.

Hudson, Lynn. "Racism Clouds Tranquil Brown University Campus." *India Abroad,* Feb. 24, 1995.

India News Network. "Digest." Feb. 6, 1995.

Islam, Naheed. "In the Belly of the Multicultural Beast I Am Named South Asian." In *Our Feet Walk the Sky,* edited by the Women of South Asian Descent Collective. San Francisco: Aunt Lute Press, 1993, 242–45.

Jensen, Joan. *Passage from India: Asian Indian Immigrants in North America.* New Haven: Yale University Press, 1988.

Major, Reginald. *A Panther Is a Black Cat.* New York: William Morrow, 1971.

Marable, Manning. "Rainbow Rebellion: Jesse Jackson's Presidential Campaign and the Democratic Party." In *Black American Politics from the Washington Marches to Jesse Jackson.* London: Verso, 1985, 247–305.

Marx, Karl. *Critique of the Gotha Programme.* New York: International Publishers, 1973.

Mathew, Biju, and Vijay Prashad. "The Saffron Dollar: Pehla Paisa, Phir Bhagwan." *Himal* 9.7 (Kathmandu, Nepal: September 1996): 38–42.

Mukherjee, Tuku. "The Journey Back." In *Multi-Racist Britain,* edited by Philip Cohen and Harwant S. Bains. London: Macmillan, 1988, 211–25.

Noble, David. "The Truth about the Information Highway." *Monthly Review* 47 (1995): 47–52.

Okihiro, Gary. *Margins and Mainstreams. Asians in American History and Culture.* Seattle: University of Washington Press, 1994.

Omatsu, Glenn. "The 'Four Prisons' and the Movements of Liberation: Asian American Activism from the 1960s to the 1990s." In *The State of Asian America,* edited by Karin Aguilar-San Juan. Boston: South End Press, 1994, 19–69.

Osajima, Keith. "Asian Americans as the Model Minority: An Analysis of the Popular Press Image in the 1960s and 1980s." In *Reflections on Shattered Windows: Promises and Prospects for Asian American Studies,* edited by Gary Okihiro, et al. Pullman: Washington State University Press, 1988, 165–74.

Paaras. "Kala Shah Kala." By Y. S. Pal. *Extra Hot 9.* Hayes, Middlesex, 1993.

Patel, Pragna. "Southall Boys." In *Against the Grain: A Celebration of Survival and Struggle,* edited by Southall Black Sisters. London: Southall Black Sisters, 1990, 43–54.

Perera, Gihan. "Heading Out to Deeper Waters." *The Ark: Membership Newsletter of the National Organizers Alliance* 7 (July 1996).

Potts, Michel W. "Welfare Bill Hits Legal Aliens: Indian Republicans Upset." *India West.* 9 August 1996.

Prashad, Vijay. "Contract Labor: the Latest Stage of Illiberal Capitalism." *Monthly Review* 46 (1994): 19–26.

Sahgal, Gita. "Secular Spaces: The Experience of Asian Women Organizing." In *Refusing Holy Orders: Women and Fundamentalism in Britain.* Ed. Gita Sahgal and Nira Yuval-Davis. London: Virago, 1992, 163–97.

SAMAR Collective. "One Big Happy Community? Class Issues Within South Asian American Homes." *South Asian Magazine for Action and Reflection.* 4 (1994): 10–15.

Shankar, S. "Ambassadors of Goodwill: An Interview with Saleem Osman of Lease Drivers' Coalition." *South Asian Magazine for Action and Reflection* 3 (1994): 44–47.

Shaliendra, Manoj. Interview with the author, Aug. 12, 1993.

Wei, William. *The Asian American Movement.* Philadelphia: Temple University Press, 1993.

Westwood, Sallie. "Red Star over Leicester: Racism, the Politics of Identity, and Black Youth in Britain." In *Black and Ethnic Leaderships in Britain*, edited by Pnina Werbner and Muhammad Anwar. London: Routledge, 1991, 146–69.

Xenus, P., et al. *Asian Indians in the U.S.: A 1980 Census Profile.* Honolulu: East-West Center, 1989.

We Will Not Be Used

Are Asian Americans the Racial Bourgeoisie?

Mari Matsuda

The Asian Law Caucus is the original public interest law firm serving the Asian-American community. It was built up from scratch by young, radical lawyers who carried files in their car trunks and stayed up all night to type their own briefs. The Asian Law Caucus has changed the lives of many—poor and working people, immigrants, and troubled youth—the least advantaged in the Asian-American community. The Caucus has also made history, successfully bringing landmark cases that have changed the law and the legal system. The supporters of the Caucus include many who participated in the civil rights and antiwar movements and who have worked all their lives in coalition with other people of color. This history is what inspired the words below, delivered at a fund-raising banquet in April 1990.

It is a special honor to address supporters of the Asian Law Caucus. Here, before this audience, I am willing to speak in the tradition of our women warriors, to go beyond the platitudes of fund-raiser formalism and to talk of something that has been bothering me and that I need your help on. I want to speak of my fear that Asian Americans are in danger of becoming the racial bourgeoisie and of my resolve to resist that path.

Marx wrote of the economic bourgeoisie—of the small merchants, the middle class, and the baby capitalists who were deeply confused about their self-interest. The bourgeoisie, he said, often emulate the manners and ideology of the big-time capitalists. They are the "wannabes" of capitalism. Struggling for riches, often failing, confused about the reasons why, the economic wannabes go to their graves thinking that the big hit is right around the corner.

Living in nineteeth-century Europe, Marx thought mostly in terms of class. Living in twentieth-century America, in the land where racism found a home, I am thinking about race. Is there a racial equivalent of the economic bourgeoisie? I fear there may be, and I fear it may be us.

If white, as it has been historically, is the top of the racial hierarchy in America, and black, historically, is the bottom, will yellow assume the place of the racial middle? The role of the racial middle is a critical one. It can reinforce white supremacy if the middle deludes itself into thinking it can be just like white if it tries hard enough. Conversely, the middle can dismantle white supremacy if it refuses to be the middle, if it refuses to buy into racial hierarchy, and if it refuses to abandon communities of black and brown people, choosing instead to forge alliances with them.

The theme of the unconventional fund-raiser talk you are listening to is "we will not be used." It is a plea to Asian Americans to think about the ways in which our communities are particularly susceptible to playing the worst version of the racial bourgeoisie role.

I remember my mother's stories of growing up on a sugar plantation on Kauai. She tells of the Portuguese *luna*, or over-seer. The *luna* rode on a big horse and issued orders to the Japanese and Filipino workers. The *luna* in my mother's stories is a tragic/comic figure. He thinks he is better than the other workers, and he does not realize that the plantation owner considers the *luna* subhuman, just like all the other workers. The invidious stereotype of the dumb "portagee" persists in Hawaii today, a holdover from the days of the *luna* parading around on the big horse, cloaked in self-delusion and false pride.

The double tragedy for the plantation nisei who hated the *luna* is that the sansei in Hawaii are becoming the new *luna*. Nice Japanese girls from Manoa Valley are going through four years of college to get degrees in travel industry management in order to sit behind a small desk in a big hotel, to dole out marching orders to brown-skinned workers, and to take orders from a white man with a bigger desk and a bigger paycheck who never has to complicate his life by dealing with the brown people who make the beds and serve the food.[1] He need only deal with the Nice-Japanese-Girl-ex-Cherry Blossom-Queen, eager to, please, who does not know she will never make it to the bigger desk.

The Portuguese *luna* now has the last laugh with this new, unfunny portagee joke: When the portagee was the *luna*, he did not have to pay college tuition to ride that horse. I would like to say to my sister behind the small desk, "Remember where you came from, and take this pledge: We will not be used."

There are a hundred ways to use the racial bourgeoisie. First is the creation of success myths and blame-the-victim ideology. When Asian Americans manage to do well, their success is used against others. Internally, it is used to erase the continuing poverty and social dislocation within Asian-American communities. The media are full of stories of Asian-American whiz kids.[2] Their successes are used to erase our problems and to disavow any responsibility for them. The dominant culture does not know about drug abuse in our communities, our high school dropouts, or our AIDS victims.[3] Suggestions that some segments of the Asian-American community need special help are greeted with suspicion and disbelief.

Externally, our successes are used to deny racism and to put down other groups. African Americans and Latinos and poor whites are told, "Look at those Asians—anyone can make it in this country if they really try." The cruelty of telling this to crack babies, to workers displaced by runaway shops, and to families waiting in line at homeless shelters is not something I want associated with my genealogy. Yes, my ancestors made it in this country, but they made it against the odds. In my genealogy, and probably in yours, are people who went to bed hungry, who lost land to the tax collector, who worked to exhaustion and ill health, who faced pain and relocation with the bitter stoicism that we call, in Nihongo, *gaman*.[4] Many who came the hard road of our ancestors did not make it. Their bones are still in the mountains by the tunnels they blasted for the railroad, still in the fields where they stooped over the short-handled hoe, and still in the graveyards of Europe, where they fought for a democracy that did not include them.

Asian success was success with a dark, painful price. To use that success to discount the hardship facing poor and working people in this country today is a sacrilege to the memory of our ancestors. It is an insult to today's Asian-American immigrants who work the double-triple shift, who know no leisure, who crowd two and three families to a home, and who put children and old folks alike to work at struggling family businesses or doing piecework until midnight. Yes, we take pride in our success, but we should also remember the cost. The success that is our pride is not to be given over as a weapon to use against other struggling communities. I hope we will not be used to blame the poor for their poverty.

Nor should we be used to deny employment or educational opportunity to others. A recent exchange of editorials and letters in the Asian-American press reveals confusion over affirmative action.[5] Racist anti-Asian quotas at the universities can give quotas a bad name in our community. At the same time, quotas have been the only way we have been able to walk through the door of persistently discriminatory institutions like the San Francisco Fire Department.[6] We need affirmative action because there are still employers who see an Asian face and see a person who is unfit for a leadership position. In every field where we have attained a measure of success, we are underrepresented in the real power positions.[7] And yet, we are in danger of being manipulated into opposing affirmative action by those who say affirmative action hurts Asian Americans. What is really going on here? When university administrators have hidden quotas to keep down Asian admissions, this is because Asians are seen as destroying the predominantly white character of the university. Under this mentality, we cannot let in all those Asian overachievers and maintain affirmative action for other minority groups. We cannot do both because that will mean either that our universities lose their predominantly white character or that we have to fund more and better universities. To either of those prospects, I say, why not? and I condemn the voices from my own community that are translating legitimate anger at ceilings on Asian admissions into unthinking opposition to affirmative-action floors needed to fight racism.

In a period when rates of educational attainment for minorities and working-class Americans are going down,[8] in a period when America is lagging behind other developed nations in literacy and learning,[9] 1 hope we will not be used to deny educational opportunities to the disadvantaged and to preserve success for only the privileged.

Another classic way to use the racial bourgeoisie is as America's punching bag. There is a lot of rage in this country, and for good reason. Our economy is in shambles. Persistent unemployment is creating new ghost towns and new soup kitchens from coast to coast. The symptoms of decay—the drugs, the homelessness, and the violence—are everywhere.

From out of this decay comes a rage looking for a scapegoat, and a traditional American scapegoat is the Oriental Menace. From the Workingman's Party that organized white laborers around an anti-Chinese campaign in California in 1877,[10] to the World War II internment fueled by resentment of the success of issei farmers,[11] to the murder of Vincent Chin,[12] and to the terrorizing of Korean merchants in ghetto communities today, there is an unbroken line of poor and working Americans turning their anger and frustration into hatred of Asian Americans. Every time this happens, the real villains—the corporations and politicians who put profits before human needs—are allowed to go about their business free from public scrutiny, and the anger that could go to organizing for positive social change goes instead to Asian bashing.

Will we be used as America's punching bag? We can prevent this by organizing to publicize and to fight racist speech and racist violence wherever we find it. More important, however, Asian Americans must take a prominent role in advocating economic justice. We must show that Asian Americans are allies of the working poor, the unemployed, and the ghetto teenager. If we can show our commitment to ending the economic upheaval that feeds anti-Asian sentiment, the displaced rage that terrorizes Asian Americans will turn on more deserving targets.

If we can show sensitivity to the culture and needs of other people of color when we do business in their communities, we will maintain our welcome there, as we have in the past. I hope we can do this so we can put an end to being used as America's punching bag.

The problem of displaced anger is also an internal problem for Asian Americans. You know the story: the Japanese pick on the Okinawans, the Chinese pick on the Filipinos, and the Samoans pick on the Laotians. On the plantation we scabbed on each other's strikes. In Chinatown, we have competed over space. There are Asian men who batter Asian women and Asian parents who batter their children. There is homophobia in our communities, tied to a deep fear that we are already so marginalized by white society that any additional difference is intolerable. I have heard straight Asian men say they feel so emasculated by white society that they cannot tolerate assertive women or sexually ambiguous men. This is a victim's mentality, the tragic symptom of a community so devoid of self-respect that it brings its anger home.

I love my Asian brothers, but I have lost my patience with malingering homophobia and sexism and especially with using white racism as an excuse to resist change. You know, the "I have to be Bruce Lee because the white man wants me to be Tonto" line. Yes, the J-town boys with their black leather jackets are adorable, but the pathetic need to put down straight women, gays, and lesbians is not. To anyone in our communities who wants to bring anger home, let us say, "Cut it out." We will not be used against each other.

If you know Hawaiian music, you know of the *ha'ina* line that tells of a song about to end. This speech is about to end. It will end by recalling echoes of Asian-American resistance.

In anti-eviction struggles in Chinatowns from coast to coast and in Hawaii, we heard the song *We Shall Not Be Moved.*[13] For the 1990s, I want to say, "We shall not be used." I want to remember the times when Asian Americans stood side by side with African Americans, Latinos, and progressive whites to demand social justice. I want to remember the multiracial ILWU,[14] which ended the plantation system in Hawaii[15] and the multiracial sugar beet strikes in California that brought together Japanese, Filipino, and Chicano workers to fulfill their dream of a better life.[16] I want to remember the American Committee for the Protection of the Foreign Born, which brought together progressive Okinawans, Koreans, Japanese, Chinese, and European immigrants to fight McCarthyism and the deportation of political activists.[17] I want to remember the San Francisco State College strike[18] and the Asian-American students who stood their ground in multiracial coalition to bring about ethnic studies and lasting changes in American academic life, changes that make it possible for me, as a scholar, to tell the truth as I see it.

In remembering the San Francisco State strike, I also want to remember Dr. Hayakawa and ask what he represented.[19] For a variety of historical and cultural reasons, Asian Americans are particularly susceptible to being used by the dominant society. Nonetheless, we have resisted being used. We have joined time and again in the struggle for democracy in America. The Asian Law Caucus represents that tradition. The caucus is a concrete manifestation of the pledge to seek a better life for the least advantaged and to work in coalition with other groups. All of you who support the caucus help keep alive a utopian vision of a world free of racism and poverty. You honor the proudest moments in our collective histories.

When I told a friend about this speech, he sent me a news clipping from the *San Francisco Chronicle* about Asian Americans as the retailer's dream.[20] It starts out, "[t]hey're young, [t]hey're single, [t]hey're college-educated, and on the white-collar track. And they like to shop for fun." Does that describe you? Well, it may describe me, too. But I hope there is more to Asian-American identity than that. I hope we will be known to history as a people who remembered the hard road of their ancestors and who shared, therefore, a special commitment to social justice.

This song is now at an end, a song of my hope that we will not be used.

NOTES

1. Dr. Haunani Kay Trask alerted me to the new *luna* phenomena.
2. See, e.g., David Brand, "The New Whiz Kids: Why Asian-Americans Are Doing so Well, and What It Costs Them," *Time*, 31 August 1987, 42. See generally Al Kamen, "Myth of 'Model Minority' Haunts Asian Americans; Stereotypes Eclipse Diverse Group's Problems," *Washington Post*, 22 June 1992, AI.

3. Cf. Harry H. L. Kitano, *Asian Americans: Emerging Minorities* (Englewood Cliffs, N.J.: Prentice-Hall, 1995) (discussing social problems facing Asian Americans).

4. "Nihongo" is the Japanese word for the Japanese language.

5. For example, individuals such as columnist Arthur Hu have opposed affirmative action admissions programs at colleges, specifically criticizing race-based admission criteria at the University of California. See Arthur Hu, "Hu's on First," *AsianWeek*, 10 May 1991, 26; 24 May 1991, 12.

6. In 1985, only 35 (2.5 percent) of the 1,380 firefighters in the San Francisco Fire Department were Asian, while Asian men comprised 19.3% of the male civilian labor force (women were not hired by the SFFD until 1987). *U.S. v. City and County of San Francisco*, 656 F. Supp. 276, 286 n. 10 (1987). A consent decree required hiring Asian Americans. As of August 5, 1990, Asian firefighters still comprised only about 4 percent of the SFFD. *U.S. v. City and County of San Francisco*, 748 F. Supp. 1416, 1428 n. 10 (1990).

7. According to 1990 census data and a report by Leadership Education for Asian Pacifics, Asian Americans are widely dispersed along the economic spectrum and face discrimination at all levels of employment. Further, Asian Americans earn less income, per capita, than whites even though they are often better educated. See generally Elizabeth Llorente, "Asian Americans Finding Many Doors Closed to Them," *Record (New Jersey)*, 23 October 1994, A1. The federal "glass ceiling report" (*Good for Business: Making Full Use of Human Capital* [Washington, D.C.; Federal Glass Ceiling Commission, 1995]) stated, "Despite higher levels of formal education than other groups, Asian and Pacific Islander Americans receive a lower yield in terms of income or promotions."

8. See, e.g., Brenna B. Mahoney, "Children at Risk: The Inequality of Urban Education," *New York Law School Journal of Human Rights*, 9 (1991): 161 (reporting the "declining numbers of urban minority high school graduates . . . pursuing postsecondary educational opportunities" and the increasing percentage of poor and minority students performing below grade level in mathematics and reading).

9. See, e.g., Augustus F. Hawkins, "Becoming Preeminent in Education: America's Greatest Challenge," *Harvard Journal of Law and Public Policy*, 15 (1991): 367 (noting that the United States is falling behind other countries in virtually all educational areas, particularly mathematics and the sciences).

10. In the 1870s, white workers, resentful of Chinese laborers (who worked for lower wages and in worse conditions), pressured politicians into enacting a series of anti-Chinese laws that culminated in the Chinese Exclusion Act of 1882.

11. U.S. Commission on Wartime Relocation and Internment of Civilians, *Personal Justice Denied: Report of the Commission on Wartime Relocation and Internment of Civilians: Report for the Committee on Interior and Insular Affairs* (Washington, D.C.: U.S. Governmental Printing Office, 1982), pp. 43–33. See also Mari J. Matsuda, "Looking to the Bottom: Critical Legal Studies and Reparations," *Harvard Civil Rights—Civil Liberties Law Review*, 22 (1987):363–68 (describing the internment of Japanese Americans during World War II and their subsequent claims for redress).

12. Vincent Chin, a Chinese American, was murdered in Detroit in 1982 by assailants (unemployed auto workers) who thought he was a Japanese person responsible for their loss of jobs. See U.S. Commission on Civil Rights, *Recent Activities against Citizens and Residents of Asian Descent* (1986), pp. 43–44 (giving a brief history of this case).

13. This popular union song based on an old hymn, *I Shall Not Be Moved*, was first sung in 1931 by miners; later versions added newer verses appropriate to the civil rights and anti-war movements. See Tom Glazer, *Songs of Peace, Freedom, and Protest* (New York: D. McKay, 1970), 332–33. For an example of anti-eviction struggle, see e.g. Chester Hartman, "San Francisco International Hotel: Case Study of a Turf Struggle," *Radical America* 12 (June 1978): 47–58 (describing activists struggling against the eviction of Chinese-American tenants in San Francisco's Chinatown).

14. The International Longshoremen's and Warehousemen's Union is a progressive, multiracial union active on the West Coast and in Hawaii.

15. See Edward Beechert, *Working in Hawaii: A Labor History* (Honolulu: University of Hawaii Press, 1985); and Sanford Zalburg, *A Spark Is Struck: Jack Hall and the ILWU in Hawaii* (Honolulu: University of Hawaii Press, 1979).

16. Thomas Almaguer, "Racial Domination and Class Conflict in Capitalist Agriculture: The Oxnard Sugar Beet Workers' Strike of 1903," *Labor History* 25 (1984): 325–50.

17. See Mari Jo Buhle et al., eds. *Encyclopedia of the American Left* (New York: Garland Publishing, 1990), 19–20 (chronicles the general history of the American Committee for Protection of the Foreign Born).

18. See generally Karen Umemoto, "'On Strike!' San Francisco State College Strike, 1968–69: The Role of Asian American Studies," *Amerasia* 15 (1989): 3–41 (recounting the events at the San Francisco State College strike and Senator Hayakawa's attempt to end it).

19. Ibid., 19.

20. John Berry, "Survey Says Asians Are Dream Customers," *San Francisco Chronicle*, 5 March 1990, C1.

THE STRUGGLE OVER PARCEL C

HOW BOSTON'S CHINATOWN WON A VICTORY IN THE FIGHT AGAINST INSTITUTIONAL EXPANSIONISM AND ENVIRONMENTAL RACISM

Andrew Leong

[T]he Coalition to Protect Parcel C for Chinatown effectively killed the garage with a skill-fully orchestrated media campaign and a series of high-profile events that painted the plan as a sellout of the community.
—LARRY SMITH, CHIEF OPERATING OFFICER, *BOSTON GLOBE*, OCTOBER 22, 1994

INTRODUCTION

For the last fifty years, Boston's Chinatown has been a shrinking community. Squeezed in by highways on two sides, its land is being gradually consumed by two medical institutions, Tufts University Medical School and New England Medical Center.[1] During the last few decades, these two medical institutions have swallowed up nearly one third of the land in Boston's Chinatown.[2] Despite this, both medical institutions want more. In its latest attempt at institutional expansion, New England Medical Center made an offer to the City of Boston in early 1993 to acquire a small plot of land in Chinatown called Parcel C, for the purposes of building an eight-story, four-hundred-fifty-five-car garage on Parcel C.

No one could have foreseen what came next—an astonishing outcry and level of protest. Almost immediately, the Chinatown community launched a fierce protest against New England Medical Center's attempt to buy Parcel C. Literally thousands in this small community came out in opposition against the hospital's proposed garage.

The Chinatown community's response to New England Medical Center's latest attempt at expansion was important, however, not just because it was vocal or widespread. Ultimately, the struggle to stop the proposed garage became more than a simple protest. It evolved into a sophisticated, but impassioned, grassroots movement, in which residents, social service organizations, activists, and college students worked arm-in-arm with environmental groups, legal services lawyers, progressive scientists, and health care advocacy groups. Not only did the Chinatown community stop a garage, it developed methods and structures for community activism and grassroots organizing that will last well beyond this struggle.

The reasons for the widespread opposition against New England Medical Center's proposed garage, by what is normally a quiet and politically inactive community, were various and complex. Part of the Chinatown community's intensely negative reaction to New England Medical Center's garage proposal stemmed from the long history surrounding Parcel C, and the always tense relationship between Chinatown and New England Medical Center over land control issues. Part of the reaction was pure self-preservation. Chinatown residents knew that New England Medical Center's garage was going to present a significant environmental hazard to their neighborhood. A great deal of the outrage, though, involved another party—the City of Boston. In approving New England Medical Center's garage proposal, the City government had broken an important promise to Chinatown.

BOSTON'S CHINATOWN

Chinatown is forty-three acres in size. It has a population of about 5,000, of which many are recent immigrants.[3] Over two-thirds of Chinatown residents speak Chinese at home.[4] Twenty-eight percent of Chinatown residents live below the federal government's poverty line.[5]

Chinatown has the distinction of being the most crowded neighborhood in Boston, with over 111 residents per acre.[6] It also has the least amount of open space per resident in Boston, at a ratio of about a half-acre for 5,000 residents.[7] There is a chronic shortage of housing in Chinatown.[8] Many recent Chinese immigrants who wish to live in Chinatown are often forced to find housing in other communities.[9]

Not surprisingly, many of Chinatown's housing problems originate from the policies of City Hall. A small, quiet neighborhood of color with very few votes, Chinatown is not a likely candidate to receive more benefits than burdens from the political establishment. In particular, like so many urban communities, Chinatown's housing and land development problems have their roots in the City's urban renewal policies of the 1960s.

During the era of urban renewal in Boston, the Boston Redevelopment Authority, which is the land development and zoning agency for the City of Boston, took basically a seize and destroy philosophy. The Authority conducted wholesale taking of homes by eminent domain in several neighborhoods, including Chinatown. The Authority demolished these homes, then sold the land to developers for upscale housing, or in Chinatown's case, institutional use.[10] In

Chinatown, it is estimated that over seven hundred Chinatown residents were displaced by urban renewal.[11] Later on, much of this land was sold to Tufts and New England Medical Center.[12]

Highways are another cause of Chinatown's problems. In the 1950s and 1960s, the federal government built two major highways, the Massachusetts Turnpike and the Southeast Expressway, straight through the heart of Chinatown.[13] Because of these highways, Chinatown suffers from serious air pollution problems.[14] Along with the medical institutions, these highways are also responsible for the chronic traffic congestion in Chinatown.[15] These problems are only predicted to worsen with the construction of one of the major exit ramps for the new Central Artery on the border of Chinatown.[16] The building of the highways are an additional reason that Chinatown has a chronic housing shortage, since their construction cost Chinatown a large portion of its land base and its housing stock.[17]

It is in this context of a severe housing shortage, serious air pollution problems, chronic traffic congestion, a critical lack of open space, and the ever-present appetite of the medical institutions for land that one must view the struggle over Parcel C. Parcel C was not just about one plot of land, or one environmental hazard. It was a reaction to history—a history in which powerful institutions and callous government agencies have continually mistreated a small and vulnerable community. It represented a critical step in the struggle for Chinatown's survival. Even if the Chinatown community did not win the battle over Parcel C, it would send a message to Tufts and New England Medical Center—that the community could, and would, fight for its survival.

BACKGROUND AND HISTORY OF PARCEL C

Parcel C is a small plot of land bordered by Oak Street, Nassau Street, May Place, and Ash Street.[18] It is in the heart of residential Chinatown.[19] Oak Street, which is the major street abutting Parcel C, is residential, and measures only thirty feet wide.[20] Yet literally hundreds of people travel Oak Street on foot every day, probably because it serves as the bridge between the western and eastern half of residential Chinatown. Oak Street is also the location of Acorn Day Care and its adjoining children's playground.

Acorn Day Care, which is the only public day care facility in Chinatown, is five feet away from Parcel C. In fact, it is so close to Parcel C that New England Medical Center's proposed garage would have been near enough to this building's fire escape to violate the fire code.[21] Across the street from Parcel C is a row of modest brick homes and a housing development under construction.[22]

About one hundred feet away from Parcel C, there is a complex that houses an elementary school, a community health center, and a social services provider.[23] This complex also contains a low-income housing development for the elderly and disabled.[24] Also one hundred feet from Parcel C is another low-income housing development.[25] As one can see from this description, Parcel C is a very hazardous place to put a 455-car garage.

The history of Parcel C extends back to the time of urban renewal. A large portion of the parcel was formed when the Boston Redevelopment Authority seized and demolished the homes of several Chinese residents.[26] After the land was taken, the Authority entered into an agreement with Tufts and New England Medical Center in which the medical institutions were given the right to buy the land.[27] Tufts and New England Medical Center made various plans for the land, but ultimately never did anything with it. For over twenty years, the land lay vacant.

On an adjoining piece of land, the Chinatown community was making good use of one of the few pieces spared from urban renewal. The Quincy School Community Council, one of the largest human service providers in Chinatown, had been renting a small three-story building from the Boston Redevelopment Authority since 1969. In that building, the group held English as a Second Language programs, conducted an after-school program, and ran Acorn Day Care.

In 1986, New England Medical Center submitted a proposal to build an 850-car garage on Parcel C. This proposal would have meant the demolition of the Acorn Day Care building and the adjoining children's playground. The concept of such a huge garage was immediately greeted with opposition by both the Chinatown Neighborhood Council, City Hall's advisory group on Chinatown matters, and the Boston Redevelopment Authority. This garage proposal was ultimately defeated.[28]

In 1988, in an effort to preserve the Acorn Day Care building for community use, the Boston Redevelopment Authority announced its decision to hand over title of the land and building to the Quincy School Community Council.[29] New England Medical Center's reaction was swift and callous. The hospital sued the Authority to stop the transfer of the Acorn Day Care building and playground.[30]

The community immediately protested New England Medical Center's decision to sue.[31] The Mayor of Boston declared that the City would not accept the hospital's attempt to interfere with the transfer of the Acorn Day Care building and would not be intimidated by the hospital's lawsuit.[32] Subsequently, a court threw out New England Medical Center's lawsuit.[33] New England Medical Center appealed, but before the appeal was heard, the City, Chinatown, and New England Medical Center negotiated a settlement.[34]

As part of the settlement, New England Medical Center agreed to sell back a plot of land neighboring Acorn Day Care and to refrain from opposing the Boston Redevelopment Authority's transfer of the Acorn building to the community. In return, New England Medical Center was given the right to buy two neighboring parcels of land.[35] Because the land faced Washington Street, a major artery, it was very lucrative. New England Medical Center immediately made plans to build two huge, nine-story buildings on these new parcels, totaling over 370,000 gross square feet.

As for Chinatown, it got the Acorn Day Care building and playground.[36] Chinatown also got a commitment from the Boston Redevelopment Authority and New England Medical Center that the remaining parcel formed out of the lawsuit's settlement would be reserved for community use.[37] Thus, Parcel C was born. The Authority promised that Parcel C would be reserved for a community center, and pledged its assistance in building this center. The Authority's first steps toward fulfilling this promise consisted of providing a $15,000 technical assistance grant and helping six community groups to incorporate as the Chinatown

Community Center, Inc.[38] The Chinatown Community Center, Inc. would be the developer of Parcel C.

A DEAL IS CUT

By 1993, things had changed. Mayor Raymond Flynn was gone. The Boston Redevelopment Authority had a new executive director,[39] and a multimillion-dollar debt.[40] The Chinatown Neighborhood Council was composed of business interests instead of community activists, and New England Medical Center was funding the Council's operating expenses.[41] The real estate boom, which was supposed to fund the Chinatown Community Center, had gone bust. The economy was still in a recession, and money was scarce.

In recognition of these realities, the Chinatown Community Center, Inc. scaled back its plans for a community center from 90,000 to 50,000 square feet. The group also approached New England Medical Center about forming a joint venture. To their dismay, New England Medical Center's only offer for a joint project was to build a small 10,000-square-foot community center in exchange for the rest of Parcel C. Yet again, New England Medical Center wanted to build a huge garage on Parcel C. To no one's surprise, the Chinatown Community Center, Inc. rejected this offer immediately.[42]

But the Chinatown Community Center, Inc. was not the only place New England Medical Center could pitch its offer. New England Medical Center approached the next logical player. The hospital made an offer to the Boston Redevelopment Authority that an agency swimming in red ink found too good to pass up—two million dollars for Parcel C and an easy approval process. Needless to say, the Authority became a major backer of the hospital's garage plans.[43]

New England Medical Center also made the same offer to the Chinatown Neighborhood Council. In return for Parcel C, New England Medical Center would build a 10,000-square-foot community center—or even better, provide $1.8 million in cash to the community. The money would be given in trust to the Council for distribution.[44]

In March 1993, the Chinatown community found out about the New England Medical Center deal. A veritable storm of criticism erupted. On May 17, 1993, when New England Medical Center formally presented its deal to the Chinatown Neighborhood Council for approval, over one hundred community members showed up to the Council's meeting. For the next several hours, speaker after speaker decried the hospital's garage proposal. Despite this intense opposition, the lure of $1.8 million proved too much. The Chinatown Neighborhood Council approved the deal that night.[45]

THE COMMUNITY ORGANIZES

With the approval of the New England Medical Center garage proposal by the Council, community activists and residents geared up for the next round of the struggle. Many were veterans of previous community struggles against Tufts and

New England Medical Center, City Hall, and other government agencies. In fact, two of the groups that belong to the Chinatown Community Center, Inc. specialized in grassroots advocacy and community organizing.[46] Experienced in protest strategies, media relations, and community mobilization, they immediately went to work in using all of these avenues to oppose the hospital's garage proposal.

Activists soon found out that the Boston Redevelopment Authority would hold a hearing on June 10, 1993 to determine whether to give preliminary approval to the hospital's garage proposal. The day before the hearing, a rally was organized in front of New England Medical Center to demonstrate the opposition of the Chinatown community to the garage proposal. Over 250 people showed up to protest.[47] It was the beginning of the community's effort to use media against the garage. Opponents of the garage knew that despite whatever angle the press would take, putting out the facts in the media alone would garner them public support.

The opposition against the garage did not simply consist of a rally. Residents and community activists also began circulating petitions well before the June 10 hearing. By the time the hearing was held, opponents of the garage had over 2,500 signatures ready to deliver to the board of the Boston Redevelopment Authority. At the June 10 hearing, community residents and activists again spoke louder against the garage. And yet again, the attraction of 2 million dollars pulled harder than the public's protest. Despite tremendous opposition from the Chinatown community, the Boston Redevelopment Authority gave its preliminary approval to the deal with New England Medical Center.[48]

Even worse, the Boston Redevelopment Authority totally discounted the community's opposition to the proposed garage. Instead, the Authority had the audacity to suggest that the Chinatown community actually favored the proposed garage because the Chinatown Neighborhood Council had approved the deal. The Authority and City Hall held out the council as the true representatives of the Chinatown community, despite the fact that 2,500 community members had registered their protest against the garage propsal.[49] Like so many minority "leaders" that are recognized as legitimate by white governments, the Chinatown Neighborhood Council acted as City Hall's puppet, approving actions that were ultimately detrimental to the Chinatown community. The Boston Redevelopment Authority believed it could shield itself against criticism by using these minority stooges.

After the June 10 Boston Redevelopment Authority hearing, the struggle against the garage looked bleak. City Hall had taken its position, and proved immune to community protest. The Boston Redevelopment Authority had its token Chinatown group to hold out as "true community representatives." The power of money appeared too strong to fight. Yet community members were not willing to give up the struggle. It was too great an injustice and harm for them to ignore. Despite what looked like formidable odds, the activists and residents prepared to continue the struggle.

The first and most critical step for activists was to have the community itself define the goals and strategies of the struggle against the garage. Too many times, an ostensibly community-based struggle leaves out the participation of the people most critical to the process—the residents, the workers, the people most affected by the outcome of the struggle. Added to that tendency was the historical exclusion of Chinatown residents, especially the elderly and recent immigrants, from the political process due to language and cultural barriers. It would be too easy for the Parcel C struggle to become a struggle of and by experienced English-speaking activists, in which the Chinatown community itself had no real ownership.

Given the level of emotion Parcel C provoked among residents, however, it was not difficult to take measures that would prevent the community from being disempowered by its own activists as well as by New England Medical Center and the City. The opposition to the garage proposal was formalized into an inclusive coalition, called the Coalition to Protect Parcel C for Chinatown. The steering committee of the Coalition was elected by community members at an open meeting. Four of the nine Coalition steering committee members were Chinatown residents. Both Coalition steering committee meetings and general meetings were conducted in Cantonese and English.

During the first open meeting, the community made clear its goal—no garage on Parcel C at all costs. The community didn't want any compromises. Residents stated very firmly that their opposition to the hospital's garage stemmed from the environmental dangers that a garage would pose to them, their families, and their loved ones. Elderly women and teenagers expressed their fears that the additional traffic generated by the garage would cause more accidents. Three residents had already died after being struck by cars near the Parcel C site.[50] Residents were also concerned that the air pollution caused by cars using the garage would harm their health. They felt no amount of additional community benefits money was worth those risks.

A structure for the Coalition was also developed during that first open meeting. The steering committee would make day-to-day decisions for the Coalition. Important decisions, it was understood, would be brought back to the community during open general meetings. Subcommittees were also formed in specific areas: media relations, legal strategy, outreach to Chinatown community members, and outreach to other communities. The Coalition was ready for a sophisticated, multifaceted, and well-orchestrated fight.

After the meeting, these committees quickly went about devising strategies in their respective areas. Many of these strategies were ultimately successful, although they took longer than the Coalition had ever imagined. It was not until the media campaign had generated over seventy-five articles and several television broadcasts, the community organizers had several rallies, after a year and a half of legal advocacy, and thousands of letters, that the Coalition had an effect. But ultimately, that effect was a victory, and well worth the effort.

THE ENVIRONMENTAL FRONT

As the mainstream public has finally recognized, communities of color are disproportionately impacted by environmental hazards.[51] Chinatown has not been spared this environmental racism. From the air pollution caused by the Massachusetts Turnpike and the Southeast Expressway to the overcrowding caused by the medical institutions' expansion, the residents of this community have always been burdened by numerous environmental dangers.[52] A garage on Parcel C seemed only to further this history of environmental injustice against Chinatown.

Chinatown residents did not need a growing nationwide awareness of the ravages of environmental racism to understand what was happening in their community. The first reaction that residents had toward the garage proposal was alarm over the environmental consequences that several thousand additional cars using a 455-car garage would generate. The burgeoning movement against environmental racism, however, did prove of great assistance in the struggle against the proposed garage.

Because of the new awareness of environmental racism, the Coalition was able to form alliances with and obtain the assistance of groups that previously would never have gotten involved in a struggle in Chinatown. Both mainstream environmental groups, such as the Sierra Club and the American Lung Association, and environmental justice groups, such as the Environmental Diversity Forum, joined with the Coalition. The Coalition was able to obtain legal support from the Conservation Law Foundation, which advocated against the proposed garage with state environmental agencies and provided advice and support to the Coalition's own lawyers. Because of the strength of their reputations with state environmental officials and their specialized knowledge of environmental issues, the support of these environmental groups proved invaluable.

One of the most difficult obstacles the Coalition faced was getting scientific and technical consultants to counter New England Medical Center's scientific studies. Most of the private consultants in the Boston area were too expensive for a grassroots organization. Fortunately, the Coalition was able to obtain the assistance of an affiliate of the Department of Environmental Health at Boston University's School of Public Health. Because of their emphasis on urban environmental problems, these experts could provide scientific information on the dangers of air pollution in minority communities. They also referred the Coalition to an inexpensive firm that conducted air pollution monitoring.

One of the most important allies of the Coalition came not from the environmental movement, but from the health care movement. Health Care for All, a Massachusetts-based advocacy organization, had been targeting the wealthy Boston teaching hospitals that were not fulfilling their obligations toward the urban communities in which they were situated. Because of the controversy over Parcel C, Health Care for All chose to focus on New England Medical Center, and joined hand-in-hand with the Coalition.[53] Health Care for All proved most effective in bringing critical public attention to New England Medical Center, especially when the group revealed that the hospital had paid thousands of dollars for antique pillow cushions for its CEO.

Finally, with a heightened awareness that acts of environmental racism were not isolated occurrences, the Coalition itself saw the advantage of establishing working relationships with other communities of color that were being threatened by environmental hazards.[54] With lines of communication now open, these communities were able to give each other technical assistance, and more importantly, moral support. The groups engaged in struggles against environmental racism were able to see that they were not alone, and to derive support from one anther's victories. When the struggles of each community group started to wear them down, that moral support was the most critical factor of all.

THE REFERENDUM

As discussed earlier, one of the most important results of the Parcel C struggle was the opportunity it provided for community members, especially the elderly and the young, to have a voice in what happened in Chinatown. Too many times, residents and community members had been denied the ability to participate in decisions affecting Chinatown. The Parcel C struggle was different—the Coalition was dedicated to ensuring that residents and community members would make the ultimate decision about the proposed garage.

The Coalition hit upon the perfect method of both providing a means for the residents and community to have their voices heard, and showing City Hall and the rest of Boston conclusively that the Chinatown community did not want a garage on Parcel C. The Coalition would sponsor a referendum over the proposed garage. It would be true democracy in action. Each and every resident and community member would be given the opportunity to vote on whether they wanted a garage on Parcel C.[55]

To maximize the credibility of the referendum, the Coalition brought in a neutral third party to run the actual voting—the American Friends Service Committee. The Coalition knew that any referendum it sponsored would be attacked by the Chinatown Neighborhood Council and New England Medical Center as unfair, but the involvement of the AFSC would enhance the legitimacy of the referendum to the media and the general public. Voting would take place over the course of two days, and would be monitored by the AFSC and volunteers approved by that group.

On September 12 and 13, 1993, over 1,700 members of the Chinatown community voted on New England Medical Center's garage proposal. By an enormous margin of 1692 to 42, the community overwhelmingly rejected the hospital's garage.[56] The Coalition was ecstatic. This proved once and for all that Chinatown did not want a garage on Parcel C. City Hall could waver on the Chinatown Neighborhood Council's approval as much as it wanted—no group of puppets could speak as strongly as the community had spoken in the referendum.

ORGANIZING IN A NON-ENGLISH-SPEAKING COMMUNITY

Because many Chinatown residents are recent immigrants, organizing in Chinatown always presents unique issues. As mentioned earlier, over two thirds of Chinatown residents speak Chinese at home. About 35 percent of Chinatown residents speak little or no English, and less than one third of Chinatown residents speak English very well.[57] Many of the strongest opponents of the garage were the elderly, who were also the least likely to speak any English. In fact, two members of the Coalition's steering committee were limited English speakers.

Fortunately, many of the activists in the Coalition were bilingual, and had extensive experience in community organizing in Chinatown. Rallies, petition drives, and letter-writing campaigns were all conducted in English and Chinese. The Coalition knew the strategies and methods to get non-English speakers, who might otherwise become very alienated from the struggle, to become active. By reaching out to Chinatown residents through the Chinese-language press and door-to-door leafleting, the Coalition was able to bring residents out en masse.

One method that the Coalition used very successfully in keeping non-English speakers and the Chinatown community as a whole informed was to hold regular community-wide general meetings, conducted in Chinese and in English. Before each of these meetings, the Coalition would publicize the meeting extensively by calling people, leafleting, and publishing notices in the Chinese press to ensure that a wide segment of the Chinatown community attended.

The Coalition used these meetings to update the Chinatown community about recent events in the Parcel C struggle, such as communications with New England Medical Center and the City, the success or failure of legal strategies, and the Coalition's own future plans. The meetings were also an optimal time for getting the residents to be proactive. Coalition members would ask those attending the meetings to write letters, sign petitions, or help in preparing events. The meetings also helped sustain the momentum of the struggle and move it forward. Most important, the meetings were critical in receiving general community input. At the general meetings, the Coalition steering committee would have residents vote on important issues. Without these regular meetings, the community would have become isolated from the struggle.

VICTORIES IN ENVIRONMENTAL LAW

One of the major victories of the Coalition's fight against New England Medical Center's garage was in the legal arena. With the assistance of Greater Boston Legal Services, the Coalition was able to persuade a state environmental agency to require New England Medical Center to conduct a full environmental review of its proposed garage. Ultimately, this environmental review took over a year. This not only forced New England Medical Center to justify its garage on environmental grounds, but it gave the Coalition the time that it needed to achieve a victory through the political process.

Because the garage proposal involved the sale of land by the Boston Redevelopment Authority, New England Medical Center had to fulfill the requirement of the Massachusetts Environmental Policy Act.[58] The hospital was required to give a preliminary environmental report to the state environmental agency. On the basis of that preliminary report, the state agency would decide whether or not to require a full environmental impact report from the hospital.[59]

In its report, New England Medical Center included scientific studies demonstrating that it did not need to prepare a full impact report.[60] The Coalition knew that it had to respond to the preliminary report. It had to convince the state agency to require the hospital to prepare a full environmental impact report. The state environmental agency offered the best chance for government intervention on the side of the community—it was a neutral party, not a city agency, and could not be bought off or pressured by the hospital. Lawyers from Greater Boston

Legal Services drafted a lengthy response to the hospital's report. Coalition members and allies, such as the Sierra Club and the American Lung Association, also sent in responses. And when the state agency held a hearing on the Parcel C garage proposal, the Coalition was prepared.

At the August 31, 1993 hearing on the hospital's garage proposal, the Coalition presented a tremendous amount of evidence against the garage to the state environmental agency—testimony from Oak Street residents that lived across from Parcel C, reports from the staff at South Cove Community Health Center, data that volunteers collected on traffic volume around Parcel C, and even a graphic picture showing the proposed garage 5 feet away from Acorn Day Care.[61] Despite their unfamiliarity with environmental law, the Coalition and its attorneys were ultimately persuasive. The community won a resounding victory when the state environmental agency ordered New England Medical Center to conduct a full environmental review of its garage proposal. Even better, the state agency ordered the hospital to focus on the areas of air pollution, traffic, and open space and recreation—the very areas that the community was most concerned about.[62]

Of course, both the Coalition and the lawyers realized that this was only an environmental review process, and could not actually stop the hospital's garage. State law only forced the hospital to study the environmental dangers of the garage and to mitigate them. Still, this victory gave the Coalition more time to conduct its political and media campaign. More important, the state environmental agency had validated the concerns of the Chinatown community about the hazards of New England Medical Center's proposal.

It took New England Medical Center until February 28, 1993 to complete the full environmental impact report. Even though the report took eight months to complete, the Coalition realized upon reading it that the report was still incomplete and full of misrepresentations. The Coalition realized that it had grounds to request a second, more complete and more accurate environmental impact report. Again, the Coalition's lawyers sent a lengthy response to the hospital's report, refuting inaccuracies and pointing out omissions page by page. Individual Coalition members, the Coalition's architect, the Conservation Law Foundation, the Coalition's scientific experts, and Health Care for All also sent in responses.

The Coalition again prevailed. The state environmental agency ruled that New England Medical Center's full environmental impact report was inadequate and deficient, and ordered the hospital to prepare a second, supplemental report.[63] The Coalition was ecstatic about this victory. Not only had the state agency validated their concerns about the environmental hazards of the proposed garage, the agency had also validated the community's long-standing sentiment that New England Medical Center had a habit of making misrepresentations and omissions. Finally, there was a government agency, unlike the City, that was not willing to let the hospital get away with it.

TRANSLATION OF ENVIRONMENTAL DOCUMENTS

One goal the Coalition developed was to have the above environmental documents translated into Chinese. The Coalition wanted the residents to be able to read and comment upon the documents for themselves. After all, there was no one better qualified to look for factual flaws in New England Medical Center's studies on traffic and environment in Chinatown than the residents who lived there. Unfortunately, the Coalition did not have the resources to translate the environmental impact report, which comprised 240 pages of text and 680 pages of appendices.[64] Therefore, the Coalition asked the state environmental agency to require New England Medical Center to translate the document.[65]

The Coalition wanted the environmental documents to be translated so that the non-English-speaking residents could meaningfully participate in the environmental review process. After all, without a Chinese translation, many of the people who would bear the brunt of the environmental ills of the proposed garage, and who were most concerned about the issue, would be excluded. On the other hand, obtaining a Chinese translation of the environmental review documents would be another step, like the referendum, toward eliminating the historical exclusion of Chinese speakers.

The Coalition prevailed in part. Because the Coalition had made its request for a translation after the full environmental report had been prepared, the state agency felt the Coalition's request was too late. The state agency, however, did decide that parts of the second, supplemental environmental report, which had not yet been prepared, should be translated into Chinese.[66] This also constituted a major victory for the Coalition and many of its member groups, since it was the first time that a government agency in Massachusetts had required the translation of an environmental document into Chinese.

Not only did the state agency require a Chinese translation of the supplemental environmental report, the agency also proposed that New England Medical Center meet with the Coalition, and come to an agreement as to which portions of the supplemental report should actually be translated.[67] Unlike City Hall, the state environmental agency was recognizing the Coalition as an equal, and as the representative of the Chinatown community. The state agency was forcing the City and New England Medical Center to deal with the Coalition.

Although the supplemental environmental report was never written, the Coalition's success in this matter alone was a significant outcome of the Parcel C struggle. The Coalition's actions set a precedent in Massachusetts: when an environmental issue affects a linguistic minority, translation of critical documents should be the norm. This was especially important to Chinatown and the Massachusetts Asian American community, because government agencies usually translated documents for these groups less often than for other non-English-speaking populations.

CONCLUSION

Ultimately, the Coalition and the Chinatown community won its battle against New England Medical Center's proposed garage. The victory took a year and a half, and was by no means complete. Although the media, the state environmental agency and the general public recognized that the Coalition was the representative body for the Chinatown community, City Hall and the Mayor's Office did not. When the

City finally reversed its decision over Parcel C, it deliberately excluded the Coalition from the process.

On October 21, 1994, the Coalition received a call from a reporter at the *Boston Herald*. Did they know that the Mayor's Office had issued a press release about Parcel C? New England Medical Center was withdrawing its garage proposal. In addition, Mayor Thomas Menino was going to sign an agreement with the Chinese Consolidated Benevolent Association over Parcel C. This agreement would preserve Parcel C for housing and would forbid all institutional use of the land. The Benevolent Association was also going to be given oversight authority over Parcel C.[68]

The Coalition was stunned. No one from the Mayor's Office had spoken to them about a settlement. No one had asked them to sit at the negotiation table or even give their input. Furthermore, the Benevolent Association was made up of the same people who sat on the Chinatown Neighborhood Council, and had approved the hospital's garage proposal less than two years ago. The Coalition had been shut out, and the community sold out.

It took a few days for the Coalition members to realize they had also won. There would be no garage on Parcel C. The Coalition had stopped New England Medical Center. It was amazing—a grassroots coalition of residents and organizations had stopped one of the most powerful institutions in Boston.

Of course, the Coalition realized there was, and still is, more work to do. Not only is the Benevolent Association made up of the same people as the Neighborhood Council, but it is notorious for squandering land and money given to it in trust for the community. Only a few years ago, the Benevolent Association had taken land that was given to them to build housing, and rented it to a supermarket. The Benevolent Association had also spent all of the rental income in mysterious and untraceable ways.[69] The Coalition and its members have the unpleasant task of ensuring that the same events do not occur with Parcel C.

Despite the victory over Parcel C, the community groups and residents that made up the Coalition have a long, hard road before there is significant success in the larger struggle—the struggle to preserve Chinatown in the face of institutional expansion. Even as the Parcel C fight was concluding, a new proposal for expansion was being advanced by Tufts University Schools of Medicine and Nutrition to build three new high-rise buildings in residential Chinatown.[70] It seems that as long as the medical institutions are around, the struggle for Chinatown's survival will continue.

NOTES

1. Historically, there is a very close relationship between Tufts University and New England Medical Center. The hospital has always been the primary teaching affiliate of Tufts University School of Medicine. Indeed, New England Medical Center and parts of Tufts University formally became one institution before 1962, when the two institutions renamed the group "T-NEMC." The entity T-NEMC was the title-holder of several pieces of real estate within the Tufts-New England Medical Center facilities. For this reason, even though Tufts and New England Medical Center later separated into two distinct entities in the mid-1980s, in many respects they still function as one institution.

2. In 1990, the two medical institutions owned 27 percent of the land in Chinatown. Boston Redevelopment Authority, Chinatown Community Plan (1990), 58 [hereinafter "Chinatown Community Plan"]. Since 1990, New England Medical Center has acquired the two parcels which were part of the settlement of its lawsuit, discussed below. These two parcels total over 370,000 gross square feet. New England Medical Center, Draft Environmental Impact Report for Parcel C Garage, 1–27.

3. The Chinatown Coalition, Chinatown Community Assessment Report, 13 (1994) (Citing Boston Redevelopment Authority's Summary of the 1990 United States Census) [hereinafter "Chinatown Coalition Report"].

4. *Ibid.*, at Appendix A, vi.

5. Chinatown Coalition Report at 13 (Citing Boston Redevelopment Authority's Summary of the 1990 United States Census).

6. Chinatown Community Plan, 64.

7. This translates into a ratio of about 9,600 persons per acre of open space. Compare this to the ratio of persons to acre of open space in the wealthy, predominantly white neighborhood of Back Bay/Beacon Hill, which has a ratio of 210 persons per acre. Chinatown is also one of the few neighborhoods in Boston without a public library branch. It has very few outdoor recreational facilities. Chinatown Coalition Report, 26–27.

8. Chinatown Community Plan, 30–36. For example, in September 1994, when a mixed-income housing development in Chinatown began to accept applications for rentals, over 1,600 people waited in line for eighty-eight units. ["1,000 Wait in Chinatown for Hours for New Housing," *Boston Globe*, August 28, 1994]. Chinatown has the lowest vacancy rate in Boston—3.2 percent. There are 1,431 units of housing for a population of about 5,000. Chinatown Community Plan, 31.

9. Chinatown Community Plan, 31–32.

10. See Kennedy, *Planning the City Upon a Hill* (Amherst: University of Massachusetts Press, 1992), 200–220.

11. Boston Redevelopment Authority, Diagnostic Report of Residents to be Relocated—South Cove Urban Renewal Project (1967), 7.

12. See 1996 Cooperation Agreement between the Boston Redevelopment Authority and Tufts–New England Medical Center.

13. Chinatown Community Plan, 23.

14. During the early 1990s the Massachusetts Department of Environmental Protection's monitor for carbon monoxide at Essex Street in Chinatown showed several violations of limits set by the Environmental Protection Agency. Furthermore, in 1987, carbon monoxide levels at the Kneeland Street portal of the Dewey Square Tunnel, adjacent to Chinatown, were estimated at eight different locations. These carbon monoxide levels were some of the highest in the City of Boston. At five out of the eight locations, modeled projections of carbon monoxide levels exceeded the EPA's limit. Massachusetts Department of Public Works, Final Supplement Environmental Impact Report for Central Artery (1-93)/Tunnel (1-90) Project, 4.11.

15. Chinatown suffers from "chronic traffic congestion, while pedestrian safety in the heavily concentrated residential areas has been threatened. Chinatown Community Plan, 18. In addition, "the neighborhood is also fragmented and isolated by heavy traffic in its midst or circulating at its borders, while it suffers from a deteriorating environmental quality." *Ibid.*, 64.

16. Palmer, "Pike Exit to Back Bay Pushed," *Boston Globe,* Nov. 15, 1994.

17. Chinatown Community Plan, 23.

18. Suffolk County Registry of Deeds, Book 16512, 171.

19. Chinatown Community Plan, 138A.

20. New England Medical Center, Draft Environmental Impact Report for Parcel C Garage, 1–4.

21. Testimony of Chia-Ming Sze, Architect, before the Executive Office of Environmental Affairs, August 31, 1993.

22. Oak Terrace, which was completed in December 1994.

23. Quincy Elementary School, South Cove Community Health Center, and Quincy School Community Council. See Chinatown Coalition Report, 29.

24. Quincy Towers.

25. Tai Tung Village, which has 240 units of housing.

26. See Suffolk County Registry of Deeds, Book 8072, 276–288; Suffolk County Registry of Deeds, Book 8094, 639–647.

27. The 1966 Cooperation Agreement between the Boston Redevelopment Authority and Tufts–New England Medical Center provides that the hospital could acquire certain parcels of land in the South Cove Urban Renewal area, including land that now makes up Parcel C.

28. Bagley, "NEMC Car Garage is Rejected by No Vote in Neighborhood Council," *Sampan*, February 1987.

29. Pantridge, "Medical Center, BRA Face Off in Chinatown," *Boston Herald*, June 30, 1988.

30. *Ibid.*

31. "Protesters Fight Medical Center Expansion Plan," *Boston Herald*, July 8, 1988.

32. O'Malley, "NEMC Files Suit to Take Oak Street Building," *Sampan*, July 6, 1988.

33. See *New England Medical Center v. Boston Redevelopment Authority.* Suffolk Sup. Ct. 88-3649 (Decision denying application for permanent injunction dated November 16, 1988), appeal denied (Appeals Ct. Docket No. 88-J-784). Further appeal of the case was dismissed by Joint Motion from all parties in 1991.

34. See Land Disposition Agreement, Suffolk County Registry of Deeds, Book 16512, 175.

35. *Ibid.*

36. *Ibid.*

37. New England Medical Center, Master Plan 1990–2000 (1990).

38. Lowe, "Center Commitments Should be Honored," *Sampan*, March 19, 1993.

39. The new Executive Director, Paul Barrett, would become well known for his promotion of massive institutional expansion projects at the expense of local communities. See Gendron, "Big Projects Pit Residents against City Hall," *Boston Herald*, July 20, 1993.

40. See Walker, "Flynn Allies May Face Layoffs," *Boston Globe*, March 31, 1994.

41. See New England Medical Center, Draft Environmental Impact Report for Parcel C Garage, 8–3.

42. Lowe, "Center Commitments Should be Honored," *Sampan*, March 19, 1993.

43. Cassidy, "Chinatown to Vote on Garage Proposal," *Boston Globe*, May 15, 1993.

44. Tong, "Chinatown Neighborhood Council Approves Controversial Garage Plan," *Boston Globe*, May 23, 1993.

45. *Ibid.*

46. These groups were the Chinese Progressive Association and the Asian American Resource Workshop.

47. See Gendron, "Chinatown Residents Protest New Garage Plan," *Boston Herald*, June 9, 1993.

48. "BRA Supports NEMC Garage on Oak Street," *Sampan*, June 18, 1993.

49. *Ibid.*

50. See "The Real Problem with Parcel C," *Boston Globe*, June 3, 1993. One of the streets near Parcel C, Washington Street, was identified as one of the twenty-six most dangerous locations for pedestrian fatalities in the City of Boston. Boston Transportation Department— Pedestrian Safety Task Force, Report on Pedestrian Safety (1992), 9.

51. See, e.g., Executive Order 12898, printed at 59 Fed. Reg. 7629 (February 16, 1994) (mandating that all Federal agencies make achieving environmental justice for minority populations a part of their missions).

52. See section A, supra, notes 12–16.

53. See Gendron, "Activists Slam NEMC Service Record" *Boston Herald*, November 10, 1993.

54. The Coalition established working relationships with the Coalition against the Asphalt Plant, Dudley Street Neighborhood Initiative, and the Environmental Diversity Forum.

55. Voting in the referendum was limited to Chinatown residents and Asian Americans in Massachusetts. The reason that all Asian Americans in Massachusetts were permitted to vote was because so many non-Chinatown residents had a stake in what happened in Chinatown.

Chinatown is really the heart of the Asian American community in Massachusetts, and in some ways, all of New England. Because of institutional expansion and urban renewal, the very ills that had brought about the Parcel C struggle, many Chinese Americans had been prevented from living in Chinatown or had been driven out. Even though these Chinese Americans lived in Quincy or Allston-Brighton, they still needed Chinatown for its groceries, its ESL classes, its employment agencies, its community health center, and its vocational training classes.

56. Gendron, "Chinatown Vote Says No to Garage," *Boston Herald*, September 15, 1993.

57. Chinatown Coalition Report, 13 and Appendix A, vi.

58. Mass. Gen. Law, ch. 30, secs. 61 and 62.

59. Code of Massachusetts Regulations, ch. 301, Part 11.

60. New England Medical Center, Environmental Notification Form for the Parcel C Garage Project (July, 1993).

61. Van Schuyver, "State Hears Opposition to Chinatown Garage Plan," *Boston Globe*, September 1, 1993.

62. Certificate of the Secretary of Environmental Affairs on the Environmental Notification Form for the Parcel C Garage (September 9, 1993).

63. Certificate of the Secretary of Environmental Affairs on the Draft Environmental Impact Report for the Parcel C Garage (April 29, 1994).

64. Actually, the Coalition did not want a full translation of all 240 pages, because the full environmental impact report was written in highly technical and obtuse language. Instead, the Coalition wanted an understandable, but thorough, abstract of the significant portions of the report. The difficulty with so many of these environmental review documents, which are supposed to be written in terms comprehensible to the general public, is that they are not understandable to the average reader.

65. This strategy was actually suggested to the Coalition's attorneys by Luke Cole, an attorney at the Center on Race, Poverty, and the Environment, who had successfully used it in an environmental struggle involving a Spanish-speaking community.

66. Certificate of the Secretary of Environmental Affairs on the Draft Environmental Impact Report for the Parcel C Garage, 7–8.

67. *Ibid.*

68. Gendron, "Menino: Developer Puts the Brakes on Chinatown Garage," *Boston Herald*, October 22, 1994.

69. "CCBA Uses Community Housing Money to Cover Its Own Expenses," *Sampan*, March 18, 1994.

70. "Tufts Plan Questioned at Chinatown Meeting," *Sampan*, August 5, 1994.

RACE MATTERS IN CIVIC

ENGAGEMENT WORK

Jean Y. Wu

In her keynote address entitled "Civic Engagement: The University as Public Good" delivered at a 2004 AACU Symposium on practicing liberal education, Nancy Cantor, Chancellor of the University of Illinois Urbana-Champaign, noted that the university has a critical role to play in civic engagement because the university has the means to foster culture-changing work in society. Cantor suggested that this work is best done when scholars and learners feel both empowered to examine their world and responsible for making change in it. At the same time, she pointed out that the most common operational aspect of civic engagement in the university—that is, service or volunteer work—while "valuable in the connections it makes and the people it helps, does not undertake to inform students about systemic sources of inequities." She went on to urge that we "immerse ourselves in environments of genuine exchange and interdependence."

I agree with Cantor's observation that civic engagement education about systemic inequality is too limited, and I would pick up where she leaves off to observe that scholars and learners cannot feel empowered to examine their society and take responsibility for action to change it if they are not solidly grounded and skilled in how to identify and analyze social systems of inequality. They will otherwise feel insecure, at the very least, about genuine exchange and interdependence. I will focus my reflections on one of the major systems of inequality in contemporary society—race—and on its relationship to civic engagement work.

W.E.B. Du Bois's (1903) declaration that the problem of the twentieth century is the problem of the colorline, though made at the beginning of that century, has not lost its relevance at the dawn of the twenty-first. While the centrality of race as a constituent element of Western modernity is widely accepted (Gilroy, 2003; Holt, 2002; James, 1996), and while the persistence of racism in U.S. society is well documented (Guinier, 2003; hooks, 1994; Matsuda, 1996; Omi and Winant, 1994; Winant, 1994 and 2004), too many scholars and teachers remain averse to critical race thinking (Matsuda, 1996; Tatum, 2003). Both intentionally and inadvertently, many avoid the explicit teaching of race and racism as they relate to their subject matter as well as to everyday lived experiences, their own and their students'. Ruth Frankenberg (1993) has named this kind of practice both race-evasive and, as a necessary consequence, power-evasive. Unfortunately, civic engagement scholars and practitioners have not escaped this aversion. Marschall and Stolle (2004) discuss such evasion and its implications for understanding and practice in their critique of Robert Putnam's (2000, 2002) works on social capital, a concept that has been central to contemporary discourse on civic engagement. They argue that Putnam's conclusions are flawed because he does not take the role of racial difference into account in his explanation for the decrease of social capital in the last three decades or more. Their view is that taking race into account would lead to different foci for research, interpretations and outcomes.

The lack of meaningful attention to race in civic engagement teaching and the resultant impact on the quality of that education have led to calls from many scholars and community activists for corrective efforts (hooks, 2004; Kivel, 2002; Matsuda, 1996; Omatsu, 2000). To a number of scholar practitioners in the academy whose work focuses on how to analyze and combat systems of inequality, it is becoming increasingly clear how important it is to teach and talk about race and especially one of its most potent social manifestations, racism, in the work of civic engagement—a crucial precept that community-based political and cultural workers know well. While the examination of race as a system of inequality itself is rarely a major focus, in recent years it has begun to be implied and included in discussions of service learning that explore the importance of diversity, consciousness of social justice, and the impact of different positionalities in service learning education and delivery (Boyle-Baise, 2000; Deans, 1999; Galura et al, 2004; Pompa, 2005; Robinson, 2000; Rosenberger, 2000). I would argue that because race is central to our individual and group identities and to our social relations, effective civic "teaching and learning" must at the very least engage us in the in-depth study of how our own assigned and chosen racial identities, privileges, and disadvantages shape the ways we engage across identity lines. For knowledge or ignorance in this area will definitely affect our ability to be effective in crossing racial and other social boundaries in our work. Yet equally important is providing a solid grounding in the history of race, its construction and how it operates as a system of inequality along with other similar systems, such as that of socioeconomic class. Only with such theoretical understanding of the social institution of race can our students be expected to make meaningful progress working on issues of racism, as a major system of inequality, in their civic engagement education.

We are living in a complexly diverse world in which racial politics increasingly are deeply contradictory. How is it, for example, that the "culture" of Asian groups, as represented in their food, music, and clothing, can be considered the height of "chic," emulated and consumed in larger society, and Asian athletes Michelle Kwan and Zhao Yang be celebrated nationally, while the brutal anti-Asian violence acted out on the bodies of Asians and Asian Americans across the nation continues to rise and to be tolerated? (Dang, 2000) How is it that even as universities and political leaders tout the positive values of diversity, multiculturalism and globalization, social groupings and communities continue to be separated along stark racial and ethnic lines, and both overt and covert racist activities pervade the lives of college students, shaping their experience both as individuals and in groups? Why do some racialized ethnic enclaves exist? Why do racial privilege and disadvantage persist despite the common postmodern insistence that race is a thing of the past and that we are in fact "post-race"? Civic engagement research and scholarship can make valuable contributions to our understanding and eventually working for change regarding these kinds of issues, but in order for this potential to be realized, race and the differential impact of race on different lives and communities must be explicitly and frankly addressed. Simply put, it is imperative that we link pedagogies of race to pedagogies of civic engagement.

In this essay I attempt two tasks. In both cases, I draw upon my experience of six years teaching and learning in an undergraduate civic engagement course within a liberal arts curriculum. First, I use my own course as a case study to illustrate how the teaching of race and its impact on lived experience is critically important to effective and ethical civic learning. Second, I step back to ruminate on my experience and speculate about the kinds of research that will be needed to improve both the effectiveness and the ethics of current work in civic engagement theory and practice.

Since there is no established definition of civic engagement in contemporary scholarship or practice, for the purposes of this writing I shall use a simplified definition of my own. It is one that has been shaped by continuing efforts to find ways to help college students understand a complex concept. I define civic engagement as the actions of informed individuals and collectives to respond to the needs created by systems of social injustice in the communities in which they live and work. These actions can take many forms, but in every case they must be requested or approved by the communities themselves, and executed in collaboration with community participants. Finally, these actions must involve some form of ethical practice within the community aiming to create a more just and humane world. Since on most campuses much of the work of civic engagement at the undergraduate level is referred to as "service learning," it is important to point out here that although the definition of civic engagement I am using may encompass activities found under the rubric of service learning (e.g., tutoring ESL [English as a Second Language] to new immigrant populations), it is, nonetheless, *distinct* from them. Not all service learning activities have as their goal addressing the underlying structural problems of social injustice, nor are they always requested and approved by, or made in collaboration with, the communities in which they take place. Civic engagement as I understand it must strive to fulfill both requirements.

. . .

Six years ago, I had the opportunity to design and teach a college-level course in which enrolled students would work regularly in Boston Chinatown on community-designated projects at nonprofit organizations, as well as participate in a weekly university seminar in which they learned theory and reflected on practice. I entitled the course "Active Citizenship in an Urban Community: Race, Culture, Power, and Politics." Its stated goal was to help students acquire the practical skills, competencies and habits of mind to be effective and ethical life-long community participants, working for a more just society. Objectives included (1) familiarizing students with the racial, economic, and political history of the community; (2) teaching them how to identify the contemporary problems confronted by the community; (3) analyzing the systems of inequality operating in the creation and maintenance of those problems; and (4) helping them develop strategies for working in and with community partners to confront the issues through direct service and advocacy. Students were expected to be willing to address community concerns through studying and applying theories, engaging in the kinds of activities assigned by community organizations and ultimately reflecting on their practice.

. . .

Boston Chinatown is located in downtown Boston. It comprises a small neighborhood in which some 5,000 residents, predominantly Asian American immigrants, currently struggle to coexist with numerous ethnic businesses serving both the community and the tourist trade, a large hospital complex, and a major medical school. Over the past four decades, much of the community's original residential housing has been torn down to make way for the institutional expansion of the hospital and medical school complex, as well as for federal and local highway projects and, in recent years, the construction of luxury high-rise condominium residences. All three forces have combined to drive property values sky high, making it increasingly difficult for low-income residents to find housing or continue to live in the neighborhood.

A special aspect of Boston's Chinatown is that it has long been both regarded and used as an urban-based center serving the social, cultural, and political needs of Asian Americans of different ethnicities within an approximately 100-mile radius of the city. As a consequence, Chinatown offers one of the very few locations in the Greater Boston and northeastern New England region in which new Asian, and occasionally even other, immigrants with limited language skills and little social and financial capital can gain a foothold from which to acquire access to life resources. Thus the problems confronting this community—and they are of crisis proportions—include but are not limited to a lack of affordable housing, of healthcare, of employment, and of many other services especially in demand among new immigrants. Environmental pollution and marginalization from city politics are harsh daily realities as well. In the view of a significant number of community workers, the community even faces the possibility of extinction, as the number of affordable residential spaces diminishes. Nonprofit community organizations that provide both direct service and advocacy work are severely understaffed and under-resourced. They welcome the assistance of informed individuals from the academy in a host of projects, as, for example, teaching adult ESL, translation services, and staffing campaigns for fundraising, for voter registration, and for environmental heath and sustainable development. Assistance in research related to community planning, sustainable development, social policy, public health, political participation, and education is valuable as well.

. . .

Students in the course range from those in their first year to seniors. They come from a variety of academic majors, and are of different racial identity locations. The majority of them identify their socioeconomic status as middle or upper middle class, and a little more than two-thirds in each class have grown up in suburban, predominantly white communities. Most come to the course without any preceding experience in civic engagement work in an urban, racialized ethnic community. Some may have volunteered in their own communities. Almost all have had no prior formal coursework on race, racial construction, and other systems of inequality. None ever have prior knowledge of the history and contemporary issues of the particular community in which they are about to enter.

The Course as a Case Study in the Process of Teaching and Learning

In this section, I employ excerpts from students' written communications to me during their involvement with the course in order to illustrate patterns of thinking, feeling, analyzing, and synthesizing that can emerge from a civic learning experience of this sort. Each student communication I have selected is also representative of a significant number of others across the six years I have taught this course. Communications range from the occasional electronic message to weekly entries in course journals and field notes. For each excerpt, I include the student's racial identity location.

Phase One: Before the Course Begins

As courses with required community involvement are relatively uncommon in the undergraduate curriculum at my institution, I receive many inquiries about the course before the first class. The following electronic mail from one student requesting information about the course is representative of an attitude I often see in students deciding whether or not to enroll:

> Hello Professor, I am told this course is about volunteering in Chinatown so I am not sure why the course subtitle is: RACE, CULTURE, POWER, AND POLITICS. Doesn't Chinatown have Chinese people in it? So why would we be talking about race and power? I can see how culture would be relevant. Actually, I want to find out what we will be reading ahead of time because I hope we do not talk about things like race and power. I had a lot of these discussions in high school and they just go nowhere and set people against people. I think we should be talking about what's positive. I am sure the students who want to take this class are not interested in race issues but are full of good will and energy. I want to be learning about the culture of the Chinese people. That's one of the reasons I want to take the course. (Latino male junior)

I hazard a guess that most readers would agree with me that were this student considering a course involving students working in a predominantly black or

African American community, he is unlikely to have made exactly the same statement. He might still have stated that he did not wish to discuss race and power in a "volunteer service" course, but he would not have questioned the fact, at least, that race, if not power, existed and was relevant to working within a black community in the United States. In the context of a course based in an Asian American community, however, this student's confusion is not extraordinary. Contemporary racial discourse in the United States continues to be dominated by a black/white paradigm (Ancheta, 1993), even though race in the U.S. has never been limited to black and white, either historically or in the present. From the perspective of the black/white paradigm, Asian Americans—neither black nor white—are frequently considered to be not "raced." In addition, it is a deeply embedded habit of mind in the U.S. to see Asians, regardless of their naturalization status, as "foreign" and "not American." The "difference" that being Asian represents is thereby relegated to a matter of "culture." In this case, it is, of course, a culture considered "foreign" to that of United States, a culture that is non-American. "American culture" is nearly always, if not always, referred back to a white European-based tradition.

During the first day of class in which students are "shopping" around for courses, an Asian American female student wrote on a student information form I collected:

> Why do you say that there is racism in Chinatown? I don't understand. Who are the bad guys? Do you mean Chinese against other Chinese? I had actually chosen this course because it wasn't going to be in a ghetto community. I am an Asian Studies major so I wanted to learn more about Chinese people and Chinese language. I am not looking for a course about race or racism. I actually don't want to study American society or Americans this semester. I want to prepare for going abroad to China next year.

A white European American student commented:

> I have always admired the Chinese race and am looking forward to my working in Chinatown. I had several friends in school who were Asian and I remember them as particularly smart and respectful so I think that I would be interested in seeing the kind of culture in their community, which must be so different from my white middle class, middle American suburb. Given the chance, I would choose to live in a culturally rich community like Chinatown.

The preceding two reflections reveal that the students clearly (1) do not include Asian Americans in their definition of "American"; (2) assume that only Chinese are to be found in Chinatown; and (3) do not consider Chinatown an American or U.S. community. Again, their confusion is quite common in the larger society. An emblematic experience of Asian America, against which it struggles constantly, is one of having Asian America conflated with Asia in the American mind. This deeply embedded habit of thinking is one of the major reasons that Asian Americans are viewed and regarded as "perpetual foreigners" or "aliens" in the United States. It results in their lived experiences of violent nativistic anti-Asian targeting as well as marginalization—if not entire omission—from the American body politic. In the case of the Asian American student, who uses the racially coded term "ghetto community" to mean a predominantly black community, "American" must be thought to apply to both black and white individuals but not to Asian Americans—even though, ironically, she herself is a second-generation U.S. citizen.

Needless to say, I have by now learned to incorporate as standard practice for the first day of class a brief definition of Asian America, its origins, its racial location in U.S. society, and its communities. The discussion ensuing from this definition inevitably includes a clarification of what the course "is" and "is not" about. It *is* about an urban U.S. community and the experience of its members as racialized "others" in U.S. society; it *is not* about China, the Chinese, a Chinese community, or Chinese culture.

Phase Two: First Contact with the Community

One of the first assignments that enrolled students must carry out is a "mapping" exercise in Chinatown. Students are dropped off in pairs at a central point in the community with a set of questions to be answered through observation and interaction with individuals that they encounter. And one of the first content lessons students receive is a formal orientation to the community, in which community-based cultural and political workers are their teachers. As students share their reactions to both learning activities, it becomes clear that ignorance about the realities of the community does not prevent students from holding and voicing some strongly pre-formed stereotypes and beliefs about the community and its residents.

A white European American student wrote:

> My image of the Chinese as very self-sufficient and clan-like is supported by the experience of walking around the community during our mapping exercise. They do not want to talk to outsiders, and though my mapping partner is Asian, she also got the brush-off. The people who did not speak English looked at us with curiosity but also with what I felt to be distrust or suspicion. I can see it's going to be difficult to break into the community since there is not much friendliness (I am comparing it to what I think I would get if I were a stranger asking for information in my own community [an upper-middle-class, predominantly white suburb southwest of Boston], and I think people would be eager to share information about the community). But I have heard that Chinese are culturally reserved, so I should not judge too much right now.

Another white European American student shared these thoughts:

> I was kind of disgusted by how dirty the streets were. I noticed that people in the community (I'm assuming they live there since they were Asian looking) didn't seem to care too much about throwing litter on the street and there was a lot of not very well packaged garbage out in front of the businesses. Some streets looked like they had not been cleaned for years. I don't understand how the hospital wouldn't want the area cleaner. I've noticed that a lot of minority neighborhoods are dirty in this kind of way and I guess I wonder if there are different cultural standards for cleanliness. Can we discuss this?

A third student, biracial African American and European American, noted:

One of the speakers giving information during the orientation seemed to be saying that there is overcrowding in the residences. I read in other places that it is not unusual for 12 or more Asian people to live in one or two rooms, so is this a standard because of larger Asian families? The speaker seemed to be saying that the overcrowding leads to unsanitary conditions and to higher rates of infectious diseases such as tuberculosis. If that is the case, then why do people continue to live in this way? Should there be regulations about how many people can live in a certain amount of space?

An Asian American student, not unfamiliar with the actual site of Chinatown, was more specific about where some of her assumptions about aspects of the community originated:

The first week of getting to know Chinatown is not without tensions for me. I've grown up going to Chinatown with my parents every other weekend to eat and get groceries, etc. But I have never considered why there is Chinatown other than some enterprising Chinese do their businesses there. My parents always referred to the people who are in Chinatown most of the time as poor Chinese, of lower class, rural "country bumpkin" type background. They also told us to be more careful down there because of higher crime and drugs and other such unsavory items. For the most part, this is what I know and what I believe about Chinatown. So I am nervous about going there regularly. My immediate questions are: How dangerous are the streets down there? And will they take advantage of me like charging me more because I am middle class and a college student?

The four statements quoted above suggest that students, regardless of their own racial locations, can come to civic engagement endeavors full of alarmingly misleading information, biases, stereotypes and myths about the community and people they will engage with. It may be obvious to many readers that what the students put forth mirrors the misinformation, cultural essentialisms and racial biases circulating in the larger society with reference to Asian Americans and "the Chinese." But it is equally important to note how their statements point to the glaring lack of any formal history and theory that might inform their attempts to make sense of lived realities very different from their own. Critical thinking and analytical skills are extremely limited. What gets drawn on are their own embedded assumptions and values, shaped by personal family experiences, popular myths, racial location, and socioeconomic class status, just to list the most important items of influence.

The confusion and ignorance revealed by students point to a dire lack of explicit education about the history of race and racial America throughout their educational experiences, both formal and informal. In discussing the way university students relate to race and racial differences, Beverly Tatum (2003) comments that one of the most common problems on contemporary college campuses is how little information students of all racial identity locations have about race and different racial histories in general. She explains that most whites, occupying racially dominant positions, have very little knowledge either about the lives and experiences of targeted or subordinate populations or about their own unmarked, unnamed white racial privilege. Some students of color in racially targeted populations may know that their white peers enjoy race privilege. They may even know of direct or indirect racist actions against people of color, including themselves. Still, these "knowings" do not translate into deep content knowledge about different racial groups' histories and experiences or about the profound impact of a racial system on our society. For many students of color, another form of racism—namely, internalized racism—leads them to hold the same essentialized racist stereotypes and myths about themselves that larger society does. Tatum argues that the only remedy for these vast ignorances is systematic pedagogy in which educators are committed to talking and teaching about race, especially as a system of inequality, in their formal curricula, without evasions and euphemisms.

Phase Three: Studying Systems of Inequality, Community History and Contemporary Realities

Early in the semester, while students are having their formal community orientations, they study the histories of Asian America in general and Boston Chinatown in particular, and they learn how to analyze current community conditions and politics by applying theories of race and economics. Toward the third week of the semester, the most common student response to the curriculum is one of shock or astonishment. The following responses illustrate the different areas in which students find themselves taken by surprise, as if unaware of their own preconceptions.

An African American student wrote about the almost universal surprise of discovering that Asian America is American, that Asians are raced in the United States, and that they experience racism:

> I had no idea that I was going to be learning about racism, and then institutionalized racism and environmental racism. I guess I had thought of this course as my "relax" course this semester—a way to get away from campus and do something fun in a cultural community. I have other courses in American history and environmental issues, and this course actually fits tightly with those, except I had never thought of Chinatown as "American" in its history and never realized it even suffered any racism!! What a surprise! I don't think I'm going to be able to relax in this course though!!!

Most students are also startled to find that Chinatowns across the nation have a long history in America and are residential enclaves born out of anti-Asian racial exclusion. A biracial Latina and white European American student wrote:

> I had no idea what to expect—all I knew about Chinatown is going there for dim sum on the weekends and sometimes at night because food is cheap and places are open late. Until the orientation and this week's readings, I didn't know that people lived there. I thought it was just restaurants and stores. I was really surprised to look up and see that people lived in apartments above the businesses and I discovered several housing projects that were quite big. I was most surprised to learn that Chinatown came about because of racial exclusion and forced segregation. I always thought that places

like Chinatowns, Koreatowns, Little Saigons exist because the Asian people wanted to segregate themselves and live together. I am familiar with the barrios and I am getting the idea that there are similarities between our communities.

An Asian American student reported both puzzlement and dismay over her lack of knowledge about the concerns that plague Chinatown communities:

> Even though I am Asian and parts of my family lived for a long time in San Francisco Chinatown, it is shockingly eye-opening for me to see how much large institutions and highways destroyed the kind of community that was in Boston Chinatown in the 40s and 50s, and how little the needs and wishes of the community are listened to, then and now. I had no idea of any of this and want to talk with my parents about what they know about the history of San Francisco Chinatown. Our readings talk about how every Chinatown in the U.S. has been targeted by gentrification and environmental racism. How could I have not known about any of this?

A fourth student, white European American, described with refreshing honesty her astonishment at her own racial and cultural biases, fueled by the omission of any examination of Asian America in her education:

> I have to admit I always thought it was in the culture of the Chinese to not care about cleanliness. I guess I always just considered Chinese restaurants to be kind of dirty and messy. I am *embarrassed* that I was so biased—where did that kind of view come from? And why didn't I consider the Asian immigrants as Americans? I have learned that black culture is not separable from the kind of racism that has dogged blacks throughout American history, so why didn't I make that link? I feel like I am just a BIG BLANK inside when it comes to thinking about Asians. I don't believe I ever had ANY information or course about Asians in any of my classes in high school or college up till now. I guess I have a lot to learn, and I better learn some of it fast before I go to work in the community and make a fool of myself and offend just about everybody around me. I really need to think about the fact that I am a white person and that I will never have to deal with what Asians have to, and I need to look hard at my own values and start changing some of them.

Clearly, the students' novel, and for the first time explicit access to curriculum content that (1) focused on the history of the racialized ethnic community, (2) articulated the impact of race and institutionalized racism within it, and (3) provided racial and economic analyses of contemporary problems was critical to the very obvious shift in their understanding. Nearly all turned from a view of the community partner as some "exotic, fun-filled cultural enclave" to one of it as a marginalized urban U.S. community of color, born of racial exclusion, and with current problems stemming from institutionalized racial discrimination. The last student's reflection underscores how crucial it is that, before students venture into their civic learning activities, the formal curricula of civic engagement not only explicitly address systems of inequality but also require students to examine their own social locations, to think about how they are shaped by these locations, and to speculate on what their own locations might imply for their interaction in the community.

Phase Four: Working in the Community

Students start working in the community a month into the semester. The readings, reflections and analyses required up to this point have given them a basic knowledge of the history and contemporary issues in the community and of theories of race, racism and systems of inequality, as well as a few opportunities to apply what they have learned to analyses of their own social locations and core values with regard to systems of inequality. As students begin their work in the field, they commonly find themselves trying to navigate unfamiliar terrain. Some face language and cultural barriers; some face a lack of resources to engage in the assigned tasks; and all experience insecurity in the face of ambiguity about the criteria by which they will be judged on their sensitivity to the community and their competence in practice. Thus, while students have by this point developed a fledgling awareness of their own race and class privileges and of several basic stereotypes and myths targeting Asians, immigrants and low-income communities, their first true encounters with the activities of civic engagement usually lead to a further surfacing of their own deeply held biases as they are pushed out of their "comfort zones" of social expectation.

A bilingual Asian American student assigned to assist in services to new immigrants wrote:

> I started doing taxes for immigrants today. I have never been so frustrated in my life. I find out that after attending hours of tax-prep training for this, the software I learned at the tax center cannot be used with the computer at the agency. The agency computers are way too old. So my supervisor asked me to do my work by hand. I was panicked. The doors opened, and immediately the lines formed, and most were older women.
>
> I was very disturbed and irritated when the older immigrant women wanted me to "just do" their taxes for them. I thought you're supposed to teach someone to fish instead of giving them the fish. That's what I learned in my high school volunteer program. I think people *should* learn to help themselves. I thought they would be curious as to how to do it and want to learn so that they are not dependent on others doing it. But when I asked them to look at the forms with me, they became agitated—and pushed it at me—saying "just do it," and "I don't want to learn this, what if I do it wrong?" When the time came for the end of my 3 hour session, I tried to tell those still in line that I had to go and if they would come back another day, someone else would help them. They got panicked and said "Just do mine—I can't take time from work again." I never expected them to be so aggressive and demanding. They seem to be demonstrating a kind of "small" mentality that is very Chinese—just take care of me. I've heard that immigrants should be forced to learn English and use it, and this is a case where it is very true.

For a Latino student, language usage triggered this response:

> I think I had a terrible day at the agency because I was eager at first and then I got upset since all the staff around me spoke mostly Chinese to one another. I found this very

rude—they know that I don't speak any Chinese. I know they can speak some English. I thought they would at least try to use some English when I'm around. When we were stuffing envelopes at the same table, I think they were talking about me. Of course I do look like I don't belong there—this college student who has weird hair and clothes and who absolutely isn't an Asian. My Asian roommate told me that Chinese people are very arrogant and rude, and maybe this is what I'm encountering. It makes it difficult to think that I am supposed to be there to help out but they don't want me there?

A number of students served as classroom aides, tutors and mentors in the only public school in Boston Chinatown. The youth they worked with, ranging from sixth to eleventh grade, were immigrants of color, or children of parents who were immigrants of color. Students' stereotypes about racial others and their own unquestioned values about the appropriateness of the behavior they witnessed, ranging from classroom deportment through educational aspirations and cultural assimilation to parental involvement, came through starkly as they reacted to their experiences working in this public school.

A white European American student wrote after meeting her after-school mentoring group:

One of the kids we're supposed to work with after school said that he couldn't attend any after-school club. We found out that his grandfather, who is from Haiti, would not let him stay after school at all. The grandfather wants the kid back at home as soon as school is over to help him with a family business in another town. I talked about this with my partner and we feel the grandfather is standing in the way of his own grandson's acculturation and involvement in American society. Since he chose to be in this country, he needs to let his family be involved here.

A white European American student was assigned to assist the teacher in classrooms. She observed:

I had a really strange introduction to the school. While I expected that the students who were going to be the least respectful were black, and they were, I was surprised to see that the Asian students were almost just as crazy. I think it's going to be a challenge for me as a white female trying to get their attention. I'm surprised at how difficult the Asian students were because I had expected that they would be easy to deal with. I have volunteered during high school in a school with a lot of African American students and I'm not surprised at their rambunctiousness but I had always assumed that Asians were the best students—quiet, well behaved and certainly not troublemakers. The Asians in my high school pretty much fit this bill.

A biracial African American and white European American student lamented:

I was upset that every student I asked told me that they didn't like school and they didn't see any real point in getting good grades and going to a good college. One kid said that he just isn't going to make it to college and become like "white people." When I asked him why, he said, "My uncle told me that I'm Chinese and people won't trust me and won't expect me to be the best in English and I just don't understand how things really work here." I think his uncle is really destructive to tell him that, maybe the guy is bitter or something, but he's killing his nephew's dreams and chances of succeeding. I expected that he would want the second generation to succeed even if he couldn't.

A biracial Asian American and white European American student reported in frustration:

> I don't know how to deal with this one student who is always acting out, always threatening about beating others up or being beaten up or running away. I found out that she is the oldest of six kids and goes home to do all the housework and cook. She is angry because of all this, and I think I would be angry too if I were in her place. Is this considered a case of abuse; it may not be physical but it could be mental?

Another biracial Asian American and African American student wrote:

> I just can't believe that so many of the parents are so uninvolved in their children's education. They don't seem to ask to see their homework and anything that the school sends home. I recall my parents were always involved and going over stuff with me. Both my parents worked full time, but they still seemed to spend a lot of time with us. The students I'm working with tell me that none of their parents have ever come to the school. All the kids I'm working with are Asian, and I guess I thought Asian parents were really intense about their kids education, almost too intense, if you know what I mean, so I'm really surprised.

Stuart Hall's (1996) observation that race often provides the language through which class conflicts find expression is present in many of the students' statements. While race and class intersect and compound many of the community youths' experiences, my students did not have the habit of mind to recognize these intersections and sort out the different components. Instead, they tended to conflate not only experiences and values related to both class and race but also to read them both as simply aspects of culture. Most commonly, students took "culture" to be the explanation for what they found unfamiliar. I have discovered that unless such conflations are thoroughly and painstakingly pointed out, and then analyzed and critiqued, students remain unaware of their problematic interpretations. In that case, their strongly embedded racist and elitist personal theories can actually be reinforced rather than dismantled by their work within the school.

Phase Five: Revelations and Reevaluations

By the middle of the second semester of the course, five to six months after their initial contact with the community, most students have had ample opportunity to gain theoretical knowledge as well as more particular insight into their own social locations and values through structured reflection on and analysis of their experiences in the field. Students have thus begun to feel much more involved in their community contexts and to infuse their work with their own talents and creativity.

Their reflections on civic learning at this point frequently refer to "what they did not know" when they started the course. They speak about which parts of the curriculum they found most useful in correcting previously held biases. Frequently, they mention titles and authors of readings that were critical in transforming their thinking, as well as activities that led them to seek alternative explanations for their encounters. Their reflections give us valuable insight into what could be not just useful but even necessary components of effective civic engagement curriculum and pedagogy.

The student who had complained about the cleanliness of the community in a quotation given above offered this reflection:

> I complained a lot about how dirty Chinatown was and how little people there seemed to care about their environment, but what I am learning about environmental racism in urban areas like the Chinatown community has totally blown me away. I never even included the city in my consideration of environment before now—it was the forests and rivers—and I had never thought of the word "racism" attached to environmental issues. I am seeing how race and especially race and class combined are so absolutely at the center of this issue. Who are the people who get to make environmental policy? Who are the people who get to choose where they want to live? Why should it surprise us that a community that is almost 100% new immigrant, with language and cultural barriers, with one of the lowest income brackets in the city, is always targeted for all the mess that people who have clout and money know how to avoid in their communities? I think these issues are right in front of our nose, except that unless we are *forced* to see them, we don't.

A white European American student who had been especially uncomfortable with and resistant to reading and discussing the role of white privilege in the system of racism reported her analysis of her own socialization and how it shaped her views:

> I was taught at home and in school to stay away from talking about controversial topics like "social injustice," so talking about racism is just one of those big no-no's. I didn't like the readings about race, especially about white privilege. If the course had not forced us to look at how race plays a major role in communities, I would have learned a totally different set of things with this community work. I think some of the biases I had—e.g., that immigrants should be forced to learn English—would have been stronger. I would have seen it as a choice whether immigrants learn English and want to participate in American society. Even the canvassing from door to door in the community would not have changed my views—it would just have made me feel that the Chinese residents were very exclusive and suspicious. The community speakers were crucial to changing my mind. After listening to them, I would go back and read about race privilege and the article from *The Possessive Investment in Whiteness* [Lipsitz 1998] and then I began to change my mind.

An Asian American student who had been especially challenged by the Asian American youth he tutored wrote about the turning point in his work:

> I think the Asian boys thought they could get away with a lot because I'm an Asian male, but once I started to call them out on their behavior, they actually calmed down

and I think I am developing a relationship with them. The article by Lisa Delpit [1995] on "Silenced Dialogues" helped me in a way that is truly *life-changing*. I grew up in the only Asian American family in an upper middle class white neighborhood and I was judging the students by what I had learned to do all my life to survive as the "other" in my own community. It took her article to wake me up. I am glad to be working with these boys because we do have a relationship and they don't get to see older Asian Americans who are teachers and professionals too often.

The student who had authored the electronic mail questioning me about the appropriateness of including the study of race and power in the course wrote specifically to address his earlier missive:

> I don't know if you remember but I'm the one who sent you an email in the summer about the course and I asked you why we had to talk about race and all that. In the beginning, I had not understood why the course had "race, culture, power, and politics" in its title and almost didn't take the course because these topics were a turn-off. Just working at the agency alone would not have convinced me that race, culture, power, and politics are required for understanding community—any community. If we had not read about how racism works against Asians and how people's race affects their access to political participation, or even just clean air and green space, I don't think I could see how the lives of the people and the existence of this whole community are all based on the inequalities of race, culture, power, and politics in our society. My own parents are immigrants in a very Latino neighborhood and I think I actually began to let myself see what they faced because of taking this course. I think maybe I was trying to deny that racism is real or that it really can affect you. I am reading another book in another class called *Savage Inequalities* by Jonathan Kozol—it is about inequality of access to education, and if I wrote a book about Chinatown, I would also call what I have seen there "savage inequalities" in access to housing, safety, space, political voice, the list goes on.

Phase Six: Reflections on a Year of Civic Learning

Finally, I turn to students' reflections at the end of their yearlong experience of civic engagement and learning. A few themes repeatedly emerge from students' written communications. Students comment frequently on the absence of information about systems of inequality in their formal education. They are able to identify these systems and analyze how they operate, and they recognize how they themselves are implicated within the systems. They identify the process of civic learning that has led them to transformed perceptions of themselves and of the community and its residents. Many students, especially seniors, share informed reconsiderations of their career and life choices.

A white European American student reflected on how his overall education had failed to provide him with critical knowledge about systems of inequality and teach the dangers of uninformed, well-intentioned "good works":

> I am one of those people who went to a diverse school and did a lot with diversity education in the school. One thing I never learned till working specifically in this community

and taking the course is that racism can be expressed in very different forms. I never learned about the institutional kind of racism, the kind that you can't see because it is just in the way that things are set up and done—in policies and laws and practices. I guess I did grow up on a diet that said that racism is mostly concentrated in those that are ignorant, uneducated, and that it's about being afraid of and hating or looking down on those that are different from you, but I realize that I never really figured out what drove it other than warped human nature. And so it is with both relief and terror that I am beginning to understand that racism is "a system of advantage based on race," that it is not just ignorant people being mean. I never saw how embedded things are in the structures of our society. So even good intentioned people like me, like other students in this class, could actually be performing out of racism and not even realize it. This is something entirely new to me. I think I've never understood this aspect of service—it's not about cleaning the streets, teaching English, getting people out to vote—I mean it is about all of these things, but that they are really individual pieces that only make real sense if you group them under the kind of action that seeks to fight to stop racism acted on one community by larger society around it.

A biracial African American and white European American senior confessed:

I have always wanted to go into law. I come from a family where there are a lot of people in law. So I still do want to go into law—I think. The only thing that is very different is the image I have in my own mind of what is possible with a law degree and what I want to do with it. My uncles all work in prestigious law firms and I guess I always thought I'd like that kind of setting. But the kind of work they do is not even remotely connected to what I've been learning about this year in community involvement. Over break I went to visit my uncles in the law firms, and I found the things they were working on to be about protecting wealth and power for those who already have it and want more—like the luxury condo developers who want to tear down Chinatown. At the same time, it is so clear to me that without the help of people who really know the law, some of the battles for community justice would have been futile. So I want to be able to use the law to do battle for community justice. That's really clear to me. I don't know how to get there yet. I can't be more blunt than that. But I do know that I want to put any education I get toward doing something that makes those who don't have access to what they need come closer to getting it. I made an appointment with the community lawyer who came to speak to us. He was incredibly down to earth but inspiring. He had mentioned that he would be willing to talk to us outside of class about the choices that he made both in and after law school.

A white European American student who had been fearful of teaching students of color appeared to have shifted her stance after her experience tutoring and mentoring:

I no longer think that I can't work with kids who are very different from me. Whenever I thought of teaching in the past, I had pictured myself teaching in a school just like my own, which I now realize is one of the richest and best suburban publics. Now I want to work in schools where there are students of color, immigrants, poor white kids, and other kids who are really "disadvantaged" by the way the school systems are set up. I don't think

I'm so naïve as to think I'll have a great time because I've seen how hard and punishing it is and how many people burn out. But I need to try to do this. I'll be teaching for a year with a program in New York where I'll be working with ESL students. I am ecstatic. I am also scared out of my mind. But I've learned in this course that it's a good thing to be scared. It will take away some of the cockiness and arrogance that I realized I have. I learned that being scared doesn't mean I can't go ahead and still do something and make it work.

An Asian American student poignantly traced the trajectory of his movement from recognizing his own internalized racism and elitism to taking on a new-found sense of responsibility for using his awareness in future work to combat racism and oppression:

I don't know what would have happened if I had gone to work in Chinatown without taking the course at the same time—the research on race and health and environmental racism made the greatest impact on me. I have been to Chinatown all my life and was very critical of those who lived there, learning these views from my parents—I always thought that the Chinese who lived in Chinatown came from poor social status and were not civic minded—that they had no concern about the larger welfare of their streets and community. I really thought that the streets were dirty because they were particularly "bad citizens," as in "I only look out for myself and my front steps." I think I've been somewhat embarrassed and apologetic about "my people" whenever I go to Chinatown to eat with my non-Asian friends and I will make comments about the people there being ignorant and uneducated. I wanted to separate myself from them.

Now that I have learned about how unequal the services are in different communities it is like seeing the world through *totally new lenses*. I was stunned to hear about how Chinatown was targeted as the place for all the highway ramps, for huge hospital complexes, for the sex industry—it is as if the residents of this community are just not considered "human" as other Americans are—this feeling that they will absorb everything because they are Asian/Chinese, poor, new immigrants without language and cultural capital, and no one will stand up and fight for this community. I realize how I didn't know anything about the history of what I now consider my own racial community here in this society. And that most people I come into contact with have no idea!! This is eye-opening because I feel very differently about this idea of working within a community. I am leaving this course feeling that given what I now know, I absolutely have a responsibility to continue to do this while I'm in this area and then wherever I go I should seek out other Chinatowns and communities like it to give my time and energy to. You had talked about life-long education and goals before, and I feel that I am really clear about these now.

RUMINATIONS ON WHAT I HAVE LEARNED AND WHERE WE NEED TO GO

Civic engagement is the most recent expression of the historic liberal arts mission of preparing students for public life as civic participants (Latham, 2003). I want to think that we have become involved in our work as scholars and teachers because one of our main goals is to swell the numbers of individuals in the generations to come who are not only willing but also intellectually and practically skilled enough to make a lifelong ethical commitment to working with communities and populations most marginalized so that in the end all involved are empowered to create more just societies. While the last few student statements in the prior section might give us some hope that our efforts toward this goal are not entirely futile, much remains to be done.

I have learned from the students I have worked with in the last six years that the transformations they underwent over the duration of the course could not have occurred without a curriculum and pedagogy "forcing" them to study community history and systems of inequality. Their comments and reflections all suggest that had they engaged in community work alone, without the more academically oriented work that helped them see the conditions they encountered in the broader context of institutionalized injustice in our society, the risk would have been very high that their experiences would have reinforced the embedded biases, assumptions, misinformation, and ignorance pervading U.S. society and, thus, their own knowledge base. Civic engagement educators and their community partners are all too familiar with a common scenario in civic engagement teaching and learning in which the unexamined biases and values that students (and teachers) bring with them into a community context result in negative interactions that engender conflict, avoidance, patronization or moralization. The result is that "well-meaning" teachers and learners avoid—perhaps even strongly oppose—forays beyond the traditional classroom into unfamiliar communities. Community partners, already stretched thin for human and material resources, find themselves suffering from the loss of time and energy they have spent educating and nurturing both outside learners and a community-academic partnership. The expectations they had that their academic partners would "do no harm" are thus shattered. Plans and projects are stalled or aborted, contributing to the development of a great deal of cynicism about any positive role for the academy and academics in the community.

I have also learned from students who caution that absent an understanding of the systems that reproduce inequality, even "positive" civic engagement work may leave underlying problematic values and gaps of knowledge unchallenged. For example, students could have a very successful experience of cleaning up neighborhoods and creating more green space in a community without ever being challenged in their belief that the residents in the neighborhood do not care about the physical environment and ultimately are the ones to blame for any poor conditions they live in. Students might therefore never come to understand institutionalized environmental racism that targets certain communities for "beautification" and others with unwanted toxic waste. Explicit theoretical instruction integrated into civic engagement education is necessary to avoid these destructive endings.

The Work Done since I Began

Six years ago, my involvement with the field of civic engagement as an educator began when a couple of administrators at my university consulted me about why a two-year-old civic engagement project they had implemented was failing. The attrition rate for the university students who had made yearlong commitments to mentor/tutor weekly in a public school program in Boston Chinatown (the same school mentioned earlier in this essay) was 60% by the end of the first semester and 90% by the middle of the spring. In a focus group I set up with the student volunteers, I learned that they had all broken their commitments out of a sense that they had nothing to contribute to the public school youth. They felt they could get the youth neither to focus on their schoolwork nor to involve themselves in after-school interest activities. They felt that the youth were "not bound for college" or were too poor at English to benefit from the help that was offered.

While the university students had been given a handbook and four hours of a tutoring workshop prior to their engagement at the school, they had no background knowledge of the students and their home communities, or of the history and culture of the school and the community in which it was located. Furthermore, the university students (all except one identified themselves as white European Americans of upper middle class backgrounds) had not been asked to consider their own social identities or those of the students they worked with (all Asian American and black/African American of working class or low-income first-generation immigrant parents) and how these different social locations influenced lived experiences. Further exploration in the focus group revealed that a plethora of misinformed and misguided assumptions and values about the race and class status of the youth—which the university students had brought with them into the project—were strongly reinforced by the actual service work in the school. In one university student's words, he had "expected the inner city poor kids would not care as much about doing well in school as middle class kids in the suburbs because parents of the two groups have different values about education"; and in fact, his time at the school "proved these expectations to be grounded in reality."

As an outcome of this consultation and the focus group, I agreed, somewhat reluctantly, to develop a yearlong course for credit in the formal university curriculum to prepare and continue to educate the next group of university students as they enlisted in this project the following year. As an instructor of comparative race studies and Asian American studies in the American Studies Program, I had two motivations for engaging in this endeavor: my sense of affiliation to and concern for the immigrant communities that the youth of the public school came from (including the Asian American community in which the school was located) and my sense that "learning through interactive and reflective practice" might be a meaningful way to educate university students about race and related social identity differences that matter in larger society. My reluctance came from my lack of experience in how to create an academic course in which civic engagement in an off-campus community played a central role.

I was well aware from my prior teaching experiences that Tatum's observation (mentioned earlier in this essay) that the majority of today's students come to university without formal education in the meaning of race and racism as institutions in society and with a great deal of misinformation about racial realities, both their own and that of their different peers. At the very least, I wanted students in my class to enter the school and its racialized ethnic community of new immigrant populations with a basic knowledge of the history of both, as well as with education not only in the meaning and impact of race and class differences on people's everyday lives but also in the cultures of social institutions.

As I embarked on research to design the course, I was both surprised and disappointed to discover the absence of race and race-related issues in the literature of civic engagement education. Moreover, the occasional reference to race invariably employed a black and white racial paradigm. In that first year of teaching, I ended up drawing on content developed in other courses I taught on comparative race in America and Asian America, adapting it (in some cases without much success) for use in the area of civic engagement. For pedagogy, I employed, with a great deal of trepidation and at high risk of disservice to the public school youth and their communities, a trial and error approach to how best to teach in order to ensure that university students would have an opportunity for meaningful learning while providing constructive and ethical contributions in this very fragile and tenuous partnership between the academy and a public school community. For the purpose of evaluating the effectiveness of both curriculum content and pedagogy, I used answers to the following questions as measures of acceptability:

1. Were the choices for theoretical and historical content and pedagogical strategies informed by the needs of the students being tutored, the school community, and the larger community in which the school was located?

2. Did the individuals, the school, and the community consider their needs served by the efforts of university students?

In the intervening years, I have come to understand that one of the many factors dissuading university faculty from taking on civic engagement projects, especially in contexts they deem unfamiliar, is the lack of readily accessible researched and tested deep-content knowledge and pedagogy to guide them in their design and implementation of this kind of educational experience.

The Work That Lies Ahead

Six years down the road, my experiences with the field of civic engagement lead me to make the following observation: As racial differences increase and their complexity of meaning deepens in our society, I am more convinced now than ever that scholars defining the field must (1) recognize the pervasiveness of racism as a system of inequality in contemporary society and (2) systematically include and pay attention to race and its impact on lived experiences as a central aspect of their research, theory construction, and knowledge production.

Several avenues of research and scholarship offer potential benefit to the field. First, exploration of the meaning(s) and practices of civic engagement in different racial/ethnic/cultural communities in the contemporary United States would generate further interest in the field and promote its usefulness among a broader and more diverse audience than is now the case. In the last two decades alone, the establishment of communities with new racial/ethnic/cultural/linguistic/religious populations has become the norm rather than the exception across the United States. Many of these communities have significant transnational populations. Do members of these new and evolving communities, for example, consider the discourse in the field of civic engagement relevant and applicable to them? How do they, for example, relate to the criteria by which traditional studies have evaluated social capital? How would they define and identify social capital in their communities? How do they react when their realities are omitted from discussions of theory, policy, and practice in civic engagement literature, and what are the implications of these omissions in their lives? How does culture-making in these new communities reshape social, economic and political culture in society at large? In this area, cooperation and collaboration between those in the field of civic engagement and those in the field of race and ethnic studies could prove exceptionally productive. Within my own field of Asian American studies, for example, the last decade has seen an abundance of new knowledge production on numerous aspects of social, political, economic, cultural and racial experiences in emergent Asian American communities across the United States. However, this scholarship can be profitably exploited only if civic engagement scholars and teachers make decisions to build it into their own knowledge base and include it in shaping their own research and formal coursework.

Second, sorely needed is critical examination of the practices of civic engagement education and dissemination of the results. We have to have empirical confirmation of precisely what procedures effectively integrate content knowledge and various pedagogies relating to race and systems of inequality. Unless scholars, educators, practitioners, and community partners are committed to continuing, systematic and active reflection on "how" civic engagement work is implemented and improved, we run a great risk of unethical practice that further harms and silences populations marginalized by institutional structures to begin with. We also stand likely to fail in the education of university learners.

Third, and finally, assessment criteria for civic engagement research, education, and practice must be developed for *all* of us in the field in order to hold us accountable for meeting our espoused goals. In this research, longitudinal studies that follow the impact of civic engagement education on learners and the communities they were or are involved in would be an important first step in allowing us to gauge whether involvement with civic engagement indeed leads to lifelong commitment to effective and ethical work. When it comes to civic engagement education, we must always keep the end in mind. What we are ultimately aiming for is productive efforts at transformative education, both theoretical and practical, through which everyone engaged, inside and outside the academy, is empowered to envision and build a more just society.

Bibliography

Ancheta, Angelo. 1993. *Race, rights, and the Asian American experience.* Piscataway, N.J.: Rutgers University Press.

Boyle-Baise, Marilynne. 2002. *Multicultural service learning: Educating teachers in diverse communities.* New York: Teachers College.

Cantor, Nancy. 2004. Civic engagement: The university as public good. Keynote speech at Association of American Colleges and Universities Symposium, Practicing Liberal Education: Deepening Knowledge, Pursuing Justice, Taking Action, January 21, 2004.

Deans, T. 1999. Service learning in two keys: Paulo Freire's critical pedagogy in relation to John Dewey's pragmatism. *Michigan Journal of Community Service Learning* 6, 15–29.

Dang, Janet. 2000. Anti-Asian hate crimes on the rise. *AsianWeek,* January 12–18.

Delpit, Lisa. 1995. *Other people's children: Cultural conflict in the classroom.* New York: The New Press.

Du Bois, W.E.B. [1935] 1997. *Black reconstruction: An essay toward a history of the part which black folk played in the attempt to reconstruct democracy in America, 1860–1880.* New York: Atheneum.

———. 1903. *The souls of black folk.* Chicago: A. C. McClurg & Co.

Foos, Cathy. 1998. The "different" voice of service. *Michigan Journal of Community Service Learning* 5, 14–21.

Frankenberg, Ruth. 1993. *White women, race matters: The social construction of whiteness.* Minneapolis: University of Minnesota Press.

Galura, Joseph A., Penny Pasque, David Schoem, and Jeffrey Howard, eds. 2004. *Engaging the whole of service-learning, diversity, and learning communities.* Ann Arbor, Mich.: OCSL Press, 2004.

Gilroy, Paul. 2003. *Against race: Imagining political culture beyond the color line.* Cambridge: Harvard University Press.

Guinier, Lani, and Gerald Torres. 2003. *The miner's canary: Enlisting race, resisting power, transforming democracy.* Cambridge: Harvard University Press.

Hall, Stuart. 1996. New ethnicities. In *Stuart Hall: Critical Dialogues in cultural studies,* ed. D. Morley and K.-H. Chen. London: Routledge.

Holt, Thomas. 2002. *The problem of race in the twenty-first century (The Nathan I. Huggins Lectures).* Cambridge: Harvard University Press.

hooks, bell. 2004. *Teaching community: A pedagogy of hope.* New York: Routledge.

———. 1994. *Teaching to transgress: Education as the practice of freedom.* New York: Routledge.

James, C.L.R. 1996. *C.L.R. James on the "Negro Question,"* ed. Scott McLemee. Jackson: University Press of Mississippi.

Kivel, Paul. 2002. *Uprooting racism: How white people can work for racial justice.* Gabriola Island, British Columbia: New Society Publishers.

Latham, Andrew. 2003. Liberal education for global citizenship: Renewing Macalester's traditions of public scholarship and civic learning. Macalester University report.

Lipsitz, George. 1998. *The possessive investment in whiteness: How white people profit from identity politics.* Philadelphia: Temple University Press.

Matsuda, Mari. 1996. *Where is your body? and other essays on race, gender, and the law.* Boston: Beacon Press.

Marschall, Melissa, and Dietlind Stolle. 2004. Race and the city: Neighborhood context and the development of generalized trust. *Political Behavior* 26, no. 2 (June): 125–153.

Omatsu, Glenn. 2000. The 'Four Prisons' and the movement of liberation: Asian American activism from the 1960s to the 1990s. In *Asian American studies: A reader,* ed. Jean Yu-wen Shen Wu and Min Song, 164–96. Piscataway, N.J.: Rutgers University Press.

Omi, Michael, and Howard Winant. 1994. *Racial formation in the United States: From the 1960s to the 1990s.* New York: Routledge.

Pompa, Lori. 2005. Service learning as crucible: Reflections on immersion, context, power, and transformation. In *Service learning in higher education,* ed. D. Butin, 173–192. New York: Palgrave Macmillan.

Putnam, Robert. 2000. *Bowling alone.* New York: Simon and Schuster.

———, ed. 2002. *Democracies in flux.* Oxford: Oxford University Press.

Robinson, Tony. 2000. Dare the school build a new social order? *Michigan Journal of Community Service Learning* 7, 142–157.

Rosenberger, Cynthia. 2000. Beyond empathy: Developing critical consciousness through service learning. In *Integrating service learning and multicultural education in colleges and universities,* ed. C. O'Grady, 23–43. Mahwah, N.J.: Erlbaum.

Tatum, Beverly. 2003. *Why are all the black kids sitting together in the cafeteria?* New York: Basic Books.

Winant, Howard. 2004. *New racial politics: Globalism, difference, justice.* Minneapolis: University of Minnesota Press.

———. 1994. *Racial condition: Politics, theory, comparisons.* Minneapolis: University of Minnesota Press.

HOMES, BORDERS, AND POSSIBILITIES

Yen Le Espiritu

When people come together voluntarily to create their own vision, they begin wishing it to come into being with such passion that they begin creating an active path leading to it from the present.

—GRACE LEE BOGGS, *LIVING FOR CHANGE*

Through my education in Ethnic Studies, I just became really empowered. I gained the knowledge. And through educational discussions and events organized by the League of Filipino Students (in L.A.) I became informed about the oppressive economic, social, and political situations occurring in the Philippines. . . . I gained the tools to really understand the world around me and to make sense of everything. And then it came to that point where I . . . wanted to apply [these tools]. For me, to do that, I felt that I needed to go back to the Philippines and participate in the liberation struggles there.

—MELANY DE LA CRUZ, SECOND-GENERATION FILIPINA

Home making is really border making: it is about deciding who is in as well as who is out. I began this project on Filipino Americans in San Diego at the border—the U.S.-Mexico border.[1] Since the mid-1970s, the militarization of the U.S.-Mexico border region has intensified. From San Diego to the Rio Grande Valley, armed U.S. federal agents patrol key border points to block "illegal" crossers—to keep "them" from invading "our" homes.[2] Since 1994, "Operation Gatekeeper," a high-profile blockade-style operation, has turned the San Diego–Tijuana border region into a war zone, pushing immigrants to attempt more treacherous crossings in the forbidding mountains and deserts east of San Diego. Since Gatekeeper's launch, an average of ninety immigrants have died per year; the most common killers are mountain cold, desert heat, and canal drownings and falls.[3] Anti-immigrant practices targeted virtually all people of "Mexican appearance"; many of my Latino students, colleagues, and friends angrily reported being stopped, harassed, and humiliated as they crossed the border. The political furor over undocumented immigration reached its nadir in 1994 when nearly 60 percent of the California electorate voted in favor of Proposition 187, a measure designed to deny almost all publicly funded social services, including education and health care, to undocumented immigrants and their children. The public relations campaign on behalf of Proposition 187 expressly targeted immigrants crossing the U.S.-Mexico border, blaming them for many of California's social, moral, and economic ills and demonizing them as "reproductive, parasitic, benefit-taking, overrunning-the-nation villains."[4]

As I watched this spectacle of border making, I was reminded of my own border-crossing experience. In 1975, when tens of thousands of Vietnamese refugees, including my own family, arrived in the United States, the majority of Americans did not welcome us. A Harris poll taken in May 1975 indicated that more than 50 percent of the American public felt that Southeast Asian refugees should be excluded; only 26 percent favored their entry. Many seemed to share Congressman Burt Talcott's conclusion that, "Damn it, we have too many Orientals."[5] Five years later, public opinion toward the refugees had not changed. A 1980 poll of American attitudes in nine cities revealed that nearly half of those surveyed believed that the Southeast Asian refugees should have settled in other Asian countries.[6] This poll also found that more than 77 percent of the respondents would disapprove of the marriage of a Southeast Asian refugee into their family and 65 percent would not be willing to have a refugee as a guest in their home.[7] Anti-Southeast Asian sentiment also took violent turns. Refugees from Vietnam, Laos, and Cambodia in many parts of the United States have been attacked and even killed; and their properties have been vandalized, firebombed, or burned.[8] The antirefugee rhetoric was similar to that directed against Latino immigrants: Southeast Asians were morally, culturally, and economically deficient—an invading multitude, unwanted and undeserving.

The rhetoric that demonizes anti-Latino and anti-Asian immigrants is disturbing not only for what it says, but more so for what it does not say. By portraying immigration to the United States as a matter of desperate individuals seeking opportunities, it completely disregards the aggressive roles that the U.S. government and U.S. corporations have played—through colonialism, imperialist wars and occupations, capital investment and material extraction in Third World countries and through active recruitment of racialized and gendered immigrant labor—in generating out-migration from key sending countries.[9] As Joe Feagin reminds us, "recent immigrants have mostly come from countries that have been substantially influenced by imperialistic efforts by U.S. corporations and by the U.S. government around the globe."[10] This portrayal of immigration stigmatizes the immigrants as desperate, undeserving, and even threatening, and delinks contemporary immigration from past U.S. corporate, military, or governmental actions abroad. It is with a deep concern over the (mis)representation of immigration to the United States—what is stated as well as what is concealed—that I began a book on Filipino Americans, *Home Bound: Filipino American Lives across Cultures, Communities, and Countries.*

The production of discourses of immigration, both popular and intellectual, is important because modes of representation are themselves forms of power rather than mere reflections of power.[11] Immigration has become a key symbol in American culture, a central and powerful concept imbued with a multiplicity of myths and meanings, capable of rousing highly charged emotions that culminate in violently unfair practices.[12] In the late twentieth century, politicians, anti-immigrant groups, media agencies, and academic researchers have colluded to create "knowledge" of an everyday "reality" that the U.S. borders are out of control and that immigration is overwhelming U.S. public institutions and threatening U.S. core values and identity.[13] In *Home Bound*, my goal was to produce a critical representation of immigration. Instead of presenting immigration (and immigrants) as a *problem* to be solved, I argued that we need to conceptualize immigration as a technology of racialization and gendering—a crucial site for the reproduction of and resistance to "scattered hegemonies."[14]

TOWARD A CRITICAL IMMIGRATION STUDY

Tayyab Mahmud, writing on the "spectre of the migrant" that haunts the modern world, states that immigration is presented in popular and scholarly debates as a "problem to be solved, a flaw to be corrected, a war to be fought, and a flow to be stopped."[15] Conceptualizing immigration primarily as a problem, the dominant theories in the field of U.S. immigration studies—theories of assimilation (including segmented assimilation), of amalgamation, of the "melting pot," of cultural pluralism—have focused on immigrant cultural and economic adaptation and incorporation and on responses by native-born Americans to the influx.[16] The debates among immigration scholars have been lively. According to immigration opponents, immigrants incur the wrath of "Americans" because they deplete the country's resources and fragment America's cultural unity.[17] In contrast, immigration proponents argue that immigrants benefit the nation's economy and enrich its cultural fabric.[18] Even as they disagree on the relative costs and benefits of immigration, both sides nevertheless approach immigration as a problem to be solved, focusing their research on the immigrants' social, economic, and cultural integration into the United States. This approach to immigration uncritically accepts U.S. white middle-class culture, viewpoints, and practices as the norm. Instead of questioning the ideological and material power of these normative standards, immigration advocates have at times sought to "prove" that immigrants are just "as hardworking or honest as native-born Americans" and that the majority "assimilate rapidly to the English language and other aspects of Euro-American culture."[19] As an example, an informative edited volume on the post-1965 second generation focuses its discussion on the following theoretical and empirical question: Will today's children of immigrants move into the middle-class mainstream or join the expanded multiethnic underclass?[20] An important question to be sure, it nevertheless leaves uninterrogated the ways in which immigration as a cultural system has constructed the "immigrant" and the "American"—the impact of which has been to *naturalize* unequal patterns of mobility and uneven integration into the nation.

Drawing on the works of ethnic studies scholars[21] such as Jose David Saldivar, David Gutierrez, Lisa Lowe, and George Sanchez, I have argued that we need to study immigration not only for what it tells us about the assimilability of the immigrants but more so for what it says about the racialized and gendered economic, cultural, and political foundations of the United States. That is, we need to conceptualize immigration not as a site for assessing the acceptability of the immigrants, but as a site for critiquing state claims of liberal democracy and cultural inclusion, for studying contestation over definition of citizenship and over terms of inclusion, and for understanding the formation and negotiation of racialized and gendered identities. Throughout *Home Bound*, I attempted to address not only the constructions of "the Filipino," which were produced through the colonial encounter in the Philippines and the migration encounter in the United States, but also how these constructions and the practices associated with them were experienced and contested by Filipinos themselves. Most immigration studies have privileged U.S.-born American responses to "distant languages and alien cultures" in their midst.[22] To counter this trend, I relied on Filipino American accounts of their experiences to better understand their subjectivity—how they have created their worlds and made meaning for themselves—and in so doing, to restore, in Amitava Kumar's words, "a certain weight of experience, a stubborn density, a *life* to what we encounter in newspaper columns as abstract, often faceless, figures without histories."[23] In the process, I pointed out the complexities of Filipino American identities, identifications, and actions. Filipino Americans, like any other group, take up many positions on a continuum between internalization of and overt resistance to oppressive discourses and practices.

BORDER IS EVERYWHERE

Hovering at the edges of the nation, immigrants call into question implicit assumptions about "fixed identities, unproblematic nationhood, invisible sovereignty, ethnic homogeneity, and exclusive citizenship."[24] As such, immigrants pose a problem to the United States, not because they are economic parasites or cultural aliens but because they reveal the gaps in the promise of liberal democracy and disrupt the fictions of cultural inclusion and homogeneity—fundamental claims of the U.S. modern state.[25] As documented in *Home Bound*, membership to the U.S. nation is regulated by strict rules of exclusion and inclusion. These immigration and citizenship restrictions—enacted to regulate the membership of the national community—send a powerful message that the United States conceives of itself as a singular, predominantly Euro-American, English-speaking culture. As Dorothy Roberts points out, many white Americans assume that "American culture is synonymous with the culture of white people and that the cultures of the new immigrants are inconsistent with a national identity."[26] In such a setting, the question of who is or is not an "American" and anti-immigrant rhetoric become entangled in revealing ways.[27]

The cultural project—the daily reproduction of symbols and myths—of representing the U.S. nation as racially and culturally homogeneous requires the construction of cultures and geographies from which the immigrants come, and therefore the immigrants themselves, as fundamentally foreign and inferior to modern American society and its citizens.[28] As an example, proponents of

Proposition 187 charged that the influx of undocumented immigrants would transform California into a Third World nation. This reference to the "Third World" must be seen as a strategic marker that "metaphorically alludes to social evolution and the threat of immigration leading to a de-evolution of 'American civilization.' "[29] In the case of Filipinos, their racial subjugation began not in the United States but in the Philippines—a U.S. colony for more than half a century and a neocolony long after that. The U.S. imperialist drive into the Philippines unleashed a consistent and well-articulated ideology depicting the Philippines and its people as requiring and even beseeching the intervention of white men from the more "civilized" United States. Drawing on ideas about gender, the racist constructions of the Filipinos as uncivilized savages and dependent children bolstered the conviction that Filipinos lacked the *manly* character needed for self-rule and justified the need for U.S. interventions to rectify the Philippine "unnatural" gender order. But these racist constructions had less to do with the Filipinos' incapacity for self-rule and more to do with U.S. imperialists' desire to cast themselves as *men* who wielded power—one of the many attempts to restore "proper" gender and racial order in the late-nineteenth-century United States.[30] In this sense, the annexation and the colonization of the Philippines must also be understood as subject-constituting projects, fashioning *both* the Filipino and American subjects in ways that were and continue to be mutually implicated in each other.

The imperialist constructions of the Philippines and its people—as inferior, immoral, and incapable—traveled with Filipinos to the United States and prescribed their racialization here. In other words, Filipino immigrant lives are shaped not only by the social location of their group within the United States but also by the position of their home country within the global racial order. In an important essay on culture and U.S. imperialism, Amy Kaplan links the study of ethnicity and immigration inextricably to the study of empire by arguing that imperialism contributes not only to the subjugation of the colonized "other" but also to the consolidation of a dominant imperial culture at home.[31] Lipsitz has made a similar point: U.S. armed conflicts against "enemies" in the Philippines and other Asian countries "functioned culturally to solidify and reinforce a unified U.S. national identity based in part on antagonism toward Asia and Asians."[32] In this sense, imperialism is not only a matter of foreign policy conducted by diplomatic elites or a matter of economic necessity driven by market forces, it is also a way of life.[33] Part of this way of life is the "possessive investment in whiteness" and the corresponding disinvestment in "undeserving" groups. Represented as being at odds with the cultural, racial, and linguistic forms of the U.S. nation, the Filipino immigrant—as a nonwhite, noncivilized body—constitutes "a moving bubble of wilderness in white political space, a node of discontinuity which is necessarily in permanent tension with it."[34] I have argued that–this "permanent tension" is the product of *differential inclusion*—a process whereby a group of people is deemed integral to the nation, but integral only or precisely because of their designated subordinate standing.[35] The designation of the Filipino as the "foreigner-within" works to resolve the contradictions between the nation's promise of equal rights and its actual practice of exclusion because it attributes Filipinos' "failed" integration to their own inability or unwillingness to assimilate into the national culture that has been defined as necessarily white.

The process of differential inclusion, then, is not about closing the physical national borders but about creating borders within the nation. In this sense, the border is *everywhere*.[36] These borders within—bolstered by political and cultural mechanisms designed to restrict the membership in the national community—set clear but imaginary boundaries between who is defined as a citizen and who is not.[37] Because Filipino and other Asian Americans are discursively produced as foreign, they carry a figurative border with them. This figurative border marks them as linguistically, culturally, and racially "outside" the national polity, and as targets of nativistic racism. Anti-Asian violence, both symbolic and physical, works to reassure "real" Americans that the national community begins and ends with them and to uphold the fiction of a homogeneous American identity.[38] Nativistic racism thus operates to regulate borders—not only the geopolitical border but the border that is everywhere.

PUSHING AGAINST BORDERS

Even though the border is everywhere, Filipino migrants, through their self-made multiple subject positions and transnational connections, repeatedly push against the borders within and between nations. Drawing on historical and oral accounts of Filipino American lives in San Diego, I have documented in *Home Bound* the multifaceted and shifting experiences of "diasporic" Filipinos as they move across and dwell within the various borders. Most scholars of immigration and transnationalism have approached transnational relations in terms of capital, labor, and political transactions—all of which privilege the activities of adult males. As a departure, I have juxtaposed the "public" world of political economy (the structural reconfigurations that accompany global capitalism) with the more "private" and domestic world of families, women, and children (the social and emotional labor and costs that sustain transnational lives).[39] My goals have been to document the impact of transnationalism on Filipino American everyday life, to understand how their own agencies are implicated in both the unmaking and remaking of the established power structure, and to identify the social relationships and regimes of truth and power in which these agencies are embedded.

I conceptualize border-crossing practices as a disruptive strategy, enacted by the migrants to challenge their differential inclusion in the United States as subordinate subjects. To discipline people under its control, the regime of the nation-state requires the *localization* of its subjects—that people be locatable and confinable, if not actually confined, to the space of the nation.[40] By living their lives across borders, Filipino immigrants, in effect, are challenging the nation-state's attempt to localize them; that is, to mold them into acceptable and "normal" subjects. As such, Filipino transnational activities must be understood in part as an act of resistance: an articulation of their deep dissatisfaction with and anger at the contradictions between official state ideals of equal citizenship and state-sanctioned forms of subordination based on class, race, gender, and sexual orientation.[41] It is also an act of resistance against the violence of globalized

capitalism, a personal resolve to provide for themselves and their families even
in the wake of the global reorganization of capitalism and to remain stubbornly
Home bound even as they are flung to the "ends of the earth" in search of work.

Whatever their class background, Filipino immigrants become integrated into
the United States as a colonized and racialized people. To contest their enforced
homelessness—their political, economic, and/or cultural subordination in the
United States—many immigrants look to the Philippines for compensation and
protection, producing and maintaining multiple layers of transnational social
connections in the process.[42] For the many migrants who have experienced downward economic and social mobility, the "homeland" becomes an important site
for establishing a sense of parity—to reclaim, reinforce, or raise their social status.
As Pierre Bourdieu points out, "struggles for recognition are a fundamental
dimension of social life," and "what is at stake . . . is the accumulation of a particular form of capital, honor in the sense of reputation and prestige." Applying
Bourdieu's insight, we can thus "read" the migrants' conspicuous spending in the
home country as an attempt to convert their economic capital into symbolic capital—that is, into status.[43] *Balikbayans*, especially home-town association leaders,
enjoy lavish welcoming receptions when they visit "home" because of their perceived and actual role as benefactors of the Philippines.[44] Even when Filipino
migrants do not physically return home, they can still remit hard-earned money
to the Philippines to help an ailing parent, finance a relative's education, or purchase property and build a house there—all actions that work to increase their status "back home" and to blunt the sharpness of life in the United States. In this
sense, many Filipino migrants, like the Tongan migrants in Small's study, left the
Philippines in order to be better Filipinos—to fulfill their obligations to their families back home and in so doing to raise their own status among other Filipinos.[45]
For all these reasons, for many migrants, the "homeland" assumes a larger-than-
life role, becoming a symbolic as well as an actual security net.

At the same time, I do not wish to overstate the frequency of Filipino transnational activities. While significant segments of foreign-born Filipinos regularly
engage in transnational activities such as sending remittances or communicating
with family members back home, most Filipino migrants I spoke to do not live in
transnational "circuits" but are instead settling permanently in San Diego.[46]
Their lived reality—their job, their church, their children's school, their social
life—is primarily local. Filipinos in San Diego have actively built community
organizations—more than 150 in all—to address the needs and advance the
interests of local Filipinos.[47] But to say that transnational activities are infrequent
is not the same as saying that they are not important. True, some Filipino immigrants harbor little desire to stay connected to the Philippines—the place they
worked so hard to leave. But they are clearly in the minority. The majority of the
immigrants I interviewed spoke longingly and lovingly of their lives in the
Philippines and would return home more often if they could. For these Filipinos,
maintaining more vigorous transnational ties remains formidable: the prohibi-
tive travel costs, unrelenting work schedules, and relentless household demands
all work to minimize their physical connections to the Philippines, however
much they desire them. So at least for now, most Filipino immigrants retain

transnational ties (through remittances, phone calls, and letters home) but remain quite locally rooted, making do instead with short visits "home," often prompted by emergency situations such as a death or illness in the family.

But transnationalism take places not only at the literal but also at the symbolic level—at the level of imagination, shared memory, and "inventions of traditions."[48] Responding to their enforced "homelessness" in the United States, many Filipino migrants have created a sense of home by memorializing the homeland, inventing traditions, and fortifying familial and hometown bonds. The idealization of the homeland, however, becomes problematic when it elicits a desire among the immigrants to replicate class and gender inequities as a means to buttress their lost status and identities in the United States. I have documented in my study the troubling ways in which immigrant parents, in the name of culture and nationalism, opted to regulate their daughters' independent choices by linking them to cultural ignorance and betrayal.[49] The practice of symbolic transnationalism is perhaps most poignant among U.S.-born Filipinos, many of whom look on the Philippines with "utopian longing"—in part out of their deep dissatisfaction with their marginalized place in the United States.[50] Given their desire to be more "authentically" tied to the Filipino culture, many young Filipinos have internalized a cultural definition of "Filipinoness" that is tied to "homeland" traditions and represented by a fixed profile of shared traits such as language and folk songs.[51] Such a conception of cultural identity—one that is imbued with stable, unchanging, and continuous frames of reference and meaning—continues to be very powerful because it is directed, in Frantz Fanon's words, "by the secret hope of discovering beyond the misery of today, beyond self-contempt, resignation and abjuration, some very beautiful and splendid era whose existence rehabilitates us both in regard to ourselves and in regard to others."[52]

In sum, transnationalism must be understood as a contradictory process—one that has the potential to break down borders and traditions and create new cultures and hybrid ways of life but also to fortify traditional hierarchies, homogenize diverse cultural practices, and obscure intragroup differences and differential relationships. In this sense, transnationalism is at best a compromise—a "choice" made and lived in a context of scarce options.[53]

SELF-MAKING: "ALTERNATIVE IMAGINARIES"

Through the lens of popular and academic discourses, we see immigrants objectified as unwanted illegal aliens, welfare dependents, and economic competitors. But what do we know about their complex personhood: their self-identity, their dreams for themselves, their hopes for their children, their "ground of being"? To ask this question is to move the field of immigration studies forward, away from focusing on how immigrants are "being made" to how they are "self-making."[54] As immigrant subjects are "being made" into "minority" subjects, their culture becomes represented as bounded, local, and limited—a reconstruction of that which, outside its relation to the dominant culture, knows no such terms.[55] To engage in the process of self-making, then, is to problematize the very authority and authenticity of the term *cultural identity* (a presumption of liberal discourse), and to assert instead that immigrant subjectivity is a production that is always in process.[56]

In a brilliant essay on diasporic identity, Stuart Hall reminds us that in defining cultural identity, we cannot speak about "one experience" or "one identity" but that we need to acknowledge the deep and significant ruptures and discontinuities that exist within any community and that are subject to the continuous "play" of history, culture, and power. Cultural identities, then, are not an essence but a *positioning*: "the names we give to the different ways we are positioned by, and position ourselves within, the narratives of the past."[57] Other scholars, especially those in ethnic studies, gender studies, cultural studies, and critical anthropology, have likewise established that identities are unstable formations constituted within webs of power relations structured along the lines of gender, race, nationality, subculture, and dominant culture.[58] Because each of these "regimes of truth and power" disciplines people under its control in different ways to form acceptable and normal subjectivities, resistance strategies to undermine the hegemonic views of one regime may have the unintended effect of supporting those of another.[59]

In my study, I have been attentive to the self-activity and subjectivity of Filipino immigrants and their children. Social movement historians have recorded Filipino active engagement in labor struggles over wages, hours, and working conditions.[60] Here I am more interested in understanding how Filipino immigrants have employed what Nonini and Ong term "alternative imaginaries" to fashion self-identities that evade, move beyond, and even invert the inscriptions and identifications made by state, capitalist, and patriarchal regimes of truth.[61] In particular, I investigate the ways in which Filipino immigrants resist the colonial racial denigration of their culture, community, and women in part by turning the tables of the colonial racial moral calculus against the dominants. In so doing, I shift attention from the otherness of the subordinate group (as dictated by the "mainstream") to the otherness of the dominant group (as constructed by the "margins"). Filipinos, both in the Philippines and in the United States, construct the United States as a land of unrivaled economic opportunity but one that is marred by licentiousness, unfettered individualism, rampant consumerism, and cultural and spiritual hollowness.[62] In contrast, they insist that the Philippines, though poor, is morally and culturally superior to the United States. In the same way, Filipino immigrants claim moral distinctiveness for their community by representing white Americans, especially white women, as morally flawed and themselves as family-oriented models and their women as paragons of morality.[63] Their invocation of family values, loyalty to elders, and female chastity and sacrifice are all pointed critiques of what they perceive as the deficient morality of America and its people. By focusing on the alternative frames of meaning that aggrieved groups employ to invert their status in relation to the dominant group, I underscore the immigrants' ability to maneuver and manipulate meanings within different domains, especially in the domains of morality and culture, in an effort to counter the fundamental assumption of inevitable white American superiority.

At the same time, I have tried to be attentive not only to cultural and ethnic resistance but also to the limitations of resistance strategies that fail to recognize the "complex *relationality* that shapes our social and political lives."[64] In *Home Bound*, I showed how idealized descriptions of virtuous immigrant daughters allow Filipinos to resist colonial denigration of their women and culture and to represent themselves as morally superior to the dominant group.[65] But this strategy exemplifies the paradox of immigrant resistance and accommodation and the relation between race, ethnicity, and gender: Filipino families forge cultural resistance against racial oppression by stressing female chastity and sacrifice, and yet they reinforce patriarchal power and gendered oppression by hinging ethnic and racial pride on the performance of female subordination. In so doing, they collapse the heterogeneous and competing (im)moral discourses and practices in the community into a stable and coherent set of collective values and goals. Along the same lines, I detailed the ways in which Filipino American men resist racist economic exploitation by reclaiming traditional definitions of manhood and sweeping aside the needs and well-being of Filipino American women and children.[66] However, I also pointed out that the denigration of Filipino women and children constitutes only one response to the stripping of male privilege. Another is to institute a revised domestic division of labor and gender relations in the immigrant family. In sum, an alternative frame of meaning is a potent counterforce to existing hegemonies, but one that is not without its own "particular mix of expansive and repressive technologies."[67]

THE *BABAES*: IMAGINING A BETTER WORLD

> We have allowed our imaginations to be so bounded so that we are left with a nation full of borders, borders that too easily become fault lines. We are left with people who live in transit, between their imaginary homelands and the mythic America. But let us not forget the power of imagination. Let us imagine, then a better community.
>
> —ROBERT CHANG, "A MEDITATION ON BORDERS"

In the above passage, critical legal theorist Robert Chang warns us about the dangers of "a nation full of borders" and exhorts us to imagine "a better community." I want to end by focusing on three second-generation Filipinas who have heeded this call to transgress borders and to imagine and participate in making a better world. All three were born in the mid-1970s, came of age during the conservative Reagan/Bush years, and attended college (University of California, San Diego) during California's "darkest days," as the state was awash with an anti-immigration and anti–affirmative action fervor.[68] All chose to respond to the urgency of the moment by drawing on their situated knowledges as Pinays[69] to enact a compelling vision of social justice. It is important to note that they understood the relationship between the local and the global—that the injustices, inequities, and indignities endured by California's racialized and gendered groups and by their own families are intimately tied to the historical and contemporary conditions of globalization. To better educate themselves about the workings of transnational capitalism, they left the United States and traveled deep into the Philippines, where they learned from the people there how to visualize alternatives to oppressive conditions and to translate these powerful visions into critical actions. This very act of border crossing is transgressive. By leaving the United States for the Philippines with the expressed intent to obtain "a better education," these young Pinays have in effect redefined what constituted knowledge and education and inverted the racialized hierarchy that privileged the United States as the world's premier center of education.

Melany de la Cruz, Jennifer True, and Strela Cervas call themselves the *babaes*, a Tagalog word for "women," to signal their cultural awareness, their political activism, and their gender consciousness.[70] They view their identities not as represented by a fixed profile of traits but as self-conscious products of political choices and actions. When a former boyfriend's brother charged that "all Filipinos look like monkeys," Melany retaliated by imbuing her identity with political weight: she became immersed in affirmative action, labor, and youth struggles. These panethnic and interethnic social movements introduced her to international labor struggles, including those waged by workers in the Philippines. From her Ethnic Studies and Urban Studies courses, Melany learned about U.S. capitalism, U.S. colonial and neo-colonial modes of development and exploitation in the Philippines, and the post-Fordist imperialism of the International Monetary Fund, the World Bank, and "free" trade. But she wanted to "apply these tools" and to "experience firsthand" the historical and ongoing exploitation of Filipino labor, women, and children. To do that, she believed she "needed to go back to the Philippines and participate in the liberation struggles there." In the summer of 1998, she traveled to the Philippines under the auspices of the Integrate/Exposure Program hosted by the Los Angeles-based League of Filipino Students (LFS). The Integrate/Exposure Program is designed to integrate and expose Americans, especially second-generation Filipino Americans, to different activist sectors of the Philippines, including the peasant, student, small mining community, urban poor, human rights, labor, and religious sectors. The program is thus structured to provide young "Integrationists" and "Exposurists"[71] with examples of already existing activism in the Philippines in the hope that they will inform and energize future struggles.[72]

Like Melany, Jennifer and Strela were drawn to the Integrate/Exposure Program because of its emphasis on activism. "I didn't want to go to the Philippines as a tourist," said Jennifer. "I wanted to see the lives and the struggles of the common Pilipino people . . . and not the megamall or the tourist spots." And Strela wanted to "know exactly what was going in the Philippines"—to concretize what she had learned through her formal and informal education in the United States. As Strela explained,

> After taking some courses on Filipino American history and immigration, I developed a sense of the Filipino population as having a history of exploitation. And . . . I wanted to experience that. I was very interested in "Third Worldism," like why the Third World exists and questions just weren't being answered for me. And then also, I wanted to know exactly why so many Filipinos, like my parents, were immigrating to the United States. I wanted to know what was pushing people out of the country.

In June 1998, Jennifer, along with Melany and another U.C.S.D. student, left for the Philippines for a two-month stay. Inspired by Jennifer and Melany's stories about their experiences in the Philippines, Strela followed suit and left for a six-month stay in the Philippines in January 2000.

Melany, Jennifer, and Strela were deeply affected by their experiences in the Philippines. On a personal level, going "home" brought them face-to-face with their transnational family: they met long-lost relatives, pored over family albums, listened to family stories, and memorized family lores—all of which gave them keener insights into their parents' lives. "I never understood why my father hadn't gone back [to the Philippines] in twenty-five years," stated Melany.

> But when I was in the Philippines, I learned something about my dad. I saw how every-body idolized my father so much because he is the only one in the U.S. My father's fam-ily constructed an image of him as someone who "made it." And I think there was pressure for him to come back wealthy, successful, and have this extraordinary ability to financially provide for everybody, no matter what it costs. But my dad was far from wealthy, and so he couldn't go home.

For Jennifer, going to the Philippines empowered her to claim a "sense of owner-ship" over her Pinay identity. As Jennifer explained,

> I gained a sense of ownership over my identity, a definite tie I could hold on to that I didn't have before. After a decade of refusing to speak Tagalog to my parents 'cuz "I don't need a language no one else around me speaks," and then running across Pilipinos who thought I wasn't Pilipino enough 'cuz I don't speak Tagalog that fluent anymore, I felt a burning sensation in my gut every time I wondered what Pilipino was, what I was 'cuz I tried so hard to be "American" for so long, I had lost my Pilipino identity. Going to the Philippines gave me the perspective, the understanding, and enlightenment I needed to find my identity. I learned the language again. I reclaimed the spirit of what the Philippines was that my parents brought to the U.S. and gave to my brother and I as chil-dren, which we lost as we grew up.

Jennifer's connection to the country and its people was so deep that she embraced the Philippines as her motherland, her home:

> Before I went to the Philippines, I saw it not as my *motherland* but as my *mother's land.* I had no ties to that [place] that my parents called home. Their home. The Philippines was just a figment of my imagination, unreal to me as a place I could feel connected to. But after I went there, I now know that it is my land too. My motherland, stretching its loving arms to me and saying "welcome to me, my child." And as its child, with tears in my eyes, in a country strangely foreign yet comforting at the same time, feeling like I am home too.

But Strela cautioned against the romanticized belief that Filipino Americans easily blend into Philippine culture and society:

> It's not always the case that we, as Pil-Ams, can blend in while in the Philippines. In fact, while trying to blend in, we oftentimes feel a sense of alienation because we realize how

removed we are from the culture and how privileged we are relative to native Pilipinos. By going to the Philippines, we attempt to reclaim our identity as Pilipinas, but we may never reclaim this identity in its entirety because in some sense, we can never be integrated into the culture entirely.

But the young women were most inspired and awed by the level of activism and political consciousness exhibited by the people and organizations in the Philippines. During their stay there, they met, worked with, and learned from numerous activist groups such as indigenous peoples fighting for scarce resources in the Cordillera, unionized urban workers fighting for a living wage in Manila, and peasant farmers fighting for their land in Hacidena Looc.[73] They learned by doing: they passed out union leaflets in the cities, planted and harvested rice in the provinces, helped organize rallies, and led discussion groups on such topics as landlessness and imperialism. Along the way, they met, befriended, and fell in love with what Jennifer termed the "spirit of the people":

> The spirit of the people [is] so strong. They fight for their land, for their family, for their survival and way of life. No matter how hard life was, they could still laugh, still had hope. The people I met were simple people, they were peasants, organizers, and indigenous peoples, but they were the most inspirational people I had ever met.

Melany, an experienced organizer, was thrilled by the level of activism that she saw in the Philippines: "The things that we participated in [in the Philippines] were things that we never saw here in the U.S., just like the mass amount of people that would protest in the streets, literally in the streets all day, instead of a couple of hours. It was just really powerful to see that kind of opposition." Armed with this collective memory, they felt ready to counter the dominant misrepresentations of the Philippines and its people as "unproductive" and "lazy." As Strela stated, "When I was there, I just saw for myself how hard people worked and how hard they fought for their rights. Especially the people in the provinces, they were just the exact opposite of 'lazy.' "Melany concurred, "Going to the Philippines strengthened me as a person and made me proud that I am a Pinay. It gave me that understanding to now defend myself when it comes to explaining my culture and my history and my people."

To remain connected to the Philippines, all three vowed to continue the social struggles here in the United States. And they have, with all three participating in various organizing efforts including the campaigns for living wage, for immigration rights, and for women's rights. Although they take seriously the power of organic solidarity based on identity, they insist on building coalitions around a common culture of activism. Going to the Philippines introduced them to the possibility of a shared struggle—the notion that people of color everywhere were engaged in a common political struggle against what Charles Mills terms the "racial contract."[74] For example, Melany discovered that the conditions faced by factory workers in the "export processing zones" in the Philippines were similar to those faced by *maquiladora* workers in Tijuana,

Mexico—that both constituted the "new" workforce within the global reorganization of capitalism:

> In Manila, I met a woman who took me to the factories where the workers were on strike and exposed me to the working conditions there. I was making connections and I was telling them about how I'd worked with the Support Committee for the *maquiladora* workers in Mexico. I was helping them to see that it was an international thing, by telling them that it was an international, by telling them that I'd seen the same conditions in Mexico.

The ability to "[tell] them that it was an international thing"—that is, to look beyond cultural and national boundaries—is a powerful resource for ordinary people because it enables new forms of "transnational grassroots politics" to emerge in response to the current conditions of transnational capitalism.[75] Such is the power, promise, and possibility of "transnationalism from below": the making of an oppositional culture based on a transformative vision that delineates the violence of global capitalism and calls on the world's people to imagine a new vision and to "create an active path leading to it from the present."[76] Melany, Jennifer, and Strela, and countless other Filipino Americans, have shown us this path. They have instructed us about the creation of new social relations, new social subjects, new connecting ideologies, and new ways of living, seeing, and fighting; these are the tools of home making.

Notes

1. Editors' note: The author is referring to her book, *Home Bound: Filipino American Lives across Cultures, Communities, and Countries* (2003), where this chapter first appeared.
2. Dunn 1996; Palafox 1996. In 1996, as an example of the escalation of military involvement in domestic law enforcement, in the San Diego sector alone, some 350 members of marine and army units helped "monitor electric sensors, staff night-vision scopes, assist with communications and transportation, and conduct aerial surveillance" (Palafox 1996:14).
3. Gross 1999.
4. Cacho 2000:402; also Hondagneu-Sotelo 1995; Lipsitz 1998:47–54.
5. Cited in Rose 1985:205.
6. Starr and Roberts 1981.
7. Roberts 1988:81.
8. U.S. Commission on Civil Rights 1992:22–48.
9. Lowe 1996; Lipsitz 1998; Ong, Bonacich, and Cheng 1994; Fernández-Kelly 1983.
10. Feagin 1997:28.
11. Smith 1992.
12. Chavez 1997:66.
13. Rodriquez 1997:225.
14. Grewal and Kaplan 1994.
15. Mahmud 1997:633.
16. For example, in 1996 the Committee on International Migration of the Social Science Research Council organized a conference entitled "Becoming Americans/America Becoming." According to the organizers, the conference was organized to provide an interdisciplinary overview and assessment of the socio-cultural and political aspects of immigrant incorporation and responses by native-born Americans. A selection of revised

conference papers was published in a special issue of the *International Migration Review* 31 (winter 1997). The organizing theme of the issue was "Immigrant Adaptation and Native-Born Responses in the Making of Americans."

17. Schlesinger 1991; Brimelow 1995.
18. Feagin 1997; Portes and Rumbaut 1996.
19. Feagin 1997:32, 37.
20. Portes 1994:634. Portes (1994:632) contends that it is the second generation, not the first, that is the key to establishing the long-term consequences of immigration. The issues to be permanently decided by the second generation include "the continuing dominance of English, the growth of a welfare-dependent population, the resilience of culturally distinct urban enclaves, and the decline or growth of ethnic intermarriages."
21. By "ethnic studies" scholars, I do not mean scholars in Ethnic Studies departments, but rather scholars who take an ethnic studies approach to their work. For a discussion on the ethnic studies approach, please see Espiritu 1999.
22. Muller 1997:109.
23. Kumar 2000:xi, emphasis in original.
24. Mahmud 1997:633.
25. Lowe 1996.
26. Roberts 1997:211.
27. Chavez 1997:62.
28. Lowe 1996:5.
29. Chavez 1997:67.
30. Espiritu 2003, Chapter 3.
31. Kaplan 1993.
32. Lipsitz 1998:70–72.
33. Kaplan 1993.
34. Mills 1997:53.
35. Espiritu 2003.
36. Chang 1997.
37. Cacho 2000:390.
38. Chang 1997:249–51.
39. Patricia Pessar (1999) has made the same point regarding immigration studies. She argues that classical theories of migration emphasize movements of capital and labor and envision migrants as adult men acting primarily from economic motives. In so doing, these theories conceptualize women and children as appendages to male migration or as occasional exceptions to the adult male model.
40. Nonini and Ong 1997:23.
41. Rosaldo 1994:239.
42. Francia 1999:205.
43. Bourdieu 1990:22.
44. Espiritu 2003, Chapter 4.
45. Small 1997.
46. Mahler (1999) and Hondagneu-Sotelo (1994) also report that most Salvadoran and Mexican immigrants, respectively, were here to stay.
47. Espiritu 2003, Chapter 5.
48. Hobsbawm and Ranger 1983.
49. Espiritu 2003, Chapter 7.
50. Francia 1999:212.
51. Espiritu 2003, Chapter 8.
52. Fanon 1963:170.
53. Espiritu 2003, Chapter 4.
54. Ong 1996.
55. Lloyd 1994:229.
56. Hall 1990.

57. Hall 1990:225.
58. Ong 1987; Williams 1989; Collins 1991; Grewal and Kaplan 1994.
59. Foucault 1991.
60. Friday 1994; Scharlin and Villanueva 1992; Fujita Rony 2000.
61. Nonini and Ong 1997:26.
62. Espiritu 2003, Chapter 4.
63. Espiritu 2003, Chapter 7.
64. Mohanty 1991:13, emphasis in original.
65. Espiritu 2003, Chapter 7.
66. Espiritu 2003, Chapter 6.
67. Ong 1997:194–95.
68. In 1994, the California electorate voted in favor of Proposition 187, a measure designed to deny medical treatment and education to undocumented workers and their families. In 1995, the University of California Regents voted to eliminate affirmative action for minorities and women in admissions. A year later, state voters passed Proposition 209 to end statewide affirmative action practices.
69. These three women prefer to identify themselves as *Pinays*, a term used to connote politically conscious Filipina Americans. As Melany explained, "To me, *Pinay* is like the term *Chicana*; it is a term used when you have a certain sense of consciousness of your history, your people, that you are respectful. It's a political term, too."
70. But they have not always been this confident about their identities. Growing up in the suburbs, Jennifer felt culturally empty: "When we moved to the suburbs, the language, the food, the culture began to disappear, and I was left empty. There's a void there full of questions of what is Filipino? You feel embarrassed 'cuz you're Filipino, but you don't know what Filipino is. A country, a land, a culture, a way of life, a language, a food?" In the same way, Melany related an "identity crisis" that she experienced during her sophomore and junior years in high school:

    I felt the pressure to *act* white because this is what would get me into college. All of my life, my best friends and people I grew up with were either Filipino or Mexican. As I started thinking about college, I realized I needed to start studying and *acting* more like the white students in my classes because they were the ones who were also pursuing a higher education. The white students were the most motivated, most prepared, and I wanted to surround myself and create relationships with those people and as a result, ended up spending less time with my friends of color.

    Unlike Jennifer and Melany, Strela attended a high school with a sizeable Filipino student population. There she helped to found Halo-Halo, the first Filipino American student club on campus. But the club did not meet her expectations: it became primarily a social space rather than an educational space where she and other Filipino students could learn about their history, language, and culture—the tangible facts and tidbits that they felt they had not been taught at home or at school.
71. These were the names used to describe participants in the Integration/Exposure Program.
72. The Exposure Program to the Philippines is about thirty years old. During the late 1960s and early 1970s, there was a strong and growing movement in the Philippines calling for an end to feudalism and fascism and U.S. imperialism in the Philippines. Movement supporters were among those Filipinos who migrated to the United States during the 1970s. These migrants took frequent trips back to the Philippines to renew and revitalize their support for the fight for the liberation of the Philippines and its people. U.S.-born and/or -raised Filipinos have also gone through these U.S.-based support groups. Their purpose was to go back to their roots, to view firsthand the conditions of the people, and to meet peasants, students, workers and others who are struggling for national democracy. Some Filipino students have gone on medical missions with pro-people health organizations. The past few years have seen an increase in the number of Filipino youth taking exposure trips. Many of them get involved in local Filipino groups that organize

locally and support the National Democratic Movement in the Philippines. The exposure trip program depends heavily on the wants and needs of the exposurists. If they want to be exposed to progressive artists, they will be programmed with an artist group as their host. If they are interested in issues affecting women and children, then their program will have that emphasis. Other programs focus on students and youth, national minorities, church, peasants, workers, teachers, medical workers. No matter what the focus is, the exposurist will be encouraged to have a minimum exposure to the peasants, workers, and urban poor. The length of the exposure depends on the exposurist. Some last for a couple of days while others have lasted for more than a year. Educational workshops, ideally before and during the trip, are an integral component of the exposure experience. These workshops give the exposurists an opportunity to learn comprehensively about the history and current economical, political, and social situation of the Philippines. As testified by Melany, Strela, and Jennifer, the exposure programs have often been life-changing as exposurists experience firsthand the harsh poverty and survival-level of life in the Philippines *and* the incredibly strong and vital movement that is transforming society. Finally, part of the Exposure Program is to understand Filipino culture and to bridge gaps between Filipinos and Filipino Americans. This means trying to ascertain where Filipino Americans fit into Filipino culture and how they can be a part of the Filipino struggle as a whole.

73. In Hacienda Looc, peasant farmers were fighting to keep their land from being converted into a golf resort—an investment venture financed by such foreign investors as Jack Nicklaus and Michael Jackson.

74. Mills 1997.

75. Smith 1994.

76. Boggs 1998:255.

REFERENCES

Boggs, Grace Lee. 1998. *Living for Change: An Autobiography.* Minneapolis: University of Minnesota Press.

Bourdieu, Pierre. 1990. *In Other Words: Essays Toward a Reflexive Sociology.* Palo Alto, Calif.: Stanford University Press.

Brimelow, Peter. 1995. *Alien Nation: Common Sense about America's Immigration Disaster.* New York: Random House.

Cacho, Lisa Marie. 2000. " 'The People of California Are Suffering': The Ideology of White Injury and Discourses of Immigration." *Cultural Values* 4 (4): 389–418.

Chang, Robert S. 1997. "A Meditation on Borders." In *Immigrants Out! The New Nativism and the Anti-Immigrant Impulse in the United States,* edited by Juan F. Perea. New York: New York University Press.

Chavez, Leo R. 1997. "Immigration Reform and Nativism: The Nationalist Response to the Transnational Challenge." In *Immigrants Out! The New Nativism and the Anti-Immigrant Impulse in the United States,* edited by Juan F. Perea. New York: New York University Press.

Collins, Patricia Hill. 1991. *Black Feminist Thought: Knowledge, Consciousness, and the Politics of Empowerment.* New York: Routledge.

Dunn, Timothy. 1996. *The Militarization of the U.S.-Mexico Border, 1978–1992: Low-Intensity Conflict Doctrine Comes Home.* Austin, Tex.: Center for Mexican American Studies, University of Texas at Austin.

Espiritu, Yen Le. 2003. *Home Bound: Filipino American Lives across Cultures, Communities, and Countries.* Berkeley: University of California Press.

———. 1999. "Disciplines Unbound: Notes on Sociology and Ethnic Studies." *Contemporary Sociology: A Journal of Reviews* 28 (5): 510–14.

Fanon, Frantz. 1963. "On National Culture." In *The Wretched of the Earth.* New York: Grove Press.

Feagin, Joe R. 1997. "Old Poison in Old Bottles: The Deep Roots of Modern Nativism." In *Immigrants Out! The New Nativism and the Anti-Immigrant Impulse in the United States,* edited by Juan F. Perea. New York: New York University Press.

Fernández-Kelly, Maria Patricia. 1983. *For We Are Sold, I and My People: Women and Industry in Mexico's Frontier.* Albany: State University of New York Press.

Foucault, Michel. 1991. "Governmentality." In *The Foucault Effect: Studies in Governmentality,* edited by Graham Burchell, Colin Gordon, and Peter Miller. Chicago: University of Chicago Press.

Francia, Luis. 1999. "Inventing the Earth: The Notion of 'Home' in Asian American Literature." In *Across the Pacific: Asian Americans and Globalization,* edited by Evelyn Hu-DeHart. New York: Asia Society; Philadelphia: Temple University Press.

Friday, Chris. 1994. *Organizing Asian American Labor: The Pacific Coast Canned-Salmon Industry, 1870–1942.* Philadelphia: Temple University Press.

Fujita Rony, Dorothy. 2000. "Coalitions, Race, and Labor: Rereading Philip Vera Cruz." *Journal of Asian American Studies* 3 (2): 139–62.

Grewal, Inderpal, and Caren Kaplan. 1994. "Introduction: Transnational Feminist Practices and Questions of Postmodernity." In *Scattered Hegemonies: Postmodernity and Transnational Feminist Practices,* edited by Inderpal Grewal and Caren Kaplan. Minneapolis: University of Minnesota Press.

Gross, Gregory Alan. 1999. "5-Year-Old Gatekeeper Is Praised, Denounced: Critics Say It Makes Border More Dangerous." *San Diego Union Tribune,* 7 June.

Hall, Stuart. 1990. "Cultural Identity and Diaspora." In *Identity, Community, Culture, Difference,* edited by Jonathan Rutherford. London: Lawrence and Wishart.

Hobsbawm, E. J., and Terence Ranger. 1983. *The Invention of Tradition.* New York: Cambridge University Press.

Hondagneu-Sotelo, Pierette. 1994. *Gendered Transitions: Mexican Experiences of Immigration.* Berkeley and Los Angeles: University of California Press.

———. 1995. "Women and Children First: New Directions in Anti-Immigrant Politics." *Socialist Review* 25 (1): 169–90.

Kaplan, Amy. 1993. " 'Left Alone with America': The Absence of Empire in the Study of American Culture." In *Cultures of United States Imperialism,* edited by Amy Kaplan and Donald E. Pease. Durham, N.C., and London: Duke University Press.

Kumar, Amitava. 2000. *Passport Photos.* Berkeley and Los Angeles: University of California Press.

Lipsitz, George. 1998. *The Possessive Investment in Whiteness: How White People Profit from Identity Politics.* Philadelphia: Temple University Press.

Lloyd, David. 1994. "Ethnic Cultures, Minority Discourse and the State." In *Colonial Discourse/Postcolonial Theory,* edited by Francis Barker, Peter Hulme, and Margaret Iversen. Manchester, England, and New York: St. Martin's Press.

Lowe, Lisa. 1996. *Immigrant Acts: On Asian American Cultural Politics.* Durham, N.C.: Duke University Press.

Mahler, Sarah. 1999. "Engendering Transnational Migration: A Case Study of Salvadorans." *American Behavioral Scientist* 42 (4): 690–719.

Mahmud, Tayyab. 1997. "Migration, Identity, and the Colonial Encounter." *Oregon Law Review* 76 (Fall): 633–90.

Mills, Charles. 1997. *The Racial Contract.* Ithaca, N.Y.: Cornell University Press.

Mohanty, Chandra. 1991. "Cartographies of Struggle: Third World Women and the Politics of Feminism." In *Third World Women and the Politics of Feminism,* edited by Chandra Mohanty, Ann Russo, and Lourdes Torres. Bloomington: Indiana University Press.

Muller, Thomas. 1997. "Nativism in the Mid-1990s: Why Now?" In *Immigrants Out! The New Nativism and the Anti-Immigrant Impulse in the United States,* edited by Juan F. Perea. New York: New York University Press.

Nonini, Donald M., and Aihwa Ong. 1997. "Introduction: Chinese Transnationalism as an Alternative Modernity." In *Ungrounded Empires: The Cultural Politics of Modern Chinese Transnationalism,* edited by Aihwa Ong and Donald M. Nonini. New York: Routledge.

Ong, Aihwa. 1987. *Spirits of Resistance and Capitalist Discipline: Factory Women in Malaysia.* Albany: State University of New York Press.

———. 1996. "Cultural Citizenship as Subject-Making." *Current Anthropology* 37 (5): 737–62.

———. 1997. "Chinese Modernities: Narratives of Nation and of Capitalism." In *Ungrounded Empires: The Culture and Politics of Modern Chinese Transnationalism*, edited by Aihwa Ong and Donald Nonini. New York: Routledge.

Ong, Paul, Edna Bonacich, and Lucie Cheng. 1994. "The Political Economy of Capitalist Restructuring and the New Asian Immigration." In *The New Asian Immigration in Los Angeles and Global Restructuring*, edited by Paul Ong, Edna Bonacich, and Lucie Cheng. Philadelphia: Temple University Press.

Palafox, Jose. 1996. "Militarizing the Border." *CAQ* 56 (Spring): 14–19.

Pessar, Patricia. 1999. "Engendering Migration Studies: The Case of New Immigrants in the United States." *American Behavioral Scientist* 42: 577–600.

Portes, Alejandro. 1994. "Introduction: Immigration and Its Aftermath." *International Migration Review* 28 (4): 632–39.

Portes, Alejandro, Luis E. Guarzino, and Patricia Landolt. 1999. "The Study of Transnationalism: Pitfalls and Promises of an Emergent Research Field." *Ethnic and Racial Studies* 22 (2): 217–37.

Roberts, Alden. 1988. "Racism Sent and Received: Americans and Vietnamese View One Another." *Research in Race and Ethnic Relations* 5: 75–97.

Roberts, Dorothy E. 1997. "Who May Give Birth to Citizens? Reproduction, Eugenics, and Immigration." In *Immigrants Out! The New Nativism and the Anti-Immigrant Impulse in the United States*, edited by Juan F. Perea. New York: New York University Press.

Rodriquez, Nestor P. 1997. "The Social Construction of the U.S.-Mexico Border." In *Immigrants Out! The New Nativism and the Anti-Immigrant Impulse in the United States*, edited by Juan F. Perea. New York: New York University Press.

Rosaldo, Renato. 1994. "Social Justice and the Crisis of National Communities." In *Colonial Discourse/Postcolonial Theory*, edited by Francis Barker, Peter Hulme, and Margaret Iversen. New York: St. Martin's Press.

Rose, Peter. 1985. "Asian Americans: From Pariahs to Paragons." In *Clamor at the Gates: The New Immigration*, edited by Nathan Glazer. San Francisco: Institute of Contemporary Studies.

Scharlin, Craig, and Lilia V. Villanueva. 1992. *Philip Vera Cruz: A Personal History of Filipino Immigrants and the Farmworkers Movement*. Los Angeles: UCLA Labor Center, Institute of Labor Relations, and UCLA Asian American Studies Center.

Schlesinger, Arthur. 1991. *The Disuniting of America: Reflections on a Multicultural Society*. New York: Norton.

Small, Cathy. 1997. *Voyages: From Tongan Villages to American Suburbs*. Ithaca, N.Y.: Cornell University Press.

Smith, Michael Peter. 1992. "Postmodernism, Urban Ethnography, and the New Social Space of Ethnic Identity." *Theory and Society* 21: 493–531.

———. 1994. "Can You Imagine? Transnational Migration and the Globalization of Grassroots Politics." *Social Text* 39: 15–33.

Starr, Paul D., and Alden Roberts. 1981. "Attitudes toward Indochinese Refugees: An Empirical Study." *Journal of Refugee Resettlement* 1 (4): 51–61.

U.S. Commission on Civil Rights. 1992. *Civil Rights Issues Facing Asian Americans in the 1990s*. Washington, D.C.: Government Printing Office.

Williams, Brackette. 1989. "A Class Act: Anthropology and the Race to Nation Across Ethnic Terrain." *Annual Review of Anthropology* 18: 401–44.

Biographical Notes

About the Editors

Jean Yu-wen Shen Wu is a senior lecturer in the American studies program at Tufts University.

Thomas C. Chen is a doctoral candidate in the American civilization department at Brown University.

About the Contributors

Angelo N. Ancheta is an assistant professor of law at the Santa Clara University School of Law.

Sucheng Chan is a professor emerita of Asian American studies and global studies at the University of California, Santa Barbara.

Monica Chiu is an associate professor of English at the University of New Hampshire, where she teaches Asian American studies.

Arif Dirlik is chair professor of Chinese history and honorary director, CUHK-Chiang Ching-kuo Asia Pacific Centre for Chinese Studies, Chinese University of Hong Kong; concurrent professor, Center for the Study of Marxist Social Theory, Nanjing University; and distinguished visiting fellow, the Peter Wall Institute for Advanced Studies, University of British Columbia.

Sara Dorow is an associate professor of sociology at the University of Alberta and has conducted a decade's worth of research on the transnational adoption of Chinese children in North America.

David L. Eng is a professor of English and comparative literature and also a core faculty member in the Asian American studies program at the University of Pennsylvania.

Yen Le Espiritu is a professor of ethnic studies at the University of California, San Diego.

Shinhee Han is a psychotherapist in private practice in New York City.

Elaine H. Kim is a professor of Asian American and comparative ethnic studies at the University of California, Berkeley.

Erika Lee is an associate professor of history and Asian American studies at the University of Minnesota.

Robert G. Lee teaches Asian American studies in the Department of American Civilization at Brown University.

Andrew Leong is an associate professor in the College of Public & Community Service at the University of Massachusetts, Boston, where he teaches legal studies and Asian American studies.

Sunaina Maira is an associate professor of Asian American studies at the University of California, Davis.

Martin F. Manalansan IV is an associate professor of anthropology and Asian American studies at the University of Illinois, Urbana-Champaign. He is also an affiliate faculty in the Unit for Criticism and Interpretive Theory and the gender and women's studies program.

Mari Matsuda is a feminist law professor and critical race theorist at Georgetown University Law Center.

Davianna Pomaika'i McGregor is a historian of Hawai'i and the Pacific, a professor of ethnic studies at the University of Hawai'i, Manoa, and a coordinator of the Protect Kaho'olawe 'Ohana.

Gary Y. Okihiro is a professor of international and public affairs at Columbia University.

Glenn Omatsu teaches at California State University, Northridge, Pasadena City College, and the University of California, Los Angeles and is active in community movements for social justice.

Michael Omi is a professor of ethnic studies at the University of California, Berkeley.

Rhacel Salazar Parreñas is a professor of American civilization at Brown University.

Hiram Perez is an assistant professor of English at Vassar College and a visiting fellow at the Center for African American Studies, Princeton University.

Vijay Prashad is the George and Martha Kellner Chair of South Asian History and a professor of international studies at Trinity College.

Louisa Schein is an associate professor of anthropology and core faculty in women's and gender studies at Rutgers University.

Nayan Shah is an associate professor of history at the University of California, San Diego.

Dana Takagi is a professor of sociology at the University of California, Santa Cruz.

Eric Tang is an assistant professor of African American studies and Asian American studies at the University of Illinois at Chicago.

Va-Megn Thoj, recipient of the Bush Artist Fellowship and the Media Arts Fellowship, is a Minnesota-based filmmaker and social justice activist.

Michi Nishiura Weglyn (1926–1999) authored *Years of Infamy: The Untold Story of America's Concentration Camps*, which fueled a movement that led to reparations for more than 80,000 Japanese Americans interned during World War II.

Howard Winant is a professor of sociology at the University of California, Santa Barbara, where he founded and directs the UCSB Center for New Racial Studies.

Ji-Yeon Yuh is an associate professor of history and director of the Asian American studies program at Northwestern University.

Helen Zia is an award-winning journalist who has covered Asian American communities and social and political movements for decades.

Copyrights and Permissions

Part Three: Culture, Politics, and Society

Part Four: Pedagogies and Possibilities

Index